RECLAIMING
THE DEAD SEA SCROLLS

THE ANCHOR BIBLE REFERENCE LIBRARY is designed to be a third major component of the Anchor Bible group, which includes the Anchor Bible commentaries on the books of the Old Testament, the New Testament, and the Apocrypha, and the Anchor Bible Dictionary. While the Anchor Bible commentaries and the Anchor Bible Dictionary are structurally defined by their subject matter, the Anchor Bible Reference Library will serve as a supplement on the cutting edge of the most recent scholarship. The new series will be open-ended; its scope and reach are nothing less than the biblical world in its totality, and its methods and techniques the most up-to-date available or devisable. Separate volumes will deal with one or more of the following topics relating to the Bible: anthropology, archaeology, ecology, economy, geography, history, languages and literatures, philosophy, religion(s), theology.

As with the Anchor Bible commentaries and the Anchor Bible Dictionary, the philosophy underlying the Anchor Bible Reference Library finds expression in the following: the approach is scholarly, the perspective is balanced and fair-minded, the methods are scientific, and the goal is to inform and enlighten. Contributors are chosen on the basis of their scholarly skills and achievements, and they come from a variety of religious backgrounds and communities. The books in the Anchor Bible Reference Library are intended for the broadest possible readership, ranging from world-class scholars, whose qualifications match those of the authors, to general readers, who may not have special training or skill in studying the Bible but are as enthusiastic as any dedicated professional in expanding their knowledge of the Bible and its world.

David Noel Freedman
GENERAL EDITOR

THE ANCHOR BIBLE REFERENCE LIBRARY

RECLAIMING THE DEAD SEA SCROLLS

The History of Judaism,
the Background of Christianity,
the Lost Library of Qumran

LAWRENCE H. SCHIFFMAN

with a Foreword by Chaim Potok

YALE

THE ANCHOR YALE BIBLE

Yale University Press
New Haven & London

THE ANCHOR BIBLE REFERENCE LIBRARY

PUBLISHED BY DOUBLEDAY
a division of Bantam Doubleday Dell Publishing Group, Inc.
1540 Broadway, New York, New York 10036

THE ANCHOR BIBLE REFERENCE LIBRARY, DOUBLEDAY, and the portrayal
of an anchor with the letters ABRL are trademarks of Doubleday,
a division of Bantam Doubleday Dell Publishing Group, Inc.

Reclaiming the Dead Sea Scrolls was originally published by
The Jewish Publication Society, Philadelphia, Pennsylvania, in 1994.
This edition published by arrangement with The Jewish Publication Society.

Book Design by Anne O'Donnell
Typeset by Circle Graphics in Trump Mediaeval

Library of Congress Cataloging-in-Publication Data
Schiffman, Lawrence H.
    Reclaiming the Dead Sea scrolls: the history of Judaism, the background
    of Christianity, the lost library of Qumran / Lawrence H. Schiffman;
    with a foreword by Chaim Potok.
        p.   cm. – (The Anchor Bible reference library)
    Previously published: 1st ed. Philadelphia: Jewish Publication Society, 1994.
    Includes bibliographical references and index.
    1. Dead Sea scrolls—Criticism, interpretation, community, etc.   2. Qumran
community.   I. Title.   II. Series.
BM487.S3128   1995   95-17280
296.1'55 – dc 20   CIP

ISBN: 978-0-300-14022-4

for
Professor Nahum M. Sarna

His word is like the word of heaven, and his teaching is according to the will of God.

מאמרה כמאמר שמין
ואולפנה כרעות אל.

Aramaic Levi Document[d]

CONTENTS

List of Tables, Charts, and Maps

AUTHOR'S NOTE

This book follows the convention used in the field of Dead Sea Scrolls studies; that is, *square brackets* denote restorations of the text where the manuscript is damaged, and *parentheses* denote explanatory additions to a translation. Readers should remember that most restorations must be based on intuition and conjecture to a great extent, which is why the meaning of some texts will always be uncertain.

FOREWORD

My first encounter with the Dead Sea Scrolls came about through the reporting of Edmund Wilson. In the late 1950s I studied some of those scrolls with Professor Jonas Greenfield in Los Angeles. The vaguest of pictures was then beginning to appear: something about a marginal sect of Second Temple Jews and the beginnings of Christianity. (And "Qumran" was becoming a word resonant with awe and apprehension, bringing some concern to historians of embryonic Christianity and slowly taking on the gravity of myth.)

Over the decades, the scrolls have produced a history of their own, some of it rather tawdry, as scholars took issue with one another over the translation and publishing rights, over the laggardly appearance of the scrolls before the public, over the self-aggrandizement of a small group of learned academics who appeared to be hoarding them, parceling them out in tightfisted fashion to their own students, and seemingly deliberately holding back the unrestricted availability of that stunning treasure.

In place of the actual scrolls came wretched journalism, tacky gossip, and the tiresome conjurings of the media, filling the void of secrecy and expectation. The popular notion was that the scrolls were relevant only to the study of nascent Christianity. Very few conceived of them as a window onto early rabbinic Judaism.

All that has now come to an end. The scrolls have become accessible to scholars everywhere. And a recently published major scroll has yielded astonishing information about, of all things, the history of Judaism in the missing period between Alexander the Great and Hillel. Scholars are now beginning to establish links between biblical and rabbinic Judaism. That between-world, the first major transition time in Jewish history, is slowly rising into focus. It is quite like the beginning of the recovery of a lost public remembrance after a sustained siege of collective amnesia.

Reclaiming the Dead Sea Scrolls is a pioneering work of scholarship by a man who has made the scrolls his life's work. Its aim is, as Lawrence Schiffman puts it, "to correct a fundamental misreading" of the scrolls and to be "the first work ever written to explain their significance in understanding the history of Judaism."

There is little doubt that the book will reverberate for a long time to come. It is with great pride that The Jewish Publication Society presents this volume to the world.

Chaim Potok
Chairman
The Jewish Publication Society
Publications Committee

PREFACE

This book aims to correct a fundamental misreading of the Dead Sea Scrolls. For some forty-five years, the scholars publishing and interpreting the scrolls have focused almost singlemindedly on the scrolls' significance for our understanding of early Christianity. This is the first work ever written to explain their significance in understanding the history of Judaism.

This book sets before the public the real Dead Sea Scrolls, our most important collection of Jewish texts from the centuries before the rise of Christianity. Only through scholarly efforts to understand what the scrolls can teach us about the history of Judaism—a project in which many of us, Jews and Christians, are now involved—can we effectively learn what they have to teach us about the history of Christianity, a religious tradition that came into being only after these texts were composed and copied.

Only recently have scrolls scholars moved toward this latter focus, beginning with the discovery of the Temple Scroll in 1967. Since the release of the entire collection in 1991, prompted in large measure by public controversy and extraordinary media attention, scholars have increasingly tended to consider the scrolls in this light. Indeed, the writing of this book would not have been possible without open access to the entire collection, which has enabled me to include here texts never before discussed. At last, the Dead Sea Scrolls can be recognized for what they really were and are: the documents of various groups of Second Temple Jews whose writings were assembled by a particular sect inhabiting the Qumran settlement during the Hasmonaean and Herodian periods, about 135 B.C.E.—68 C.E.

Although this description of the corpus may seem obvious, its full implications for our understanding of both Judaism and Christianity have only recently been recognized. The popular press, however, is far behind the scholars, who despite disagreements on many specific matters of interpretation have reached virtual consensus on this central point. In fact, the media continue to provide a forum for exaggerated and irresponsible claims that the scrolls belong primarily in the Christian domain, a view that ignores their value in illuminating the history of Judaism. Almost all of the numerous books that have appeared promote impossible theories about the origins of the scrolls, and more books like these are sure to come. To a great extent, we can attribute such unfounded theories to the unfortunate secrecy that surrounded the scrolls for so long.

The study of the Dead Sea Scrolls, and their reevaluation after the granting of full access to the documents, must be conducted as an integral part of the study of the Bible. These scrolls are infused throughout with the traditions and language of the Hebrew Bible, and can be of great help in the interpretation of the authoritative religious literature of Judaism and Christianity. The appearance of this book in the Anchor Bible Reference Library, which seeks to make available the best and most recent of approaches to biblical studies, is therefore most fitting.

The first of its kind, this comprehensive study of the Dead Sea Scrolls is based on previous scholarship as well as more than twenty years of my own research and that of many colleagues. It is my hope that this study will enable readers to draw intelligent conclusions about the Dead Sea Scrolls, perhaps the most important archaeological discovery of the twentieth century.

ACKNOWLEDGMENTS

I could not have written this book without the help of many people. Much of this work was accomplished while I was a fellow of the Institute for Advanced Studies of the Hebrew University in Jerusalem in 1989-90 as part of a Qumran research group headed by Emanuel Tov and Moshe Weinfeld. I thank them for their invitation and express my appreciation to the Institute for its support then and for making its facilities available for my research in the years since then. I also want to express my thanks to Esti Eshel, who served as research assistant for our group. Soon afterwards I was appointed to join a similar group as a Fellow of the Annenberg Research Institute in 1992–93. I am grateful to the Institute (now the Center for Judaic Studies of the University of Pennsylvania) for its support. Dean C. Duncan Rice of New York University was instrumental in making possible my participation in this program, and I thank him for his generous support of my work. During those years as a Fellow I benefited from discussions with many colleagues: I especially must thank Joseph Baumgarten, Moshe Bernstein, George Brooke, Magen Broshi, Devorah Dimant, Hanan Eshel, Jonas Greenfield, Bilhah Nitzan, Émile Puech, Elisha Qimron, Eileen Schuller, John Strugnell, Shemaryahu Talmon, Emanuel Tov, Eugene Ulrich, and James VanderKam. Many ideas found in this book emerged from the presentations my colleagues gave in our seminars. I have tried to document their contributions in the Reference Notes. I cannot overstate my debt to them as well as to participants in all of the academic conferences on the scrolls, from whom I have learned so much.

The intellectual genesis of this book lies to a large extent in my reaction to the announcement of the existence of the *Halakhic Letter (Miqsat Ma'ase ha-Torah)* in a 1984 paper by Elisha Qimron and John Strugnell. Thereafter, they were kind enough to make available to me the draft of their commentary to the legal material in this text and to encourage my research on it. I have benefited immeasurably from the opportunity to read this commentary, which shaped my views on this text in many ways.

My colleagues at New York University, in the Skirball Department of Hebrew and Judaic Studies and the Hagop Kevorkian Center for Near Eastern Studies, have put up with much as a result of the Dead Sea Scrolls controversy, but they have been most helpful and understanding of all of its demands. I want to especially thank Robert Chazan, Chairman of the Skirball Department, Baruch Levine and Elliot Wolfson, with whom I have shared many discussions and who have given me both of their expertise and their encouragement. Frank Peters, especially during his years as Chairman of the Department of Near Eastern Languages and Literatures, was extremely supportive of my work. Erik Larson of NYU has worked with me on the publication of Qumran texts and has made a significant contribution to the preparation of the Reference Notes and Bibliography for this book. My students at NYU have responded with enthusiasm to the study of the smallest of fragments and have helped in my quest to get some grasp of the corpus of Qumran manuscripts as a whole.

As always, my wife Marlene has accompanied this research from its earliest beginnings through the editing of the last draft, contributing untold hours to the improvement of the book. In its final stages, Dr. Ellen Frankel, editor-in-chief of the Jewish Publication Society, the original publisher, helped to give this book its final shape and style. Rabbi Michael Monson, executive vice president of the Society, has been most helpful as well. Virtually all translations of biblical passages follow the New Jewish Publication Society translation. I wish to thank Dr. Chaim Potok for providing the Foreword to this volume.

I wish to express my gratitude to Doubleday for its decision to include the paperbound edition of this book in the prestigious Anchor Bible Reference Library. I am certain that appearance in this series will greatly stimulate interest in the reevaluation of the scrolls that this book seeks to engender.

I wish to thank the Israel Antiquities Authority, Department of Antiquities of Jordan, Israel Museum, West Semitic Research, the Ancient Biblical Manuscripts Center (ABMC), the Jewish Theological Seminary of America, Cambridge University Library, and the Biblical Archaeology Society for their help in making available the illustrations. I am particularly grateful to Marilyn Lundberg of West Semitic Research and the ABMC for her assistance. Special thanks to Bruce and Ken Zuckerman for the use of their photographs. I wish to thank Clifford A. Rieders, Esq., of Rieders, Travis, Mussina, Humphrey and Harris for legal evaluation of selected text.

The volume is dedicated to Professor Nahum M. Sarna, who first introduced me to the study of the Dead Sea Scrolls when I was an undergraduate at Brandeis University and who guided my doctoral research on the scrolls. He must have instinctively known back then that the scrolls were fertile ground for my combined interest in biblical and talmudic studies. It was he who initially suggested that I write this book for The Jewish Publication Society, long before the scrolls attained their recent popularity. From him I learned not only the methods of scholarship but also how to live the life of a scholar. No one could rival his dedication to students and community and to the tradition of objective study and teaching, to which he has dedicated his life.

INTRODUCTION

During the first week of April 1984, some 1,200 scholars assembled in Jerusalem for the first International Conference on Biblical Archaeology. I had been invited to participate in a session on Jewish law in the Dead Sea Scrolls. Already on the airplane, I ran into excited colleagues who could talk of nothing else but the upcoming conference. When I reached Jerusalem, I found the city bustling with talk of ancient ruins and arcane texts. By the time my session came around, I had been dazzled for days by fascinating presentations. Now it was finally my turn to share my research with colleagues, an opportunity I had looked forward to as the highlight of my trip. But I was in for a surprise.

Scheduled to speak at my session were the prominent scrolls scholars Elisha Qimron and John Strugnell, slated to present a joint paper entitled "An Unpublished Halakhic Letter from Qumran." Rumor had it that Qimron was going to reveal a new Dead Sea Scroll text from the still secret cave 4 materials. I had also heard that for political reasons, Strugnell would not be at the conference.

Unassumingly, Qimron ascended the podium to give his presentation. For the first time, a spellbound audience heard about a *Halakhic Letter*, a collection of legal rulings representing a foundation document for the Dead Sea sect. In his talk, Qimron claimed that this document took positions paralleling those of the Sadducees, a priestly sect from Maccabean times. In the view of Qimron and Strugnell, this document was a letter from the Teacher of Righteousness—the religious leader of the Dead Sea sect—to his opponents in Jerusalem.

It is hard to describe the audience's shock. We now realized that for forty years, this text, holding the key to many mysteries of the Dead Sea Scrolls, had been hidden from us in the recesses of the Rockefeller Museum's scrollery. As Qimron continued his presentation, we took frantic notes on the passages he quoted, so that we could bring home at least a fragment of this scroll to study even before publication of the full text.

What was so extraordinary about Qimron's revelation?

Certainly not the fact that this text had been kept from us—we all knew that much of what was in the cave 4 lot was still unpublished by the official editorial team. No, what galvanized us was the unexpected *significance* of this particular scroll. For years we in scrolls research had grudgingly accepted the status quo of withheld information and limited access for those outside the editorial team. Our hands tied, we had contented ourselves with studying the available corpus of Dead Sea Scroll texts—admittedly impressive—published in the initial years after the discovery.

But Qimron's revelation of this extraordinary scroll shattered our customary complacency. When we realized that a document so central to the history of the Qumran sect and, indeed, of Second Temple Judaism, had been withheld from the academic community for so long, we were outraged. Qimron's disclosure made us acutely aware of the unfair distribution of texts, of the existence of haves and have-nots among Dead Sea Scrolls scholars.

For the rest of the conference, all we could talk about was this amazing document. On our bus tours of archaeological sites and in the halls of the conference, those of us for whom the scrolls were our major subject of research found it impossible to talk about anything else.

Yet even we insiders did not appreciate how much this revelation would change the field of Qumran studies.

I now realize that the disclosure of even this small part of the *Halakhic Letter* played a major role in triggering the release of the entire scrolls corpus to scholars and to the public. But its greatest effect on me was to recast in a radical manner the work I had already been doing for years on the Dead Sea Scrolls and, in particular, on their relevance to the history of Jewish law. In many ways, the book that follows is strongly influenced by this text. The recent release of the entire corpus, spurred in large part by this text's disclosure, has made possible the publication of this volume. Indeed, now that the entire Qumran corpus has become available to us, we can appreciate how much the scrolls tell us about the history of ancient Judaism. Here for the first time is this vital chapter of the scrolls' story.

Discovery of the Scrolls

In 1947, a young Bedouin shepherd, searching for a lost goat, entered a cave near the shore of the Dead Sea and found seven nearly complete scrolls encased in clay jars. Immediately below the caves lay the ruins of Khirbet Qumran, a site scholars guessed was connected with the scrolls. That initial discovery touched off a widespread search by both Bedouin and archaeologists for other materials.

The most extensive find came in 1952 with the penetration of cave 4, wonderfully filled with some 550 manuscripts. The cave was located just opposite the site of Qumran itself. These were the manuscripts that provoked so much controversy, because so many of them remained unpublished and closed to most researchers for the next forty years. Among those fragmentary manuscripts lay hidden some of the most important biblical and Second Temple Jewish texts ever discovered.

My own involvement with the Dead Sea Scrolls started some twenty-five years ago with a foray into scrolls research for my senior honors thesis at Brandeis University. By the time I had completed my work, I was inescapably captivated. After graduation, I wrote a doctoral dissertation on Jewish law in the scrolls and produced several books thereafter.

What was it about the scrolls that fascinated a young Judaic scholar who had pursued biblical and talmudic studies so extensively? Why are the scrolls so important for the study of Judaism in late antiquity? What do the scrolls teach us about the origins of the rabbinic consensus that was to lay the foundation of modern Judaism?

In a nutshell, what captured my imagination was the opportunity to uncover the unknown missing links between the Judaism of the Bible and that of the Talmud and to trace the links between prophet and priest on the one hand and talmudic rabbis on the other.

In the Jewish tradition, the Oral Law—the unwritten, revealed tradition—bridges this chasm. This Oral Law, when it was finally committed to writing in the third century or later in a text known as the Mishnah, preserved traditions from a much earlier period, but unavoidably, it filtered them through the perspective of those who compiled the material centuries later. Up until the discovery of the Dead Sea Scrolls, no contemporary documentary evidence existed for the intermediate period.

Suddenly, with this discovery, we had material from that dark age: the fourth century B.C.E. through the first century C.E.—the years from Alexander the Great to Hillel. These ancient fragments speak to us across the millennia, helping us to illuminate a period about which previous generations could know very little.

The Dead Sea Scrolls Explained

In laying adequate groundwork for the exploration of the ancient library that will follow, it is important to define clearly what the Dead Sea Scrolls are—and what they are not. It is also important to explain the two ways in which the term is used. Most often, "Dead Sea Scrolls" refers specifically to the Qumran scrolls, that collection of documents discovered in the caves at Qumran, an archaeological site on the Dead Sea some eight miles south of Jericho.

But the term is also sometimes used to designate the entire corpus of materials discovered in the Judaean Desert region. According to this second definition, the Dead Sea Scrolls include several groups of documents, listed here in chronological order: (1) the Wadi el-Daliyeh papyri from the fourth century B.C.E.; (2) the Qumran corpus including scrolls copied between the third century B.C.E. and the first century C.E.; (3) the Masada texts, all copied before the destruction of Masada in 73 C.E.; (4) the Bar Kokhba documents, including letters from the revolt of 132–135 C.E. and earlier legal documents; and (5) Greek, Christian Aramaic, and Arabic materials from the Byzantine period found at Khirbet Mird (Horqaniah).

Since the Qumran scrolls are the focus of this book and of the recent controversies erupting in the news media, we will use the term "Dead Sea Scrolls" here to refer only to this collection of texts. (Occasionally, and in one of the concluding chapters, we discuss those other texts as they relate to Qumran research.)

How did this particular group of documents find their way to the Qumran caves?

Scholars agree that the Dead Sea Scrolls were probably gathered together by a sectarian group occupying a building complex at Qumran adjacent to the caves. These scrolls, containing primarily biblical texts, apocryphal literature, prayer texts, and sectarian documents, were composed over a very long period. The earliest compositions are ancient biblical materials such as the Torah—the Five Books of Moses. The collection also includes texts composed at various times during the Hellenistic period, from the fourth century B.C.E. on. It is widely recognized that most of the Aramaic documents found at Qumran were composed before the sect even came into being and then were imported to Qumran after the sect occupied the settlement. Scholars have come to term such texts "pre-Qumranian."

We must carefully distinguish between the dates the texts were *composed* and the dates they were *copied*. The documents were composed over many centuries, from the earliest days of Israelite history (before 1000 B.C.E.) up through the end of the Second Temple period (70 C.E.). They were gathered into the Qumran collection between approximately 150 B.C.E. and 68 C.E., when the Qumran settlement came to an end. The date of composition is critical to an understanding of the context of many texts, and helps us identify the historical allusions concealed in some of them. Other texts, if ordered chronologically, can help us construct a history of the thought of this unusual sect.

Although a few of the Qumran texts were copied as early as the third century B.C.E., most were copied between the second century B.C.E. and the early first century C.E. Indeed, this was the heyday of the sect and its building complex at Qumran. The community was most probably destroyed at the hands of the

Romans in 68 C.E. as part of the military campaign to crush the Great Revolt of the Jews against Rome (66–73 C.E.).

What exactly is in this collection of texts? The collection can best be described as a library. A large percentage of the scrolls come from cave 4, an artificially hewn cave only a five-minute walk from the buildings that served as the center of sectarian activity.

Judging from the regularly spaced rows of holes found in the cave's walls, we can infer that the cave had wooden shelves of some type. When the cave was abandoned, the shelves eventually rotted and collapsed, leaving the scrolls on the floor of the cave. This explains their damaged and fragmentary condition. Fortunately, other scrolls survived with little damage. These were found in neighboring caves, some in protective jars, apparently placed there to save them from destruction shortly before the conquest of Qumran by the Romans.

As in any library, the collection contains a wide variety of works valued by its collectors, not simply books composed or even copied by them. Accordingly, the Qumran caves have yielded various works providing information on the texts the sectarians valued and the views they and their opponents held, as well as those of related but not identical groups in the complex landscape of Second Temple Judaism. For this reason, not only do the scrolls let us reconstruct the views of those who gathered them, but they also shed light on a variety of trends in ancient Judaism.

Let me say a few things about what the scrolls are not. First, they are not the library of the Jerusalem Temple. Clearly, if there is anything that unifies this collection, it is its owners' *opposition* to the practices and procedures of the Temple in the hands of the priestly leadership. These, then, are the documents of the Temple's opposition, not of its leaders.

Second, the scrolls are not the documents of an early Christian sect. Contrary to claims by certain sensationalists, the scrolls never mention Jesus, John the Baptist, or James the Just, the "brother" of Jesus. Further, the scrolls in no way reflect Christian beliefs. The only way to make such an outrageous claim is to radically redefine Christianity to accord with the scrolls. In fact, the most recent carbon-14 testing has confirmed the dating that had already been established by paleography, which is the study of the shapes of Hebrew letters and of other ancient writing. Since all the material was composed before the rise of the early church, the Dead Sea Scrolls cannot refer to those events.

WHAT THE SCROLLS TEACH US

The Dead Sea Scrolls—the earliest Hebrew and Aramaic Jewish documents composed after the books of the Hebrew Bible—are our main source of information about the history of Judaism between the Bible and the Mishnah. Little other contemporary information about this period exists. Therefore, from these ancient texts it is possible to learn a great deal about the history of the Jews and Judaism in the Second Temple period as well as about the Jewish background of early Christianity.

It is my belief that the scrolls were gathered in Qumran by a sect whose members left Jerusalem in the aftermath of the Maccabean revolt. When the victorious Hasmonaean rulers (Judah the Maccabee's family) adopted the rulings of the Pharisees (forerunners of the talmudic rabbis) regarding the conduct of the Temple in about 152 B.C.E., the loyal opposition—a band of pious Sadducees—retreated to the desert, taking up residence at Qumran.

Our primary source about the Sadducean origins of this sect is the extremely important text known as the *Halakhic Letter* (*Miqṣat Maʿase ha-Torah*, or, more simply, MMT), the hidden text revealed by Elisha Qimron in 1984. From that text we have discovered that the religious legal tradition of the Dead Sea sect was primarily Sadducean. Knowing this, we can begin to reconstruct from the scrolls the nature of this priestly group's system of biblical interpretation and law, of which we knew almost nothing before. Further, it is now clear that the Dead Sea sect underwent a gradual process of development and radicalization, transforming it into the community we recognize from the sectarian scrolls. Although most scholars identify this community as the Essenes, we would like to argue that the term "Essenes" encompasses a much wider movement than this one particular sect.

The *Halakhic Letter*, along with the text known as the *Temple Scroll*, contains many polemical arguments against the Pharisees. Such arguments help us deduce numerous Pharisaic legal teachings, from which we learn that many laws enshrined in the Mishnah in about 220 C.E. already existed in the Hasmonaean period. Other texts enable us to confirm and expand on the history of the Pharisees already known from Josephus and rabbinic tradition. And this is only a small part of what we can learn from the Qumran scrolls about the major Jewish sects in Second Temple times.

In the documents specific to the Qumran sect itself, we find evidence of a highly dualistic Judaism, dividing individuals into predestined lots of good and evil. Evildoers were to be destroyed at the End of Days, expected to dawn immediately. The sect organized itself in preparation for this messianic period, closely studying the Bible for guidance and strictly adhering to Jewish law as they interpreted it.

The sect also gathered the texts of related groups, placing them in its library along with approximately 225 biblical texts. Those other compositions, some previously known, others unknown, were preserved here in the original Hebrew or Aramaic. Numerous prayer texts, those of either the sect or other groups of Jews, were also preserved, as were tefillin and mezuzot, which are quite similar to those in use today.

Thus the entire collection of scrolls makes available to us a broad range of information about the years between the close of the Hebrew biblical period (c. 400 B.C.E.) and the compilation and editing of the Mishnah (c. 220 C.E.). The scrolls provide us with a much needed perspective on this era, filling in the gaps left by the small amount of information we have about this formative period from Josephus and the talmudic sources.

Such are the secrets unlocked by the recent release of the remaining Judaean Desert manuscripts. For me, and for other scholars of ancient Judaism, these materials significantly advance our efforts to reconstruct the complex history of Judaism in this period. Although unconscionable delays in publication have slowed the progress of our research, we now can move ahead in the wake of the scrolls' release. Each new scrap of information helps us refine our theories and deepen our understanding.

QUMRAN STUDIES AT THE CROSSROADS

The field of Dead Sea Scrolls research is currently undergoing a major transformation. With the release of the entire corpus of manuscripts and the widening of the publication process, many previous interpretations and theories now must be reevaluated in light of new scholarly research.

The first generation of scrolls scholars, primarily Christians interested in either the Hebrew Bible or the New Testament, did not understand the scrolls for what they really were: documents illuminating the history of Second Temple Judaism. The few Jews who did enter the field and make contributions failed to get a fair hearing for that approach. To some extent they were hindered because many of them published only in Hebrew. Such was the case with most Israeli scholars. In addition, all Jewish scholars were denied access to the materials in Jordan because of the ongoing hostilities in the Middle East.

Accordingly, research during the first period of scrolls studies focused primarily on what the scrolls said, or could be claimed to say, about the background of Christianity. What resulted, therefore, was a Christianized interpretation of the scrolls.

More recently, both Jewish and Christian scholars have adopted a different approach, attempting to understand the scrolls in their original Jewish context. Even within New Testament studies, such an approach has become widely accepted as the only valid way to deal with these ancient texts. In light of this changed attitude, scholars have finally turned to the Jewish character of the scrolls. It is to that purpose that this book is dedicated. For the first time, we are mining these Jewish scrolls specifically for what they reveal about the history of Judaism.

There is a myth within the scrolls studies industry that even today most scrolls studies build upon a scholarly consensus originating with the earliest editorial team. Nothing could be further from the truth. Those who read the many articles on the Dead Sea Scrolls published today in scholarly journals or who attend academic conferences on the subject quickly discover that such consensus extends only to a few fundamental background facts: the dating and the archaeology of the scrolls. Some scholars have recently tried to challenge even this basic foundation of information, arguing that archaeology, paleography, and even carbon-14 dating do not constitute scientific evidence.

This book cannot silence those who prefer controversy to scientific method. But this book's job is rather to use the tools of scientific textual and historical scholarship to piece together a giant jigsaw puzzle from the minute details found on hundreds of tiny scraps of ancient leather. We will then seek to frame the emerging picture within a historical context crafted out of genuine, scholarly consensus.

Is This Book Revolutionary?

In light of the present scrolls mania, especially when it comes to exaggerated claims regarding Christianity, it is indeed revolutionary to propose that the scrolls can be understood only in the context of Jewish history.

It is revolutionary to argue that only by reading and examining a wide variety of texts from the scrolls collection can one even begin to discuss this topic.

And it is revolutionary to suggest that we should determine the scrolls' origins not through external evaluation and theoretical criteria, but rather through examination of the specific contents of the manuscripts.

It is this revolution that began for me some twenty-five years ago when I started my research on the scrolls. I invite you now to join me on this exciting intellectual journey. Here you will encounter the real Dead Sea Scrolls, not some fantastic construct invented to storm the Bastille of Christian consensus. Through an honest and responsible examination of hundreds of tattered manuscripts, we will reconstruct the past of the Jewish people and their religious tradition, coming to a new understanding of the unique approach to God and humanity that the Jews have bequeathed to the world.

The Dead Sea Scrolls Speak to Us Today

The Dead Sea Scrolls have more to offer us than obscure knowledge about ancient history and antiquarian curiosities. They have come to life anew in our own day, specifically because they indirectly address issues confronting us in our own times. This in large measure explains the intense public interest in the scrolls and in the scholars who study them.

The scrolls speak to us across the centuries about the issue of pluralism in Judaism. Through them, we gain a glimpse of an era characterized by several competing approaches to Judaism, each claiming a monopoly on the true interpretation of the Torah. All these approaches, with the exception of the extreme Hellenizers, demanded observance of the Torah's commandments. They differed only on certain theological issues and in the particular rulings of the Law and its interpretation. Yet although their disputes are different from those dividing our communities today, we can benefit by studying how these groups interacted with each other and negotiated their diverse approaches.

The scrolls can also help us clarify our own relationship to the Land of Israel. As with every major archaeological find in Israel today, the discovery of these ancient scrolls binds contemporary Jews to their past through the land. For it was there that so much of ancient Jewish history took place. And it is there that the future of the Jewish people is now being shaped. As archaeology rediscovers the past, it is also creating the present. The issues that the Dead Sea Scrolls raise—God, Torah, messiah, holiness—still powerfully resonate as the modern state of Israel gropes toward its own identity.

Finally, the scrolls can help us forge better relations between Jewish and Christian communities. Now, after two millennia of strife, the two faiths, so deeply linked by common origins, are establishing a new relationship in the aftermath of the Holocaust. Here the scrolls speak to us again, showing precisely how Christianity emerged from currents in ancient Judaism much more widespread in the period than we previously imagined. This new understanding calls on Christians to continue the process of the shedding of anti-Semitism and to join with Jews in eradicating it. At the same time, the new understanding calls on Jews to respect, even when they do not accept, aspects of their neighbors' faith, since these aspects derive more from ancient Jewish roots than we once thought.

Yet, we should be careful not to take these comparisons with modern times too far. We are still obligated to study the scrolls within the context in which they were composed, copied, and gathered. And we must base these studies on the most scientific approaches possible, for the job of the scholar of antiquity is to reconstruct ancient reality as authentically as possible, not to shape the past in the image of the present. The reconstruction of the ancient Jewish past is precisely the intention of the present study.

SCOPE AND METHOD OF THIS BOOK

Since the time of the full release of the "hidden" scrolls, and in light of the growing recognition of their Jewish content, it is now especially appropriate to study what the scrolls reveal to us about the history of Judaism. Such a study must be based on an understanding of the historical context of the nonbiblical texts, the history of the sect itself, the archaeology of Qumran, and a description of the scope and contents of the library as a whole. Further, the study must seek to avoid the prejudices of the previous generation of Qumran scholars, to eschew the influences of confessionalism (the tendency to reach scholarly judgments based on one's own religious beliefs), and to provide a balanced picture of the content and significance of the scrolls.

We will begin with the dramatic discovery and publication history of the Dead Sea Scrolls. Then we will turn to the archaeology of the Qumran site and the historical background of Second Temple times. Next we will examine the contents of the documents themselves, investigating the sect and its beliefs. These texts provide the key to understanding what the sectarian library can tell us about other groups of Jews and other approaches to Judaism in that period. Here are the real aims of this book: To interpret the Qumran materials within the context of the wider history of Judaism and then to use these materials to understand the religious situation of the rest of Israel at this time.

In that spirit, we will discuss what the scrolls reveal about such topics as the history of Jewish biblical interpretation. Not only do the Qumran documents illuminate the tradition of biblical interpretation practiced at the time they were gathered, but they also point forward to interpretive approaches that shaped the later history of Judaism.

In addition, the scrolls cast new light on our understanding of ancient Jewish law and messianism, each the focus of substantial discussion within the book. Toward the end of the volume, we will look at the sect's distinctive notions about the nature of the Jewish people and its holy city. Finally, we will show how the Masada and Bar Kokhba documents clarify the shift from sectarianism to consensus in the aftermath of the destruction of the Temple in 70 C.E.

Because the Qumran texts represent primarily the teachings of groups that only indirectly influenced the development of rabbinic Judaism, we have to avoid oversimplified judgments. Nevertheless, these materials show much greater interrelation of the various approaches to Judaism than has previously been assumed. In fact, we can learn much from the sect's polemics with its neighbors. Because much of the polemical literature opposes the Pharisees—the spiritual and intellectual ancestors of the talmudic rabbis—we can now better understand the prehistory and early history of rabbinic traditions, which are based on the Pharisaic approach.

The scrolls have indeed been rediscovered, and the excitement they generate today is no less than when they were first unearthed almost half a century ago. A new generation of scholars, both Jewish and Christian, is now engaged in their publication and interpretation. As research progresses and as the remaining texts are published, we will understand much better how rabbinic Judaism is rooted in Pharisaism and how Jewish belief and practice were translated into Christianity and other sects.

Indeed, these ancient scrolls hold out great promise. They can provide us with a much deeper and more sophisticated appreciation of the various approaches to Judaism current in the Second Temple period and of the crucial role they played in the unfolding history of the religious traditions of the Western world.

PART I

Discovery and Disclosure: Liberating the Scrolls

CHAPTER 1

Shepherds and Scholars:
Secrets of the Caves

To understand the mystique of the Dead Sea Scrolls, we need to begin with the strange saga of their discovery and the abortive attempt to publish them. It will then become clear how the finds themselves and the strange events surrounding the publication process are intimately linked both with the way the scrolls have been read and interpreted and with the question of who was given access to them.

DISCOVERY AND ACQUISITION, 1947–1956

The Dead Sea Scrolls were not discovered all at once in 1947. We have several accounts from antiquity and the Middle Ages about scrolls discovered in the region of Jericho. These previously discovered scrolls may have reached certain circles that influenced Karaism, a medieval Jewish sectarian movement that has certain parallels to the Dead Sea sect.

In modern times, the earliest scroll materials to be discovered were two partial medieval manuscripts of the *Zadokite Fragments*, also called the *Damascus Document* by many scholars. These manuscripts came to the attention of Solomon Schechter in 1896, when he retrieved them from the Cairo *genizah*, a storehouse for old books and documents in the Ben Ezra Synagogue in Fustat, Old Cairo. Manuscripts of the very same text were later found in the Qumran collection. It is now clear that this document was a central sectarian text.

The story of the discovery of the first hoard of Dead Sea Scrolls in cave 1 at Qumran by a Bedouin shepherd has been rehearsed often. Despite the momentousness of the occasion, the story actually pertains only to the first seven scrolls. That initial discovery was followed by many more. Ultimately, the collection included fragments of some 850 scrolls from Qumran, not to mention the other Judaean Desert sites where scrolls were found by Bedouin or archaeolo-

Medieval Manuscript A of the *Zadokite Fragments*   The finding
of the *Zadokite Fragments* among the manuscripts of the Cairo
genizah provided information on the Dead Sea sect even before
the scrolls were discovered at Qumran. This page, referring to the
earliest history of the sect, was thought to be the beginning of the
composition, but we now know from the Qumran manuscripts
that at least one page preceded it. *With permission of the Syndics
of the Cambridge University Library (U.L.C. 10.K.6).*

Manuscript Finds in the Judaean Desert

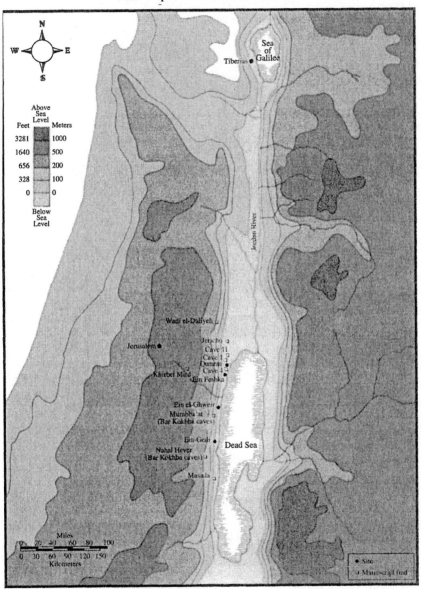

gists. The spectacular controversy over unreleased documents that was to erupt years later involved only the finds of cave 4, discovered in 1952.

In the winter of 1947 (perhaps fall 1946), a Bedouin shepherd named Mohammed edh-Dhib from the Ta'amireh tribe went searching for a lost goat near the shore of the Dead Sea. Chancing upon the opening to a cave, he threw in a stone and heard the sound of the stone's hitting pottery. In the cave, he found seven almost complete scrolls encased in protective pottery jars. Realizing that they might be able to sell these scrolls, the Bedouin shepherd and his friends brought them in the spring of 1947 to a shoemaker in Bethlehem named Khalil Eskander Shahin, who also doubled as an antiquities dealer. Kando, as he was popularly known, soon became the agent for the Bedouin as they continued to recover scrolls from the Judaean Desert.

In July 1947, Kando sold four of the scrolls to the Syrian Metropolitan Athanasius Yeshue Samuel of St. Mark's Syrian Orthodox Church in Jerusalem. Since the scrolls' antiquity was not yet recognized, they were sold for a pittance. At the same time, another antiquities dealer, Feidi Salahi, offered two scrolls for sale to the Jerusalem archaeologist Eleazar L. Sukenik. Sukenik, father of the prominent Israeli archaeologist Yigael Yadin, had founded the Institute of Archaeology at the Hebrew University and was the leading expert on Jewish antiquities in the Jewish community of Palestine. He immediately recognized the antiquity of the texts from their script, which resembled that of some Second Temple period inscriptions he knew. He succeeded in buying these two scrolls, as well as several fragments, on behalf of the Hebrew University and the Jewish Agency. On December 22, Sukenik acquired another scroll from the same source.

He had acquired, then, three of the seven scrolls found by the Bedouin in cave 1: a manuscript of the biblical Book of Isaiah; the *Thanksgiving Hymns,* a collection of sectarian hymns; and the *Scroll of the War of the Sons of Light against the Sons of Darkness,* a manual for the messianic battle expected by the Qumran sect.

The initial identification of the scrolls by Sukenik took place between the November 1947 UN vote in favor of the Partition Plan for Palestine and the Declaration of Independence of the State of Israel on May 14, 1948. By this time, in the difficult months leading up to the Declaration of Independence of the new state, relations between Arabs and Jews were at best strained. Taking great risks, Sukenik doggedly continued his pursuit of the scrolls.

In late January 1948, Sukenik was shown the other four scrolls by Anton Kiraz, an associate of the Metropolitan. The four consisted of another scroll of Isaiah; *Rule of the Community,* a sectarian rule book; *Pesher Habakkuk,* a sectarian scriptural commentary; and *Genesis Apocryphon,* a retelling of parts of the Book of Genesis. On February 6, Sukenik returned the scrolls to Kiraz, telling him that he wished to purchase them for the soon-to-be-declared state of Israel. But Sukenik had trouble organizing the purchase, and in the meantime, intervening political changes made it impossible for him to continue the negotiations. Eventually, these scrolls were acquired by his son, archaeologist Yigael Yadin, but not until 1954.

Rather than going ahead with the sale to Sukenik, the Metropolitan continued to investigate other possibilities. In late February 1948, the Metropolitan's assistant took three of the same scrolls to the American Schools of Oriental Research (ASOR) in East Jerusalem to get another opinion. The American Schools in Jerusalem, now known as the Albright Institute (in memory of the late William Foxwell Albright, dean of U.S. biblical archaeologists), was and still is a major center for U.S. archaeological activity in the Land of Israel. In the absence of the director, the scrolls found their way to a young graduate student, John C. Trever, who was an expert in photography. Trever concluded that they appeared ancient, although his own memoirs reveal that he had little real knowledge of Hebrew. He succeeded in getting the Metropolitan's permission to photograph three scrolls (excluding *Genesis Apocryphon*). He took the photographs in both black and white and color, demonstrating consummate mastery of his craft.

By the time archaeologists began to investigate the location from which the scrolls had come, the state of Israel had been declared on May 14, 1948, and the War of Independence had begun.

The results were of great importance for the future of the Dead Sea Scrolls. The area of Qumran, the provenance of the scrolls, had previously been part of British Mandatory Palestine. When Israel's Arab neighbors invaded immediately after the Declaration of Independence, the Jordanian Arab legion swarmed across the Jordan River and occupied the West Bank. From that moment until the transfer of territorial sovereignty after the Six-Day War, Qumran manuscript purchases and archaeological excavation remained in the hands of officials of the Jordanian Antiquities Department and those designated by them.

Locating cave 1 for archaeological study was a difficult task, especially since the Bedouin, who still expected to find additional treasures nearby, were reluctant to talk. The cave was found by a detachment of British and Jordanian troops after a seventy-two-hour, meter-by-meter search of the cliffs. In February 1949, G. Lancaster Harding, director of the Jordanian Antiquities Department, and Roland de Vaux of the École Biblique—the French biblical and archaeological school in Jerusalem—undertook the excavation of cave 1.

In the spring of 1950, ASOR published photographs and transcriptions of two of the scrolls in the possession of the Metropolitan; editions of the *Isaiah A Scroll*, which preserved virtually the entire biblical Book of Isaiah; and *Pesher Habakkuk*. A year later, ASOR published *Rule of the Community*. In order to

Solomon Schechter taught at Cambridge University and was later president of the Jewish Theological Seminary in New York. At the end of the nineteenth century he discovered what was later identified as the first Dead Sea Scroll text, the *Zadokite Fragments*, in the Cairo *genizah*. *Courtesy of the Ratner Center for the Study of Conservative Judaism of the Jewish Theological Seminary of America.*

Eleazar L. Sukenik was the first to recognize the antiquity of the Dead Sea Scrolls after their discovery in 1947. He had founded the Institute for Archaeology of the Hebrew University and had published numerous studies on ancient synagogues. Shown here examining the *Thanksgiving Hymns*, Sukenik was also the first to connect the scrolls with the Essenes. *Photograph by Fred Csasznik. Courtesy of the Institute for Archaeology of the Hebrew University.*

Roland de Vaux (center, with beard) and his editorial team conducted the archaeological excavations at Qumran and began the process of piecing together the fragmentary scrolls. On de Vaux's right is J. T. Milik; on his left is Jean Starcky; John Allegro is to the far right of the picture. *Courtesy of the executors of the estate of John Allegro.*

The Qumran Caves

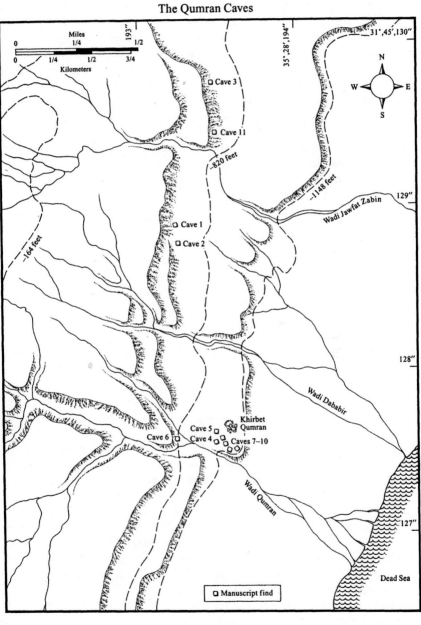

convince the Metropolitan to permit publication of his scrolls, ASOR had assured him that publication would raise their monetary value. This promise turned out to be a pipe dream.

After completion of the excavation of cave 1, it was natural to turn to the excavation of Khirbet Qumran (*khirbeh* is Arabic for "ruin"). From November 24 through December 12, 1951, de Vaux and Harding conducted the first season of excavations there. Their efforts yielded coins and pottery, confirming the connection between the caves from which the scrolls had come and the adjoining site, as well as establishing the dating of the scrolls.

By this time, the Bedouin, realizing the value of these fragments, had stepped up their efforts to locate additional caves. The biggest treasure came to light in the first part of September 1952, when Bedouin discovered caves 4 and 6 at Qumran. Once the materials were finally pieced together, cave 4 would yield a bountiful harvest: fragments of some 550 manuscripts. Ironically, archaeologists working only about a five-minute walk away from this cave had missed it entirely.

In 1952, the growing volume of manuscript finds and excavated artifacts prompted the Jordanian authorities to arrange for analysis and publication of the scrolls. Harding appointed de Vaux to the post of editor in chief. The work was thereafter subsidized by the Palestine Archaeological Museum (PAM), now the Rockefeller Museum. In 1954, a large donation was secured for this purpose from John D. Rockefeller, who agreed to fund the project for six years, defraying the expenses of the scholars in Jerusalem, the secretarial staff, photography, and preservation. Large sums were also provided for the purchase of material by the PAM. The materials were to be stored and restored in the PÅM and to be published by Oxford University Press in the series Discoveries in the Judaean Desert.

Almost all of the photography was done by Najib Anton Albina, mainly during the years 1954 to 1960. Originally the photographer for the PAM, he devoted himself almost exclusively to the production of photographic plates of the Judaean Desert texts during those years. After mastering the techniques of infrared photography, he took three sets of photos of each of most of the texts, representing different stages in the process of sorting and joining the fragments. In many cases, these photographs remain the best documentation we have of the texts, some of which have since deteriorated or lost letters around the edges during various stages of storage, research, and preservation.

The conditions in the PAM during that period were primitive at best. Scholars working on the scrolls never had enough room to work, and there were no assistants provided. Worst of all, no attention was paid to conservation and preservation. Scholars used Scotch tape or the gummed edges of postage stamps to attach fragments as they were being assembled. Sunlight streaming into the room bathed the ancient manuscripts, leading to further decay. Coffee cups and cigarettes were a common sight, and we can only imagine what toll they may have taken on the fragile scrolls.

EARLY PUBLICATION EFFORTS, 1953–1967

De Vaux limited the initial assignments for publication to his colleagues at the École Biblique: Pierre Benoit, Jozef T. Milik, and Maurice Baillet. The three were responsible for archaeological reports, the sorting of the jigsaw puzzle of cave 4 fragments, transcription, and publication of the texts. By the spring of 1953, the enormous volume of materials had led to the formation of the International Team, a group of scholars made up of representatives of various archaeological schools and missions then active in Jordanian East Jerusalem. As might be expected, the group included no Israeli or Jewish scholars. Each of the scholars was expected to find individual financial support and remain in Jerusalem for an extended period in order to edit and publish the manuscripts.

The Protestant and Catholic scholars of the ASOR, the École Biblique, and a variety of other Christian institutions in East Jerusalem were assigned lots of manuscripts to prepare for publication. Institutional and interdenominational politics no doubt played a major role in determining which institutions sent representatives to the team. Many have argued that such considerations also helped to decide who would be among the fortunate few. Yet the evidence suggests that in some cases, de Vaux did not even know the members of the team before their arrival. Apparently, little thought had gone into the planning of ways to organize the vast amount of data, who was best qualified for the project, what kind of funding would be necessary, and what would happen in the event of unreasonable delays.

The popular media has characterized the group as overwhelmingly Catholic. In fact, however, the original team of cave 4 editors consisted of four Protestants and four Catholics, although one of the Protestants, John Allegro, was already an agnostic, and another, John Strugnell, would later convert to Catholicism. The exclusion of Israelis and even of Diaspora Jews from that process has been linked to the political situation at the time or the anti-Semitic sentiments of some of the scholars involved. Indeed, most of the editors openly aligned themselves with the Arab cause until well after the 1967 war.

The first scholar to become involved in the new team was Frank Moore Cross Jr., who went on to become an eminent professor at Harvard. Cross was assigned responsibility for the publication of most of the biblical scrolls. His most important contribution to Qumran studies was his paleographic analysis of the history of the scripts, published in 1961. That analysis made possible the dating of fragments with such accuracy that when the more precise method of carbon-14 dating was later applied, Cross's dates were more or less confirmed.

In fall 1953, Milik and Cross began working together on the cave 4 material in the "scrollery," the room where scroll fragments were being sorted. Milik had a large lot of fragments assigned to him, including tefillin (phylacteries), mezuzot (small parchment scrolls), Targum (Aramaic Bible translation), pseudohistorical texts, rule books, benedictions, calendrical materials, apocrypha and pseudepigrapha, and business documents. Milik went on to publish more than any of the other scholars. But even his extraordinary productivity could not compensate for the fact that he was assigned many more texts than was reasonable.

By November, it had become apparent that the Jordanian government lacked the necessary funds to keep this important historical treasure from falling into the hands of private collectors. Accordingly, the authorities decided to invite foreign academic institutions to purchase fragments. Between 1954 and 1959, manuscripts were purchased by McGill University of Montreal, the Vatican, the Universities of Manchester and Heidelberg, McCormick Theological Seminary in Chicago, All Souls Church in New York, and Oxford University.

By the time 1953 drew to a close, the scholars working in the PAM had identified some seventy manuscripts from among the cave 4 collection. Additional manuscripts continued to come in as archaeological excavations proceeded.

Then the Syrian Metropolitan decided to redouble his efforts to sell the four large manuscripts in his possession. Although he had tried for years to peddle his scrolls, he had met with little success. He had even exhibited them at the Library of Congress in an attempt to attract buyers. Despite ASOR's assurances to the contrary, the publication of these texts had in fact lowered their value. Stymied, the Metropolitan placed an advertisement in the *Wall Street Journal* of June 1, 1954, suggesting that the scrolls "would be an ideal gift to an educational or religious institution."

The advertisement was brought to the attention of Yigael Yadin, then on a lecture tour of the United States. With the assistance of the Israeli government, Yadin immediately made arrangements to purchase the scrolls through an intermediary. Before the purchase was finalized, Harry Orlinsky of Hebrew Union College–Jewish Institute of Religion in New York, using an assumed name and under conditions of great secrecy, inspected the scrolls and authenticated them. On July 1, 1954, the scrolls came into the possession of the State of Israel. Soon after, the cost of those scrolls, the sum of $250,000, was donated by Samuel Gottesman of New York, allowing Yadin to repay the loan with which he had paid for the scrolls. The texts were eventually housed in the Shrine of the Book of the Israel Museum, where they remain today.

At about the same time, John Strugnell of Jesus College of Oxford University joined the scrollery. Beside Milik, he was the most consistent in his scrollery work in the 1950s. His assignment was a large lot of paraphrases of the Pentateuch, pseudoprophetic texts, hymns, and liturgical and sapient texts. Since he

Yigael Yadin, a soldier, statesman, and archaeologist, was also Israel's leading scrolls scholar. He edited the *Genesis Apocryphon* with Nahman Avigad, the *War Scroll*, and the *Temple Scroll*, which he is here shown examining. In his excavations, Yadin also uncovered the Masada scrolls in addition to numerous Bar Kokhba letters and documents. *Photograph by Zev Radovan. Courtesy of the Institute for Archaeology of the Hebrew University.*

John Strugnell, first of Oxford University and later of Harvard, was a member of the original scrolls editorial team and was appointed editor in chief in 1984. Together with Elisha Qimron, he edited the *Halakhic Letter* and produced an extensive commentary on it. The announcement of that text was a critical factor in the call for release of the scrolls. *Photograph by Lawrence H. Schiffman.*

Frank M. Cross and Eugene Ulrich are shown here at the Madrid Scrolls Congress held in 1991. Cross, of Harvard University, was one of the members of the original editorial team; he dated the biblical scrolls based on paleography and was later proven correct by carbon-14 dating. Ulrich, of the University of Notre Dame, had reorganized the publication of the biblical scrolls even before public demand for access to the scrolls began. *Photograph by Lawrence H. Schiffman.*

had managed to publish only very few of them himself, Strugnell eventually turned many of these over for publication to his students at Harvard, where he taught for many years. Strugnell was eventually to rise to the position of editor in chief. It was during his tenure that the pressure for full release of all of the scrolls came to a head.

In 1955, Sukenik's edition of a scroll of Isaiah (*Isaiah B*), the *Thanksgiving Hymns*, and the *War Scroll* was published posthumously. Thus, by 1955, all of the scrolls in the possession of the Israelis had been published except *Genesis Apocryphon*, which, owing to its fragile condition, was not successfully unrolled until 1956.

In the winter and spring of 1955, excavations revealed four additional caves which had collapsed—caves 7–10. These caves yielded small numbers of texts. January 1956 brought the discovery of cave 11 by Bedouin. The Jordanian government sold to various institutions the rights to publication as a means of financing the purchase. The main purchasers were ASOR—through the generosity of the Bechtel family—and the Royal Academy of the Netherlands. Among the ASOR lot was an *Ezekiel Scroll*, which could never be opened because of its poor state of preservation, and the *Psalms Scroll*, which was published by James A. Sanders in 1965. The Dutch purchased the *Job Targum* and a number of other extremely important manuscripts. The largest of the cave 11 scrolls, the *Temple Scroll*, was acquired by Yadin for Israel from Kando only after the Six-Day War.

In 1956, de Vaux and his colleagues undertook a preliminary investigation at Ein Feshka, near the Dead Sea. (This site was eventually identified as an offshoot and industrial zone of the inhabitants of Qumran. It was officially excavated in 1958.) On June 1 of that same year, the *Copper Scroll*, a list of buried treasures allegedly hidden in the Judaean wilderness, was revealed to the public after it had been sawed apart and deciphered.

That year, the politics of the Middle East and the Arab-Israeli conflict once again interfered in Dead Sea Scrolls research. As a direct result of both Egypt's nationalization of the Suez Canal and Arab raids into Israel, together Israel, Britain, and France attacked Egypt in the 1956 Sinai Campaign. That military confrontation led to the dispersal of the International Team. For the duration of the hostilities, the scrolls were temporarily removed to Amman for safekeeping.

In the fall of that year, the five legible columns of *Genesis Apocryphon*, the last of the Israeli scroll acquisitions to be published, appeared in the edition prepared by Yigael Yadin and Nahman Avigad. With the publication of that volume, Israeli scholars had completed their obligation to publish the Qumran scrolls in their possession.

Research on the scrolls was now sufficiently advanced to necessitate creation of a concordance—an index of all the occurrences of each word—to aid in interpretation of the material. In July 1957, Joseph Fitzmyer began to compile the concordance on index cards. He was joined by Raymond Brown and William G. Oxtoby. Their project was halted in 1960, when Rockefeller's funding ended, except for some additions by Javier Teixidor. Both Fitzmyer and Brown went on to become distinguished contributors to Qumran studies, Fitzmyer emerging as a leading expert on the Aramaic materials and on the relationship of the scrolls to the New Testament. It was that concordance that would eventually lead to the International Team's undoing and the end of their monopoly.

In July 1958, the last of the cave 4 texts were purchased from Kando by the Jordanian authorities, bringing to a close an important stage in the history of Qumran research. Those fragments, however, would wait years before seeing the light of day and, indeed, are only now being published.

Throughout that period, Israeli archaeologists had watched with great interest as Bedouin continuously unearthed scrolls in the Jordanian-controlled part of the Judaean Desert. In March 1955, the first season of an archaeological survey was carried out at Masada, the Herodian desert fortress farther south on the shore of the Dead Sea. Participating in this project were the Hebrew University, the Israel Exploration Society, and the Israel Department of Antiquities. Masada had been the last stand of the rebels in the Jewish revolt against Rome in 66–73 C.E. Archaeologists would find at Masada some of the same texts found at Qumran.

In the spring of 1960, John M. Allegro published his edition of the *Copper Scroll*. He had gained access to the scroll because as a member of the International Team, he had supervised its unrolling in Manchester. Even though this scroll had been officially assigned to Milik for publication, Allegro preempted him by publishing an unauthorized edition. Not surprisingly, Allegro's edition caused great friction within the team, whose members never forgave him for this betrayal nor for his exaggerated claims that the scrolls had explosive implications for the Christian faith. That same spring, Allegro conducted an expedition to try to find the treasures mentioned in the scroll, but he came up empty-handed. This quest continues even to the present day.

When funding by the Rockefeller family came to an end in June 1960, the members of the International Team scattered to their various universities. By this time, the work of sorting the entire collection had been basically completed. Almost all of the texts had been transcribed in preliminary fashion. Had publication followed quickly, members of the International Team would have emerged as heroes, acclaimed for their expert and speedy work. But such was not to be the case. The many delays that occurred after they left Jerusalem, coupled with the denial of access to other scholars, eventually led to intense controversy.

When the International Team disbanded, de Vaux wrote letters to the various institutions that had purchased scrolls, informing them that work on the scrolls was now complete. The next step was for those institutions to apply to the Jordanian government for export permits. On July 27, 1960, that government made the wise decision to cancel such arrangements, deciding instead to keep the scrolls in Jordan and to reimburse the various institutions for their contributions toward purchase of the scrolls.

By June 1961, 511 manuscripts of cave 4 had been identified, arranged on 620 museum plates; 25 plates of material remained unidentified. The final series of photographs was also completed at that time.

In November 1966, the Jordanian government, in an effort to control its national archaeological treasures, decided to nationalize the Palestine Archaeological Museum. The following spring, when Israel conquered East Jerusalem in the Six-Day War, its Department of Antiquities assumed control of this important collection of unpublished Dead Sea Scrolls.

In the aftermath of the war, Yadin acquired the *Temple Scroll* from Kando. That purchase ended a drama begun in 1960. At that time, a certain Reverend Joe Uhrig had offered the scroll to Yadin, supplying him a small sample and securing in return a deposit of $10,000. Yadin never heard from Uhrig again. In 1967, Yadin learned that the scroll was now in Kando's hands. In the early days of the war, Yadin sent a detachment of soldiers to Kando's house in Bethlehem, where they seized the scroll, thereby saving it from the rot that was destroying it under Kando's floorboards. Later, Kando was compensated with a payment of $108,000.

Although the conquest of East Jerusalem in the 1967 war was originally not the aim of the Israeli government, it changed its plans when Jordan began shelling Israeli West Jerusalem. In the wake of the bombing, the Israelis pressed on to capture and unify Jerusalem. During intense hand-to-hand fighting, Israeli soldiers entered the Palestine Archaeological Museum, where they found virtually all of the Dead Sea Scrolls safe and intact. Soon after the war, the museum was reopened to the public and renamed the Rockefeller Museum in commemoration of the major financial support the Rockefeller family had provided in the past. A few scrolls on exhibit in Amman when the war broke out still remain there along with the *Copper Scroll*.

CHRISTIANIZATION OF THE SCROLLS

From its beginnings, the publication process was profoundly affected by the physical location of the scrolls and the politics of the scholars involved. Perhaps the most serious cost was the exclusion of Jews, and certainly of Israelis, from the editorial team from the 1950s through the late 1980s.

The silencing of Jewish scholars had a number of negative ramifications for the interpretation and publication history of the scrolls. Until Jewish scholars entered the conversations about the scrolls' contents, an entire genre of Christianizing studies was being published, interpreting the material as if it were a collection of proto-Christian rather than Jewish texts. Furthermore, because many

Jewish scholars best trained in the reading of Hebrew manuscripts and in their analysis were not included in this work, the pace of publication was seriously retarded. When the controversy finally erupted in 1991, some 50 percent of the titles—but actually only 25 percent of the material—still remained unpublished.

Perhaps most important, the texts considered most Jewish in nature—legal texts and other such documents—were the last to be edited, because the scholars charged with editing and publishing the scrolls were most at home with the Bible, but least comfortable with these Jewish legal texts.

In light of some of the accusations that have appeared in the popular media, it is important to maintain a proper perspective on the matter. I am not claiming that the scholars who eventually composed the International Team deliberately hid the scrolls because of any fears about the scrolls' possibly explosive effects on Christianity. Nor am I arguing that those scholars sought to unduly distance the material, either chronologically or theologically, from Christianity. On the contrary, it is my contention that they attempted all too much to describe the material in Christian terms, never really confronting the Jewish character of the corpus.

So why were the scrolls kept secret for so long?

The answers are, in reality, rather prosaic. Those who were supposed to publish them failed for a variety of reasons: Their efforts were insufficiently funded. Some lost interest. Some succumbed to alcoholism. Some died. Some lacked sufficient linguistic skills to do the job in a reasonable amount of time. Selfishly, they continued to believe both that only they could do the job correctly and that they and the students they chose had rights to the material in perpetuity.

Another consequence of the Christianizing approach has been the tenacity of the Essene theory. Soon after the Qumran scrolls were unearthed, it became the prevailing view that the sect described in the scrolls was none other than the elusive sectarian group termed the Essenes—a theory previously championed based on evidence from the *genizah* manuscripts of the *Zadokite Fragments*. First suggested by Sukenik, that theory was fully developed in a series of works, the most important of which was that written by Cross. The theory took its cue from descriptions of the Essenes by the ancient authors Philo Judaeus, Josephus, and Pliny the Elder. Numerous parallels to the Dead Sea Scrolls could be cited in their descriptions pointing to this identification. However, important differences were ignored. Scholars used the material from Philo, Josephus, and Pliny as a means of interpreting the scrolls and vice versa, thus giving rise to a circular process. This amalgam of material was then used in searching for Christian origins that, the theory held, might be found in the library of the Essenes.

It is hard to believe that this approach prevailed for so long. Even the most casual reader of the scrolls can see that they are clearly Jewish texts. Yet that self-evident fact has not stopped some scholars from producing an entire genre of materials describing and analyzing the texts as though they were precursors of Christianity. These studies also largely ignore the legal materials, placing emphasis instead on such notions as eschatology—the doctrine of the End of Days. Although it is true that the scrolls illuminate much about the background of Christianity, it is not true that they are proto-Christian documents. Despite this fact, however, confessionalists often picture the sect in terms derived from the New Testament, interpreting the New Testament in light of the scrolls. By importing the terminology of the early church into Qumran, many scholars have created the false impression that the sect and early Christianity were much closer than they in fact were.

To show how important terminology can be, let me present a composite portrait of the sect as drawn from these Christianizing analyses:

The monks of Qumran were ascetics who practiced a baptismal rite and were led by a Teacher of Righteousness. They ate together in a refectory after taking ablutions, and they shared a Eucharist of bread and wine. After the teacher died, they were led by an *episkopos* (bishop). They practiced community of goods and dedicated themselves to the healing of the sick and the clothing of the poor. They composed hymns in which they praised God, and they eagerly awaited a savior who combined priestly and Davidic aspects. The monks copied manuscripts in the scriptorium, leaving us the Dead Sea Scrolls.

Correspondingly, the same community could be reconfigured in Jewish terms:

The inhabitants of Qumran were observant Jews who practiced ritual purity and were led by their Rabbi, a Teacher of Righteousness. They ate communal meals in their dining room after immersion in the *mikveh* (ritual bath). They recited *ha-motzi* over the bread before the meal and made a special *berakhah* (blessing) over wine. After the teacher died, they were led by another Rabbi. They were always willing to lend their possessions to others and dedicated themselves to the *mitzvah* (commandment) of healing the sick and giving charitable donations to clothe the poor. They composed prayers in which they praised God, and they eagerly awaited a messiah who combined priestly and Davidic aspects. The scribes among the sect copied their most important texts for their library, leaving us the Dead Sea Scrolls.

Both of these descriptions, made up by me, demonstrate how easy it is for language and terminology to influence our perception of the scrolls.

Christianizing the scrolls is not, as previously mentioned, the only way Christian readers have interpreted the scrolls. In fact, there has been something of an internal Christian debate over the scrolls' meaning. Conservative Christians, wanting to accent the uniqueness of Jesus and his contribution to the rise of the Christian church, emphasize the Jewish character of Qumran, even its halakhic nature.

More liberal Christians, on the other hand, tend to see Christianity as closer in origin to Judaism, experiencing its birth pangs even before Jesus. To them, Jesus emerged out of the circumstances that gave rise to the messianic movement he represented, although they probably would not state it so strongly. To these scholars, Qumran can best be understood as closer in spirit and practice to early Christianity. Therefore they neglect the specifically Jewish elements, like law, purity, and other practices.

For the first twenty years of scrolls studies, the internal Christian debates were carried on almost as if the Jewish elements in the scrolls were meaningless. The only issue that mattered was how Christian the scrolls were. It was that issue that largely determined the public agenda. Jewish scholars who contributed to scrolls research, such as the talmudist Saul Lieberman, were relegated to the sidelines, skirting around the edges of scrolls scholarship. Even the seminal work of Sukenik became insignificant as new editions appeared. Jacob Licht's masterful Hebrew commentaries on the *Thanksgiving Hymns* and the *Rule Scroll* were not read, and Yadin's *War Scroll*, a definitive work, was honored but not really fathomed. Although Chaim Rabin's edition of the *Zadokite Fragments* became standard, the impact of his commentary and accompanying studies was minimal. Every other element was emphasized save the uniquely Jewish one, the aspect that could illumine the later development of Judaism.

Much of the interpretive confusion would not have come about had the texts been published in a different order. But because the most characteristically Jewish material was kept for last, it is the Christian interpretation of the scrolls that has dominated until now. When the whole is out, scholars will no doubt recognize the untenability of that approach, but by then that view may have irreversibly penetrated and permeated popular literature. So are myths created and preserved.

The Six-Day War of 1967 marked the turning point in scrolls studies. The return of the scrolls to the Jewish people was not a merely administrative matter; it profoundly affected the texts' interpretation and the matter of access to them. It is to this story that we now turn.

CHAPTER 2

Scholars, Scrolls,
and Scandals

The Israeli conquest of East Jerusalem set off a chain of events that ultimately led to the release of all of the Dead Sea Scrolls and made it possible for us to understand more fully the secrets of the ancient library at Qumran. But when Israel took control of the scrolls in 1967, that understanding still lay almost twenty-five years into the future. Not until the 1990s would the publication project be reorganized and the Qumran documents made available for general scholarly research. And even after full release of the scrolls, we have yet to see within the scholarly and popular understanding the reassertion of their Jewish character.

THE DISPUTE OVER PUBLICATION AND RELEASE, 1967–1991

Immediately after the Six-Day War, Israeli officials agreed to let the Christian scrolls scholars continue their work, expecting that the work would soon be completed. In retrospect, this constituted a clearly naive decision. It was impossible for the scholars ever to finish their task, for their allotments were simply too large for publication within a reasonable time. Some were even assigned to publish more scrolls than any individual could handle in a lifetime. Some died, bequeathing their texts to their students, who themselves failed to publish them. Yet the editorial team refused anyone else access to the remaining unpublished documents. Like misers, they hoarded the scrolls as currency to enrich their careers and those of their students.

With the acquisition of the *Temple Scroll* in 1967, scrolls studies reached a major watershed. When Yigael Yadin revealed the *Temple Scroll*, first in a series of public lectures and then in a published edition in 1977, he capped a process already observable earlier: interpretation of Qumran materials within a Jewish context. The *Temple Scroll*, a text the same size as the Book of Isaiah, comprising Jewish law exclusively, was now on the reader's table. The agenda had shifted. All eyes turned to the new scroll, which, for some, raised false expectations that it would solve virtually all of the problems of Qumran studies. Yadin used his sense of drama and publicity to draw attention to this text. Indeed, one senses that Yadin fully understood the role we are attributing to him here.

In retrospect, we can see that research had been moving in this direction for some time. Joseph M. Baumgarten, a rabbinic scholar at Baltimore Hebrew University, had been contributing studies in the area all along. My own works were beginning to come to fruition as well at the same time. Yadin's new find helped to spur on this research and re-Judaize the scrolls. At last, the significance of these texts for the study of Jewish law—halakhah—was becoming clear. Because Yadin had definitively identified the authors of the *Temple Scroll* with the Qumran sectarians, publication of his new scroll led to full recognition, even among Christian scholars, of the halakhic character of this group, that is, their grounding in Jewish law.

Temple Scroll **after Unrolling of Outer Part** The *Temple Scroll* remained in the possession of the antiquities dealer Kando until 1967. Because it was stored poorly, it deteriorated greatly. Painstaking work was required to unroll it, and much of the writing was preserved on the back of the columns. *Courtesy of the Shrine of the Book of the Israel Museum.*

New Testament scholars suddenly found themselves waiting for scholars of Jewish law to interpret the scroll texts. And then the authority of Judaic researchers was heightened still further by the ironies of Middle Eastern history. In the aftermath of the Yom Kippur War (1973), Yadin was appointed to the Agranat Commission to investigate Israel's military performance during the war. Yadin's new commitment necessarily led to a delay in the publication of the English edition of the *Temple Scroll*.

For more than six years (1977–83), the *Temple Scroll* remained closed to those who did not read modern Hebrew. Although German, French, and Spanish translations were published before the English, they offered little in terms of commentary, and the expansive nature of Yadin's introduction and notes made the Hebrew edition a hidden boon of secret lore known only to Jewish scholars and a few fortunate Christians. Now for the first time, the tables were turned: A scroll was opened to Jews and not to Christians. The recognition that only scholars trained in Second Temple literature and rabbinic texts could deal adequately with the new and now preeminent scroll promoted a completely new perspective on the Qumran finds in general and even on the background of early Christianity.

In September 1971, Pierre Benoit succeeded de Vaux as editor in chief of the International Team and the Discoveries in the Judaean Desert series. Although several publications did appear, much of the work, especially on the cave 4 texts, was not really proceeding at all.

These problems were already clear in September 1984, when Benoit retired and the Israeli Department of Antiquities confirmed John Strugnell of Harvard as editor in chief of the scrolls publication project. Objections from a number of quarters were raised to the appointment of Strugnell, both because of the historically long delays in his own publications and because some accused him of harboring anti-Semitic views. Desiring to be confirmed, Strugnell suggested expanding the team. The group now grew to some twenty members, including a number of Israelis—Devorah Dimant, Elisha Qimron, and Emanuel Tov—whom Strugnell invited to participate in the work. It is indeed ironic that Strugnell, who was later to give an interview to an Israeli newspaper which was widely viewed as anti-Semitic, was instrumental in inviting Jews to participate in the publication of the scrolls. He also furnished a timetable to the Israeli Department of Antiquities (which in the meantime had become the Israel Antiquities Authority), but the deadlines he specified were not kept and could not be enforced. The abortive attempt to maintain that timetable set the stage for the struggle over open access to the scrolls that would occur some years later.

The eventual confirmation of Strugnell's appointment did not stem the rising tide of opposition to the status quo in scrolls research and publication. Qimron's revelation of a few lines of the *Halakhic Letter* at the 1984 International Conference on Biblical Archaeology greatly stimulated curiosity about what other such bombshells might still lie hidden in the unpublished corpus of Qumran texts.

Hershel Shanks, as editor of the *Biblical Archaeology Review* (BAR), campaigned tirelessly to open the scrolls to all qualified scholars. He has been the major force in bringing the battle over the scrolls to international attention. Shanks was sued by Elisha Qimron in an Israeli court for publishing his edition and reconstruction of the *Halakhic Letter* without Qimron's permission. *Photograph by Beverly Rezneck.*

Shemaryahu Talmon of the Hebrew University has been active in scrolls research for many years, training Israel's young scholars. His research has dealt with messianism, biblical texts, and the Qumran calendar. He is editing the texts from Masada, a task entrusted to him after the death of Yadin. He was appointed to the Israeli oversight committee, established after scholars began to complain about the slow pace of publication. *Photograph by Lawrence H. Schiffman.*

Jonas C. Greenfield, of the Hebrew University, is a member of the Israeli oversight committee; he has been assigned to publish the Aramaic documents from the Bar Kokhba caves as well as some of the Aramaic texts from Qumran. Greenfield has contributed important studies on the Aramaic of that period, especially dealing with the legal formulary and its links to Jewish law. *Photograph by Lawrence H. Schiffman.*

Robert Eisenman, of California State University, Long Beach, was the first scholar to go public when his request for access to the unpublished scrolls was denied by former editor in chief Strugnell. He has advocated the view that the scrolls are closely linked to early Christianity, an approach that has gained few adherents. *Photograph by Lawrence H. Schiffman.*

Ben Zion Wacholder, of Hebrew Union College, was frustrated by the inability to gain access to all the scroll texts. He and his student Martin G. Abegg reconstructed the cave 4 materials by computer, based on the concordance produced by the editorial team. Wacholder's and Abegg's publication effectively broke up the monopoly, thus leading to the release of the scrolls to the wider scholarly community. *Photograph by Thomas Kristich. Courtesy of Nina Wacholder.*

Elisha Qimron, of Ben Gurion University of the Negev, published extensively on the grammar of Qumran Hebrew. He joined the scrolls editorial team under the direction of Strugnell and worked with the latter on the official edition of the *Halakhic Letter.* He sued Hershel Shanks when BAR published his edition of that text without his permission. An Israeli court upheld his view, but the case has been appealed. *Photograph by Lawrence H. Schiffman.*

Scarcely a year later, at the New York University Conference on the Dead Sea Scrolls in Memory of Yigael Yadin, the late Morton Smith delivered an impassioned plea for immediate publication of photographs of the entire corpus. Ben Zion Wacholder, a then 67-year-old scholar, stated that if he waited patiently much longer, he would never see the texts before he died. Hershel Shanks, editor of *Biblical Archaeology Review (BAR)*, took up the struggle in his popular magazine. He editorialized extensively on the issue and began his campaign in earnest to liberate the scrolls.

The call for release and publication of all of the documents became almost deafening, resounding regularly at scholarly conferences and in the press. Such attention prompted the Israel Antiquities Authority to reconsider its policies. During the academic year 1989–90, while participating as a fellow of the Institute for Advanced Studies of the Hebrew University in a Dead Sea Scrolls research group, I met with members of the Israeli oversight committee and Amir Drori, director of the Israel Antiquities Authority. We discussed numerous plans for speeding up the rate of publication. Yet change was slow in coming.

Not that it mattered, for the monopoly was soon to be broken by the efforts of scholars themselves.

The clamor for open access intensified when Robert Eisenman and Philip Davies formally requested to read the *Zadokite Fragments*, one of the unpublished documents in the Rockefeller Museum, and were rebuffed by Strugnell. Shanks published their exchange of letters in *BAR*.

Then, in 1990, Stephen A. Reed of the Ancient Biblical Manuscripts Center in Claremont came to Jerusalem to prepare the first complete catalog of scrolls materials and negatives. He made use of an earlier catalog by Qimron that had circulated privately. Reed's catalog clarified the extent of the still unpublished material. More important, it helped spur reorganization of the material and drew attention to the need for its proper conservation and restoration.

The official editorial team—significantly widened by 1990 to include some thirty scholars, Jewish and non-Jewish and of all nationalities—was still controlling exclusive access to texts and producing text editions much too slowly for use by other researchers. Many disenfranchised scholars proposed that access be granted to any and all on the basis of research or university affiliation. Shanks stressed this point in his journal and to the Israel Antiquities Authority, suggesting that in lieu of extensive and time-consuming transcriptions, translations, and commentaries, the authority should distribute easily prepared photographs of the texts.

In November 1990, Strugnell's health sharply deteriorated. In an interview published subsequently in the Israeli newspaper *Haaretz*, Strugnell made disparaging remarks about Judaism. After a period of intense negotiations, his colleagues on the editorial team decided to relieve him of his position as editor in chief—for health reasons, it was explained. At that point, the Israel Antiquities

Authority stepped in to appoint Emanuel Tov of the Hebrew University as the new editor in chief of the International Team and head of the Discoveries in the Judaean Desert (DJD) series. Émile Puech of the École Biblique, Eugene Ulrich of the University of Notre Dame, and Tov were designated the general editors by the members of the team. The International Team was expanded by them to fifty-five editors, in the hope that the work would proceed promptly and that the entire corpus would soon be published. Since then, the pace of publication of additional volumes of DJD has been stepped up, and the long-awaited volume on the Halakhic Letter has just been published. It is clear that the new team will succeed in publishing the Dead Sea Scrolls in excellent editions within a reasonable amount of time.

This new team had barely gotten to work when events overtook them. In September 1991, only a few days after Tov returned from leave in Holland, newspapers around the world carried reports of the computer-aided reconstruction of the still-hidden texts by Ben-Zion Wacholder and Martin G. Abegg of Hebrew Union College in Cincinnati. Wacholder's and Abegg's edition had been produced from the privately distributed concordance prepared by the original editorial team, in a limited edition of about thirty copies. The Biblical Archaeology Society published it with a preface by BAR editor Shanks. Release of the reconstructed edition was timed to precede a PBS "Nova" television documentary that had been in the works for more than a year.

Only a few weeks later, on September 22, the Huntington Library in San Marino, California, announced that it would release a full set of photographic negatives of the scrolls. The Huntington had originally intended to make this announcement around the time of the television program on October 15 but, scooped by the release of the Wacholder-Abegg edition, the library decided to advance its announcement.

A photographer from the Huntington had originally taken those photographs as part of a project to ensure the scrolls' preservation in case of war in the Middle East. After official copies were distributed with the permission of the Israel Antiquities Authority, an extra set of negatives ended up in a vault at the Huntington. Initially, Israeli reaction to the Huntington release was very strong, including threat of legal action, but Israeli authorities soon adopted a more conciliatory stance, seeking to open up access to the collection.

On October 15, 1991, the "Nova" documentary "Secrets of the Dead Sea Scrolls" appeared on nationwide television. Reaching an audience of 13 million, it detailed the discovery of the scrolls and the controversies surrounding their delayed publication. By making viewers aware of the controversy and stimulating further press coverage, the "Nova" program demonstrated the instrumental role played by the media in the release of the scrolls.

The actions of the Huntington Library together with the edition by Wacholder

Emanuel Tov, of the Hebrew University, succeeded Strugnell as head of the editorial team in 1991 and serves as editor of *Discoveries in the Judaean Desert*. He reorganized the publication process, and assigned texts to a much wider group of scholars. His own research has led to an entirely new picture of the history of the biblical text. Lawrence H. Schiffman, of New York University, has concentrated on the study of Jewish law in the scrolls. He is an editor of the planned *Oxford Encyclopedia of the Dead Sea Scrolls* and of the journal *Dead Sea Discoveries*. From the Collection of *Lawrence H. Schiffman*.

James C. VanderKam, of the University of Notre Dame, is an expert on the Ethiopic books of Jubilees and Enoch. Together with J. T. Milik, he is currently engaged in publication of the Jubilees manuscripts from Qumran. He is an editor of the newly established journal *Dead Sea Discoveries* and of the *Oxford Encyclopedia of the Dead Sea Scrolls*, which is in preparation. *Photograph by Lawrence H. Schiffman.*

Joseph Baumgarten recently retired from Baltimore Hebrew University and is now devoting his time to editing the Qumran manuscripts of the *Zadokite Fragments*. His many published studies on Jewish law as contained in the scrolls emphasize the value of Talmudic sources for the scrolls' interpretation. *Photograph by Lawrence H. Schiffman.*

George **Brooke,** of the University of Manchester, was a student of William H. Brownlee, an expert on *pesher;* Brooke is continuing the study of biblical interpretation in the Qumran scrolls. He is a member of the reorganized publication team, an editor of *Dead Sea Discoveries,* and has organized several scrolls conferences, editing the proceedings for publication. *Photograph by Lawrence H. Schiffman.*

Devorah **Dimant,** of the University of Haifa, began her career by doing research on the Book of Enoch and was appointed by Strugnell to the editorial team. She is now editing the difficult pseudoprophetic texts. Her articles include groundbreaking studies of the Qumran library as a whole. *Photograph by Lawrence H. Schiffman.*

Esti **Eshel** is a doctoral student at the Hebrew University and one of many young people who constitute the next generation of Qumran scholars. She has written several articles on new textual finds from the Judaean Desert, including "Prayer for King Jonathan." Here she is seen deciphering and preparing another text for publication from photographs. *Photograph by Lawrence H. Schiffman.*

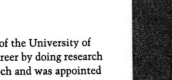

and Abegg effectively ended the editorial team's privileged status. In a world growing increasingly democratic, freedom of information must inevitably triumph over all other considerations, even legitimate scientific concerns. Although the official publication program, had it been pursued with vigor and haste, might have provided a sounder basis for future scholarship, it had now become impossible to delay publication any longer. Despite the genuine intentions of Tov and his associates to advance the pace of publication and solve the problem of scholarly access, the world—nervously expecting bombshells that would shake the foundations of Judaism and Christianity—would not wait.

I welcomed the full release of all the documents, for it gave me the chance to test my theories by studying all the texts. After more than twenty years of research, the conclusions I have reached, and subsequently published in books and articles, can now be supplemented. My students are now able to work with the full set of manuscripts and to write their doctoral dissertations without having to fear that they can be disproven by some unpublished text in the hands of a student of one of the editors. We are no longer dependent on the information furnished to us by others—often ones less competent to study the material than we.

Beginning in 1990, new technological advances and aids to scholarship not only opened up the scrolls to all scholars but also facilitated better readings of the manuscripts. In that year, carbon-14 tests of a selection of manuscripts were run that generally supported the paleographic and archaeological dating previously proposed. Several editions of photographs were released that offered varying degrees of usefulness. Unfortunately, the microfilms of the Huntington, though striking a blow for liberation of the scrolls, were available only on interlibrary loan and proved not to be of sufficient quality for serious research.

At about the same time, copies of photographs of the unpublished fragments were reaching Robert Eisenman, chairman of the Department of Religious Studies at California State University, Long Beach, from an undisclosed source. Eisenman was a natural conduit for such photographs because he had been so outspoken in demanding release of the scrolls. Together with James Robinson of the Center for Antiquity and Christianity at Claremont, he organized those photographs for publication in a two-volume set preceded by a foreword by Hershel Shanks, who discussed the publication controversy and related his role in it.

These publications forced the Israel Antiquities Authority to reformulate its own policies on access to photographs of the scrolls. Since October 1991, the authority has allowed open access to all photos, but it asks scholars to refrain from publishing editions of texts assigned to others for editing. Open access to all photographs available in Jerusalem, Claremont, and Oxford is now the norm.

Along with the photographs, Shanks published a transcription of the *Halakhic Letter*, at that time being prepared for publication by Qimron and Strugnell. Qimron then sued Shanks in Israeli court for copyright violation and won. At this writing, however, the case is being appealed by Shanks before the Supreme Court of Israel.

With the release of the Huntington microfilms and the Eisenman-Robinson-Shanks facsimiles, it became clear that high-quality, properly indexed photographs of the entire Judaean Desert corpus would have to be issued. The Dutch publishing house E. J. Brill, with the cooperation of the Israel Antiquities Authority, issued a set of positive microfiches in 1993. It is a project of extremely high quality and when projected produces much clearer images than the Eisenman-Robinson-Shanks photographs. And it is the most complete set of photos ever issued. Today, anyone who can read Second Temple Hebrew and Aramaic texts in the texts' original scripts can study the entire corpus. At long last, this important part of humanity's heritage is available to all.

With the full release of the documents behind us, we must now set aside the politics that have wracked the field for so long. Those of us who have been waiting decades for this material can now go back to our real work: using the scrolls to reconstruct the history of Judaism in Second Temple times so that we can better understand the development of rabbinic Judaism and the background against which Christianity arose. As we continue our work, we must now prove ourselves capable of the major strides finally made possible with the opening up of these manuscript treasures.

Contents of the Library

Only now that the entire corpus is at last available to scholars is it possible to gain an accurate sense of the nature and significance of the entire collection. Indeed, the present book would have been impossible to produce before the release of the scrolls.

The collection of documents salvaged from the Qumran caves is both extensive and varied. Some of the most important questions scholars have had to answer about these documents concern their age: When were they written? copied? gathered together into a library?

Dating the Scrolls

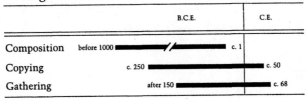

Archaeological and paleographic examination and carbon-14 tests have established that the manuscripts were *copied* in a few cases in the third century B.C.E., for the most part in the second and first centuries B.C.E., and in a few cases in the first century C.E. The manuscripts were *composed* during the period beginning with the Torah's composition—during Israel's earliest history—until about the turn of the common era, when the last of the Qumran texts were composed. The manuscripts were *gathered* at Qumran—for the most part in cave 4—sometime after 134 B.C.E., when the sect established a center at Qumran, and before 68 C.E., when the Qumran area was destroyed by the Romans during the Great Revolt of 66–73 C.E.

Most of the texts are in Hebrew, with some 20 percent in Aramaic and a few in Greek. This picture already indicates that the community that collected and used these manuscripts was only minimally affected by Hellenism—the influ-

Carbon-14 Dating of the Dead Sea Scrolls

	No. of Samples	Description of Scroll	Calibrated Age Range(s)	Paleographic or Specified Age
1.	3	Wadi el-Daliyeh	405–354 B.C.E. 306–238 B.C.E.	352 or 351 B.C.E.
2.	4	Testament of Kohath	388–353 B.C.E.	100–75 B.C.E.
3.	3	Rewritten Pentateuch	339–324 B.C.E. 209–117 B.C.E.	125–100 B.C.E.
4.	4	Book of Isaiah	335–327 B.C.E. 202–107 B.C.E.	125–100 B.C.E.
5.	5	Testament of Levi	191–155 B.C.E. 146–120 B.C.E.	Late 2nd cent.–early 1st cent. B.C.E.
6.	2	Book of Samuel	192–63 B.C.E.	100–75 B.C.E.
7.	4	Masada–Joshua	169–93 B.C.E.	30–1 B.C.E.
8.	2	Masada–Sectarian	33 B.C.E.–74 C.E.	30–1 B.C.E.
9.	5	Temple Scroll	97 B.C.E.–1 C.E.	Late 1st cent. B.C.E.– early 1st cent. C.E.
10.	4	Genesis Apocryphon	73 B.C.E.–14 C.E.	Late 1st cent. B.C.E.– early 1st cent. C.E.
11.	5	Thanksgiving Hymns	21 B.C.E.–61 C.E.	50 B.C.E.–70 C.E.
12.	3	Wadi Seyal	28–112 C.E.	130–131 C.E.
13.	3	Wadi Murabba'at	69–136 C.E.	134 C.E.
14.	2	Khirbet Mird	675–765 C.E.	744 C.E.

Adapted from Bonani, et al., *'Atiqot* 20 (1991), 30.

Comparison of Carbon-14 and Paleographic Dating

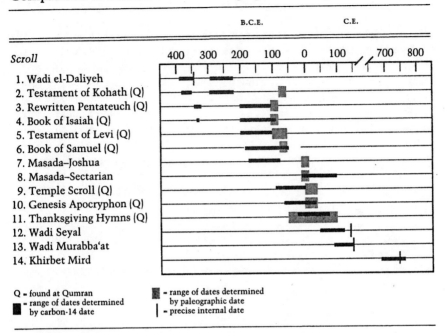

	B.C.E.	C.E.

Scroll

1. Wadi el-Daliyeh
2. Testament of Kohath (Q)
3. Rewritten Pentateuch (Q)
4. Book of Isaiah (Q)
5. Testament of Levi (Q)
6. Book of Samuel (Q)
7. Masada–Joshua
8. Masada–Sectarian
9. Temple Scroll (Q)
10. Genesis Apocryphon (Q)
11. Thanksgiving Hymns (Q)
12. Wadi Seyal
13. Wadi Murabba'at
14. Khirbet Mird

Q = found at Qumran
■ = range of dates determined by carbon-14 date
▦ = range of dates determined by paleographic date
| = precise internal date

Adapted from *BAR* 17 (Nov./Dec. 1991), 72.

ence of Greek culture. For the most part, the texts used both Hebrew and Aramaic, the languages most common among Jews in the Land of Israel at that time.

Over and over in this study we will distinguish between texts that were brought to the community and texts that were composed by its members. Essentially, there are three classes of texts in this corpus. Each one constitutes roughly one-third of the collection, if we exclude unidentified materials.

First are the biblical texts, covering some part of every book except Esther, which is probably missing only by chance. Many of them were certainly copied outside the domain of the sect. Second are the apocryphal compositions and other texts that were part of the literary heritage of those who formed the sect or that were composed by similar groups. They were composed outside the sectarian center and brought there, although some of them may have been copied there. The third group of texts we can describe as sectarian. They describe the teachings and way of life of a specific group of Jews, apparently some of whom lived at the sectarian center excavated at Qumran. They include texts outlining the beliefs of the sect, rules for entry to the sect, legal codes, and liturgical compositions. We cannot be sure that all of them, or even most of them, were copied at Qumran.

This threefold division of the materials had been recognized early on. But it was not evident—until the opening up of the entire corpus—how much Jewish literature of the period, not specific to the Dead Sea sect, the collection contained. This recent appreciation has helped greatly to provide a more accurate sense of the meaning of these documents for our understanding of the general history of Judaism.

The biblical manuscripts, as mentioned, include parts of the entire corpus of Scripture, except for Esther. The Qumran biblical texts represent a number of different text types. A large number of manuscripts resemble the later, Masoretic (received), biblical text used by the Jewish community throughout the ages. A fair number represent biblical texts written in a specific dialect of Hebrew used by the Qumran sect, and these must have been used within the community. A few represent the Hebrew text type from which the Greek translation of the Bible (Septuagint) was made, and a few represent forerunners of the Samaritan text of the Bible.

The specific documents of the Qumran community form a substantial part of the collection. They constitute some 249 manuscripts, or about 115 works (some works are represented in multiple manuscripts). These texts are distinguished by a number of characteristics: they generally reflect the practices and organization of the Qumran community, the history of the community and its own self-image, and the theological views and specific biblical interpretations of the community. Although parallels to many of these ideas can be located outside the community, what makes these documents unique is the combination, within a

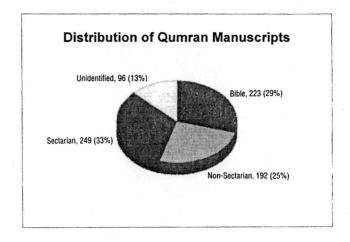

Distribution of Qumran Manuscripts

Unidentified, 96 (13%)

Bible, 223 (29%)

Sectarian, 249 (33%)

Non-Sectarian, 192 (25%)

text, of these particular aspects and the specific linguistic character of Qumran sectarian compositions. It is that special character that clearly marks these as distinctively Dead Sea sectarian documents.

On the other hand, many of the Qumran texts reflect the general literature of the period. The contents of these texts parallel those found in the Masada excavations, which certainly cannot be identified with the Qumran sect. Rather, the communities occupying Qumran and Masada, together with most Jews in the Second Temple period, shared a literature in common: apocryphal and pseudepigraphic documents, some known before the discovery of the scrolls in other languages and now known in the original Hebrew or Aramaic. This class of texts has great significance for us because it can teach us not only about the Qumran sect but also about a variety of Jewish groups of the period. Texts common to all Jewish groups in Second Temple times are an important tool in our work.

Now that we have gained a sense of the ancient library and its contents, we turn, as did the scholars who first worked with the scrolls, to the historical issues pertaining to origins. But origins can be understood only within the archaeological context. Accordingly, our next task is the undertaking of a survey of the archaeology of Qumran.

CHAPTER 3

The Archaeology of Qumran

If we are to reconstruct the history of the Qumran sect and its way of life, we must build upon the substantial archaeological evidence available to us from the settlement at Qumran, close to the caves where the scrolls were discovered. Almost all research on the scrolls confirms the conclusion reached by early investigators: that the site and building complex of Qumran, immediately below the cliffs, were intimately linked with both the caves and the scrolls found within them.

Such a relationship can be conclusively established by comparison of the dating of the ruins with the scroll-dating derived by paleography and more recently from carbon-14 tests. We can also gather evidence by comparing what the ruins tell us about the Qumran community's way of life with what we learn from the literary texts.

The story about publication of the excavation reports is very similar to that of the scrolls themselves. But there is one major difference: Whereas the entire collection of written texts is now available in photographic form to all scholars, the results of the excavations conducted by de Vaux and his team have still been published only in preliminary reports and in a summary volume. The specific, detailed records and plans are just now, more than twenty years after de Vaux's death, being prepared for publication. It is expected that Jean-Baptiste Humbert of the École Biblique in Jerusalem, where de Vaux was based, will publish the records and plans of the architecture. Robert Donceel and Pauline Donceel-Vaute, a Belgian husband-and-wife team, have undertaken to publish an analysis of the pottery.

In a sharp departure from the prevailing scholarly consensus, the Donceels seek to present a new reconstruction of the site, depicting Qumran as an aristocratic dwelling rather than a sectarian center. Humbert has taken this view one step further, suggesting that the buildings at Qumran were initially a Maccabean outpost, converted later into an Essene settlement and cult center. Some support for his theory is coming now from excavations by Itzhak Magen and Amir Drori. Although some doubt the validity of their conclusions, as long as these archaeologists have privileged access to the data, we cannot conclusively prove them wrong. In fact, until full publication of the excavation records and the records' reinvestigation by other scholars, the details of whatever we say here must to some extent remain tentative.

THE RUINS OF KHIRBET QUMRAN

Along the western shore of the Dead Sea, on the plain between the sea and some of the caves where the scrolls were found, lies an ancient ruin called Khirbet Qumran, which looks out over a wadi (stream bed) that extends from the cliffs above down to the Dead Sea. When the Jordanian Department of Antiquities and archaeologists in East Jerusalem learned of the location of cave 1, where the first seven scrolls were found, they realized that this ruin, so close to the caves, demanded closer scrutiny.

The ancient site had been surveyed previously, in 1940 and 1946, but had been mistakenly identified as dating from Byzantine or even Arab times. After the scrolls were discovered in nearby cave 1, detailed archaeological excavations were conducted at the site between 1951 and 1956. Although those excavations were never published in full in proper scientific manner, de Vaux's survey volume provides us with a basic outline of the chronology and character of the site.

From the earliest occupation of Qumran in the period of the divided Israelite monarchy (eighth to seventh centuries B.C.E.), there remain a large round cistern, still clearly visible, and some walls. In this early stage, the site may have served as an outpost of the Judaean military.

When the area came to be inhabited again in the Hellenistic period, the Iron Age remains at the site most probably became the basis for constructing the next stage of the building, in use during the time known as period Ia. The new occupants introduced two main changes: improvement of the water supply by means of a channel to bring water into the settlement and the addition of a few extra rooms to the structures surviving from the Israelite period. They also installed potter's kilns. Although it is difficult to date the initial stage of occupation of the site, we know it ended by period Ib, which began with the reign of Alexander Janneus (103–76 B.C.E.) and possibly may have begun during the reign of John Hyrcanus (135–104 B.C.E.). In general terms, we can fix this first occupation during the Hellenistic period either around the time of the Maccabean Revolt (168–164 B.C.E.) or early in the Hasmonaean period—the years of the Maccabean dynasty.

The most active building at Khirbet Qumran occurred during period Ib, when

Wadi Qumran and the Ruins Eastward view from the cliffs
overlooking Qumran toward the Dead Sea. The wadi (dry river
bed) unfolds below. The runoff from the cliffs was channeled to
the Qumran water system when the torrential winter rains filled
the wadi. Caves 10, 4, and 5 are visible on the left. *Photograph by
Lawrence H. Schiffman.*

Archaeological Periods at Qumran

Israelite		8th–7th centuries B.C.E.
Hellenistic	Ia	before c. 134 B.C.E.
	Ib	c. 134 B.C.E.–31 B.C.E.
Roman (Herodian)	II	c. 31 B.C.E.–68 C.E.
Roman	III	after 68 C.E.–c. 73 C.E.
Bar Kokhba Revolt		c. 132–135 C.E.

the occupants built the basic structure we see today. To the north of the two-story building often called the "tower" stands the main entrance, still visible today. A pathway from the north once led up to the gate. Other entrances faced the northwest and the east. To serve the needs of the inhabitants during that period, the building comprised a complex of rooms and courtyards, including storage areas, workshops, the "tower," a kitchen, and pottery installations. There may also have been a stable for animals. The recent excavations at Qumran in connection with Operation Scroll—the systematic search of Judaean Desert caves undertaken by the Israel Antiquities Authority—revealed that an installation thought to be a winepress was actually used for the production of date-honey. In addition, storage areas for grain were found below the plateau on which the Qumran buildings sit. These discoveries are further proof that the community inhabiting the site had a developed economy.

An extensive water system was fed by an aqueduct designed to catch the water at the top of Wadi Qumran and bring it to the site through tunnels. The system incorporated a variety of cisterns, including that surviving from the Israelite period, all of which were filled by winter rains. The water system also fed

Plan of the Settlement at Khirbet Qumran at the Time of the ►
Earthquake (31 B.C.E.) (1) corners of the 8th- to 6th-century B.C.E. enclosure; (2) tower; (3) stairs leading to the room identified by the excavators as the scriptorium on the upper floor; (4) room with low benches around its walls; (5) room designated by the excavators as the scriptorium; (6) kitchen; (7) dyer's shop; (8) laundry; (9) pottery; (10) potter's kilns; (11–11) wall separating the settlement from the cemetery; (12) meeting hall; (13) pantry; (14) workshops; (15) junction of the aqueduct with the canals of the settlement; (16) main canal; (17) large cisterns; (18) earthquake fault; (19) stables; (20–20) retaining wall along the western edge of the plateau. *From J. T. Milik*, Ten Years of Discovery in the Wilderness of Judaea. *London: SCM Press, 1963, facing p. 48.*

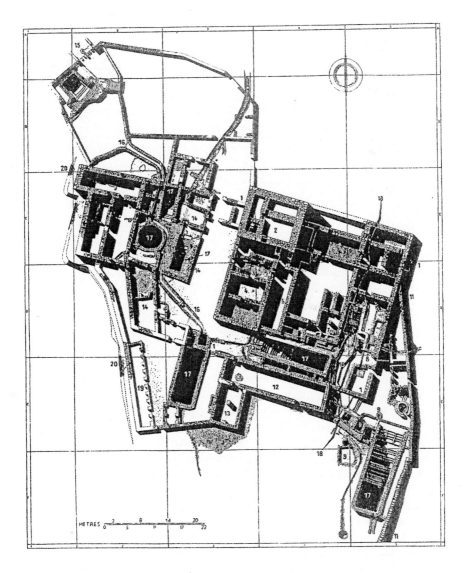

METRES

Mikveh A number of *mikva'ot* (ritual baths) were scattered throughout the Qumran buildings. Fed with the flowing water supply and lined with plaster, these baths were considered proper for fulfilling the various purification rituals prescribed by the Torah. *Photograph by Lawrence H. Schiffman.*

several ritual baths (*mikva'ot*), which definitely match the design of *mikva'ot* known from other sites. The system was designed so that water flowed from the point of entry at the northwestern corner throughout the settlement. Thus all the pools would have qualified as ritual baths from the standpoint of Jewish law. The cisterns could hold enough water to remain in use during the hot, dry summer. Purification basins at various points emptied the water of its silt and dirt as it flowed through the system. Any excess spilled out at the southern side, where the system came to an end.

Despite such an extensive water system as well as the large kitchen and dining facilities—suitable for a sizable group—there are very few areas that could under normal circumstances have served as living quarters. Today we still do not know where those living quarters were. Three possible locales have been suggested: nearby caves, tents, or the upper story of the building complex.

That the inhabitants lived in the caves surrounding Qumran is impossible,

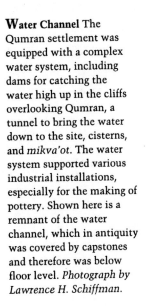

Water Channel The Qumran settlement was equipped with a complex water system, including dams for catching the water high up in the cliffs overlooking Qumran, a tunnel to bring the water down to the site, cisterns, and *mikva'ot.* The water system supported various industrial installations, especially for the making of pottery. Shown here is a remnant of the water channel, which in antiquity was covered by capstones and therefore was below floor level. *Photograph by Lawrence H. Schiffman.*

because the caves are too small and dank to have served this purpose. (This is true even though many caves in the area show evidence of occupation, probably because they were used as places of refuge during times of war.) The tent theory is indeed possible although we have no way of confirming or disproving it. And it is equally likely that people occupied living quarters in the upper story of the complex, because only ruins of the bottom story remain.

Some rooms appear to have been used for assemblies of small groups. One particular room stands out in such a context. It is 72 feet (22 meters) long by 15 feet (4.5 meters) wide. At one end stands what some have identified as a kind of circular-shaped, speaker's podium. Apparently, those using this room cleaned it by bringing in water through a pipe and letting it wash down along the inten-

Dining Room This large room, located toward the southern end of the building complex at Qumran, has been identified by excavators as a dining room. Adjacent to it was a pantry with a large number of dishes still neatly stacked when the site was destroyed. The dining room was equipped with a drainage system, which allowed the floor to be washed easily. It is generally believed that the Qumran sectarians ate their communal meals in this room. *Photograph by Lawrence H. Schiffman.*

tionally sloped floor to the other end. Because of this cleaning system (which parallels the system used to clean the floor of the Second Temple in Jerusalem), most scholars have concluded that this room served as a dining hall. An adjoining room contained more than a thousand eating vessels, consisting of neatly stacked jars, jugs, bowls, and dishes. As many as 708 bowls were found neatly arranged in dozens. That collection of pottery represents the equipment needed to serve a typical mass meal in Hellenistic-period Palestine. The stack of dishes gives us a general idea of how many people ate there. Obviously the dining room fed more than a single family.

From these finds we can also derive evidence disproving the Donceels' theory that Qumran was an aristocratic settlement. No aristocratic family would have been so large. But those supporting the "villa" theory have offered a second piece of evidence to prove their case: the original excavators' discovery of pieces of fancy glassware at the site. By setting up the ascetic Essenes as straw men— would those sworn to poverty use such fancy glassware?—the "villa" theorists have claimed validation of their hypothesis.

The theory is, however, built on faulty assumptions: To be sectarian, the Qumran group need not have been Essene. But even if it were, there is absolutely no literary evidence to associate with poverty the Essenes' communal, shared way of life. Essenes could very well have used expensive glassware. It is also possible that a villa could have been converted to sectarian use after its construction. Such was the case, for example, at Masada, where the *sicarii*, a Jewish rebel group taking its name from the short dagger (Latin *sica*) carried by its members, occupied the Herodian royal palaces in the last years of the Great Revolt against Rome.

We also can derive evidence of large-group occupation from the considerable number of bones of edible animals found buried between the buildings in pottery containers, a practice otherwise unknown in Jewish tradition. It is important to stress that these bones could not have been the remains of sacrifices, because the literary evidence strongly indicates that ritual sacrifice at Qumran would have been unacceptable to the sectarians. Furthermore, no altar or other sacrificial equipment has been found at Qumran.

During period Ib there were also some workshops at Qumran. One in particular was used for making pottery. It had facilities for washing the clay in a shallow tank, a potter's wheel, and kilns. It is likely that much of the pottery found at Qumran, which represents a particular, consistent, yet unique collection of styles, was made in this workshop. The pottery, along with lamps and coins, helps to date period Ib as being at the end of the Hellenistic period.

Numismatic evidence helps to further refine the dating of the settlement, although there has been considerable debate over its meaning. From such numismatic evidence, it can be ascertained that the site was occupied in the Hasmonaean period—during the reign of Alexander Janneus (103–76 B.C.E.). It is probable that the buildings were used earlier in the time of John Hyrcanus (134–104 B.C.E.), as can be gathered from literary and historical evidence as well. There are too few Seleucid coins to warrant a dating earlier than the era of John Hyrcanus.

The excavators of the site have maintained that the occupation came to an end by way of earthquake and fire in 31 B.C.E. The evidence can be seen most dramatically in the broken steps of a cistern and in other ruins as well. Evidence for the fire comes from the layer of ash found in a number of buildings, resulting from the burning of roofs made of wooden beams and reeds. Even though most scholars regard the earthquake and fire as simultaneous, some believe that the earthquake completed the destruction of buildings that had been previously

Coins from Qumran Numismatic evidence was of great help in dating the layers of occupation of the Qumran settlement. A hoard of 561 silver coins was found in three pottery vessels between levels Ib and II. The earliest exemplars were from 136–135 B.C.E., and most of the coins dated to after 126–125 B.C.E. Shown here are 24 Tyrian *shekalim* and half-*shekalim* minted between 103–102 B.C.E. and 10–9 B.C.E. *Courtesy of the Israel Antiquities Authority.*

damaged by fire. The fire might have occurred during the Parthian invasion of 40–39 B.C.E. or at the hands of the Parthians' Hasmonaean ally Antigonus, who reigned during 40–37 B.C.E. Most likely there was a short period of abandonment before the inhabitants returned at the beginning of period II.

Period II involved only minor modifications of the site, presumably because the same community used it. Much of the debris cleaned out by the returnees was discarded around the outside of the buildings as well as in the ravine to the north of the ruins. A number of buildings had to be strengthened or repaired, and others, when the destruction was too extensive, had to be condemned and abandoned. Some additional rooms were added, perhaps to replace those that could no longer be used. The large dining room continued in use, although its cleaning system was no longer functioning. Nonetheless, dishes found on the floor indicate that this room was still used during that period for dining. Additional deposits of animal bones also date to this period. The original water system was

Scriptorium The excavators of Qumran, incorrectly assuming that all the Dead Sea Scrolls had been copied at Qumran, identified a particular location as the scriptorium—the scribes' workshop. That identification was encouraged by the finding of inkwells and strange tables on the floor of the room. Actually, the tables must have been located in the room above, falling onto the floor below when the building was destroyed. *Photograph by Lawrence H. Schiffman.*

cleaned out and slightly modified, although some portions were never restored to use. Some new industrial installations were put in as well, including a mill for grinding grain.

Dating from this period is the controversial scriptorium. A scriptorium is a facility for copying manuscripts and is usually organized for production of multiple copies. A large room in the Qumran ruins has been identified as such a facility because archaeologists found some furniture in it assumed to be tables used by scribes, as well as two inkwells buried in the debris. These items probably had fallen from the floor above, where the scriptorium might have been located.

The debate over this room has centered on the shape of the tables—16 feet (5 meters) long, 1.3 feet (40 centimeters) wide, and only 1.6 feet (50 centimeters) high. Some scholars point out that ancient scribes generally did not write at ta-

Tables These strange tables were assumed by the excavators of Qumran to be those upon which the scrolls were copied. Yet as far as we know, ancient scribes sat cross-legged and rested the parchment on their laps. No satisfactory explanation has yet been given for the way in which these tables might have been used. For this and a variety of other reasons, serious question has been raised about identification of the room in which they are found as a scriptorium. *Courtesy of the Israel Antiquities Authority.*

bles. Though some parallels for the use of tables have been noted, none of them solves the problem of the tables' low height. Nevertheless, those scrolls that articulate both the Qumran group's distinct sectarian ideas and their particular spelling and linguistic structure had to be copied somewhere. I see no reason not to entertain the possibility that this or some other room in the complex was furnished and outfitted for scribal activity.

The pottery unearthed at Qumran from period II is very similar to that of first-century C.E. Roman Jerusalem, although it is apparently of local manufacture. Specific dating of this stage of the occupation, however, is based on numismatic evidence. It seems that the reoccupation took place during the rule of Herod Archelaus, son of Herod the Great, who reigned from 4 B.C.E. to 6 C.E. It is possible but not likely that it may have occurred somewhat earlier.

This period came to an abrupt end with the community's destruction at the hands of the Romans. The archaeological evidence here is irrefutable: Thick debris from the ceilings and upper floor filled many of the buildings. A layer of carbon indicates that the roofs burned in the destruction of the site. Archaeologists have also found iron arrowheads at this level. Because the last coins date from the Great Revolt against Rome, it seems that the Qumran complex was destroyed during that war. Evidence from the specific coins found there points to destruction by 68 or 69 C.E. From other sources, we know that Vespasian was at Jericho in the spring of 68. It is likely that during that time he attacked and sacked Qumran. So ended the sectarian community and its unique culture. From that point on, coins testify to the beginning of a new period—period III.

It is generally believed that when the Romans destroyed Qumran, they entered caves 4 and 5 and there ripped up the scrolls in an anti-Jewish orgy. Recent studies have shown, however, that such was not the case. The fragmentary condition of the scrolls in cave 4, by far the largest portion of the materials, can be attributed only to natural conditions. The patterns of destruction observable in the preserved fragments indicate that this was the case. The Romans never destroyed these scrolls; it was the vicissitudes of time and climate that took their toll.

It is often claimed that some Qumran survivors fled to Masada, where the Jewish rebels made their last stand against Rome. Those making this claim point to the fact that *Songs of the Sabbath Sacrifice,* one of the compositions found in several manuscripts at Qumran, was also found at Masada. Today, with the publication of much more material from Masada and Qumran, we recognize that these texts were part of the general literature of the times and were shared by many communities. Qumran was not the only source for such documents.

Period III marks the short occupation of the site by Roman garrisons during the remainder of the revolt. During the years the Romans besieged Masada, Qumran served as an outpost and an observation post. The two-story tower was reinforced and adapted for the purpose. Although the Romans made some other alterations, they left most of the complex in ruins. They depended upon a greatly simplified water system. Thus, this period involved no facilities for assemblies, no industrial production, and no cooking of large quantities of food. We cannot be sure when the site was abandoned, but it seems to have happened shortly after the fall of Masada in 73 C.E. A few coins found on the surface indicate that Khirbet Qumran served briefly as a refuge for followers of Bar Kokhba during the abortive revolt of 132–135 C.E.

INTERPRETATION OF THE SITE

The data we have presented thus far, based primarily on excavations by de Vaux, make it clear that for most of its active history, the site was occupied by a group engaged in certain communal activities and religious rites. It is also clear that the scrolls, caves, and building complex were intimately linked. Despite all claims to the contrary, this interpretation remains the most plausible in light of the archaeological and historical evidence. Those rejecting this view are isolated voices whose theories have gained no adherents except the authors themselves.

The archaeological evidence plainly disproves the theory that Qumran was a military outpost not related in any way to the scrolls, an argument put forward to prove that the scrolls originated in Jerusalem. In fact, not a single trained archaeologist agrees that Qumran was a fortress. The evidence also disproves the proposed Christian provenance of the scrolls, for such a theory calls for later dating for the documents than is warranted by the scientific evidence. Older alternative theories, such as the Zealot hypothesis, which dates the community to the years of the Jewish revolt against Rome in 66–73 C.E., are likewise untenable. The notion that the site was an aristocratic dwelling, recently put forward, has also been discredited.

Accordingly, we will accept the conclusions of the excavators and the majority of the scholarly community that the scrolls, caves, and sectarian community that inhabited the building complex were intimately connected. Our next job, then, is to imagine how this site would have served the community whose life is described in the sectarian scrolls.

Our tour of the Qumran ruins has provided both a chronological framework for the sect's occupation of the site and some evidence for the sect's way of life. We can even at this point sketch in some aspects of the group's history.

Sometime after 152 B.C.E., the sect came into being and then went through a period of formation and solidification. By the reign of John Hyrcanus, the sectarians were fully established at what had already been an inhabited site. Apparently, they adapted the site to their own use and expanded it. Their lives included communal meals in a large room, which contained facilities for preparing food for large numbers of people. The sectarians occupied themselves extensively with ritual purity. They engaged in making pottery, examples of which were found at Qumran, and they may have had an area for preparing manuscripts—a scriptorium.

The sect, as an organized group, apparently broke up sometime during the Great Revolt, in the aftermath of the destruction of Qumran in 68 C.E. Some scholars have tried to link the phases of occupation of Qumran with the specific internal history of the sect, assuming that the different phases represented stages in the sect's history and ideology. To bolster this theory, they have relied excessively on the excavators' conclusion that there was a hiatus in occupation after the earthquake of 31 B.C.E.

From my point of view, such precise explanations cannot be verified. First, we cannot be certain whether there was indeed an interruption or for how long. Second, it has not been conclusively proven that the break in occupation between periods Ib and II was caused by the earthquake. Finally, although the rebuilding of the site at the start of period II may have involved certain changes, we cannot prove that such changes signal a change in the nature or constitution of the community. Thus, even though the excavations reveal facilities that were ideal for the kind of group described in the sectarian scrolls, more exact conclusions seem unwarranted.

A recent theory tries to explain the Qumran ruins differently. Jean-Baptiste Humbert, accepting that the scrolls and the caves are linked with the buildings, has suggested that Qumran was originally founded as a Hasmonaean fortress. This facility was supposedly surrendered to the Essenes soon after the rise of Herod, in about 37 B.C.E. It then served the Essenes as a cult center, complete with Temple and sacrifices, until the Essenes abandoned sacrifice with the approach of the destruction of Judaea at the hands of the Romans.

While we have no problem with the notion that the original construction of the Qumran site may have been for purposes other than as a sectarian center, we still cannot accept this view. First, it makes the assumption that the sect is to be identified with the Essenes, an issue which we regard as still unresolved. Second, the presence of so many ritual baths in the Hasmonaean period ruins means that a religious group must have made use of this facility already in the Hasmonaean period. Finally, we reject categorically the claim that sacrifices were performed at Qumran, and we cannot accept the analysis of the archaeological evidence as a basis for this claim.

THE CEMETERIES

Particularly important for our understanding of the archaeological evidence are the cemeteries, which have been regarded as pivotal in proving or disproving the possible celibacy of the sect. I argue, based on the literary materials, that the sect was not celibate. But to be fair, let us take a detailed look at what the cemetery excavations reveal about the sect.

In a cemetery located 55 yards (50 meters) to the east of the building complex and extending down toward the Dead Sea, are 1,100 graves in neatly arranged rows. Piles of stones mark each of the graves, which are oriented north/south. Twenty-six of the graves were excavated while Qumran was under Jordanian occupation. All of the bodies were buried in the same position in individual graves. Other than a few small ornaments, nothing was placed in the graves with the dead.

Of those excavated so far, the main cemetery has yielded only male graves, but women and children have been found in graves outside the main cemetery. In addition, there were two secondary cemeteries used apparently by members of the Qumran community. One, to the north of Khirbet Qumran, contained twelve graves. Two were excavated—one male and one female. Another ceme-

Cemetery To the east of the Qumran ruins, stretching toward the Dead Sea, are the remains of a cemetery containing some 1100 graves. All of the well-ordered graves are oriented from north to south. Only a small number were excavated, but the proportion of those graves that are women's and children's is large enough to cast serious doubt on the prevailing notion that the sectarians were celibate Essenes. *Photograph by Lawrence H. Schiffman.*

tery located to the south of Wadi Qumran contains thirty graves: one of them contained a woman; three were children's graves.

Although examination of the mode of burial does not help us pinpoint the dating of the tombs, archaeologists have found sufficient numbers of shards in the grave fill to conclude that the cemetery was used by those who inhabited the ruins and that the building complex and the cemetery were in contemporaneous use in both periods Ib and II, essentially the period generally identified with the sectarian occupation of Qumran.

Evidence from the cemetery confirms that the site was used for a considerable period of time, long enough for 1,100 people to have been buried there, probably more than could have occupied the site at any one time. Further, it is clear that there were women and children at Qumran. Such evidence counters the claim that the inhabitants practiced celibacy, although it is not sufficiently convincing without the textual evidence of the scrolls.

If the Qumran community did not practice celibacy, why then are its cemeteries filled with a disproportionate number of men? The most probable explanation is that Qumran served as a study center for the sectarians and that men left their families for periods of time to study there. Only the limited number of inhabitants who lived there permanently had families, and it is they who account for the women and children buried at Qumran.

THE CAVES

Cave 1, discovered by a wandering shepherd boy seeking a lost sheep, is located high up in the rocky cliffs. This almost invisible natural cave, where the first scrolls were found, is half a mile (1 kilometer) or so from Qumran and looks down on the wadi. It is 26.6 feet (8 meters) long, 13.3 feet (4 meters) high and from 2.5 to 6.5 feet (.75 to 2 meters) wide. The manuscripts removed by the Bedouin from this cave were seven virtually complete scrolls, consisting of two copies of Isaiah, *Rule of the Community, Thanksgiving Hymns, Pesher Habakkuk, Genesis Apocryphon,* and the *War Scroll.* This small sample already contained the major categories of Qumran manuscripts: Bible, pre-Qumranian Second Temple literature, and sectarian compositions. During later excavations, fragments of sixty-seven additional texts were found in cave 1, including pieces of the same manuscripts offered for sale by the Bedouin, thus confirming that this cave was where these scrolls originated.

The seven original texts, wrapped in cloth, were stored in clay jars by the sectarians, which is why they survived almost intact. Such special storage was exceptional in the Qumran caves. Unfortunately, cave 4, from which the largest number of texts came, had no such jars.

Apparently, cave 1 was not used as a library. Rather, the few scrolls found inside were placed there for safekeeping, probably toward the end of the sectarian occupation of the area, after the start of the Great Revolt in 66 C.E., and before the destruction of Qumran in 68 C.E.

After the scrolls were removed, cave 1 was excavated again, this time yielding scraps of cloth, pieces of wood, olive and date stones, phylactery cases, and shards. The pottery assemblage included parts of jars and covers such as those used to store the scrolls; household pottery from the Hellenistic period; and lamps from the Hellenistic and Roman periods. Because this pottery exactly matches the inventory found at Qumran in the building complex, the excavators quickly concluded that the cave had been used by the same group occupying the adjacent settlement.

Cave 2 was discovered by Bedouin, who removed and sold thirty-three manuscripts from this cave. This second discovery alerted scholars that more finds could be forthcoming. Cave 2 is a small natural cave, uneven in shape, with chambers on two levels. The archaeologists who followed the Bedouin found about six jars, one lid, and three bowls. Again, this pottery matched material from the Qumran site. Because the jars in this cave resembled those containing scrolls found in cave 1, it would seem that this cave, too, served as a hiding place for texts, but not as a library from which scrolls could be obtained.

In cave 3, located somewhat to the north of cave 1, archaeologists found several inscribed fragments of hide and papyrus. But the most important find was the *Copper Scroll*, a document written on sheets of copper riveted into the shape of a scroll. The *Copper Scroll*, originally found in two rolled pieces, is written in a Hebrew dialect closer to Mishnaic Hebrew than the rest of the scrolls, although it has many affinities to Qumran Hebrew. The scroll describes a list of buried treasure that some scholars identify as the Temple treasury. At one point, it mentions the hiding of a text. A large quantity of pottery was also found in cave 3: jars, lids, jugs, and a lamp.

In addition, excavators found quite a number of caves that might have been temporarily inhabited, many with pottery similar to that found at Qumran. A number of other scroll caves were discovered as well. Cave 6 yielded fragments of thirty-one manuscripts and a jar and bowl similar to those in the building complex. Cave 11, located a little to the south of cave 3, contained a number of very important and well-preserved texts, such as the *Psalms Scroll* and the *Temple Scroll.*

After a while, the Bedouin turned their attention to the marl terrace directly opposite the settlement to the west. There they chanced upon the most important cave of all, cave 4. This cave yielded fragments of approximately 550 manuscripts, which together constitute the vast majority of unpublished texts recently released. Cave 4, artificially hollowed out of the limestone, is located immediately opposite the Qumran settlement on the other side of the ravine to the west. It is easier to get to than any of the other caves and seems to have been the only one that served as a library. The cave consists of an oval chamber opening onto two smaller chambers.

As always, the archaeologists came too late, following close on the heels of the Bedouin. They discovered additional manuscript fragments but very little pottery: parts of a few jars and lids, bowls, two jugs and a pot, a juglet, and a lamp. The Bedouin had already removed most of the manuscript material, but the archaeologists also found fragments of about one-fourth of the manuscripts, establishing beyond a doubt that the hoard put up for sale by Kando had actually come from this cave.

Of all the caves, cave 4 has yielded the most valuable finds, which have provided keys to unlocking the entire library. Here were found parts of 223 biblical

Cave 4 The largest collection of texts was found in cave 4, which yielded fragments of some 550 manuscripts. This cave was artificially hewn into the limestone and fitted with wooden shelves, which were mounted in the holes that can be seen all around the cave. This cave—the one closest to Qumran and probably accessible by a wooden causeway in ancient times— served as a library for those who inhabited the building complex at Qumran. *Photograph by Lawrence H. Schiffman.*

scrolls; numerous apocryphal compositions, many of them previously unknown; many types of unknown sectarian writings; and some economic documents. These materials, because of their fragmentary condition, have posed a tremendous challenge to scholars. In fact, the bulk of work on the scrolls in our generation will be directed at conserving, piecing together, editing, analyzing, and translating the documents.

A few points about this cave need to be stressed. First, its inside chambers were hewn out of rock. Such an ambitious project would only have been undertaken to serve the needs of the adjoining settlement. Second, its construction clearly took planning and considerable time. It is therefore impossible to argue, as some scholars do, that this cave was used to stash the Temple library while the Romans were closing in on Jerusalem. Furthermore, since so much of the material in the cave directly opposed Temple practice of the time, it seems implausible that those responsible for the precious Temple library would have chosen to store it here. Rather, it seems most likely that this entire cave was constructed to serve as a library for the inhabitants of the nearby building complex.

Cave 4 provides us with another clue to support this theory. On the sides of the cave's main chamber—at specified intervals and at a uniform height—are holes clearly intended to hold wooden supports to accommodate the scrolls. When the cave, with its treasure of scrolls, was abandoned, the wooden planks rotted, spilling the entire collection onto the floor, where the cave's natural conditions—dampness, animal droppings, and climate—took their deadly toll. As the scrolls deteriorated, they broke into 80,000–100,000 subfragments, many of them as small as a third of an inch by a third of an inch (a centimeter by a centimeter), producing the greatest jigsaw puzzle in history. Unfortunately, because cave 4 was an active library, no scrolls here were stored in jars—hence, the vast number of fragments.

Close by, somewhat to the north of cave 4, was cave 5, containing manuscript fragments but no pottery whatsoever. In time, archaeologists excavating caves 7, 8, and 9 found some manuscript fragments, parts of a tefillin (phylactery) case, date stones, ropes, a bit of leather, and a few pieces of pottery. Curiously, cave 7 contained only Greek manuscripts, a phenomenon that still remains unexplained. In cave 10, very close to cave 4, excavators found a floor mat, a Hebrew ostracon (inscribed piece of pottery), date stones and desiccated dates, part of a lamp, and some shards typical of Qumran.

What can we learn from the evidence of the caves? First, that the caves are really of two types: The majority of them served as hiding places for scrolls endangered by the invading Roman forces, which eventually succeeded in destroying Qumran. Cave 4 served a special function as the sect's library, housing an entire collection of biblical, apocryphal, sectarian, and economic texts. This book is concerned primarily with the cave 4 library and what it can tell us about various approaches to Jewish thought and practice in the Second Temple period.

We can also conclude from the evidence that the caves and the documents found there were intimately related to the Qumran settlement. Scientific analysis of the pottery found in the caves and in the settlement incontrovertibly establishes their close similarity. The cylindrical jars are of a type not found anywhere else. (Only one has been found outside Qumran.) Furthermore, Qumran lies physically at the center of the line along which the caves are located.

The excavations also disprove the theory that the scroll collection in cave 4 might have been a *genizah*, a repository of damaged texts piled up in the order in which they were discarded. On the contrary, the evidence shows that the Qumran documents were stored on shelves or in carefully packed jars, indicating either constant use or storage for future use. What we have is indeed what Frank Moore Cross aptly called the "ancient library of Qumran."

In thinking about the finds at Qumran, one always questions: Are there any more surprises awaiting us? Will new caves or more manuscripts be found in the future?

Such discoveries are unlikely—but not impossible. For forty-seven years so far, the caves have been minutely examined and sifted by native would-be antiquities dealers and archaeologists alike. "Operation Scroll," a detailed search conducted by the Israel Antiquities Authority, failed to unearth scrolls in the Qumran area. Although it is possible that some manuscripts or antiquities were removed from the caves before archaeologists surveyed Qumran and have not yet surfaced on the market, it is likely that the significant finds from Qumran have been brought to light already.

EIN FESHKA AND EIN EL-GHWEIR

It remains for us to discuss two other locations that may have been satellite settlements of the main Qumran community. From the documents of the sect, especially the *Zadokite Fragments*, we learn that other such communities existed. In fact, it is generally assumed that sectarians in small numbers were scattered throughout the Land of Israel. As far as we know, there were two such satellites in the immediate vicinity of Qumran.

The first, Ein Feshka, 2 miles (3 kilometers) south of Qumran, is today the location of a swimming beach on the shore of the Dead Sea. Visitors pass the ruins on their way into the parking lot. Just as Qumran was apparently chosen because the nearby wadi provided a plentiful water supply once its runoff was harnessed, so Ein Feshka (literally, "spring of Feshka") was chosen because of its natural freshwater supply. The ruins of Ein Feshka consist primarily of a large building with an enclosure and shed on its south and a courtyard equipped with basins on the north.

The main building is a rectangle of 79 by 59 feet (24 by 18 meters). Its two entrances, leading to different parts of the complex, may have been segregated for human use and for animals kept in the courtyard. In the corners of the courtyard were smaller buildings—one apparently a storeroom and the other containing some waterworks for draining the courtyard. Two main rooms with fine doorways were found: one had a paved floor and two recessed cupboards, and the other had a partial flagstone floor and one such cupboard. Another storeroom and two paved rooms were also excavated. A stairway led to an upper story with a terrace or veranda. Archaeological evidence has definitely established that there was a second floor.

The most logical conclusion regarding the complex as a whole is that it contained living quarters and storerooms. The building as we know it reflects its latest stage, built upon a previous stage that had been abandoned earlier. This rebuilt structure, dating from period II, came to an end by fire. After this destruction, the building was apparently partly reoccupied.

The chronology of the building seems to match that of the Qumran complex. Period II of Ein Feshka coincides with period II of Qumran. The small pottery of the two occupations corresponds, although none of the large jars found at Qumran was found at Ein Feshka. Numismatic evidence confirms the dating. One interesting object is an almost complete limestone vase typical of Herodian-period Qumran and of Jerusalem, 2.25 feet (.7 meter) high, which had a two-line inscription beginning: "in the first year." Unfortunately, we cannot restore or decipher the second line.

Less can be said about the dating of the earlier occupation, during period I. Only some pottery and a few coins have been found. The coins allow us to conclude that period I of Ein Feshka corresponds to period Ib of Qumran, dating to the Hasmonaean period.

Period III apparently dates from between the two Jewish revolts against Rome and, as was the case at Qumran itself, constitutes only a partial reuse of the complex. As opposed to Qumran, it does not appear that Roman troops were garrisoned at Ein Feshka immediately after the area was conquered in 68 C.E.

The conclusion of the excavators is fairly definite: These two sites—Qumran and Ein Feshka—are somehow related and were both occupied by similar inhabitants. Although Ein Feshka was not in use during the earlier stage of Qumran—period Ia—it was occupied during Qumran's periods Ib and II.

The disagreement over the end of period Ib at Qumran has spilled over to Ein Feshka. If Qumran was in fact destroyed by an earthquake, then we have to assume that for some reason Ein Feshka escaped a similar fate, for there is no evidence there of destruction by earthquake. If, instead, the Qumran site was destroyed by enemies and abandoned, then we can understand the break between periods I and II at Ein Feshka. Perhaps publication of the complete excavation report will shed light on this question.

To the southwest of the building stands an enclosure about 48 square yards (40 square meters), which in period II was equipped with a small shed, perhaps for drying dates or storing reeds. In this desert region, the only large-scale cultivation possible is that of the date palm. Date culture is mentioned extensively in connection with Ein Gedi and is documented in texts from the Bar Kokhba caves. Though palm wood and leaves were used for building roofs at Qumran and though date stones were found there as well, there is no way conclusively to determine how the shed was used. The enclosure was most probably intended for livestock.

A second enclosure was built in period II at the northwestern corner of the building, measuring 75.5 by 131 feet (23 by 40 meters). In the eastern half is a series of plastered basins and small channels served by a water supply system. A sewage system to draw away wastewater was also built there. It is probable that this area was used for the processing of hides. Although no residue from the chemicals necessary for processing hides has been found in these installations at Ein Feshka, such chemicals were not used in the preparation of skins for writing scrolls. It has been suggested that the basins found there were used for rearing fish, but these installations are much too small for any significant fish farming. Whatever the case, the place was obviously some form of industrial facility. Preparing hides remains the most likely explanation. This installation was not reused in period III.

Why is this site important? Because this nearby settlement was occupied during the main periods that the sectarian community occupied Qumran, we can learn more about the activities of the sect. It seems likely that the people living in the area were engaged in raising livestock and had considerable stores. The area may have housed the sect's tannery, where skins used for some of the scrolls were prepared. It would make sense for the sect to locate its industrial processes at a distance, especially since such processes required a fresh water supply and also because the tanning process generated noxious odors. In any case, it seems that this outpost was part of the Qumran community. It must have been one of the "camps" mentioned in the *Zadokite Fragments*.

Another site in the area, Ein el-Ghweir, is also probably relevant. As its name indicates, it is located on a spring, 9 miles (15 kilometers) south of Qumran. A rectangular building has been excavated there, measuring 64 by 141 feet (19.5 by

43 meters). It was occupied in two strata, which are separated by a layer of burnt material. The coins that have been recovered indicate that this site was in use during period II of the other two locations.

About half a mile (.8 kilometer) north of this building was a small cemetery. About twenty graves have been excavated there, containing twelve men, seven women, and a boy. Burial was in the same form as at Qumran. The pottery in the fill proves that the graves were contemporaneous with the building. One grave contained a jar inscribed with the name Yehohanan.

Although it is possible that this building and cemetery were also connected with the Qumran group, numismatic evidence suggests that occupation of this site may have begun later and ended earlier than at the Qumran site. Because Ein el-Ghweir is some distance from Qumran, we must be cautious in regarding this as an offshoot of the Qumran settlement. As is the case also with Ein Feshka, no scroll or document has been found in this area. Nevertheless, Jews definitely inhabited this area in the Second Temple period, and it is possible that their settlement could have been connected with Qumran.

It is helpful to say something here about the livability of Qumran and the surrounding region. Visiting the site today, one finds a most inhospitable area, hostile to human habitation. How then did the ancient community survive?

First of all, the inhabitants certainly had a sophisticated knowledge of irrigation techniques. They were adept at catching and retaining an adequate water supply during the rainy season; for that purpose they used large underground cisterns, which survive to this day. In addition, the area has always supported sheep and goat herding, and in the oasis of Ein Feshka, palms could easily have been grown with minimum irrigation facilities. Barley does grow on the hill above Qumran, and grindstones have been found in the ruins there. The reeds growing naturally in the region could have been made into baskets and mats and been used for thatching of roofs as well. Salt and bitumen could be mined from the Dead Sea. Asphalt has also been found in the excavations of Qumran and at Ein Feshka. Apparently, other industries connected with agriculture or shepherding were practiced at Ein Feshka. Pottery was also a successful venture, as evidenced by the kilns and potter's workshops found at Qumran. Brushwood for fuel, especially for baking, could be gathered in the area. We know that the area also was occupied in Israelite and Byzantine times, and the economic basis must have been similar in all these periods.

What emerges from this survey of the archaeology of Qumran is a picture of a sophisticated and resourceful community. Those who hid the scrolls in the caves occupied the building complex at Qumran from sometime after 152 B.C.E. until Qumran was destroyed by the Romans. They amassed the bulk of their manuscripts in cave 4, which served as the group's library that adjoined the set-

tlement, affording them easy access to their manuscripts. Apparently, the sect also made use of Ein Feshka for herding and for industrial purposes, and it may also have maintained other "camps" in the desert area. There the sectarians developed an economy that sustained their particular way of life. To understand that way of life and how it emerged, we must first more fully understand certain aspects of Jewish history and Judaism in the Hellenistic period.

PART II
The Community
at Qumran

CHAPTER 4

Judaism, Hellenism, and Sectarianism

The Qumran corpus began in the distinctive historical experience of a sectarian group, one that emerged out of Second Temple Judaism and then withdrew to Qumran, where it accumulated a library. The sect came into being the moment the group came together as a recognizable movement with its own self-consciousness and self-definition. At that point, the group's distinct ideological stance distinguished it as separate from others.

Although the sect's early ideology emerged out of the religious culture of Second Temple Judaism, the group that finally bequeathed us the manuscripts at Qumran was nevertheless unique in many respects. Therefore, we must seek to establish historically when and how the group arose and what specific conflicts shaped its history and ideology.

The Qumran sect inherited many texts and traditions that helped generally to formulate its teachings, and with the aid of recently released material, we can now establish specifically the main influences. In particular, a new text, the *Halakhic Letter*, offers us vital information not only on the ideologies of that time but also on the era's political realities. Let us now review the political and religious situation in Judea so that we can understand how the *Halakhic Letter* fits into the history of the sect.

The corpus of scrolls we will study illumines primarily the period from the conquest of Palestine by Alexander the Great in 332 B.C.E. through the Great Revolt of the Jews against Rome in 66–73 C.E. During those crucial years, the Jewish people entered into a confrontation with Hellenism, laid the groundwork for the Second Commonwealth, and reestablished their national existence, only to see it extinguished by their Roman conquerors. It is out of this historical and cultural background that the Qumran scrolls arose. In particular, the information the scrolls provide us is most relevant to the years between the Maccabean Revolt of 168–164 B.C.E. and the turn of the era.

In 538 B.C.E., immediately after his conquest of Babylonia, Cyrus (II) the Great, king of Persia and Media, decreed that the Temple of the Jews in Jerusalem was to be rebuilt and that all the exiles who wished might return home. This decree inaugurated the period of the Second Temple, also known as the Second Commonwealth.

The Persian period was formative for the Second Jewish Commonwealth. During that time, Jerusalem was rebuilt and its sacrificial ritual reconstituted in the Second Temple. Equally significant was the granting of temporal—not just religious—authority to the high priesthood. This system of government survived into the Hasmonaean period after the Maccabean Revolt, becoming an object of protest in the Dead Sea Scrolls and in other contemporary literature.

The Hellenistic period began formally with Alexander's conquest of Palestine. However, the date of conquest does not mark the beginning of Hellenistic influence in the region. Already in the fourteenth century B.C.E., the Near (Middle) East as a whole, and Palestine and its Jewish residents more particularly, came under the sway of increasing Aegean influence.

Due to increased trade connections, that influence became much more extensive during the Persian period, when Greek coinage became the standard in the Land of Israel. The cultural phenomenon we call Hellenism exercised such power in ancient Judea that it left a lasting imprint on Judaism and the Jewish people. Indeed, the phenomenon of sectarianism in Judaism, to which the scrolls are our best witness, was largely the indirect result of forces set in motion by the influence of Hellenism.

UNDER PTOLEMIES AND SELEUCIDS

After the death of Alexander the Great in 323 B.C.E., his generals, known as the *diadochi* (successors), were unable to maintain the unity of the empire. Individual generals claimed control over specific areas. Palestine found itself caught in a tug of war between Ptolemy, ruler of Egypt, and Seleucus, ruler of Syria, until 301 B.C.E., when Ptolemy finally secured his hold on Palestine. In the shadow of this political instability, local Jewish autonomy and the already significant role of the high priest grew stronger. This continuing instability also retarded the inroads of Hellenism.

During the third century, Ptolemaic and Seleucid armies conducted five major battles in Palestine, but the Ptolemies maintained control. Because the country was often beset by Seleucid attacks and Bedouin incursions, Ptolemaic military units were stationed throughout Palestine. Many Greek cities were established as military colonies, and many of the soldiers stationed there married native women. In addition, an extensive Ptolemaic bureaucracy existed in Palestine to manage the affairs of government, taxation, and the economy. Ptolemaic presence allowed Hellenism to gain a more secure foothold in Palestine, but Judaea continued to be governed by the high priest and the priestly aristocracy.

The Hellenistic Period

332 B.C.E.	Alexander the Great conquers Palestine
323	Alexander's death and division of Empire
301	Ptolemaic rule over Palestine established
201–198	Seleucid conquest of Palestine
175–164	Antiochus IV Epiphanes
175–171	Jason High Priest
c. 175	Hellenistic Reform
171–167	Menelaus High Priest
168–164	Maccabean Revolt
167–166	Antiochus decrees persecution
166–160	Judah Maccabee leads rebellion
164	Judah conquers Jerusalem and rededicates Temple
160	Judah defeated and killed
157	Jonathan enters Jerusalem
152	Jonathan establishes independence and is appointed high priest
143	Jonathan murdered
142	Simon assumes rule
140	Public assembly confirms Simon as high priest and ruler
134	Murder of Simon
134–104	John Hyrcanus
104–103	Aristobulus I
103–76	Alexander Janneus
76–67	Salome Alexandra
67–63	War between Hyrcanus II and Aristobulus II
63	Roman conquest by Pompey

In 201 B.C.E., the Seleucid king Antiochus III invaded Palestine and quickly conquered it. Although Antiochus affirmed the right of the Jews to live according to their ancestral laws, Hellenism was by now firmly established in Palestine.

HELLENISM AS A CULTURAL PHENOMENON

Hellenism represented the synthesis of Greek culture with the native cultures of the Near East. In a dynamic process, the ever-evolving Hellenistic culture, itself an amalgamation of the Greek and the native, became the raw material for further synthesis with other native cultures not yet under the sway of Hellenism.

Indeed, it was not even the Greeks themselves who spread their own culture to the East, but the Macedonians, whose own civilization derived from that of the true Hellenes, who greatly intensified the process leading to Hellenism's eastward spread. And as it penetrated the Near East, it merged with the native culture. Over many centuries, Hellenistic culture evolved into many different forms in the Near East. Alexander's conquest completed the process of contact and union between East and West.

The Greek city-state, known as the *polis*, was the vehicle for the assimilation and Hellenization of the natives. Such city-states, populated mostly by native Near Easterners, were the cultural melting pots of the East, the home of institutions that promoted the Greek way of life: schools, theaters, and gymnasia. They also expressed Greek culture through athletic contests, Greek language and literature, architecture, and philosophy. Native Near Easterners gravitated to the arts and sciences of the Hellenic world, soon taking the lead in such disciplines as literature and philosophy. The Greek emphasis on physical culture and beauty also spread throughout the Near East. The religion of the Greeks gradually fused with native religions in the form of many different local cults. The official cult of the polis encouraged the constant symbiosis of Greek and Near Eastern elements.

Reacting to this overwhelming influence, natives often redefined and reinterpreted their own traditional cultures in light of what they considered their modern civilization. This process of reinterpretation gave rise to several varieties of Hellenistic Judaism—and to a bitter struggle over how much accommodation to Hellenism each group would tolerate.

HELLENISTIC TRENDS IN PALESTINIAN JUDAISM

During the two centuries before the Maccabean Revolt (168–164 B.C.E.), the new amalgamation of Hellenic and native cultures severely challenged the traditional Jewish way of life. However, that confrontation had differing effects both within Palestinian Jewish society and throughout the country.

The Jewish group least affected by the process of Hellenization was the peasantry, who visited the cities mainly to sell their produce or to make religious pilgrimages to Jerusalem. In the cities they certainly came into contact with more Hellenized Jews and with non-Jews. Yet their language and culture remained Hebraic, and Hellenism's influence on them was restricted largely to the use of Greek words for the various new items they encountered. On the whole, these common people had no intention of abandoning their ancestral way of life for the new cultural symbiosis.

The situation of the urban masses was very different. Although artisans and traders lived in predominantly Jewish cities, the extent of their contact with the

Greek world was much greater than that of residents in rural areas. Literature such as the Book of Ben Sira (Ecclesiasticus), parts of which were found at Qumran and Masada, testifies to the moderate influence of Hellenistic culture on traditional and pious Jews in the early second century B.C.E.

The urban population found itself forced to use the Greek language simply to be understood. Increasingly, throughout the third and second centuries B.C.E., Hellenism exercised a greater and greater influence on architecture and cultural life even among traditionally pious Jews. Certain aristocratic families connected closely with the priesthood were more Hellenized than most other Jews in these cities, perhaps as a result of their greater contact with the wider Hellenistic world or for political and economic reasons.

Those Jews who were interested in an even greater form of Hellenization gravitated to the Greek cities, mostly on the seacoast and in the area later known in Roman times as the Decapolis, located in the northern Jordan valley and Transjordan. In these regions, Greek was the everyday language, and the dominant culture was Hellenistic. Such Jews compromised with the pagan cults primarily by interpreting the city liturgies as extensions of their monotheistic Judaism. Indeed, they radically reinterpreted the Jewish Scriptures to be consistent with these pagan cults. In order to ease the transition from the ancient Near Eastern life of the Palestinian Jew to the new, cosmopolitan life of the Hellenistic Jew, this Jewish group tried to remake Judaism into a subculture of the Greek cosmos.

These trends coexisted for a time within Judaean society until they came into open confrontation. Beginning in the late second century B.C.E., extreme Hellenizers of the type previously known only in the Greek cities took control of the Jerusalem priesthood and attempted to transform Jerusalem into another Hellenistic polis. This event set the stage for the Maccabean Revolt.

THE MACCABEAN REVOLT

The ascension of Antiochus IV Epiphanes (175–164 B.C.E.) to the Seleucid throne continued to fuel the political instability in Palestine that had resulted from the constant Ptolemaic-Seleucid warfare. In a move certain to provoke the Jewish population, Antiochus sold the office of high priest, traditionally a hereditary succession, to Jason, the highest bidder. Jason also bought the right to establish in Jerusalem a gymnasium and an ephebion (a Hellenistic school), intending, through such centralized educational and cultural institutions, to turn the city into a Hellenistic polis. The right to live according to the Torah, granted to the Judaeans by Antiochus III, was now rescinded. In its place, the Jews were to live under the law of the Greek city. Jews suddenly found themselves second-class citizens under an oligarchy. The Hellenized aristocracy, on the other hand, saw many benefits to the new reforms: citizenship in a Greek city, trade with other such cities, the minting of coins, and other advantages particularly attractive to the wealthy and powerful.

Even with these political and commercial changes, the Temple and its rituals continued according to the ancient tradition. Yet Jason's brand of Hellenization was not enough for some. Amidst violent struggles between moderate and extreme Hellenizers and political intrigue connected with the supporters of Ptolemies and Seleucids, foreign deities were introduced into the Temple, creating further friction. To extreme Jewish Hellenizers, the ancestral God of Israel was simply another manifestation of the supreme deity known in Syria as Baal Shamin (Master of Heaven) and in the Greek world as Zeus Olympius.

The earliest attempts at organized rebellion were probably led by the Hasidim, a group of pietists who found the religious compromises in Hellenistic Jerusalem totally unacceptable. Rebellion was mounting, and Antiochus acted to stem it.

To do so, he enacted the infamous persecutions. Understanding all too well that the only way to defeat the rebels was by attacking the forces that inspired them—the Torah, the commandments, and the culture of the Jewish people—Antiochus struck at the heart of Jewish practice. But his actions had precisely the opposite effect from the one he intended. After years of struggle and insurrection, fueled by the Jewish Hellenizers' attempts to foist their way of life on the entire nation of Israel, the Jews reached their boiling point and struck back.

Antiochus's persecutions were enacted in the winter of 167–166 B.C.E. Foreign idolatrous worship and cultic prostitution were introduced into the Temple in December 167 B.C.E. Throughout Palestine, the Sabbath and Festivals were to be violated. High places were built where unclean animals were to be offered. Circumcision was outlawed. The laws of kosher food were not to be observed. The penalty for violating these ordinances was death.

Throughout the land Jews found themselves confronted by officials who sought to enforce the new regulations with a vengeance, burning Torah scrolls and executing those who hid them. The stage was now set for confrontation of two opposing forces—the Jewish people and the Seleucids. The appearance of the Hasmonaean (Maccabean) family would soon ignite the flames of full-scale revolt.

Several thousand rebels coalesced around the Hasmonaean family, led by Judah the Maccabee and his brothers John, Simon, Eleazar, and Jonathan. This army began to take control of villages throughout the countryside. By 166–165 B.C.E., they had taken Judaea.

Under Judah the Maccabee (hammer), the Jewish armies defeated successive Seleucid generals, who attempted to put down the uprising. In December of 164 B.C.E., Judah and his men took Jerusalem, and on the 25th of the Hebrew month of Kislev, Judah purified the Temple and reorganized the sacrificial worship to conform to the Jewish tradition. This event is commemorated in the Jewish holiday of Hanukkah (rededication). The main objective of the revolt—elimination of the persecutions and restoration of Judaism to the nation—had been achieved.

Next, Judah undertook wars throughout the Land of Israel to extirpate paganism from the country and eliminate Hellenizing rivals. Judah was killed in battle against the Seleucids in 160 B.C.E. The Hasmonaeans now rallied around Jonathan, his brother. Again the Hellenized Jews sought to rule, and again the Hasmonaeans plagued them on all sides. For several years, the post of high priest remained vacant as war raged. Finally, responding to competing offers from both sides vying for succession to the Syrian throne, Jonathan, with the support of the Syrian pretender Alexander Balas, appeared in the robes of the high priest on the Festival of Sukkot (Tabernacles) in the year 152 B.C.E. A dynasty had dawned that would rule the Jewish people until the coming of the Romans in 63 B.C.E.

HASMONAEAN TAKEOVER OF THE TEMPLE

Immediately following the revolt, there occurred a crisis in the Jewish priesthood that had a direct impact on the formation of the Qumran sect and its establishment in the Judaean Desert.

The Zadokite priests, tracing their ancestry to Zadok, high priest in the time of King Solomon, had occupied the high priesthood virtually without interruption up to the Maccabean revolt. Yet members of this group, known as Sadducees, were also among the extreme Hellenists who had perpetrated the Hellenistic reforms and opened up Judaea to the interference of the Seleucids, the Antiochan persecutions, and the Maccabean wars. However, many Sadducean priests during this period continued to be pious, maintaining the ancient traditions of the Temple in Jerusalem.

As a result of the revolt, the Zadokites lost control of the high priesthood to the Hasmonaeans, the Maccabean family. When the dust of the revolt had settled, Jonathan the Hasmonaean, not of the Zadokite line, had been proclaimed high priest. Hasmonaean takeover of the high priesthood was made permanent only later at an official assembly in the time of Simon: "forever, until a trustworthy prophet should arise" (I Maccabees 14:41).

The change must have been welcome to many elements of the Jewish population. After all, the Zadokites had led the people astray by their corruption in the last years before the revolt. The Hasmonaeans, on the other hand, were looked upon as reformers, ready to maintain the purity and holiness of the Temple and Jerusalem, for which they had fought so valiantly. Only later would those hopes also be dashed, as the Hasmonaean rulers themselves became increasingly Hellenized. But in the flush of victory, the Jews of Palestine hailed the rise of the Hasmonaean high priesthood as signaling a return to the purity of Israelite worship.

However, it is unlikely that the entire population greeted the new regime with unqualified acceptance. The old Zadokites, especially the pious priests, must have bitterly resented Hasmonaean control of the office of high priest. Even more objectionable to them were the changes in Temple practice introduced by the

The Hasmonaean Family

Mattathias
d. 166/165 B.C.E.

Simon	Judah	Jonathan
d. 134 B.C.E.	d. 160 B.C.E.	d. 143 B.C.E.

John Hyrcanus I
d. 104 B.C.E.

Aristobulus I	Alexander Janneus —— Salome Alexandra
d. 103 B.C.E.	d. 76 B.C.E. d. 67 B.C.E.

Hyrcanus II	Aristobulus II
d. 30 B.C.E.	d. 49 B.C.E.

Alexandra	Alexander	Antigonus
d.? 28 B.C.E.	d. 49 B.C.E.	d. 37 B.C.E.

Aristobulus III	Mariamme	Daughter who married
d. 35 B.C.E.	d. 29 B.C.E.	Antipater III, son of
		Herod the Great

Hasmonaeans under the influence of the Pharisees. From Josephus and talmudic sources, we know that the Pharisees at this time held both political power and religious authority and that their views probably played a large role in the conduct of both government and priesthood, although that role was not as great as the Pharisees themselves might have wanted. Additional proof of Pharisaic hegemony comes from the Dead Sea Scrolls, as we will see.

JEWISH SECTS IN THE AFTERMATH OF THE MACCABEAN REVOLT

In this historical setting, we first meet, in the writings of Josephus, the three major sects of the period—Pharisees, Sadducees, and Essenes. The group that collected the Dead Sea Scrolls also arose at that time, being yet another response to these events. Though scant direct information exists about most of these sects, the Dead Sea sectarians have left us their ancient library, which is now reshaping our understanding of all of the groups of Second Temple Judaism.

For our purposes, a sect can be defined as a religious ideology that may develop the characteristics of a political party in order to defend its way of life. The way the term is generally used in the study of ancient Judaism differs from its usual usage in religious studies, wherein "sect" commonly denotes a group that has somehow split from a mainstream movement. Thus, in the Second Temple period, we refer to all Jewish groups as sects, regardless of size or importance.

Competing sects each sought adherents among the people. Although all were Jewish and regarded the Torah as the ultimate source of Jewish law, each had a different approach or interpretation of Jewish law and considered other groups' approaches illegitimate. The various sects also held differing views on such theological questions as the nature of God's revelation, the free will of human beings, and reward and punishment. They also took different stands on how much acculturation or assimilation to Hellenism they were willing to tolerate.

The greatest conflict arose over the most important symbol of Jewish life—the Temple itself. When one group would brand as illegitimate sacrifices made by the priestly caste in charge of sacrifices or would accuse them of conducting services improperly, fierce intersectarian conflict would erupt. The Pharisees and Sadducees each sought to control the temporal powers that gave one sect or another the right to determine how the priests would minister in the Temple.

Sadducees and Pharisees were the major participants in the Jewish religious and political affairs of Greco-Roman Palestine. In fact, the gradual transfer of influence and power from the priestly Sadducees to the learned Pharisees went hand in hand with the transition from Temple to Torah that characterized the Judaism of this period.

At the same time, a number of sects with apocalyptic or ascetic tendencies also contributed to the texture of Palestinian Judaism. Some of these sects played a crucial role in creating the backdrop against which Christianity arose. Others encouraged the messianic visions that twice led the Jews into revolt against Rome. Still others served as the locus for the development of mystical ideas that would eventually penetrate rabbinic Judaism. Each of these groups was characterized by its adherents' extreme dedication to its own interpretation of the Torah and the associated teachings it had received.

SADDUCEES

The Sadducees were a recognizable group by about 150 B.C.E. Predominantly aristocratic, they were mostly either priests themselves or had intermarried with the high-priestly families. They tended to be moderate Hellenizers whose primary loyalty was to the religion of Israel but whose culture was greatly influenced by the Greek environment in which they lived.

The Sadducees derived their name from Zadok, the high priest of the Jerusalem Temple in the time of Solomon. The Zadokite family of high priests served at the head of the priesthood throughout First Temple times—except when foreign worship was brought into the Temple—and then during Second Temple times—until the Hasmonaeans wrested control of the high priesthood from them. Ezekiel had assigned the priestly duties exclusively to this clan (44:9–16).

The Sadducees rejected the "traditions of the fathers" that the Pharisees considered law. For this reason, later rabbinic sources picture them as rejecting the Oral Law. However, the notion promulgated by some church fathers that the Sadducees accepted only the Torah as authoritative, rejecting the Prophets and the emerging corpus of Writings, is unsubstantiated by any earlier sources.

It is difficult to date the many differences that early rabbinic texts ascribe to the Pharisees and Sadducees, especially because some of this information is preserved only in very late, posttalmudic sources. The differences discussed in the earlier Mishnaic materials are of particular interest. We learn from these sources that the Sadducees required compensation for injuries done by a person's servant, whereas the Pharisees required compensation only in the case of one's animals, according to their interpretation of the Torah's laws (Exodus 21:32, 35–36). The Sadducees required that false witnesses be executed only if the accused had already been put to death as a result of such false testimony (Deuteronomy 19:19–21). The Pharisees imposed this penalty only when the accused had not been executed. The Sadducees criticized the inconsistencies in the Pharisaic interpretation of the purity laws, and the Pharisees regarded Sadducean women as menstrually impure because they followed improper interpretations of these laws. In general, the Sadducees regarded the purity laws as applying exclusively to the Temple and the priests, and they refused to extend those laws into the daily life of all Jews. To the Pharisees that extension was fundamental to their approach.

Why did the Sadducees disagree so extensively with Pharisaic tradition? What made the two diverge on so many matters of Jewish law?

Later Jewish tradition claimed that all the differences revolved around the Sadducean rejection of the Oral Law. Based on this assumption, modern scholars have argued that the Sadducees were strict literalists, who followed the plain meaning of the words of the Torah. Yet such an approach does not explain most of the views on legal matters attributed to the Sadducees.

The Sadducees also differed from the Pharisees on theological questions. They denied the notions of reward and punishment after death and the immortality of the soul, ideas accepted by the Pharisees. They did not believe in angels in the supernatural sense, although they must have acknowledged the "divine messengers" mentioned in the Bible. To them, because of human beings' absolute free will, God did not exercise control over human affairs.

It is difficult to pinpoint the precise beginnings of the Sadducees party. The priestly aristocracy, tracing its roots to First Temple times, had increased greatly in power during the Persian and Hellenistic periods because it controlled both the temporal and spiritual affairs of the nation. Although some priests had been involved in the extreme Hellenization leading up to the Maccabean Revolt, most of the Saducean lower clergy had remained loyal to the Torah and the ancestral way of life.

In the aftermath of the revolt, a small, devoted group of Saducean priests probably formed the faction that eventually became the Dead Sea sect. Unwilling to tolerate the replacement of the Zadokite high priest with a Hasmonaean, which took place in 152 B.C.E., they also disagreed with the Jerusalem priesthood on many points of Jewish law. Recent research indicates, as we will see, that soon after the Hasmonaean takeover of the high priesthood, this group retreated to Qumran.

Other moderately Hellenized Sadducees remained in Jerusalem. It was they who were termed Sadducees, in the strict sense of the word, both by Josephus in his descriptions of the Hasmonaean period and by the later rabbinic traditions. They continued to play a key role in the Hasmonaean aristocracy, supporting the priest-kings and joining with the Pharisees in the governing council. After dominating that body for most of the reign of John Hyrcanus and Alexander Janneus, they suffered a major political setback when Salome Alexandra turned so thoroughly to the Pharisees. In the Herodian era, the Sadducees regained power when they made common cause with the Herodian dynasty. In the end, it was a group of Saducean lower priests who, in deciding to end the daily sacrifice for the Roman emperor, triggered the full-scale revolt against Rome in 66 C.E.

Closely allied to the Sadducees were the Boethusians, who seem to have held views similar to those of the Sadducees. Most scholars ascribe the origin of the Boethusians to Simeon ben Boethus, whom Herod appointed high priest in 24 B.C.E. so that Boethus would have sufficient status for Herod to marry Boethus's daughter Mariamme (II). This theory, however, is completely unproven. In fact, certain parallels between Boethusian rulings and material in the Dead Sea Scrolls argue for a considerably earlier date. Although there certainly were some differences between the Sadducees and the Boethusians, the latter appear to have been a subgroup or an offshoot of the Saducean group.

As recorded in rabbinic literature, the primary dispute separating the Sadducees from the Pharisees pertained to the calendar. The Sadducees held that the first offering of the Omer (barley sheaf; Leviticus 23:9–14) had to take place not on the second day of Passover, as the Pharisees claimed, but rather on the first Sunday after Passover, in accord with Leviticus 23:11, "on the morrow of the Sabbath." To ensure that this Festival was observed on the proper day of the week, the Sadducees adopted a calendar that, like the one known from the Dead Sea sect and the Book of Jubilees, was based on both solar months and solar years. Following that calendar, the holiday of Shavuot would always fall on a Sunday.

Even though this approach seemed to accord better with the literal interpretation of the words "on the morrow of the Sabbath," the Pharisees could accept neither the innovative solar calendar (the biblical calendar was based on lunar months) nor the interpretation on which it was based. To them, "Sabbath" here meant Festival.

The Sadducean approach had a major impact on political and religious developments in the Judaism of the Second Temple period. Sadducean offshoots played a leading role in the formation of the Dead Sea sect. There is even evidence that some Sadducean traditions remained in circulation long enough to influence the Karaite sect, which came to the fore in the eighth century C.E. Yet despite their important role in these phenomena, the Sadducees ceased to be a factor in Jewish history with the destruction of the Temple in 70 C.E. The sacrificial system, in which they had played such a leading role, was no longer practiced. Their power base, the Jerusalem Temple, was gone, and their strict legal rulings augured poorly for the adaptation of Judaism to the new surroundings and circumstances of the years ahead.

PHARISEES

The Pharisees derived their name from the Hebrew *perushim*, meaning "separate." This designation probably refers to their self-imposed separation from ritually impure food and from the tables of the common people, later termed 'am ha-'aretz (people of the land) in talmudic sources, who were not scrupulous regarding laws of Levitical purity and tithes. Originally, the name may have been a pejorative term used by their opponents.

Talmudic sources describe those who observed the laws of purity as *haverim* (associates), and groups of such people as *havurot* (fellowships). The *haverim* are contrasted with the 'am ha-'aretz. Although most historians assume that those *havurot* were Pharisaic, the sources never associate the terms "Pharisee" and *haver.*

In rabbinic sources, the Pharisees are sometimes identified as the "sages," an anachronism resulting from the Rabbis' view of themselves as the inheritors of the Pharisaic tradition. Although the Pharisees' influence grew steadily until they eventually came to dominate the religious life of the Jewish people, scholars estimate that they numbered only six thousand in Herodian times.

Who were these Pharisees and where did they come from? Because the Pharisees first appear by name in the extant sources during the reign of Jonathan, brother of Judah the Maccabee (about 150 B.C.E.), many scholars have tried to identify them with the Hasidim, the allies of Judah in the Maccabean revolt. That theory, however, cannot be substantiated, because our information about the Hasidim is very limited. It is probable that the Hasidim were not a sect or party but rather a loose association of pietists, as denoted by the term in later talmudic literature. Equally unsupported is the notion that the pre-Maccabean Hasidim gave rise to the Essenes.

Rabbinic sources trace the origins of the Pharisees back even earlier—to the Persian and early Hellenistic periods, when the Men of the Great Assembly were said to have provided Israel's religious leadership. Some modern scholars have identified the Men of the Great Assembly with the *soferim* (scribes), thereby making them the forerunners of the Pharisaic movement.

Unfortunately, the historical evidence does not allow us to draw any definite conclusions here. All we know is that the Pharisees appear suddenly, as a distinct entity, in the Hasmonaean period and that Pharisaic theology and organization must have been developing somewhat earlier. How much earlier and in what form we simply cannot say.

The Pharisees appear in Hasmonaean times as part of the governing council in coalition with the Sadducees, with whom they sought to advance their vision of how the Jewish people should live and govern themselves. Under the Hasmonaean rulers John Hyrcanus (138–104 B.C.E.) and Alexander Janneus (103–76 B.C.E.), conditions led the Pharisees further and further into the political arena. As the Hasmonaeans became increasingly Hellenized, the Pharisees expressed greater opposition to them. Under John Hyrcanus, there was a decisive Hasmonaean tilt toward the Sadducees. By the time of Alexander Janneus, the Pharisees were in open warfare with him, and he was consequently defeated by the Seleucid king in 88 B.C.E. That rout led to a reconciliation between Alexander Janneus and the Pharisees. This entire story is recounted in the Dead Sea Scrolls, as we will see. During the reign of Salome Alexandra, the Pharisees were the dominant political element—in control of the affairs of the nation—although the extent of their influence has been exaggerated by many scholars.

The Pharisees themselves were divided over the question of how best to respond to the Hellenizers in power. Some advocated an accommodationist policy toward the government, so long as it allowed them to practice Judaism according to the Pharisaic view. Others, maintaining that no government was acceptable unless it was controlled by Pharisees, advocated revolt. This dispute, a leitmotif throughout the history of Pharisaism and continuing in rabbinic Judaism, became central in the two Jewish revolts against Rome.

By and large, the Pharisees had three major characteristics: First, they represented primarily the middle and lower classes. Second, and perhaps as a consequence of their lower social status, they really did not become Hellenized but seem to have remained primarily Near Eastern in culture. To be sure, they may have adopted Greek words or intellectual approaches, but they viewed as authoritative only what they regarded as the ancient traditions of Israel. Third, they accepted what they termed the "traditions of the fathers"—nonbiblical laws and customs believed to have been passed down through the generations. These teachings supplemented the written Torah and were part of what the Rabbis later would call the Oral Law. They are said to have been extremely scrupulous in observing the Torah and to have been expert in its interpretation.

In a number of significant teachings, the Pharisees espoused views that were later incorporated into the rabbinic tradition. Primary among these were beliefs in the immortality of the soul, reward and punishment after death, and angels, as well as the idea of divine providence. The Sadducees rejected all of these ideas. Unlike the Sadducees, who totally denied the notion of divine interference in human affairs, the Pharisees believed that God could play a role there. To the Sadducees, free will was complete and inviolable; to the Pharisees, it was circumscribed. The Essenes, in contrast, maintained a belief in predestination, as did the Dead Sea sect.

Although Josephus, our only source describing the theological disputes between these groups, dresses these various sectarian views in Greek philosophical garb, it is obvious that these disputes emerged from varying interpretations of biblical tradition. Therefore, the basic outlines of the controversy may be accepted as authentic.

How seriously should we take later rabbinic claims that the Pharisees dominated the ritual of the Jerusalem Temple? That question has sparked considerable controversy. Recently, scholars have been inclined to discount such reports as a later reshaping of history in light of post-destruction reality. We will see, however, that the *Halakhic Letter,* found at Qumran, proves that the views assigned to the Pharisees in a number of Mishnaic disputes are exactly those in practice in the Jerusalem Temple. Whether the dominance of the Pharisaic view was due to their political power or whether their views were indeed widely held in the Hasmonaean period cannot be determined with certainty.

Repeatedly, Josephus stresses the popularity of the Pharisees among the people. Given his firsthand knowledge of the last years of the Second Temple period, we should credit this view, although we also need to acknowledge Josephus's definitely pro-Pharisaic prejudices. The Pharisees' popularity, together with their unique approach to Jewish law, laid the groundwork for their eventual ascendancy in Jewish political and religious life. The Oral Law concept that grew from the Pharisaic "traditions of the fathers" allowed Judaism to adapt to the new and varied circumstances it would face in talmudic times and later. In time, Pharisaism would become rabbinic Judaism—the basis for all subsequent Jewish life and civilization.

ESSENES

The Essenes, a sect noted for its piety and distinctive theology, were known in Greek as *Essenoi* or *Essaioi.* Although numerous suggestions have been made about the etymology of the name, none has achieved scholarly consensus. The most recent theory, and also the most probable, holds that the name was borrowed from a group of devotees of the cult of Artemis in Asia Minor, whose demeanor and dress somewhat resembled those of the group in Judaea.

Since the discovery of the Dead Sea scrolls, most scholars have identified the Qumran sect with the Essenes. In fact, the only information we have about the group is gleaned from Greek sources, primarily Philo, Josephus, and Pliny the Elder. The term "Essene" does not appear in any of the Qumran scrolls.

According to the testimony of Philo and Josephus, there were about four thousand Essenes—scattered in communities throughout Palestine—although there is some evidence that they avoided the larger cities. The Roman author Pliny identifies an Essene settlement between Jericho and Ein Gedi on the western shore of the Dead Sea. For those scholars identifying the Essenes of Philo and Josephus with the Dead Sea sect, that location—in the vicinity of Qumran—has been regarded as decisive proof of their claims. As we shall soon see, identification of the sect is a much more complex issue.

ESSENE PRACTICES

Essene children were educated in the ways of the Essene community, but only adult males could enter the sect. The community was organized under officials to whom obedience was required. A court of one hundred could expel from the community any members who transgressed.

Aspiring members received three items—a hatchet, a loin-cloth, and a white garment—and had to undergo a detailed initiation process that included a year of probation. They were then eligible for the ritual ablutions. After that stage, candidates had to undergo a further two years of probation, after which they had to swear an oath—the only oath the Essenes permitted. In the final stages of their initiation, the candidates bound themselves by oath to be pious toward God, just to men, and honest with their fellow Essenes, and to properly transmit the teachings; to be kept secret were the names of the angels. The initiates were then allowed to participate in the sect's communal meals and were considered full-fledged members.

The Essenes practiced community of property. Upon admission, new members turned their property over to the group, whose elected officials administered it for the benefit of all. Hence, all members shared wealth equally, with no distinctions between rich and poor.

Members earned income for the group through various occupations, including agriculture and crafts. The Essenes avoided commerce and the manufacture of weapons. All earnings were turned over to officials, who distributed funds to buy necessities and to take care of older or ill members of the community. Not only did the Essenes provide aid for their own members, but they also dispensed charity throughout the country. Special officers in each town took care of traveling members.

Characteristic of the Essenes were their moderation and avoidance of luxury. They viewed income only as a means of providing the necessities of life, and that approach guided their eating and drinking habits as well as their choice of clothes. It also explains why they did not anoint themselves with oil. Indeed, they saw oil as transmitting ritual impurity. Asceticism manifested itself most strongly among those Essenes who were celibate. But it appears that in many cases celibacy may not have been absolute, but instead practiced later in life, after the individual had had children.

The Essenes' attitude toward the Jerusalem Temple was ambivalent. Whereas they accepted the notion of a central place of worship in Jerusalem, they disagreed about how the Temple authorities understood purity and sacrifices. They therefore sent voluntary offerings to the Temple but did not themselves participate in its sacrificial worship.

The Essenes began their day with prayer, after which they worked at their occupations. Later, they assembled for purification rituals and a communal meal prepared by priests and eaten while wearing special garments. After the members silently took their places, the baker and the cook distributed the food, according to the order of the diners' status. The community then returned to work, coming together once again in the evening for another meal. At sunset, they recited prayers once again. Though some of these practices were common to other Jews of the period as well, the Essenes' unique manner of practice separated them from their fellow Jews.

Ritual purity was greatly emphasized. Ablutions were required not only before communal meals but also after relieving oneself and after coming in contact with a nonmember or a novice. Members were extremely careful about attending to natural functions modestly. They immersed often in order to maintain ritual purity and refrained from expectorating. They customarily wore white garments, regarding modesty of dress as very important. Noteworthy was their stringency in matters of Sabbath observance.

Essene teachings were recorded in books that the members were duty bound to pass on with great care. Essenes were reported to be experts on medicinal roots and the properties of stones, the healing powers of which they claimed to have derived from ancient writings.

According to Greek sources, the Essenes embraced several fundamental beliefs. One was the notion of unalterable destiny. Another was their belief in the immortality of the soul. According to Josephus, they held that only the soul survived after death. Josephus asserts that in that respect their belief was very close to that of the Pharisees.

Josephus first mentions the Essenes in his account of the reign of Jonathan the Hasmonaean (152–143 B.C.E.), when describing the religious trends of the time. He says that the Essenes participated in the war against Rome in 66–73 C.E. and that some were tortured by the Romans during the revolt. With the destruction of the country following that unsuccessful uprising, the Essenes disappeared.

Ever since the discovery of Qumran cave 1 in 1947, scholars have attempted to identify the Qumran sect with one of the groups known to have existed in Second Temple times. Those who seek to identify the sect with the Essenes tend to gloss over points of disagreement, pointing only to similarities between the two groups. Yet, important differences do exist between descriptions of the Essenes and Qumran sectarian teachings, regarding details of the initiation process and of Jewish law.

The major sects of Second Temple times participated in religious and political ferment throughout their existence. The results of that ferment would eventually determine the future of Judaism. The failure of the Great Revolt and the destruction of the Temple in 70 C.E. settled once and for all some of the most volatile issues. The Sadducees lost their power base; the Essenes and the Dead Sea sect were physically decimated; extreme apocalypticism had been discredited. The Pharisaic approach alone was left to accommodate itself to Roman rule and post-Temple worship, in time becoming the Judaism known today. The legacy of the other sects, however, lives on in their rediscovered writings, in the sectarian teachings that influenced the medieval Karaites, and in some aspects of the new theology of Christianity.

One of the sects that disappeared was the Dead Sea sect. Now, after almost two thousand years of silence, its writings have been rediscovered. How did it fit into this picture of sectarian strife in the Second Commonwealth? And from its library what can we discover about what happened so many years ago?

Examining the origin and early history of the sect will help us to understand the forces that operated after the Maccabean Revolt and how various Jewish groups reacted to those forces. While some sects were accommodating themselves to the new order in various ways, the Dead Sea group decided it had to leave Jerusalem altogether in order to continue its unique way of life.

CHAPTER 5

Origins and Early History

To understand the schism that gave birth to the Dead Sea sect, we need to frame it against the background of Jewish history and sectarianism in the Hellenistic period. But we now have even more specific information about the particular conflicts, mostly over sacrifices and ritual purity, that led the sectarians to break away and form a distinct group. Indeed, we will see that the origins of the sect are to be traced to the internal priestly turmoil associated with Hellenistic reform, the Maccabean Revolt, and the rise of the Hasmonaean dynasty and high priesthood.

EVIDENCE OF THE *HALAKHIC LETTER*

A Qumran text, today known as the *Halakhic Letter*, demonstrates quite clearly that the root cause that led to the sectarian schism consisted of a series of disagreements about sacrificial law and ritual purity. The full name of this document is *Miqṣat Ma'ase ha-Torah* (some legal rulings pertaining to the Torah). The writers of its text list more than twenty laws that describe the ways their practices differed from those prevailing in the Temple and its sacrificial worship. But even more important, the document reveals more precise information than we have previously had about the origins of the sect.

The *Halakhic Letter* begins with a statement about its own intent:*

> These are some of our (legal) rulings [regarding Go]d's [Torah] which are [some of the] rulings of [the] laws which w[e hold, and a]ll of them are regarding [sacrifices] and the purity of. . . . *(HALAKHIC LETTER B1–3)*

---

* Information on this and all texts quoted or cited in this book is found in the Guide to Dead Sea Scrolls Texts Cited at the back of the book. All translations presented here are by the author, except for biblical texts, which for the most part follow the New Jewish Publication Society translation. *Square brackets* are used to indicate restorations made by scholars to fragmentary scroll texts. *Parentheses* are used to indicate explanatory material added to the translation.

The first sentence announces that what follows are some of "our (legal) rulings" that "we hold." Throughout the letter the authors refer to themselves in the plural. What then follows is a list of twenty-two halakhic matters over which the sectarians disagree with the addressee of the letter. For most of these, the text includes both the view of the writers as well as that of their opponents. Such phrases as "but you know" and "but we hold," indicate the polemical nature of the text. Later we will look at one of the document's specific laws, which demonstrates unquestionably that this group adhered to the Sadducean trend in Jewish law.

The second part of the letter returns to general principles, presenting the writers' general views on the schism now under way. The authors state:

> [You know that] we have separated from the mainstream of the peo[ple and from all their impurities and] from mixing in these matters and from being involved w[ith them] regarding these matters. But you k[now that there cannot be] found in our hands dishonesty, falsehood, or evil.
> (HALAKHIC LETTER C7–9)

The writers here state that in accepting the aforementioned rulings, they had to withdraw from participation in the rituals of the majority of the people. The purpose of this document was to call on their erstwhile colleagues in Jerusalem and the Hasmonaean leader to effect a reconciliation that would allow them to return to their role in the Temple. Needless to say, reconciliation meant accepting the views this document puts forth. Accordingly, the authors make the general statement that the addressees know that the members of this dissident group are reliable and honest, meaning that the list of laws is indeed being strictly observed as stated by the authors.

At this point, the letter plainly explains its purpose:

> [For indeed] we have [written] to you in order that you will investigate the Book of Moses [and] in the book[s of the P]rophets and of Davi[d . . . , in the deeds] of each and every generation. (HALAKHIC LETTER C9–11)

The sectarians have written to the addressee (now for the first time in the singular) in order that "you" will examine the words of the Torah, the Prophets, and David (presumably the biblical accounts of the Davidic monarchy), as well as the history of the generations.

The text now turns to what is to be found in those particular documents, that is, the Scriptures that the sectarians want their opponent to search. The addressee is told (again in the singular) that it has been foretold that he would turn aside from the path of righteousness and, as a result, suffer misfortune. The text of the *Halakhic Letter* then predicts that in the End of Days, the ruler will return to God. All of it is in accord with what is written in the Torah and in the

Halakhic Letter The announcement of the existence of a
foundation document of the Qumran sect, now known among
scholars as MMT, helped to trigger the campaign for release of the
scrolls. The document, shown here in one of its six manuscripts
(E), is an epistle purportedly sent to the Jerusalem Temple
leadership by the founders of the sect. Its positions on matters of
Jewish law demonstrate that the founders of the sect were
Sadducees in origin. *Courtesy of the Israel Antiquities Authority.*

Prophets. This time the authors do not mention the Writings, probably because
the relevant blessings and curses do not occur there.

The text now returns to the discussion of the kings, recalling the blessings
fulfilled during the time of Solomon, son of David, and the curses visited on Israel
from the days of Jeroboam, son of Nebat (c. 922–901 B.C.E.), through the time of
Zedekiah (597–586 B.C.E., last king of Judah).

Next the writers state that in their view some of the blessings and curses have
already come to pass:

> And we recognize that some of the blessings and curses which are written in
> the B[ook of Mo]ses have come to pass, and that this is the End of Days when
> they will repent in Isra[el] for[ever . . .] and they will not backsli[de].
> (HALAKHIC LETTER C20–22)

Here the authors reveal their belief that they are currently living on the verge of
the End of Days, a notion that later became normative in Qumran messianic
thought. It is also clear that they considered their own age the period foretold by
the Bible as the final repentance of Israel.

In light of these beliefs, the authors exhort the addressee (singular) to recall the
events surrounding the reigns of Israel's kings, to examine their deeds, and to
note that those who observed the laws of the Torah were spared misfortune, their

transgressions forgiven. Such was the case with David, whom the addressee is asked to remember.

The authors then sum up why they sent this text to the addressee:

> And indeed, we have written to you some of the rulings pertaining to the Torah which we considered were good for you and your people, for [we have seen] that you have wisdom and knowledge of the Torah. Understand all these (matters) and seek from Him that He correct your counsel and distance from you evil thoughts and the counsel of Belial, in order that you shall rejoice in the end when you find some of our words correct. And let it be considered right for you, and lead you to do righteousness and good, and may it be for your benefit, and for that of Israel. (HALAKHIC LETTER C26–32)

Here the phrase *Miqṣat Ma'ase ha-Torah* (some of the rulings pertaining to the Torah) appears. The authors state that the letter is intended for the benefit of the addressee and the nation. The addressee is credited with being wise and having sufficient knowledge of the Torah to understand the halakhic matters presented in the letter. The writers call on him to mend his ways and renounce all of his incorrect views on matters of Jewish law. Doing so will lead him to rejoice at the end of this period (the End of Days), for he will come to realize that the writers of the letter are indeed correct in their views. His repentance will be judged a righteous deed, beneficial both for him and for all Israel.

One of the interesting features of the *Halakhic Letter* is the way the grammatical number of addressees shifts. In the introductory sentence, the letter is addressed to an individual, but in the list of laws, the authors engage in a dispute with a group ("you," plural). When the text returns to its main argument—at the conclusion of the list of laws—it shifts back to the singular. We will see later that the plural sections are addressed to priests of the Jerusalem Temple, and the singular to the Hasmonaean ruler.

To understand the nature of this text, we will consider an example of one of its halakhic controversies—the law regarding liquid streams:

> [And even] regarding (poured out) liquid streams, we sa[y] that they do not have [pu]rity. And even the liquid streams do not separate between the impure [and the] pure. For the moisture of the liquid streams and (the vessel) which receives from them are both considered one identical moisture. (HALAKHIC LETTER B56–58)

This enigmatic rule refers to questions of ritual purity in the pouring of liquids from one vessel to another. In a case when the upper vessel is pure and the lower one is not, the question in our text concerns whether the upper vessel—the source of the liquid stream—can be rendered impure when the stream itself links the two vessels together. The text of the *Halakhic Letter* asserts that the entire entity is "one moisture," that is, that the impurity does rise back up the stream, against the direction of the flow, so as to render the upper vessel impure.

This law has a close parallel in the Mishnah. There, in reporting a number of disputes between the Pharisees and the Sadducees, the Mishnah states:

> The Sadducees say: "We complain against you Pharisees. For you declare pure the (poured out) liquid stream." (M. YADAYIM 4:7)

In contrast to our text and the Sadducean view implied in the Mishnah, the Pharisees ruled that in such cases the stream did not impart impurity to the pure vessel from which it was being poured. To them, the impurity of the lower vessel could not flow up, against the flow of the stream, to render the upper vessel impure. Because the Sadducees, in this and many other cases, share the same positions we find in the *Halakhic Letter*, we can convincingly show, using this and other Qumran texts, that the Qumran sect had a substratum of Sadducean halakhic views.

It appears that this letter was written to the head of the Jerusalem establishment, the high priest. The comparisons with the kings of Judah and Israel must have been particularly appropriate to someone who saw himself as an almost royal figure. In the letter, the ruler is admonished to take care lest he go the way of the kings of First Temple times. Such a warning could be addressed only to a figure who could identify, because of his own station in life, with the ancient kings of biblical Israel.

The *Halakhic Letter* makes no mention of the Teacher of Righteousness or any other leader or official known from the sectarian documents. Because the sect's own official history, presented in the *Zadokite Fragments*, claims that their initial separation from the main body of Israel took place some twenty years before the coming of the teacher, we can conclude that the *Halakhic Letter* was written by the collective leadership of the sect in those initial years. This explains why the teacher does not appear in this text.

HISTORICAL RAMIFICATIONS

The *Halakhic Letter* has wide ramifications for our understanding of Jewish history in the Hasmonaean period. In the letter, the views ascribed to the opponents of the emerging sect are the same as those usually attributed in rabbinic literature to the Pharisees or the early Rabbis. When mishnaic texts preserve Pharisee-Sadducee conflicts over the same matters discussed in the *Halakhic Letter*, the views of the letter's authors match those of the Sadducees.

Only one possible explanation can be offered for this phenomenon: The earliest members of the sect must have been Sadducees unwilling to accept the status quo established in the aftermath of the Maccabean revolt. The Maccabees, by replacing the Zadokite high priesthood with their own, reduced the Zadokites to a subsidiary position for as long as Hasmonaean rule lasted. Even after leaving Jerusalem, the Dead Sea sect continued to refer to itself or its leaders as the "Sons of Zadok." Our text makes clear that the designation "Sons of Zadok" is to be taken at face value. These were indeed Sadducees who protested the imposition of Pharisaic views in the Temple under the Hasmonaean priests.

That interpretation explains why the writers of the *Halakhic Letter* constantly assert that the addressees know the authors' views to be correct. The founders of the sect aimed their halakhic polemics (addressed to a plural opponent) at their Sadducean brethren who continued to serve in the Temple and accepted the new reality. It was these remaining Jerusalem Sadducees who now followed views known to us from Pharisaic-rabbinic sources and who, in the view of the authors of this letter, knew very well that the old Sadducean practices were otherwise than what they were now observing.

Although it may be hard for us moderns to conceive that a schism of such magnitude could occur over what appear to be minor aspects of ritual law, we must remember that to the various factions in the Jerusalem priesthood and to the Jewish people in ancient times, the correct conduct of sacrificial worship was the primary guarantor of their welfare. Indeed, they regarded the sacrificial system as the prime connection of the people of Israel to God, the source of blessing for the land and its inhabitants. Had not many Jews only recently risen up in arms in the Maccabean Revolt in order to ensure the purity of that worship against foreign, pagan influence? Now, in the aftermath of that rebellion, no one was willing to accept easily the conduct of this worship in any way inconsistent with his own particular views.

Thus, when Temple worship was entrusted to a usurper—the Hasmonaean high priest who acted according to already existing Pharisaic views—some pious Sadducees formed a sect and seceded from participation in the ritual of the Jerusalem Temple. At first the sect sought a reconciliation. When that failed, the members experienced disappointment and confusion.

The dissonant Zadokite priests increasingly saw themselves as a sectarian group. We can date the true beginnings of our sect to the moment the Qumran Zadokites' moderate attempts at reform failed, convincing them that Hasmonaean succession was not temporary but permanent.

Some have challenged this theory of the sect's Sadducean origins, arguing that it does not explain the group's more sectarian or radical tendencies, especially the animated polemic and xenophobia so often found in later sectarian texts. But those later texts reveal the eventual effects of the earlier schism. After they failed in their initial attempts, exemplified by the *Halakhic Letter*, to reconcile and win over the Hasmonaeans and the remaining Jerusalem Sadducees to their own system of Temple practice, the Qumran Zadokites gradually developed the sectarian mentality of the despised, rejected, and abandoned outcast. Accordingly, they began to look upon themselves as the true Israel, condemning and despising all others.

Another challenge to this theory is the incongruity between some of the beliefs of the sect in its heyday with teachings Josephus attributes to the Sadducees. However, Sadducean priests were not uniform in their degree of Hellenization nor in all their beliefs. Josephus's descriptions concern only the somewhat Hellenized Sadducees of the Roman period. Moreover, I am not claiming that the Dead Sea sect as we know it is Sadducean, only that its origins and the roots of its halakhic tradition lie in the Sadducean Zadokite priesthood.

The *Halakhic Letter* is a sectarian document from the earliest stage in the sect's development, when its members still hoped to return to participation in Temple worship. It is not even certain that the letter postdates the beginning of the self-imposed exile of the sect. In this document we learn of the disagreements about Jewish law that led to the formation of the sect. It was only later that the Teacher of Righteousness and other leaders, most probably priestly, developed the group that was to produce the complete corpus of sectarian texts. Another Qumran text—the *Temple Scroll*, essentially a rewritten Torah into which the author has inserted his own views on Jewish law—is also composed of sources deriving from the Sadducean tradition. Indeed, the finds at Qumran are now providing us with insights into this tradition never before available.

The revelations contained in the *Halakhic Letter* demand that we reevaluate some of the older theories identifying the sect with known Second Temple groups. First, the theories that seek to link the sect and its origins with the Hasidim (pietists) must now be abandoned. Other theories tying the emergence of the sect to some subgroup of the Pharisees are certainly no longer tenable. The dominant Essene hypothesis, if it is to be maintained at all, requires radical reorientation. Those holding this theory must now argue that the term "Essene" came to designate the originally Sadducean sectarians who had gone through a process of radicalization until they became a distinct sect. Alternatively, they must broaden their understanding of the term to include a wide variety of similar groups, of which the Dead Sea sect might be one.

The notion that the collection of scrolls at Qumran is not representative of a sect but is a balanced collection of general Jewish texts must also be rejected. There is by now too much evidence proving that the community that collected those scrolls emerged out of sectarian conflict and that that conflict sustained it throughout its existence. The *Halakhic Letter* characterizes the conflict as a disagreement over points of Jewish law with those in control of the Temple in Hasmonaean Jerusalem. Further, the nature of the collection, even if it contains many texts not explicitly sectarian, which might have been acceptable to all Jews in Second Temple times, is still that of a subgroup with definite opposition to the political and religious authorities of the times.

THE EXODUS TO QUMRAN

When the group who composed the *Halakhic Letter* decided to move to Qumran, the members took a decisive step in their own evolution. They now defined themselves as a dissenting group struggling against an unsympathetic majority. This was not a sudden step, however. It seems likely that the Qumran center was established after a period of groping that lasted about a generation. Only then did the sect retreat to Qumran. The Teacher of Righteousness, whose leadership had been established sometime after composition of the letter, probably influenced the decision.

How can we determine the nature and date of the exodus to Qumran? Our conclusions must rest on the archaeological finds at Khirbet Qumran and on the literary evidence of the sectarian texts. And central to an understanding of the event is familiarity with the text known as the *Zadokite Fragments*, the first scroll discovered by Solomon Schechter among the manuscripts of the Cairo *genizah*. Today, we know of at least nine additional manuscripts of this text, which were found at Qumran. Affinities in language and ideology indicate that this document belonged to the Qumran sectarians. Further, other sectarian texts contain excerpts from that text, indicating that it indeed was a document central to the thought of the Qumran sect. Modern scholars refer to this text also as the *Damascus Document* or *Damascus Covenant* due to its symbolic reference to Damascus as the land of the sect's exile.

The text is divided into two parts: the Admonition and the Laws. (Our discussion focuses first on the Admonition. We will return later to the Laws when we discuss the subject of Jewish law in the Dead Sea Scrolls.) Although the Qumran manuscripts of this text indicate that there was additional material at the beginning of the *Zadokite Fragments*, they preserve very little significant material from that section, which must at one time have been part of a much longer passage. The text of the *Zadokite Fragments* as preserved in medieval manuscripts begins by declaring that in ancient times, Israel went astray. As a result, God "hid His face" and allowed the destruction of the First Temple (dated in modern scholarly chronology to 586 B.C.E.). Yet a remnant of the defeated people remained, and it was they who ultimately formed the sect. In this narrative, the sectarians regard their way of life and belief as a direct continuation of biblical tradition, claiming to be the tradition's true recipients.

The text presents its understanding of the formation of the sect as follows:

> And in the period of wrath, three hundred ninety years after He had handed it (the Temple) over to Nebuchadnezzar king of Babylonia, He remembered them (Israel) and caused to grow from Israel and Aaron the root of a plant (i.e., the sect). (*ZADOKITE FRAGMENTS* 1:5–7)

Qumran Manuscript of the *Zadokite Fragments* The discovery of the Dead Sea Scrolls made it immediately clear that the *Zadokite Fragments* (or *Damascus Document*), which had come to light previously in two medieval manuscripts, was closely related to the new documents. Subsequently, nine fragmentary manuscripts of this composition were found at Qumran, and they have greatly increased the extent of the preserved text. Shown here is a portion of a late-first-century B.C.E. manuscript, which discusses marriage, among other things. Note the stitches at the left where this sheet of parchment was connected to the next. *Courtesy of the Israel Antiquities Authority.*

This official chronology, written by the sectarians themselves, poses problems for scholars. If we calculate from the modern scholarly dating of the destruction of the First Temple, we arrive at 196 B.C.E. for the founding of the sect. This dating does not square with the archaeological data, however. Further, based on evidence in the *Halakhic Letter*, the sect must have formally separated itself after the Maccabean Revolt of 168–164 B.C.E.

Nevertheless, there is evidence that ancient Jews did not have a chronology that matches ours for dating the destruction of the First Temple. Because of a vast gap in the chronology of the Persian period, it is doubtful whether ancient Jews could have made such a calculation with any degree of accuracy. Therefore, we can only assume that we have approximate information from the period. We therefore must be content to date the founding of the sect sometime in the second century B.C.E.

The text of the *Zadokite Fragments* then tells about a period of confusion followed by the rise of the sect's leader, the Teacher of Righteousness:

> Then they understood their transgression and knew that they were guilty. They were like blind (men) groping on the road for twenty years. Then God paid attention to their deeds for they sought Him whole-heartedly, and He set up for them a Teacher of Righteousness to direct them in the way of his (the teacher's) heart. *(ZADOKITE FRAGMENTS 1:8–11 = Dᵃ 2 I 12–15)*

It appears that during an initial period—perhaps of twenty years—the sect was leaderless and perhaps even formless until the Teacher of Righteousness established his leadership over it. Only with the teacher's emergence and his assumption of control did sectarian teachings and a distinctive way of life take shape.

From what we learned earlier from the *Halakhic Letter*, we can accept as reliable the account in the *Zadokite Fragments* that describes this initial period between the schism and the emergence of the teacher's leadership. It was during that period, most probably, that the *Halakhic Letter* was sent and a reconciliation attempted. After their failure to win over the Jerusalem Sadducees and the Hasmonaean high priest the sect became a permanent entity, no longer expecting to rejoin the Jerusalem establishment.

The Teacher of Righteousness assumed leadership of the sect and introduced his teachings; at that time or shortly thereafter the sect moved to its site in the wilderness at Qumran. Both the archaeological dating of the site and the literary materials about Damascus confirm the fact.

The *Zadokite Fragments* has a portion that has become known as the "Well Midrash" (6:3–11), which prominently features the Damascus imagery. It is an excellent example of *pesher* interpretation, a form of biblical interpretation that reads biblical verses as prefigurations of contemporary events. Here a verse from Numbers is interpreted: "A well which the officers have dug, which the notables of the people have dug . . ." (Numbers 21:18).

The *Zadokite Fragments* explains:

> The well is the Torah and those who dig it are the returnees (or: penitents) of Israel who leave the land of Judaea and who live in the land of Damascus. *(ZADOKITE FRAGMENTS 6:4–5)*

On the face of it, this text seems to refer to an exodus of the sectarians from Judaea to Damascus, where they settled, at least for a time. Below this, on the same page, the sectarians are described as:

> those who enter the new covenant in the land of Damascus. *(6:19)*

Again this text refers to an exodus to Damascus.

Before continuing, I would like to comment on the expression "new covenant." In several texts the sectarians term themselves "those who have entered the covenant," referring to the new covenant they entered when they constituted or joined the sect. This idea derives from Jeremiah 31:31–32, which speaks of a renewal of God's covenant with Israel in the End of Days. The term as it is used in this text must be sharply distinguished from the Christian concept of a new covenant, that is, a New Testament, which will replace the old covenant (so-called Old Testament) with a new scripture.

In another *pesher*-type exegesis, the text interprets Amos 5:26–27, "And you shall carry . . . the star of your God which you have made for yourselves, and I will exile you beyond Damascus." There we find:

> And the "star" (Amos 5:26) is the interpreter of the law (the sectarian official who interprets Torah for the sect with divine inspiration) who comes to Damascus. (ZADOKITE FRAGMENTS 7:18–19)

A literal reading of this passage would suggest that the interpreter of the law left Judaea and joined his fellow sectarians at Damascus. Later on, in describing sectarians who ceased to live according to the ways of the sect, the *Zadokite Fragments* speaks of:

> those people who had entered the new covenant in the land of Damascus and have turned away and rebelled, and turned aside from the well of living waters. (ZADOKITE FRAGMENTS 19:33–34)

The "well of living waters" is God's Torah as correctly interpreted by the sectarians. The Damascus theme is continued further on when the text describes those:

> . . . who have despised the covenant and the agreement to which they swore in the land of Damascus, which is the new covenant.
> (ZADOKITE FRAGMENTS 20:11–12)

Writing before the *Halakhic Letter* was known, many scholars deduced from these passages that after the initial schism, there was an actual exodus to Damascus. This theory further claims that in Damascus the sect took shape and set down the foundation of its teachings. From there, it is assumed, the group moved on to the sectarian settlement at Qumran. Some have actually sought to locate a historical event that might have led to that exodus. Others have suggested excavation of modern-day Damascus in an attempt to find the remains of this group.

What then is Damascus? Is it a real place or a metaphorical term? We know that the sectarians, especially in the *Zadokite Fragments*, often spoke in code words. We find all kinds of pseudonyms for actual personages, yet almost never a personal name that would allow a definite identification. The Jewish sects of the day are never mentioned by name even though we see numerous references to them designated with code words in the sectarian texts. Why then should we fall into the trap of taking place names literally? Rather it is more likely that "Damascus" is a code word for Qumran.

The notion is strengthened even more by the use of Damascus as a symbol in other texts of the period. The New Testament pictures Paul receiving a vision of Jesus on the road to Damascus (Acts 9:3–6). It is likely that the symbolic meaning of Damascus as an eschatological stopover would have led to its use here. Indeed, even in Amos 5:27 it is connected with the destruction of syncretist Israelites— those who had mixed worship of the God of Israel with pagan ways—in the End of Days.

In addition, we should mention the suggestion that Damascus was actually at one time the name of the toparchy (administrative district) in which Qumran was situated. This suggestion assumes that Qumran, even though it is located on the western shore of the Dead Sea, was at one time part of the same adminis- trative unit as Damascus and could, therefore, bear its name.

In any case, these possibilities all taken together allow us to regard Damascus as a symbol. Accordingly, we need not seek any specific exodus to Damascus. Rather, we can assume that the desert settlement of Qumran was the Damascus to which the sectarians referred and that it was there that the sect established its settlement at about the same time as the Teacher of Righteousness (perhaps the very same first interpreter of the law) came to the fore.

It is indeed curious that the sectarian texts from Qumran contain no mention of the name of the site; Khirbet Qumran is the Arabic name. Some scholars have theorized that it may be the biblical place Secacah (Joshua 15:61), although this is probably an iron age site located 4 miles (7 kilometers) southwest of Qumran. In any case, it was to Qumran, not to Damascus, that the sect migrated.

There is one additional text, *Rule of the Community*, that must be considered here because it makes the connection between the sectarians' separatism and the desert. *Rule of the Community*, also known as *Manual of Discipline* (a Christian monastic term imposed on the text), was one of the first seven scrolls discovered in cave 1. This almost intact document lays out the basic theology of the sect as well as its rules of admission and initiation and its code of punishments. At one point, the scroll speaks of the separation of the Qumran sectarians from the main body of Israelites:

> When these form a community in Israel, according to these rules they shall be separated from the midst of the settlement of the people of iniquity to go to the desert, to clear there the road of the Lord, as it is written, "In the desert clear the road of the Lord; straighten in the wilderness a highway for our God" (Isaiah 40:3). This is the interpretation of the Torah [which] He com- manded through Moses to observe, according to everything that is revealed from time to time, and as the prophets have revealed by His holy spirit.
> *(RULE OF THE COMMUNITY 8:12–16)*

The passage appears to refer directly to the exodus to the desert. But in fact, this separatism is to be understood symbolically as fulfilling the command of Isaiah 40:3 to prepare a way through the wilderness as part of the preparations for the End of Days. The passage then goes on to tell us how to interpret that preparation. To prepare the way in the desert means to interpret the Torah, specifically to explain it according to sectarian interpretations.

Despite its mention of the wilderness, the text makes no direct connection between the sect and the desert region. Nonetheless, it is only against the background of the sect's settlement at Qumran that such desert imagery makes sense. In fact, the desert motif is extremely prominent in sectarian literature. The sectarians saw themselves as living a pristine life like that of the Israelites in the period of desert wandering. Further, they saw themselves as having gone into the desert to receive the Torah, just as Israel had in the period of the Exodus. All this is to be expected from a group that had left the more thickly settled areas of Judaea to relocate in the wilderness, there to maintain its own standards of sanctity and purity.

The sect came into being, then, after the Hasmonaeans had taken over the high priesthood, about 152 B.C.E. Thereafter, they attempted, as we can see from the *Halakhic Letter*, to reconcile with their Zadokite-Sadducean brethren who continued to serve in the Jerusalem Temple, as well as with the Hasmonaean leaders. When this failed, they still were leaderless until, at some point, the Teacher of Righteousness arose to lead them. It was he who gave the sect shape and direction. Eventually he led the group from its Sadducean origins toward its intensely apocalyptic, sectarian mentality and toward the many beliefs that differentiated the sect from the Sadducees. Probably during the early years of the teacher's career—within a generation or so after the founding of the sect—the members of the group established the sectarian center and library at Qumran. The next chapter discusses what kind of community ultimately developed there.

CHAPTER 6

The Character
of the Community

We have already established that the Qumran sect began in the period immediately after the Maccabean Revolt, and we have sketched its origins and early history. In this chapter, we take a look at the sect's organizational patterns and way of life.

All of the various aspects of sectarian life were intended for one purpose—the achievement of a life of purity and sanctity in the present to prepare for the End of Days. Although it has been suggested that some characteristics of the sect derive from the Hellenistic milieu in which it functioned, it is more likely that its organizational patterns arose primarily from the needs and aspirations of the sect to fulfill the commands of the Torah as the members understood them. It was, after all, for this very purpose that the sect was constituted. To ensure the continuity and integrity of the sectarian way of life, the sect developed specific initiation rites, a strict discipline of ritual purity, and strict regulations governing behavior and property.

ORGANIZATIONAL PATTERNS

INITIATION RITES

One of the most singular aspects of sectarian life among the variety of Jewish groups in the Second Temple period was the practice of initiating members into the group. A number of sources give specific evidence for such an initiation process. The Qumran scrolls, particularly *Rule of the Community* and the *Zadokite Fragments*, describe such a process, and Josephus and Philo mention that the Essenes also had such a rite. Further, it is known that such practices existed in the fellowship (*ḥavurah*) described in rabbinic sources.

Primarily, initiation rites mark a dividing line between those inside and outside a group. Study of initiation rites also yields much information on group

Rule of the Community The Dead Sea sectarians were guided in
their lives by a text entitled *Rule of the Community*, which set
out how members were to be accepted, members' obligations, the
conduct of the affairs of the sect, basic theological beliefs, and the
code of punishments. This scroll was one of the original seven
scrolls found in 1947, and it serves as a basic text for the study of
the sectarian community that gathered the Dead Sea Scrolls.
*Photograph by John C. Trever. Courtesy of the School of Theology
at Claremont.*

structure and group purpose. Indeed, the hierarchy of the Qumran sect, the individual's place in the sect, the privileges an individual was accorded or which were withheld from him, and the initiation rites themselves were all intimately connected with the founding principles of the sect and its aspirations.

Many of the laws on this topic can be found in *Rule of the Community* and the *Zadokite Fragments.* We can also compare evidence from accounts about the Essenes and from rabbinic sources dealing with the *ḥavurah.* After examining these materials, we can draw some conclusions about how the initiation process functioned and what role it played in Qumran sectarian life.

EVIDENCE FROM *RULE OF THE COMMUNITY*

Rule of the Community contains the fullest prescriptions for entry into the Qumran sect. Entry consisted of a complex process comprising several stages. The first step involved examination by a sectarian official followed by instruction in the regulations of the group:

> As to every one of Israel who volunteers to join the council of the community, the man who is appointed at the head of the assembly (literally, "many") shall examine him regarding his understanding and deeds. If he is capable of grasping the instruction, he (the official) shall bring him into the covenant to return to truth and to turn from all iniquity. Then he shall instruct him in all the regulations of the community.
>
> *(RULE OF THE COMMUNITY 6:13–15)*

After this examination and instruction, the candidate for membership advances to the next step, which occurs after an unspecified interval; he is brought before the general community or its assembly:

> When he comes to stand before the assembly, then everyone shall be asked regarding him. Then according to the decision that shall come forth from the council of the community, he shall be brought near or kept away. When he approaches the council of the community he may (still) not come in contact with the pure food of the community until they examine him regarding his spirit and his deeds, until he has completed a full year. Nor may he mingle (his property) with the property of the community.
>
> *(RULE OF THE COMMUNITY 6:15–17)*

The text makes clear that during the one-year initiatory period the candidate is a conditional member. He still may not touch pure food, not even the pure solid food that is less susceptible to ritual impurity than the liquid food. Furthermore, his property may not be made available for communal use, a privilege extended only to full members.

The next stage in the initiation takes place after a year and involves an examination by the assembly, apparently led by the priests and those associated with them:

> And when he completes a year in the community, the assembly shall be asked regarding him, according to his understanding and his observance of the Torah. And if the decision shall go forth regarding him to draw near to the council of the community, according to the priests and the men of their covenant, they shall bring near both his property and his labor into the hand of the man who is the examiner of the property of the community. Then he (the examiner) shall write it (the property) in the accounting with his own (the examiner's) hand, but he (the examiner) may (still) not spend it for the community. *(RULE OF THE COMMUNITY 6:18–20)*

During this time the sectarian is still only conditionally admitted. He becomes more integrated into the sect but is still not a full-fledged member until a second year passes, culminating in another examination by the assembly:

> He may not come in contact with the liquid food of the community until he completes a second year among the men of the community. Then, if the decision shall go forth for him to bring him near to the community, then he (the examiner) shall register (literally, "write") him in the list, in his proper place among his fellows, for Torah, judgment, and purity, and to mingle his property. Then his counsel shall be for the community as well as his judgment. *(RULE OF THE COMMUNITY 6:20–24)*

When he finally is fully accepted into the sect, the new member may come into contact even with the pure liquids of the community, which are more susceptible to impurity than solids. And he can now share in the communal property and the work of the group, and so his property is mingled. He also is entitled to participate in the sectarian assembly and to contribute his counsel to the community. This final acceptance by the entire assembly adds his name to the roster that was used, among other things, for mustering the able-bodied into battle array.

EVIDENCE FROM THE ZADOKITE FRAGMENTS

The *Zadokite Fragments* sets out a second set of rules regarding entry into the sect:

> And thus is the ruling for the entire period of wickedness for everyone who turns from his corrupt way: On the day when he speaks with the examiner who is over the community, they shall muster him with the oath of the covenant which Moses made with Israel, his promise to re[turn] to the Torah of Moses with all (his) heart and [with] a[ll] his soul, to that which has been derived to do in a[ll] the period of his drawing near. But let no one make known to him the (sectarian) regulations until he stands before the examiner, lest he turn out to be a fool when he examines him. And when he takes upon himself (or "swears") to return to the Torah of Moses with all (his) heart and with all (his) soul, they (the sectarians) are innocent of him if he transgresses. *(ZADOKITE FRAGMENTS 15:6–13 = Dᵃ 17 I 1–4; Dᵉ 10 II 6)*

This text effectively describes a two-stage novitiate: According to this version, after presenting himself to the examiner, the recruit is mustered and takes an oath. From this point on, he is a conditional member and so may not be taught the true teachings of the group—the sectarian law—until he completes a second test. At that point, he may be admitted to that knowledge. One must presume that the examiner, when presented with the new recruit, can, if he wishes, reject him, although this is nowhere mentioned. After a period of low status, the recruit is once more probed by the examiner. Presumably, at this point he becomes a permanent member.

There seems to be a fundamental disagreement between this text and the material from *Rule of the Community*. Although both texts require an oath upon one's initial entrance, only *Rule of the Community* explicitly requires at this point an examination by the official. And according to *Rule of the Community*, the second examination, after an initial period of instruction, takes place in front of the assembly, whereas in the *Zadokite Fragments*, it occurs in front of the same examiner. In the *Zadokite Fragments*, it is explicitly forbidden to teach the recruit the secret laws and lore of the sect until he is inducted even further. A similar idea is only hinted at in *Rule of the Community* (9:17). Unlike *Rule of the Community*, the *Zadokite Fragments* does not even mention either further induction of the recruit or his gradual access to pure solid food after a year and liquid food only after a second year.

Theoretically, a number of possible explanations might be offered for these differences. It is possible that *Rule of the Community* was written later and therefore presents a more complex or simply a modified system of initiation. But it is more likely that *Rule of the Community* legislates specifically for the sectarian center at Qumran, and the *Zadokite Fragments* for groups scattered in camps throughout the Land of Israel. That explains why the *Zadokite Fragments* discusses only the first two stages of the novitiate: because sect members in the regional communities could attain only this minimal status. Members could be inducted to full membership, including the right to touch pure solid and liquid food, only under the rigorous standards maintained, as far as we know, at Qumran alone. Furthermore, full admission was available only to those who had devoted themselves to much more complex and prolonged study than what was available in other, scattered sectarian communities. Only at Qumran was there an assembly, which explains why in the *Zadokite Fragments* the examiner must substitute for the assembly.

If so, we have reached a very important conclusion about the nature of the sect: Its members were scattered throughout Palestine, not just organized in one place, and the regional centers would send their members to study at the main location, apparently in Qumran. Members would go to Qumran for periods of study so as to attain the highest levels of sectarian purity and to complete their initiation into the group.

RITUAL PURITY

The entire process of sect admission is intimately linked with issues of ritual purity and impurity. A recruit, even after examination by the official, instruction in some sectarian teachings, and reexamination by the community, was considered ritually impure and was not permitted to come in contact with any of the sect's victuals. After a second public examination, possible only at the sectarian center, he was allowed to touch the solid pure food of the community for a year. Apparently, even after being permitted to touch solid food, he was not considered entirely free of the danger of ritual impurity until he passed the final examination before the sectarian assembly. After that final examination a year later, he was allowed to touch even the liquid foods of the community. Only then did he become a full member of the group and was he considered ritually pure.

The sect's approach is based on a concept of purity similar to that found in rabbinic halakhah. The very term for "liquid" in our text, *mashqeh*, is used in Mishnaic terminology to designate a liquid fit for human consumption that may be rendered ritually impure. According to rabbinic legislation, purity regulations regarding such liquids are in certain senses stricter than those regarding solid foods. Even the smallest amount of liquid that has been rendered impure can in turn render clothing, food and drink, or vessels impure. In contrast, solid food is capable of rendering other substances impure only if it occupies the volume equivalent of an egg.

There is yet a further stringency in regard to liquids: whereas solid foods decrease in their levels of impurity as the impurity is passed from one object to another, the impurity of liquids does not decrease regardless of how many times the impurity is transferred from liquid to liquid.

It is likely that the Qumran sectarians based their initiation process on a set of regulations similar to those we have just described for the early Rabbis. The Rabbis, too, were stricter regarding contact with liquid foods than with solids. To understand the reasoning behind this system, we must remember that one who eats or drinks impure food will, according to these regulations, become impure in the same degree as the food one has consumed. Indeed, this attempt to extend purity regulations into the everyday life of the sectarian was part of the larger tendency in Second Temple Judaism to bring the sanctity of the Temple into the home and family.

Based on those considerations it is now possible to understand the initiation rites. One who is not a member is impure at the highest level of impurity possible. Only a dead body has greater impurity. During the first year, a candidate is impure in the first degree. In his second year, he is impure by being prohibited from touching the liquid food of the sect. Only after becoming a full member of the group is he presumed entirely pure and is he then permitted to touch both liquid and solid food.

What emerges from study of sectarian material is an understanding of the unique relationship between repentance, initiation into the sect, and ritual purification. To the sectarians, ritual purification was no more than a symptom of spiritual purification. Indeed, the sect believed that no amount of lustration or ablution would render pure anyone who was still an unrepentant transgressor (*Rule of the Community* 3:4–6):

> He will not be purified by atonement rituals,
> nor will he become pure in waters of lustration.
> He will not be sanctified in seas or rivers,
> nor will he be purified in any waters of ablution.
> Impure, impure he will remain as long as he despises the divine regulations,
> so as not to be disciplined by the counsel of His community.

To the sect, then, ritual purity and impurity were symbolic manifestations of the moral and religious state of the individual.

Although the ritual purity rules followed by the sect might not have been identical to those put forward in rabbinic sources, the aspects treated here were common to both. These observations give us a clue to the observances of the Pharisaic forebears of the Rabbis, allowing us to infer that the Pharisees did observe many of the purity laws found in later sources. Once again the scrolls have taught us about Pharisaic Judaism as well as about the Qumran sect—not through the lens of polemic, but by demonstrating commonly held practices of ritual purity.

COMPARISON TO THE ESSENES

Now that we have analyzed the initiation laws of the sect in two versions, we can compare two other bodies of evidence: the procedures for entry into the Essene sect and those in use by the *ḥavurah.*

Initiation into the Essene sect is described by Josephus. The Essenes required that the candidate first study Essene teachings for a period of one year. During that period, he received the Essene equipment—the hatchet, loincloth, and white raiment. The hatchet was used as a digging tool to make holes for excrement; the loincloth and raiment were the normal garb of the members of the Essene community. If a candidate proved acceptable during this period, he was allowed to proceed to the next step.

For a period of two years the recruit's character was further tested, but he was also taught more and permitted access to the "purer kind of holy water." He was still not permitted to touch the common food or to attend community meetings. After this two-year period, he was again judged and, if found acceptable, was expected to undertake a series of oaths to obligate himself to the principles of the group. Thereafter, he became a full member.

Interpreting what is meant by admission to the "holy water" is difficult. Most scholars interpret it to refer to admission to the ritual baths, assuming that before attaining a certain level of membership, candidates were not permitted to use the Essene sect's purification facilities. It is also possible to understand "holy water" as referring to the liquid food of the sect, in which case we would have to assume some confusion on the part of Josephus. In all likelihood, the Essenes would first have admitted members to the solid food and later to the liquid, because solid food is less susceptible to impurity.

Although this process of the Essenes is somewhat similar to that described by the Qumran texts, there are important distinctions. In the Qumran materials, a novice takes an oath at the beginning of the process; in Josephus's description, he does so at the end. In the Qumran texts, he is admitted to common meals at an earlier stage than Josephus's Essenes, who can eat with members only at the very end of the process.

Of course, one of the central questions in Qumran studies concerns the relationship between the Essenes of Philo and Josephus and the sect. In order to show that the Essenes and the Qumran sect were not one and the same, we would need more evidence than that provided by a few minor differences in their admissions procedures. Despite Josephus's claim that he himself went through the process of Essene initiation, it may be that historical changes or the coexistence of different groups under the general heading "Essene" might make the situation much more complex.

THE ḤAVURAH

Early rabbinic sources mention a *ḥavurah*—best translated as "fellowship"—that was formed to enable members (*ḥaverim;* singular, *ḥaver*) to properly observe the laws of tithes and Levitical purity. Sources describe these *ḥaverim* as part of the community of Mishnaic sages. In the scholarly literature it has become customary to describe this group as "the Pharisaic *ḥavurah*," although there is no direct reference to the Pharisees within the texts. Indeed, the Rabbis responding to the anonymous descriptions of the *ḥavurah* in the sources all lived in the early second century C.E., thus casting some doubt on the assumption that the *ḥavurah* dates to Second Temple times. Nonetheless, these regulations indicate that groups such as this one existed in rabbinical circles in the early centuries of the common era. It is possible, therefore, that such groups were found among the Pharisees in the Hasmonaean and Herodian periods, but no definitive evidence can be cited. Therefore, to avoid drawing conclusions without any evidence, we refer to them simply as the *ḥavurot* described in rabbinic sources.

From passages in the Mishnah, Tosefta, and the Palestinian and Babylonian Talmuds, it is possible to reconstruct the pattern of admission into the *ḥavurah*. The procedure seems to have been as follows: The novice took an initial oath or declaration to accept the group's rules of ritual purity and to eat only food that he knew for certain was properly tithed. This process conferred on the initiate the status of a "reliable person."

After some undisclosed period, there was another initiatory oath or declaration in order to become a *ḥaver*. There followed a period of twelve months during which the recruit observed some of the regulations and was taught. Finally, the *ḥaver* was examined, and if accepted, was permitted to share common, solid food. After another twelve months (or one month according to another opinion), the new *ḥaver* could be admitted to membership as far as liquid foods were concerned. The candidate was now a full member of the fellowship.

When we compare these regulations with those of the Qumran sect, we can see many parallels, such as the required initial oath, the three-stage process, instruction as part of the process, and the sequence of admission to the solid, then liquid, food. But there are also some differences. For example, in the *ḥavurah*, the initial oath was already public; at Qumran, it was taken only before the examiner. In the *ḥavurah*, there were two oaths taken; at Qumran, only one.

Comparing the initiation rites of the Qumran sect with those of the *ḥavurah*, we are reminded of similar comparisons between the Qumran sect and the Essenes as described by Josephus. Differences in the evidence provided by the scrolls versus that in the rabbinic material regarding the *ḥavurah* indicate that despite their similarities, the two groups did not practice the same initiation rites and were therefore not identical. Indeed, in the Judaism of this formative period, numerous groups of this kind existed, and these documents provide but three examples of how such groups inducted members. Yet despite many differences, all the Jewish groups of this period shared much more in common than is usually assumed.

Some parallels to the Qumran initiation procedures have been cited from evidence about the Hellenistic guilds. And though we do not doubt that such parallels existed, they provide only partial analogies to the sectarian system. Most important, these Hellenistic initiation procedures did not include a system of progression through increasing levels of purity. In contrast, the Qumran sect, Essenes, *ḥavurah*, and all other such Jewish groups did include such a system, because all of their rituals were designed to help them fulfill Jewish law. The initiation process practiced by the Qumran sect and other Jewish groups is in no way analogous to those used by Hellenistic guilds, although they do share some details in common. It is also interesting to note that no such initiation rites were required to enter the early Christian community. Only later did such rites become prominent in Christian monastic orders.

COMMUNAL USE OF PROPERTY

One of the most commonly held beliefs about the Qumran community is that it practiced communism of property, that is, that all property was corporately owned. Those subscribing to that view and to the notion that sect members were celibate (a subject to be discussed in a later chapter) presume that the sect prefigured the early church that was to emerge in the second half of the first century C.E. To test the theory, we examine the passages that deal with the issue of property in the sectarian texts.

As in so many other matters, the text of the *Zadokite Fragments* discusses issues about property from a different viewpoint from that of *Rule of the Community*. Whereas *Rule of the Community* presents regulations applicable only to the sectarian center, the *Zadokite Fragments* addresses the smaller communities located throughout the country.

The material in the *Zadokite Fragments* shows beyond a doubt that the society envisaged there was to be based on private property and private enterprise. Indeed, not even a hint of any aspect of communal property can be found in the work.

Numerous references in the *Zadokite Fragments* confirm the practice of private ownership in the sect. In one passage, there is explicit reference to the system of voluntary offerings to the Temple (*Zadokite Fragments* 16:14–15), a practice that assumes the existence of private property. Another passage (*Zadokite Fragments* 16:16) actually mentions donation of a private field to the Temple.

A set of laws about doing business with non-Jews (discussed in detail in a later chapter) is extremely significant to our discussion because it suggests the widespread private ownership of property among sect members (*Zadokite Fragments* 12.8–11). This passage forbids the sale of animals lest they be used for pagan sacrifices. Likewise, untithed produce could not be sold to non-Jews lest it then be resold to a Jew who was unaware it was untithed Jewish produce. Finally, the sale of slaves that had begun the process of conversion to Judaism (the status the Rabbis called the "Canaanite slave") was also prohibited.

The economic structure depicted here was the typical rural economy of Palestine of the Hasmonaean period. Grain crops and slaves were the private property of the individual. Similar economic activity in the Judaean Desert area is known from the legal documents found in the Bar Kokhba caves. The threshing floor and winepress mentioned in this text, however, need not necessarily have belonged to the sectarians. In most areas of Palestine, private individuals brought their own produce to be processed in communally owned installations such as threshing floors and wine and olive presses. Taken altogether, these references in the *Zadokite Fragments* attest to the private possession of produce by sect members.

Clearly, members of this group participated in wider trade, even with non-Jews. Otherwise, laws regulating these activities would have been unnecessary. As for trade with Jews who were not members of the sect, the text declares:

> Let no man, from any of those who have entered the covenant, do business with the men of the pit except hand to hand (i.e., for cash). And let no man do anything in business unless he has made it known to the examiner and done (it) with (his) counsel, lest they err. (ZADOKITE FRAGMENTS 13:14–16 = D^a 18 II 1–4)

Here we have several regulations. First, there is the requirement that any business done with nonmembers of the sect, that is, with other Jews, be conducted only in the form of cash transactions. The only likely reason for that rule is to avoid violating any of the Torah's prohibitions on charging interest to one's fellow Jew (Exodus 22:25, Leviticus 25:36–37, Deuteronomy 23:19–20). Apparently, the sect regarded the regular methods for conducting business through credit, then current in Palestine, as a violation of those laws. This impression is also supported by evidence from later rabbinic sources and from the complex contracts found in the Bar Kokhba caves.

The second regulation requires that a member obtain the approval of the examiner before entering into any business deal. This measure was intended as a safeguard against error and against the violation of some commercial law of the Torah or the sect's laws. Again we see that this text presumes a free economy, with buying and selling (albeit not on credit) with outsiders.

The group described in the *Zadokite Fragments* taxed the salaries of its members regularly in order to fulfill its obligations of social service:

> And this is the rule for the community to provide for all their requirements: two days' salary per month mi[ni]mum. And they shall give (it) to the examiner and the judges. From it they shall give for their tribulation and from it they shall sustain the poor and needy, the old man who is bent over, the man who is afflicted, the one who is taken captive by a foreign people, the young woman who has no close relative, and the youth for whom no one cares. (ZADOKITE FRAGMENTS 14:12–16 = D^a 18 II 5–9)

The sectarians had to pay a tax of 8 percent of their personal income to be distributed to the needy by the examiner and the judges. We do not know whether the poor and needy mentioned here were expected to be members of the sect. The sect's practice of charitable behavior clearly recalls the traditional Jewish law that requires every community to care for the needs of those less fortunate in its midst.

Many specific details in the Sabbath code of the Qumran sect also assume that members own property and private houses; these passages do not fit the setting of a communal settlement. Indeed, as we have seen, the society envisaged in the *Zadokite Fragments* is definitely based on private property and enterprise. Nowhere is there any mention of communal ownership or use.

Yet if we consult *Rule of the Community*, we learn that there may have been different arrangements at the sectarian center at Qumran or elsewhere. For the Qumran community, our basic information comes from the process of admission into the sect. Since we have studied this process in detail earlier, we need only isolate and review certain details relevant to property.

If a recruit passed the second examination, before the assembly, he still was not permitted to mingle his property with that of the sect, just as he was still forbidden to touch the pure food. A year afterward, if he was again approved by the same assembly, his property and labor (or income) were registered by the examiner, who still could not spend any of the funds. After a second one-year period and another examination (the third by the assembly), the recruit became a full member, and his property was to be mingled.

Two observations can already be made. First, as the new member climbed the ladder of ritual purity, property was increasingly mingled. Thus, there was some connection between the two aspects. Further, the community required a record of this property. In the intermediate period, the funds were held in escrow until it was determined whether or not the sectarian was to attain full status. It is already clear that at the Qumran center, for those who had progressed to full membership, there was some kind of pooling of property.

The first regulation in the sectarian penal code refers to property:

> If there is found among them (the sectarians) a man who lies regarding property, they shall separate him from the midst of the pure food of the community for one year, and he shall be fined one-fourth of his food ration.
> *(RULE OF THE COMMUNITY 6:24–25)*

Apparently, the problem of individuals' withholding property from communal use was serious enough to require legislation. This same problem existed in the early Christian church, which also required the surrender of goods to the group (Acts 5:1–11).

We should pause to explain that the penal code is found in both *Rule of the Community* and the *Zadokite Fragments*. The manuscripts of *Rule of the Community* give evidence of at least two recensions of this code. Whereas the medieval manuscripts of the *Zadokite Fragments* preserve only an abbreviated code, there is a longer one in the Qumran fragments of this text. These various versions demonstrate that such a code was in force during the entire history of the sect, both in the sectarian center and in the so-called camps. The text evolved as penalties were modified over time.

This first provision of the penal code already reveals another aspect of the issue. The penal code contains a series of regulations that prescribe the docking of one-fourth of a miscreant's food ration for some specific period. In order for the community to dock or reduce an individual's rations, it would have to permit

Sectarian Offenses and Punishments

OFFENSE	PUNISHMENT
Misuse of the divine name	Permanent expulsion
Informing against the sect Complaining against the teachings of the sect	Expulsion
Rebelling against the teachings of the community	Separation from pure solid food for 1 year Reduction of food ration by one-fourth for 2 years Separation from pure drink for 2 years
Speaking angrily against the priests Intentionally insulting another Knowingly lying about money Gossiping against one's fellow	Separation from pure food and reduction of food ration by one-fourth for 1 year
Replying stubbornly to a superior sect member	Reduction of food ration by one-fourth for 1 year
Accidentally speaking angrily against the priests Speaking deceptively to one's fellow Bearing a grudge against one's fellow Walking about unclothed Complaining about one's fellow unjustifiably	Reduction of food ration by one-fourth for 6 months
Speaking obscenely	Reduction of food ration by one-fourth for 3 months
Dealing deceitfully with the property of the community	Restitution with penalty or reduction of food ration by one-fourth for 60 days
Falling asleep during the assembly Missing a vote Spitting in the assembly Exposing one's genitals Laughing loudly and foolishly	Reduction of food ration by one-fourth for 30 days
Interrupting one's fellow Absence without reason from the assembly for three days in a session Gesticulating with one's left hand during conversation	Reduction of food ration by one-fourth for 10 days

individuals to possess their own food. However, food allocation is not the same as a full-blown concept of private ownership. But it does indicate that the Qumran sect subscribed to a concept of individual possession, for without such a concept, allocating food and imposing fines would make no sense.

This system of punishments was equivalent to a process of demotion. When one transgressed, one was regarded as ritually impure and, therefore, was forbidden access to the pure food. Such a ban placed one on the same level as a recruit who had not yet completed the process of initiation. In fact, reduction in the transgressor's food ration was almost a reversal of the mingling of his property, which had marked his induction into the sect.

Some scholars have regarded these fines as evidence that the community described in *Rule of the Community* practiced the same system of private property as the community depicted in the *Zadokite Fragments*. Such, however, is not the case. Rather, what *Rule of the Community* describes is a system designed to make property available for common use. But even if the community could use this property, individuals still possessed differing personal allocations, which could be altered by the levying of penalties. In order for members to be fined, their individual property had to be recorded. All this clearly bespeaks the fact that private ownership in the Qumran community was retained.

Thus, upon entrance into the sect, members made their property available for common use but did not fully surrender ownership, for that would violate the principle of private ownership enshrined in the Bible. This two-tiered economic system explains why the same text describes both private ownership and communality of property. Put simply, use was communal but ownership was private.

RELATIONS WITH OUTSIDERS

Among the oaths that bound sectarians upon entrance into the group, according to *Rule of the Community*, is the following:

> . . . that he will not enter into community with him (the outsider) regarding his work or his money lest he cause him (the sectarian) to be guilty of transgression, for thus it is written, "From every deceitful matter you shall keep afar" (Exodus 23:7). . . . That he not eat of anything belonging to them, nor drink, nor buy from them anything which is not for cash, as it is written, "Stay away from man who has living breath for in what manner is he considered?" (Isaiah 2:22). For all those who are not counted in His covenant, one must keep them away and all that belongs to them.
> (*RULE OF THE COMMUNITY 5:14–18*)

Although property was used in common by members of the sect, members were to forswear similar commercial and work relationships—partnerships, so to speak—with those outside the group. The above-cited text specifies the reason:

the avoidance of deceitful dealings. A very similar ruling appears in the *Zadokite Fragments* (20:7–8). Presumably, doing business with those who did not adhere to sectarian interpretations of Jewish law about business and commerce would lead sect members to violate those laws. In the second part of this text, we are told that nothing may be taken from outsiders unless it is paid for. One must separate from outsiders completely.

The abstention from food and drink was legislated most likely because the sect followed different laws of ritual purity and impurity from those of other Jews. And the prohibition of all noncash transactions with nonmembers can only be explained, as already noted, as a special safeguard against potential violation of sectarian law that was likely to occur if members followed the credit and loan practices then current in Palestine.

These texts give us important insights into the economic structure of the society to which *Rule of the Community* applied. Such insights make clear that members could enter into a variety of transactions or partnerships with outsiders. How then can we reconcile the apparent contradiction between these laws and the mingling of property described in the initiation process? We can conclude only that the mingling referred to communal use, not ownership, of property. Members of the sect thus continued to own their own property and could exercise over it the normal jurisdiction and powers of an owner.

That members of the sect were forbidden to enter into transactions with outsiders that would involve the mingling of property is reiterated in another passage:

> As to the property of the men of holiness who live (literally, "walk") in per-
> fection, let them not mingle their property with the property of the men of
> deceit who have not purified their way to separate from iniquity and to walk
> in the perfect path. (*RULE OF THE COMMUNITY 9:8–9*)

"Men of deceit" refers here to Jews who were not members of the group.

Thus, the *Zadokite Fragments* presumed complete private use and private ownership of property, whereas *Rule of the Community* described a society built on the principle of communal use but private ownership of property. This explanation fits in well with the comparison of the two documents and their social settings previously proposed. Just as the *Zadokite Fragments* allowed initiates to progress through only the second stage of purity, so too it made no provision for the conversion of members' property to communal use. It is thus clear that members of the scattered sectarian contingents in the towns of Palestine never became full members of the sect.

On the other hand, *Rule of the Community* sets out the more elaborate initia-tion process leading to the highest level of membership in the sect. After attain-ing full membership, the property of the new member was mingled and was thus made available for use by any sect member who had attained full membership. However, members retained ownership of their property and could use it for business purposes. Of course, the sectarian was expected to conduct his business affairs while mindful of the various restrictions embedded in sectarian legislation.

Sectarian life was formulated into a complex system of initiation procedures, similar to parallel processes followed by the Essenes and the ḥavurah. Those procedures were intertwined closely with the attainment of higher states of ritual purity. Behind the procedures lay the notion that ritual purity was a symbol of the inner spiritual purity of the sectarian and of his closeness to God. As he progressed up the ladder of ritual purity, he progressed spiritually. In the main sectarian center, it was possible to progress to the highest level of full membership, although in sectarian communities located elsewhere, it was possible to attain only the first two stages. For this reason, the mingling of property for communal use was practiced at Qumran, but not in the other camps. Even within the main center, aspects of the biblical notion of private ownership persisted, as can be seen in the commercial laws of the sect.

The Qumran group had come into being under the leadership of Zadokite priests. It soon developed thereafter under the leadership of the Teacher of Righteousness and a variety of other leaders and officials. We now turn to those leaders and their role in the history of Jewish communal and religious leadership.

CHAPTER 7

Leadership

The Qumran sectarian texts mention a number of leadership positions. The forms of leadership did not necessarily exist at the same time, so it is possible that the use of various terms indicates different historical periods in the life of the sect. The study of the nature of leadership elites in religious groups in general, and in Jewish ones in particular, is crucial to an understanding of the nature of such groups and their teachings. We therefore have much to learn about the Qumran community by examining its primary forms of leadership as described in sectarian documents and the role of each form in the life of the sect. As we learn about these leaders and offices, we should remember that the sect shared the general tendency of Second Temple Judaism to move from priestly to lay leadership—a transfer of authority best exemplified by the evolution of the Pharisaic sages into the talmudic Rabbis.

ZADOKITE PRIESTS

At the very founding of the sect, Zadokite priests played a leading role. Yet even though we have considerable documentary evidence about their prominence in the sect, the role of the Zadokite priests may have been largely ceremonial or even anachronistic. As founders of the sect, the Zadokite priests probably passed from actual to ceremonial leadership as the sect attracted lay Israelite followers with the passing of time. Nonetheless, the Zadokites were certainly the initial leaders until the Teacher of Righteousness assumed control. If we accept the claim of the *Zadokite Fragments* that the period before the Teacher of Righteousness lasted only twenty years (*Zadokite Fragments* 1:9–11), then this part of the history of the sect lasted no more than a generation or so. Apparently, the Zadokite priests continued to play a leadership role for sometime after, although it is not clear for how long or how extensively.

These priests were clearly at the heart of the sect's early ideology. The

Zadokite Fragments describes in metaphoric terms the establishment of the sect as the remnant, that is, the only Israelites who truly maintained the commandments when everyone else in the Jewish community had gone astray (*Zadokite Fragments* 3:12–20). Then it quotes the promise of God through Ezekiel:

> This is in accord with what God promised them through Ezekiel the prophet, saying, "The priests and the Levites and the Sons of Zadok who maintained the service of My Temple, when all Israel went astray from Me, they shall offer Me the fat and blood" (adapted from Ezekiel 44:15). "The priests": these are the penitents of Israel who leave the land of Judaea and those who join them. "And the Sons of Zadok": they are the chosen ones of Israel, the renowned men, those who arise in the End of Days.
> (*ZADOKITE FRAGMENTS 3:20–4:4*)

This text is an interpretation of a passage in Ezekiel chosen for its reference to the Zadokite priests. In this interpretation, the phrase "the priests . . . the Levites . . . the Sons of Zadok" has been broken apart in order to describe three separate groups. First are the priests (who are certainly Zadokites), identified as the repentant ones who have abandoned the land of Judaea, probably referring here to Jerusalem. Ezekiel's "Levites," originally an adjective modifying "priests," here is understood to refer to those who have joined the priests. Finally, the Sons of Zadok are identified as the chosen of God, those who will inherit the End of Days.

That these obviously anachronistic ideas are raised at all in biblical commentaries requires some explanation. The *pesharim*, as mentioned previously, are not commentaries as we know them, but rather contemporizing interpretations of specific biblical material. In them, the sectarian writers interpreted the visions of the prophets of the Hebrew Bible as referring to events in their own time. They searched for—and found, albeit sometimes in a very veiled manner—allusions to events and personages relevant to their current circumstances.

From this complex *pesher* interpretation (of which more examples are discussed in a later chapter), this author deduces that the sect was initially formed by Zadokites, who were then joined by others. In other words, the initial leaders were the Zadokite priests who left Jerusalem.

Rule of the Community also testifies to the primacy of this priestly group:

> This is the rule for the men of the community who volunteer to turn aside from all evil and to hold fast to all which He has commanded according to His will: to separate from the congregation of the men of iniquity to be a community as regards Torah and property. And they shall answer according to the Sons of Zadok, the priests, who observe the covenant, and according to the majority of the men of the community who hold fast to the covenant. According to them shall go forth the decision regarding every matter of Torah, property or judgment. (*RULE OF THE COMMUNITY 5:1–3*)

Then follows a series of obligations for the sectarian. The text next goes on to describe the oath of admission to be taken by new members, a topic treated earlier. For the moment, we shall look at only one portion of this text.

> He shall take upon himself with a binding oath to return to the Torah of Moses, according to everything which He commanded, with all his heart and all his soul, according to everything which is revealed of it (i.e., the Torah) to the Sons of Zadok, the priests, who maintain the covenant and seek (or study) His will, and according to the majority of the men of their covenant who volunteer together for His truth, and to conduct themselves according to His will. *(RULE OF THE COMMUNITY 5:8–10)*

Here the Sons of Zadok appear as leaders of the sect, but not as the sole seat of power. Rather, they are in association with the majority of the men of the community, who together are expected (as we know from other texts) to make all decisions regarding financial matters or Torah for the members of the sect.

The prominence of this group, based as it was on the Zadokite-Sadducean role in the founding years of the sect, took its cue as well from biblical tradition regarding this priestly clan. Zadok was one of Solomon's two high priests. The Bible gives precedence to him, because his priestly colleague Abiathar was eventually banished (I Kings 2:26–27). It was therefore natural for a sect so closely linked to and inspired by biblical tradition to place the Zadokite priests in a position of leadership and authority. The sect found further validation for the legitimacy of the Zadokites in the vision of the future Temple and the sacrificial service described near the end of Ezekiel, which sets out an entire code of priestly service, limiting the priesthood to Sons of Zadok (Ezekiel 44:9–31).

The introduction to *Rule of the Congregation,* a messianic text from cave 1 (not to be confused with *Rule of the Community),* indicates that in the End of Days, the Zadokite priests would retain at least their ceremonial role:

> And this is the rule for all the congregation of Israel in the End of Days: when they assem[ble as a community to li]ve according to the regulation of the Sons of Zadok, the priests, and the men of their covenant who have [turned away from living in the way of the people] . . . *(RULE OF THE CONGREGATION 1:1–3)*

The Assembly of the End of Days will be conducted under the direction of the Zadokite priests and their followers. Though it is possible that this role for the Sons of Zadok is only titular and ceremonial in this text, it is a role that acknowledges their initial function as founders and leaders of the sect. And though other officials would clearly join the Sons of Zadok in leading the community of the End of Days (*Rule of the Congregation* 1:23–25), the Zadokite priests would conduct the meetings of the Assembly (*Rule of the Congregation* 2:1–3).

Rule of Benedictions, which I believe was part of the ritual of mustering the sectarians in the End of Days, contains a blessing to be recited in honor of the Zadokite priests:

> . . . whom God chose to strengthen His covenant [eternally and to ex]amine all of His laws in the midst of His people and to instruct them as He commanded, and who established [His covenant of tr]uth, and in righteousness commanded all of His laws and lived a[s] He had chosen.
> *(RULE OF BENEDICTIONS 3:22–25)*

In this passage, the Zadokite priests fulfill their role as instructors of the law and of its correct, that is, sectarian, interpretation. The sect believed that the Zadokites had been chosen from among God's people to fill this role. The passage also confirms beyond a doubt that the term "Sons of Zadok" did not refer to the sect in general, but rather to a segment of the group entrusted with teaching and interpreting the law to others. It also shows that the sectarians expected that leadership role to continue in the End of Days.

The expectation that the Zadokite priests would play a messianic role seems to challenge the assumption that their leadership eventually became simply symbolic or anachronistic. In fact, the entire text of *Rule of the Congregation* is a rehearsal in the present for what was to occur at the End of Days. That is, the sect regarded its present behavior and procedures as instrumental in bringing to realization its dreams and aspirations for the future. Accordingly, the text suggests that when it was authored at least, the Zadokites still maintained an important role in the conduct of the sect's affairs.

Such a leadership structure would fit well with the sect's self-image as a replacement Temple. Because the Zadokites considered the current conduct of the sacrificial system in Jerusalem illegitimate, it makes sense that they would include priests among their core leadership group, replacing their former role in sacrificial worship with that of leaders of the sect. Indeed, the sect saw its entire religious life and communal existence as a substitute for the Temple worship in which they no longer participated.

Other priestly leaders may have also played a significant role in the life of the sect. A number of passages refer to Aaronide priests. For example, *Rule of the Community* specifies:

> Only the sons of Aaron shall have control over law and property, and according to them shall the decision go forth for every norm of the men of the community. *(RULE OF THE COMMUNITY 9:7)*

In that text, and in others of its type, it is most likely the Zadokite priests who are intended, for in other passages that have been quoted here, sectarians appear to have delegitimized all others.

Yet we cannot be certain that other priests did not have a role in the sect, especially in light of numerous biblical traditions to that effect. After all,

Deuteronomy 17:8–13 enjoins that in difficult cases requiring further investigation, the litigants are to go up to the chosen city to be judged by "the Levitical priests and the judge." Deuteronomy 21:5, perhaps reflecting an idealized command, requires that all lawsuits be decided by priests. The priest was also expected to be a teacher of Torah, as is clear from Deuteronomy 33:10, and to render decisions in matters of impurity and diseases. Indeed, we cannot be sure if all of the priestly officials of the sect were Zadokite. Certain legal passages mention only the Sons of Aaron.

TEACHER OF RIGHTEOUSNESS

No Qumran figure has been more frequently discussed than the Teacher of Righteousness. Although his sobriquet also may be translated as the "correct teacher," the current translation has become almost a technical term in the field of Qumran studies and cannot be easily replaced. The "teacher" has been credited with so much that he is often falsely identified as the author of texts to which he has no explicit relationship. Assuming that only direct references to this figure can be taken to concern him, I will attempt to reconstruct all that legitimately can be said about him. It is also possible that the term may have designated not only one but a series of figures who occupied the role of sectarian leader over a period of time.

The *Zadokite Fragments* makes a few references to the Teacher of Righteousness. We have already seen in our study of the origins of the sect that according to this text (*Zadokite Fragments* 1:11), the teacher was believed to have been sent by God to lead the sect after its separation from the Jerusalem religious establishment.

An extended passage in the *Zadokite Fragments* refers to the role of the teacher as legislator. In referring to the fate of members who have held fast to the teachings of the sect, the text states:

> All those who have held fast to these regulations, to [g]o out and to come in according to the Torah, shall listen to the voice of the teacher (or and who have listened to the voice of the teacher) . . . (*ZADOKITE FRAGMENTS 20:27–28*)

Only a bit farther down the same page, this teacher is explicitly identified as the Teacher of Righteousness. The text refers to:

> . . . those who have been instructed in the original regulations by which the men of the community were judged, and who have listened to the voice of the Teacher of Righteousness . . . (*ZADOKITE FRAGMENTS 20:31–32*)

The context of this passage indicates that it is speaking about the age of tribulation, what the Rabbis would later call "birthpangs of the messiah." The sect hoped to emerge from the age of tribulation into the future age of messianic perfection.

From these two passages we learn that the teacher is expected to show his followers how to put the Torah into practice and that it is his wise instruction that all must obey. The sect believed that Jewish law consisted of two complementary parts: the revealed, written Torah (*nigleh*) and the hidden or secret (*nistar*), known only to the sect. It was this second body of law with which the teacher had endowed them. Therefore, his teachings had the same validity as the Torah itself.

At least part of the *Zadokite Fragments* was authored after the teacher's death, as is clear when the text speaks of the period:

> From the day when the teacher of the community was gathered in (passed away) until the arising of a messiah from Aaron and Israel.
> (*Zadokite Fragments* 19:35–20:1)

In this text, although the teacher has died, the sect still looks forward to the speedy coming of the messiah. Thus, contrary to the claims of many scholars, the teacher himself was not regarded as a messianic figure, even though he had arisen on the eve of the End of Days (*Zadokite Fragments* 6:11).

Though it is difficult to be specific on this matter, it seems that the sect suffered a crisis with the death of its first primary leader. It had expected that the messianic era was soon to dawn and that no successor to the Teacher of Righteousness would be needed. Nonetheless, the sect weathered this crisis and was able to replace its leader with various officers, who later managed its affairs.

The *Pesher Habakkuk*, the sectarian commentary on the biblical Book of Habakkuk, contains much information about the teacher and his career and tribulations. The teacher was opposed by the Man of Lies (*Pesher Habakkuk* 2:2). In interpreting the words of Habakkuk 1:5, following the textual reading "See O treacherous ones . . ." (see verse 13), the scroll writes:

> [The interpretation of the matter concerns] the treacherous ones together with the Man of Lies. For they did not [listen to the words of] the Teacher of Righteousness from the mouth of God. (*Pesher Habakkuk* 2:1–3)

Here the teacher is depicted as a sectarian leader and messenger of God opposed by those who reject his teachings. Later we will see that these opponents are probably the Pharisees, the predecessors of the talmudic Rabbis.

This same theme appears in Habakkuk 2:2, which discusses the writing of a vision on tablets "in order that the reader would be able to read it [literally, "run"] quickly." *Pesher Habakkuk* says:

> Its interpretation concerns the Teacher of Righteousness, to whom God made known all the mysteries of the words of His servants the prophets.
> (*Pesher Habakkuk* 7:3–5)

According to this passage, God granted the teacher the ability to understand the true meaning, that is, the sectarian interpretation of the words of the canonical prophets. The teacher therefore could understand the historical processes unfolding at that time as well as the true interpretations of Jewish legal matters and the Torah about which so much friction existed between the sect and its opponents.

The sect always believed that it would be rewarded for its steadfast adherence to the teacher's authority. Interpreting Habakkuk 2:4 ("But the righteous man shall live by his faith"), the text states:

> Its interpretation concerns all those who observe (lit. "do") the Torah in the House of Judah (the sect), whom God will save from the place of punishment because of their toil and their faith in the Teacher of Righteousness.
> (PESHER HABAKKUK 8:1–3)

Later on, the teacher is mentioned in an interpretation of Habakkuk 1:13 ("Why do you look on, treacherous one, [and] keep silent when an evil man swallows up one more righteous than he?"):

> Its interpretation concerns the House of Absalom and the men of their council who were silent during the reproof of the Teacher of Righteousness and who did not help him (the teacher) against the Men of Lies. (PESHER HABAKKUK 5:9–12)

This text depicts an experience of the teacher when he was verbally abused by the Man of Lies. A certain group, called here the "House of Absalom," stood by and did not come to the teacher's assistance. Apparently, the group's name derives from the biblical story of Absalom's rebellion against his father, David (II Samuel 15–18). We learn here of the teacher's dispute with the leader of an opposing group.

The teacher was also plagued by a Wicked Priest, certainly a designation for one of the early Hasmonaean rulers. On Habakkuk 2:8 ("For crimes against men and wrongs against lands, against cities and all their inhabitants"), *Pesher Habakkuk* relates:

> Its interpretation concerns the [Wi]cked Priest, whom, because of (his) transgression against the Teacher of Righteousness and the men of his council, God handed over into the hand[s] of his enemies to afflict him . . .
> (PESHER HABAKKUK 9:9–10)

The sect saw the suffering of the Wicked Priest as a direct result of his persecution of the teacher.

In the interpretation of Habakkuk 2:15 ("Ah, you who make others drink to intoxication as you pour out your wrath, in order to gaze upon their nakedness"), we find a more specific explanation of the nature of the Wicked Priest's transgression. Our text reads the final phrase as if it said, "in order to gaze upon her appointed times":

> Its interpretation concerns the Wicked Priest, who pursued the Teacher of Righteousness to swallow him up with his wrathful anger to the place of his exile. And at the time of the day of rest of the Day of Atonement, he (the Wicked Priest) appeared before them, to swallow them up and to make them stumble on the day of the fast of their abstention from work. (PESHER HABAKKUK 11:4–8)

The teacher led the people in a "place of exile," that is, when they were already at their sectarian center. Although it cannot be proven that this is a reference to Qumran, it is the most probable location for these events. The Wicked Priest pursued and attacked the sect "with his wrathful anger" as they were celebrating the most holy Day of Atonement—one of the appointed times—and disrupted their fast and prayers.

The seriousness of the attack against the teacher and his followers is magnified by its occurrence on the Day of Atonement. But it is important to point out that it was this sect's Day of Atonement, not that of the rest of the Jewish people. This most important detail indicates the sect's adherence to a different calendar, a point to be taken up further in a later chapter.

One final characteristic of the teacher may be gleaned from *Pesher Psalms*. In interpreting Psalms 37:23 ("The steps of a man are prepared by the Lord"), the text states:

> Its interpretation refers to the priest, the Teacher of [Righteousness, whom] God [pr]omised would arise, fo[r] He (God) prepared (i.e., predestined) him (the teacher) to build for Him a congregation . . . (PESHER PSALMS A 1 III 15–16)

This text completely accords with the notion in *Pesher Habakkuk* that God gave the teacher the gift of an almost prophetic message. Here we learn that the teacher was a priest. If this detail is true, it would fit well with the historical picture previously suggested. We can easily imagine that out of the Zadokite priestly leadership, one priest would emerge to take control of the sect and give it shape and form. We could then easily comprehend the competition between him and the Wicked Priest. It is curious, however, that only this text identifies the teacher as a priest.

We can see from the preceding discussion that the Qumran documents do not give us very much information about the teacher. Nevertheless, some scholars have assumed him to be the author of various texts and have increased his role far beyond what is warranted by the documents we have studied. They see him, for example, as author of *Rule of the Congregation* and *Thanksgiving Hymns*. Some of the early Qumran scholars were inclined to see in him a proto-Jesus. A similar view has recently been espoused by some who wish to claim that the scrolls refer directly to the early Christian movement. This view, as I previously maintained, is impossible to accept on chronological grounds. In fact, the sources allow us to say little more than that the teacher led the sect in its formative period after the initial schism and period of uncertainty, that he was probably a priest, that he had confrontations with the Man of Lies, and that he was persecuted by the Wicked Priest. But most important, the sect believed that his leadership derived from his God-given ability to interpret the words of the prophets and to formulate the beliefs and halakhic norms of the sect.

Although the Teacher of Righteousness died at some point during the life of the sect, the sect continued to adhere to its principles, expecting the End of Days and the coming of the messiah. The teachings of the sect's preeminent leader were still considered authoritative and determined the sect's pattern of behavior long after his death.

MEVAQQER

Most likely the various sectarian leadership roles did not all coexist at the same time, but rather represent different stages in the organizational history of the sectarian community. The role of the Teacher of Righteousness may have been inherited after his death by the *mevaqqer* (examiner), to whom we now turn our attention.

This important figure in the sectarian leadership appears in both the *Zadokite Fragments* and *Rule of the Community*. The term *mevaqqer* has been variously defined as "examiner," "overseer," or, in some anachronistic and confessional presentations, "bishop." Instead of seeking a literal translation of *mevaqqer*, we shall examine his function, hoping in this way to understand his role in the sect's life.

Almost all of the references to this official occur in the *Zadokite Fragments*. However, reference to this office in *Rule of the Community* as well suggests that it functioned in sectarian communities both at Qumran and elsewhere in the Land of Israel.

The examiner was considered sufficiently important to merit an entire halakhic section in the *Zadokite Fragments:*

> This is the rule regarding the examiner of the camp: He shall instruct the community in the deeds of God and teach them His wondrous mighty acts. And he shall relate before them the events of eternity in its details. And he shall have mercy upon them, like a father to his sons, and heal their diseases. Like a shepherd to his flock, he shall loose all the fetters of their bonds, so that there shall not be (anyone) oppressed or downtrodden in his congregation. And anyone who joins his congregation, he shall examine him as regards his deeds, his wisdom, and his strength, his might, and his property. And he (the examiner) shall inscribe him in his place, according to his inheritance in the lot of truth. No one from the people of the camp shall decide to bring any

person into the congregation without the permission of the examiner who is
(in charge of) the camp. . . . And let no one do anything in regard to buying or
selling unless he has made (it) known to the examiner who is (in charge of)
the camp, and does so with (his) counsel, lest they e[rr. And thus] for a[ny]one
who ma[rr]ies a wo[man], i[t] (must be) [with] (his) counsel. And thus (also) for
one who divorces (his wife). And he (the examiner) shall [instruct their sons
and their daughters with a spirit of] of humility and with lovingkindness. He
may not harbor a [grudge] against them. [He should forgive] their sins.
(ZADOKITE FRAGMENTS 13:7–19)

This long passage certainly places the examiner at center stage in sectarian life. In
fact, it seems as if he must have been the inheritor of the duties, and perhaps the
powers, of the Teacher of Righteousness, although such a claim cannot be
proven.

What precisely were the examiner's responsibilities?

First and foremost, the examiner was a teacher and a guide to his followers, responsible for their spiritual and physical welfare. He tested new members and
had to approve their entrance into the community. He supervised all members'·
business transactions, probably deriving the prerogative from the rights of communal use exercised by the sect over individuals' property. He was responsible
for approving marriages and divorces (evidence that the sect was not celibate, a
matter to which we will return later), and he was required to treat his people
with love and kindness.

Apparently, a number of individuals fulfilled this office for smaller groups of
sectarians and one was in charge of the entire sect. His age and qualifications are
carefully specified:

The examiner who is in charge of all the camps shall be from thirty years old
[and] up to fifty years old. (He must be) experienced in every secret (known) to
men and in every language. . . . According to him shall the men of the congregation enter, each in his turn. And regarding every matter which any man
should have to say, he should speak to the examiner regarding any dispute or
judgment. (ZADOKITE FRAGMENTS 14:8–12)

This official, with his wisdom, understanding, and knowledge of languages, was
to organize the sectarians in order of their ranks. The system of ranking served
both for the mustering ceremony at the annual covenant renewal and for determining the order of speaking in the sectarian assembly, where senior members
were given first opportunity to speak. (This same practice was followed in the
Sanhedrin, according to rabbinic sources, except in capital matters, when junior
judges voted first.)

As we have already seen, the examiner was heavily involved in the process of
accepting new members, and he had an important function in the sectarian legal
system as well. It appears from our study that the examiner occupied an office

that was to a great extent designed to serve as a substitute for the Teacher of Righteousness after the teacher's death. However, because other officials also carried on some of the teacher's tasks, the examiner alone did not wield exclusive power.

PAQID

Rule of the Community places an official known as the *paqid* (appointed one) at the head of the community. It was the job of the *paqid* to administer the initial test for those wishing to join the sect:

> And whoever volunteers from Israel to join the council of the community, the one who is appointed (as *paqid*) at the head of the community shall investigate him as regards his understanding and his deeds . . .
> *(RULE OF THE COMMUNITY 6:14)*

A passage in the *Zadokite Fragments*, which can now be correctly and definitely restored with the aid of the fragments from cave 4, mentions the same official, there called the "priest who musters at the head of the community":

> And the priest who shall muster at the head of the community shall be from thirty to sixty years old, learned in the Book of Hagu/i and in all the regulations of the Torah to pronounce them according to their regulation.
> *(ZADOKITE FRAGMENTS 14:6–8 = D^b 11 II 10–13)*

The Book of Hagu is probably the Torah, and the regulations are the sectarian laws that emerged from the sect's interpretation of the Torah. This priest, whatever his functions—and we are not really certain what they were—had to be from thirty to sixty years old. Because the upper age limit differs from that of the examiner, it is not possible to suggest that they are the same official. It is also difficult to speculate further on the role of this priest, for our information is too scanty.

MASKIL

It is difficult to define precisely the role of another leadership type, the *maskil*. The word itself derives from a verb, meaning, "to enlighten," and it might be translated literally as "enlightener," that is, "instructor." No doubt the use of the term was influenced by Daniel 12—a chapter known to have been influential in Qumran sectarian texts—in which the term appears twice (verses 3 and 10). For reasons of convenience, and because of the dual usage of this term at Qumran to denote both the enlightened nature of the *maskil* and his role in enlightening others, we have chosen to leave the term untranslated.

A very general description of the role of this leader states:

> It is for the *maskil* to explain and to teach all the Sons of Light the nature of all men: all the types of their spirits, their signs, according to their actions in their generations, and the visitation of their plagues, as well as their periods of peace. (*RULE OF THE COMMUNITY 3:13–15*)

According to sectarian teachings, humankind has been predestined to be divided into the Sons of Light, the sectarians, and the Sons of Darkness, the rest of the Jewish people and the other peoples of the world. The job of the *maskil* was to teach the sectarians the nature of the spirits of light and darkness, as well as the way these two spirits manifest themselves in human history. He was to explain how interaction between these two spirits could lead both to misfortune in the world and to peace as well. Presumably, the *maskil* was responsible for conveying the ideology and theology of the Qumran community to other members of the group.

Another passage emphasizes the *maskil* as possessor of legal knowledge:

> These are the statutes for the *maskil* according to which he should conduct himself with every living being, according to the measure of each and every period, and according to the value of each and every person, to do the will of God according to everything that is revealed from time to time, and to learn all the knowledge which is derived according to the times, and the law of the time. (*RULE OF THE COMMUNITY 9:12–14*)

The *maskil* was expected to be a master of the sectarian legal tradition as it applied to the various periods of time. He was supposed to apply it properly in his dealings with others according to their status and level within the sect. Each member of the group had a particular status, determined by the order in which the sectarians were mustered.

This "legal" wisdom is also stressed in a very similar passage in the *Zadokite Fragments*, which serves as the conclusion to a list of laws:

> These are the statutes for the *maskil* according to which he should conduct himself with every living being, according to the regulation for each and every time. And according to this regulation shall the descendants of Israel conduct themselves so that they not be cursed. (*ZADOKITE FRAGMENTS 12:20–22*)

Neither of these last two passages speaks about the teaching or leadership role of the *maskil*. It is therefore possible that, in time, a class of scholars became a class of leaders, although this theory cannot be proven. What is most interesting about the *maskil* is that this learned leader did not have to be a Zadokite or even a priest. He appears to have been a lay member of the sect—knowledgeable about its law, but not born into his status.

Another passage from the same text should be mentioned because it is now possible, with the help of the newly released Qumran manuscripts of the *Zadokite Fragments*, to reconstruct it fully. It, too, serves as the conclusion for a list of laws:

> And these are the statutes for the *maskil* according to which he should conduct himself [when God brings visitation (punishment) on the] earth, when [the] matter takes [place] about which He (God) said, "There will come [upon you days the likes of whi]ch have not come [since] the day when E[ph]raim turned away from [Judah" (approximately Isaiah 7:17). And all those who con]duct themselves according to these (statutes), the covenant of God is dependable [for them to save them from all sn]ares of the [p]it, "for the f[oo]ls violated (these statutes) and were punished . . . " (Proverbs 27:12).
> (*ZADOKITE FRAGMENTS* D^b 11 II 1–4 = 13:22–14:2).

Here again we see the *maskil* connected with knowledge about how to live correctly according to the Torah. Those who knew these laws were to be saved from the coming visitation, which would be the greatest catastrophe since the split of the kingdom after Solomon's death. But others—the "fools" who violated the Torah—would suffer greatly.

The *maskil* took the lead in reciting the blessings found in *Rule of Benedictions*. I maintain that these were to be recited in the eschatological mustering ceremony. The text begins with the blessing for those who fear the Lord (*Rule of Benedictions* 1:1). Further on, the text presents a blessing for the Zadokite priests (3:22–28) and the Prince of the Congregation (5:20–29).

The *maskil*, an expert in the law, was expected to share this knowledge with his fellow sectarians and to set an example by his own way of life. Yet nowhere do we find specific administrative functions assigned to this person or class.

SECTARIAN OFFICIALS AND JEWISH LEADERSHIP

The various types of sectarian leaders and the roles they played tell us much about the basic transitions Judaism was undergoing at that time. Initially, the sect was led by Zadokite priests who started the breakaway group in protest over the Hasmonaean takeover of the high priesthood sometime after 152 B.C.E. But their leadership seems to have been augmented soon after by the Teacher of Righteousness as well as an examiner and by a priestly official known as the *paqid*. These other officials played an administrative role in the sect, which allowed legislative and judicial functions to pass into the hands of the entire community, called "the priests, the Sons of Zadok, and the men of their covenant." The last group consisted of the Levites and Israelites who made up the majority of the sect. Thus, just as the council of elders in Jerusalem, which served as the Hasmonaean council of state, included both priestly and lay elements, so lay leaders at Qumran shared authority with the sectarian priests.

In addition to giving us insight into the ways that lay officials and other Israelites entered into decision-making roles, the *maskil* closely resembles the lay Pharisaic sages who eventually became the teachers of the Mishnah. The *maskilim*, like the early Pharisaic lay sages, were experts in the law and its interpretation and, in some cases, involved themselves in its dissemination. Clearly, lay influence on communal and legal decision-making in Jewish life was already making inroads in Second Temple times, not only among the Pharisees but among other groups as well, even among so priestly a group as the Qumran sect.

When the Temple was destroyed in 70 C.E., the Jews of Palestine found themselves facing a vacuum of communal authority. As with so many other developments of that period, the nonpriestly rabbinic leadership that rose to fill that vacuum already had its antecedents not only among the Pharisees, but also among the wider Jewish community in the Land of Israel.

The texts we have discussed so far might leave the false impression that women had nothing to do with the life of the sect and were ignored in the documents collected at Qumran. Nothing could be further from the truth, as we will see in the next chapter.

CHAPTER 8

Women in the Scrolls

Since the earliest years of Qumran research, most scholars have assumed that the Dead Sea sect was made up only of men who lived a celibate life, forswearing marriage and sexual relations. That view has been conditioned by certain ancient accounts of the Essenes, who were assumed to be identical to the Dead Sea sect. Furthermore, certain approaches to studying early Christianity led some scholars to import the monastic model and impose it upon the Qumran discoveries.

This issue needs to be discussed anew for a variety of reasons. First, even partial excavation of the cemeteries at Qumran has yielded the graves of some women and children. Second, though the conditioned view of the Qumran community might have been consonant with the information contained in *Rule of the Community*, it is flatly countermanded by numerous texts, including the *Zadokite Fragments* and *Rule of the Congregation*. Finally, if we take a new look at the account of Josephus, we find ourselves questioning the nature of even Essene celibacy.

CELIBACY OF THE ESSENES

Assumptions that the Dead Sea sect was celibate and that women were not accepted into its ranks represent to a great extent the legacy of classical writers' descriptions of the Essenes. Based on that received tradition, most scholars in our own time have concluded that the Dead Sea sect is therefore identical with the Essenes. For that reason, it is useful to review ancient accounts describing Essene celibacy so that our investigation has a context.

We begin with the accounts that unquestioningly portray Essenes as celibate. Pliny the Elder (23–79 C.E.), who wrote soon after Destruction of the Temple and defeat of the Jews at the hands of the Romans, describes Essenes in his description of the Dead Sea region. There he says of the "tribe of the Essenes" that "it has no women and has renounced all sexual desire" (*Natural History* 5, 73). A number of passages in Greco-Jewish literature provide additional information. Philo the Alexandrian Jewish philosopher writes:

> Furthermore, they abstain from marriage because they plainly perceive it to be the only or the primary danger to the maintenance of the communal life, as well as because they especially practice continence. For no Essene takes a wife, because a wife is a selfish creature, addicted to jealousy and skilled at beguiling the morals of her husband and seducing him by her continued deceptions. *(Hypothetica 11, 14)*

This discussion presents several supposed reasons for Essene celibacy. First, marriage was perceived, Philo tells us, as a danger to the structure of the community. In other words, the Essenes set aside the Bible's command to "be fruitful and multiply" (Genesis 1:28) so that the sect could conduct its affairs in an orderly fashion, something impossible to do in the company of women. Second, Philo tells us that Essenes practiced abstinence from sexual relations. Finally, he presents a negative view of women that is familiar from some Hellenistic sources but not common in Palestinian Judaism. We cannot know how Philo got his ideas about Essene celibacy, but it is clear that they were to some extent influenced by the Hellenistic environment in which he lived.

The most important material on this subject comes from Josephus (37–100 C.E.), for he had firsthand acquaintance with the Judaean sects, at least those of the latter part of the Second Temple period. Josephus writes of the Essenes:

> They avoid pleasures as a vice and regard continence and the control of the desires as a special virtue. They disdain marriage. . . . They do not actually on principle reject wedlock and the propagation thereby of humanity, but they want to protect themselves from promiscuous women, since they are convinced that none of them preserves her fidelity to one man. *(War 2, 120–121)*

First, Josephus tells us that Essenes shunned sexual relations in order to control their passions. Then the text gives us yet another reason: they feared that a wife would engage in illicit relations with others. Thus, if they were to have relations with their wife after she had been unfaithful, they would in some way become defiled. This account echoes the same notion expressed by Philo and may not really involve direct knowledge of the group, because Josephus's account here seems to be influenced by that of Philo. Elsewhere, Josephus writes that Essenes do not "bring wives into the community" since it "opens the way to a source of dissension" (Antiquities 18, 21).

Josephus also writes of "another order of Essenes":

> They believe that those who refuse to marry negate the chief purpose of life—the propagation of humanity—and that furthermore, if everyone were to adopt the same approach, the entire (human) race would very quickly become extinct. But they subject their wives to three years' probation and marry

them only after they have by three periods of ritual purification demonstrated proof of fertility. They do not have sexual relations with them during pregnancy, thus showing that their purpose in marriage is not pleasure but the assurance of posterity. *(War 2, 160–161)*

Various strange interpretations have been offered for this passage, even suggesting that Essenes lived together with their wife-to-be before marriage.

The most plausible explanation, however, is to understand the text as describing a three-year period of betrothal, designed to verify that the bride-to-be was appropriate, followed by a three-month investigation to confirm that the woman was at least on the surface able to give birth. The reason for these practices, the text goes on to say, is that this group regarded nonprocreative sexual relations as forbidden. Rabbinic sources give evidence of a similar idea held by some early Jewish pietists (B. Niddah 38a).

We cannot cite any parallels in the Qumran sectarian documents that echo the negative views toward women that are attributed to nonmarrying Essenes, although we encounter references to evil women in other Second Temple texts that are preserved at Qumran. Nor can we find parallels to the view that the only purpose in marriage is procreation. Furthermore, we cannot be sure that the Essenes described by Josephus, or even by Philo, held such negative views about women, because such ideas were commonplace in the Hellenistic milieu and may simply reflect the desire of these Greek writers to describe Jewish sectarian practices in terms understandable to non-Jewish readers.

All we can know for certain is that some Jews who were extremely vigilant about fidelity within the marriage relationship held views somewhat different from those of the mainstream regarding even sexual relations within marriage but nonetheless still married and had children. It is possible that Josephus's "marrying Essenes" are identical with our sect.

Indeed, in the passage, Josephus shows that the term "Essene" may have been an inclusive term encompassing a number of groups. It is then possible that our sect, which certainly does exhibit some valid parallels with the Essenes as described by Philo, Josephus, and Pliny the Elder, would fall under this wider heading.

EVIDENCE FROM THE *ZADOKITE FRAGMENTS*

Let us now turn to the internal evidence in the Qumran sectarian texts themselves. In regard to the identification of the sect with a specific group, we have already noted that these texts do not use the name "Essenes" or any other such name to refer to the sect. Neither do they list any regulations mandating celibacy for sect members.

On the contrary, the *Zadokite Fragments* contains many indications of a society in which marriage and family were the norm. This document constitutes a good starting point for investigation of the role of women in the sect, although it is generally believed that the text describes members who were scattered in camps throughout the Land of Israel rather than those at Qumran. (We take up the Qumran community later.) So the passages discussed here probe only that group within the larger Dead Sea sect (or perhaps the Essenes) who practiced marriage and family life.

The *Zadokite Fragments* wages a spirited attack on polygamy and other practices that the sect considered violations of Jewish marriage laws, but they never criticize, let alone negate, the institution of marriage itself.

The text attacks opponents of the sect for practicing polygamy:

> They are caught . . . in fornication, by taking two wives in their lifetime. But the foundation of creation is "male and female He created them" (Genesis 1:27) and those who entered the ark, "two of each, [male and female,] came [to Noah] into the ark" (Genesis 7:9). And regarding the king it is written, "He shall not have many wives" (Deuteronomy 17:17). *(Zadokite Fragments 4:20–5:2)*

This passage has given rise to many interpretations. Central to the dispute has been the question of whose lifetime is meant by "their lifetime"—the men's or the women's? I take the passage to categorically forbid polygamy and, furthermore, to forbid a man to take another wife during his current wife's lifetime. In defining marriage as a lifetime commitment, the text's author clearly interpreted the biblical right of divorce to permit separation but not remarriage. The man or woman had to wait until the other died before taking a new spouse. The passage also quotes the law of the king in Deuteronomy to show that the king serves as an example to his subjects. Just as he is not permitted to have more than one wife, so others are not. The *Temple Scroll* contains an especially strong prohibition against the king's having more than one wife.

Here is incontrovertible evidence that polygamy is prohibited but marriage is not. Yet the passage does not prove that marriage was actually the norm in the sectarian community. The text goes on to prohibit marriage with one's niece— a point of contention between the Pharisees and other Jewish groups in Second Temple times—and to complain about the observance of purity regulations by other Jews who apparently disagreed with the author's views:

> And they also render impure the Temple since they do not separate according to the Torah, and they have sexual relations with one who experiences her blood flow. And they marry each (his niece) the daughter of his brother and the daughter of his sister. *(Zadokite Fragments 5:7–8)*

This passage goes on to reason that the marriage of a niece ought to be prohibited by logical deduction because the Torah explicitly prohibits a woman from marrying her nephew (Leviticus 18:13). Although the text here protests the violation of the purity laws and the laws of consanguinity, it does not even hint that marriage itself is undesirable or proscribed.

Later on, a man is commanded "not to transgress against his wife and to abstain from fornication" (*Zadokite Fragments* 7:1). He is also commanded:

> Let a man not have sexual relations with a woman in the city of the sanctuary so as to render the city of the sanctuary impure by their defilement.
> (*ZADOKITE FRAGMENTS* 12:1–2)

This prohibition surely proscribes relations in Temple precincts, although other scholars have suggested that it refers to the entire city of Jerusalem. In any case, the text does not imply total prohibition of sexual relations, only restrictions in a specific area surrounding and including the Temple itself. Parenthetically, it should be noted that despite the sect's abandonment of Temple worship, which it regarded as impure, it continued to legislate for the perfect society in which it would conduct Temple ritual in accord with its views.

Another passage, preserved only in the Qumran fragments of this text, specifically takes up the laws of ritual purity as they relate to women:

> [And if a man has sexual relations with her (a menstrually impure woman), the pen]alty (i.e., the impurity) of menstrual impurity will be upon him.
> (*ZADOKITE FRAGMENTS* D^a 9 II 1–2)

The text goes on to explain how women could be purified: by waiting seven days and immersing in the ritual bath. Then, on the eighth day, women could enter the Temple. Again, laws concerning relations with women assume the legitimacy of sexual unions.

In another passage, the text addresses the issue of family life explicitly:

> If they live in camps according to the custom of the land, and they have taken wives and had children, then they should live according to the Torah . . .
> (*ZADOKITE FRAGMENTS* 7:6–7)

The passage then addresses the issues of oaths and vows and the right of the father or husband to annul those of his daughter or wife:

> [Regar]ding a (married) woman's oath: As to that which He (God) said to the effect that her husband may annul her oath, the husband may not annul an oath about which he does not know whether it ought to be carried out or annulled. (*ZADOKITE FRAGMENTS* 16:10–11 = D^f 2 II 10–11)

The law of oaths and vows in the *Zadokite Fragments* expands upon that of Numbers 30:14–15, which states that a husband could cancel an oath that his wife had taken, or, if he had no objection to it, he could let it stand. For our purposes, this passage simply confirms that married women were a common feature of the society described in this text.

A similar text from the *Temple Scroll* repeats this law, but adds:

> But as to any vow (made) by a widow or divorcee, whatever she has imposed upon herself shall be binding upon her, according to everything which comes forth from her mouth. *(TEMPLE SCROLL 54:4–5)*

Here we have evidence not only for marriage but for divorce as well. The widow or divorcee had complete control over her legal actions; her husband or father could not intervene on her behalf, and anything she swore was binding.

We have already mentioned that among the tasks of the examiner was approval of marriages and divorces among the members. The examiner was apparently expected to serve as counselor and guide in those matters.

Perhaps most interesting is a passage that speaks of making sure that a bride-to-be is appropriate. To this end a person is commanded to reveal any of her imperfections or blemishes to an unsuspecting groom:

> . . . all of her blemishes he should relate to him. Why should he bring upon himself the punishment of the curse which He (God) said, "[Cursed be] he who misdirects a blind person on his way" (Deuteronomy 27:18)? And also, he should not give her to one who is not appropriate for her, for it is a forbidden mixture, [like (plowing with) "an o]x and an ass" (Deuteronomy 22:10) and wearing "wool and linen together" (Deuteronomy 22:11).
> *(ZADOKITE FRAGMENTS D^f 1 I 8–10 = D^e 5 14–16 = D^d 9 1–3)*

In addition, this passage forbids the father from marrying off his daughter to one who was inappropriate to her, considering such a marriage a violation of the law of forbidden mixtures.

After a broken section that is difficult to interpret, the text resumes with a passage restricting members of the sect from marrying women of questionable moral standards:

> And whoever had sexual [relations (literally, "knew to perform the act") in the house of] her father, or a widow who had sexual relations after she was widowed, or any (woman) about [whom] there was about her a bad name (i.e., a claim of nonvirginity) during her (period of) virginity in her father's house, let no man marry her. Except with the supervision of reliable women and definite facts according to the instruction of the examiner who is over [the assembly of the many, he may not] marry her.
> *(ZADOKITE FRAGMENTS D^f 1 I 11–15 = D^e 5 18–21 = D^d 9 4–7)*

This text certainly legislates for a society in which marriage was acceptable, and it seeks to protect the male sectarian from contracting marriage with a woman who had engaged in illicit relations, that is, relations out of wedlock. In addition, women were considered reliable to certify the virginity of a prospective wife.

Therefore, these texts, and others that could be cited as well, demonstrate conclusively that the society described by the *Zadokite Fragments* was to be based on marriage and family. If this document were our only source for the Qumran sect, no one would ever have suggested that women were not a part of the community. But as we will now see, it is not the only one.

RULE OF THE CONGREGATION

Rule of the Community, one of the first seven nearly complete scrolls to be recovered from cave 1, is generally accepted as the most important document describing the structure and organization of the community at Qumran. Significantly, this scroll does not itself contain any mention of women or children.

Among other texts recovered later from that same cave were two documents that we now know were definitely copied on the same scroll as *Rule of the Community*. The first of these associated documents, written immediately after *Rule of the Community*, is called *Rule of the Congregation*, or, sometimes, *Messianic Rule*. This second rule describes the messianic community embodying the perfect holiness of the End of Days. This same text, which provides an eschatological mirror image of *Rule of the Community*, anticipates that the life of the sectarians in the End of Days will involve children and family and, as explicitly stated, sexual relations.

In the introduction to this text, we read that in the End of Days

> they shall assemble all those who join (the sect), women and children . . . .
> (*RULE OF THE CONGREGATION* 1:4)

This description of the only true Israel of the End of Days, the perfect sectarian community, includes women and children, who, according to the text, will participate in the reenacting of the covenant renewal ceremony commanded by Deuteronomy from which this description derives its language (Deuteronomy 29:10). Other Qumran sources tell us that the premessianic sect at Qumran engaged in the very same covenant renewal ceremony on an annual basis (*Rule of the Community* 1:1–3:12). Many scholars believe it occurred on Shavuot, the Festival identified by the Pharisaic-rabbinic tradition as the time the Torah was given at Sinai.

Further on, the same text outlines the life stages of a sectarian in the messianic community. There we learn that marriage and sexual relations are the expected norm:

> And at twenty year[s of age he shall pass among the mu]stered to enter into full status along with his fam[il]y, to join the holy congre[gation]. He shall not [approach] a woman to have sexual relations with her until he reaches the age of twe[nty], at which time he knows [good] and evil.
> (*RULE OF THE CONGREGATION* 1:8–11)

Stages of Life for Men
in the Sectarian Community

Age in Years	Activities and Obligations
Early childhood (up to 10)	Studies Book of Hagu/i Studies laws of covenant
20	Participates in mustering ceremony Makes one-time payment of half-shekel May marry and have sexual relations May serve as witness
25	Minimum age for military service Minimum age for judicial service
30	May serve as official May serve as *paqid* or *mevaqqer* Minimum age for skirmishing troops
40	Minimum age for serving in battle array
45	Maximum age for skirmishing troops
50	Minimum age for camp prefect Maximum age for serving as *mevaqqer* Maximum age for serving in battle array
60	Maximum age for judicial service Maximum age for serving as *paqid* Maximum age for camp prefect

In the view of the sect and in wider circles in Palestinian Judaism in our period, twenty was the age of physical and legal maturity. It was also the age of sexual maturity, denoted by the phrase "knows good and evil." This, indeed, may be the meaning of the phrase in the recounting the story of the Garden of Eden, wherein the eating of the tree causes Adam and Eve to become sexually aware (Genesis 3:5, 8). In any case, here is explicit evidence that in the ideal messianic community of the sect, women were to be not only present but also wives and partners in sexual and family life.

A problematic excerpt from this same text has sometimes been interpreted as proving that women gave testimony according to the Qumran halakhic system, a practice for the most part forbidden in the Pharisaic-rabbinic system. Literally translated, the text would indeed seem to support such a reading:

> And at that time she will be received to bear witness of him (concerning) the judgment of the law and to take (her) pl[a]ce in proclaiming the ordinances.
> (RULE OF THE CONGREGATION 1:11)

It would be attractive for our argument to be able to claim that women even testified in the sectarian legal system. However, then we would have a text allowing

134

women to testify about one and only one thing: the conduct of their husbands. Imagine what marriages this would have made! Clearly, the text has been corrupted through scribal error and must be emended (substituting *yqbl* for *tqbl* and *'lpy* for *'lyw*) to read: "And at that time he shall be received to testify in accordance with the laws of the Torah and to take [his] place in hearing judgments." Those familiar with how limited women's roles were in ancient Jewish and general legal proceedings would understand why this emendation makes more sense.

If the sectarians anticipated in the End of Days a society based on marriage and family and if that society represented for them the perfection of what already existed in their own world and their own community, then it is hard to escape the conclusion that the Qumran sectarians lived in a normal society that included marriage and family. If such is the case, then we still need to explain why so many fewer women and children than men were buried in the graves excavated at Qumran.

We know that the Qumran settlement and building complex constituted the center of a larger group scattered throughout Israel. At the regional locations, it was possible to proceed only through the first two steps in the novitiate, and only by going to the Qumran center and completing the requisite studies could one enter fully into the sect. Since this stage required concentrated study, sectarians may have left their wives and families for periods of time to accomplish the goal. After completion of their novitiate, they were free to return home. Therefore, only permanent settlers at Qumran, probably few in number, would have had families living at the site—hence, the few women and children buried in the Qumran graves.

MARRIAGE RITUAL

Cave 4 has yielded a document dubiously labeled *Ritual of Marriage*. Because its formulation seems to have little to do with matrimony, however, it is highly doubtful that this text actually was a marriage ritual. On the other hand, the alternative suggestion that the text is an old-age ritual for honoring the elders of the sect seems just as unlikely. The truth is that we do not really understand what purpose this text was designed to serve.

The surviving material is extremely fragmentary, consisting of about one hundred and fifty fragments, most of which bear little more than a few incomprehensible letters. But a few expressions found in the text are significant: "and his wife"; "to make seed"; "daughter of truth . . . his wife" (fragments 1–3). God is praised repeatedly for giving joy to the sect, or "joy together" (fragments 7–9). Also mentioned are "sons and dau[ghters]" (fragment 14); "seed of blessing, old men and old [women . . . young men] and virgins, boys and gi[rls] . . ." (fragment 19); and "for the fruit of the w[omb]" (fragment 20).

Whatever the overall contents and character of this text, it certainly involves families' rejoicing together. Far from describing a celibate community, these fragments convey a sense of the true joy of generations' celebrating the continuity of the Jewish family.

WOMEN IN THE *TEMPLE SCROLL*

The *Temple Scroll* sketches out an ideal paradigm for holiness in the present, pre-messianic era. It is probable that this text was not composed entirely by the Qumran sect, for it depends heavily on sources derived from Sadducean circles and differs in many respects from the Qumran sectarian corpus. Nonetheless, it reflects a way of thinking quite close to that of the sectarians, who preserved it and most probably edited it. Certainly, this text assumes marriage, sexual relations, and childbirth as part of its ideal society. Because women are potentially agents for either sanctification or defilement, they are the focus of legislation in this scroll. The selected laws that follow demonstrate once again how basic the institution of marriage is to the social fabric of a document which was cherished by the sect.

Several laws deal with prohibited and permitted marriages. In the case of marriage between a man and his niece, the *Temple Scroll* is stricter even than the legislation of the Torah:

> A man may not marry his brother's daughter or his sister's daughter, for it is an abomination. (*TEMPLE SCROLL 66:15–17*)

According to Leviticus 18:12–13, a man is prohibited from marrying his aunt; the *Temple Scroll* reasons that if a woman may not marry her nephew, then a man may not marry his niece. This very same ruling appears in the *Zadokite Fragments* (5:7–11), as previously mentioned. However, the Rabbis allowed a man to marry his niece and even encouraged it. But the *Temple Scroll* agrees with the Qumran sectarians, Samaritans, early Christians, and Karaites in forbidding such marriages.

The scroll also deals with the various ritual purity rules and their relevance to women. It is extremely strict in separating menstrually impure women from the community at large:

> In each and every city you shall set aside places for . . . women when they are in their period of impurity and when they have given birth, so that they not defile in them (the cities) during their period of impurity.
> (*TEMPLE SCROLL 48:14–17*)

During a woman's "period of impurity," she was forbidden to enter cities. In order to enter the Temple City, she had to undergo purification rituals beforehand.

Temple Scroll This scroll was recovered by Yigael Yadin in the aftermath of the Six-Day War in 1967. It is almost completely preserved to a length of almost 9 meters. The text is a reworking of the laws of the Torah that advocate the author's approach to the Temple and its ritual, the government, the army, and the legal system of the Jewish people. The document as a whole calls for thoroughgoing reform of the existing religious and political order of the Hasmonaean period. *Photograph by Bruce and Kenneth Zuckerman, West Semitic Research. Courtesy of the Shrine of the Book of the Israel Museum.*

In the Second Temple, described by Josephus and the Mishnah, women were permitted to enter the outer of the two Temple courts. In the ideal Temple described in this scroll, the Temple would be surrounded by three courts instead of two; women who were ritually pure would be permitted into only the outer of the three courts. Thus, in the actual Second Temple, and later in rabbinic halakhah, women were permitted physically nearer the holy area where priestly ritual was performed than they were in the ideal sanctuary described in the *Temple Scroll*. As in the case of women, men too were moved one court outward, permitted to enter only into the middle court rather than into the closer inner court of the actual Second Temple.

Concern with female purity also expresses itself in another passage, which deals with captive women who have been acquired in war. Like Deuteronomy 21:1–9, the *Temple Scroll* allows a soldier to bring home a woman captured from the enemy and to marry her, but he must cut her hair, pare her nails, give her new clothes, and offer her the opportunity to mourn her parents. The *Temple Scroll* adds:

> Afterward, you may have sexual relations with her, and she shall be your wife. But she may not touch your pure food for seven years. Nor shall she eat a whole-offering until seven years pass; then she shall eat (it).
> (TEMPLE SCROLL 63:10–15)

Like the *Zadokite Fragments* and *Rule of the Community*, the *Temple Scroll* excludes from contact with the pure food a person who is regarded as impure. A non-Jewish wife is not allowed to partake of the pure foods for a period of seven years. Although this time frame is different from that which applied to a novice seeking admission into the sect, the concept is the same. Only those who were full members of the community had access to the pure food. Note, however, that there is no distinction made here between solid and liquid food, in contrast to the distinction made in the system of sectarian initiation.

The special section of the *Temple Scroll* known as Law of the King maintains especially strict marital regulations for the king: He may not marry more than one woman. She must be a Jewish woman of his own clan. He may not divorce her and remarry as long as she lives; however, he may remarry if she dies.

This scroll, then, certainly the largest halakhic text found in the scrolls corpus, assumes marriage and family, and it legislates on that assumption. In setting out an ideal plan for a future society, but not one that is messianic, the scroll expects that women and family will occupy their natural place. Whether this document was edited in the sectarian community or imported from a related but different group, it is obvious that its readers must have felt no discomfort about the society described here; it was, as the *Zadokite Fragments* said, "the custom of the land" (*Zadokite Fragments* 7:6).

IMAGE OF WOMEN IN QUMRAN POETRY

A few poetic texts found at Qumran portray women in erotic contexts. Even though those texts show no evidence of having been composed by the sectarians, and in some cases were definitely not, they are important to this discussion because their presence in the Qumran collection suggests that they were of interest to the group and constituted part of the literary and religious heritage the sect had received. Accordingly, they help to create a context for the material analyzed earlier, and they give us a sense of how women were portrayed and understood. We will encounter several basic archetypes here: woman as seductress, leading men astray; woman as symbol of wisdom, the acquisition of which is described in erotic terms; woman as birth mother of the messiah and the messianic era; and woman as beautiful erotic partner. In fact, all these images of women derive directly from the Hebrew Bible but appear here greatly expanded and enriched.

A Qumran document in the wisdom text genre discusses the wicked woman who leads men astray. Some have interpreted this harsh condemnation as indicative of the sect's negative view toward women. In reality, the poem simply rehearses an ancient biblical-wisdom trend that warned against the dangers of a wanton woman who entices even the best of men.

Preserved in a first century B.C.E. manuscript, this is a text that, in fact, need not have been authored within the Qumran community, for it evinces no particular sectarian features. Some scholars have read it as an allegory, depicting such ideas as the evils of false doctrine. I prefer to see it as a wisdom exhortation—in the style of Proverbs 7 and other passages in the Bible—that sets forth the timeless truths that some women use their feminine charms irresponsibly and that men need to guard against their own proclivities to fall into the traps laid for them.

The poem, known as *Wiles of the Wicked Woman*, is too long to quote in full, but following are some representative portions:

> [From] her [mouth] she brings forth vanity,
> and on [her tongue she expresses nou]ght.
> Error shall remain always [on her lips],
> she shall [make] smooth [her] words with ridicule and flattery. . . .
>
> Her hands have taken hold of the Pit,
> her legs have descended to do evil,
> and to go in (the way of) [guilty] transgressions,
> [and to probe] the foundations of darkness. . . .
>
> For she is the beginning of all the ways of iniquity,
> trouble (and) misfortune to all who possess her. . . .
>
> For her ways are the ways of death,
> and her paths are the paths of sin. . . .
>
> Her [g]ates are ga[t]es of death,
> at the entrance to her house she steps [into] Sheo[l].
> [Those who enter it will not] return,
> and all who possess her have gone down to the Pit. . . .
>
> [Her feet] hurry [always],
> her eyes search to and fro.

To se[e] a righteous [man] so that she can ensnare him,
and a man of [perfec]tion so that she can cause him to stumble.
The upright to turn (them) aside from the path,
and those chosen for righteousness from the observance
of the commandment . . . ,
so they not [wa]lk in the paths of uprightness.
To cause men to go astray in the ways of the Pit,
and to seduce with lies the sons of man.

A poem bearing certain similarities to this one appears in the Book of Ben Sira
(c. 180 B.C.E.) and also appears as part of the additional, noncanonical material included in the *Psalms Scroll*. The presence of this poem in the Qumran *Psalms
Scroll* suggests that it had attained a measure of status among the sectarians.

This poem is actually the converse of the one just previously examined: Here
the erotic imagery dramatizes the pursuit of wisdom. The man's seduction results not from going astray after the vices of an evil woman, but rather expresses
his deep, erotic attraction to the secrets of wisdom, symbolized as a beautiful and
sensual woman. The man's consummation of the sexual act is not a transgression and fall as in the first poem, but is rather a symbol of the highest level of personal attainment. The following is the preserved portion of the poem in the
translation of James A. Sanders (*Psalms Scroll* 21:11–17):

I was a young man before I had erred when I looked for her.
She came to me in her beauty when I finally sought her out.
Even (as) a blossom drops in the ripening of grapes, making glad the heart,
(So) my foot trod in uprightness; for from my young manhood have
I known her.
I inclined my ear but a little and great was the persuasion I found.
And she became for me a nurse; to my teacher I give my ardor.
I purposed to make sport: I was zealous for pleasure, without pause.
I kindled my desire for her without distraction.
I bestirred my desire for her, and on her heights I do not waver.
I spread my hand(s) . . . and perceive her unseen parts.
I cleansed my hand(s). . . .

To understand this poem, we need some familiarity with the erotic language of
ancient Israel. Both the "foot" and the "hand" are often euphemisms for the male
sexual organ. The verb to "know" often connotes sexual relations, and to "make
sport" means to make love. What we have here is the learning process pictured in
totally erotic images. Wisdom, portrayed in the poem as a woman, is the greatest

of all acquisitions. Curiously, the Greek translator of this poem as it appears in the Septuagint was so pious that no trace of eroticism comes out in his rendering. He speaks only of the acquisition of wisdom.

The positive image of women and sexuality, used here to portray wisdom, is possible only in the context of a positive attitude both to male-female relationships and to sexuality. The same attitude underlies the portrayal of a woman as giving birth to the messiah, an image found in another beautiful poem in a clearly sectarian poetry collection.

The *Thanksgiving Hymns* (3:6–10) describe a woman in labor with her first child. This difficult birth represents the birth pangs of the messianic era:

> They caused [me] to be like a ship on the deeps of the [sea],
> and like a fortified city before the [enemy].
> [And] I was in pain like a woman in travail with her firstborn child,
> upon whom pangs have come and grievous pains in her throes,
> to cause (her) to writhe with anguish in her womb.
> For the children have come to the throes of death,
> and she who gives birth to a man labors in her pains.
> For amidst the throes of death she shall bring forth a male,
> and amidst the pains of hell there shall spring from her womb
> a Marvelous Counselor in his strength;
> and a man shall be delivered from out of the throes.

This graphic poem depicts the birth of the messiah. This birth is not to be unnatural in any way, but rather, following certain biblical traditions, is to be preceded by tremendous suffering, here pictured as a difficult birth that endangers the very life of the child. In the end, the messianic era will dawn and the Marvelous Counselor will lead his people.

What interests us here is, again, a positive picture of woman. She herself gives birth to the End of Days. We are here shown not a world without women, but one that recognizes the difficult, indeed painful, role of women in the eschatological process. Though clearly we deal here with poetic imagery, it is imagery based on the assumption that birth is a positive and creative process.

Yet in this context we must note that some passages in *Thanksgiving Hymns* picture the female sexual and reproductive organs in a negative light. These passages place the origins of mortal man in the filth of the birth canal and may tend toward the notion found in early Christianity that sexuality is inherently sinful. However, despite the presence of such imagery, found occasionally in rabbinic tradition as well, we consider the vast majority of Qumran sectarian passages we have surveyed as affirming a positive view of women.

An idealized picture of women's beauty is found in the *Genesis Apocryphon*. In retelling the story of Abram and Sarai in Egypt (a passage to be discussed in a survey of the apocryphal texts), the king is told how beautiful Sarai is, and he sends for her and desires to wed her. The text goes to great lengths to describe Sarai's beauty, elaborating on the brief account in Genesis 12:14–15: "When Abram entered Egypt, the Egyptians saw how very beautiful the woman was. Pharaoh's courtiers saw her and praised her to Pharaoh, and the woman was taken into Pharaoh's palace."

The Aramaic text of the *Genesis Apocryphon* here turns poetic, borrowing images from the Song of Songs. Here is the courtiers' description of Sarai as told to Pharaoh (*Genesis Apocryphon* 20):

> How splen[did] and beautiful is the appearance of her face!
>
> How . . . fine are the hairs of her head!
>
> How lovely are her eyes!
>
> How desirable her nose and all the radiance of her countenance . . .
>
> How fair are her breasts and how beautiful all her whiteness!
>
> How beautiful are her arms and how perfect her hands,
>
> and how [attractive] all the appearance of her hands!
>
> How fair are her palms and how long and slender are her fingers!
>
> How comely are her feet, how perfect her thighs!
>
> No virgin or bride who enters the marriage chamber is more beautiful than she;
>
> she is fairer than all other women.
>
> Truly her beauty is greater than theirs.
>
> Yet together with all this grace she possesses abundant wisdom,
>
> so that whatever she does is perfect.

As in rabbinic midrash, Sarai is here depicted as the most beautiful of women. In this idealized portrait of feminine beauty, the author of the poem not only describes Sarai's beautiful face and slender fingers but also praises parts of a woman's body usually covered, such as her breasts and thighs, and imagines her being led to the marriage chamber. After describing her physical appearance, he adds that she also possesses wisdom. Thus, a woman, provided she is suitably wise, is to be praised for her beauty and sensuality. Sarai, the archetype of the Jewish woman, is indeed endowed with such characteristics. The beauty of the matriarch is pictured in terms both feminine and erotic.

There is no question that this text was composed before the Qumran sect came into being. This is the case with all the Aramaic texts preserved at Qumran. Some individual sectarian lovingly stored the text in a jar, wrapped in protective cloth. And clearly, the sect must have treasured its contents.

The Qumran scrolls envisioned women in many guises—as wives, mothers, temptresses, and beautiful captives—and as possessing purity or impurity, wisdom or guile. The texts portray women variously as the embodiment of sexuality, the desired bride, the woman in childbirth. They mandate laws regulating women's ritual purity. In all cases, we can see that women were very much a part of the lives of most Second Temple men, who indeed expected to marry and build families. In the same way, I would argue, they were part of the life of the Dead Sea sect. There simply is no evidence that the sectarians of Qumran were celibate.

Now that we have established the structure of the sect, its social framework, and its leadership, we turn to its theological views. We will see that the Qumran sectarians had distinctive ideas about the nature of God and his relationship to the world and the Jewish people.

CHAPTER 9

Faith and Belief

Until the Middle Ages, Jews for the most part avoided direct and systematic discussion of theological matters. All kinds of descriptions of God and God's actions occur in Jewish texts, but these were generally not brought together or systematized. Only under the influence of medieval philosophical trends did Jews turn to systematic discussion of theology.

However, in biblical and postbiblical texts of antiquity and late antiquity, certain basic beliefs were assumed: God was one—the creator of the universe and its eternal master. Human beings were therefore obligated to serve God and to fulfill God's decrees. Yet beyond these assumptions, different perspectives existed.

The Qumran sectarians had very specific views on these topics. Indeed, theological issues, though not the immediate cause of the schism that created the sect, must have encouraged it greatly. Perhaps the most interesting part of our discussion will focus on just how extensively theological issues engaged the Qumran community and were discussed in the literature. The Qumran community was not simply a group of religious automatons mechanically pursuing Jewish observances. Rather, the members were deeply concerned with the nature of God and humanity, and they sought to use Jewish law and observance to teach and express their theological beliefs. Qumran was surely a community of faith.

Much informative material on this topic is available from *Thanksgiving Hymns*, which was one of the original scrolls found in cave 1. Although *Thanksgiving Hymns* has been identified by some as liturgical, there is no actual evidence for its liturgical use. More plausibly, it is a series of poems forming a body of introspective devotional poetry. Therefore, it is a centrally important text for determining the theological ideas of the sectarians. Some scholars have identified the Teacher of Righteousness as the author of this scroll. Of course, there is no way to prove such an assumption. What is clear from many of the excerpts quoted here are the *Thanksgiving Hymns'* author's particularly personal religious and spiritual experience and his desire to convey his views through poetry.

Thanksgiving Hymns is also tied in to other sectarian compositions, chiefly, *Rule of the Community.* Our basic theological picture of the sect emerges primarily from these two documents. In addition, we can gain theological insights by comparing the sect's views, when applicable, with Josephus's descriptions of ancient Jewish sects.

The Nature of God

In their external appearance, the sectarian manuscripts themselves already testify to a tremendous respect for God. The sectarians generally avoided use of the tetragrammaton—the four-letter divine name YHVH—traditionally pronounced "Adonai" by Jews and translated "Lord" in most Bible translations. They often substituted other divine names for YHVH in nonbiblical manuscripts, mainly, "El," translated as "God." Some scrolls write the divine names in paleo-Hebrew script, the ancient script of the First Temple period, in order to give them greater emphasis and, perhaps, sanctity. Underlying these scribal and literary conventions is the desire to recognize the unique sanctity of God and God's name, which symbolized the essence of God in ancient Hebrew thought.

The sectarians' sense of reverence for the divine name goes hand in hand with their textual emphasis on God's majesty and glory. This point is most prominent in *Thanksgiving Hymns.* In the following excerpt (10:8–11) God is seen as all-powerful:

> Behold, You are the prince of the angels and king of the honored ones,
>
> Lord of every spirit and ruler over every creature.
>
> Without You nothing is done, and nothing can be known without Your will.
>
> There is none beside You, and no one shares power with You.
>
> Nothing compares to Your glory, and Your strength is beyond comparison.

In this poem, the author declares that none can compare to God and nothing can be known without God's will. This nexus of the will, the knowledge, and the power of God is repeated over and over in the Qumran sectarian corpus. Human beings are left virtually powerless in this system; they can do nothing except with God's knowledge and approval.

God's majesty brings with it the notion of a divine retinue—the angels. Angels appear in various forms—as rulers over the hosts of heaven and as living among the Qumran sectarians in their messianic community. The prevalence of angels is characteristic of many Second Temple period texts; the sectarians were not unique in that regard.

The Qumran group also believed that God created the world for God's own glory. The division of the human race into the righteous and the wicked—the basic dualistic principle of Qumran sectarian thought—was made for the same reason:

> ... so that You may be glorified through judgment of the wicked, and show Yourself mighty on my behalf before the children of mankind.
> (THANKSGIVING HYMNS 2:24)

God's glory is demonstrated to humankind through God's punishment of the evildoers and reward of the righteous.

God is of course the unquestioned creator of all:

> Praised are You O Lord ... all things are Your work.
> (THANKSGIVING HYMNS 16:8)

Indeed, as creator, God predestined the future of all God's creations:

> And before they were established He knew their deeds ... and He knew the years of their existence and the set times and exact epochs of all that have come into being and those which will come into being forever—what will happen in their periods—for all the years of eternity.
> (ZADOKITE FRAGMENTS 2:7–10)

Everything is foreknown by God, a doctrine that is, in fact, typical of ancient Jewish theology and found in the Bible and in later rabbinic literature. What is new at Qumran is the notion that everything has been predestined and that human beings really have no choice over the way their affairs will play out, either in individual terms or in the national and cosmic senses:

> From the God of knowledge comes all that is and will be, and before they came into being He predestined all their thoughts. And when their appointed times come according to His glorious plan, they will fulfill their function with no change. (RULE OF THE COMMUNITY 3:15–16)

All has been set forth by the divine plan; predestination is absolute. Again, this sectarian formulation goes way beyond the notion of a divine plan as articulated in other Second Temple literature.

God has also imposed order on the universe and on nature. The divine role is set forth in a beautiful poem in the *Thanksgiving Hymns* praising God as the creator:

> And You stretched forth the heavens for Your glory,
> [and] all [which is in them You pre]destined according to Your will ... ,
> The luminaries according to their mysteries,
> the stars in [their] orbits,
> [And all the storm winds] for their task,
> meteors and lightning for their service (1:9–12).

God's orderly placement of the astral bodies and their orbits was extremely important to the sectarians, for these were the basis of their distinct, sectarian calendar. The calendar is seen as just another in a series of proofs that all has been set forth by God and predestined. The divine plan set forth for the universe is known only to God, not to humankind. It is therefore often called a mystery. The orbits of the heavenly bodies are often referred to as secrets, as are the processes of history.

God is the God of history, as made clear already in the Hebrew Bible. This concept finds many expressions in the scrolls. For example, God controls the national fate of Israel and precipitated the destruction of the First Temple:

> For because of their transgression, in that they abandoned Him, He hid His face from Israel and from His Temple, and handed them over to the sword. (ZADOKITE FRAGMENTS 1:3–4)

He is also responsible for Israelite military successes and will give the sectarians victory in the great eschatological battle, a notion mentioned repeatedly in the *War Scroll* (11:1–3, 9–10).

God is the embodiment of righteousness and will judge and punish the wicked:

> For You are righteous and all Your chosen ones are truth, and all iniquity [and e]vil You will destroy forever. (THANKSGIVING HYMNS 14:15–16)

But if one repents, God receives that repentance and spares the individual from punishment:

> [I have] leaned upon Your kindnesses and Your abundant mercies, for You will grant atonement for transgression, and to pur[ify man]kind from guilt in Your righteousness. (THANKSGIVING HYMNS 4:36–37)

The problem of how to square this notion of repentance with the concept of complete predestination is one to which we will return later.

God's abiding righteousness guarantees that sectarians will be treated with mercy. This notion is stressed in the *Rule of the Community* in a poem (11:13–15) that brings that document to a close, a composition with many parallels to *Thanksgiving Hymns:*

> In His mercies He brought me near,
> and in His kindness He will bring about my vindication.
> In His truthful righteousness He has judged me,
> and in His great goodness He will grant atonement for all my transgressions.
> And in His righteousness He will purify me from all human impurity,
> and (from) the sin of mankind.
> So that I will give thanks to God for His righteousness,
> and to the exalted One (for) His glory.

God's goodness, righteousness, and forgiveness are here all associated with one another. These attributes will become manifest in the End of Days when the sectarians as individuals and as a group will be victorious with God's help. Then God's justice will be manifest to all humanity.

One of the basic difficulties with any system that posits God as absolute and good is that it must explain the existence of evil. Sectarians dealt with that problem by accepting a kind of extreme ethical dualism. Picking up on the prophet Isaiah's description of God as the one "who forms light and creates darkness, makes weal and creates woe" (Isaiah 45:7), the sect believed that God was indeed the author of both good and evil. But neither the good nor the evil attributes could derive from God directly. So the sectarians, or those from whom they drew, developed the idea of two spirits, the good and the bad, who acted as God's agents in the management of the world.

In *Rule of the Community*, a very detailed section explains that dualistic approach, outlined as follows:

> And He created mankind for dominion over the earth, and He set over him two spirits, so that he (man) could follow them until the time of His visitation. These are the spirits of truth and iniquity. From the dwelling place of light are the origins of truth, and from the source of darkness are the origins of iniquity. In the hand of the Prince of Light is the dominion of all the sons of righteousness; they walk in the ways of light. But in the hand of the Angel of Darkness is the entire dominion over the sons of iniquity; and they walk in the ways of darkness. (*RULE OF COMMUNITY 3:17–21*)

The passage goes on to explain the basic doctrines of this remarkably elaborated system: God created the two spirits at the time of creation, and the affairs of the world are dependent on them. The good spirit, loved by God, is connected with light, truth, and righteousness. The evil spirit, often known as Belial (literally, "of no worth"), is connected with darkness, sin, and evil. Belial appears as a prince of evil spirits in the *Testaments of the Twelve Patriarchs*, occasionally in later Jewish mystical literature, and in the New Testament (II Corinthians 6:15). He is hated by God, Who is nonetheless his creator.

Each of these spirits has a group of human and angelic followers, called the "lot." And one's entire pattern of behavior is determined by one's belonging to one of those two groups. The evil spirit, assisted by demonic angels, causes all transgressions. These spirits are predestined to have dominion at different times, so that the ultimate triumph of the spirit of good can be anticipated. Since God is the creator of both powers, the dualism described here is not absolute as in some Eastern religions or in Zoroastrianism. Rather, it is tempered by the power of God as the ultimate and only creator.

The ethical and religious dualism proposed in this text is very similar to the rabbinic idea of the good and evil inclinations. The primary difference is that in the rabbinic system, these inclinations are internal psychological urges that compete within one human personality. In sectarian doctrine, in contrast, they are external powers that compete for dominion over the entire cosmos. Other texts of the Dead Sea sect, however, may indicate that the concept is indeed one representing an internal, personal struggle.

The messianic war will eventually result in victory by the spirit of good. But until then, the struggle will go on uninterrupted:

> For God has placed them side by side until the final age, and He has set eternal enmity between their divisions. *(RULE OF THE COMMUNITY 4:16–17)*

The war that will finally resolve this struggle is described in the *War Scroll*. In those final battles, human and angelic armies of the Sons of Light and the Sons of Darkness will engage in a war of some forty years, from which the sect—the Sons of Light—will emerge victorious.

Part of the plan of predestination is that God determines to which group a person belongs. Speaking of the two spirits, *Rule of the Community* says:

> And He knew the performance of their deeds for all the periods of [their performance], and He has caused them to be inherited by mankind so that they would know good [from evil and] to assign lots for every living thing according to His spirit in [His division until the time of the] visitation. *(RULE OF THE COMMUNITY 4:25–26)*.

God, then, has decided, indeed predestined, the assignment of humankind into lots.

A number of scholars have suggested Zoroastrian or other Iranian influence on the dualistic doctrine of the Qumran sectarians. However, no such influence has actually been proven, especially since sources for the religions in question occur actually much later than the Qumran texts. On the other hand, there can be no question that these religious traditions grew from a common soil that might have contributed to the development of Qumran sectarian views.

IN SEARCH OF GOD

One of the themes most emphasized in the sectarian scrolls concerns humanity's lowliness and depravity. Though it is true that such a characterization of the human race is found later, in the Musar ("ethics") literature of East European Jewry, this image of human beings is otherwise exceptional in Jewish teachings, and probably exerted its influence more fertilely on early Christianity.

According to the sectarian view, the human being is a lowly creature made of clay (or dust) and molded with water. This idea is especially emphasized in *Thanksgiving Hymns* and may reflect to a great extent the personal experience of the author, who many scholars have surmised was the Teacher of Righteousness.

Just one sample from the text (*Thanksgiving Hymns* 12:24–26) will bring together those dominant motifs:

> But I have been ta[ken] from dust [and] form[ed from clay],
> into a fount of impurity and the nakedness of shame,
> a source of dust and knea[ded with water,
> a place of gui]lt and a dwelling of darkness.
> And a return to dust is (the destiny) of a creature of clay,
> at the time which is [appointed for it,
> and] its [end] is in the dust,
> to the place from which it was taken.

Over and over the author stresses his own feelings of inadequacy when standing before God. But the author goes even further: the terms translated "fount" and "nakedness" refer to female reproductive organs. The language of this and many other passages makes clear that the author of *Thanksgiving Hymns* regarded those organs as always impure, even during birth. This approach points away from the traditional Jewish view that sexuality is positive, and it instead upholds the idea, later taken up by early Christianity, that sexuality is basically an impure and undesirable feature of human existence. Such a notion can be contrasted with the generally positive view of women that we saw previously.

In a number of passages, "flesh" is associated with the humbleness of human beings, for example:

> What is flesh that it should understand [Your mysteries, and a creature] of
> dust that it should be able to guide its steps? (THANKSGIVING HYMNS 15:21)

This notion of the lowly nature of flesh, although not emphasized in premedieval Jewish literature, was certainly present in early Jewish thought. It exerted a major influence on some early Christian views of sexuality and of the physical dimension of the human being. What we need to emphasize here is that these Qumran texts do not reflect a dualistic notion pitting flesh against soul but rather condemn flesh when it is not endowed with the divine spirit that elevates it to holiness.

In the view of the author of the *Thanksgiving Hymns* (4:29–30), human beings are essentially sinful:

> And he (man) is in sin from the womb,
> and until old age he is in the guilt of faithlessness.
> And I know that man cannot attain righteousness,
> nor can a person (achieve) perfection of the way.

According to this text, human beings are endowed with an innate proclivity to sin and are unable to free themselves of transgression. But such proclivity is never blamed on original sin (Adam's and Eve's transgression in eating of the tree of knowledge in the Garden of Eden). Rather, human sinfulness derives from the influence of the two spirits, as explained previously. Only God can be wholly righteous.

Yet the situation is not hopeless, because forgiveness is available (*Rule of the Community* 3:6–9):

> For through the spirit of the counsel of the truth of God
> are the ways of man atoned. . . .
>
> And through the spirit of holiness of his community of truth
> he will be purified of all his sins.
>
> And through a spirit of uprightness and humility
> will his sin be cleansed,
>
> and through subordinating himself to all the laws of God
> will his flesh be purified.

Nonetheless, all atonement is subject to the predestinarian doctrine of the sect. It is only possible for one to repent if one is predestined to be among those who turn away from iniquity and join the community. On the other hand, if it has been predetermined that a person belongs to the lot of Belial, then one will not repent of one's transgressions. Indeed, everyone's final fate has already been predetermined:

> You alone have [cre]ated the righteous and from the womb You have predestined him for the appointed time of Your choice. . . . And You created the evildoers for [the periods of] Your [wr]ath, and from the womb You have set them aside for the day of slaughter, for they have walked in a path which is not good, and they have despised Yo[ur] covenant.
> (*Thanksgiving Hymns* 15:14–18)

The elect, those predestined to be part of the good lot, have been blessed with knowledge by God:

> And I, through my understanding, have come to know You, my God, through the spirit which You placed within me. . . . In Your holy spirit You have [o]pened to me knowledge of the mystery of Your understanding.
> (*Thanksgiving Hymns* 12:11–13)

God has vouchsafed knowledge of the divine mysteries to the elect. Through this knowledge, the members of the community—the elect or "chosen ones" of God—can discern the correct path and follow the divine will. (Some have sought to see in this emphasis on knowledge the influence of Gnosticism, the diverse religious movement that challenged orthodox Christianity in the early centuries of the common era. However, if there was any mutual influence, it was the Dead Sea sectarians or groups like them that influenced the Gnostics, because Gnosticism apparently postdates Qumran ideology.)

Once a person has been selected for the lot of the Sons of Light and has assumed the obligations of membership in the sect, then that person must meet numerous behavioral requirements, encompassing both ritual and ethical Jewish norms consonant with the teachings of the sect. The purposes of the Sons of Light are:

> To illumine the heart of mankind, and to straighten before him(self) all the ways of true righteousness, and to cause his heart to fear the regulations of the Lord, and a humble spirit and patience, and great love and eternal good, and understanding and discernment, and mighty wisdom, sustained by all the deeds of God and dependent on His great kindness and a spirit of knowledge of the plan of every creature, and zealousness for just judgments, and a thought of holiness with a stable personality, and great love of all the people of truth, and glorious purity, despising all the disgusting impurities, and walking humbly with knowledge of all, and concealing the truth of the mysteries of knowledge. *(RULE OF THE COMMUNITY 4:2–6)*.

The text then immediately attributes to the Sons of Darkness the opposite character traits and actions.

The sectarian ideal calls for development of the entire personality as well as observance of the ethical and religious requirements of the Torah. Such a personality exemplifies equanimity and stability, which the passage bespeaks. We also learn here that sectarians are required to keep the group's teachings secret from outsiders. This requirement apparently applied both to theology and to matters of Jewish law.

Whereas the sect expected to be rewarded for its piety in the End of Days, it also expected a reward in the present age for such piety and for following the way of the Sons of Light:

> And the visitation of all those who walk in it will be for health and great well-being with long life, and fertility, with all the eternal blessings, and eternal joy in eternal life, and a crown of glory with splendid raiment in eternal light. *(RULE OF THE COMMUNITY 4:6–8)*

This reward seems to include eternal life. Some have suggested that since the sectarians expected to see the coming of the End of Days in their lifetime, their theology lacks belief in resurrection of the dead. On the other hand, a few texts, most probably not written by the sectarians themselves but included in their library, do speak of resurrection, a notion found in the biblical Book of Daniel as well as in a variety of Second Temple period texts.

Josephus and Second Temple Theology

Josephus's descriptions of Jewish sects in the Second Temple period have been instrumental in the quest to identify the Dead Sea sect. In light of this, it is useful to examine Josephus's descriptions to see how the beliefs prevalent in the sectarian doctrines compare with what Josephus says about other groups of the period, especially the Essenes, whom so many scholars have identified with the sect. We will see that facile comparisons cannot be made. In fact, the subject turns out to be quite complex.

Here is Josephus's summary of the most prominent theological differences between the groups:

> Regarding the Pharisees, they say that certain events are the work of fate, but not all. Regarding other events, it depends upon us as to whether they will take place or not. But the view of the Essenes states that fate is the mistress of all things, and that nothing happens to people unless it is in accordance with her decision. But the Sadducees do away with fate, believing that there is no such thing, and that human actions are not determined in accordance with her decision, but that all things are within our own power, so that we ourselves are responsible for our well-being, while we suffer misfortune as a result of our own folly. (Antiquities 13, 171–173)

Thus, according to Josephus, the groups hold three distinctly different views about how "fate" interferes in human life: For the Pharisees, providence—what Josephus means by "fate"—controls human destiny only in partnership with our own free will. For the Sadducees, there is no providence; we are masters of our entire life. For the Essenes, however, there is complete predestination.

Later on in the Antiquities, Josephus again characterizes Jewish sects. About the Pharisees he says:

> Though they assert that everything is brought about by fate, they still do not deprive the human will of the pursuit of what is in man's power, since it was God's desire that there should be a combination and that the will of man with his virtue and vice should be permitted to enter the council chamber of fate. They believe that souls have the power to survive death and that there are rewards and punishments under the earth for those who have led lives of virtue or vice. (Antiquities 18, 13–14)

Here Josephus seems to understand the Pharisees a bit differently, implying that they basically agree that God has complete control, but they understand that control as tempered by human free will. Josephus seems intent on attributing to the Pharisees the belief that even though God has the capacity to control everything, God chooses not to exercise it. Up to this point, this statement repeats Josephus's earlier description of the Pharisaic position.

However, Josephus now adds a new piece: that the Pharisees believe in the immortality of the soul and in reward and punishment after death.

About the Sadducees mentioned in the same passage, Josephus states:

> The Sadducees believe that the soul perishes along with the body.
> (ANTIQUITIES 18, 16)

As opposed to the Pharisees, Sadducees do not believe in the immortality of the soul. Therefore they cannot have a concept of punishment after death. God's punishments must befall humankind in this world.

Regarding the theology of the Essenes Josephus says:

> The teaching of the Essenes tends to leave everything in the power of God. They regard the soul as immortal and believe that they should especially strive to draw near to righteousness. (ANTIQUITIES 18, 18)

So the Essenes take the view that all is in the hands of divine providence. This view opposes the one attributed to the Sadducees, but it shares with the Pharisees the notion that God is ultimately able to control all human affairs (while granting a role to human free will). And like the Pharisees, the Essenes believe in the immortality of the soul. Given that the text juxtaposes the Essenes' desire to strive for righteousness with the mention of the soul's immortality, it is reasonable to assume that Essenes also believed in reward and punishment after death. However, the passage does not say so explicitly.

Josephus goes into greater detail in his account in *War*. There he writes about the Essenes:

> For it is a definite belief of theirs that the body is destructible and that its constituent matter is temporal, but that the soul is immortal and imperishable. (WAR 2, 154)

Here he repeats that to the Essenes, the soul survives after death. He then goes on to present a Hellenistic description of Essene views involving the body and soul that he claims parallel the views of the "sons of Greece." He also puts forward a Hellenized version of reward and punishment after death that resembles beliefs common in Greek thought. Here in this section, Josephus is clearly trying to convince his Greek readers that at least some Jews embrace Greek religious ideas. For the purposes of this study, we can discount Josephus's exaggerated claims.

About the Pharisees he says: ·

> [They] attribute everything to fate and to God. They believe that to act properly or otherwise (is a decision which) rests, indeed, for the most part with men, but that fate plays a role in each action. Every soul, they maintain, is imperishable, but only the soul of the good passes into another body, while the souls of the wicked suffer eternal punishment. (WAR 2, 162–163)

For the most part, Josephus says nothing new here. Pharisees see human affairs as decided in partnership with divine providence. The soul after death passes to another life. The notion of the transmigration of the soul introduced here seems out of place but may again reflect Josephus's desire to make this entire description conform to Greek ideas.

Of the Sadducees he says:

> [They] do away with fate altogether and separate God not only from the commission of evil but even from the very sight of it. They maintain that man has the free choice of good and evil and that it rests with each man's will whether he will follow the one or the other. As for the survival of the soul after death, penalties in the underworld, and rewards, they will have none of them. *(WAR 2, 164–165)*

Sadducees are again described as believing in complete free will, but this time the ramifications of such a view are spelled out: God can in no way be connected to or blamed for the existence of evil. Evil can only be the fault of those who commit it. Further, because they do not believe in the immortality of the soul, Sadduccees can have no concept of reward or punishment after death.

How do these ideas compare with those that the scrolls attribute to the Qumran sect? Can these accounts in Josephus help us to identify the sect?

The sectarians, according to their own documents, believed in absolute predestination, as the Essenes did. Here or there, like the Pharisees, they seem to see a role for personal repentance in ensuring the future of an individual, although we get the distinct impression that this ability to repent is also conditioned by God's will. Scholars do not agree about whether the Qumran sect believed in the immortality of the soul as did the Pharisees and the Essenes. Some texts in the scrolls definitely imply that it did. It is likely that once the sectarians realized they themselves would not live to see the messianic era, they did adopt such beliefs.

From evidence in the scrolls it certainly seems that the sect believed in reward and punishment after death, as did the Essenes and the Pharisees. But we need to understand that although Josephus emphasizes the immortality of the soul and reward and punishment in describing the Essenes, those notions are only secondary concerns in the sectarian scrolls.

What we now understand from examining the two sets of documents is that the sectarian views were similar to but not exactly the same as those that Josephus attributed to the Essenes. Those who continue to maintain that the sect was in fact Essene explain away the discrepancies between the two groups as resulting from Josephus's biased emphasis on precisely those aspects most impressive to his Greek readers. Yet it is these very differences that argue against the facile identification of the sect with the Essenes.

An even greater challenge posed by Josephus's account of the theological differences between the Jewish sects is that the account seems to dispute the Sadducean origins of the sect, a cornerstone of this book's argument. How could the Qumran sect develop out of the Sadducees if the sectarian theology shares so much in common with Josephus's Essenes and opposes the central beliefs of the Sadducees?

This objection is in no way decisive, however. First, we have to remember that Josephus wanted to cast these sects in the framework of Hellenistic philosophies. Second, the Sadducees themselves went through complex historical development. By Josephus's time, they were highly Hellenized. Josephus's description of Sadducean theology exactly matches that of the Epicureans, who saw God as playing no role in the world. But it is impossible to accept this as the fundamental Sadducean view, because the Sadducees were devoutly committed to the biblical tradition, which certainly militates against such a view. In my opinion, the Sadducees who participated in events leading up to the schism and the creation of the sect would certainly have believed in a divine role in the world.

Both groups of Sadducees—those who left the Temple to become the sectarians, perhaps included in the term "Essenes," and those who remained in Jerusalem—underwent profound changes thereafter. One became the Dead Sea sect described in the sectarian writings. The other gradually became Hellenized and, together with the Hasmonaeans and later the Herodians, led the nation in a completely opposite direction. Only the eventual breakdown in Roman-Jewish relations and the rise of Pharisaic-rabbinic hegemony would eventually reverse that process.

The Dead Sea sect had a unique set of theological views. It believed that the world was divided into the two realms of good and evil and that God had predestined all the affairs of humankind. It saw humanity as inherently sinful and lowly, and it believed that only through God's mercy and the practices of the sect could that lowliness be in any way mitigated. For the sectarians alone was there hope of a brighter future—in the messianic era. Sectarians believed in reward and punishment in this world, even if transgression were predestined by God's placement of a person in the wrong lot. In addition, they probably also accepted the notions of immortality of the soul and reward and punishment in the next world.

Now that we have studied the structure and basic beliefs of the sect, we shall examine the biblical texts preserved in the sect's library and try to understand how these texts were interpreted. In the next chapter, we shall see that the scrolls teach us not only about the Qumran sect but also about the relation of the wider Jewish community to the Bible and the Bible's central role in Judaism.

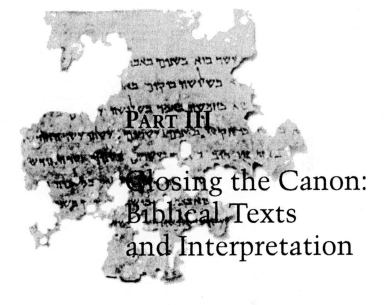

PART III

Closing the Canon: Biblical Texts and Interpretation

CHAPTER 10

Bible, Canon, and Text

To understand the development of Judaism in the Second Temple period, we need to examine the history of the biblical canon and its text. By "canon" we mean the collection of biblical writings that formed the core of Jewish literature for all Jews, regardless of their "sectarian" affiliation. Because the canon constituted the authorized record of God's revelation, direct or indirect, to humanity, the process of determining its contents represented nothing less than identifying the divine word.

Once the accepted body of divinely inspired books—the biblical canon—is defined, the authoritative, standardized text of the Bible must be established. One aspect of this task is the determination of the exact wording and linguistic character of the text, a matter not completely settled for many Jews in the Hellenistic period. Then there are questions about the copying of the Bible as well as about the script, the writing materials, scribal characteristics, methods of correcting errors, and many other such halakhic (Jewish legal) matters. All these issues are covered by the term "history of the biblical text."

Regarding both canon and text, a number of exaggerated claims have been made about the Qumran corpus, chief among them that the Qumran sect had an open canon—a view that we will see is very questionable—and that the scrolls show that the Hebrew text found in our Bibles today—the Masoretic (=received) Text—was only one of three equally prominent text types in Second Temple times. In truth, there was a specific canon of holy texts, and the Masoretic text was the dominant text type. This chapter examines the biblical material itself and challenges those claims, showing definitively how much the Qumran biblical manuscripts contribute to our understanding of the Bible's role in Second Temple Judaism.

Because the Qumran collection was copied in the Greco-Roman period, it necessarily reflects the character of the Bible and its text from that time. Hence, the scrolls can tell us nothing about the history of the Bible in the First Temple and early Second Temple (Persian) periods, except insofar as the texts copied in the later Hasmonaean and Herodian periods reflect the Bible inherited from earlier generations. Similarly, we cannot extrapolate from the Dead Sea Scrolls some imagined, original Bible—what scholars call an *Urtext*—because the scrolls date to a period much later than the composition of virtually all the biblical books. And, of course, the Dead Sea Scrolls cannot "prove" or "disprove" the truth or falsehood of traditional beliefs concerning the divine inspiration of biblical books or the historical and historiographical accounts in the Hebrew Bible.

THE BIBLICAL CANON

The term "canon" is borrowed from the debates of the fourth century regarding the actual contents of the collection called the New Testament, that authoritative body of Christian scriptures. The term is derived from a Greek word, in turn derived from Sumerian, meaning "reed" or "rod," hence a measuring stick or ruler. It later came to refer to a rule, standard, or limit. Eventually, it became the term describing the list of authoritative scriptural books. Although that designation may be handy for us, it reflects a concept of scriptural authority that differs from the one formulated in Jewish sources.

The only direct Jewish discussions of the canonicity (authoritative scriptural quality) of specific works are found in rabbinic sources. In mishnaic times the Rabbis debated about the status of a number of books. These debates were framed in the context of a strange law, indeed one not satisfactorily explained to this day. The Rabbis held that if a particular book were sanctified as part of the biblical canon, then contact with that book rendered a person's hands impure, requiring that one wash after touching the book. On the other hand, a noncanonical book, or a canonical book written in a manner violating the appropriate laws of scribal practice, did not render the hands impure. In the case of the Song of Songs, the debate over canonicity also extended to the holiness of the book's contents, demonstrating that theological sanctity, ritual impurity, and the question of canonicity went hand in hand.

Although it is widely held that soon after the destruction of the Temple the Rabbis held a canonical convention at the rabbinical academy at Yavneh (Jamnia), on the coast south of what is today Tel Aviv, the textual evidence does not support that claim. In fact, the final catalog of the biblical collection was fixed except for those few books of the Writings, the late date of which left them in question. Thus, the Rabbis debated only about a few books, namely, Song of Songs and Ecclesiastes, and perhaps Esther. Because mishnaic Judaism had already inherited a tradition, predating the Yavnean period and ordaining which books were part of the biblical canon, the Rabbis at Yavneh had only to make a few final rulings to complete the corpus. And even for this rather limited agenda there is no evidence that any such meeting ever took place at Yavneh.

Can the Qumran manuscripts inform us about the status of the biblical canon relative to the Qumran sect itself or other groups of Second Temple Jews? Indeed it can. And comparing this information with what we know from later rabbinic material will tell us a great deal about how the Bible came down to us in its present form.

To begin on the most elementary level, we will take a count of how many Qumran manuscript copies exist for each of the various biblical books. Although the vast majority of these texts consists of small fragments, we can assume that at an earlier point the entire manuscripts existed, of which only small parts have been preserved.

Following is a table of the various books and the numbers of Qumran manuscripts found, presented for convenience in the order in which the books appear in medieval and modern Jewish Bibles.

Qumran Manuscripts of Books of the Bible

CANONICAL SECTION	BOOK	NUMBER OF QUMRAN MANUSCRIPTS
Torah	Genesis	18 + 3?
	Exodus	18
	Leviticus	17
	Numbers	12
	Deuteronomy	31 + 3?
Former Prophets	Joshua	2
	Judges	3
	I–II Samuel	4
	I–II Kings	3
Latter Prophets	Isaiah	22
	Jeremiah	6
	Ezekiel	7
	Twelve (Minor) Prophets	10 + 1?
Writings	Psalms	39 + 2?
	Proverbs	2
	Job	4
	Song of Songs	4
	Ruth	4
	Lamentations	4
	Ecclesiastes	2
	Esther	0
	Daniel	8 + 1?
	Ezra-Nehemiah	1
	I–II Chronicles	1

The table shows that every book except Esther is represented at Qumran in some form. While several explanations are possible for the absence of Esther, the most likely is simply chance. A finding of zero copies is neither surprising nor statistically meaningful, for several other books of the Writings are found in only one or two copies. Alternatively, it is possible that the members of the sect did not consider that book, or the holiday of Purim, as authoritative parts of their own Jewish life and observance. Yet despite the book's absence, we have reason to believe that the sectarians knew and read the Book of Esther. Expressions from it show up here or there in compositions in the Qumran sectarian corpus. One apocryphal work in Aramaic, termed *Proto-Esther*, is clearly related to it.

We cannot assume simply because the same books considered canonical in later rabbinic tradition are present in the Qumran caves that these books were considered authoritative by members of the sect or by other Second Temple period Jews. After all, many other books besides the particularly sectarian materials were also collected at Qumran. Before we can determine the canonical authority of these Qumran texts, we will have to establish a useful definition of "canon." Then we can ask whether there was indeed a biblical canon at Qumran or if such a concept even existed. We also have to allow that the situation at Qumran may or may not have been typical of the general situation in the Land of Israel.

We have several indications that already in the Second Temple period some Jews had a sense of a tripartite division of the Holy Scriptures. Such a division, standard from the rabbinic period on, comprises the sections (1) Torah (Five Books of Moses), (2) Prophets (Nevi'im), and (3) Writings (Ketuvim). The three together, constituting what we now call the Hebrew Bible, are traditionally referred to by the acronym TANAKH.

In about 180 B.C.E., the apocryphal Book of Ben Sira speaks of "the law of the Most High," "the wisdom of all the ancients," and "prophecies." Ben Sira's grandson, who translated the book into Greek from the original Hebrew in about 132 B.C.E., mentions "the law and the prophets and the other books of our fathers" in his prologue. A similar division is probably referred to in 2 Maccabees 2:2–3 and 13 wherein there is reference to "the law," the "kings and the prophets," and "the writings of David." Luke refers to the same division when he speaks of the "the law of Moses and the prophets and the Psalms" (Luke 24:32, 44–45).

Apparently, then, in Second Temple times, many Jews accepted the idea of a fixed group of holy texts. Yet we also see from the evidence just cited that the final contents of the Writings were not yet fixed, for that collection, including those books authored latest, is referred to in various ways. This observation dovetails nicely with early rabbinic texts that discuss controversies over the canonical status of some books of the Writings.

Some evidence exists for a similar division in the Qumran corpus, although it is not as clear as we might like. A number of passages juxtapose Torah and Prophets. One passage in *Rule of the Community* refers quite clearly to these two divisions:

> This is the interpretation of the Torah [which] He (God) commanded through Moses to observe, according to everything that is revealed from time to time, and as the prophets have revealed by His holy spirit.
> (*RULE OF THE COMMUNITY 8:15–16*)

This text also tells us that the Prophets are to be considered a source for Jewish law, a matter that contrasts with rabbinic tradition.

The same notion about the authority of the Torah and Prophets is alluded to at the very beginning of *Rule of the Community*, requiring the sectarian:

> to do that which is good and upright before Him (God) as He commanded through the agency of Moses and through the agency of His servants the prophets. (*RULE OF THE COMMUNITY 1:2–3*)

Here the authority or canonicity of these books is clearly assumed, because in the view of the sect, they determine upright behavior, the fulfillment of the command of God.

This same distinction can also be found in a difficult passage in *Zadokite Fragments* 7:15–16, which similarly juxtaposes "the books of the Torah" with "the books of the Prophets." Thus, to the Qumran sectarians, the Torah and the Prophets were certainly granted canonical authority. But what about the Writings?

There has been much debate about the cave 11 *Psalms Scroll*, which contains a mixture of canonical psalms and other poetic texts. In my view, this scroll was a liturgical text, not a literary collection like the canonical Book of Psalms. Among the nonbiblical elements in the scroll is a passage describing the compositions of David:

> The Lord gave him a spirit of wisdom and enlightenment and he composed psalms . . . [there follows a description of his 4,050 compositions]. All these he spoke through prophecy which was given to him from before the Most High. (*PSALMS SCROLL 27:3–11*)

Here we see that the sectarians considered the Psalms, including many apocryphal prayers, divinely inspired like prophecy. The phrase "spirit of wisdom and enlightenment" fits the characterization of the divine inspiration of the Writings as it was later understood by the Rabbis. This passage suggests that the sect considered the Writings canonical, as the Prophets were. From this passage, however, we know nothing of any other Writings besides the Psalms.

The recently released *Halakhic Letter* provides us with significant new evidence about the development of the biblical canon, documenting notions preva-

David's Compositions from the *Psalms Scroll* From cave 11,
this is among the best-preserved scrolls discovered. Besides
biblical Psalms, it includes extrabiblical material. Pictured here is
a passage found toward the end of the scroll, describing the
hymnic compositions of David, who is said to have composed
through prophecy a total of 4,050 hymns and songs. *Courtesy of
the Israel Antiquities Authority.*

lent in the earliest years of the sect's history. Appealing to the addressee, the
sectarian authors explain:

> We have [written] to you in order that you should understand the Book of
> Moses (the Torah), [and the words of the Pro]phets, and Davi[d, and the
> chronicles of each] and every generation. *(Halakhic Letter C 9–11)*

Most likely we are dealing here with an allusion to the tripartite canon. The
authors refer explicitly to the Torah and the Prophets. The "words of David" are
probably the Psalms, and "the chronicles" probably refers to the Books of Chronicles, perhaps to Ezra and Nehemiah as well. So here again we encounter the
Writings, although we do not yet have a fixed name for them. Nor can we be
certain that this third part of the canon has been finally closed. ⊢

What we have established so far then is that the founders of the sect had a tripartite canon, even though later sectarian texts, especially *Rule of the Community* and the *Zadokite Fragments*, emphasize only the authority of the Torah and Prophets. Ben Sira, Maccabees, and the New Testament also attest to a similar three-part division of the canon. It is most likely, therefore, that such division was standard among most Jews at that time regardless of sectarian predilections.

Some scholars maintain that the Sadducees considered only the Torah canonical. However, that view reflects the opinion of a later church father. In light of the mention of the tripartite canon in the *Halakhic Letter*, it seems to me that this view was mistaken. Perhaps the error resulted from confusing the Sadducees with the Samaritans—those remnants of the North Israelite kingdom who intermarried with the nations brought into Judaea by the Assyrians and who maintained a Judaism based only on the Torah. But if the founders of the sect were in fact Sadducees in origin, they certainly accepted the Torah, the Prophets, and some Writings as part of their Bible.

The Samaritans did indeed hold only the Torah as canonical, although they have preserved a medieval Arabic account of the narratives of Joshua, which recounts the historical tradition of this period. Since the Samaritan schism occurred so early—in my view at the time of Ezra and Nehemiah in the fifth century B.C.E.—this sect did not regard the Prophets or Writings as canonical. The Samaritans separated from the Jewish people before individual books were canonized and before these two collections took final shape.

I maintain, therefore, that the Dead Sea sect and most Jews of this period accepted the concept of a canon. The prophetic division was already closed, and the notion of a collection of Writings firmly entrenched, although we are not totally certain if this section of the scriptures was yet closed.

We have some evidence that two other books—the Testament of Levi (or *Aramaic Levi Document*) and Jubilees—may also have been considered canonical by the Qumran sect. These books are explicitly quoted a few times, and passages are preceded by the same quotation formulas—usually "as He (or it) said"—used before quotations from the Hebrew Bible. Many scholars believe that the sectarians' use of these same formulas may indicate that these books were regarded as canonical.

Although rabbinic sources quote the Book of Ben Sira with the same formula used for biblical books, the Rabbis explicitly prohibit its public reading. This evidence raises serious questions about quotation formulas as reliable indicators of a book's canonical status. On the other hand, the need to prohibit public reading of the Book of Ben Sira demonstrates that the book had achieved almost canonical status among some Jews.

We can also attack the issue of canonicity from another direction. Much ancient and medieval Jewish literature was composed by the reuse of materials found in the canonical Scriptures. The most familiar example of this process can be found in the liturgical poetry of the synagogue that is made up of snatches of biblical passages often recast to express ideas found in later midrashic literature. The Qumran sect and many of the other Jewish groups of the Second Temple period composed their texts in the same way. The reuse of material this way is based upon the assumption that it is divinely inspired and that it has religious authority. Only texts accorded such canonical status served as the raw material for new sacred compositions. Determining which texts provided this raw material for derivative texts will reveal which books the authors considered authoritative.

At Qumran all the biblical books, that is, those in our canon of the Hebrew Bible, are used in this way, but such is not the case with any other books. Therefore, it is highly probable that the biblical canon at Qumran was the same as that of the later Rabbis. This means that the Pharisees must have shared this canon with the Sadducean elements who formed the sect. In other words, the only Palestinian group to dispute the canon was the Samaritans. This was not an issue between Pharisees and Sadducees; nor did the Qumran sect take a divergent position on the question.

So far we have discussed the canonicity of biblical books, but what about their content? How similar to the traditional text of the Hebrew Bible were the individual books found in the Qumran caves? We will discover that certain biblical books preserved at Qumran raise fascinating issues regarding their form in antiquity.

We have interesting evidence about several books from the Greek Bible, usually termed the "Septuagint." The translations in this text include additions to canonical books, specifically Esther, Daniel, and Jeremiah. The Greek Jeremiah contains a letter, entitled the Letter of Jeremiah, that purports to be the letter sent by Jeremiah to the exiles taken to Babylonia in 597 B.C.E. (Jeremiah 29:1). In Esther we find prayers, so conspicuously missing in the Hebrew version, supposedly recited by Mordecai and Esther. The Greek Daniel includes the prayer of Azariah and the Song of the Three Young Men, as well as the stories of Susanna and Bel and the Dragon. Do we find similar variations at Qumran?

The Book of Daniel found at Qumran has often been cited as one such canonical book with additional material. It is alleged that certain pseudo-Danielic materials formed part of a loose collection of "uncanonized" Danielic literature gathered at Qumran, some of which was ultimately excluded from the canonical book. The pseudo-Danielic texts are apocalyptic texts foretelling the final succession of world empires, leading up to the messianic era. (One of these compositions has become known as the Son of God Text.)

Some scholars have cited this evidence to bolster their claim that the canon was still open at Qumran. They have also pointed to the theory shared by most modern scholars that this book was completed in the Maccabean era. However, of all the manuscripts of the Book of Daniel at Qumran, not one of them contains any of these so-called additions. Further, the manuscripts of the pseudo-Danielic texts do not include any of the canonical text of Daniel. In fact, some of the material shows no definite link at all to Daniel or to the Book of Daniel. So this extracanonical material does not prove the existence of a still fluid or "open" book.

The other case usually cited as an example of a still undefined book is Psalms. Some scholars, pointing to the various texts in the *Psalms Scroll* not found in the canonical Book of Psalms and citing the scroll's reference to additional psalmodic compositions in the section entitled "David's Compositions," have concluded from this evidence that the canon was still open-ended at Qumran. They maintain that the sect did not sanction a closed corpus of holy books, such as our Hebrew Bible, but rather regarded the Holy Scriptures as an evolving collection open to additions as time went on. Therefore, they conclude, because the Book of Psalms was still not closed, additional materials were added to the Qumran manuscripts. That view is predicated on the assumption that the *Psalms Scroll* and other texts with such additional materials are in fact manuscripts of the biblical Psalms.

A more satisfying explanation of this variant text is to recognize the *Psalms Scroll* as a liturgical text, a sort of prayerbook. The collectors and copyists chose to include in it certain of the canonical Psalms, already accepted as part of the Writings, as well as some of the apocryphal psalms. If this were the case, then this scroll, too, is irrelevant to the question of the canonicity of Psalms in the Second Temple period.

Thus, despite certain differences in biblical books to be discussed later, nothing in the Qumran corpus suggests that the contents of canonical books had not yet been fixed. Rather, by this time, the books constituting the Bible were fixed and closed. The Torah and Prophets and most of the Writings were fully canonized. Only a few books of the Writings remained in dispute, and their status would be resolved early in the mishnaic period, soon after the destruction of the Temple in 70 C.E.

TEXT TYPES AND FAMILIES

Despite the fact that the Qumran corpus shows no signs of fluidity regarding the basic contents of biblical books, we do find some fluidity in the nature of the texts preserved there. In order to understand this phenomenon, we need some information about what scholars call the "witnesses" to the biblical text, which were known before the discovery of the Qumran materials. By "witnesses," we mean the sources providing direct or indirect evidence about the state of the text in late antiquity.

Before the discovery of the Dead Sea Scrolls, the only form of the biblical text known in the original Hebrew was the Masoretic text. "Masoretic" is an adjective derived from the Hebrew *mesorah,* "tradition," meaning a received, traditional text. The Hebrew text as we have it today includes vowel points and accents that were added in the early Middle Ages. The consonantal text, however, was fixed as authoritative in antiquity. Despite a few textual variants known in the medieval texts and even in the modern printed Hebrew Bibles, this text was essentially standardized by the second century C.E.

A somewhat different recension (textual version) is the Septuagint, the Greek translation of the Bible. Technically, the term "Septuagint" applies only to the translation of the Torah, the Five Books of Moses. In antiquity, a legend circulated that the Torah had been translated by seventy-two Jewish elders (Latin *septuaginta* means "seventy"). But in reality, the various books were translated over a long period of time that spanned the third through second centuries B.C.E. Regarding several of these books, research has shown that the Greek was translated from a Hebrew text different in general shape or in specific readings from the Masoretic Hebrew text. Although many of these differences are exegetical or may result from translation errors or from scribal errors in the original text, called the Vorlage, many are genuine textual differences.

The third major witness to the biblical text in antiquity is the Samaritan Torah. The sect of the Samaritans was a remnant of the population of Northern Israel who remained after the exile in 722 B.C.E. and intermarried with the foreigners brought into the country by the Assyrian conquerors. They accepted only the Torah as canonical.

The Samaritan Torah texts differ in two respects from the Masoretic text. One group of variants is of little importance to our discussion, for these variants were intentionally introduced into the Torah by the Samaritans to establish Mount Gerizim, located in Samaria, as the holiest place in the Land of Israel. The other stratum of variants represents an earlier stage in the history of the Samaritan text. Some are genuine variants from the Masoretic text, consisting of differences in spelling or wording that resulted from the process of transmission and copying. The other differences are what we call harmonistic variants, resulting from the tendency of scribes to level the differences between parallel or related biblical texts.

When the Qumran scrolls were first investigated, scholars proposed that the biblical materials in the Dead Sea caves exemplified these three versions of the biblical text: Masoretic, Septuagint, and Samaritan. In the case of the Septuagint, it was concluded that some Qumran manuscripts provided the Vorlage, the Hebrew text that had served as the basis for the Greek translation.

This theory further gave rise to a geographic division of the biblical materials: A so-called Palestinian text was assumed as the basis of the Samaritan version, that is, the text to which the intentional sectarian variants were added. Based on the assumption that the proto-Masoretic text came from Babylonia, the scholars referred to this text as Babylonian. And the supposed Vorlage of the Septuagint was dubbed Alexandrian, since it was considered the text current in Alexandria, Egypt, when the Septuagint was translated from Hebrew.

Although this theory tells part of the story, several problems require that it be modified. First, no evidence exists for the geographical assumptions made here. According to the accounts in the *Letter of Aristeas* (a Hellenistic Jewish text composed in Greek) and in the Talmud—which describe how the Septuagint was translated—the so-called Alexandrian text was originally brought from Palestine. And the notion that the Masoretic text has its origins in Babylonia is totally without foundation. Whatever text types we are talking about already existed in Palestine in late antiquity, which is why they turned up in the collection assembled and deposited at Qumran. In this ancient library, we have for the first time a full complement of Hebrew biblical texts revealing the state of the Hebrew Bible in Second Temple times.

In addition to the three already known text families, there exist at Qumran biblical manuscripts of a type unique to this collection. Many Qumran manuscripts are written in an orthography (spelling system) and morphology (grammatical form) characteristic of the Qumran sect. This writing method is used in virtually all the documents that can be directly attributed to the sect and that contain its teachings. Texts composed elsewhere but preserved at Qumran do not exhibit the special characteristics of the language of Qumran.

It stands to reason that the biblical texts written in the unique Qumran style were copied by the sectarians, perhaps at Qumran, although the geographic location cannot really be proven and is not of great importance. The theory of three basic text families fails to adequately explain these sectarian biblical materials and the linguistic structure they share with the other sectarian documents. Yet these sectarian biblical manuscripts constitute about one-fifth of the total biblical material.

Scrolls scholars should have realized long ago that these sectarian-type Bible texts challenged the three-text theory. The few scholars who did focus their attention on these texts, especially on the *Isaiah A Scroll*, suggested that their many variations revealed an attempt to create a vulgar text for the populace—a simpler text they could understand more easily. Whereas that explanation fell short, it at least recognized that these sectarian-type texts were important and needed to be explained. It also emphasized the independence of this group of manuscripts.

Even more damaging to the three-text theory is the finding that the manuscript types in the Dead Sea Scrolls are not evenly distributed. Of the texts available for analysis, some 60 percent are proto-Masoretic, that is, closely related to the Masoretic text; another 20 percent, reflecting the system of writing and grammar prevalent among the Qumran sectarians, were clearly copied by them.

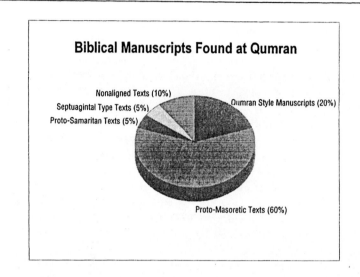

Biblical Manuscripts Found at Qumran

Nonaligned Texts (10%)
Septuagintal Type Texts (5%)
Proto-Samaritan Texts (5%)
Qumran Style Manuscripts (20%)
Proto-Masoretic Texts (60%)

Of the remaining texts, only a few may be considered proto-Samaritan or Septuagintal texts. And a few are nonaligned.

Examining the Qumran text type, we discover that it is originally based on proto-Masoretic texts. The same can be said of the proto-Samaritan text types that have as their basis the early proto-Masoretic text. What we learn from this distribution is that already when the texts found at Qumran were being copied, the proto-Masoretic text type was dominant outside the sect. The sectarians wrote texts for their own use in their particular text type. But even their manuscripts show a high degree of Masoretic dominance despite divergences from the Masoretic text in many details. When we study the few variant texts of the Septuagintal or Samaritan type, we discover that although the process of standardization and dominance of the proto-Masoretic was already quite advanced by the Hasmonaean period, the other types of Hebrew biblical texts did exist to some extent. Their disappearance among all Jews except the Samaritans would still take about a century.

The continuation of this development can be observed in the materials from Masada and the Bar Kokhba caves. The biblical manuscripts from Masada, the last fortress to fall to the Romans in the Jewish revolt (destroyed in 73 C.E.), are all proto-Masoretic in character, reflecting a higher degree of standardization in this respect than the Qumran collection does.

When we move to a slightly later period, looking at the material from the Bar Kokhba caves, deposited during the second Jewish revolt of 132–135 C.E., we find that this material has been fully standardized in the form of the Masoretic consonantal text. By that time, an effort was under way, even in Greek texts used by

Jews, to bring all texts of the Bible into harmony with the Hebrew Masoretic text. The *Greek Twelve Prophets Scroll*, dated to the latter half of the first century B.C.E., shows this tendency. There we see a Greek translation deriving from the Septuagint that has been edited to agree with the Hebrew text then used in Palestine—essentially the Masoretic consonantal text. These observations fully support the well-documented rabbinic evidence about the state of the biblical text in Second Temple and mishnaic times, and the Rabbis' efforts to stamp out all texts other than the one they regarded as most accurate and authoritative—the consonantal Masoretic text.

The view I present here is somewhat different from the dominant scholarly view. Most scholars tend to accept the three-text theory at Qumran and then cite the Masada and Bar Kokhba materials as evidence of a later process of standardization. Accordingly, they date the process of standardization in the first two centuries of the common era. The evidence of the Qumran scrolls, however, shows that this process was much further advanced in the Hasmonaean period than has previously been recognized. By the second century B.C.E., proto-Masoretic texts were dominant outside the sect—and to some extent within.

SIGNIFICANT VARIANT MANUSCRIPTS

A few manuscripts deserve our attention precisely because of their particular variations from the Masoretic text. I have singled out some of these to discuss, not because they are representative, but rather because they are exceptionally interesting.

THE ISAIAH TEXTS

The first biblical texts discovered in the Qumran caves by the Bedouin shepherd were the two *Isaiah Scrolls* of cave 1 (*Isaiah A* and *Isaiah B*). These scrolls came into the possession of the State of Israel, one in each of the two lots of texts acquired from cave 1. The *Isaiah A Scroll*, essentially complete, had been published in 1950 by the American Schools of Oriental Research. The *Isaiah B Scroll* was quickly published by the Israeli scholar Eleazar L. Sukenik. This latter scroll preserves portions of Isaiah 10–66, but it is fragmentary at many points, and whole chapters are missing.

Looking at the two texts, we immediately recognize the coexistence of differing versions. *Isaiah B* represents a proto-Masoretic text, with only minor variation from the traditional Hebrew text as we now know it. On the other hand, *Isaiah A* represents the sectarian type, for it uses Qumran linguistic forms and, therefore, was most probably copied by members of the group.

In addition to these unique forms, this text also has many linguistic "modernizations"—forms and words common when it was copied (rather than when it was composed)—as well as simplifications. Some scholars have concluded, therefore, that the *Isaiah A Scroll* was intended for study and not for worship and that it represents a sort of common text, often termed "vulgar." The Book of Isaiah was so popular that eighteen fragmentary manuscripts of this book have been identified in the collection from cave 4.

Although there are many minor textual variations in the Isaiah texts from Qumran, each of which would be instructive for our discussion, one particular example will be cited here, because it provides hints that some variants may tell us something about the literary history of the Bible.

In the Hebrew Bible that has come down to us, II Kings 20 and Isaiah 38 contain parallel accounts of Isaiah's healing of King Hezekiah. Verse 7 in the chapter in Kings appears out of sequence because it assumes that the king has been healed, whereas in verse 8, he is still hoping to be cured. The problematic verse 7 does not appear in the parallel account in Isaiah 38:1–8 but instead is postponed until the end of the chapter as verses 21–22.

In the *Isaiah A Scroll*, the problematical text of verse 7, initially omitted by the scribe, was later added at the end of the line (after verse 6), continuing into the margin. For the scribe, then, there must have been some question about the proper placement of this verse. The scribe must have been aware of an alternative placement designed to solve the problems this text raises. What we will never know is whether the original scribe had a text of Isaiah without this problematical passage or whether the scribe simply made an error, which was then corrected by another scribe. To say the least, because of examples like this, study of the Book of Isaiah will never be the same after the finding of the Qumran scrolls.

SAMUEL

One of the Samuel manuscripts from Qumran, the *Samuel B Scroll*, has been identified, along with the *Jeremiah A Scroll*, discussed later, as one of the earliest biblical manuscripts in the collection. The *Samuel A Scroll* has been dated to about the last quarter of the third century B.C.E., previous to the founding of the Qumran community. This scroll, therefore, must have been brought to Qumran. This text is basically of the proto-Masoretic type.

Varying considerably from the Masoretic text is the *Samuel C Scroll*. This manuscript preserves only parts of the first two chapters of I Samuel. The script has been dated to the first century B.C.E.

Clearly, the most interesting of these texts is *Samuel A*. In many of its variations from the Masoretic text, this manuscript seems to accord with the Septuagint and provides clues about the type of Hebrew text that would have stood behind it. However, the text shows evidence of being mixed, for it also reflects elements that are clearly proto-Masoretic. Although the manuscript clearly demonstrates that a Hebrew original of this text lies behind many of the variations found in the Septuagint, it also appears that the Book of Samuel has been interpreted to bring elements of the historical account it presents into harmony with the legal requirements of the Torah.

This scroll has become legend because of the claim that it includes material missing in the Masoretic Hebrew text that supposedly was part of the original Book of Samuel. Further, scholars have argued that this manuscript preserves the original text, whereas the Masoretic version represents a shortened text. In particular, the *Samuel A Scroll* adds a prologue at the beginning of chapter 11:

> [And Na]hash, king of the children of Ammon, sorely oppressed the children of Gad and the children of Reuben; and he gouged out a[ll] their right eyes and struck ter[ror and dread] in Israel. There was no one left among the children of Israel bey[ond the Jordan who]se right eye was no[t go]uged out by Naha[sh king] of the children of Ammon; except (for) seven thousand men (who had) [fled from] the children of Ammon and entered [J]abesh Gilead. About a month later . . .

What follows is the text of I Samuel 11:1. In verse 2, Nahash proposes the gouging out of the right eyes as a condition for entering into a treaty, since the men of Jabesh Gilead had previously escaped this fate. Such a condition would make no sense without the context provided by the addition of *Samuel A* at the start of the chapter. Since this passage is so specific to these historical events and is clearly not derivative of other biblical materials, it appears to be original. And because this addition was known to Josephus, we have to say at the minimum that it was part of the Samuel text of some Jews in Second Temple times and may actually have been part of the original book.

Although this example is quite convincing, it stands alone in the entire Qumran biblical corpus as a piece of original composition, rather than an explanatory addition. In other cases in which Qumran texts have additions, they usually cannot have been part of the original text but are rather to be explained as the result of biblical interpretation.

JEREMIAH

The Book of Jeremiah is preserved only in small fragments of six manuscripts, Jeremiah A through E, and the cave 2 *Jeremiah Scroll*. Two of these, *Jeremiah B* and *Jeremiah D*, are especially significant because they represent a Septuagint text type. These two manuscripts have been dated to the first half of the second century B.C.E. or to the Hasmonaean period. Whereas the cave 2 text of Jeremiah reflects the sectarian style of language but adheres textually largely to the Masoretic text, *B* and *D* appear to represent the kind of text that underlies the Greek translation in the Septuagint. In fact, of all the texts found at Qumran, these two Jeremiah manuscripts are the closest to the Septuagint version.

⊣ Even before the discovery of the Qumran manuscripts, it was known that the Greek text of Jeremiah differed from the Hebrew in two fundamental ways. The Greek is shorter by approximately one-sixth, and it represents a somewhat different order of chapters. The most prominent of the changes in order concerns the placement of the prophecies against the nations. In the Masoretic text, and in the other ancient biblical versions, these chapters appear at the end of the book in chapters 46–51, before the historical section, chapter 52. In the Greek Bible, they occur in the middle of Jeremiah, after Jeremiah 25:13.

Jeremiah B and *D* display both of these features—the shorter text and the different order. On the other hand, *Jeremiah A* and *C* are clearly proto-Masoretic. They follow the order and the text that we know from the Hebrew Bible. The *Jeremiah A* text has been dated to 275–175 B.C.E., and *Jeremiah C* as no earlier than the end of the first century B.C.E.

The discovery of the *Jeremiah B* and *D* texts at Qumran helps to prove a longstanding scholarly theory: Scholars had long been of the opinion that the variant Greek text had not been the result of internal Greek revision, but rather that it was based on a Hebrew text which was considerably different from the Hebrew of the Masoretic text. Here we have absolute proof that this is the case for Jeremiah. We cannot really be sure how this happened, but it is clear that in biblical times there circulated two versions of Jeremiah's prophecies. Both, in the original Hebrew, have survived in fragments from Qumran. |—

PALEO-EXODUS

Among the most interesting questions raised by the Qumran corpus is how extensively the Samaritan Torah reflects earlier textual traditions. This question has been asked especially of the Qumran manuscripts copied in the paleo-Hebrew script. This script was used in ancient Israel until the period of the return (sixth to fifth centuries B.C.E.), when there was a shift to the Aramaic script, called Assyrian by the Rabbis. The Samaritans continued to use the ancient script, either because they split from the rest of the Jewish community before the script changed or because they deliberately wanted to archaize their text to assert their claim as the true continuators of the biblical tradition.

Study of the Qumran manuscripts written in paleo-Hebrew script has shown that they have no special character. Use of the old script does not signify closeness to the proto-Samaritan Torah text. This finding is illustrated clearly in the *Paleo-Leviticus Scroll* from cave 11, which is virtually identical to the Masoretic Hebrew text, even though it is written in the old Hebrew script. In fact, texts at Qumran displaying a relationship to the Samaritan Torah come in both the old and new scripts, and some texts written in the old script are even proto-Masoretic.

Paleo-Exodus The *Paleo-Exodus M Scroll* from cave 4 is an example of the type of biblical text that underlies the Samaritan Torah. A few such texts are found at Qumran, and they are characterized by expansions based on other biblical passages. This well-preserved scroll shows the use by some scribes of paleo-Hebrew (old Hebrew) script even after the later "square" Jewish script had become the norm. *Photograph by Bruce and Kenneth Zuckerman, West Semitic Research, in collaboration with Princeton Theological Seminary. Courtesy of the Department of Antiquities of Jordan.*

However, one text, the *Paleo-Exodus Scroll,* is quite interesting because it is both a proto-Samaritan manuscript and is written in the old Hebrew script. This text is well preserved, with fragments of forty-three or forty-five consecutive columns extant, ranging from Exodus chapters 6 to 37. It was originally fifty-seven columns long. The manuscript has been dated to between 100 and 25 B.C.E.

Like the later Samaritan Torah, this scroll contains a text with numerous expansions, which are generally constructed out of other parts of the Torah and attempt to harmonize with those other verses the passage in question. For example, Exodus 32:10 contains God's request that Moses stop entreating Him so that He can destroy the people of Israel for the sin of the golden calf. At this point, the *Paleo-Exodus Scroll* adds:

> [Moreover, the Lo]rd [was angry with Aaron,] enough to have destroyed him; so Moses interceded for A[aron].

This addition is taken from Deuteronomy 9:20, the parallel description of the golden calf incident, in which Moses says, "Moreover, the Lord was angry enough with Aaron to have destroyed him; so I also interceded for Aaron at that time." Such additions are typical of this text and of others with similar harmonizing tendencies.

This scroll has three major features that characterize the Samaritan Torah: the old script, a text in the proto-Samaritan tradition, and the extensive use of vowel letters. The tenth commandment of the Samaritans, requiring the erection of an altar on Mount Gerizim, is not found. This manuscript shows that earlier Hebrew texts provided the textual base for the Samaritan modifications. Such texts existed in the Hasmonaean period and found their way into the Qumran collection.

PSALMS

Much of the debate about canon at Qumran has swirled about the question of the contents of the *Psalms Scroll* from cave 11. This scroll contains excerpted portions of the last part of the Book of Psalms interspersed with other noncanonical materials, in the following order: Psalms 101–103, 109, 105, 146, 148, 121–132, 119, 135–136, 118, 145, Apocryphal Psalm II, the Plea for Deliverance, Psalms 139, 137–138, Ben Sira 51, Apostrophe to Zion, Psalms 93, 141, 133, 144, Apocryphal Psalm III, Psalms 142–143, 149–150, Hymn to the Creator, II Samuel 23:7, David's Compositions, Psalms 140, 134, and the Apocryphal Psalms 151 A and B. Based on this text, scholars claimed that the contents of the Book of Psalms were still fluid in the Hasmonaean period.

I reproduced the extensive list above to show that this text is not merely a Psalms scroll with a few additions. Prominent here are certain liturgical features. First, the Psalms included in this scroll are for the most part ones we know were prominent in the liturgy of the Jerusalem Temple or in early Jewish synagogue ritual. Second, in the case of Psalm 145, recited regularly in the synagogue service, liturgical refrains that are not part of the biblical text have been introduced, and these accord with what rabbinic texts tell us about the use of refrains in Second Temple ritual. After each verse of the Psalm, an addition appears:

> Blessed be the Lord and blessed be His name forever. *(PSALMS SCROLL 16:7–17:17)*

Third, the order of the chapters has been rearranged, obviously to fit the liturgical needs of some community. Finally, the additions are mostly liturgical poems. For example, the Hymn for the Creator has a close relationship to later Jewish liturgical poetry of the synagogue service. For these reasons, I consider the entire scroll a liturgical composition, a view espoused by Israeli scholars since the publication of the text.

This view is supported by an excerpt that appears close to the end of the scroll, entitled by modern scholars David's Compositions. This text speaks of the liturgical role of the Psalms but includes many actual or presumed apocryphal poems:

> And David the son of Jesse . . . composed 3,600 psalms; and songs to sing before the altar over the daily burnt offering for each and every day; for all the days of the year, 364; and for the Sabbath sacrifices, 52 songs; and for the sacrifices of the new moons and for all the Festival days and the Day of Atonement, 30 songs. And all the songs which he spoke were 446, and songs for making music over the stricken, 4. And the total was 4,050. All these he spoke in prophecy which was given to him from before the Almighty.

This text certainly regards the Psalms as a liturgical genre. Its presence toward the end of the *Psalms Scroll* lends support to identification of this scroll as a sort of prayer book.

That view is supported by the existence of another Psalms scroll from cave 4, the *Psalms F Scroll*, which includes three apocryphal compositions immediately after Psalm 109. The first is the Apostrophe to Zion, which occupies a different position from that in the *Psalms Scroll*. Then follow an unidentified poem and what has been termed an Apostrophe to Judah, that is, the land of Judaea. This, like the larger cave 11 *Psalms Scroll*, is also a liturgical collection. A variety of such texts, separate from "canonical" Psalters, apparently existed at Qumran and, perhaps, in the wider context of Second Temple Jewish life as well.

That these are liturgical collections is highlighted by the presence of other manuscripts of Psalms at Qumran that are just that: biblical manuscripts. The *Psalms B Scroll* is such a text. This Hasmonaean period manuscript preserves much of Psalms 91–94, 99–100, 102–103, 112–116, and 118. Psalms 104–115 were apparently omitted from this manuscript, although they are preserved in other Qumran Psalms scrolls. This text is presented in columnar form according to the poetry of the Psalms and is very close to the Masoretic text.

The *Psalms A Scroll* is arranged without poetic lines and preserves Psalms 5–6, 36, 33, 35–6, 38, 71, 53–4, 66–67, and 69 in an order different from that of the canonical Psalter. Psalm 32 was clearly omitted. Psalms 38 and 71 appear here as one psalm. This text is simply a copy of the Psalms, which, like all ancient Bible manuscripts, represents the period in which some fluidity in text and arrangement is still found. But this type of biblical text can be clearly distinguished from a liturgical scroll. Other Qumran manuscripts represent the canonical Book of Psalms. The *Psalms C Scroll* is written in the Qumran system of writing and grammar and was, therefore, prepared for use by the community. The proto-Masoretic type texts were most probably brought from outside the community.

This survey shows that there did not exist an open canon at Qumran for the Book of Psalms. Rather, there are two types of Psalms texts in the Qumran corpus: canonical Psalms scrolls and liturgical collections. By this time, the Psalms were playing a central role in both Temple and non-Temple Jewish worship, and other poems were already beginning to become part of the liturgy of various groups as well.

What has been demonstrated by even this cursory survey of the biblical manuscripts from Qumran is at odds with the conventional wisdom that denies the existence of a biblical canon among the Qumran sectarians. It is clear from the evidence that there indeed was a canon of specifically authoritative materials that served as the basis for other compositions. The proto-Masoretic text type was dominant, even though alongside it were texts of sectarian-type as well as a few proto-Samaritan or Septuagintal-type texts. The scrolls, when taken together with the finds from Masada and the Bar Kokhba caves, reveal a process of standardization of this dominant recension, which is attested in rabbinic literature. The process was completed by the time biblical manuscripts were deposited in the Bar Kokhba caves, some sixty-five years after abandonment of the Qumran collection.

The Bible in turn gave rise to numerous apocryphal texts in late antiquity that sought to expand or interpret the canonical Scriptures. Sometimes these compositions were difficult to distinguish from earlier biblical works. At other times, the tendency of these works to rewrite biblical texts must have been obvious to ancient readers. It is to this body of literature, most of which was part of the common heritage of Second Temple Jews, that we now turn.

CHAPTER 11

Apocryphal Literature

Many compositions found at Qumran, especially those composed in Aramaic, preexisted the Qumran community. Material of a similar nature was found at Masada as well. Given that the defenders of Masada were Jews who seem to have practiced the Pharisaic approach to Jewish law, rather than the sectarian approach that was essentially Sadducean in origin, the presence of these texts at both Qumran and Masada suggests that they were widespread among various elements of the Jewish population. These documents were apparently part of the wider literature of Second Temple period Judaism.

The genre of apocryphal compositions is related directly to the canonical Bible. Much of it may be thought of as "rewritten Bible," for it represents a retelling or supplementing of the biblical text. These texts are not represented as commentaries or supplements, but rather as independent works.

Apocryphal material is important for several reasons. First, it enlightens us about the period that led up to the momentous events of the Hellenistic reform and the Maccabean Revolt. Second, these texts were apparently highly valued by the Qumran sect and influenced sectarian thinking on a variety of issues. Third, some of these materials influenced the development of Jewish mysticism, apoca-lypticism,* and messianism, and they thus help us to understand these powerful trends in their later forms. Finally, comparison of the fragmentary remains of these works with the various translations available from antiquity and the Middle Ages proves the general reliability of these translations, a finding that surprised scholars when the Qumran material was first made known.

This chapter concentrates on a few examples of this kind of writing from the Qumran corpus. Later chapters present other examples. In addition to the texts from Qumran, we know of other apocryphal books in versions transmitted in

---

* "Apocalypticism" is a term used to classify a trend of Jewish thought that produced a body of materials typified by the revelation of heavenly mysteries or secrets of the end of days, often as part of a guided tour of heaven.

translation or otherwise passed down by various Eastern churches. Such works collectively demonstrate how prevalent apocalyptic and sectarian tendencies were in Second Temple Judaism.

ENOCH

One of the earliest examples of such Bible-related literature can be found in the Enochic traditions preserved in Aramaic fragments found at Qumran, in Greek fragments discovered in Egypt, and more fully in the Ethiopic translation of the Book of I Enoch that was brought to Europe in the eighteenth century. These traditions appear at least as early as the third century B.C.E. Three basic themes run through this material: the fall of the watchers (angels) and the violent deeds of their sons, the giants; revelation of heavenly secrets to the human race by the watchers; and Enoch's ascent to heaven, where he becomes a prophet and scribe.

Apparently, much speculation surrounded the figure of Enoch, Adam's descendant who, according to Genesis 5:24, "was no more, for God took him." That enigmatic biblical statement led to the belief that Enoch was translated alive into heaven, where he saw apocalyptic visions. This speculation gave rise to the Enochic literature that developed in antiquity. We now know, from fragments discovered at Qumran, that the original language of this material was Aramaic. Virtually without exception, all Aramaic texts found at Qumran were authored before the rise of the sect. Such works came into the collection because they constituted part of the heritage of Jewish literature familiar to the sect. All of the sectarian compositions, on the other hand, were composed in Hebrew.

The Aramaic Enochic materials found at Qumran by and large parallel I Enoch. Generally, I Enoch is understood to have five parts. The first, the Book of the Watchers, portrays the End of Days and the final Judgment, and it relates the story of the fallen angels and various visions of Enoch. The second, the Parables (or Similitudes), deals with the coming Judgment, the son of man (taken by many scholars to be the agent of God's salvation in the End of Days), paradise, resurrection, and the punishment of the fallen angels. The third, the Book of Astronomical Writings, is a treatise dealing with the reckoning of time by a solar calendar of 364 days, a calendar virtually identical to that advocated by the Qumran sect. The fourth, the Book of Dream Visions, includes visions of the future (from Enoch's perspective) of the world, Israel, and the Flood, up to the coming of the messiah. The fifth part, the Epistle of Enoch, is a testament discussing the blessedness of the righteous and the punishment of sinners. This section includes the Apocalypse of Weeks; in which the history of the world is schematized in ten consecutive "weeks," extending from the time of Enoch through the Last Judgment. In ancient times, various books of Noah—small treatises filling in the details of his life or of the Flood—circulated. One such text or part of one is appended at the end of I Enoch.

After the discovery of the Qumran fragments, ideas about the history of the Book of Enoch changed radically. Now it has been accepted that the parts of this book were originally separate collections. This understanding of the book explains why only four parts of the existing Ethiopic I Enoch were found at Qumran. The section known as the Parables was not found, and it is now generally regarded as a later composition. In addition to the four other sections represented in the Aramaic fragments, there were remnants of a Book of Giants, previously known in a Manichaean version (Manichaeanism is an Eastern dualistic religion) preserved in various languages, among the Qumran Aramaic fragments.

Each of the so-called books is itself a composite work with a literary history. The Aramaic fragments show that in Hasmonaean times, Enoch as we now have it had not yet taken final shape. Further, at Qumran, we have recovered the ancient Book of Giants, of which only quotations existed in the Manichaean text. It is also important to note that the Book of Jubilees, an extremely popular book at Qumran, apparently is based somewhat upon I Enoch. We should note parenthetically that II Enoch, preserved only in Slavonic, is itself based on I Enoch and other traditions and is not otherwise relevant to the scrolls. The so-called III Enoch is an early medieval Hebrew mystical text.

A few examples will show how the Enoch material relates to the biblical tradition: I Enoch 6–11 is a reflection of two independent traditions regarding the origin of sin and God's reaction to it. The first of these recasts Genesis 6:1–9, portraying Shemihazah as the main angelic rebel. This section is preserved in Aramaic in *Enoch A* and *Enoch B:*

> And these are the [names of their leaders]: Shemihazah who [was their chief]. . . . Those and their leaders [all took for themselves] wives from whomever they chose; and [they began to have sexual relations with them, and to defile themselves with them] and to teach them sorcery. . . . And they became pregnant with them and bore [giants . . .].
> (ENOCH A 1 III 5–16 = I ENOCH 6:7–7:2)

In this account, evil stems not from humankind but from angelic rebellion and the subsequent relations of the angels with the daughters of men. This union produces the giants who bring evil into the world. As a result, God must send the angel Sariel to instruct Noah as to how to escape the coming Flood. Michael is then sent to destroy the fallen angels and the giants who are the cause of the evil on earth. Behind this narrative is the author's view of the coming destruction of evil followed by a new eschatological beginning for humanity. In effect, therefore, we have here an apocalypticized recasting of the Genesis story.

A second strand of tradition embodied in the same passage from Enoch attributes the revolt to a different chief angel, Asael:

> Asael taught [men to] make swords of iron and breastplates of brass, [and he showed] them (metals) which are mined, [and how] they should work gold to fashion it . . . and concerning silver . . . [for adornments] of [women].
> *(Enoch B 1 II 26–27 = I Enoch 8:1)*

This version is based on Genesis 4:22. Here the revolt involves revealing to human beings the arts of metallurgy and mining, thus making possible the production of instruments of war, a story reminiscent of the Prometheus myth. In both traditions, the reworking of Genesis material has as its purpose not simply the interpretation of the material in its original context but also its application to the historical context of the author in the author's time.

Somewhat similar is the adaptation of the birth of Noah story, an appendix to the Book of Enoch (I Enoch 106–107). Here the Noah narrative begins with a miraculous birth story—a sine qua non for any legitimate biblical hero—but which, in Noah's case, was not provided in the canonical Book of Genesis. Part of this section survives in a very fragmentary Qumran Aramaic manuscript:

> [And when the boy was born, his flesh was whiter than snow and] redder [than a rose, and all his hair was as white as pure wool, and thick and bright. And when he opened his eyes he illumined the] entire [house like the sun, and the whole house was very bright]. *(Enoch C 5 I 28–30 = I Enoch 106:2)*

The miraculous appearance and actions of the child cause his father, Lamech, to seek an explanation from his own father, Methusaleh, who in turn asks Enoch, who is already in heaven. The resulting oracle explains the coming of the Flood (cf. I Enoch 6–7) and the role of Noah in saving the world from destruction. Accordingly, he is told to call his son "Noah" (rest), "for he shall be your rest . . . from the corruption of the earth." Enoch also foretells the decline that would again ensue after the Flood.

Similar rewriting of the Noah story occurs in II Enoch (Slavonic Enoch) and in the *Genesis Apocryphon,* an Aramaic rewriting of Genesis that was one of the first seven scrolls discovered at Qumran. In addition, there is a text found at Qumran called the Book of Noah. In this story Noah is elevated to the status of a truly righteous man, already intended for that role from birth. He may provide a paradigm for a messianic redeemer to save the world from the present evils that beset it in the age of the author.

Also to be considered here as a possible part of the Noah literature is an Aramaic work often termed *Messianic Aramaic* or *Elect of God.* While some have taken this as a description of the miraculous birth of the messiah, it is properly to be seen as describing the birth of Noah. Indeed, according to numerous traditions from this period, Noah's special birth already foreshadowed his future role. After interpreting certain physical signs as proof of an unusual birth, the text suggests that Noah has been endowed with special wisdom:

> Counsel and prudence will be with him, [and] he will know the secrets of man. And his wisdom will reach all the peoples and he will know the secrets of all living things. [And a]ll their plans against him will come to nothing although the opposition of all living things will be great . . . , because he is the elect of God. (ELECT OF GOD I 7–10)

Despite his wisdom, Noah will face ridicule and opposition from his neighbors as he toils in building the ark. Yet his being God's chosen one, as evident already from his miraculous birth, will ensure his success.

Closely linked to the Enoch literature and to the stories we have been discussing is the Book of Giants, which deals with the giant sons of the rebellious angels Shemihazah and Barakel. The text, attempting to supply details regarding the giants mentioned in Genesis, relates an entire mythology. The giants receive a vision of the coming judgment and of the destruction of evil and ask Enoch to interpret it. In a very fragmentary passage, Enoch foretells the coming destruction and exhorts the giants to pray:

> Let it be known to you that . . . and your deeds and those of your wives [. . .] themselves [and their] children and the wives of [their children . . .] by your fornication on the earth. [. . . And the earth complains] and accuses you, and regarding the deeds of your children also . . . [of] the corruption by which you have corrupted it. (GIANTS A 8 6–11)

The text then goes on to foretell the destruction and concludes:

> And now, loosen your bonds which bind [you] and pray (lines 14–15).

Apparently, the author sees prayer as the only possible way to avert the catastrophe that has been foretold.

The exact relationship of this work to I Enoch is not yet certain. It may have originally formed part of a cycle of Enoch books, or it may be dependent on I Enoch, as is the later II Enoch. Whatever the case, the recovery of the original Aramaic of substantial parts of I Enoch and of the long lost Book of Giants greatly enriches our knowledge of the literature of the Second Temple period.

JUBILEES

A more extensive rewriting of the Book of Genesis and the beginning of Exodus (through chapter 14) is the Book of Jubilees, usually dated to the second century B.C.E. Twelve Qumran manuscripts of this text have been identified. Jubilees is quoted in the *Zadokite Fragments* (dated to c. 100–75 B.C.E.); Qumran copies are at least as old as the first century B.C.E. Jubilees probably refers to the Hellenistic reform, so if it postdates those events, it was completed by c. 168 B.C.E.

Although parallels exist between Jubilees and some Qumran material, it is certain on both historical and philological grounds that the work was not composed at Qumran. Indeed, it seems to have predated the Qumran sect somewhat. Its Hebrew is not of the dialect familiar to us from the various texts composed by the members of the sect. Nonetheless, the work had an influence on the life of the Qumran sect and may even have had canonical status for its members.

Jubilees claims to have been dictated to Moses on Sinai by an angel:

> And Moses went up to the mountain of the Lord. . . . And God revealed to him both what (was) in the beginning and what will occur (in the future). . . . And He (God) said, "Set your mind on every thing which I will tell you on the mountain, and write it in a book . . ." *(JUBILEES 1:2–5)*

This same revelation later appears in the form of heavenly tablets being copied for Moses by the angel of presence (Jubilees 1:27–29). As such, it presents itself as a sort of alternative to the canonical Torah, a supposedly more accurate picture of the true divine revelation. Obedience to this Torah will bring the End of Days. The author follows the Torah closely, sometimes repeating it word for word, sometimes omitting material and, for the most part, rewriting it extensively. He imposes on the biblical account (and from this it derives its name) a scheme of chronology based on Sabbatical and Jubilee cycles of seven and fifty years, respectively. This historical sequence culminates with the entry of the Israelites into the Land of Israel in the first year of the fiftieth Jubilee (2,451 years from creation).

A consistent theme informing the additions to the book is Jewish law. The author attempts throughout to claim that the patriarchs and other heroes of Genesis observed all the laws later to be given at Sinai, especially the ritual calendar of Festivals. The author inserts numerous points of Jewish law into the patriarchal narratives where they do not appear in the canonical Torah. For example, he says that Abraham observed the Festival of Shavuot:

> In the fifth year of the fourth week (i.e., Sabbatical cycle) of that Jubilee in the third month, in the middle of the month, Abram made a feast of the first-fruits of the harvest of grain. And he offered up a new sacrifice upon the altar . . . *(JUBILEES 15:1–2)*

From the parallel text in the Torah (Leviticus 23:15–16) it is clear that this is the Festival of Shavuot. But it is worth noting that situating this Festival in the middle of the third month (Sivan, in rabbinic parlance) is in accord with the sectarian, not Pharisaic, calendar.

The Festivals, in the view of the author of Jubilees, are to be determined based on a three-hundred-and-sixty-four-day calendar made up of solar months and solar years. The Qumran sect accordingly called this book the "Book of the Divisions of the Times According to the Jubilees and Their Weeks" (*Zadokite Fragments* 16:2–4). A number of sectarian groups in the Second Temple period advocated using such a calendar.

The author places certain of his teachings in the mouths of the patriarchs, for example, the prohibition of intermarriage:

> And if there is any man in Israel who wishes to give his daughter or his sister to any man who is from the seed of the gentiles, let him surely die. . . . And also the woman will be burned with fire because she has defiled the name of her father's house . . . (*JUBILEES 30:7*)

The author's strong stand against intermarriage should be seen in the context of the extreme Hellenization going on in those contemporary times. Nonetheless, the author is echoing the traditional Jewish prohibition of mixed marriage, to which he has added extremely harsh penalties, as is his tendency throughout.

The author makes additions also for didactic purposes, similar to what the Rabbis called Aggadah, explaining that the Flood resulted because the angels intermingled with the daughters of men, giving rise to the demonic world. The author also adds apocalyptic messianic additions. In addition, the author stresses the revelation at Sinai, repentance, and the belief that soon the wicked will be destroyed. The text also attributes various ethical teachings to the patriarchs. Abraham is seen as a paragon of virtue, wisdom, and insight. To a great extent the author homogenizes the features attributed to a patriarch at one point in the biblical narrative and applies them to his behavior elsewhere. This form of analogical exegesis is common throughout. Indeed, the source for many of the additions to the Bible is the biblical material itself.

The vast majority of modifications of the canonical book are for halakhic purposes. Many of the laws in this text parallel other sectarian laws of the Dead Sea sect or of the *Temple Scroll,* but there are also many divergences. It is not possible to identify the author's legal tradition with that of the Sadducees, although there are certain points of contact. Some of the laws seem to be directed polemically against the practices of the author's own age.

Jubilees was composed in Hebrew, and substantial portions of the original Hebrew have been preserved at Qumran. Before the discovery of the Qumran fragments, it was known in an Ethiopic translation brought to Europe in the eighteenth century, in Greek quotations, and in parts of a Latin translation. Fragments have also been recovered from Masada, confirming the popularity of this text.

From Hebrew, Jubilees was translated into Greek, but the Greek survives only in fragments of quotations and summaries. The Ethiopic text, however, itself translated from the Greek, survives in its entirety. A Latin translation, also from the Greek, is often helpful in interpreting difficult passages in the Ethiopic version. Study of the Qumran fragments has generally confirmed the accuracy of the Greek translation and, in turn, of the Ethiopic text derived from it.

It is likely that the author of Jubilees was a Palestinian Jew from a priestly family. That author's pietistic views have led some to suggest that he was part of the Essene or Hasidic group. While this seems oversimplified, it is clear from the high status accorded this work by the Qumran sect that it can be traced to circles the sect regarded as its spiritual forerunners. Nonetheless, we must note that in certain respects, the theology of Jubilees, like its halakhah, differs from what we encounter in the Qumran sectarian writings.

Similar to the Book of Jubilees are three manuscripts from Qumran that are called *Pseudo-Jubilees A–C.* These texts closely follow the approach of Jubilees and are closely related to it. *Pseudo-Jubilees A,* for example, retells the story of the binding of Isaac. Here, as in Jubilees (17:16), the angel Mastema, prince of evil, who is similar to Belial known from many Qumran texts, challenges God to test Abraham by asking him to sacrifice Isaac, his only son:

> Then the prince Ma[s]tema came [to G]od and accused Abraham regarding Isaac, and so [G]od said [to Abra]ham, "Take your son, Isaac, your onl[y son]" *(Genesis 22:2). (Pseudo-Jubilees A 2 1 9–11)*

As in Jubilees, the angel Mastema is put to shame when Abraham stands up to the challenge to his faith.

Whatever the exact relationship of this and other texts like it to Jubilees, they all show that there was in antiquity a lively tradition of such retellings, replete with the kinds of details mentioned here. This material is definitely a forerunner of the later rabbinic Aggadah, which also expanded on the biblical text in order to draw out ethical, moral, and religious lessons.

GENESIS APOCRYPHON

One of the works found in cave 1 among the original scrolls was the previously unknown *Genesis Apocryphon.* Fragments were later found in cave 4 as well. This scroll retells the patriarchal narratives, at least as far as the text has been preserved, covering the period from Lamech to Abraham. It is one of the four relatively complete scrolls purchased by Yadin from the Syrian Metropolitan Athanasius Samuel. It is only partially preserved and published, and the unpublished sections have deteriorated, so that for the most part, little can be read. Recently devised scientific techniques of spectral imaging have helped scholars read a previously illegible word, so it is possible that this approach will yield further material from this text.

Genesis Apocryphon Found among the first seven scrolls in 1947, *Genesis Apocryphon*, from cave 1, is written in Aramaic and was composed before the Qumran sect came into being. The text consists of a retelling and an expansion of stories in the Bible and is in a style similar to that of the Book of Jubilees. Much of the text cannot be read because of the deteriorated state of the scroll. *Courtesy of the Shrine of the Book of the Israel Museum.*

The text is written in Aramaic and is largely in the first-person singular. There are no parallels in this text to either the beliefs or the teachings of the Qumran sect, nor is there any reason to associate its composition with that group. Neither are there any apocalyptic teachings, at least in the preserved portions of this scroll. We should remember that it is almost an ironclad rule that texts found at Qumran that were composed in Aramaic are part of the heritage of Second Temple literature brought to Qumran.

The author presents a running narrative parallel to that of the Book of Genesis. Sometimes this work repeats the Bible, and sometimes it paraphrases it. Often it has substantial additions, some of which are parallel to material in other compositions such as the Book of Jubilees, which may have been one of its contemporaneous sources. *Genesis Apocryphon* also contains parallels to later texts such as the Targumim (the Jewish Aramaic translations of the Bible) and Midrashim.

Like I Enoch, this book contains a story of the miraculous birth of Noah except that the protagonist is Lamech, not Enoch (columns 2–5). Columns 6–17 recount the Flood story and its aftermath and display a number of parallels to Jubilees. We also find Noah observing the laws of the Torah. Here Noah is the narrator:

> I and all my sons began to cultivate the earth and I planted a vineyard . . .
> on Mt. Lubar. And in the fourth year it produced wine for me. . . . And I
> began to drink (from) it on the first day of the fifth year.
> (GENESIS APOCRYPHON 12:13–15)

A very similar tradition is found in Jubilees (7:2). In this passage, Noah is observing the legislation of the Torah regarding the fruit of new trees or vines (Leviticus 19:23–25). Accordingly, he does not drink of the produce of the fourth year until the beginning of the fifth year. While this interpretation is at variance with later rabbinic tradition, requiring that fourth-year produce be offered as a sacrifice, it is clear that this text is reflecting an alternative approach to fulfilling that law. The complete text, in its original form, must have included many more such halakhic details.

From column 18 the scroll tells the story of Abraham. Also here, there are parallels with Jubilees. Abraham dreams of people trying to cut down a cedar and a date palm—symbolizing himself and his wife, Sarah. The danger he senses in his dream serves in the story to justify the lie he tells, claiming that Sarah is his sister. The poetic description of Sarah's beauty is influenced here by Song of Songs, using the analogic method of exegesis to fill out the details of the biblical narrative. (Both of these passages are discussed in greater detail in other chapters.) Abraham is portrayed as a seer, interpreter of dreams, and healer. The portrayal of the character of Abraham has clearly been influenced by the biblical stories of Joseph and Daniel.

TOBIT

The Book of Tobit, known previously only in Greek and various secondary translations, has been discovered at Qumran in four fragmentary manuscripts of what was apparently the Aramaic original, and in one Hebrew adaptation. Because the book is part of the Apocrypha, it has been preserved in the Septuagint Greek Bibles. Tobit most probably dates to the third century B.C.E., because the author seems to have written before the Maccabean Revolt and the building of the Herodian Temple. Some claim that this book was composed in the Diaspora.

Tobit is a fanciful tale set in the Assyrian period, although it can be argued that its real message and date of composition should be placed in the Hellenistic period. Like other such Aramaic apocryphal literature found in the Qumran collection, it was part of the literature of Second Temple period Judaism eventually collected at Qumran.

The main character is Tobit, son of Tobiel of the tribe of Naphtali, who had been taken captive to Nineveh in Assyria, where he lived with his wife, Anna, and son, Tobias, according to the laws of the Torah. The names, all based on the Hebrew word *tov*, "good," are designed to convey the goodness of the family. Tobit was a charitable man devoted to burying Jews who had been left unburied. While sleeping in the courtyard after performing one such burial, he was blinded by the droppings of a bird.

Off in distant Ecbatana in Media lived a Jewish woman named Sarah who had had seven husbands killed by the demon Asmodeus on their wedding night. Because Tobit had deposited some money in Ecbatana, he sent Tobias to recover the money. Guided by Raphael, the angel of healing, Tobias arrived at Ecbatana, where he wed the seven-times widowed Sarah. With instructions from Raphael and by means of some magical paraphernalia, he warded off the demon on his wedding night. Tobias and his wife returned to his parents' home, where Tobias cured his father's blindness, again with Raphael's help. Both Tobit and Tobias lived to ripe old ages.

The message of this book is that adherence to the law will be rewarded, even if at times it appears otherwise. At the height of his tribulations, Tobit prays:

> Righteous are You O Lord. All Your deeds and all Your ways are mercy and truth, and You render true and righteous judgment forever. Remember me and look favorably upon me. Do not punish me for my sins and for my unwitting offenses and for those which my fathers committed before You. (TOBIT 3:2–3)

The piety of Tobit and his family, even in the Diaspora, is rewarded: they triumph over adversity, are cured, and are able to cure others. Further, the book deals with the suffering of the righteous as well as with God's orchestration of human affairs and those of the people of Israel, who are ultimately to be restored to a rebuilt Jerusalem.

TESTAMENTS

Common in Second Temple literature is a genre usually termed testaments. These are essentially the last words of famous personages, in the form of discourses delivered before death. The classic examples begin with a frame narrative declaring that what follows is the testament of the relevant character. Often, these texts, like the last words of Joseph or Moses in the Torah, include revelations of the future of the Jewish people or calls for repentance. The main collection of such texts consists of the Testaments of the Twelve Patriarchs, of which only those of Levi and Naphtali appear at Qumran.

TESTAMENTS OF LEVI AND NAPHTALI

The Testaments of Levi and Naphtali are traditionally placed in the context of the Testaments of the Twelve Patriarchs, a collection of twelve such texts preserved in Greek. The Greek text is surely not the original version, for throughout there are Christian additions. That at least some of the twelve testaments were originally Jewish, not Christian, has been proven conclusively by the finding at Qumran of an Aramaic version of the Testament of Levi and a Hebrew text of the Testament of Naphtali. Some of the messianic material in these texts, previously believed to be Christian, is now understood to be Jewish, reflecting various messianic doctrines evident in the Qumran texts, sectarian and otherwise. Further, it seems that for the entire collection of testaments, the Christian interpolations are actually secondary additions to a Jewish core. The testaments are most likely dated to the Hasmonaean period, although some books are earlier, perhaps emanating from circles that preceded the Qumran sect. Noteworthy is the presence in the Greek Testaments of the Twelve Patriarchs of the idea of two messiahs—one descended from Aaron and one from Israel—a notion prominent among the Qumran sectarians.

Qumran fragments of the Aramaic Testament of Levi have been found in caves 1 and 4. These Qumran texts are sufficiently different from the previously known Testament of Levi to have earned them the name *Aramaic Levi Document*. These texts are in turn related to versions of the text that evidently circulated among some Jews in the Middle Ages and that were also found in several manuscripts in the Cairo *genizah*.

Among the most outstanding passages, preserved both in the Qumran fragments and in a *genizah* copy, is this description of a sage:

> He who teaches wisdom, all his days shall be lo[ng] and great shall be [his re]putation. In every place or city into which he enters, he has a friend [and he will not be like] a stranger there, nor will he be an unfamiliar person there, nor will he be like a [foreigner]. [F]or all of them will give him honor [s]ince all are desirous of learning from his wisdom. His friends are many, and magnates seek his peace. And they seat him on a seat of honor, in order to hear his words of wisdom. Wisdom is a great treasure of honor for those who know it, and there is treasure in it for all those who acquire it.
>
> (*ARAMAIC LEVI DOCUMENT A 4 I 13–20 = MS CAMBRIDGE*)

Here we see presented the same idea of the respect that is due sages and their wisdom as found in other Second Temple sources. Similar ideas are found in the Book of Ben Sira as well.

Parts of the Hebrew Testament of Naphtali from cave 4 preserve a parallel to the Greek Testament of Naphtali 1:6–12. A medieval Hebrew text of Testament of Naphtali circulated as well in two versions. However, it does not seem to be the same text as that found at Qumran. Yet it shows that the tradition embodied in this text did continue to circulate among Jews. It is no small coincidence that the two testaments found at Qumran are the very same ones that circulated in medieval Jewish versions. At least these two must have emerged from a Semitic milieu and survived independently, in the original languages of composition, beyond the incorporation of their Greek versions into the collection known as Testaments of the Twelve Patriarchs.

The Qumran version of the Testament of Naphtali included a section that evoked ideas typical of the sect and its literature:

> For the period of evil is ending and all evil will dis[appea]r. The period of [righ]teousness is coming and the earth is full of knowledge and the praise of God is in it . . . in order that [every person] shall understand the ways of God and His mighty deeds . . . and every person shall bow down to Him. . . . For he [predestined] their actions before He created them and the work of righteousness. . . . For the reign of righteousness (and) goodness is coming.
>
> (*TESTAMENT OF NAPHTALI 1 IV 3–9*)

Except for the notion of predestination, this text expresses messianic ideas typical of Second Temple Jews, indeed of Judaism throughout the ages. Yet with the addition of predestination, it betrays the thinking of Qumran sectarian circles that must have produced this Naphtali document. It is possible that the text mentions the "throne of the [messiah]" in a subsequent passage; not at all surprising in such a text.

Both the Levi and Naphtali documents, as well as other testaments, refer to a Book of Enoch, but these passages cannot be identified with our extant books of Enoch. There is also some connection with Jubilees. The *Zadokite Fragments* (4:14–18) may also include a quotation from the Testament of Levi.

TESTAMENT OF KOHATH

An Aramaic text found in cave 4 can probably be identified as a Testament of Kohath, son of Levi and father of Amram. The manuscript is part of a group that was subjected to carbon-14 dating. While virtually all the other materials tested corroborated the paleographic dating (based on the history of the script), the Testament of Kohath turned out to be earlier than had been predicted. Although scholars had previously dated its copying to some time in the late second century B.C.E., tests showed that the skin that served as the writing material dated back to the fourth or third century B.C.E. If this finding is correct, the text is the product of the early Hellenistic period. The text appears to be dependent on the Testament of Levi, although its scientific dating may lead to reevaluation of that conclusion.

Kohath appears here as a narrator, presenting his testament. He first tells his children to maintain the tradition they have inherited from their forefathers:

> And now my sons, be careful with the inheritance which has been given to you, which your forefathers have given you. And do not give over your inheritance to foreigners, nor your heritage to destructive men, lest you be regarded as lowly and disgraced in their eyes. *(Testament of Kohath 1 I 4–6)*

If they act this way, Kohath tells his children, they will cause Abraham, Isaac, and Jacob to rejoice (presumably in the next world), and they will prevent their patrimony—the office of the priesthood—from falling into the hands of strangers. The book then tells of the impending judgment of the wicked and their utter destruction, a motif common in much of this literature.

At the end of this well-preserved fragment, Kohath entrusts Amram, his son, with all the books he received from Levi, who in turn had received them from his forefathers. A similar notion—Levi's inheriting the books of Jacob—appears in Jubilees 45:16. If, as has been suggested, this Qumran Testament of Kohath was the source of the Jubilees notion, then the Testament of Kohath would predate Jubilees. However, that argument is insufficient to prove such a dating, for it is equally possible that this idea was part of the aggadic lore of the day. Nonetheless, because Aramaic compositions found at Qumran generally date back to the third century B.C.E., this theory may very well be correct.

The Testament of Kohath, like parts of the Testament of Levi, seeks to establish the legitimacy and authority of the Levitical priesthood. The text shares the dualism of light and darkness with the Testament of Levi, the *Visions of Amram* (a text describing Amram's advice to his sons on his deathbed), and the Qumran sectarian works. Whatever the date of this work, it was intended to advance the claims of the Levitical priesthood against others whom those in the priesthood considered usurpers.

Fragments of a number of other testaments also have been identified in the Qumran corpus, although these identifications are extremely tentative. It has been proposed that there are both Aramaic and Hebrew fragments of a Testament of Judah and Aramaic fragments of a Testament of Joseph. These texts show only partial parallels with the Greek Testaments of the Twelve Patriarchs. The dating and history of this Greek work will certainly undergo radical reevaluation after full publication and analysis of all of the Qumran documents.

This chapter has limited itself to materials that form part of the literature already in existence before the advent of the Qumran sect, collected by the sectarians and placed in their library. These texts were also read throughout Palestine, and they influenced other Jewish movements as well, some texts even surviving into the Middle Ages whether in the original or in translation. Eventually these texts influenced the aggadic tradition of the Rabbis. Many ideas and motifs contained in them were later enshrined in the various midrashic compositions. The Qumran corpus has provided us with original texts for much of this literature as well as new compositions in the genre. Thanks to Qumran research, we have more accurate views of the religious literature read by Jews in the Second Temple period and of how these texts influenced the subsequent history of Judaism.

At the same time as the apocryphal texts were elaborating upon biblical traditions, another genre of literature represented in the Qumran library was continuing and expanding upon the wisdom heritage of the Hebrew Bible. We turn now to the study of the wisdom literature found in the Qumran collection, itself another bridge between the Bible and the Dead Sea sect.

CHAPTER 12

Wisdom and the
Mysteries of Creation

Among the vital contributions that ancient Near Eastern culture made to the history of Judaism was the tradition of wisdom thought and literature. Virtually every ancient Near Eastern civilization participated in a common tradition based in what modern scholars call wisdom schools, many apparently for the training of scribes. The schools emphasized practical wisdom, often unrelated or only minimally related to the specific religious traditions of the local region and culture.

In Israel, that tradition entered the Bible through such books as Proverbs and Ecclesiastes and through certain Psalms. Some scholars also include Job in this category. Even though the interconfessional, cross-cultural nature of much of this material remains in the Hebrew version, the wisdom expresses a distinctly Jewish tone. It is clear that the biblical tradition oriented Israelite wisdom toward a distinctly Jewish religious consciousness.

That development continued into Second Temple times. We have already seen how the *Aramaic Levi Document* praised the sage, a figure of increasing importance in Israel. The wisdom sage may in fact have marked a phase in the development of the Pharisaic-rabbinic sage—the religious leader par excellence of the Jewish people—a role not fully realized until after the Destruction of the Temple. Second Temple wisdom texts show the strong influence of the biblical wisdom texts that some of them seek to imitate.

Further, the living wisdom tradition continued to progress in the Second Temple period. For example, the Book of Ben Sira emerges in the second century B.C.E. out of an actual wisdom school. At the same time, the Dead Sea Scrolls have opened up to us, particularly in the newly released documents, an entire corpus of wisdom literature, known as *Sapiential Works*, never known before. Taken together with the *Mysteries* texts from the Qumran corpus, these fascinating new texts illuminate the ways this literature developed in ancient times. Research on the newly released scrolls will eventually recast our understanding of this literary genre totally, as we uncover the influence of the Second Temple period wisdom tradition on both the New Testament and the rabbinic corpus.

The Book of Ben Sira

Chief among the Second Temple period wisdom texts before the discovery of the Qumran scrolls was the Book of Ben Sira. This work was preserved in Greek as part of the Apocrypha of the Septuagint—the Greek Bible. Ben Sira is also known as Ecclesiasticus, not to be confused with the biblical Book of Ecclesiastes, Kohelet in Hebrew. When the manuscripts from the Cairo *genizah* began to reach Europe in the late nineteenth and early twentieth centuries, manuscripts of a Hebrew version of Ben Sira were found among the fragments. These texts sparked a vigorous debate. While many scholars maintained that they were indeed manuscripts representing the original Hebrew text of Ben Sira, others considered them no more than a medieval Hebrew translation from the Greek or from a Latin translation based on the Greek.

This debate was conclusively settled with the discovery of fragments of Ben Sira in cave 2 at Qumran, a portion of the book cited in the *Psalms Scroll*, and an independent manuscript of Ben Sira, preserving substantial portions of the last part of the book (chapters 38–44), at Masada. These manuscripts showed beyond a doubt that the medieval texts were for the most part descended from the original Hebrew, even though they showed signs of some revision and textual variation. Now, after combining the ancient and medieval fragments of this book, we can be fairly certain that the vast majority of it is now in our hands in a Hebrew text.

Early rabbinic tradition prohibited the reading of the Book of Ben Sira, presumably as part of a public ritual. Indeed, rabbinic teaching forbade the reading of any noncanonical apocryphal books. This ban derived from the Rabbis' effort to assert the exclusive sanctity and canonicity of the biblical books. Yet since rabbinic literature quotes some verses from Ben Sira in Hebrew or Aramaic, this book obviously influenced the rabbis and was at least partially known to them.

Fascination with this book in the Middle Ages led to the composition of various pseudepigraphical Ben Sira texts, such as the Alphabet of Ben Sira, all of which are essentially aggadic works. These texts have no real connection with the original book but were composed by authors who knew of the sage and his reputation and sought to fill the void caused by the virtual loss of the book to the Jewish community.

The prologue to the Greek translation of the book explicitly states that the author, named Joshua (or according to some manuscripts Simeon) ben Sira, composed the book in Hebrew in the Land of Israel in about 180 B.C.E. and that his grandson subsequently translated it into Greek in about 130 B.C.E. These dates have been universally accepted as accurate by scholars. From the book, we can gather that the author functioned as a wisdom teacher in pre-Maccabean Jerusalem and ran a school to which young students came. Much of the text was no doubt composed for or based upon the lessons he gave those students.

Ben Sira is essentially a wisdom anthology, much of it composed in the style of the biblical Book of Proverbs. It provides practical advice on interpersonal relations, especially concerning the family, the raising of children, the conduct of business, and a variety of ethical teachings. A typical passage is Ben Sira 42:1–5, from the *Ben Sira Scroll* from Masada:

> [B]ut regarding these do not be ashamed,
> and do not respect persons so that you end up sinning:
> Regarding the Torah of the Exalted and the law,
> and regarding judgment to convict the evildoer.
> Regarding reckoning with a partner or a fellow traveler,
> and regarding dividing an inheritance or property.
> Regarding the dust on the scales or balance,
> and regarding the shaving of measures and weights.
> Regarding a purchase whether large or small,
> [and regarding] the price of a purchase from a merchant.

Here the text suggests that an individual must stand up for principles, ensuring that God's law be observed, and that honesty and integrity reign. At the same time, the text clearly instructs readers not to allow themselves to be mistreated in commercial situations.

Much has been written about Ben Sira's attitude toward women. In my view, the book reflects the cautions and experiences of a man of ancient Palestine and should not be judged too harshly. Regarding the experience of raising a daughter, another passage preserved in the *Ben Sira Scroll* from Masada cautions (Ben Sira 42:9–11):

> [A daughter] to a father is a decep[tive] treasure,
> [and worry over her will pre]vent sleep.
> In her youth lest she be despised,
> and when she get older lest she be [forgot]ten.
> In her virginity lest she be defiled,
> and when she is a wife [lest] she be accused of adultery.
> In her father's house lest she become pregnant,
> and when [she] is married, [lest she remain ba]r[ren.
> [My son,] watch carefully over a daughter,
> [le]st she [make for you a bad reputation].

Ben Sira Text from the *Psalms Scroll* Among the nonbiblical passages found in the *Psalms Scroll*, from cave 11 at Qumran, was Ben Sira 51:13–30. Ben Sira circulated widely in Second Temple times, which helps to explain its quotation in rabbinic literature. The Hebrew version preserved here parallels the very similar medieval text of this passage discovered in the Cairo *genizah*. In the original Hebrew, it is possible to detect the erotic imagery behind this passage, which is obscured by the Greek translation in the Septuagint. *Courtesy of the Israel Antiquities Authority.*

This advice also reveals much about the contemporary situation of urban Jews, whose traditional Jewish values were seriously threatened as the process of Hellenism took its toll.

The wisdom that the book proffers is said to come from God, who created everything and rules over the cosmos (Ben Sira 39:16):

> All things are the works of the Lord for they are very good,
> and whatever He commands will be done in His time.

To Ben Sira, God is omnipotent and all His actions are for the good. Elsewhere in the book, we are told that God rewards the righteous and punishes the guilty.

As is the case with much of the wisdom tradition in Judaism, wisdom is here identified with the Torah. In this passage (Ben Sira 24:8–12), the speaker is wisdom personified:

> Then the Creator of all things gave me a commandment,
> and the One who created me assigned a place for my tent.
> And He said, "Make your dwelling in Jacob,
> and in Israel receive your inheritance."
> From eternity in the beginning He created me,
> and for eternity I shall not cease to exist. . . .
> So I took root in an honored people,
> in the portion of the Lord Who is their inheritance.

Here we learn that wisdom, the Torah, created by God before the world itself, is eternal. Indeed, Ben Sira is the first author to identify wisdom with the Torah, a notion that later became standard and permeates rabbinic literature. This concept identifies the Torah, God's revelation, as the expression of divine wisdom, predating even creation.

The author argues strongly for the need to observe God's commandments and to resist the rising trend of foreign influence, which he strongly opposes. Hellenism by this time was increasingly affecting the Jews of Palestine. Ben Sira favors observance of the sacrificial obligations but opposes meaningless sacrifice unaccompanied by true ethical and moral behavior. In the liturgical poem found toward the end of the book, he champions the priestly House of Zadok and its exclusive rights to the high priesthood.

The author praises all of Israel's biblical heroes, concluding with the high priest Simeon II, who served in his own day. He describes Simeon in language that conjures up the mishnaic description of the high priest on the Day of Atonement (Yoma 7:4) and a fourth- or fifth-century Jewish ritual poem incorporated in the High Holiday liturgy. This section reveals how the author conceived of the biblical canon, for it alludes to all the books of the Hebrew Scriptures except Daniel and Esther. Perhaps the canonical status of these books was still under debate in his time. Probably only part of the Book of Daniel was then in circulation.

Considering that these various manuscripts and versions of the text were found among the Qumran collection, it is somewhat surprising that Ben Sira had little influence on the Qumran sectarian texts or, for that matter, on the sectarian ideology. We might have expected to see it quoted and alluded to—but it is not even mentioned.

The Ben Sira Scroll from Masada The apocryphal book of Ben Sira, composed ca. 180 B.C.E., was known only from its Greek translation until medieval manuscripts were identified in the Cairo *genizah*. At Masada, this ancient manuscript was found containing chapters 39–44 in the original Hebrew. Shown here is Ben Sira 42:15–43:8, with parts of the preceding and following columns as well. On the left, the stitching between sheets is visible. *Courtesy of the Shrine of the Book of the Israel Museum.*

THE SAPIENTIAL TEXTS

We next look at a set of wisdom texts that had a somewhat different history. Known only through the Qumran collection, these texts seem to have been more closely related to the sectarian texts and to have had an influence upon their vocabulary and ideas.

In the cache of texts that became available only a few years ago after full release of the scrolls, perhaps the biggest surprise was a collection of texts, termed in the catalogs *Sapiential Works*, constituting previously unknown wisdom literature. Although the study of these texts is still in its infancy, with only preliminary publications available, they already have opened up a new window on the development of wisdom literature and thought. And even though we must be somewhat tentative in what we can say about them at this point, they are too important to ignore while we await the results of further study.

Fourteen manuscripts have at one time or another been given the title *Sapiential Work*. By the time these texts are formally published, some of them will no doubt be renamed, but for the moment we shall use the names given them by the original editorial team. These works cover a wide variety of topics, only a few of which we will touch on here.

Because the texts are often quite fragmentary, they are difficult to follow. Like the *Mysteries* material, to be taken up also in this chapter, these texts call upon their reader to "investigate" things:

> . . . and I will teach you wisdom. And investigate the ways of mankind and the actions of peop[le. . . . For when] God [created] man, He gave him a great inheritance of His true knowledge. And to the extent that he despises it, all evil [. . . in the h]earing of his ears or the sight of his eyes, it will not be. And now . . . and investigate the years of ge[neration] after generation, as God revealed . . . *(SAPIENTIAL WORK [413], 1 1–4)*

This text cites the need to investigate the past in order to understand human actions and their consequences. The ability to understand such things is part of God's gift of knowledge to us, a concept we likewise found in the *Thanksgiving Hymns*, which indeed have many points in common with this wisdom literature. Those who detest evil, the text declares, will avoid it as much as possible. To bolster one's efforts to do so, one must develop a strong antipathy to evil deeds by acquiring wisdom.

The secrets of which the texts speak are engraved in heaven and may be seen as the representation of the divine will:

> And then you will know the [eternal] glory [wi]th His wondrous secrets and His mighty deeds. And you will understand the beginning of your actions in the remembrance of the ti[me, for] in it the law is engraved and the entire

command is incised. For it is engraved (and) incised for God . . . and the book
of remembrance is written before Him, for those who observe His command.
(SAPIENTIAL WORK I⁻ 2 I 13–16)

This wisdom, then, is built into the order of creation and engraved on heavenly
tablets. The "book of remembrance" alludes to Malachi 3:16, which speaks of
"a book of remembrance for those who fear the Lord and esteem His name."
According to our text, one can understand one's early actions when they are filtered through a later perspective, "the remembrance of time."

The author tells us that God is master of the world, controlling nature and
judging humankind:

[. . . and He will judge] all of them in truth and punish fathers and sons of the
[nation]s with all their countrymen . . . visiting the seasons of the summer
and harvesting their cro[ps at the correct time . . . (SAPIENTIAL WORK V 5 5–6)

The seasons and the times of harvest are in God's hands. God alone judges the
nations.

These texts assert that all, rich and poor, should seek the hidden wisdom:

. . . If you are poor, do not say I am destitute, and therefore I will no[t] seek
knowledge. To every teaching put your shoulder, and in every [lesson] join
your heart, and (then) your thoughts will be with much understanding.
(SAPIENTIAL WORK I⁻ᵇ 2 III 12–14)

Such wisdom will lead one to separate oneself from evil, since those whom God
has endowed with His knowledge should perceive the evils of sinfulness:

He has separated you from the spirit of mankind, so you should separate from
everything which He despises and abstain from all abominations of the soul.
[Fo]r He made everything and He apportioned them, each to his inheritance,
and He is your portion and your share among people, and He has made you to
rule over His inheritance. And you, honor Him in this, by sanctifying your-
self to Him as He has made you the holiest of the holies.
(SAPIENTIAL WORK I⁻ᵈ 81 1–4)

Those who have become adepts at wisdom have an obligation to reciprocate
God's largesse. Because God has chosen them, placing them in the lot of the
wise—here again we find the sectarian notion of predestination—they must
reciprocate by abstaining from evil and sanctifying themselves. The text then alludes to the special inheritance of the tribe of Levi, to which God has allotted no
territory in the Land of Israel, because "I am your portion and your share among
the Israelites" (Numbers 18:20). Levi's singular holiness is its portion. The wise,
too, have a special holiness: they are the holy of holies.

Like Proverbs and Ben Sira, much of the advice in the sapiential scrolls is simply good common sense gained by studying wisdom:

> Investigate the mystery that is coming to be and study all the ways of truth and look carefully at all the roots of iniquity. Then you will know what is more bitter for a person and what is sweet for a man. The glory of your father should be upon your head, and of your mother in your steps. For his father is like a teacher to a man, and his mother is like a master. For they are the crucible of your birth . . . and as He (God) has opened your ear to the mystery that is coming to be, honor them for the sake of your own honor . . . for the sake of your life and the length of your days. *(SAPIENTIAL WORK I^b 2 III 14–19)*

Honoring one's parents is presented here as more than just good advice; it is part of the "mystery that is coming to be." This mystery, never fully explained in any of the wisdom or *Mysteries* texts, is the hidden wisdom vouchsafed by God. The promise of long life as a reward for honoring one's parents is based upon the Fifth Commandment (Exodus 20:12, Deuteronomy 5:16). Throughout, these texts assume a society based on marriage and family life, as is evident in this passage. They cannot have emerged from a celibate community.

Pithy sayings abound in these texts:

> [A person who is] hard of hearing do not send to seek judgment, for he will not be able to judge fairly the dispute between people. For like one who winnows in the wind [grain] which is not purified, so is one who speaks in an ear that does not hear, or speaks to one who is slumbering deeply under the spirit of [sleep]. *(SAPIENTIAL WORK II 33–35)*

Strings of aphorisms like this hark back to the ancient wisdom tradition. In ancient wisdom schools, such epigrammatic style was the norm.

The text also advises against vowing, which is discouraged not only in the Qumran texts but also in the New Testament and rabbinic literature:

> Do not add a vow or free wil[l offering] . . . . And any binding oath to vow a vow, you should cancel at the time it comes forth from your mouth, and according to your free will cancel [it]. *(SAPIENTIAL WORK I^b 2 IV 7–9)*

The author no doubt would have advised that a man should follow the same practice when it comes to canceling his wife's or daughter's vows. Because failing to discharge vows properly constitutes a major transgression against God, vows should always be canceled to avoid the risk of violating them.

Another halakhic passage reminds readers of their obligation, twice stated in the Torah (Leviticus 19:19, Deuteronomy 22:9–10), to keep separate different types of seeds, to avoid wearing a mixture of linen and wool, and to refrain from plowing with mismatched animals (*Sapiential Work I^a 103 II 7–9*). These texts stress that following the ritual requirements of Judaism is a prerequisite to gaining wisdom.

In many ways, this literature points toward ideas found in the sectarian texts. It teaches that knowledge comes from God, and it casts wisdom in a profoundly religious light as God's revelation to humankind. The *Mysteries* texts, which we consider next, went one step further. These texts include terms typically used by the sectarians to describe their particular religious ideas. Many of those special terms and the ideas they represent are also found in the *Thanksgiving Hymns*, which share much in common with the *Sapiential Works*.

The Book of Mysteries

Another set of manuscripts, very similar to the *Sapiential Works*, have been entitled *Mysteries*. These documents, sharing many of the same ideas and language used in the wisdom materials, contain even more sectarian terminology. When read together with the *Thanksgiving Hymns*, the *Mysteries* seem more integral to the Qumran sectarian corpus than the other sapiential texts.

The *Mysteries* consist of four manuscripts. Three of these—the cave 1 *Book of Mysteries* and the cave 4 *Mysteries A* and *Mysteries B*—are one and the same text. But the fourth, *Mysteries C*, although classified by the original editors as part of this same composition, shows no definite overlap with these other texts. It does, however, show parallels to the poetry of early Jewish mystical literature. Because such parallels are found in this text but not in the other three manuscripts, we need to be more cautious about identifying it with the others. We will, therefore, refer to a *Book of Mysteries*, represented in at least three manuscripts. This book is poetic, belonging to a type of reflective (that is, nonliturgical) poetry typical of many compositions in the Qumran library.

The *Mysteries* share much in common with the so-called *Sapiential Works*, especially *Sapiential Work I^c*. They belong to a similar genre, and share similar content and terms. However, the fact that their texts do not overlap at all, considering how much material we have recovered from both documents, makes it extremely unlikely that these constitute parts of the same text.

The *Mysteries* get their name from the term, *raz*—"mystery"—a word of Persian derivation that appears in the Book of Daniel as well as in these texts. Numerous studies compare the use of the term *raz* in Qumran literature to the use of "mystery" in the New Testament. These similarities indicate that Christians derived their ideas from Jewish sources, not from Greco-Roman mystery religions.

In the *Mysteries* and *Sapiential Works*, *raz* refers to the mysteries of creation, that is, the natural order of things, and to the mysteries of the divine role in historical processes. The source of these mysteries is divine wisdom. Therefore, all natural phenomena and historical events are part of the divine wisdom.

The largest single unit of text in this group of manuscripts is a long poem reconstructed from three of the texts. Following is a composite rendering that will convey the flavor of the composition. The text begins by explaining why wisdom was given to mankind (Book of Mysteries 1 I 3 = Mysteries B 3 2–3):

> . . . in order that they would know (the difference) between good and evil,
> (that they would understand the) mysteries of transgression (with) all their wisdom.

This wisdom should have led human beings to righteous behavior, but its lessons were ignored (Book of Mysteries 1 I 3–4):

> But they did not know the mystery of that which was coming into being,
> and the former things they did not consider,
> nor did they know what was to come upon them.
> And so they did not save their lives,
> from the mystery that was coming into being.

Despite clear evidence of major cosmic changes, human beings did nothing to prepare themselves. Although they should have realized that God's plan for the End of Days, the mystery, was soon to unfold, they ignored the signs (5–7):

> And this shall be the sign to you that it is taking place:
> When the begotten of unrighteousness are delivered up,
> and wickedness is removed from before righteousness,
> as darkness is removed from before light.
> (Then,) just as smoke wholly ceases and is no more,
> so shall wickedness cease forever,
> and righteousness shall be revealed as the sun
> (throughout) the full measure of the world.
> And all the adherents of the mysteries of [Belial] will be no more.
> But knowledge shall fill the world,
> nor shall folly ever[more] be there.

These mysteries clearly describe the coming of the End of Days, at which time the wicked will be destroyed. Signs have already begun to make its impending arrival clear (Book of Mysteries 1 I 8–12 = Mysteries A 1 1–4):

> The thing is certain to come,
> and true is the oracle.
> And from this you will know that it will not be reversed:
> Do not all the people]s hate iniquity?
> But it goes on at the hands of all of them.

> But does not the truthful report (issue) from the mouth of all the nations?
> Is there a language or a tongue which upholds it (truth)?
> What nation desires that a stronger one should oppress it?
> (Yet) what nation (is there) which has not stolen property (of another)?

It is precisely humanity's complete dishonesty and the nations' struggles with one another that bear witness to the imminent dawning of the End of Days.

Although God had granted human beings the wisdom to distinguish between good and evil, truth and falsehood, human beings had failed to heed that wisdom. They did not realize what would ultimately happen to them in the future, because they did not properly grasp the significance of past events. Therefore, God was now announcing that the End of Days was about to dawn, when all the wicked and evil itself would be eliminated and cease forever, and when knowledge of God would fill the earth. How would one know that the End of Days was really at hand? God would send unmistakable signs; the hypocrisy of all the nations would reveal itself—although all nations would denounce evil, they themselves would commit it against their neighbors. This last notion is reminiscent of rabbinic teachings that on the eve of the messianic era, "impudence will be abundant" (M. Sotah 9:15).

Although humankind has failed to grasp this fateful message, God has made these mysteries manifest as part of His order of creation:

> He causes everything [which comes into being]. H[e is from be]fore eternity;
> the Lord is His name, and for e[ternity . . . the p]lan of the time of birth He
> opened be[fore them . . .] for He tested our heart, and He caused us to inherit
> [. . .] every mystery and the tribulations (that would come) upon every
> creature. (MYSTERIES A 2 II 11–15)

The text emphasizes the omniscience of God, who determines the fate of all humanity. And God has given human beings the means to understand these secrets. In this passage we encounter the familiar sectarian concept of predestination: that God is the cause of everything, governing a person's life with a divine plan from the moment of birth.

To a great extent, the divine wisdom is sealed so that human beings cannot uncover it, except when God grants understanding in reward for a person's righteousness. When contemplated properly, these divine signs apparently can be understood, if we can judge from this extremely difficult and fragmentary passage:

> . . . the mag]icians (?) who are skilled in transgression, say the parable and re-
> late the riddle before it is discussed. Then you will know if you have consid-
> ered, and the signs of the heav[ens . . .] your foolishness. For the [s]eal of the
> vision is sealed up from you, and you have not considered the eternal myster-
> ies, and you have not come to understand wisdom. The[n] you will say [. . .]
> for you have not considered the root of wisdom, and if you open the vision it

will be clo[sed to you . . .] all [yo]ur wisdom, for yours is the [. . .] His name, for [wh]at is wisdom (which is) hidden [. . . sti]ll there will not be [. . .] the [vis]ion . . . *(MYSTERIES B 1 II 1–5)*

The magicians are called upon to explain the hidden meaning of the parable or riddle to see if they have properly understood the signs. But the text makes clear that they cannot, since the true vision, perhaps that of prophecy, is hidden from them and they do not understand the mysteries of God. The text seems to expect them to acknowledge their lack of understanding. And even if they were to uncover the vision (the text goes on), they would still not understand it, because their wisdom is valueless. They are then summoned to hear what the true hidden wisdom is.

As in the *Sapiential Works*, this hidden wisdom, vouchsafed only to the righteous, takes the form of extensive moral advice, for example:

. . . and what man is more exalted than a righteous [person . . .], and there is nothing more poisonous before Him than one who takes vengeance by bearing a grudge without [. . .] His judgment, like the na[me] of One Who is righteous in all [His ways . . . what] is more evil than hating . . . *(MYSTERIES B 7 1–4)*

Evil is the worst course of action; justice, the best. Bearing a grudge poisons a person's moral state. Nothing is worse than hating one's fellow. God is righteous and just. The use of rhetorical questions here is common in this literature, as it is in the genre of wisdom literature in general. .

As already mentioned, it is not at all clear whether *Mysteries C* is actually part of the same document, especially because it contains a poetic text strongly reminiscent of some later Jewish mystical hymns. The poem is characterized by a sequence of adjectives describing the majesty and greatness of God such as, "Great is He/Exalted is He."

An additional feature is the use of certain sectarian terms, such as "chosen ones" and "period of evil." That kind of terminology affirms the familiar sectarian scenario: The present age is a time of evil, to be followed by a sectarian victory in the war of the Sons of Light against the Sons of Darkness. The preserved portion of the poem (*Mysteries C* 3 4–8) follows:

. . .] and honored is H[e] in His sl[ow]ness to anger,
[and gr]eat is H[e] in [His] great anger.
And exalted is He in the multitude of His mercies,
and awe-inspiring is He in the plan of His anger.
Honored is He [in] . . . and in which the earth is His rule.
[And ho]nored is God by His holy people,
and exalted is H[e for] His chosen ones,

and exalted [is He in the heights of] His [holi]ness.
Great is He in the blessings [. . .] their glory and [. . .],
when there comes to an en[d] the period of evil . . .

This poetic text begins by praising God in a series of opposing pairs: God is long-suffering but also wrathful; extremely merciful, yet willing to pour out His anger. Furthermore, He is both an exalted, transcendent God and an immanent God, who is close to His people. His true greatness will ultimately be revealed in the End of Days, when evil will be entirely destroyed.

In other passages of the *Mysteries* texts, we read about the knowledge of what came before and what will come after the world as we know it. As in the rabbinic esoteric tradition, part of the hidden wisdom concerns what happened before creation and what will happen in the End of Days. This text, together with the related *Sapiential Works*, encourages the reader to investigate these mysteries, as opposed to Ben Sira and the Rabbis, who discourage such speculation.

The *Mysteries* texts and the *Sapiential Works* open to us a new genre of wisdom literature. In that literature, hidden secrets, unlocked by way of a proper understanding of the past, spell out the future, but such secrets are available only to a select group endowed with an ability to interpret the signs. Unlike biblical wisdom literature, the hallmark of which was commonsense advice, these texts proffer wisdom of a deeply religious character. What we have here is a wedding of wisdom and prophecy—not only a new literary genre, but further testimony to the religious creativity of Second Temple Judaism.

Like the apocryphal texts, the wisdom literature found at Qumran can in some ways be seen as the continuation of the biblical tradition. We next look at how the Bible itself was interpreted in the Qumran texts, examining the ingenious methods developed by Second Temple Jews to adapt what they saw as God's eternal word to their own times and circumstances.

CHAPTER 13

Biblical Interpretation

In nearly all of its ancient manifestations, the Jewish tradition was significantly grounded in the interpretation of a set of Scriptures that we know today as the Bible. Already within the biblical corpus itself, especially in Second Temple literature, we find evidence that exegesis was used as a means of deriving laws and reinterpreting earlier biblical accounts for didactic purposes. This pattern, which continued without interruption throughout the Second Temple period, eventually culminated in the great midrashic works that contained the halakhic and aggadic interpretations of the talmudic Rabbis.

The texts in the Qumran corpus reveal many types of interpretation that were practiced by the Qumran sect as well as by other contemporary Jewish groups. In the scrolls collection, we find the earliest examples of Bible translation, including fragments of the Greek Septuagint and Aramaic Targum. These translations share certain formal elements and literary techniques. The scrolls also reveal early attempts to explain the plain sense of Scripture (termed *peshat* by the later Rabbis). We also find books like *Genesis Apocryphon* and Jubilees, which retell— or rather, reinterpret—the biblical stories and which reflect the specific hermeneutics (exegetical methods) of each author.

The sect inherited a method of legal interpretation we find represented in the *Temple Scroll* and underpinning some of the laws in the *Halakhic Letter*. We can also see aspects of such an interpretive approach in the harmonizing tendencies found in the expanded Torah scrolls known as *Rewritten Pentateuch*. This interpretive technique was most probably based on that of the Sadducees. In addition, the sect had its own method of halakhic exegesis that gave rise to much of its legal teachings. Alongside these other methods was a form of contemporizing biblical interpretation called *pesher*, that interpreted prophetic texts as referring to present events and the history of the sect itself.

Although biblical interpretation runs through this book as a constant leitmotif, I would like to present here a comprehensive picture of the exegesis in the scrolls in order to highlight the different genres. Perhaps it is most important to realize that this corpus thoroughly documents the role of biblical interpretation as a vehicle for the development of Judaism at that early date. The selection of examples that follows concentrates on interpretive method and the literary form it takes. *Pesher*, because of its central role in the thought of the Qumran sect, is reserved for separate discussion in the next chapter.

THE EARLIEST TRANSLATIONS

THE SEPTUAGINT

Perhaps the best place to start is with texts that present biblical text in an almost literal translation. The earliest such translation known is the Septuagint, the Greek translation. The Septuagint (often abbreviated LXX, for "seventy") is the Hellenistic Jewish version of the Bible. Its name derives from a legend preserved in both the Letter of Aristeas (a Greek work probably from the late second century B.C.E.) and in talmudic sources attributing its translation to seventy-two elders brought from Jerusalem to Alexandria, Egypt, by Ptolemy II Philadelphus (285–246 B.C.E.). After this translation was abandoned by the Jews, it was preserved by the church. The canon of the Septuagint was wider than that of the Hebrew Bible, including various apocryphal works, some of which have been previously discussed.

The Septuagint translation, which began to take shape in the third century B.C.E., was made as a response to the needs of the Egyptian Jewish community in Alexandria. Its initial purpose was to provide a version of the Torah for worship and study. By the second century, the books of the latter prophets, then the former, were translated as well. Although some of the Writings were translated by the beginning of the second century B.C.E., others were not translated into Greek until the first century.

The Septuagint was not simply a literal translation. In many passages, the translators used terms from Hellenistic Greek that made the text more accessible to Greek readers, but they also subtly changed its meaning. Elsewhere, the translators introduced Hellenistic concepts into the text. At times, they translated from Hebrew texts that differed from those current in Palestine, a matter now made clearer through the evidence of the biblical scrolls from Qumran. At other points, the Septuagint reflects knowledge of Palestinian interpretive traditions enshrined in rabbinic literature.

Qumran cave 7, containing a peculiar collection of only Greek texts, included two Septuagint fragments written on papyrus—one of Exodus and one of the Letter of Jeremiah, an apocryphal composition containing the prophet's letter to the exiles in Babylon (Jeremiah 29:1), a text that does not appear in the Hebrew version. Cave 4 also has yielded fragmentary Septuagint manuscripts—two to

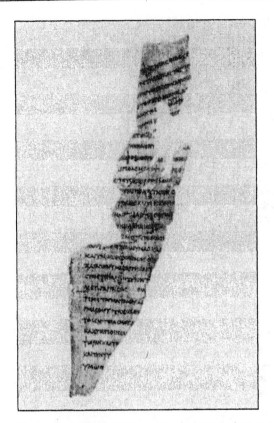

Cave 4 Septuagint Fragments Among the documents from cave 4
were fragments of the Septuagint—the Greek translation of the
Torah—to Leviticus, Numbers, and Deuteronomy. Pictured here
is the text of *Septuagint Leviticus A* to 26:2–16. The top and
bottom margins are easily visible, and evidence of stitching is
preserved on the left, indicating that even the Greek biblical
texts were copied on scrolls. *Courtesy of the Israel Antiquities
Authority.*

Leviticus and one each to Numbers and Deuteronomy. These manuscripts, dating
to the first two centuries B.C.E., generally represent a text close to that of the later
Septuagint textual tradition. However, they also contain some readings indicating that the later texts were somewhat revised from the original, usually termed
the Old Greek. In the case of the Numbers manuscript, the text of an earlier
Greek version was quite extensively revised to accord with a version of the Hebrew text very close to the Masoretic text.

The Septuagint seems to have had no role in the Qumran community. So far no one has satisfactorily explained why there was a collection of Greek texts in cave 7. In any case, the importance of the Septuagint for Jews began to wane once it was adopted by Christianity. Eventually it was replaced by other Jewish translations into Greek that adhered more closely to the Masoretic text.

THE TARGUM

The earliest translations composed in Palestine are the Targum texts, which are important because later on, such Aramaic translations, most notably that of Onkelos, were used in synagogues to translate the Torah readings for Jews who used Aramaic as their primary spoken language. Later Targums, such as the Palestinian Targum and Pseudo-Jonathan, provided a more midrashic exegesis of the Bible, including various aggadic traditions paralleled in the midrashim. The earliest forms of these translations—literal Targumim—are those of Leviticus and Job found in the scrolls.

The *Leviticus Targum* survives only in a small fragment from cave 4, in a manuscript dated to the second or, less probably, to the first century B.C.E. Although the remnants found at Qumran are certainly from a complete scroll, all that survives is Leviticus 16:12–15 and 18–21.

The passage preserved in this fragment relates to the sacrifice for the Day of Atonement. With a few exceptions, the Targum follows the biblical passages literally. Exceedingly important is the translation of the word *kaporet,* often rendered in Christian translations as "mercy-seat," assumed to be part of the ark. In this Qumran Targum, it is translated as "cover," in accord with some later Jewish traditions. In verse 20, referring to the priest's having completed "purging the Shrine," the term for shrine literally means "holiness." Our text adds "house of" to clarify that the ritual here is intended to atone for the Temple itself. This interpretation is reflected as well in later rabbinic exegesis.

The overall impression here is of a translation in accord with various Jewish interpretations, some of which became part of the later rabbinic tradition. In this text there is no hint of any sectarian interpretations, such as those provided for the very same passages of Leviticus in the *Temple Scroll* (25:10–27:10).

The other Targum from Qumran, much better preserved, is to the Book of Job. Found in cave 11, the *Job Targum* is dated generally to the late Herodian period, namely to the early first century of the common era. The twenty-eight preserved columns cover chapters 17–37 and portions of 37–42 of the Book of Job.

For the most part, this Targum is also literal. The translator, using a text of Job very similar to the later Masoretic text, comes up with a translation quite close to that text. As would be expected, there are a few textual differences reflected in the Targum. Occasionally, these minor differences stem from different vocalizations of the biblical text, which, until the Middle Ages, had no vowel points. If we discount these minor differences, we can see that the translation is generally a literal one, based on what scholars term the translator's Vorlage, the text he had before him.

The text does include some exegetical renderings, however. For example, for the verse, "Why do the wicked live on, prosper and grow wealthy" (21:7), the translator translates the last part of the verse ("and grow wealthy") as "and increase (their) possessions." This is a case of an interpretive translation, because the translator has chosen to define the Hebrew *ḥyl* as referring to wealth, not to strength or power, which it can also mean.

Sometimes the translator sought to eliminate difficulties in the grammatical structure of the original, sometimes even adding words to make the text understandable or to express his own particular interpretation of it. For example, for the verse, "Who closed the sea behind doors, when it gushed forth out of the womb . . . ?" (38:8), the translator translated "out of the womb" as "the womb of the deep," thus explaining that the "womb" from which the sea gushed was the depths of the sea itself, so that no one would mistakenly think that this verse referred to the mythological birth of the sea god, Yamm, prominent in ancient Near Eastern mythology.

Often the text adds pronominal suffixes for clarity. In translating Job 21:5—literally, "Look at me and be appalled, and clap hand on mouth"—the translator rendered the second half of the verse as "and clap your hands [on your mouth]." Needless to say, in lexical matters, the translation of all Hebrew words reflects the translator's own interpretation. It is hard to tell whether the occasional shortening of a text by combining parallel lines of poetry was for exegetical or literary purposes or whether it resulted from textual variation.

Rabbinic tradition speaks of the hiding of a Targum to Job by Rabban Gamaliel during the days of the Temple. It is difficult to know if this is indeed the very same Targum. Like the *Leviticus Targum* found at Qumran, there is no indication that this is a sectarian text. What these two Targum texts show is that the Targum method and specific Targum texts were known to the sectarians and that they were in existence at the time the scrolls were gathered at Qumran. In general, Aramaic texts found at Qumran are pre-Qumranian; that is, they existed before the rise of the sect. Although we cannot be certain that is the case with these Aramaic translations, it is probable. Targum was already an exegetical form in Jewish literature in the Hasmonaean period, and it is therefore not surprising that as Hebrew speaking became less common over time, Targum should become a major repository for Jewish interpretive literature in Aramaic.

PLAIN SENSE COMMENTARY

One text, the *Genesis Commentary*, also termed *Pesher Genesis* or *Genesis Florilegium*, represents a form of interpretation very close to the plain sense of Scripture, falling somewhere between the dry translation of most of the Targum material and the more expansive genre of rewritten Bible. Among the newly released documents, this text has attracted a tremendous amount of attention; numerous works have already been written about it. It is for the most part a retelling of the biblical Flood story, squaring its chronology with the solar calendar advocated by the sectarians. Another point in common with the Qumran sectarian approach is represented by the document's messianic teachings.

However, two particularly interesting expansions occur in regard to other parts of Genesis. After Noah exited the ark, he soon became drunk, and his son Ham saw his nakedness. His other sons covered him up and let him sleep off his drunkenness in his tent. The Bible then tells us that upon awakening, Noah cursed Canaan, son of Ham (Genesis 9:25–26). The obvious question is, Why curse Canaan, who committed no offense, rather than his father, Ham, who had committed the indignity to his own father, Noah? The text explains:

> He (Noah) did not curse Ham but rather his son, for God had blessed the sons of Noah. (GENESIS COMMENTARY II 6–7)

This interpretation refers to God's blessing of Noah and his sons earlier in the Genesis narrative (9:1–2). It provides a simple and direct explanation about why Ham is not cursed: Because Ham was already blessed, God could not reverse His blessing. The simplicity and directness of this answer and of other explanations given in this text have led one scholar to suggest that this is the first biblical commentary attempting to provide the plain sense of the biblical text.

The text continues by adapting the biblical, "May God enlarge Japheth and let him dwell in the tents of Shem" (Genesis 9:27):

> And he will dwell in the tents of Shem, (namely) the land which God gave to Abraham his beloved. (GENESIS COMMENTARY 1 II 7–8)

Here again the text supplies a simple interpretation to identify the "tents of Shem." It refers to the Land of Israel.

A final example is found in the section headed, "Blessings of Jacob." Here the text comments on the difficult passage, "For when you mounted your father's bed, you brought disgrace—my couch he mounted!" (Genesis 49:4) by saying:

> Its interpretation is that he (Jacob) reproved him (Reuben) because he had sexual relations with Bilhah his (Jacob's) concubine. (GENESIS COMMENTARY 1 IV 5–6)

This is widely held by modern biblical scholars to be the plain sense of this verse. It alludes to the fact that Reuben, earlier in Genesis, "went and had sexual relations with Bilhah, his father's concubine; and Israel (i.e., Jacob) found out" (Genesis 35:22). Here again, the Genesis Commentary provides the direct interpretation of the biblical text.

Although this text retells biblical stories, it should not be regarded as a precursor of the aggadic type of interpretation, as is the case with the Genesis Apoc-

ryphon. Rather it belongs to the genre of plain sense interpretation often found in the early midrashim, interspersed with the Aggadot. This kind of interpretation is conceptually more complex than the Targum type, since it deals with larger issues rather than simply interpreting words, the usual procedure in the Qumran Targum texts.

RETELLING THE BIBLE

The previous chapter detailed certain apocryphal-type texts that involve retelling the Bible. Now we look at some of this material from the point of view of biblical exegesis, for whenever a biblical tale or account is retold, we encounter a form of interpretation. In Second Temple times, such retellings were quite common; they have come down to us in both Hebrew and Aramaic. Although the texts representing this approach in the Qumran documents were in some cases presectarian, in others they agreed strongly with sectarian views and may actually have stemmed from the group itself.

We turn first to *Genesis Apocryphon,* a retelling of the Book of Genesis, which, like other Aramaic texts in the scrolls corpus, probably predates the Qumran sect, going back to sometime during the pre-Maccabean period. Among the best-preserved sections of the scroll are those dealing with Abraham and Sarah.

In Genesis 12:10–13 we are told matter-of-factly that Abram (his name before God changed it to Abraham as a symbol of the covenant) had to go down to Egypt because of the famine in the Land of Canaan. As Abram and his wife neared the border, he told his wife to say that they were brother and sister, so that he would not be killed, for Sarai (Sarah's name was also still unchanged) was such a beautiful woman. The text seems to assume that the Egyptians would kill Abram in order to take his wife. Commentators have pondered this story since ancient times, unable to understand by what right Abram could tell such a lie that would leave his wife subject to violation by the Egyptians in any case.

Genesis Apocryphon seeks to solve this problem in its retelling of the biblical story by relating the following incident not found in the biblical text:

> Then I, Abram, dreamt a dream on the night I entered the land of Egypt. And I saw in my dream [that there wa]s a cedar, and a very beautiful date palm. Then some men came and they wanted to cut down and to uproot the cedar, and to leave the date palm by itself. . . . At night I awoke from my sleep and said to Sarai, my wife, "I dreamt a dream [and I] am frightened by this dream." . . . [And I made known] to [her the meaning of this] dream [and] s[aid], "[There are those] who will seek to kill me and to spare you. [No]w this is the entire favor which you must do for me:] wherever [we shall be, say,] 'He is my brother.' Then I shall live because of you and my life will be saved because of you." *(GENESIS APOCRYPHON 19:14–20)*

To answer the question of why Abraham would suddenly ask his wife to lie about their relationship, the text explains that he did it to save his life. Yet in the process the author fills in details of the story. Indeed, this kind of biblical retelling, typical also of the Hebrew Book of Jubilees, shares this tendency with later rabbinic Aggadah, a sort of expository narrative interpretation that on the surface seems merely a collection of legends about the Bible. When investigated carefully, however, the Aggadah turns out to be an attempt to fill in the interstices in the text, the gaps left blank by the biblical narrative but crying out for interpretation. This form of narrative retelling of the Bible, found in presectarian documents in the Qumran corpus, proves that this approach was developing extensively in pre-Maccabean times.

Harmonizing Interpretation

Another type of interpretation common in Qumran writings, this time in both the presectarian and sectarian compositions, is harmonizing exegesis. In that type of interpretation, a text is interpreted in light of a similar one, so that the two are harmonized so as to say essentially the same thing. Underlying this method is the assumption of a fixed body of holy texts, a canon, so that the writings of one text can be used to interpret the other. We have already seen this kind of interpretation used in the creation of textual variants in certain biblical texts, specifically those of the proto-Samaritan variety. The later Samaritan biblical text is full of such interpretations, which have effectively created an expanded Torah text.

Sometimes such harmonizations are used in texts pertaining to Jewish law so as to eliminate ambiguities. For example, in the *Temple Scroll*, in a section toward the end of the scroll adapted from Deuteronomy, the following command is given:

> And you shall not sacrifice to Me an ox or a sheep in which there is any serious defect, for they are an abomination to Me. *(Temple Scroll 52:3–5)*

This text is simply an adaptation of Deuteronomy 17:1. However, the original verse in Deuteronomy had a problematic formulation, literally, "which has a defect, anything serious." In reformulating those words, the author was influenced by a parallel expression, elsewhere in Deuteronomy: "any serious blemish" (Deuteronomy 15:21). In this way, the text has harmonized Deuteronomy 17:1, the author's primary text, with the secondary reading from Deuteronomy 15:21, creating a new, "harmonized" text that is smoother and less ambiguous.

In this case, it is the interpreter's deliberate intention to remove ambiguity. Therefore, we should consider the interpreter's revision interpretive as opposed to the purely textual harmonization we discussed in connection with the biblical texts from Qumran. In the latter case, harmonization results from the process of textual transmission, for scribes tend, subconsciously, to level variations and harmonize texts.

Harmonization, especially in the *Temple Scroll*, can apply even to entire biblical commands, where one is understood in light of another. An excellent example concerns the New Year Festival, discussed in a section of the scroll known as the Festival Calendar because it lists all the Festivals and their sacrifices. In general, the section includes, by various techniques of harmonization and biblical interpretation, a number of Festivals not mentioned in the Bible. There we find a springtime New Year not mentioned in the Torah's Festival sequence:

> And on the first of the [first] month [(there shall be) the beginning of the months. It shall be for you the first of the months] of the year. [You may not do] any laborious w[ork. And you shall prepare a he-goat as an expiation offering.] By itself, it should be offered to aton[e for you. Then you shall offer a burnt offering: one young bull,] one ram, [seven] male lambs [a year o]ld [which are perfect . . .] [be]si[des the bu]r[nt offering of the new month].
> (TEMPLE SCROLL 14:9–13)

Through interpretation, the scroll has created a pseudobiblical text. Although the Bible tells us that the first day of the first month (Nisan 1) is the "beginning of the months . . . the first of the months of the year" (Exodus 12:1), it nowhere specifies any ritual for this "new year." So the author of the scroll (or a predecessor, because a similar holiday is also found in Jubilees) interpreted this text as analogous to the description of the autumnal New Year (Rosh Hashanah), the ritual for which appears in detail in the Torah (Numbers 29:1–6). Our author then harmonized these two biblical passages, appropriating from the autumnal New Year all of its sacrificial procedures as well as the requirement that "You may not do any laborious work" (Numbers 29:1). In that way, the author harmonized the autumnal New Year Festival of Numbers with the springtime New Year that the author understood to be described in Exodus. Over and over in the various compositions of the Qumran corpus dealing with Jewish law, we find examples of this technique, similar to the method of analogy used later in rabbinic exegesis and by the medieval sect of the Karaites.

HALAKHIC MIDRASH

Halakhah, Jewish law, has always used a technique of midrashic interpretation that figures prominently in the scrolls as well. For our present purposes, Midrash may be narrowly defined as the interpretation of one biblical passage in light of another. In the Books of Ezra and Nehemiah, such techniques are used to harmonize variant biblical passages on the same theme. The problem of apparently contradictory biblical texts confronted the Jews in the early Second Temple period because the Torah was already circulating as a unified whole. In the sectarian halakhic texts, this technique is quite developed.

Somewhat rare in the scrolls is a technique of halakhic Midrash in which the biblical text is quoted explicitly. A complex example, involving a number of biblical passages, is the sectarian understanding of the required reproof of transgressors found in the *Zadokite Fragments:*

> As to that which He (God) said, "You shall not take vengeance or bear a grudge against your kinfolk" (Leviticus 19:18), any man from among those who have entered the covenant (i.e., the sect) who shall bring a charge against his neighbor which is not with "reproof" before witnesses . . . is taking vengeance and bearing a grudge. Is it not written that only "He (God) takes vengeance on His adversaries and bears a grudge against His enemies" (Nahum 1:2)? But if he kept silent about him from day to day and (then) accused him . . . , his (the accused's) guilt is upon him (the accuser) since he did not fulfill the commandment of God, Who said to him, "You shall surely reprove your neighbor, lest you bear guilt because of him" (Leviticus 19:17).
> *(ZADOKITE FRAGMENTS 9:2–8)*

In this text we have a string of biblical verses all interpreted to yield a unique sectarian legal interpretation.

The Bible's prohibition on bearing a grudge (Leviticus 19:18) is understood here to refer to one who improperly observes the requirement of giving "reproof," the subject of verse 17 in Leviticus. As we know from other passages, the sectarians understood reproof as a formal process executed before witnesses. Unless reproof had been made and recorded for a previous offense, the offender could not be punished at a later date. This procedure was designed to ensure that an offender knew that offending actions were in fact prohibited and that therefore the individual was a purposeful transgressor. To support its claim that grudges are not permitted, the text quotes the prophetic passage from Nahum, interpreting it to mean that only God, not man, may take vengeance. The end of Leviticus 19:17, "lest you bear guilt . . ." is thus understood to mean that if one accuses a neighbor of a crime without having first executed reproof, one is liable for the same penalty for which the transgressor would have been liable.

These conclusions all emerge from interpreting two verses in Leviticus as referring to each other and from interpreting a verse in Nahum as sanctioning the requirement of sectarian reproof. Implicit in this interpretation is an unstated verse: Numbers 30:15, "if he kept silent about her from day to day," referring to the law that if a husband does not object to his wife's vows on the day they are made, the vows are considered valid. The sectarian text has borrowed this language to create the clause, "But if he kept silent about him from day to day." It is this uncited verse from Numbers that informed the sectarians that reproof was comparable to canceling a wife's vow and that it had to be executed on the same day. A variant text of the *Zadokite Fragments* (D^b 10 1–3) reads, "[But if he kept silent about him] from month to month." If this version is correct, then we would have to restrict the influence of the Numbers passage on our text only to the supplying of some biblical expressions.

My interpretation of this passage was challenged when I first presented it, some scholars arguing that reproof was simply an ethical action, not a formal legal procedure. However, one of the newly released documents proves that my view is correct. One of the texts, probably a document prepared by the examiner according to sectarian procedures, records an actual reproof process in the Qumran community. Although extremely fragmentary, the relevant bits of text support my conclusions:

> . . . their soul, and to reprove . . . the [c]amp of the many . . . Yohanan son
> of . . . because he was short tempered . . . And (as to) Hananiah son of Notos,
> he reproved him . . . [to cor]rupt the spirit of the community . . .
> (*Decrees of Reproof 2 I 2–3, 2 II 3–6*)*

Here we have a court docket regarding reproof for offenses against the sectarian way of life. With this document in hand there can no longer be any question that Qumran reproof was a formal, legal procedure.

Other legal interpretations in the sectarian scrolls never mention the biblical sources of a law but weave the source into the language of the text in such a way that it can be teased out by close textual analysis. In these cases, the biblical texts that are being interpreted are not quoted. An example of this type of exegesis can be cited from the Sabbath laws:

> No one shall walk about in the field to do the labor of his business on the
> Sabbath. (*Zadokite Fragments 10:20–21*)

This sentence seems to be a simple declarative statement of the law—what biblical scholars call an apodictic law. It prohibits one from taking a Sabbath walk in one's field for the purpose of determining what work needs to be done during the coming week. But detailed study of the words in this passage reveals that it is based on a biblical text. Several times the prophets rail against doing business on the Sabbath. A passage in Isaiah (58:13–14), literally translated, begins, "If you turn back your foot from the Sabbath, from pursuing your business on My holy day." Our sectarian law is an interpretation of the passage in Isaiah: "turning back your foot" means "not taking a walk"; "from the Sabbath" means "on the Sabbath"; and "business" refers to labor in connection with one's business, prohibited on the Sabbath. But the key to this sectarian law is the interpretation of the Isaiah passage as referring to the planning on the Sabbath of business to be

---

* A passage farther down on this fragment was read so as to refer to an offense of masturbation and translated, "he loved his bodily emissions." This reading is completely unfounded. The correct reading would yield, "he loves his relative." What a difference!

done afterward. This interpretation is fundamental to the sectarian legal text. In this case, the resulting law is exactly in accord with the later talmudic halakhah, but the interpretive route leading to it is different.

One feature of this interpretive method will seem strange to those who know the talmudic sources. Whereas the Rabbis avoid using prophetic passages and those from the Writings, instead limiting themselves almost exclusively to the Torah to derive Jewish law, the Qumran sectarians had no compunctions about interpreting non-Torah passages for this purpose. It is most likely that the Rabbis avoided using this material from Prophets and Writings because Christians were drawing on it to justify their claims regarding the messiah. In reaction, therefore, the Rabbis shied away from using these texts for authoritative derivation of law. Because the sectarian corpus, and for that matter other documents found at Qumran as well, were entirely pre-Christian, they reveal no such hesitation.

The interpretations outlined here are quite complex, representing only a small sample of the many such interpretations found in the sectarian legal corpus. Indeed, it is my view that this form of interpretation together with harmonizing interpretation typifies the Sadducean trend of biblical exposition alluded to in rabbinic sources. In any case, examples like these certainly prove that complex legal interpretation of the Bible was already quite developed in Second Temple times, well before the Destruction of the Temple and the creation of the great literary classics of talmudic Judaism.

The scrolls found at Qumran, some from the literary heritage preserved by the sectarians and some composed by them, present a variety of forms of biblical interpretation. Some attempt to establish the plain sense of the biblical text, some to expand upon it. Some retell the Bible, seeking to fill the spaces between the words—to fill in, as it were, the white spaces between the black letters. The more expansive, interpretive texts involve various types of harmonizations, midrashic interpretations, and detailed legal exegesis. Evaluated as a whole, the corpus offers forerunners and parallels to all the types of interpretation we find in the later Jewish tradition as transmitted by the rabbinic sources: Targum, the Aramaic translation of the Bible; direct, simple interpretation of the sense of Scripture; aggadic expansion; and halakhic Midrash. All these techniques were available when the Pharisees were competing with the various sectarians to dominate the religious scene in Hasmonaean Palestine. We have no reason to doubt the Rabbis' statements about the crucial role played by these types of interpretation during the period when Pharisaic Judaism was evolving into the form it would later bequeath to the Judaism of the Mishnah, Midrash, and Talmud. But one more type of interpretation still needs to be investigated. It is *pesher*, the unique historicizing and contemporizing interpretation developed by the sect and through which it saw itself and the events of its time as the fulfillment of God's prophecy to Israel.

CHAPTER 14

The Prophets in
the Hands of Men

A completely different system of interpretation is that known as *pesher*, a method particular to the Qumran sect itself although it has some parallels in New Testament exegesis of the Hebrew Bible and in aggadic Midrash. *Pesher* interpretations of isolated statements are found embedded in the *Zadokite Fragments* and other sectarian compositions. Strings of *pesher* interpretations, often called *pesharim*, are usually arranged in the order of a biblical book. Sustained, running commentaries on biblical texts, mostly from the latter prophets and psalms, have survived. These read like commentaries but are constructed out of the unique type of *pesher* interpretation.

The term *pesher* is derived from the Hebrew root *p-sh-r*, meaning, "to explain" or "expound." This term, used in both its Hebrew cognate and its Aramaic equivalent, *p-t-r*, refers to the interpretation of dreams. In the ancient Near East, and in particular in the biblical narratives of Joseph (Genesis 37:5–11, 40:1–41:57) and Daniel (Daniel 7), the practical effect of dreams was intimately bound up with their interpretation. For a dream to come true it must first be properly interpreted. *Pesher* interpretations regard the biblical prophecies in the same way. The efficacy of prophecy depends on its correct interpretation. *Pesher* provides such interpretations.

One more feature of this type of exegesis is that it contemporizes, meaning it interprets the prophecies of old as if they refer directly to the time and place of the interpreter. Although Jewish tradition, in virtually all its phases and approaches, has understood the message of the prophets to apply in each and every generation, it has nonetheless acknowledged the true historical context of prophecies in the biblical period.

In *pesher* interpretation, on the other hand, the original historical context is nonexistent. Habakkuk or the Psalms are understood as applying in their original sense to the time of the sect and foretelling its history. Indeed, in that sense, *pesher* shares a common element with much of the quotation and interpretation of the Hebrew Bible found in the New Testament. Early Christians regarded the works of the ancient prophets as referring to the events of their own day.

This feature of *pesher* exegesis leads to its importance as a historical source. Since it often seeks to tie the words of the Scriptures to "modern-day" (i.e., contemporary) events, it alludes directly to real people who lived in the Hasmonaean period. Together with other documents found in the Qumran materials, lists of names, and a few business documents, these materials are the only direct historical allusions that the scrolls provide.

We can state with certainty that the *pesher* texts are of sectarian provenance because they express the specific beliefs and theology of the Qumran sect, use its characteristic terminology, and are written in the peculiar Hebrew of the sect. Because the *pesher* material illumines so many important aspects of the thought of the Qumran sect, it will be helpful to attack it from a number of points of view, first in terms of the method of exegesis itself, and then in terms of the various texts and their historical significance.

The Literary Genre

In general, *pesharim* are distinguished by a specific form and style. First, a biblical passage is quoted, and then follows an interpretation, often preceded by the words *pesher ha-davar*, "the interpretation of the matter is," or *pishro*, "its interpretation is."

Pesharim may be roughly divided in terms of their literary form into three categories: (1) For some of the prophets, as well as for Psalm 37, we have "continuous *pesharim*," that is, essentially sustained, verse by verse, interpretations of the biblical material, in the style we would call a commentary. (2) A second type is usually termed "thematic *pesharim*," in which verses relating to a central theme, such as the End of Days, are interpreted within the framework of a defined text. (3) Finally, there are "isolated *pesharim*"—*pesher*-type interpretations embedded within larger texts on other subjects. Some have theorized that whenever a *pesher*-type interpretation appears in another kind of text, these passages may be drawn from *pesher* texts that no longer survive. Still unresolved is the question of whether the *pesher* form of interpretation was limited to the Prophets and Psalms, for these are the only texts that have survived.

Certain of the exegetical techniques—that is, the hermeneutical rules setting out the system of interpretation—used in the *pesharim* are also used in rabbinic Midrash. Nevertheless, the basic characteristic of the *pesher*, reading contemporary historical events and eschatological interpretations of present-day events into the words of the biblical prophecies, is not found in the rabbinic Midrashim except to a very limited extent. Therefore, despite parallels that may be cited regarding interpretive technique, the basic distinction between Qumran *pesher* and rabbinic Midrash remains firmly in place. Although from the perspective of literary genre we cannot class New Testament interpretations of the Hebrew Bible as *pesher*, we can legitimately point to common use of contemporizing exegesis, a method found much more frequently in early Christian materials than in rabbinic Midrash.

THE THEOLOGICAL BASIS

The theological link binding prophecy and *pesher* has been explained in full by the sectarian authors themselves. In interpreting Habakkuk 1:5, "Look among the nations . . . ," *Pesher Habakkuk* seems to have based itself on a biblical text that read, "Look at the traitors. . . ." Among the three definitions given for the "traitors" there, we find the following:

> for they did not [hearken to the words of] the Teacher of Righteousness from the mouth of God. *(PESHER HABAKKUK 2:2–3)*

Here we find that the teacher has received his teaching from the mouth of God. It is against this teaching that the traitors have rebelled. The text clearly affirms the divine inspiration of the teacher's interpretations. Later on in the same passage we learn the significance of this concept more clearly:

> They did not believe when they heard all that which was hap[pening to] the last generation from the mouth of the priest in whose [heart] God had put the [know]ledge to interpret (*p-sh-r*) all the words of His servants the prophets, [in who]se hands God recounted all that which was happening to His people and [to the nations]. *(PESHER HABAKKUK 2:6–10)*

The reference to the "priest" here is to the Teacher of Righteousness, who was indeed a member of the priestly clan. He was given the power to properly interpret the words of the prophets, who prophesied the future of the people of Israel and the nations. In other words, the sect regarded prophecy as a two-stage process. The first stage took place when God delivered His prophecies to the prophets. Yet they did not really understand their own prophecies. Only the contemporary interpreter can explain their true meaning through divinely inspired interpretations, the *pesharim*. Further, it is these correct interpretations that ensure the validity of the prophecies. This approach compares to what we find in the study of the sectarian halakhic system. There, too, the authority of interpretations results from their being seen as divinely inspired.

The very same point is made in another passage. In interpreting Habakkuk 2:2, in which the prophet is commanded, "Write the prophecy down, inscribe it clearly on tablets, so that it can be read easily," the text states:

God commanded Habakkuk to write down all that was happening to the final generation. But He did not make known to him the end of the period. And as to that which He said, "So that it can be read easily" (Habakkuk 2:2), its interpretation (*pesher*) concerns the Teacher of Righteousness, to whom God made known all the secrets of the words of His servants, the prophets.

(*PESHER HABAKKUK 7:1–5*)

Again we find that the teacher has been entrusted with the true interpretation, the secrets, that underlie the words of the prophets. We are told explicitly that God did not reveal to the prophet "the end of the period." It was made known only to the sectarian teacher. Revelation, to the authors of the *pesharim*, is clearly a two-stage process in which the sectarian leader completes the process started by the biblical prophet.

In this notion we can discern also that one of the basic beliefs of the Qumran sect is that all of history has been foreordained by God. In contrast, the Pharisaic-rabbinic tradition eschewed that notion, believing instead in human free will. Furthermore, this view elevates the authority of the sectarian teacher so that the teacher effectively controls divine revelation. The meaning of that revelation becomes clear only because the teacher participates in the interpretive process. Although such a notion may seem unique, we should note that the Pharisaic-rabbinic tradition effectively gave the Rabbis a similar kind of gatekeeper authority over biblical law by grounding the authority of biblical law in its correct interpretation as handed down by the Rabbis. For this reason, in rabbinic halakhah, the Bible is binding only according to the interpretations of the Rabbis of the Mishnah and Talmud.

THE MAJOR TEXTS

A brief survey of the major texts containing *pesher* and their basic themes will be helpful as a first step in understanding the *pesher* method and its contribution to Qumran thought and exegesis. We will reserve for separate treatment an analysis of the historical significance of these texts.

PESHER HABAKKUK

Among the first scrolls discovered in cave 1 by the Bedouin was *Pesher Habakkuk*. For this reason, and because it is so well preserved, this text had a profound, indeed even an exaggerated influence on attempts to reconstruct the history and teachings of the Qumran sect. The manuscript, written by two scribes, has been dated to between 30 and 1 B.C.E. The actual composition of the text can be dated on contextual grounds to the last years before the Roman conquest of Palestine, c. 84–63 B.C.E.

The main theme of the text concerns the early history of the sect. It describes

Pesher Habakkuk This ancient commentary on Habakkuk
was found among the complete scrolls from cave 1. The text
understands the words of the biblical prophet as referring
specifically to events experienced by the sect and its leaders.
The ruling lines from which the letters are suspended, as
well as the markings of the side margins, are visible. The
Tetragrammaton (four-letter divine name) is written in paleo-
Hebrew script in this and many sectarian manuscripts.
*Photograph by John C. Trever. Courtesy of the School of
Theology at Claremont.*

the struggle between the Teacher of Righteousness and his opponents—the Man of Lies (also termed the Spouter or Preacher of Lies) and the Wicked Priest. The Spouter is pictured as heading a community. The dispute between the teacher and the Spouter seems to have been based on matters of religious interpretation and law.

The Wicked Priest is said to have begun his rule in truth but then to have abandoned the way of truth. He then persecuted the teacher, confronting him on the holiest day of the year, the Day of Atonement. The text expects a warlike people called Kittim to attack from the islands of the sea and to punish the priests of Jerusalem. There is no question that Kittim, originally a designation for Cyprus, became a designation or code word meaning "Romans" in sectarian texts as well as in other contemporary sources. It was used because Romans were understood to come from the west, the direction of Cyprus.

PESHER NAHUM

Pesher Nahum survives only partly in a manuscript from the late Hasmonaean or early Herodian (Roman) period. The surviving text appears to be incomplete. Because certain of the passages deal with each of the three chapters of the biblical book, the original text must have covered the entirety of Nahum. From one allusion, it appears that the text must be dated after the Roman conquest in 63 B.C.E. The text mentions two specific historical personages—an Antiochus and a Demetrius—and events from the early first century B.C.E. We shall return later to interpretation of these events.

Demetrius is described as allied with the "seekers of smooth things," a term better translated "those who interpret (Scripture) falsely," a sobriquet used to denote the Pharisees. The Lion of Wrath is also allied with Demetrius. Because the text speaks of different sects within Judaism, termed here Ephraim, Menasseh, and Israel or Judah, the document is very important for an understanding of the history of the Jewish movements of the Hasmonaean period.

PESHER PSALMS

Pesher Psalms is represented in three manuscripts. Because these manuscripts do not overlap, we cannot be sure that they represent the same text, although it is most likely they do. *Pesher Psalms* from cave 1 includes scattered verses from Psalms 57 and 68. From cave 4, *Pesher Psalms A* covers parts of Psalms 37, 45, and 60, and *Pesher Psalms B* preserves material on Psalms 118, 127, and 129. The text did not cover the entire Book of Psalms, at least not in the present order, as is apparent from the fact that it moves directly from interpretation of material from Psalm 37 to Psalm 45. The manuscripts of *Pesher Psalms* can be dated to the Roman period.

Pesher Psalms A reads the controversy of the sectarians with their opponents into the biblical Psalm 37, which itself discusses the destiny of the righteous and the wicked. This text also mentions the familiar dramatis personae: the Teacher of Righteousness, termed "the priest"; the Wicked Priest; and the Man of Lies. The Wicked Priest persecuted the teacher and sought to kill him. The Man of Lies led people astray. The groups designated as Ephraim and Menasseh have both opposed the sect.

This text describes the destruction of the wicked at the End of Days and the peace that the righteous will enjoy in the soon-to-dawn final age. We should also call attention to the mention of the same "nets of Belial"—temptations to transgress—cited in the *Zadokite Fragments* (4:15), indicating the common sectarian character of these compositions.

PESHER ISAIAH

Six different manuscripts preserve fragments of a *pesher* on Isaiah. We cannot be certain whether these manuscripts represent parts of the same text or whether there was more than one composition dealing with this book, which was so seminal for the sect and its ideology. We have evidence of the special significance of this book for the sect in that twenty-two manuscripts of it were found among the documents. On the other hand, it may simply be coincidental that one complete scroll of this book and a second very substantial portion of a scroll survive.

Pesher Isaiah A deals with parts of Isaiah 10 and 11, interpreting the march of the Assyrians as referring to contemporary events and apparently referring to the invasion of Judaea by Seleucid Syria during the reign of Alexander Janneus (104–76 B.C.E.). This text, however, has recently become more important because it contains a parallel to the so-called pierced messiah text, actually called the *War Rule*, which, as will be shown in a later chapter, in reality has nothing at all to do with an executed or crucified messiah. It does, however, mention the sectarian leader termed Prince of the Congregation, who is expected to lead the sect into the End of Days, and the defeat of the Kittim, the enemies of the sect. This text is important for our discussion of the messianic idea in the scrolls. It should be noted here that the text refers only to one messiah, a "shoot of the branch of David," not sharing the two-messiah concept, priestly and lay, found in some other Qumran and Second Temple documents.

Pesher Isaiah B, probably copied in the immediate pre-Herodian period, survives only for parts of chapter 5 of Isaiah. The sect's opponents in this text are termed "the scoffers in Jerusalem," who may be the followers of the Wicked Priest.

Pesher Isaiah C is dated paleographically to the early first century B.C.E. and may therefore be the earliest extant copy of a *pesher* text. As preserved, it includes comments on portions of Isaiah 8, 10, 14, 19, and 29–32, also quoting other prophets, namely Zechariah and Hosea. In that respect it differs from the other continuous *pesharim*. It may, in fact, have dealt only with parts of Isaiah. The text refers to the sect's enemies, the "seekers of smooth things," generally accepted as denoting the Pharisees, with whom the sect disagreed on matters of law and biblical interpretation, not to mention politics.

The fourth Isaiah *pesher* from cave 4, *Pesher Isaiah D*, composed in the early Hasmonaean period, is preserved in a copy from early Herodian times. It is extant only for Isaiah 54:11–12. It applies Isaiah's vision of a New Jerusalem to the sect, interpreting the precious stones mentioned there to refer to different groups within the sect. The text refers to a group of twelve, either priests or Israelites, that governs the sect or the eschatological community. Attempts have been made to draw parallels from this text to the twelve apostles of early Christianity.

OTHER CONTINUOUS *PESHARIM*

Some fragments of two manuscripts—*Pesher Hosea A* and *Pesher Hosea B*—preserve *pesher* exegeses on a few passages in Hosea. Both manuscripts date to the Herodian period. The text castigates wicked Jews who spurned the commandments by observing gentile feasts. Hence, they were punished by God. The *pesher* refers to a "furious young lion" and to a "last priest," who will attack Ephraim—a symbolic term for the Pharisees.

A few fragments survive of *Pesher Micah*. They interpret Samaria to refer to the Spouter of Lies and Judah and Jerusalem to refer to the Teacher of Righteousness and the council of the sectarian community.

THEMATIC *PESHARIM*

A number of works have been classified as thematic *pesharim* because they string together a series of *pesher* interpretations on a common theme, which are derived from various biblical passages. Two examples of this phenomenon will be discussed here.

A text known as *Florilegium* was found in cave 4. Its name derives from the Latinized form of a Greek term for "anthology," and this is indeed an anthology of biblical passages with messianic implications, at least as interpreted here. The manuscript has been dated to the end of the first century B.C.E. It is organized around selected biblical verses from a number of books: II Samuel (or I Chronicles), then Exodus, Amos, Psalms, Isaiah, Ezekiel, and, again, Psalms. It may be that this text is actually derived from earlier *pesher* texts of which this is an anthology.

Florilegium discusses three temples: the eschatological one to be built by God, the present one that is depicted as desecrated, and the "temple of man"—a reference to the sect that for its members replaces the Temple in the present age. The text goes on to discuss the Davidic messiah, who is expected to appear together with the eschatological interpreter of the law, probably to be seen as a sort of messianic Teacher of Righteousness.

Melchizedek is preserved in an early Herodian period manuscript found in cave 11. The author presents a series of *pesher*-like interpretations of various biblical texts from Leviticus, Deuteronomy, Isaiah, Psalms, and Daniel, in that order. The freedom of the biblical Jubilee is seen as symbolic of the eschatological redemption at the End of Days. Apparently the author understood time as divided into ten Jubilees, with the dawning of the End of Days to take place in the last. The biblical figure of Melchizedek, "priest of Salem, . . . priest of God Most High" (Genesis 14:18; cf. Psalms 110:4), is the main actor in the eschatological drama. He destroys the forces of evil and liberates and expiates the Sons of Light (the members of the sect).

Some of these texts will be considered again when we discuss the messianic aspects of Qumran literature. For our purposes now, it is important to observe that these texts use a variety of biblical passages dealing with messianic themes, which are interpreted symbolically in a manner very close to that of the *pesharim*. Unlike the *pesharim*, however, they do not contain historical references to the immediate life of the sect and its history.

HISTORICAL RELEVANCE OF THE *PESHARIM*

The texts that have just been surveyed, together with a few related documents, like the Admonition—the first part of the *Zadokite Fragments*—provide most of what we know of the sect's internal history and its relations with and attitudes to opposing groups of Jews. But, as already mentioned, these texts speak in difficult allusions, depending on interpretation of the biblical texts and on a particular set of terms and symbols used by the sect to express its self-image and its view of its opponents.

Further, we have to reckon with the possibility that we are dealing here not with historical reality, but with a conception constructed by the sect of its own history as well as that of the Jewish and non-Jewish world outside. Perhaps this portrayal is not in any way realistic. In that case, we would be learning exclusively about the sect's self-image and the historiosophy underlying its approach to Judaism and its communal structure.

Because almost no names are mentioned, many of the interpretations presented in what follows are matters of scholarly debate. We will try to present the most plausible interpretation of these difficult data, pausing occasionally to explain opposing points of view.

The material in the *pesharim* covers three primary periods of sectarian history: the early days of the sect; the years immediately preceding, and perhaps following, the Roman conquest in 63 B.C.E.; and the final stages of the End of Days. The last is dealt with primarily in the thematic *pesharim*.

Whereas the *Zadokite Fragments* begin their account of the sect's history with the period before the rise of the Teacher of Righteousness and his leadership of the sect, we first encounter the sect in the *pesharim* under the leadership of this figure, whom God has sent to lead the sect. Interpreting Psalms 37:24, "for the Lord gives him support," *Pesher Psalms A* states:

> Its interpretation concerns the priest, the Teacher of [Righteousness, wh]om God [ch]ose to arise, f[or] He set him up (or: predestined him) to build for Him a congregation [of His chosen ones in truth]. *(Pesher Psalms A 1–10 III 15–16)*

The teacher was specifically designated, indeed perhaps predestined, for his role in building the community. In addition, it was he who revealed to them the meaning of the prophets' words.

But he found himself, presumably as a result of his teachings, in conflict with the Man of Lies. A group called the House of Absalom did not support the teacher in his confrontation with the Man of Lies. The *pesher* explains Habakkuk 1:13, which in the Masoretic text reads, "Why do You countenance treachery, and stand by idly while the evil one devours one who is more righteous than he?" as follows:

> Its interpretation is concerning the House of Absalom and the men of their council who kept silent when the Teacher of Righteousness was rebuked and did not help him against the Man of Lies, who rejected the Torah in the midst of all their con[grega]tion. *(Pesher Habakkuk 5:8–12)*

Clearly, the verse has been taken to refer to an episode in the sect's history during which the teacher was publicly rebuked by the Man of Lies. The House of Absalom was a group the teacher could have expected to defend him. Some have suggested that the group might be the Pharisees; others believe they were a group within the sect. From the point of view of the community, this event showed that the Man of Lies had effectively rejected the Torah and its laws.

In commenting on Habakkuk 1:5, "Look among the nations and observe well," read by the *pesher* as, "Look O traitors and observe well," the *pesher* states:

> [The interpretation of the matter concerns] those who are traitorous with the Man of Lies, for [they] did not [hearken to the words of] the Teacher of Righteousness from the mouth of God. *(Pesher Habakkuk 2:1–3)*

The traitors, apparently led by the Man of Lies, were most probably straying members of the group or a competing group. In any case, this passage shows that the teacher faced opposition not only from the official priesthood, but from others as well.

The main opponent of the teacher was the Wicked Priest. It was he who confronted the teacher and challenged him in the presence of the members of the group. That confrontation is described in an interpretation of Habakkuk 2:5–6,

"How much less then shall the defiant go unpunished, the treacherous, arrogant man . . . who has harvested all the nations and gathered in all the peoples":

> Its interpretation concerns the Wicked Priest who was called by the name of truth at the beginning when he arose. But when he ruled over Israel, his heart became haughty and he abandoned God, and he rebelled against the laws for the sake of wealth. And he stole and gathered the wealth of the men of violence who had rebelled against God. And he took the wealth of the nations to add to it the guilt of transgression. And he conducted himself according to abom[in]able ways with all impurity. *(PESHER HABAKKUK 8:8–13)*

The Wicked Priest began his career with the support of the sectarians, but he quickly lost his way and began to transgress in order to increase his wealth. The sectarians regarded this depredation as stealing. The Wicked Priest made war against the other nations and had a conflict with the "men of violence," most likely the Pharisees.

Further, he violated the laws of ritual purity and defiled the sanctuary, as is explained in reference to the extremely difficult Habakkuk 2:17, the end of which says, "For crimes against men and wrongs against lands, against cities and all their inhabitants." To this the text comments:

> Its interpretation: The city is Jerusalem in which the Wicked Priest undertook abominable actions, and he defiled the Temple of God.
> *(PESHER HABAKKUK 12:7–9)*

This interpretation must refer to legal rulings and ritual procedures in Temple worship regarded by the sectarians as violations of the Torah. A similar theme recurs in the *Zadokite Fragments,* the *Halakhic Letter,* and elsewhere in the sectarian corpus.

The Wicked Priest went so far as to lie in ambush for the Teacher of Righteousness. In interpreting Psalms 37:32, "The wicked watches for the righteous, seeking to put him to death," the text states:

> Its interpretation concerns [the] Wicked [Pr]iest who wa[tched out for the Teach]er of Righteous[ness and sought to] put him to death.
> *(PESHER PSALMS A 1–10 IV 8–9)*

Although the Wicked Priest sought to kill the teacher, he did not succeed.

Various theories have sought to identify the teacher with Jesus, claiming that he was executed by the Wicked Priest. Had that been the case, the text would not have gone on to explain how God took vengeance against the priest by turning him over to the "ruthless ones of the nations" (lines 9–10). And according to this text, the teacher certainly survived this ambush. Indeed, the entire passage is an interpretation of Psalms where the text continues, "The Lord will not abandon him (the righteous) into his hand (the wicked); He will not let him (the righteous) be condemned in judgment (by the wicked)" (Psalms 37:33).

This passage from *Pesher Psalms A* is probably a reference to the very same event described in *Pesher Habakkuk* where we are told about the Wicked Priest that:

> He pursued the Teacher of Righteousness to swallow him up in his intense anger at the place of his (the teacher's) exile. And at the time of the festival of their abstention from labor he appeared before them to swallow them up and to make them stumble on the day of the fast of the Sabbath of their abstention from labor. *(PESHER HABAKKUK 11:5–8)*

This account has likewise been interpreted as if it describes the death of the teacher, but it simply describes a painful confrontation. The "fast of the Sabbath of their abstention from labor" is the Day of Atonement, called in the Bible a "Sabbath" but also a fast. The Wicked Priest confronted the sectarians on this day of their holy Festival, but for him evidently it was not the Day of Atonement. This passage highlights that the sect used a different calendar from that used by the majority of Jews, a solar calendar. Thus, the Jewish holidays fell on different days from the days they would have fallen in the calendar used by the Wicked Priest.

Ultimately, however, the Wicked Priest was punished:

> . . . because of his transgression against the Teacher of Righteousness and the men of his counsel, God gave him over into the hand[s] of his enemies to afflict him with disease so as to destroy (him) with mortal suffering because he had acted wickedly against His chosen one. *(PESHER HABAKKUK 9:8–12)*

The Wicked Priest's enemies tortured him, which represented divine punishment for his attacks on the Teacher of Righteousness. The sufferings of the Wicked Priest are even more graphically described in another passage:

> [And all his enemies arose and ab]used him in order [for] his sufferings to be (fit) punishment for his evil. And they inflicted upon him horrible diseases, and acts of vengeance in the flesh of his body. *(PESHER HABAKKUK 8:17–9:2)*

The one who suffered was the Wicked Priest, not the Teacher of Righteousness. The enemies of the Wicked Priest, the nations against whom he had made war, are said to have tortured him, so that his life ended in mortal disease and affliction.

Various theories have been suggested to identify the Wicked Priest and to place these events within the context of what we know of Second Temple period history. In many cases, those theories have not been anchored sufficiently in paleography, archaeology, or the general historical sources. However, when these are all taken into consideration, it becomes abundantly clear—and this is unquestionable—that the events described in the texts just surveyed herein must be placed in the early Hasmonaean period—in the years soon after the Maccabean Revolt.

In our study of the *Halakhic Letter*, we established that the sect was founded in this same period. We also saw that the Teacher of Righteousness must have emerged as the sect's leader some years after the initial break that occurred soon after 152 B.C.E. The career of the Wicked Priest must be similarly dated. Most scholars now agree that the Wicked Priest is either Jonathan (160–143 B.C.E.) or Simon (142–134 B.C.E.), brothers of Judah the Maccabee, who were the first two rulers of the Hasmonaean priestly dynasty.

We have additional information from a text found in cave 4 (not technically a *pesher*) called *Testimonia*, an anthology of biblical verses. The identical passage occurs also in another apocryphal work, called *Psalms of Joshua*.

Here is the text as it appears in *Psalms of Joshua*, with the breaks in the manuscript filled in with the help of *Testimonia*:

> When Joshua finished praising and giving thanks in his psalms, he said, "Cursed be the man who builds this city. He shall lay its foundations at the cost of his firstborn and set up its gates at the cost of his youngest" (cf. Joshua 6:26). And behold, a cursed man of Belial who arises to be a fowler's trap to his people and a cause of destruction to all his neighbors. And . . . arose [and ruled (?)], so that both of them were instruments of violence. And they rebuilt [th]is [city] and they set up a wall and towers for it to make it a stronghold of evil in Israel and a horror in Ephraim and in Judah . . . great [e]vil among the sons of Jacob and they s[pilled blood and com]mitted abomination in the land, and great blasphemy. (They spilled blood) like water on the rampart of the daughter of Zion and within the boundaries of Jerusalem.
>
> (PSALMS OF JOSHUA B 22 II 7–4 = TESTIMONIA 21–30)

Scholars have tried to identify the historical events outlined in this adaptation of Joshua 6:26. According to this text, someone tried to rebuild Jericho despite Joshua's curse. In doing so, he lost both of his sons, who themselves had become evildoers, in the view of the author. He himself led his people astray and died, only to be replaced by another ruler, who followed the same course. They were both guilty of shedding the blood of Jews in Jerusalem.

Two theories have been put forward. One holds that this text describes Simon the Hasmonaean (brother of Judah the Maccabee). Simon and his two sons (one of whom was probably his eldest and one his youngest) were on a tour of the kingdom and attended a banquet at the newly built fortress of Jericho in 134 B.C.E.

There they were murdered by the local commander, who attempted a coup. Simon's remaining son, John Hyrcanus, was warned and was thus able to escape danger. He then reasserted control and ruled from 134 to 104 B.C.E.

A second theory places this event after the death of the two Hasmonaean scions Antigonus and Aristobulus I in 103 B.C.E. At that time, work on the palaces and fortifications of Jericho was in full swing, as can be shown by recent excavations. The author of the text believed that Joshua's curse was visited on John Hyrcanus when he lost his two sons while rebuilding Jericho. His son Antigonus murdered his own brother Aristobulus I and then died himself shortly afterward. John Hyrcanus would be the accursed man of the text, who led his people astray and paid for his transgressions with the lives of his sons.

In the absence of any firm historical evidence, it is not possible to decide to which Hasmonaean ruler—Simon or his son John Hyrcanus—this dually preserved text applies. The text shows us that even after the lifetime of the Wicked Priest, the Qumran sectarians continued to be anti-Hasmonaean, considering the descendants of the Maccabees as transgressors who led their people astray. This was an underlying view of the Qumran sect and is reflected in quite a number of sectarian texts.

We next encounter historical information in the *pesharim* in *Pesher Nahum*, which describes a somewhat later period. This material is virtually unique in that it describes actual people known from the pages of history. In this period the ruler is the Lion of Wrath, clearly an allusion to another of the Hasmonaean priests who by this time were styled as kings. There we hear of the "interpreters of false laws" (usually translated literally as "seekers after smooth things") and their alliance with:

> [Deme]trius, king of Greece, who sought to enter Jerusalem with the counsel of the interpreters of false laws, [but God had not given Jerusalem over] into the hand of the kings of Greece from Antiochus until the rise of the rulers of the Kittim . . . but (later) the city was given into the hand of the rulers of the Kittim. (*PESHER NAHUM 3–4 I 2–4*)

This Demetrius, a ruler of the "Greek" empire, tried with the help of the interpreters of false laws to invade Jerusalem but did not succeed. In fact, from the time of Antiochus until the time of the Kittim (Romans), no one succeeded in conquering Jerusalem.

The result of the attack of Demetrius is also recorded:

> [. . . Demetrius who made war] against the Lion of Wrath so that he smote his nobles and the men of his council. (*PESHER NAHUM 3–4 I 5–6*)

After the war was over and the Lion of Wrath was victorious, he took his revenge:

> ... against the interpreters of false laws in that he hanged men alive [which was never done] in Israel before ... *(PESHER NAHUM 3–4 I 7–8)*

Most scholars understand this passage to mean that the Lion of Wrath punished his enemies by crucifying them, a punishment never before practiced by the Jewish people.

The events in this *pesher* text can be thoroughly decoded by drawing upon the evidence provided for the later Hasmonaean period in the works of the ancient Jewish historian Josephus. We can identify all the dramatis personae in this text. The Kittim are the Romans, a designation common in the scrolls. Demetrius is Demetrius III Eukerus (95–88 B.C.E.). His designation "king of Greece" refers to the Seleucid empire, often referred to as Greece in Jewish literature. The Antiochus from whose time Jerusalem was never conquered by a foreign king was most probably Antiochus III the Great (223–187 B.C.E.). The Jews voluntarily opened the gates of Jerusalem to him in 198 B.C.E. because of their disenchantment with Ptolemaic rule. The interpreters of false laws are the Pharisees, about whom we will learn much more from this text in another chapter. The Lion of Wrath, ruler of Judaea, is the Hasmonaean king Alexander Janneus (104–76 B.C.E.), grandson of Simon the brother of Judah the Maccabee.

The events described here are narrated in greater detail by Josephus (Antiquities 13, 372–383). The story begins with public protest over the sacrificial procedures followed by Alexander Janneus. Although Josephus gives no specific information, a Mishnaic parallel (Sukkah 4:9) indicates that he followed Sadducean practice, rejecting the water libation required by the Pharisees. A riot ensued as well as objections to his legitimacy as a priest, indeed to that of the entire Hasmonaean dynasty. Josephus says that as a result, he killed six thousand people. After a military setback, he was severely criticized by his subjects, which in turn led him to make war against them. Josephus gives the probably exaggerated figure of fifty thousand Jews killed during this conflict with their own king. When he tried to convince the people to make peace, they told him that they wanted him dead. Desperate to throw off the yoke of this cruel ruler, they sent for Demetrius III Eukerus to assist them. He invaded the country. On each side fought both Jews and Hellenized pagans, each appealing to the other to desert. In the ensuing battle, Alexander Janneus was forced to flee. Some Jews came to his aid, persuading Demetrius to withdraw, apparently convinced that the Jewish people was, in fact, divided in its attitude to Alexander Janneus. The battles continued until Alexander was able to retake Jerusalem and reassert his power. After reestablishing himself, Alexander feasted with his concubines while eight hundred Jews were crucified and their wives and children slaughtered as they watched. His opponents, numbering eight thousand, were forced to flee into exile.

This is exactly the story told in the *Pesher Nahum*. But from the *pesher* we learn that Janneus's enemies were the Pharisees, which agrees with the account of the Mishnah, which claims that the trouble began over his following Sadducean legal practices. "His nobles" were the Sadducean leadership with whom Janneus (the Lion of Wrath) closely cooperated. This horrible Jewish civil war is the subject of the historical allusions in *Pesher Nahum*.

Some scholars see direct allusions in this text to the end of the Hasmonaean dynasty, specifically to the time of Salome Alexandra (76–67 B.C.E.) and her sons, the Hasmonaean brothers Hyrcanus II and Aristobulus II (67–63 B.C.E.), but these figures cannot be definitely identified in this text. We do find clear reference, however, to the Roman conquest of Judaea in 63 B.C.E.

Before we leave this story in *Pesher Nahum*, it would be helpful to say a few words about a text that is not a *pesher* but is relevant to the historical account derived from the *pesher* texts. After its difficult semicursive writing was deciphered, this curious text was recently identified as a *Prayer for King Jonathan*. Although it is possible that this Jonathan is the brother of Judah the Maccabee, it seems much more likely that it is Alexander Janneus, whose name, "Janneus," is a Greek form of the Hebrew Jonathan ("Yannai" would be shortened from "Yonathan"). If so, we find in the Qumran library a prayer offered for the welfare of this king.

The text includes some liturgical poetry, also found in the *Psalms Scroll*, as well as the following prayer:

> Holy One, watch over (or: Arise O Holy One on behalf of) King Jonathan and all the congregation of Your people Israel who are in the four corners of heaven. May peace be on all (of them) and upon Your Kingdom. May Your name be blessed! *(Prayer for King Jonathan B1–9)*

Prayer for King Jonathan This manuscript, of which nothing more than what is shown here is preserved, has both an excerpt from one of the Apocryphal Psalms contained in the *Psalms Scroll*, from cave 11, and a prayer for the welfare of a King Jonathan, whom most scholars have identified as Alexander Janneus, the Hasmonaean ruler (104–76 B.C.E.). The tab on the right side originally anchored a thong, which was used to tie the manuscript closed when it was not being used. *Courtesy of the Israel Antiquities Authority.*

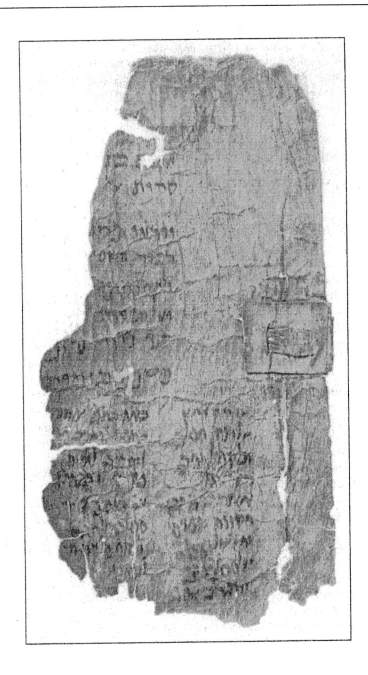

This beautiful prayer asks for the welfare of King Jonathan. How can we explain its presence in the Qumran corpus? According to *Pesher Nahum*, the sectarians were opposed to Jonathan. Two possible answers may be suggested. First, it is possible that the sectarians initially regarded this king favorably, only later changing their mind as he followed policies they did not accept. Or it is possible that this text simply testifies to the heterogeneous nature of the Qumran collection. It may have happened that a text presenting an opposing view simply ended up there—an exceptional occurrence, but not impossible.

It is worth noting that a few other historical personages are mentioned in the scrolls. These names occur in *Mishmarot* texts, which are calendrical documents that furnish no actual information about these people or their historical context. The name "Shelomzion," the Hebrew name of Queen Salome Alexandra (76–67 B.C.E.), for all intents and purposes the last Hasmonaean ruler, appears in *Mishmarot* C^a 2 4 and C^e 1 5. "Hyrcanus the king," who appears in C^a 2 6 with Shelomzion, may be either John Hyrcanus (134–104 B.C.E.) or Salome's son Hyrcanus II, who served as high priest from 76 to 40 B.C.E. Although he tried to assert himself as Hasmonaean king in 67 B.C.E. after the death of his mother, he was defeated by his brother Aristobulus II, who ruled until the Roman conquest in 63 B.C.E. A text tells us that "Aemilius killed" in *Mishmarot* C^d 2 4, 8. This most likely refers to Aemilius Scaurus, the first Roman governor of Syria (65–62 B.C.E.). We may have here an allusion to a massacre that Scaurus perpetrated. The mention of Scaurus in the *Mishmarot* texts is most interesting, for he supported the claims of Aristobulus II against those of his brother and rival Hyrcanus II, suggesting that the "Hyrcanus" of our text is indeed Hyrcanus II. Yet the title "king" is more appropriate to John Hyrcanus, who actually reigned over the Hasmonaean state. However, we should note that these texts are basically calendrical or astronomic. It is thus possible that these names designate heavenly bodies rather than actual people.

Virtually all of these historical allusions are found in the context of *pesher* interpretation, a technique unique to the Qumran sect. Although later Christian tradition reflects certain parallels, and rabbinic literature and even medieval Jewish writings occasionally feature such contemporizing interpretation, it was certainly not common in later Judaism. In obliterating the original historical context of the words of the prophets, *pesher* marks a radical departure from normative Jewish biblical interpretation.

To the Qumran sect, *pesher* was a powerful tool in forging the sect's emerging self-definition. As such it reveals much about the early history of the sect, enabling us to trace the interaction between certain shadowy but very important figures in the history of the Jewish people. It shows us that the sect was essentially anti-Hasmonaean, a notion confirmed also by other sectarian documents

Far from being an isolated, monastic community, the Qumran sect was actively involved in the affairs of the times. Finally, *pesher* literature provides one more example of how the word of God can be molded in human hands to provide a sacred history for an emerging religious group.

How did interpretation shape Jewish law, both within the sect and beyond it? To answer that question, we first need to understand the theological principles underlying the various approaches to Jewish law in Second Temple times.

PART IV
To Live as a Jew

CHAPTER 15

The Theology of Jewish Law

From the very first discovery of what we now know to be a Qumran text—the *Zadokite Fragments* found in the Cairo *genizah*—it was clear that the new material would be of great importance for our understanding of the history and development of Jewish law. When the Qumran library itself was discovered, the presence of multiple copies of that text, as well as other halakhic material, made clear that the new texts had much to teach us in this area of research.

However, the order in which these texts were published greatly minimized progress on this front. Work on the cave 4 manuscripts of the *Zadokite Fragments*, as well as on texts entitled *Halakhah* (law) and *Toharot* (purification rituals), was delayed. These texts apparently posed great difficulty to the publication team, which had little experience with postbiblical Jewish law. Because at that time Jews were excluded from the publication process, qualified scholars for this work could not be recruited. Furthermore, the editorial team gave priority, whether intentionally or not, to materials that seemed to support the description of the sect as a proto-Christian group. These factors certainly contributed to the delay in publication of the *Halakhic Letter*, the fragments of the *Temple Scroll*, and related compositions. With publication of the *Temple Scroll* and subsequent revelation of the *Halakhic Letter*, research in this area has made great strides.

THE STUDY OF QUMRAN LAW

Initially, scholars focused their efforts on studying the law of the Qumran sect itself, about which we have much significant information. But the texts from Qumran also tell us a remarkable amount about the more general state of Jewish law in the Hasmonaean period, not only about the nature of the law within the sect itself. Through these documents, we are constructing a fuller picture of Pharisaic and Sadducean law, of attitudes toward the authority of the Torah during that period, and of the sect's views in this regard. Thus, we are able to understand better the development of Jewish law that plays so important a role in mishnaic and talmudic Judaism and into our own day.

Law has always been central to Judaism. Throughout history and up until the onset of the modern period, all forms of Judaism were grounded in the principle that the obligation of each and every Jew was to fulfill the word of God as revealed in the Torah. To carry out this obligation, all groups of Jews adhered to a system of Jewish law. Although they may have disagreed about how to interpret and fulfill the Torah's legislation, they nevertheless all accepted that these laws were binding. Furthermore, because they did often differ on theological issues, their common adherence to Jewish law often gave the Jews their distinct character in the eyes of others. This was certainly true in the Greco-Roman period, when the Jew was distinguished most prominently for observing the Sabbath, abstaining from pork, and circumcising male children.

We are accustomed to using the term "halakhah," literally "the way," or according to another interpretation, "the required portion," to refer to a set of regulations espoused by the Rabbis in the Mishnah and Talmud. Unfortunately, halakhah is often treated as if it were monolithic, as if the various legal materials did not stem from different periods and express differing views. Nothing could be further from the truth. And even in its broader definition, the term usually designates the law only of the Pharisaic-rabbinic Jews. We will see that in Second Temple times things were much more diverse.

Although technically the term "halakhah" refers exclusively to Pharisaic-rabbinic law, excepting other groups including the Sadducees and the Dead Sea sect, scholars generally use it to refer to non-Pharisaic or nonrabbinic trends, because it captures so well the mix of ritual, civil, and moral law constituting the Jewish legal system in all its forms.

THE AUTHORITY OF THE LAW

At the heart of any system of Jewish law is the source of authority that motivates it. All premodern systems of Judaism agreed that the written text of the Torah was that source. But because the Torah text itself did not provide full guidance about how to live as a Jew but left much open to interpretation, supplementary laws had to be developed. Therein lay the problem. All systems of ancient Judaism had solved the problem in some way; the scrolls provide much information about how it was done.

One of the fundamental issues in Second Temple Judaism consisted of how to incorporate extrabiblical traditions and teachings into the Jewish legal system and how to justify their inclusion theologically. Although in antiquity and late antiquity Jews (except in the Hellenistic Diaspora) engaged in little theoretical theology, issues of Jewish belief were of central importance and often lie behind other, more clearly expressed disputes.

THE REVEALED AND THE HIDDEN

The bulk of the materials we shall discuss are sectarian, and thus we begin by laying out their basic views. Then we turn to additional materials in the collection and to the sect's polemics against other approaches in order to learn about other contemporary systems of Jewish law.

The legal materials of the sect are to a great extent derived from biblical interpretation, an activity that took place at regular study sessions as part of sectarian life, most probably in the main center at Qumran. The decisions reached at such sessions were recorded in lists of sectarian laws called *serakhim*. Indeed, collections of laws or regulations of this type constitute the component parts of *Rule of the Community* and the *Zadokite Fragments*.

Where did these laws come from? In what ways were the laws not directly found in the Torah to be tied to God and His revelation? How did the sect view the process of interpretation that lay behind these laws?

When we examine the sectarian laws in detail, we will see that they were for the most part made up of snatches of biblical phraseology woven together. Only rarely do we find explicit quotation. By examining these paraphrases, we can discover the biblical basis upon which the sect arrived at its own particular views.

The sect divided the law into two categories—the *nigleh*, "revealed," and the *nistar*, "hidden." The revealed laws were known to all Israel, for they were manifest in Scripture, but the hidden laws were known only to the sect and were revealed solely through sectarian exegesis:

> Everyone who joins the council of the community shall enter the covenant of God in the presence of all the volunteers, and shall take upon himself through a binding oath to return to the law of Moses, according to everything which He (God) commanded, with all (his) heart and with all (his) soul, in respect of everything which has been revealed (*nigleh*) from it to the Sons of Zadok, the priests who guard His covenant and seek His will, and to the majority of the men of their covenant who volunteer together for His truth and to live by His will. And he shall establish by a covenant upon himself to separate (himself) from all men of iniquity who walk in the path of evil. For they have not been reckoned in His covenant, for they did not search and did not study His laws, to know the secrets (*nistarot*) in which they erred, incurring guilt, and the revealed (*niglot*) they did (violate) defiantly . . . (*RULE OF THE COMMUNITY* 5:7–12)

In this passage the revealed laws refer to those explicitly stated in the Torah. All Israel was expected to know and observe these laws. Although the hidden laws were known only to the sect, the other groups were nonetheless held responsible for not observing them.

In general, the revealed laws left little room for debate about their observance. However, the hidden laws required the help of divinely guided exegesis to enable sect members to discover their correct interpretation. This process involved searching in the law, an activity not practiced by the sect's opponents. Hence, the opponents did not have the correct views. These hidden laws had been revealed to the Sons of Zadok—the members of the Zadokite high priestly family—who founded and first led the sect.

That these hidden laws are those of the sect is emphasized in a passage in the *Zadokite Fragments:*

> And with those who hold fast to the commandment(s) of God, who remained of them, God established His covenant with Israel eternally: to reveal to them hidden laws (*nistarot*) in which all Israel erred. His holy Sabbaths, His glorious Festivals, His righteous testimonies, His truthful ways, and the desires of His will, which man shall observe that he may live, He opened before them. (*Zadokite Fragments 3:12–16*)

Not only were these halakhic mysteries divinely revealed to the sect through study sessions, but these laws and the revelation behind them would change and develop over time. Such a concept is emphasized several times in *Rule of the Community.* One passage provides that sectarians who join are:

> To walk before Him perfectly in all that has been revealed (*niglot*) for their appointed times. (*Rule of the Community 1:9*)

In another passage, the *maskil*—the sectarian teacher—is expected:

> To do the will of God according to everything that is revealed from time to time and to learn all the knowledge which is derived according to the times and the law of the time. (*Rule of the Community 9:13–14*)

The hidden laws were thus progressively revealed and changed with the times. The sectarians held a similar view about the revealed law, that is, the law of the Bible itself:

> This is the interpretation of the Torah [which] He commanded through Moses to observe, according to everything that is revealed (*nigleh*) from time to time, and as the prophets have revealed by His holy spirit. (*Rule of the Community 8:15–16*)

The text intimates here that the prophetic books also represented a modification of the words of the Torah over time. The sectarians indeed believed that it was legally valid to use statements from the Prophets to derive laws. Later rabbinic tradition rejected this practice almost entirely.

The notion of revealed and hidden laws discloses to us a system of sectarian legal theology. The revealed law—that is, the Torah and the words of the Prophets—was known by all of Israel, who, nonetheless, violated it. The hidden, on the other hand, was known only to the sect. These hidden laws constituted the very points of disagreement around which the sect coalesced. The written

Torah, originally revealed by God, had been modified later by His prophets through their divine visions. The hidden law, the *nistar*, had also developed over time and would continue to change, but it did not originate at the same time as the revealed Torah. Rather, it represented God's constant, ongoing revelation of Torah interpretation disclosed to the sectarians during and through their study sessions. These two types of law complemented each other and together made up the system of Jewish law as understood and practiced by the sect.

PHARISEES AND SADDUCEES

Not only can we understand the legal theology of the Qumran sect from the scrolls, but also we can gather from them a great deal of information about the legal views of the Pharisees and Sadducees, supplementing what we already know from rabbinic sources and Josephus.

What we learn about the Pharisees comes indirectly from the sectarian polemics against their views. By evaluating this material carefully and then judiciously comparing the later evidence from Josephus and the rabbinic tradition, we can reconstruct many Pharisaic attitudes. Here we will be concerned not with the content of Pharisaic halakhah but with its basic theoretical underpinnings.

The Admonition, which opens the *Zadokite Fragments*, includes a list of transgressions attributed to:

> The builders of the wall who followed (literally, "walked after") the "commander." The "commander" is the preacher about whom He (God or the prophet) said (Micah 2:6), "They shall surely preach."
> (*ZADOKITE FRAGMENTS* 4:19–20)

Who are the builders of the wall? Who is the commander or preacher? Clearly, they are the villains. Buried in the text are two biblical allusions that make these references clear. One is to Hosea 5:10–11: "The commanders of Judah have acted like shifters of field boundaries. On them I will pour out My wrath like water. Ephraim is defrauded, robbed of redress." A different passage states, " 'Stop preaching!' they preach. 'That is no way to preach' " (Micah 2:6). The commanders of Judah are equated here with Ephraim, a sectarian term for the Pharisees. They are the builders of the wall who follow the teachings of the commander. This same commander is the one who preaches improperly, hence defrauding his listeners. The sect regarded the Pharisees as preaching falsely and misleading their followers.

Thereafter appears a series of laws with which the sectarians disagreed, constituting the views of the preacher who here again refers to the Pharisaic leader and the "builders of the wall." The designation "builders of the wall" apparently derives from a concept found in the mishnaic tractate Avot, generally known as Ethics of the Fathers, which instructs, "Build a fence around the Torah" (M. Avot 1:1).

To "build a fence" refers to the Pharisaic-rabbinic concept of creating more stringent laws than those found in the Bible in order to safeguard biblical laws from violation. For example, to uphold the Torah's prohibition against laborious work on the Sabbath, the Rabbis, and the Pharisees before them, prohibited handling even the implements used to do such work. Although talmudic sources consider this "fence" (*siyyag* in mishnaic Hebrew) a positive feature of rabbinic halakhah, the authors of the *Zadokite Fragments* oppose this approach, not only because they disagreed with the specific laws that resulted but also because they did not accept expanding the law in this manner in the first place.

That the differences of opinion between the sect and the Pharisees went to the heart of many *halakhot* is clear from this continued critique of the Pharisees:

> They even rendered impure their holy spirit and in blasphemous terms opened (their) mouth against the laws of the covenant of God, saying, "They are not correct." And they spoke abomination about them.
> (*ZADOKITE FRAGMENTS 5:11–13*)

To the sectarians, the Pharisaic polemic was not only fierce, but worse—an abomination.

We find another mention of the Pharisees' lack of understanding, here again referring to them as "builders of the wall," later in the *Zadokite Fragments:*

> All these things the builders of the wall and the daubers of plaster did not understand. For one who raises wind and preaches falsehood preached to them, because of which God became angry with His entire congregation. (*ZADOKITE FRAGMENTS 8:12–13; cf. 19:24–26*)

As a result:

> Since He hated the builders of the wall, He became angry. (*ZADOKITE FRAGMENTS 8:18; cf. 19:31*)

When false preachers—"windbags"—stirred up the people with their false message, God's anger blazed against them, causing the people of Israel to suffer.

Over and over again in the scrolls, the sect characterizes Pharisaic halakhah by its tendency to derive laws not directly from scriptural sources but through their own interpretations. In this spirit the Pharisees are called *dorshe halaqot*, literally "seekers after smooth things," but correctly translated "interpreters of false laws." This phrase is based upon the biblical expression "smooth things," referring to lies or falsehood, as in "Speak to us falsehoods" (Isaiah 30:10).

Dorshe halaqot puns on the Hebrew *dorshe halakhot*, "interpreters of the laws." The use of this pun in Qumran texts indicates that the term *halakhot* (laws) was already in use in Pharisaic circles. During this period, Pharisaic teaching was indeed distinguished by traditions and laws not having a direct basis in Scripture, a body of law called by the Pharisees the "traditions of the fathers" or "elders." Thus, the Pharisaic laws certainly included nonbiblical laws.

On the first page of the Admonition, the *Zadokite Fragments* clearly refers to the Pharisees when speaking of the followers of the Man of Scoffing, apparently some Pharisaic leader:

> . . . they interpreted false laws (*dareshu be-halaqot*) and chose delusions, and sought out breaches (opportunities to violate the law), and chose luxury, and declared innocent the guilty and declared guilty the innocent; and they violated the covenant and annulled the law, and banded together against the soul of the righteous. (*ZADOKITE FRAGMENTS 1:18–20*)

Here the Pharisees are accused of following those false laws, finding ways around the requirements of the law, and pronouncing false verdicts in legal cases—practices leading to the virtual annulment of Jewish law in the view of the sect. Indeed, the very existence of such laws constitutes an annulment of the Torah, because it replaces Torah laws with the laws of the Pharisees.

It may be that the *Thanksgiving Hymns* refers to the Pharisees when it speaks of the author's adversaries:

> They planned evil (literally, "Belial") against me to replace Your Torah which You taught in my heart with smooth things (i.e., false laws) (which they taught) to Your people. (*THANKSGIVING HYMNS 4:10–11*)

To the sect, the very notion of adding laws to the divinely given laws of the Torah was forbidden. They permitted themselves to derive laws from the Torah only by means of inspired exegesis, discovering what they termed the "hidden" laws.

Similar ideas about the Pharisees are discussed in *Pesher Nahum*. We have already noted that this text as a whole cannot be dated earlier than the last years of the Hasmonaean period. For our purposes here, one phrase in this text is extremely important. In the course of interpreting Nahum 3:4, "Because of the countless harlotries of the harlot . . . who ensnared nations with her harlotries," *Pesher Nahum* states:

> [Its] interpretation [con]cerns those who lead Ephraim astray, whose falseness is in their teaching (talmud), and whose lying tongue and dishonest lip(s) lead many astray. (*PESHER NAHUM 3–4 II, 8*)

Elsewhere in this text we discover that Ephraim is a code word, symbolizing the Pharisees. (Menasseh represents the Sadducees.) There is no question that our author is referring to them in this passage.

At the beginning, the text refers to "those who lead Ephraim astray," that is, the leaders and teachers of the Pharisees. The text likens them to the harlot mentioned in Nahum 3:4; their offense is teaching falsely. The text refers to their teaching by the Hebrew term "talmud," the same word later used to designate the "Talmud," the rabbinic work also known as the Gemara, the commentary and discursive discussion on the Mishnah.

In the early years of scrolls study, some scholars argued that the presence of this Hebrew word in the text proved the Karaite origins of the scrolls and the medieval dating of the material. Unfortunately, they mistakenly took "talmud" here to refer to the later rabbinic text by the same name.

Yet the matter is even more complex. In early rabbinic literature, the term "talmud" referred to the Pharisaic-rabbinic method of study that allows the deduction of laws from one another. It is precisely that method of study that the sectarians are excoriating in this text. What this scroll text proves is that such a method of legal argumentation already existed in the Hasmonaean period, at least in the latter half.

If both the Pharisees and the Qumran sect deduced laws from the Torah, why then was the former's method considered illegitimate by the latter? After all, interpretation of the Bible underlay the legal traditions of both groups. How precisely did they differ?

Apparently, a substantial difference did exist between these two modes of interpretation. Although the method, known as "talmud," used by the Pharisees in this period certainly seemed to yield laws derived from biblical exegesis, the Pharisees did not regard such exegesis as divinely inspired. They may have readily acknowledged the involvement of human interpretive creativity in the process, perpetrating, in the sect's view, further falsehood. Even more serious, the laws resulting from the Pharisaic method of "talmud" did not agree with those of the sectarians.

The Sadducees

Unfortunately, the scrolls give us much less direct material about the legal theology of the Sadducees than about the Pharisees. We can only tentatively sketch the outlines of their point of view by using material from the scrolls. Our sources are so indirect that we have no choice but to start with the evidence of Josephus:

> For the moment I wish only to explain that the Pharisees had passed on to the people certain regulations handed down by former generations and not recorded in the Law of Moses, for which reason they are rejected by the Sadducean group, who say that only those regulations should be considered obligatory which were written down (in Scripture), and that those which had been handed down by the fathers should not be observed. And regarding these matters the two parties came to have disputes and serious differences . . .
> (Antiquities 13, 297–298)

Like the sectarians, the Sadducees rejected the nonbiblical laws of the Pharisees. It is not that the Sadducees did not have their own interpretations of the Bible; what they rejected were regulations with no scriptural basis.

The only way we can corroborate this information in the Qumran material is to posit a series of probable assumptions. As we have already seen, the *Halakhic*

Letter, Miqṣat Ma'ase ha-Torah, reflects the view of the sect's Sadducean fore-runners, who could not accept the Maccabean takeover of the high priesthood and the attendant Pharisaic influence in the Temple. In several cases, laws mentioned in rabbinic sources in the name of the Sadducees appear there as those espoused by the authors, who are the founders of the Qumran sect. Because a number of laws in the *Halakhic Letter* are similar to the presectarian sources of the *Temple Scroll,* we can generally conclude that the sources of the *Temple Scroll* represent teachings of the Sadducees, arguing for their beliefs and interpretations regarding the Temple.

If this theory is correct, and it is still only a theory, then the approach by the author of the *Temple Scroll* to the questions we have been discussing would indicate to us something about the Sadducean point of view. If the *Temple Scroll,* Josephus, and rabbinic sources all agree, we can at least consider this theory to be logical. Let us investigate this line of reasoning to try to derive a probable set of Sadducean principles on the issues of divine revelation and the provenance of extrabiblical laws. It is to this difficult task that we now turn.

In the *Temple Scroll* we find a point of view very different from either the Pharisaic materials or the sectarian documents from Qumran. Essentially, the approach used by this author (or by the author's sources to the extent that they can be isolated) is to regard all laws as derived from a onetime experience of revelation at Sinai. In order to make this point, the author carefully weaves together his own legal views so that they seem to speak in the language of the Torah. Even when the author has no choice but to compose entire sections himself, he does so through imitation so as to present both the canonical Torah and his own Torah as if constituting one divine revelation. Indeed, even the intermediacy of Moses is eliminated so that the revelation of the Torah to Israel is direct. Furthermore, by rewriting the Torah in a certain manner, the author eliminates the impression that there was a series of revelations. After all, the Torah itself speaks of revelations at Sinai, on the plains of Moab, and in the Tent of Meeting. But to this author all is from God—even the author's own interpretations—and the laws were presented all at once at Sinai.

In contrast to the other two approaches we have encountered, this text does not recognize any other body of material—interpretive, traditional, or otherwise. What to us is clearly the author's interpretation is presented here as God's Torah itself. Such an approach is probably closest to that of the Sadducees. If so, we can now conclude that the Sadducean legal system accepted only laws regarded as actually implicit in the Torah, which were seen as integral to the Sinaitic Torah and directly revealed by God. Although we cannot know for sure whether the views expressed in the *Temple Scroll* are totally Sadducean or merely close to the Sadducean approach, it is clear that thanks to this document and the *Halakhic Letter* we are a lot closer to Sadducean views than ever before.

Halakhic Letter The text of the *Halakhic Letter* was
reconstructed by Qimron from six fragmentary copies. These
fragments of manuscript C concern laws pertaining to the
impurity of skin diseases, purification rituals, condemnation of
sexual immorality, and mixed marriages. On matters such as
these, the laws within this document were often in agreement
with those in the *Temple Scroll*, and both texts polemicized
against the views of the Pharisees. *Courtesy of the Israel
Antiquities Authority.*

All Jewish groups in the Second Temple period tried to assimilate extrabiblical
teachings into their way of life. The Dead Sea sect did so through the concept of
the *nigleh* ("revealed") and *nistar* ("hidden"). All Jews were permitted access to
the revealed, that is, the simple meaning of Scripture and its explicit commandments. Only the sect possessed the hidden knowledge, discovered through inspired biblical exegesis, regularly conducted by members of the sect. Tradition
had no authority, since all Israel had gone astray. The true way had only been rediscovered by the sect's teacher. The rules and the interpretations upon which
the rules were based taught the sect how to follow the Torah correctly in the
present, premessianic age.

On the other hand, the Pharisees observed traditions "handed down by the
fathers" as well as "unwritten laws." These included various legal traditions of

great antiquity as well as interpretations of the biblical texts. Indeed, the Pharisees were known as expounders of the Torah and seem to have excelled in the application of the laws of the Torah to their own circumstances and times. Somewhat later, the successors to the Pharisees, the early Rabbis, the teachers of the Mishnah, would stress that these traditions had been revealed by God to Moses on Sinai as a second Torah. Thus, the Rabbis asserted, God had given two Torahs to Israel, the written and the oral. For the Rabbis, this view essentially elevated the oral Torah to a sanctity and authority equal to that of the written.

The common claim that the Sadducees were strict literalists represents a misunderstanding of their approach, to a great extent predicated on late rabbinic sources and on a parallel misunderstanding of the medieval Karaite movement. The Sadducees apparently regarded only the written law as authoritative, although they admitted the need to interpret it. Their interpretations attempted to adhere as closely as possible to the plain meaning of Scripture.

Against this background, we can now understand the approach of the author/redactor of the *Temple Scroll*. Seeking to assimilate extrabiblical traditions, the author contends that his new, rewritten Torah properly expresses the will of God as revealed in the original document. The author further claims that the correct meaning of the divine revelation at Sinai, apparently left vague in the canonical Torah, is to be found in the *Temple Scroll*. Thus, like the sectarians of Qumran, the author has no dual Torah concept such as that of the Rabbis. Neither does he accept the sectarian notion of a continuous, inspired revelation through biblical exegesis. Rather he affirms only a onetime revelation at Sinai of a single Torah, the true contents of which are expressed in the scroll he has authored and redacted. We will now take a closer look at this scroll and its unique system of law and biblical interpretation.

CHAPTER 16

The Enigma of
the *Temple Scroll*

The *Temple Scroll* of cave 11, at 28.5 feet (8.75 meters) the longest of the preserved Qumran scrolls, consists of nineteen sheets, mostly of three or four columns each. The handwriting of the scroll, the work of two different scribes, is clear and unbroken except for some damaged or missing lines on the top edges. Although much research has been done on this scroll, its place in the sectarian corpus still remains somewhat enigmatic.

The author/redactor* of this scroll called for a thoroughgoing revision of the existing Hasmonaean order, advocating its replacement with a Temple, sacrificial system, and government representing his own understanding of the law of the Torah. This author's rather utopian vision is expressed in a section called the Law of the King (*Temple Scroll* 56:12–59:21). Since this section is incorporated into the fully redacted scroll, we can safely date the scroll as a whole no earlier than the second half of the reign of John Hyrcanus, to which the scroll's polemics apply. That would yield a date sometime after 120 B.C.E.

THE *TEMPLE SCROLL* AND THE QUMRAN CORPUS

The scribal techniques and script of the *Temple Scroll* are typical of the other Qumran manuscripts. It has even been suggested that sect members may have regarded this scroll as "a veritable Torah of the Lord," since the divine name is written in the same square script as the rest of the scroll, characteristic only of the canonical biblical books found at Qumran. Yet in certain linguistic features and in its legal terminology, the scroll exhibits more affinities to rabbinic Hebrew than do most of the sectarian scrolls.

Significantly absent from the *Temple Scroll* are the polemical language and

---

* We use this term to designate the final compiler of the scroll, who edited and revised (redacted) a variety of sources available to him and then authored new material on his own as well.

terminology distinctive to the Qumran group. The *Temple Scroll* does not mount a sustained polemic against the priestly establishment in Jerusalem with which the sect argued. And as we have already seen, the underlying theological principle for deriving law in the *Temple Scroll* is different from that found in the rest of Qumran literature and from the other contemporary systems of Jewish law. It is likely that this view is linked with that of the Sadducees, for it appears that Sadducean sources form a substratum to parts of the scroll. If so, it may be that this kind of approach is synonymous with the Sadducean denial of Oral Law. The Sadducees, like our author, may have believed that the Torah revealed the whole law to those who understood it properly. Hence, they would have denied notions of dual or continuous revelation, instead claiming that their own views had in fact already been revealed at Sinai as part of the written Torah given to Israel by God.

The *Temple Scroll* concerns matters that are, for the most part, not treated elsewhere in the scrolls. Although the sacrificial service and the sanctuary were not part of the life of the sect, the scroll nonetheless seeks to define their details. Ironically, the *Temple Scroll* is curiously silent about carrying on Temple practice through observing ritual purity in everyday life, a central concern of the sect.

From the earliest analysis of this scroll, scholars have been aware of some commonality between the law in this scroll and that revealed in the *Zadokite Fragments*. Yet they have also noted startling incongruities between the two texts, such as in the laws of idolatry or oaths and vows. Those incongruities, along with other evidence, have led to the conclusion that the *Temple Scroll* cannot be identified simply as a Qumran sectarian document.

How can we explain the relationship of this enigmatic scroll to those authored by the Dead Sea sect? How can we account for the silence of the *Temple Scroll* on precisely those matters that were of greatest concern to the sect? It is probable that despite its presence at Qumran and its many similarities to the sectarian literature, the *Temple Scroll* was not authored by members of the sect. Ever since its publication, I have suggested that the *Temple Scroll* may have emerged from a related group either contemporary with or earlier than the Qumran sect. Other scholars have sought to place it much earlier, which in my view confuses elements of the source material with the completed scroll. And so the enigma remains. To this day, we still do not know who wrote the scroll or why. Neither do we know how it made its way to the Qumran caves.

CONTENTS OF THE *TEMPLE SCROLL*

The scroll presents itself as a rewritten Torah, beginning with the renewal of the Sinaitic covenant of Exodus 34 and then turning to the building of the Temple in Exodus 35. After these two chapters, the scroll continues in the order of the canonical Torah. In this document, the author/redactor tried to compose a com-

Temple Scroll Deterioration of the tops of the columns of the *Temple Scroll* has led to the need to restore large parts of the first six to eight lines of each column. In many sections, parts of the text adhered to adjacent columns, and the writing was read by combining traces from the front and back of the scroll. This damaged passage details the sacrificial procedure for the ordination of priests, a ceremony that was to be performed annually according to the scroll. *Photograph by Bruce and Kenneth Zuckerman, West Semitic Research. Courtesy of the Shrine of the Book of the Israel Museum.*

plete Torah that expounded his views on the sanctity of the Temple, the land, and the Jewish people, as well as on his ideal conception of government and society. Working through the Torah in order, he gathered all the pertinent material at the first occurrence of a topic. In this way he reedited and reredacted legislation of the Pentateuch, inserting at the appropriate places the preexistent collections of laws at his disposal. To give the impression that his Torah was a complete body of law, he appended at the end a selection of laws from Deuteronomy, some of which deal only tangentially with the theme of his scroll. This collection is not simply a paraphrase of Scripture. Rather, it includes numerous halakhic and exegetical changes, as well as full-blown midrashic interpretations.

After the introductory columns, the *Temple Scroll* continues by discussing the structure, furnishings, and equipment of the Temple, according to the order of the Torah, and the offerings involved with these items. In the process, it covers the architecture of the Temple and its precincts, the laws of sacrifice, priestly dues and tithes, the ritual calendar, Festival offerings, ritual purity and impurity, the sanctity of the Temple, the laws of the king and the army, prophecy, foreign worship, witnesses, the laws of war, and various marriage and sex laws.

However, this "new Torah" never claims to be messianic. The author tells us explicitly that the scroll describes the Temple in which Israel will worship before the End of Days:

> These [you shall offer to the Lord at your Festivals, besides your votive and freewill offerings] for your burnt offerings and your libations [. . .] in the Temple upon which I [cause] My name [to dwell . . .], the burnt offerings [of each day] on that day, according to the law of this regulation, always from the children of Israel . . . , which they shall bring Me for acceptance for th[em]. And I will accept them, and they will be My people, and I will be their (God) forever. [And] I will dwell with them forever and ever. And I will sanctify My [Te]mple with My presence when I cause My presence to dwell on it, until the Day of Blessing (or: of Creation) when I will create My Temple, to establish it for Me for all times, according to the covenant which I made with Jacob at Bethel. *(Temple Scroll 29:2–10)*

This is an ideal Temple, built upon the principles of scriptural interpretation and the beliefs of the author or authors. The text expects that this Temple will be replaced in the End of Days (the Day of Blessing or Creation) with a divinely created sanctuary, as God had promised Jacob at Bethel when he dreamed his vision of the ladder (Genesis 28:10–22). Until that time, this scroll represents the correct way to build and operate the Temple.

The scroll also demonstrates a distinct form of harmonistic exegesis, in some ways similar to the Midrash of the later Rabbis, employed to reconcile the differences between the various texts of the Pentateuch so as to create a unified and consistent whole. At times, it makes minor additions to clarify its legal stance. In a few places, extensive passages appear that are not based on our canonical Scriptures. In this way the scroll presents its own views on the major issues of Jewish law. It is this exegetical and legal approach that makes the *Temple Scroll* so central for understanding the history of Jewish law and midrashic interpretation. In addition, the scroll contains allusions to contemporary events, shedding valuable light on the sects of the Second Temple period.

Although the authors of the various sources as well as the author/redactor of the finished composition drew from the canonical Torah, it is clear that their textual substratum was not in all respects identical to the Masoretic text. In noting these innumerable minor variants in the substratum, we must be careful to distinguish these from the intentional changes made by the author or the author's sources to convey their halakhic or exegetical views.

Because he wanted to claim that the law had been handed down directly by God without the intermediacy of Moses, the author altered the commandments of Deuteronomy, wherein God speaks through Moses, but preserved the language of Exodus, Leviticus, and Numbers, wherein God speaks directly in the biblical text.

Many unique features distinguish the *Temple Scroll* from other biblical or Second Temple literature. The architecture of the Temple proposed here differs from biblical accounts—although the author claims to base himself on those accounts—as well as from descriptions of the Second Temple in Josephus and the Mishnah. Most interesting is the extension of the "Temple City" to encompass a third courtyard, so large that it would have encompassed most of what was then Jerusalem.

In addition, the sacrificial Festival calendar includes a number of festivals not part of the biblical or rabbinic cycle. As mentioned in a previous chapter, a second New Year Festival is celebrated on the first of Nisan, in the spring, and it is followed by an annual celebration of the eight days of priestly ordination. Besides the Omer Festival for the barley harvest (the second day of Passover) and the first fruits of wheat (Shavuot), the scroll adds two more first-fruits Festivals, each at fifty-day intervals, for oil and wine. The wood offering is also celebrated as an annual Festival in the summer.

Extensive laws deal with the sacrificial procedure and with ritual purity and impurity. Here we see a general tendency to describe additional ways to protect the sanctuary from impurity. This brief survey does not even begin to represent the rich nature of the scroll's biblical interpretation and the many details of Jewish law in which the text diverges from the views of other sectarian documents or rabbinic literature.

Even in the scroll's present form, it is not difficult to discern that the *Temple Scroll* has been redacted from a number of sources, actually units or sections that the author/redactor knitted together. To these he added his own Deuteronomic paraphrase at the end (*Temple Scroll* 51:11–56:21, 60:1–66:17). In view of the parallels between the *Temple Scroll* and the *Halakhic Letter* and between both of these documents and descriptions of the Sadducees in rabbinic literature, it is most likely that the sources of the *Temple Scroll* stem from the Sadducean heritage of those who founded the sect.

If this is the case, we can reconstruct a variety of Sadducean laws not previously available to us. Further, if the polemics of the *Temple Scroll* are indeed directed against the views of the Pharisees, it would confirm the early dating of many Pharisaic-rabbinic laws known otherwise only from the later rabbinic corpus.

In addition, we learn from the *Temple Scroll* that the practice of interpreting

Scripture in order to derive Jewish law—what the Rabbis later called Midrash—was already a central part of the Judaism of the Hasmonaean period. This interpretive method produced highly developed legal teachings, demonstrating that among some groups of Second Temple Jews, strict adherence to a living and developing tradition of Jewish law was already normative.

The scroll also informs us about the views of those Jews who objected strenuously to the conduct of the Hasmonaeans in the religious, political, and military spheres. Opponents of the Hasmonaeans were at the forefront of the movement represented by the Qumran sect. Among the texts they brought with them to Qumran were the sources of the *Temple Scroll.*

Theology of the *Temple Scroll*

Certain basic theological notions, forming the core of all approaches to Judaism in Second Temple times, undergird much of what appears in this scroll. The author no doubt regarded these beliefs, which he appropriated from the Torah, as constituting a uniform theology. To the author and his sources, God is the creator, the ultimate legal authority, and the object of worship. However, we find here none of the characteristic theology of the Qumran sect: no dualism, determinism, or even messianism. Rather, the scroll makes explicit only a few specific theological notions that motivate the author's polemic against the dominant views of the Pharisees and of the reigning political and religious order in Hasmonaean Palestine.

Implicit in the literary style of the *Temple Scroll* is a theological claim about the authority of the laws presented here. Although the author derives his laws through a type of midrashic interpretation of the canonical (and, therefore, authoritative) Torah, he presents them as actually deriving directly from Sinaitic revelation. In one passage this notion is stated explicitly:

> And do not become impure by (contact with) those (sources of impurity) which I relate to you on this mountain. *(Temple Scroll 51:6–7)*

Although the passage refers directly only to purity regulations, it is unquestionable that the author/redactor regards his entire "Torah" as divine.

In order to emphasize this point, the text regularly excises Moses from the picture, constantly rewriting the scriptural text to eliminate Moses as intermediary. In one passage the author/redactor seems to have slipped, allowing an indirect reference:

> And the en[tire] right side of the gate of Levi and its left side you shall apportion to the sons of Aaron, your brother. *(Temple Scroll 44:5–6)*

But the overall picture presents God directly revealing the author's legal views to the entire people standing at Sinai.

The *Temple Scroll* begins with the covenant between God and Israel found in Exodus 34:10–16. The Land of Israel is to be given by God to Israel as part of a covenant requiring separation from the nations and from their idolatrous practices:

> [For that which I] am do[ing for you is awe-inspiring. I am about to drive out from before you] the A[morites, the Canaanites, the Hittites, the Girgash]ites, the Pe[rizzites, the Hivites, and the Jebusites. Take c]are of yourself, lest you enter a cove[nant with the inhabitants of the land] to whom [you are] going lest they become a sn[are among you]. *(TEMPLE SCROLL 2:1–5)*

The scroll emphasizes that Israel's tenure on the land is conditional on its avoidance of idolatry. Perhaps the author identified idolatry with Hellenism, intending to polemicize against the Hellenizing tendencies already observable under John Hyrcanus (134–104 B.C.E.) and Alexander Janneus (104–76 B.C.E.). It was during the reign of one of these kings that the *Temple Scroll* was compiled. Alternatively, the original source on which the scroll is based may have been targeting the extreme Hellenizers of the early second century B.C.E. But of course in the original biblical text, the dangerous idolators were the Canaanites.

Basing itself on passages in Exodus and Deuteronomy, the text continues:

> [Indeed] you must tear down their [altar]s, [smash their] pillars, cut down their [Asherim], and [burn] the graven images of [their] god[s with fire. You must n]ot covet (their) silver or gold, les[t you be ensnared by it, for it is an abomination to Me. You may not] take of it, so that you do not bri[ng (this) abomination into your house and become] accursed like it. (Rather,) you shall utterly dete[st and abhor it, for] it is an accursed thing. *(TEMPLE SCROLL 2:5–15)*.

These words are in reality no more than an explicit quotation from the Bible. Probably the author has here chosen to stress pure monotheism to protest the syncretism inherent in the views of the more Hellenized Jewish groups.

At the top of column 3 (which is missing from the scroll) may have stood some adaptation of Exodus 25:8, "And you shall make Me a sanctuary so that I can dwell in their midst," commanding the Jews to build the Temple. This notion is certainly one of the major themes of the scroll, derived from Deuteronomy 12:10–11. Here the scroll specifically commands that when the enemies of Israel give them rest in the land which God has given them, then they shall build the Temple in the place where God shall choose to place His name, that is, the sacred place of God's presence. This new Temple, the fulfillment of God's command in Deuteronomy, is to be even more perfect than the Temple of Solomon. It is this Temple alone that will be appropriate for the indwelling of God's presence.

The notion of this perfect Temple, repeated numerous times in all sections of the scroll, most probably represents the ideology of the author/redactor who imposed it upon his sources, or it may have been an idea already shared by all the sources used in the composition of the *Temple Scroll*.

The main purpose of this text is to prescribe the sacrificial worship that may take place in this Temple and nowhere else. The author of the *Temple Scroll* stresses that only if sacrifices are conducted according to the particular ritual calendar of the text, including its added Festivals dependent on the solar calendar, will God cause His name, that is, His presence, to dwell in the Temple. The sacrifices are intended to bring God's favor upon Israel, both strengthening the bond between God and His people and bringing about atonement for transgression.

The sacrificial rites outlined here are intended for the present age and the present Temple. In the End of Days, God will create a new Temple to replace the present one. Such a Temple is actually mentioned in *Florilegium* 1:2–3, where it is distinguished from that of the present age.

Ritual Purity and the Presence of the Lord

In an independent literary unit, the *Temple Scroll* presents a series of purity regulations, consisting of laws designed to insure the purity of the Temple precincts and the land (columns 46–47). The passage sets out the need for a barrier, apparently consisting of a wide, empty space of about 150 feet (45.75 meters), located beyond the Temple structure:

> And you shall construct a barrier around the sanctuary one hundred cubits wide which shall divide between the holy sanctuary and the city, so that they will not enter suddenly into the midst of My sanctuary, so that they not profane it. And they shall consider My sanctuary holy and revere My sanctuary because I dwell in their midst. (TEMPLE SCROLL 46:9–12)

This barrier was intended to separate the Temple and its courtyards from the rest of the Temple Mount. Its function was to ensure the holiness of the three courtyards surrounding the Temple. The text specifically informs us why it is needed: so that the Temple (here the entire precincts) will not be defiled by sudden entry into the courtyards.

In this context, the *Temple Scroll* articulates its notion of sanctity: the worshiper's awe of the sanctuary where God's indwelling presence resides. This presence and the sanctity it engenders radiate from the Temple to the rest of the Land of Israel, thus endowing it and the people who dwell on it with holiness and sanctity.

The scroll returns to this same theme in the next column:

> And the city which I will sanctify to cause My name and My sanctu[ary to dwell within it] shall be holy and pure from every type of impurity by which one can become impure. And everything which shall enter it shall be pure. (TEMPLE SCROLL 47:3–6)

The city in which God's presence dwells must be holy and free of all impurity. This law extends to everything in it and everything brought into it. The text goes

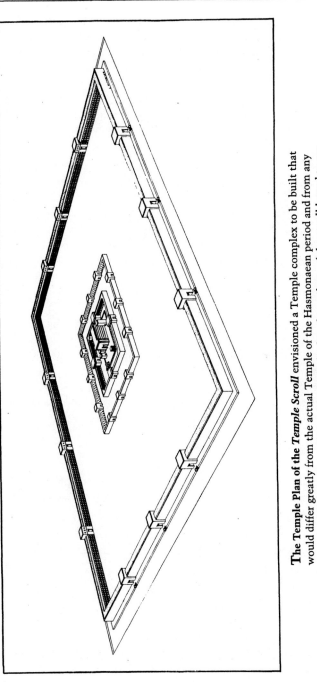

The Temple Plan of the *Temple Scroll* envisioned a Temple complex to be built that would differ greatly from the actual Temple of the Hasmonaean period and from any other Jewish Temple we know. The Temple that the authors of the scroll hoped to see built was of an ideal construction, intending to duplicate within Temple precincts the camp of Israel around the Tabernacle in the desert. It was to have three concentric courtyards, in addition to gates apportioned to all the tribes and priestly families. *Reconstruction copyright Leen Ritmeyer, Ritmeyer Archaeological Design.*

on to require the purity of foodstuffs and to prohibit bringing into the Temple area the skins of animals not sacrificially slaughtered, for it is impossible to expect that God will coexist with impurity of any kind.

Even the hides of animals made into bags or sacks for transporting goods must be pure:

> Therefore, all pure food for the Temple you shall bring in hides of (animals slaughtered in) the Temple so as not to render impure My Temple and My city, in which I dwell, with the hides of your abominations.
> (*Temple Scroll 47:17–18*)

The author, much like the compilers of the *Halakhic Letter*, carried on a sustained polemic against both the Hasmonaeans and the Pharisees. However, his polemic had a unique style. Instead of condemning his opponents and castigating them, the author/redactor articulated his ideas in the form of an imitation Torah so as to present those ideas as the word of God, revealed directly to Israel at Sinai.

Against the Hasmonaeans, in the section termed by scholars the Law of the King, he argued for a new system of government and for separation of the roles of kingship and priesthood. Against the Pharisees, he argued about numerous legal matters and interpretations of Scripture, sometimes espousing views we know to be Sadducean.

Yet his polemic went even further. He called for a new Temple building and for new settlement patterns as well. In discussing the Temple building, settlement patterns, and his approach to the Land of Israel, the author took a distinctly utopian view. His plan envisioned concentric spheres of holiness, beginning with the Temple complex at the center and extending outward to the tribal allotments, to the cities of Israel, and into the houses where the people dwelled. He was also concerned with the sanctity of the entire land as sacred space.

The Land of Israel and the Temple

The *Temple Scroll* claims that Israel is given the land only conditionally. In order for the people to merit the land, they must uphold the highest judicial standards. Bribery and corruption in judgment must be avoided:

> . . . in order that you live, and come and take (or: retain) possession of the land which I am giving you as a possession for ever. (*Temple Scroll 51:15–16*)

If they violate these principles, the land will experience destruction, and the people, exile. Only after repentance will Israel return again to its land (59:2–11).

For the author of the *Temple Scroll*, the center of the Land of Israel was the Temple and its surrounding complex. The scroll presents a Temple plan of very different proportions from that which existed in First or Second Temple times. This new Temple plan envisions the Temple building enclosed by three concentric courtyards. This Temple, of course, was never built.

The Inner Court (*Temple Scroll* 36:3–7) was to measure some 280 cubits square, with an outside dimension of 294 cubits. (A cubit is approximately one and a half feet or half a meter.) The gates of the Inner Court would be located on each of its four sides. By extrapolating from the apportionment of chambers on the inside wall of the Outer Court, we can surmise that these gates represented the four groups of the tribe of Levi: the Aaronide priests on the east, the Levites of Kohath on the south, Gershon on the west, and Merari on the north. This arrangement corresponds exactly to that of the desert camp as described in Numbers 3:14–39. The courtyards and their gates would represent the Israelite encampment in the wilderness. The entire Temple plan was intended to re-create the experience of the desert period, when sanctity radiated to all Israel from the sanctuary at its epicenter.

The Middle Court (*Temple Scroll* 38:12–15) was to surround the Inner Court, 100 cubits farther out, covering an area 480 cubits square, with three gates on each side. Each of the twelve tribes would have its own gate (*Temple Scroll* 39:11–13).

The Outer Court (*Temple Scroll* 40:5–11), a concentric enclosure surrounding the Middle Court with sides measuring some 1,600 cubits, would also have twelve gates corresponding exactly to those of the Middle Court. Equally important were the chambers in the outer wall that faced inward. These areas, three stories high, were to be apportioned to the various tribes as well as to the priestly and Levitical groups. Aaron was assigned two groups of chambers in recognition of his status as a sort of "ritual firstborn," entitling him to a double portion (*Temple Scroll* 40:13–45:2).

This unique Temple plan does not follow the plans of any of the biblical sanctuaries—either the Tabernacle, the Solomonic Temple, or the descriptions at the end of Ezekiel. Neither does it match the pre-Herodian or Herodian Second Temple structures. Rather, its layout represents a synthesis of the Tabernacle and the desert camp. Through this design, the architect sought to grant the tribes access to the Temple and even symbolic dwelling places for them within the Temple courtyards. Each tribe would enter the Temple precincts through its assigned gate and proceed first to its designated chambers. From there all members of the tribe or Levitical clan could circulate in the Outer Court. Those not disqualified from entry into the Middle Court could then proceed into that court, again through their respective gates. Only priests and Levites could proceed to the Inner Court through their gates where the Temple and its furnishings were located.

This entire plan envisions the Temple as the center of sanctity, accessible by entering further and further into the concentric spheres of holiness. The scroll repeatedly makes clear that what grants the Temple its special level of sanctity is the indwelling of the divine presence there. According to many passages throughout the text, God is to dwell in the Temple among the children of Israel forever.

This motif, expressed in all of the possible sources for the scroll, is among its most dominant themes.

Beyond the Temple City were a few installations designed to ensure the sanctity of the holy place. Among them would be the place for the latrines, constructed as "roofed houses with pits within them." These structures were to be located northwest of "the city," that is, the Temple City, at a distance of 3,000 cubits (46:13–16).

Further, the scroll requires (46:16–47:1) that outside the Temple City, specific locations be assigned to the east for three groups that are impure: those with the skin disease ṣaraʿat (usually mistranslated as "leprosy"), gonorrhiacs, and those who have had a seminal emission. The intention of the scroll is to locate the entire residential area of Jerusalem outside the Temple City. Those who came to Jerusalem in a state of impurity would not be allowed to enter the Temple until the seven-day purification rites were completed. They were to stay in these outside areas during the rituals, after which they could enter the Temple to offer their sacrifices in a state of purity.

Beyond the Temple City, which symbolized the desert camp, was the hinterland of Israel. There the territory of each tribe would be located, directly opposite its gate. Indeed, it was through these gates that the tribal territories would be tied to the sanctity of the central shrine and the divine presence that dwelled there.

We cannot be certain exactly how the tribal allotments were to be shaped. They may have been conceived as radiating from the epicenter, so that the tribes essentially dwelled in a circle around the Temple. Probably the scroll treated the Land of Israel as a square, with the tribes distributed in equivalent positions, each occupying square or rectangular areas. Only such a model could provide all the tribes with equal access to the Temple through their respective gates and at the same time accord with the scroll's predilection to square structures.

Since the author expected all the tribes of Israel to dwell in the land as ideally constituted, it appears that he assumed the return of the lost tribes, although this is nowhere stated directly. Throughout the scroll, in numerous cultic and other contexts, the twelve tribes as a whole play a role corresponding to that reflected in the architecture of the Temple and the apportionment of the land. In this respect, the Temple functions as a microcosm of the Land of Israel, with each tribe having its appointed place in the sanctuary.

THE LAW OF THE KING

The collection of laws pertaining to the king constituted a separate unit that the author incorporated into the *Temple Scroll*. The text first discusses the obligation of setting up a monarchy:

> When you enter the land which I am giving you, and you take possession of it and dwell in it, and you say, "I will set a king over me like all the nations who are around me," you shall set as king over you the one whom I choose. (TEMPLE SCROLL 56:12-14)

This passage is virtually identical to Deuteronomy 17:14-15, except that, as is his general habit, the author or redactor has replaced the third person—"which the Lord your God is giving you"—with the first person, to suggest the unmediated authority of the text.

The requirement that a king be appointed is most likely intended as a critique of the early Hasmonaean rulers, who, while serving as high priests, arrogated to themselves the temporal powers of the king. Our passage requires that the monarchy and the high priesthood be two separate offices with two distinct incumbents.

The *Temple Scroll* goes on to require that the appointed king be Jewish and that he have written for him a special copy of the Torah for his edification. Adapting Deuteronomy 17:16-17, the scroll continues with a series of prescriptions that limit the power of the monarch:

> But he may not keep for himself many horses nor may he send the people back to Egypt for war in order to accumulate for himself horses, silver and gold. For I have said to you, "You may never go back that way again." Nor may he have many wives lest they turn his heart from following Me, nor may he accumulate for himself silver and gold to excess. (TEMPLE SCROLL 56:15-19)

Josephus gives us a hint about the dating of this section. He reports that the unrest in Syria "gave Hyrcanus leisure to exploit Judaea undisturbed, with the result that he amassed a limitless sum of money." No doubt Hyrcanus's extensive military campaigns outside the boundaries of Judaea also contributed to his wealth. It is likely that this text, in repeating here the Torah's law against the king's sending his people to war to increase his own wealth, is reacting to conditions during the period of John Hyrcanus.

The king is obligated to raise an army and provide a royal guard:

> He (the king) shall choose for himself from them (those he has mustered) one thousand from each tribe to be with him, twelve thousand warriors, who will not leave him alone, lest he be captured by the nations. And all those selected whom he shall choose shall be trustworthy men, who fear God, who spurn unjust gain, and mighty men of war. They shall be with him always, day and night, so that they will guard him from any sinful thing, and from a foreign nation, lest he be captured by them. (TEMPLE SCROLL 57:5-11)

The king is also required to select twelve thousand men, one thousand from each tribe, to serve as a palace guard. They must never leave him, lest he be captured by foreign enemies. The members of the guard are to be honest, God-fearing men, of the highest military prowess.

The author of this text may have based his number of twelve thousand men on the twelve thousand warriors who went out against the Midianites (Numbers 31:3–4) or the twelve thousand horsemen of Solomon (I Kings 5:6, 10:26). This description of the royal guard is in direct contrast to its Hasmonaean counterpart, which was manned by foreign mercenaries. The author requires for the royal guard not only trustworthy Jews but also those who will keep the king from transgressing. Apparently, the author is here criticizing the Hasmonaean rulers for being overly influenced by their foreign mercenaries.

The purpose of the guard was to prevent the capture of the king. These elaborate arrangements for the royal guard only make sense against the background of the last days of Jonathan the Hasmonaean ruler—namely, the years 152–143 B.C.E.—who while traveling with three thousand guards, was captured by Trypho, a Seleucid pretender, and later murdered.

The *Temple Scroll* further required that the king constitute a council of twelve princes, twelve priests, and twelve Levites to consult in matters of judicial rulings (*Temple Scroll* 57:11–15). He is forbidden to act without their advice. Historical sources inform us that a council of elders functioned in Judaea both before and after Maccabean times. To ensure the influence of religious leaders in government, the *Temple Scroll* here requires the inclusion of priests and Levites. A further passage mandates that the king may not pervert the system of justice nor confiscate any of his subjects' property unlawfully (*Temple Scroll* 57:19–21).

The Law of the King concludes with an admonition. A king who turns aside from God's laws will find his kingdom taken from him. But as for the king who observes the Torah and rules justly:

> . . . none of his sons shall be cut off from sitting on the throne of the kingdom of Israel forever. I will be with him, and I will save him from the hand of his enemies and from the hand of those who seek to take his life.
> (*Temple Scroll 59:17–19*)

Here the author, pronouncing the end of the royal line for a king who does not govern according to the Torah, clearly implicates the Hasmonaean dynasty.

In this scroll, compiled during the Hasmonaean period, the author/redactor presents his utopian vision of the present, premessianic era: an ideal Temple, located in the sacred Land of Israel, settled by the twelve tribes in their allotments. Such idealistic hopes are also reflected throughout other sections of the scroll, probably from preexistent Sadducean sources. Indeed, this overall plan expressed the author's dream of a complete reform of the polity and worship of the Jewish people in the Hasmonaean period.

The complete, edited scroll may be seen to a large extent as a polemic against the policies of the Hasmonaeans on the one hand and against the rulings of the Pharisees on the other. A similar polemic underlies the *Halakhic Letter*, confirming that Pharisaic rulings were being followed in the Temple in the early Hasmonaean period. Also composed during this period, the *Temple Scroll* called for a total reconstruction of the Temple and redistribution of the land around it, a rededication to strict purity laws, and the appointment of a high priest and a king who would uphold the holiness of the Temple and the Land of Israel. Only in this way, the author believed, would the future of Israel upon its land be guaranteed.

The scroll's plan, as we have examined it here, bears little relationship to the teachings of the Qumran sect as they are known from the sectarian texts. Further, the architecture of the Qumran structures reflects no attempt to follow any ideal blueprint. In this respect, the preceding study supports our general conclusion that some of the sources of the *Temple Scroll* are in fact pre-Qumranian and that the author/redactor, regardless of his own affiliation, was not reflecting the ideas of the Qumran sect.

It appears that the Sadducean sources of the scroll included laws dating back to pre-Maccabean days, a theory confirmed by comparing this scroll to the *Halakhic Letter*. Whatever may eventually be decided about the many enigmatic issues surrounding this scroll, it is clear that its final author truly believed that the observance of Jewish law and sacrificial ritual brought the worshiper into the presence of God. This belief, common to all expounders of Jewish law throughout the ages, certainly was shared by the compilers of the legal material of the Dead Sea sect, the subject of the next chapter.

CHAPTER 17

The Law of the Sect

We have already seen that the Qumran sect divided laws into two types: the revealed and the hidden. Because the revealed law, the Torah, was accessible to all Jews, the sectarians did not concern themselves with it very much. Therefore, following their lead, we will focus primarily on the hidden law.

From the moment of the sect's founding, legal issues played a pivotal role in determining the character and political fate of the group. The *Halakhic Letter* clearly demonstrates this. After the letter failed to achieve its aims, the sect went its own way, at some point relocating at Qumran. From that point on, the sect's halakhic views began to diverge from those of the Sadducean group, becoming distinct but retaining a link to the Sadducean texts and halakhic method, as evidenced in the *Halakhic Letter* and the *Temple Scroll*. We will now take a look at some of the laws transmitted in the sect's own documents.

THE LAWS OF THE SECT

A major source of Qumran legislation is the sectarian law code known as the *Zadokite Fragments*. But how can we be certain that this document, found in medieval copies and at Qumran, indeed represents the teachings of the Qumran sect? First, the sectarians themselves attached this code to the Admonition, a sort of sectarian manifesto outlining the early history of the sect and its basic arguments with the Jerusalem establishment. Second, the Laws—the legal section forming the second part of the *Zadokite Fragments*—frequently turns, without even a pause, from mention of laws applicable to all Jews to mention of regulations bearing exclusively on the organization and conduct of sectarian life. The considerable extent to which these two aspects are integrated in this text amply demonstrates that these laws represented the sect's views.

The nine copies of the *Zadokite Fragments* found at Qumran confirm the general reliability of the medieval copies of this text. At the same time, the Qumran manuscripts have doubled the size of the preserved text known to us. The new material has shown the same integration of halakhic and sectarian concerns.

Scholars have observed that the *Zadokite Fragments* reflects the way of life of satellite sectarian communities scattered throughout the country. No distinctions in religious law would have existed between these offshoot communities and the sectarian center at Qumran. In fact, we could even go one step further and assert that the law of the sect was part of a wider trend of Sadducean law. It is likely that many of these rulings were observed not only by the sectarians in and outside Qumran but also by other groups related in their legal tradition to the Sadducean priestly approach.

It is thus clear that the laws in the *Zadokite Fragments* and in the other sectarian legal documents did not all originate among the sectarians at Qumran. No doubt the sect's first members brought many of these laws into the newly formed group. And many of the laws may have been shared by other Jewish groups close to the Sadducean approach, the sect's source of origin. But it is difficult to establish the original provenance of these laws by studying the *Zadokite Fragments*, because the legal material is embedded in the literary framework of a sectarian text.

Numerous topics are covered in the fragments: oaths and admission to the community, witnesses, judges, court procedure, Sabbath regulations, ritual purity, and organizational issues relative to the community. This collection of laws was not intended to be complete, however. The text lists only a number of those laws that the sectarians wished to emphasize, perhaps those they felt were not being properly followed by the Jewish people as a whole.

Rule of the Community contains other legal materials, although these are vastly outnumbered by sectarian organizational regulations. That these sectarian laws are so similar in language, form, and content to those presented in the *Zadokite Fragments* proves beyond a doubt both that we are dealing here with the same group and that the sectarian laws are meant to function in the society described in the *Rule*. Although the *Zadokite Fragments* deals with the satellite communities while the *Rule* deals with the main center, together these texts describe a unified society living by common sectarian laws.

The *War Scroll*, a text that addresses eschatological matters, lists various laws pertaining to conscription into the army, purity of the camp, sacrificial worship, prayer, and thanksgiving rites. *Rule of the Congregation* concerns many halakhic aspects of the messianic age, including ritual purity, and presents an eschatological mirror image of the sect's current way of life. Because sectarians saw themselves as living on the verge of the End of Days, they sought to practice its laws in their present life. In a later chapter, we will take a look at aspects of the sect's messianic halakhah.

Other legal documents include calendar texts (often termed *Mishmarot*) describing the sect's calendrical calculations and listing the holy days. We can also glean valuable information from a number of prayer and ritual texts as well as tefillin (phylacteries) and other evidence of scribal law in the scrolls. A variety of important smaller texts reflects the same halakhic approaches as the larger ones.

To illustrate the sect's legal teachings and method, we will treat a few examples of these complex legal discussions in detail. In particular, we will examine topics addressed in two of the legal lists (*serakhim*): the Sabbath and issues of civil law. When we study these laws closely, we discover their remarkable similarity to the later topical codes of the mishnaic tractates. I also hope to convey here a sense of the complexity of this distinctive legal system and its process of legal interpretation. But since whole books have been written on this subject, I present the material here only to exemplify this singular system of Jewish law that sometimes harmonizes with and other times clashes with that of the later Rabbis. The ritual of the sect, including its calendar, prayers, tefillin, and mezuzot, will be treated in a separate chapter.

As we study sectarian law, it is important to keep in mind that the vast majority of Jewish laws and practices were shared by Torah-observing Jews of the Second Temple period; debates and even conflicts arose over only a small number of issues. That is why it is not surprising that here as well as elsewhere we find so much agreement.

THE SABBATH CODE

The Sabbath code, clearly marked as a discrete literary unit by its heading, is one of the primary legal sections in the *Zadokite Fragments*. It contains a list of laws—called a *serekh*. We will briefly discuss some of its laws, noting how these laws derive from the Torah and how they compare to the views of other Jewish groups, most importantly to the rabbinic tradition of halakhah

We begin with the first prescription in this code:

> No one shall do work on Friday from the time when the sphere of the sun is distant from the gate (by) its (the sun's) diameter, for this is (the import of) that which He said (Deuteronomy 5:12), "Observe the Sabbath day to sanctify it." (ZADOKITE FRAGMENTS 10:14–17 = D^e 10 V 1–3)

For ritual purposes, the Jewish day begins at sunset the night before. The Rabbis derived this approach from various scriptural sources. From the foregoing passage we learn that this understanding of the day was normative in Second Temple times. But sectarian law goes even further. The sect effectively agrees with the later talmudic sources requiring that the observance of the Sabbath begin even before actual sunset—that is, on Friday afternoon. According to most views in rabbinic literature, such a measure was only an added stringency, designed to show greater appreciation for the Sabbath by extending its beginning and end. But our text and one rabbinic opinion maintained that the Torah indeed *required* such an extension of the Sabbath. It is likely that in Second Temple times all Jews began the Sabbath early, when a set of trumpet blasts in Jerusalem announced the time to stop work. Even those who did not consider this precaution required by the Torah probably followed this practice in order to avoid accidentally violating the holy day.

This text has sparked a curious debate. One scholar has suggested that Sabbath in Qumran began on Saturday morning, a practice that would fit in with the solar calendar used by the sect. However, that theory flies in the face of the explicit prescription found in our Qumran Sabbath code. To account for the contradiction, the theory's advocates have claimed that a medieval copyist added this prescription to the *genizah* manuscripts of the *Zadokite Fragments*. But since the discovery of cave 4, especially since the release of these documents in 1991, it has become clear that this supposedly late medieval addition was unquestionably part of the original text (*Zadokite Fragments* D^e 10 V 1–3). Although one scholar has continued to promote the idea of a Saturday morning onset for the Sabbath, any fair reading of the text must acknowledge that the sectarians shared with the rest of the Jewish people the notion that the Sabbath began on Friday at sunset.

Two laws deal with Sabbath limits, meaning, the distance one is allowed to walk beyond the city limits on the Sabbath. The first law sets a general limit:

> Let him not walk about outside his city more than a thousand cubits.
> (*Zadokite Fragments* 10:21)

The medieval scribe was sufficiently surprised at the one thousand–cubit limitation that he wrote the last part of the sentence in large letters. Later on, the text includes a law specifying a two thousand–cubit limit, similar to that known from mishnaic law:

> No one shall walk after an animal to pasture it outside his city more than two thousand cubits. Let him not raise his hand to strike it with a fist. If it is stubborn let him not take it out of his house. (*Zadokite Fragments* 11:5–7)

According to the first text, on the Sabbath one was permitted to walk only one thousand cubits (about 1,500 feet or 450 meters) beyond the city limits. But the second text notes an exception: in order to pasture an animal, one could go another thousand cubits, reaching a total of two thousand cubits, about three thousand feet (900 meters).

These prescriptions are based on the prohibition of travel on the Sabbath found in the Book of Exodus, "Let everyone remain where he is: let no person leave his place on the seventh day" (Exodus 16:29). During the Second Temple period this verse was generally understood to prohibit long journeys. According to the third-century C.E. church father Hippolytus, the Essenes did not leave their beds on the Sabbath, a view not supported by earlier sources. Yet we do know that both Samaritans and Falashas refused to leave their home on the Sabbath, except to go to synagogue. Clearly, our sect did not subscribe to such a limiting interpretation of Exodus 16:29. Like the Rabbis, the sect allowed walking about within one's immediate city limits. What was debatable was how far and under what circumstances one might extend that limit.

The sect reached its decision about Sabbath limits through a kind of midrashic interpretation. We can conclude from the way these laws are formulated that they depend on an interpretation of Numbers 35:5, which sets out the boundaries of the Levitical cities, prescribed by the Torah as homes for the Levites. There we find an early version of urban planning, the requirement that areas be set aside for "town pasture" for animals.

This biblical passage specifies two limits for the size of the pastureland surrounding the cities: one thousand and two thousand cubits. Selecting the larger number, the Rabbis ruled that the limit for Sabbath travel was two thousand cubits. Therefore travel for all purposes was limited to that distance. Sectarian law, however, chose the stricter view, ruling that one could travel only one thousand cubits, except when one needed to pasture animals. To sectarians this interpretation seemed to accord completely with the Torah, because Numbers specifies two thousand cubits as the pasture area. Although the sectarians and the later Rabbis disagreed on this matter because of their different interpretive approaches, we see that they both based their legal rulings on this text from Numbers, applying to the question of Sabbath limits a case seemingly unrelated to Sabbath law.

A few regulations in this scroll are virtually identical to those in rabbinic law, suggesting that all Jewish groups in the Second Temple period shared the great bulk of Jewish law. One example is the following prescription about carrying on the Sabbath:

> No one shall carry (anything) from the house to the outside, or from the outside into (the) house. And if he is in the *sukkah*, let him not carry (anything) out of it or bring (anything) into it. (ZADOKITE FRAGMENTS 11:7–9)

As in rabbinic law, sectarian law prohibited carrying anything on the Sabbath from a private to public domain. This law is stated explicitly in Jeremiah 17:21 and 22: "Guard yourselves . . . against carrying burdens on the Sabbath day. . . . Nor shall you carry out burdens from your houses on the Sabbath day, or do any work. . . ." Here the sectarians derived their law from prophetic texts, whereas the Rabbis stretched to avoid using this passage.

Formulating the law in its own words, the sect added here the case of the *sukkah*, referring either to any temporary dwelling or, more likely, to the *sukkah* connected with the Festival of Sukkot. This Festival posed a particular problem for those who abstained from carrying on the Sabbath, as it still does today: when the *sukkah* is in a field, or in a yard next to the house, it constitutes a separate domain; therefore, food cannot be carried from the house to the *sukkah*. For rabbinic Jews, the solution to this problem lies in the *eruv*, a legal institution designed to create a wider "home" by enclosing large areas and designating a loaf of bread as a symbolic common meal, thereby making carrying permissible on the Sabbath. Did Qumran sectarians accept this procedure? Talmudic sources tell us that the Sadducees did not. Unfortunately, our sources simply do not provide this information. But certainly the Pharisees, Sadducees, and Qumran sectarians all agreed that carrying from domain to domain was forbidden on the Sabbath.

In the headlong rush by many scholars to compare the scrolls to the New Testament, the halakhic material has been generally ignored. Yet a number of laws demonstrate that the views of the sectarians were very different from those of the early Christians as recorded in the New Testament. One such case is the following:

> No one shall deliver an animal on the Sabbath day. And if it fall into a cistern or a pit, one may not lift it out on the Sabbath. (ZADOKITE FRAGMENTS 11:13–14)

This text deals with two similar cases, both involving the question of whether one can set aside or otherwise relax the Sabbath laws to aid an animal on the Sabbath. Both cases concern issues about caring for domesticated animals on the Sabbath.

The prohibition against delivering a newborn animal on the Sabbath applies specifically to removing the fetus from the uterus. This action is prohibited by rabbinic law. In fact, the Rabbis prohibited any other help to the animal on the Sabbath. In this case, the Qumran sectarians agreed with rabbinic halakhah. Although both the sectarians and the Rabbis set aside the Sabbath restrictions to save a human life, including providing aid during childbirth, they did not set these restrictions aside for the benefit of animals.

The second part of this law concerns an issue apparently common in the agrarian everyday life of Second Temple times: animals that have fallen into pits. The Rabbis ruled that if an animal falls into a pit on the Sabbath, it should be given food to keep it alive. The later talmudic sages understood this ruling even to permit placing pillows or other devices there to allow the animal to climb out.

But rabbinic law still prohibited lifting the animal out of the pit, even if its life were endangered by remaining there. If rising water in the pit threatened to drown the animal, the case assumed here by the later Rabbis, it would be no different from the case of an animal's giving birth, during which the life of both the mother and the offspring was at risk. The ruling was still the same: Sabbath rules could not be suspended or relaxed to save an animal.

Qumran Cistern Essential to the complex water system that made life possible at Qumran was a series of large cisterns. They were lined with plaster and usually were built with stairs to allow easy access. We have to assume that they were covered with reed mats or similar devices to prevent evaporation. *Photograph by Lawrence H. Schiffman.*

In this matter, the sectarians again agreed with the view expressed in later rabbinic texts. But the New Testament indicates that the early Christians disagreed, perhaps reflecting a more lenient view common among other Palestinian Jews in this period. We know from Matthew 12:11 and Luke 14:5 that early Christian tradition considered it acceptable to draw animals directly out of a pit on the Sabbath. In this case, the sectarians and the Rabbis agreed; the sectarians and early Christians did not.

Closely related to this issue is the question of violating the Sabbath to save a human life. Did the sectarians accept such violation as permissible? This issue, long under debate, can at last be resolved with the help of the newly released cave 4 documents. The text of the medieval manuscript of the *Zadokite Fragments*, partly confirmed by a Qumran manuscript and in one case slightly emended, reads:

And as to any human being who falls into a place of water or into a reservoir,
let no one bring (him) up with a ladder, rope, or instrument.
(Zadokite Fragments 11:16–17 = D' 3 I 10–11 = D' 10 V 19–20)

If one looks at this text with no preconceptions, it appears to outlaw setting aside
the Sabbath restrictions to save a life. Apparently one may not use tools and
equipment normally forbidden for Sabbath use even to save a life, for then one
would be engaged in forbidden labor. Most scholars, including myself, have
always refused to accept this understanding of the Qumran law, because it is so
antithetical to the spirit of Judaism. Furthermore, the context of this law suggests
that the sect did in fact accept violation of the Sabbath to save a life, because it is
presented in contrast to the ruling immediately preceding, which forbids relaxing
Sabbath rules in the case of an animal.

The idea of setting aside the Sabbath is a pillar of rabbinic Sabbath law. The
Bible says about the laws of the Torah, "by the pursuit of which man shall live"
(Leviticus 18:5), meaning that the commandments were given to ensure life, not
to bring death. Further, the Rabbis, enlisting additional support from various
verses, argued that it was better to violate one Sabbath in order to make sure that
many more would be observed.

This principle was promoted by the Maccabees after a group of Hasidim
(pietists) gave their lives early in the Maccabean Revolt rather than defend themselves on the Sabbath. Refusing to handle work-related equipment to block the
entrances to their hiding places, the Hasidim proved that they regarded this prohibition as inviolable (I Maccabees 2:29–41). After the revolt, this law seems to
have been firmly in place among virtually all Jewish groups.

To establish that the sect refused to violate the Sabbath to save a life, some
scholars have argued that this law did not specifically concern using equipment,
but rather was listing the ways people were usually saved. In effect, they regarded
this law as a blanket prohibition against saving people. I have argued in response
that what the law demanded was that one should not use those prohibited articles—ladder, rope, or tool—to save the life, but if possible should find another
means that would not require setting aside the Sabbath rules concerning these
tools. When I initially made my arguments, I was criticized for being apologetic
and for harmonizing the sect's laws with rabbinic sources. However, when the
documents from cave 4 began to appear, I learned that I had been proven correct.
Among the cave 4 fragments is a text called *Serekh-Damascus*. This document,
an interesting piece of evidence about the history of sectarian literature, brings
together some of the laws in the *Zadokite Fragments* with the Penal Code of
Rule of the Community. In addition, it contains other laws not known from
other texts. Its composite nature demonstrates that sectarian law was a living,
developing phenomenon constantly giving rise to new compilations of lists of

laws (*serakhim*). In this document we find a parallel to the Sabbath code we have been studying:

> And if it is a human being who falls in[to] the water on the Sabbath [day,] he (the rescuer) should extend to him his garment to bring him up with it, but he should not pick up an instrument. (*SEREKH-DAMASCUS 7 I*)

Here we see the rescue prescribed according to the sectarian legal system; the sectarians do in fact believe that the Sabbath is to be set aside to save a life. The text contrasts this ruling with the preceding lines, which, as in the text of the *Zadokite Fragments*, concern an animal, which is not to be saved on the Sabbath. As I had originally suggested, the rescue was to be accomplished without the use of forbidden utensils, if possible. But if such utensils provided the only way to save a person's life, we can be certain that the sect would have allowed their use. In this passage, sectarians were simply proposing that this be avoided—if at all possible.

Parenthetically it may be noted that here again we have come upon an incongruity between the sectarian approach and that of the early Christians. The New Testament (Matthew 12:1–8, cf. Mark 2:23–28) regards even feeding the hungry as a form of "saving of life," permitted on the Sabbath. It argues that this positive commandment sets aside the negative one, that is, violating the Sabbath. In this case, the early Christians were the most lenient, but the Pharisees, with whom they argued, accepted this principle only when an actual risk existed. And the sectarians were even more strict by requiring that the use of forbidden utensils be avoided whenever possible.

Once again we see that the law of the sect can be understood only in the context of what we know about Jewish law in this period. Certain basic principles, such as the need to override the Sabbath to save a life, were shared by all groups, from the Hasmonaean period on.

We can now sum up the Qumran Sabbath law, including other laws not treated here, to create a general picture of sectarian Sabbath practice. Like the mishnaic treatise of Shabbat, the Sabbath code of the *Zadokite Fragments* deals primarily with labors forbidden on the Sabbath, not with the positive actions that are required as well.

The sect began its Sabbath on Friday night, some time before sunset, to be sure there would be no violation of the Sabbath. Any discussion of business was forbidden, including all financial matters and the planning of work to be done after the Sabbath. For this reason, it was forbidden to walk in the field on the Sabbath to plan further work. It was probably also forbidden to enter a partnership on the Sabbath.

The sect had two Sabbath limits: One permitted a person to walk only one thousand cubits beyond the city; if one were pasturing an animal, one could go an additional thousand.

All food had to be prepared before the Sabbath, including not only cooking (as in rabbinic law) but all aspects of preparation as well. Containers had to be opened in advance, and vegetables had to be peeled. Food and drink could be consumed only within the "camp," the settled area. Other food and drink were regarded as not prepared before the Sabbath.

To avoid carrying on the Sabbath, a person on a journey had to drink directly from a water source since it was forbidden to draw water. Even within the camp, it was forbidden to carry from domain to domain. Children, likewise, could not be carried on the Sabbath. Nor were women permitted to wear ornamental perfume bottles. It was forbidden to have non-Jews do labor on one's behalf on the Sabbath. A servant could not be instructed to do even permitted labor. It was expected that members of the sect would wear clean, deodorized clothes on the Sabbath. It may have been forbidden to fast on the seventh day.

Although the Sabbath limit was extended in order to pasture animals, nevertheless one was forbidden either to help deliver an animal being born or to draw it out of a pit on the Sabbath. In fact, the Sabbath could never be profaned for the sake of material possessions. The sect allowed violation of the Sabbath to save a life, but it demanded that such rescue be undertaken if at all possible without using instruments or tools forbidden to be handled on that day. Handling rocks and earth on the holy day was forbidden because these were objects not suited to the spirit of the Sabbath. The sect forbade spending the Sabbath anywhere other than in a Jewish environment and prohibited, apparently, the offering of sacrifices except for the Sabbath offering.

Even though the sect had separated from the Temple because the sectarians regarded Temple procedure as improper, they still legislated for Temple worship on the assumption that they would resume their participation after their approach had triumphed over that of their opponents. The Rabbis likewise continued, in the Mishnah and Talmud, to legislate for sacrifice long after the Temple had been destroyed.

COURTS AND TESTIMONY

The *Zadokite Fragments* contains also a full set of legislation regarding civil law, dealing with the same topics that are treated in the mishnaic order of *Nezikin* (Damages), although the topics are not discussed in as much detail. Even though the sectarian court system, laws of witnesses, and testimony are derived from biblical interpretation, we will find in the case of civil law much greater divergence from early rabbinic approaches than we saw in the case of Sabbath law. Further, in this area of law we will also encounter a greater nexus between the halakhic issues under discussion and the way the sect was organized. These laws clearly address the sectarian community, albeit one with private ownership, marriage, and family.

Because the foundation of any system of law is the judiciary, it is not surprising that the sect had very specific laws regarding courts and judges:

> And this is the rule for the judges of the congregation, according to the time, four of the tribe of Levi and Aaron, and from Israel six, learned in the Book of Hagu and in the teachings of the covenant, from twenty-five years old to sixty years old. (*ZADOKITE FRAGMENTS 10:4–8*)

This text describes a court of ten, certainly not the norm in any other Jewish source we know. This court was to be composed of four members of the tribe of Levi, one a priest descended from Aaron the brother of Moses, and the other three to represent each of the other Levitical clans of Gershon, Kohath, and Merari.

The judges were to have studied the Book of Hagu (perhaps read "Hagi"), which was either the Torah or some particular sectarian book of laws. Various theories have tried to link this book with known compositions from the Qumran library. There is, however, no basis for identifying that text as the *Temple Scroll*. Nor should it be identified with one of the recently published *Sapiential Works*, as has also been suggested.

In addition to the laws of the Torah, these judges also had to know sectarian law. They were limited in age from twenty-five to sixty. In the Torah, twenty-five was the minimum age for Levitical service. Probably because the sect regarded itself as a substitute Temple, sectarians selected this number as the starting age for judicial service. The retirement age of sixty could have been derived only from the maximum age of valuation stated in Leviticus 27:3. This age was considered applicable, for as the text explains, it supposedly marked the onset of senility.

These judicial laws contrast markedly with later rabbinic usage. Although some early sources refer to groups of ten that performed certain legal functions, the Rabbis make no mention of a court of ten. The most prominent group of ten in Jewish tradition, of course, is the minyan, the group of ten Jewish adult males that makes up the quorum for public worship. Rabbinic law does not specify ages for judicial service. Although some rabbinic sources require that priests and Levites be part of the Great Sanhedrin, the high court of seventy-one members, this passage goes much further, assigning a greater judicial role to priests and Levites. Of course, this requirement is understandable coming from a group founded by dissident Zadokite priests.

Witnesses must also meet specific requirements:

> Let no witness be accepted by the judges to put someone to death by his testimony whose days are not sufficient to pass among the mustered (and who is

not) God-fearing. Let no man be trusted as a witness against his neighbor who violates any commandment intentionally, until (his deeds) have been purified (sufficiently for him) to return. *(ZADOKITE FRAGMENTS 9:23–10:3)*

Here we learn that witnesses were to be at least twenty, the age of majority in the sect, when young men were mustered and took an oath of adjuration to abide by the sectarian way of life. They were to be God-fearing—meaning, members of the sect. Finally, if they were not totally observant of the commandments, they could not be trusted as witnesses unless they had undergone a process of repentance. Although some have attempted to claim that the sectarians accepted women as witnesses, a view we considered in the chapter on women, that view must be rejected because it is based on a corrupt text and does not accord with the role of women described in other Qumran documents.

Even though other Jewish sources do not specify twenty as the minimum age for witnesses in capital cases, we have some indications that twenty might have been a general age of majority in Second Temple times. The age of thirteen, commonly termed Bar Mitzvah, meaning "obligated to observe the commandments," was considered the minimum age for physical maturity, bringing with it ritual obligation and, hence, religious majority. By twenty, maturity could be confidently ensured, and, therefore, testimony could be accepted. This way of thinking, however, was at odds with that of the Pharisaic-rabbinic tradition.

This text accepts as witnesses only members of the sect, those who are "God-fearing." Here we see the connection between legal requirements and the sectarian life. For if righteousness were attainable only through the sect's way of life, then only those who observed that way of life were qualified to serve as witnesses. Others, obviously untrustworthy, had to be excluded. The law of witnesses, then, in its present form, was applicable only to the sectarian community.

An issue of considerable controversy among scholars is the number of witnesses required in legal cases. The section of text discussing this issue (*Zadokite Fragments* 9:16–23) is so difficult that its translation and analysis would take us far afield. Suffice it to say that in my view, the sect required two witnesses for financial matters and three for capital matters. Further, witnesses were permitted to testify before the examiner about independent occurrences of the same transgression, provided that the violator had been informed of the gravity of the transgression prior to committing the offense and that the offense had been duly recorded by the sectarian official. This is the process termed "reproof" that we examined in the chapter on halakhic midrash.

These laws are peculiar to the *Zadokite Fragments* and disagree with rabbinic halakhah. Although the requirement of three witnesses has some Second Temple parallels, it is not known as a legal requirement anywhere else but in our text. Furthermore, later talmudic law considered and rejected the notion of cumulative testimony to separate repeated occurrences of the same offense.

An exceedingly illuminating feature of the sectarian legal system was its method of attempting to recover lost or stolen property. In this regard, the *Zadokite Fragments* provides:

> But anything which is missing and it is not known who stole it from the property of the camp in which it was stolen, its owner shall swear an oath of adjuration. Whoever hears, if he knows and does not tell, is guilty.
>
> (*ZADOKITE FRAGMENTS 9:10–12*)

This law states explicitly that it applies to a situation in which a sect member steals property within the "camp," a term in the *Zadokite Fragments* for the sectarian settlements located throughout the country. The law thus addresses the case of theft specifically among sectarian group members. Further, this text, as well as for that matter the entire civil law code, assumes that sectarians have private property. Because of these features, many scholars claim that the law in this document applies only to those in the "camps" who did in fact own their own property. Consequently, they would claim that these laws did not apply in the Qumran center. However, we have shown that even in the Qumran center the system of property ownership provided for private ownership and communal use. So this restricted view of the law cannot be justified.

If property were missing, the sect employed an oath of adjuration to effect its recovery. Sectarians derived this procedure from the command found in Leviticus 5:1, "If anyone sins in that he has heard a public adjuration, and he is able to testify . . . , if he does not speak, then he shall be subject to (punishment for) his offense." According to the sectarian interpretation of this passage, a person who heard such an adjuration was obliged to come forward and reveal the location of the lost or stolen property.

Therefore, anyone who knew the whereabouts of the missing property would, upon hearing this oath pronounced in public, feel compelled to reveal it. Although there is no similar law in rabbinic sources, we encounter such a procedure in medieval Jewish law. Unfortunately, we have no way of knowing whether the medieval parallel is simply coincidental or whether it is a survival into the Middle Ages of an ancient sectarian practice documented in the Qumran scrolls. We should note that rabbinic sources do describe an oath employed to cause recalcitrant witnesses to testify, but that procedure functions only to compel testimony, not to recover stolen or lost property.

Since "oath of adjuration" is a term used specifically in the Bible to describe the oath administered to the woman suspected of adultery, it is most probable that this biblical legal procedure (Numbers 5:11–31) enabled sectarian legal scholars to fill in various missing details not even hinted at in Leviticus 5:1. From the law of the suspected adulteress we learn that suspicion alone was enough to require the oath. The sectarian oath was probably formulated as follows: Those adjured swore not only that they did not know the location of the stolen property but also that they accepted upon themselves a dire curse should they be hiding the truth. Probably the hearers of the oath were compelled to recite "Amen, Amen," indicating that they too were bound by the oath, since such a requirement applied to the adjuration of the suspected adulteress.

The last of these civil laws that we shall examine discusses the restoration of property to an owner who cannot be located or determined. Here again, we may observe the priestly orientation of the law and the community it assumes:

> (Regarding) every amount to be repaid which does not have an owner, the one making restitution shall confess to the priest and everything shall be his (the priest's) except for the ram of the guilt-offering. And likewise, any lost object which has been found and has no owner shall go to the priests, for its finder does not know the regulation pertaining to it. If no owner is found for it, they (the priests) shall guard it. *(Zadokite Fragments 9:13–16)*

This passage first deals with how to make restitution in a case in which the rightful owner cannot be located or identified. This law is based on the Torah's legislation dealing with the restitution of property kept by means of illegal and dishonest legal claims, most probably by means of false oaths (Numbers 5:6–8 and Leviticus 5:21–26). In such a case, the sect ruled that the restitution be made to the priest who received the money and the added penalty of one-fifth prescribed by the Torah. In addition, the sacrifice of a ram as a guilt-offering was to be made by the person making restitution.

The Rabbis understood these verses completely differently, taking them to refer to the property of a proselyte, a convert to Judaism. They believed that the words "If the man has no kinsman to whom restitution can be made" (Numbers 5:8) referred to a proselyte, because there could be no other Jew who could possibly have no relatives as heirs. Accordingly, for the Rabbis this biblical passage did not offer a general rule about the disposition of lost property.

In a case in which the owner was unknown, the sect required that the object be given to the priests for safekeeping, a practice probably adopted due to the complex questions, also discussed in the Mishnah, of how to care for the property and what to do if the property had a maintenance cost that could consume its value, as in the case of feeding a lost animal. It was assumed that the average person, no matter how well-meaning and upright, simply could not adjudicate these difficult matters.

But this entire procedure is difficult to understand in light of the requirement of Deuteronomy 22:2 that such property be kept by the finder until the owner can be located. Indeed, the mishnaic approach, whereby the finder keeps the property until the owner or his heir is located, seems much more consistent with the biblical prescription.

Then how did the sect come to this conclusion? Probably it understood the requirement—to take it to "your house" (bayit; Deuteronomy 22:2)—to refer not to the finder's home but to the Temple, often designated as bayit, the house of God. Based on this understanding, the sect mandated that the lost property be given to the priests. In their own community, in which they did not participate in the rituals of the Temple, this ruling would make even more sense.

These examples have shown that the sectarians developed an extensive and detailed system of civil law to deal with the affairs of their members. Although their system varied in many ways from the later rabbinic one, it agreed in many matters as well.

Before we leave this topic, it will be worthwhile to summarize this system as a whole: The basic court had ten members. Judges were to be trained both in Scripture and in sectarian legal teachings. Specific age requirements ensured the competence of judges. Witnesses had to be members of the sect and, in capital matters, had to be older than twenty. Whereas two witnesses were sufficient for financial matters, three were required for capital cases. The testimony of fewer witnesses sufficed for the imposition of sectarian sanctions even when the testimony was insufficient for conviction. It was possible to make use of the cumulative testimony of single witnesses to successive commissions of the same crime, provided that the offense was duly recorded. All trials had to be preceded by the required formal reproof in the presence of witnesses before conviction was possible. In cases of lost or stolen property, laws provided for the use of oaths of adjuration that aided in the return of missing items. When illegally gained property was to be returned but the owner was absent, the property could be returned to the priests. If no one claimed lost property, it was entrusted to the priests for safekeeping.

This set of laws has been examined in order to show how in matters concerning Sabbath law, civil law, and even in some cases the conduct of sectarian affairs, the sect derived its laws differently from the ways other groups of Second Temple Jews and the later Rabbis did. In many cases, the differences resulted from differing interpretations of relevant biblical laws. Early Christianity, we noted, tended to be on the opposite side of the spectrum from the Qumran sect, representing a more lenient group than the Pharisees, whereas the sect tended to be still stricter. And we found that, in many aspects of the law, the sect's views were either the same as or very similar to those of the rabbinic tradition. Even where they differ, they indicate a common agenda and even some common conclusions, alongside their many differences.

The next chapter examines the religious way of life of the Dead Sea Scrolls community and allied groups. Here we will observe the life of the sectarian not from the abstract point of view of legal codes, but from the evidence of actual practice.

CHAPTER 18

Prayer and Ritual

For all Jews in the Second Temple period, the question of how to serve God was of utmost importance. This was a period when the Temple still stood in Jerusalem, and Jews flocked there to offer sacrifices and experience the divine presence. To the people of Israel, Temple and sacrifice represented the fulfillment of God's commandments, the guarantors of cosmic order, and the pipeline through which God's blessing might flow to His people in return for their service to Him.

But at the same time, for all groups of Second Temple Jews, prayer was increasing in importance, as were a variety of other religious practices centered in the home. Today, with historical hindsight, we can see that during the Second Temple period, Judaism was gradually moving away from sacrifice. Thus, by the time the Temple was destroyed, the Jewish people were prepared to function in the new age, serving God in new ways.

However, for the Jews of the Hellenistic period, this major transition had not yet dawned. They regarded prayer and ritual as either mere accompaniments to sacrifice, substitutes for those located too far away from the Temple, or, in the case of sectarian groups like the Qumran sect, as replacements for a Temple ritual they judged impure. Nevertheless, we can observe through the scrolls the rise of prayer and other religious institutions familiar to us in later Judaism and thereby learn much about the history of their development.

It is from this point of view that we approach the early history of Jewish liturgy as reflected in the Qumran scrolls. We will attempt to evaluate the liturgical patterns in evidence at Qumran and to compare them with what is known of the early rabbinic traditions. Once we have assembled a considerable list of parallels, we will discuss their significance and the conclusions we can draw from them.

Temple and Synagogue

The sect that left us the Dead Sea Scrolls removed itself voluntarily from Hellenistic Jerusalem and forswore participation in the Jerusalem sacrificial service, regarding the conduct of that service's priestly rituals no longer acceptable. Sect members maintained that violations of the law marred the Temple and that its priests were illegitimate. Presumably, the founders of the sect believed that the Jerusalem cult no longer served as a vehicle for contact between Israel and its God; therefore, they saw no value in their continued participation in it. Whether retiring to Qumran or living in "camps" throughout Palestine, they were left with a Judaism devoid of Temple and sacrifice, a Judaism in which prayer, purity, study, and the sectarian life itself would have to serve as a replacement for the Temple. The sect thus viewed itself as a sanctuary that brought its members into the same intimate contact with God that members formerly had experienced through cultic worship. Despite the claims of some scholars, sacrifices were not performed at Qumran.

The situation facing the Rabbis soon after the Destruction of the Temple, when the mishnaic sages assembled at Yavneh on the Mediterranean coast, was very similar. Judaism had long been based on sacrificial worship, which ensured Israel's relationship with God through the proper and orderly conduct of the rites required by the Levitical codes. Now, in the aftermath of the Great Revolt of 66–73 C.E., the Temple was gone. The priests no longer sacrificed; the Levites no longer sang; Israel no longer made pilgrimages to the holy Temple. Henceforth, only prayer and the life of rabbinic piety could ensure Israel's continued link to their Father in Heaven.

It is naive to assume that this catastrophe came upon Pharisaic-rabbinic Judaism with no warning. Indeed, it is clear to us now that throughout the Second Commonwealth period, sacrificial ritual was on the wane, and prayer and liturgy on the rise. Gradually, prayer made greater and greater inroads even in the Temple. Those distant from the Temple turned increasingly to prayer during the Second Commonwealth period. Pharisaism, in displacing Temple purity to the home and table, had helped to free the later sages from the inexorability of sacrifice. The Qumran sect, too, had long before demonstrated how to live a Jewish life without a Temple. Sectarians had, as we shall see, developed both a liturgy and an ideology to compensate for their absence from the Temple.

Throughout its days, the sect yearned not for the restoration of the Temple, which still stood and functioned albeit improperly, but for the return of their priestly leaders to leadership of the Temple and its ritual. This, to them, was tantamount to the Temple's restoration, which would result in establishment of the New Jerusalem and renewal of the bonds uniting the people of Israel and its God. Then, in the End of Days, the sect's priests would officiate at the Temple, properly carrying out its practice and ensuring its utmost purity. It is probable that to

Synagogue at Masada The earliest synagogues known in the
Land of Israel are the bleacher-type structures found at Masada,
Herodion, and Gamla. These synagogues are all to be dated to the
first half of the first century C.E., and they represent adaptations of
previously existing buildings. Certain early discussions of
synagogue ritual in rabbinic sources refer to structures like
these. *Photograph by Zev Radovan. Courtesy of the Biblical
Archaeology Society.*

many of the sectarians, the *Temple Scroll,* with its dream of an expanded Temple
and greater levels of sanctity for the Temple and its sacrifices, expressed their
hopes for the premessianic Temple. But until such a Temple were established, or
until the coming of the divinely built sanctuary at the End of Days, they would
have to be satisfied with the efficacy of prayer and with the study of texts dealing
with the worship and cult of the Temple at which they would neither serve nor
offer sacrifice.

The *Zadokite Fragments* refers to some kind of place of worship:

> And anyone who enters the house of prostration let him not come in a state
> of impurity requiring washing. (*ZADOKITE FRAGMENTS 11:21–22*)

Although the remainder of the passage is difficult to decipher, the text seems to
indicate that sectarians who were scattered in the towns and cities of Palestine
established permanent places of sanctity for the conduct of sacred services.

However, we find in the archaeological remains from Qumran no evidence of the establishment of a synagogue or a fixed place of prayer. In fact, the Qumran settlement predates the earliest excavated synagogues in Palestine—at Masada, Herodion, and Gamla—all from the first century C.E. References to earlier synagogues in the Hellenistic Diaspora probably signify Jewish communal organizations, not buildings used for ritual purposes. It seems, therefore, that community prayers, certainly part of the life of the sectarians at Qumran, were conducted in premises used for other purposes, perhaps in the dining hall. A special building for worship would not have been necessary at the sectarian center at Qumran, for the entire settlement was dedicated to this purpose. Such a house of worship would be needed only by those sectarians who lived elsewhere in the Land of Israel.

Liturgy of the Qumran Sect

The basic prayer times observed by the Qumran sect are presented in a poem concluding the *Rule of the Community*. From this poem we learn that a specific series of liturgical texts existed for the various times of prayer. The beginning of the poem mentions the need to pray evening and morning (*Rule of the Community* 10:1–3):

> [I will praise Him] at the times which He has ordained:
> At the beginning of the rule of light in its time,
> and when it is gathered to its appointed place.
> At the beginning of the watches of darkness,
> when He opens His storehouse and sets out the darkness,
> and at its end when it is gathered before the light.
> When the lights appear from the holy heaven,
> when they are gathered to the place of honor.

This text refers to prayers for the morning and the evening. Based on this passage, one theory maintains that the sect prayed three times each day and three times each evening. But it seems more likely that the series of synonymous lines in the poem is simply imitating the ancient Hebrew poetic form of parallelism, whereby the same ideas are repeated for effect. If so, this text, like the *Daily Prayers* found among the cave 4 texts, would require prayer each morning and afternoon, at times corresponding to the required sacrifices of the Temple ritual.

The poem then lists various special occasions that require additional prayers (*Rule of the Community* 10:3–8):

> When the seasons begin on the days of the New Moon,
> when together at their end they succeed one another. . . .

> At the beginnings of the months in their appointed times,
> and holy days at the times appointed for their remembrance. . . .
> At the beginnings of the years and the times of their Festivals. . . .

It is difficult to ferret out the allusions in this poem and in the verses that follow. Yet from other sources we know that the sectarians observed a complex ritual calendar, which included not only the Festivals required in the Torah—the New Year, Day of Atonement, Sukkot, Passover, Shavuot, and the New Month days— but also some additional holy days such as the extra harvest Festivals mentioned in some texts, mostly in the *Temple Scroll*. This poem makes clear that there were special prayers for these occasions.

Central to the liturgy of later Judaism is the proclamation of Jewish faith, Shema Yisrael: "Hear, O Israel, the Lord our God, the Lord is One" (Deuteronomy 6:4). The term "Shema" has come to designate a complex of biblical passages (Deuteronomy 6:4–9, 11:13–21; Numbers 15:37–41) recited according to Jewish tradition morning and evening. According to the Mishnah, this prayer was already central in Second Temple times (M. Tamid 5:1). We can identify allusions to the reading of the Shema in the poem at the end of *Rule of the Community* (10:10):

> With the entry of day and night I will enter the covenant of God,
> and at the exit of evening and morning I will speak of His laws.

The expressions "enter the covenant of God" and "speak of His laws" are direct allusions to the major theme of the Shema: the confirmation of the Jew's covenant with God and the requirement to speak of His commandments.

A number of expressions from elsewhere in this poem are suggestive of the language of the Amidah prayer. The Amidah (literally, "standing" prayer) is the core of the service in rabbinic Judaism. Because it originally contained eighteen benedictions, it is also known as the Shemoneh Esreh (eighteen). Talmudic traditions maintain that this prayer was authored in the time of Ezra and the Men of the Great Assembly, a body of sages said to have functioned from the fifth through the third centuries B.C.E. Because we have no direct evidence that the text of this prayer existed during the Qumran period, it is quite interesting to find in the scrolls parallels to its language, although we cannot conclude from such evidence that the prayer as we know it was recited by the sectarians.

DAILY PRAYERS

Numerous fragments found in the Qumran caves have been classified by scholars as liturgies. Whereas many of the earlier-known fragments were at best insubstantial, more recently published material has changed the picture radically. Now we have prayer texts for daily prayers and Festivals as well as various supplicatory prayers. These texts show that numerous rituals and liturgies, similar in scope to those of talmudic tradition, were associated with the sectarians of Qumran.

Among the prayer texts dating to the Hasmonaean period (100–75 B.C.E.) is a text scholars have entitled *Daily Prayers*, found in cave 4. It consists of a series of prayers to be recited on the various days of the month. The liturgical materials found here are too short, however, to have constituted the entire liturgy. These prayers appear to have constituted a small section of the worship service, which changed on a daily basis throughout the month and perhaps throughout the year.

Specific texts are designated for evening and morning, although no specific nighttime prayer appears to be included here. The material for each day of the month represents a discrete literary unit, and the days are numbered according to lunar months.

Each day's entry begins:

> On the x of the month, in the evening, they shall bless, recite and say: Praised be the God of Israel Who. . . . May peace be upon you, O Israel.

Then the text takes up the morning prayer:

> When the sun goes forth to illumine the earth they shall bless, recite and say: . . . They shall bless and recite: Praised be the God of Israel. . . .

The text is very fragmentary and no complete unit survives or can be reconstructed with certainty. Nonetheless, we can gather some sense of the text from this otherwise broken excerpt:

> . . . the light of day for our knowledge . . . in the six gates of ligh[t . . . and we,] the sons of Your covenant, will prais[e Your name] with all the troops of [light . . . al]l the tongues (endowed with) knowledge, bless . . . the light of peace [upon you O Israel. . . . On the seventh of [the month in the evening, they shall bless, recite and sa]y: Praised be the God of Is[rael Who . . . right-eousness . . . al]l [th]ese things we knew. . . .] Blessed be [the G]od [of Israel] . . . *(DAILY PRAYERS 7–9 IV 1–8)*

In the rabbinic liturgy, the Shema is preceded by two benedictions and followed by one in the morning and two at night. Of the two benedictions before the Shema, for both morning and night, the first benediction deals with the heavenly luminaries, and the second with God's revelation of the Torah to Israel and the commandments. It is most likely that the benedictions preserved here, focusing on the cosmic order and the heavenly luminaries, were expanding upon a precursor of this first benediction before the Shema.

As we mentioned earlier, the Mishnah dates the recitation of the Shema to Second Temple times. In the same passage, the Mishnah notes that in the view of the Rabbis, some benediction was associated with the Shema already in Temple times. We can therefore conclude that an early version of the blessing on the heavenly luminaries—the first benediction before the Shema—must have then been in use. Although in rabbinic tradition this benediction varied only for morning and evening, with passages added later for Sabbaths and Festivals, the version used at Qumran varied each day of the month.

This text speaks of "gates" or "portals" of light. The same idea is found in the rabbinic morning benediction for the Sabbath: "The God Who opens every day the doors of the gates of the east, and opens the windows of the firmament . . . and gives light to the entire world and its inhabitants." The image here depicts the gates in the heavenly dome through which the lights shine during the appropriate parts of the day.

Another significant parallel with rabbinic liturgy is in the benediction:

[Praised be the God of Israel W]ho cho[se] us from among all [the] nations.
(DAILY PRAYERS 24–25 VII 3–4)

This benediction is almost identical to that recited today over the reading of the Torah in the synagogue: "Blessed are You, O Lord our God, King of the Universe, Who chose us from all the peoples. . . ." Much of the vocabulary of these prayers is also found in the rabbinic liturgy.

Our text speaks of twice-daily prayer—morning and evening (late afternoon). Later talmudic tradition regarded prayer as a substitute for the Temple sacrifices only after the Temple had been destroyed. Accordingly, regular daily prayer by individual Jews should not have been widespread before the Destruction of the Temple. However, some earlier Rabbis argued that these daily services were already being conducted in the Second Temple, corresponding with the times of the daily sacrifices. Still others maintained that the prayers were instituted by the patriarchs—Abraham, Isaac, and Jacob—who had each prayed once at one of the designated times. In the Bible, we are told that Daniel prayed thrice daily (Daniel 6:11). The later sages explained that even if the three prayer services had originated with the patriarchs, their exact times were set only later to correspond to the schedule of sacrificial worship.

The link with sacrificial worship was apparently considered central. How else can we explain why the status of the evening service, to which no Temple sacrifice corresponded, was debated throughout the mishnaic period? Indeed, it was eventually decided that in terms of halakhah, the evening service was optional. Because no evening sacrifice was offered in the Temple, it is likely that the evening prayer had an inferior status relative to the other two services—hence its optional standing. Even the rabbinic argument that the burning of the limbs and fats of sacrificial animals throughout the night constituted the equivalent of an evening sacrifice was not sufficient to elevate the evening prayer to the status of a required daily service.

Since our Qumran text mentions only two required prayer times, we can conclude that during this period, at least some Jews prayed only twice a day. In fact, our text supports the view of some Rabbis that originally, twice-daily prayer was the norm. These prayers from Qumran provide definite evidence that well before the Temple was destroyed by the Romans in 70 c.e., some Jews in the Second Temple period found their path to God through the service of the heart.

THE QUMRAN SUPPLICATION TEXTS

Certain parallels to what rabbinic liturgy calls *Taḥanun* (supplication texts) have also been identified in the caves. The *Lament* of cave 4 was copied in about 50–25 b.c.e. This text appeals to God to remember the downtrodden condition and disgrace of Israel and not to hand over the land to foreigners. God is asked to avenge the wrongs that the nations have perpetrated against his nation:

> Do not give over our inheritance to strangers and our legacy to foreigners. Remember that [we are the . . .] of Your nation and the abandoned ones of Your inheritance. Remember the children of Your covenant who are destroyed. . . . Look and see the disgrace of the children of [Your people . . .].
> *(LAMENT 1–2, 5–6)*

Although this text is extremely fragmentary, we can still identify parallels in theme and content to the rabbinic supplication recited on Mondays and Thursdays (*We-Hu' Raḥum*). Although the *Taḥanun* prayer in its present form has been dated to the Middle Ages, it apparently had ancient antecedents and probably drew from a tradition of previous prayers. Both the Qumran *Lament* and the rabbinic prayer clearly depend upon Joel 2:17, "Let not Your possession become a mockery, to be taunted by nations! Let not the people say, 'Where is their God?'"

A similar composition is the *Words of the Luminaries*, preserved in three copies. The name of the text actually appears within the manuscript, a rare phenomenon in the Qumran library. Scholars have described this text as a collection of liturgical hymns for use on specific days of the week. Indeed, Wednesday, the "day of the covenant," and the Sabbath, the "day of praise," are explicitly mentioned. The passage preceding the Sabbath material identifies Friday—assuming this is the day described—as the "day of confession of sins." Because the text is so fragmentary, we can presume that the other days are mentioned in sections that were not preserved.

Central to this text is the notion that although God had to punish his people for their transgressions, he spared them from complete destruction:

> . . . and they worshiped a foreign god in their land. And also their land was destroyed by their enemies. For Your anger has been [pou]red out and Your wrath with the fire of Your zealousness, to destroy it so that there is no more

traveler or passerby. Even so, You did not despise the descendants of Jacob nor revile Israel to destroy them and to cancel Your covenant with them. For You alone are a living God and there is none like You. And You remembered Your covenant that You had taken us out (of Egypt) in the presence of the nations and You did not abandon us among the nations.

(WORDS OF THE LUMINARIES A 1–2 V 3–11)

This passage reflects notions of sin, destruction, mercy, and return found in the rebuke passages of Deuteronomy (29:23–30:6). These same notions are also prominent in the final section of the *Halakhic Letter*.

Also significant is the theme of asking forgiveness:

> [. . . and ca]st [off] from [u]s all ou[r] transgressions, and pu[r]ify us from our sins, for Your own sake. For Yours O Lord is righteousness, for You have created all these. And now, at this time, for our hearts are submissive, we have paid the penalty for our sins and for the sins of our forefathers, because we sinned and because we lived rebelliously.
>
> *(WORDS OF THE LUMINARIES A 1–2 VI 2–6)*

This text draws on the confessional formula—"we have sinned, we have transgressed . . ."—antecedents of which are known from the Bible (Ezra 9:6–15) and from various Qumran documents and which was prominent in the Day of Atonement service in the Temple and later became part of the synagogue liturgy.

We can therefore identify this text as a series of daily supplications for liturgical use, one for each day of the week. The supplication for the Sabbath apparently avoided topics judged improper for the Sabbath day, specifically references to the tragedies that had befallen the people of Israel. This text would have been recited as part of an organized ritual. It is not possible to tell if this particular text was written for Temple service or for worship away from the Temple.

Although we cannot claim based on this evidence that rabbinic *Taḥanun* texts go back to Second Temple times, we can state with assurance that some Jews, whose works are preserved at Qumran, were already reciting prayers with similar motifs as part of their prayer services in the first century B.C.E. Specific selections were used for the various days of the week. Already by the time the *Words of the Luminaries* was composed, a special version had been created for the Sabbath, acknowledging the day's uniqueness as well as the inappropriateness of bringing up certain motifs on this holy day.

FESTIVAL PRAYERS

Prayers for Festivals are preserved in three manuscripts from cave 4—*Prayers for Festivals A, B,* and *C*—and another fragment from cave 1. The cave 4 manuscripts have been dated to the beginning of the first century C.E. (*Prayers for Fes-*

tivals A and *B)* and the end of the Hasmonaean period, about 70–60 B.C.E. (*Prayers for Festivals C*). The preserved portion of the text specifically mentions the Day of Atonement and the Day of First Fruits (Shavuot). A plausible reconstruction of the text organizes it according to the entire Jewish ritual calendar, beginning with the New Year on the first of Tishre, followed by the Day of Atonement, Tabernacles, Offering of the Omer or Barley Harvest, perhaps the Second Passover, and Shavuot. The New Moon is also mentioned. A reference to Passover has not been identified in the surviving fragments of the text.

It is impossible to reconstruct exactly the ritual calendar described in this text and the prayers for each occasion because the manuscript is not preserved well enough to allow it. In addition, we cannot determine whether this ritual calendar is similar either to that known from rabbinic Judaism or to the expanded calendar of the *Temple Scroll.*

One line particularly stands out in this text for its parallel to the rabbinic liturgy:

> And may You assemble our banished at the time of . . . and our dispersed [ones] may You soon gather (cf. Isaiah 11:12). *(PRAYERS FOR FESTIVALS C 3 I 3–4)*

This passage strongly resembles the words of the Festival Musaf (additional service) of later rabbinic tradition, "Gather our scattered ones from among the nations, and our dispersed ones bring together from the corners of the earth." This parallel suggests that the prayer for restoring the Diaspora to the Land of Israel, recited on Festivals, may go back as early as the first century B.C.E.

These supplicatory texts clarify an interesting issue: What was the attitude of the Jews of the Second Temple period to the Destruction of the First Temple? After all, the Jerusalem Temple had been reestablished and was functioning in their own day. Did Second Temple Jews still mourn the First Temple? Did they pray for the restoration of an independent Jewish state? It is clear from these texts that they did indeed long for and pray for a return to the ancient glories of the united monarchy of David and Solomon and that they continued to pray for the ingathering of the exiles.

It is not possible to determine the exact function of the *Festival Prayers.* They do not refer to the sacrificial system nor do they suggest that they were intended as a substitute for it. Nor is there any indication that they were to be recited along with sacrificial rites. Because happiness and rejoicing are explicitly mentioned, it is probable that these prayers were meant to be recited as part of the celebration of the Festivals at Qumran or elsewhere.

The texts examined here contain prayers for each day of the month to be recited morning and evening, daily supplicatory prayers, and specific prayers for each Festival. These together constituted a cycle of prayer texts that suggests that already before the Destruction of the Second Temple, a fairly developed liturgy was practiced by some if not many Jews. Although we cannot be sure that all these were recited by the same people, it does seem likely that the sect practiced a regular order of prayer.

PURIFICATION RITUALS

Another manuscript to be considered here, *Purification Rituals*, has been dated to the early first century B.C.E. The text discusses a number of issues: sexual impurities, purity of the cultic servitors, the laws of skin diseases for both persons and houses, and contact with the dead. In addition, the text explicitly mentions the obligation to purify oneself for Sabbaths and Festivals, for the equinoxes and solstices, and for the harvest Festivals and the New Moon.

In this text we find certain rulings on halakhic matters pertaining to ritual purity and impurity. What concerns us here, however, is the text's liturgical features. Each person engaged in a personal purification ritual was to recite a prayer beginning with the clause: "Blessed be You, God of Israel, Who . . ." (frag. 41:3; frag. 42–44:3).

The evidence in this text can help us dispel a common misconception about the Jewish laws of ritual purity and impurity—that they lack ethical and religious dimensions. Critics claim that these rites are mechanical at best and that they actually represent taboos. But in the Qumran *Purification Rituals* we find clear evidence that at least by the first century B.C.E., this Jewish group emphasized the spiritual and religious meaning of such rituals, believing that ritual purification must be preceded and accompanied by an inner turning, a dedication to the goals and aspirations sought by Judaism. One example is the following:

> And he shall bless and reci[te] and say: Praised are You [God of Israel Who has saved me from al]l my transgressions and has purified me from contact with menstrual impurity, and You have granted atonement, so that I may go [. . .] purification, and the blood of the burnt offering of Your acceptance and the remembrance of the sweet sav[or . . .], Your holy incense, [and the swe]et sav[o]r of Your acceptance . . . *(PURIFICATION RITUALS 29–32 VII 6–9)*

Indeed, what made the purification rituals work was repentance. In fact, when these rituals were performed with genuine feelings of spiritual purification, they apparently served as a substitute for the sacrifices no longer being offered by the sectarians. This idea is enshrined in *Rule of the Community* (2:26–3:12), which required proper repentance by anyone who wished to enter the waters of purification. Thus, purification was a deep spiritual process of self-improvement, not a mere cultic rite.

Other Liturgical Texts

A text that may provide information about organized liturgy at Qumran is the *Psalms Scroll*. This scroll, as we have already explained, contains canonical and noncanonical psalms, as well as numerous other poetic prayer texts. Many of the canonical psalms in this text are exactly the same as those incorporated into later rabbinic liturgy. Even the organization of the psalms in the scroll seems to parallel the conceptual framework of the later rabbinic prayer book. Most important, many of the selections discussed in the Talmud as part of the prayer services appear here. One psalm, Psalm 145, has liturgical responses included in it as well. Clearly, these same psalms, most notably Psalm 145 (preceded in Jewish liturgy by the verses beginning with the word "Ashre"), were used in liturgical context by the Qumran sect.

One particular noncanonical poem included in the scroll, the Hymn to the Creator, may be of great significance in this regard (*Psalms Scroll* 26:9–15). It is a poetic hymn of praise to God:

> Great and holy is the Lord,
> holiest of holies from generation to generation.
> Before Him majesty goes,
> and after Him the rush of many waters.
> Mercy and truth surround His presence,
> truth, justice and righteousness are the foundation of His throne.
> He distinguished light from darkness,
> the morning He established with the knowledge of His heart.
> Then all the angels saw and they sang,
> for He showed them what they did not know.
> He crowns the mountains with produce,
> good food for every living being.
> Blessed be the One Who creates the earth with His strength,
> Who established the earth with His wisdom.
> With His understanding He stretched forth the heavens,
> and He took out [the wind] from [His store]house.
> He made the [lightning for ra]in,
> and He raised up the clou[ds from] the end(s) [of the earth].

This poem certainly resembles the early Jewish mystical hymn El Adon, which eventually found its way into the rabbinic liturgy. El Adon, recited on Sabbaths and Festivals, contains a number of the same motifs. Among the many parallels we can cite are these two: "knowledge and understanding surround Him" and "merit and uprightness are before His throne, kindness and mercy are before His glory." But in one important respect, the two poems differ: whereas the Qumran hymn portrays God as the creator of the entire world, the rabbinic hymn speaks of God only as the creator of the heavenly luminaries.

It is tempting to regard the *Thanksgiving Scroll* as a series of hymns for public worship. But we have no evidence that this material was in fact liturgical. These poems are individual plaints, perhaps composed by a leader of the sect—some scholars claim by the Teacher of Righteousness himself—concentrating on serious matters of theology and belief. The *Thanksgiving Hymns* were certainly not part of a regular order of prayers. Rather, they belong to a genre of devotional, introspective poetry.

The same is the case with the *Songs of the Sabbath Sacrifice*, also called the *Angelic Liturgy*. This text describes how the angelic hosts daily praise God in the heavens according to fixed rituals. As we will see in a later chapter, this is a mystical text describing the angels' praise of God in the heavens, not songs of praise for us to recite on earth. Therefore, this text cannot actually help us understand the ritual of the sectarians or of other ancient Jews.

CALENDAR CONTROVERSIES

Because the calendar used by Jews in this period and the controversies surrounding it run as a leitmotif throughout our discussion of prayer, sacrifice, and the Temple in Qumran texts, it is appropriate here to outline this controversy and its ramifications.

Numerous texts in the Qumran sectarian corpus castigate the sect's opponents for observing the holidays on the wrong dates. Among the instructions to the sectarians is the following:

> And to observe the Sabbath day according to its specification and the Festivals and the day of the fast according to that derived by the members of the new covenant in the land of Damascus . . . (*ZADOKITE FRAGMENTS 6:18–19*)

Clearly, this text alludes to observance of the Festivals and the Day of Atonement (Yom Kippur) according to the calendar of the Dead Sea sect.

We learn more about the calendar dispute from the description of the confrontation between the Teacher of Righteousness and the Wicked Priest (*Pesher Habakkuk* 11:4–8), discussed earlier. This text describes the Wicked Priest's appearance at the sectarian center, presumably Qumran, and the ensuing confrontation. Significantly, the text records that this confrontation occurred on the Day of Atonement, when all Jews would have shunned travel, clearly forbidden on a day of rest. However, we are told that the Wicked Priest traveled to the

The Festivals According to the Calendar of the Sect of the Scrolls

First Month	Second Month	Third Month	Fourth Month	Fifth Month	Sixth Month	Seventh Month
1 W *Beginning of Days of Consecration*	1 F	1 Su	1 W	1 F	1 Su	1 W *Day of Memorial*
2 Th	2 Sa	2 M	2 Th	2 Sa	2 M	2 Th
3 F	3 Su	3 T	3 F	3 Su *Feast of First Fruits of Wine*	3 T	3 F
4 Sa	4 M	4 W	4 Sa	4 M	4 W	4 Sa
5 Su	5 T	5 Th	5 Su	5 T	5 Th	5 Su
6 M	6 W	6 F	6 M	6 W	6 F	6 M
7 T	7 Th	7 Sa	7 T	7 Th	7 Sa	7 T
8 W	8 F	8 Su	8 W	8 F	8 Su	8 W
9 Th	9 Sa	9 M	9 Th	9 Sa	9 M	9 Th
10 F	10 Su	10 T	10 F	10 Su	10 T	10 F *Day of Atonement*
11 Sa	11 M	11 W	11 Sa	11 M	11 W	11 Sa
12 Su	12 T	12 Th	12 Su	12 T	12 Th	12 Su
13 M	13 W	13 F	13 M	13 W	13 F	13 M
14 T *Passover*	14 Th	14 Sa	14 T	14 Th	14 Sa	14 T
15 W	15 F	15 Su *Feast of First Fruits of Wheat*	15 W	15 F	15 Su	15 W *Feast of Booths*

16 Th	16 Sa	16 M	16 Th	16 Sa	16 M	16 Th
17 F	17 Su	17 T	17 F	17 Su	17 T	17 F
18 Sa	18 M	18 W	18 Sa	18 M	18 W	18 Sa
19 Su	19 T	19 Th	19 Su	19 T	19 Th	19 Su
20 M	20 W	20 F	20 M	20 W	20 F	20 M
21 T	21 Th	21 Sa	21 T	21 Th	21 Sa	21 T
22 W	22 F	22 Su	22 W	22 F	22 Su *Feast of Oil*	22 W *Eighth Day of Assembly*
23 Th	23 Sa	23 M	23 Th	23 Sa	23 M *Beginning of Feast of Wood Offering*	23 Th
24 F	24 Su	24 T	24 F	24 Su	24 T	24 F
25 Sa	25 M	25 W	25 Sa	25 M	25 W	25 Sa
26 Su *Day of Waving the Sheaf*	26 T	26 Th	26 Su	26 T	26 Th	26 Su
27 M	27 W	27 F	27 M	27 W	27 F	27 M
28 T	28 Th	28 Sa	28 T	28 Th	28 Sa	28 T
29 W	29 F	29 Su	29 W	29 F	29 Su	29 W
30 Th	30 Sa	30 M	30 Th	30 Sa	30 M	30 Th
		31 T			31 T	

Yadin, *Temple Scroll*, 1:118.

teacher's place of exile on Yom Kippur. We can make sense of this text only if we assume that these two groups were using different calendars so that the sacred Festivals fell on different days.

We have considerable evidence about the peculiar sectarian calendar, and we also know that it was used by other groups of Second Temple Jews as well. Drawing upon a variety of Qumran texts, most only recently released, we can reconstruct the sect's calendar in its entirety. We know from talmudic sources that the Boethusians, a group of Second Temple Jews closely linked to the Sadducees, as well as the authors of the apocryphal books of Jubilees and Enoch, advocated this same calendar.

The calendar consisted of three hundred sixty-four days, divided into twelve months of thirty days each. The months were calibrated according to the cycle of the sun. At the equinoxes and solstices at the end of each three-month cycle, a thirty-first day was added to that month.

This calendar helped the sectarians solve a thorny problem: establishing the date for the holiday of Shavuot. According to the Bible, the Israelites were to bring the Omer sacrifice, the sheaf of barley, beginning on the morrow following the "Sabbath" after Passover (Leviticus 23:15). From that day, they were to count forty-nine days, and on the fiftieth day they were to celebrate the holiday of Shavuot, the Festival of first fruits of wheat.

Followers of the Pharisaic-rabbinic tradition began their counting on the day after the first day of the Festival, because they understood "Sabbath" to mean "Festival," referring in this case to the first day of Passover. In contrast, the Dead Sea sect and the Boethusians interpreted "Sabbath" literally, so that they began their count on a Sunday. We now know from the Qumran evidence that this was the Sunday after the last day of the Festival. Under this system, the first day of the counting as well as the holiday of Shavuot always fell on a Sunday. The sectarian solar calendar guaranteed the sectarians' legal interpretation of the Torah.

But this calendar had one major disadvantage: it was short by a day and a quarter each year. We have no idea how the sect dealt with this problem. Scholars are divided over the question, some theorizing a system of intercalation—that is, adding extra days—that would equalize this otherwise imprecise calendar. It is more likely, however, that this calendar was never really put to the test except perhaps for a short period on the part of some of the sectarian groups.

In contrast, the calendar of the Pharisaic-rabbinic tradition, still in use today, used such a system of intercalation. That calendar consisted of twelve lunar months, totaling three hundred fifty-four days, to which every three years or so a month was added, thus bringing the calendar into harmony with the solar year and aligning the Festivals with their proper seasons.

Which calendar—solar or lunar—represents the original calendar of biblical Israel? Various evidence points to the lunar (Pharisaic-rabbinic) calendar, although we have no direct information about the process of intercalation in biblical times. The Hebrew language itself provides a clue. The Hebrew term for month, ḥodesh, refers to the new moon; another word for month, yeraḥ, is derived from yareaḥ, which denotes the moon itself. How else can we understand these terms except in the context of a lunar calendar system? Furthermore, it is unlikely—over the long biblical period—that a solar calendar for which no intercalation system is known would have functioned successfully.

But despite these arguments, some scholars claim that the biblical calendar was a solar one, and that the lunar (Pharisaic-rabbinic) calendar was an innovation. This theory implies that the sectarian groups continued to use the ancient calendar even after the Pharisees had changed it. In my view, evidence from the *Halakhic Letter* has decisively challenged the plausibility of this theory. For if such were the case, why did the sectarians in all their various polemics against their Pharisaic opponents not accuse the Pharisees of changing the calendar?

At the beginning of one manuscript of the *Halakhic Letter*, we find a three-hundred-sixty-four-day calendar. At the end of the calendar, just before moving on to the *Halakhic Letter*, the text says:

> And (thus) is the year completed, three hundred and six[ty four] days.
> (*HALAKHIC LETTER* A20–21)

Apparently, the scribe regarded this issue as so central to the founding of the sect that he appended a calendar text to the *Halakhic Letter* to fill in what he felt was missing. But why is this calendar missing in the text of the letter itself? We must conclude that the sect's founders did not accuse the Pharisees of changing the calendar because the Pharisees were in fact following the ancient calendar inherited from biblical times.

For reasons we cannot know, various groups of priests and others in this period apparently wanted calendar reform, replacement of the lunar calendar with a solar one. This demand was shared by a number of groups represented in the Qumran caves. However, the solar calendar is not the only one represented at Qumran. The *Daily Prayers* apportioned for the days of the month are in fact keyed to a lunar month. Did the Qumran sect use both calendars? Or do the materials based on the lunar calendar reflect the views of others outside the sect? Some scholars have suggested that the sect did indeed use both calendars and had developed a system for synchronizing them.

TEFILLIN AND MEZUZAH

Central to the religious life described in talmudic sources are tefillin and mezuzah. The tefillin, usually called phylacteries in English (a misnomer derived from the Greek word meaning "amulet"), are leather boxes containing parchments, each with certain biblical passages. The boxes are attached with leather thongs to the head and arm. The mezuzah (plural, mezuzot) is a similar parchment enclosed in a container and is attached to the right doorpost of doors and entryways. Previous to the discovery of the Qumran corpus there was much debate about the dating and extent of these practices in ancient Israel. The finding of large numbers of tefillin and mezuzot at Qumran has certainly shown that these practices date back at least to Hasmonaean times. But we still have questions about which groups practiced these commandments and how.

In dealing with the tefillin, we need to discuss several separate issues: how the leather boxes enclosing the scriptural texts were constructed, which passages were placed in the boxes, and how these passages were written.

In construction, the Qumran tefillin are generally similar to those known from rabbinic halakhah and traditional Jewish practice. The head tefillin, comprising four compartments, consists of a cube with its strap passing immediately below the cube. Each of the compartments contains one piece of parchment on

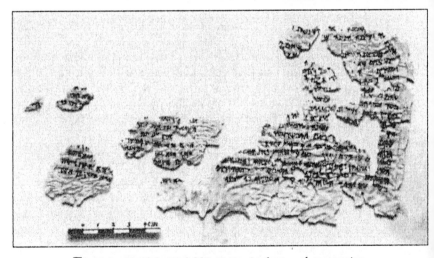

The Calendar of the *Halakhic Letter* At the top of manuscript A of the *Halakhic Letter* is the conclusion of a 364-day solar calendar such as that found in the books of Jubilees and Enoch, as well as in Qumran sectarian documents and in the *Temple Scroll.* It is most likely that the calendar was not originally part of the *Halakhic Letter* but that it was copied above it by a scribe who saw the calendar as intimately linked to the halakhic issues that led to the founding of the Qumran group. *Courtesy of the Israel Antiquities Authority.*

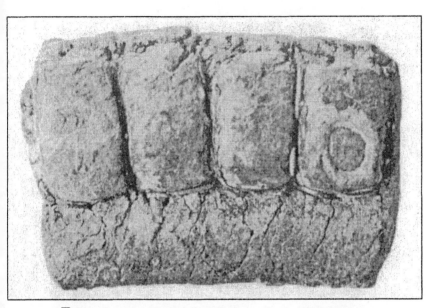

Tefillin, Outside View Tefillin (phylacteries)—the small, black leather boxes that contain scriptural portions to be fastened to the head and arm—were found in the Qumran caves. This example of a head tefillin is the only one in which the box was found intact. As is the case in later rabbinic tefillin, there were four sections in the head tefillin, each of which contained a separate parchment with biblical text. *Courtesy of the Shrine of the Book of the Israel Museum.*

which is written one or (in the case of some Qumran tefillin) more biblical passages. The arm tefillin contains passages all of which are written on one parchment enclosed in a single compartment. The arm tefillin, worn on the forearm, is arranged differently from the head tefillin, consisting of a cube sitting atop a rectangular base, the strap passing through the rectangle at its upper end. (In contrast, both head and arm tefillin today consist of cubes resting on rectangular bases.) In both head and arm tefillin, the leather compartment is stitched closed. All of the tefillin are made of blackened leather with the hair side facing out.

Everything described so far appears to have been acceptable both to the sectarians at Qumran, who certainly used these tefillin, and to the Pharisees, if we can judge by what the later Rabbis required. But such is not the case regarding what the tefillin contained. Virtually all the tefillin found at Qumran contain the four cardinal passages that were understood to mention tefillin—the same ones re-

Tefillin, Inside View When opened, the Qumran tefillin
contained four parchment strips containing biblical passages. It
was determined that the one on the left, clearly smaller than the
others, had been substituted by the seller—hence its different
appearance. *Courtesy of the Shrine of the Book of the Israel
Museum.*

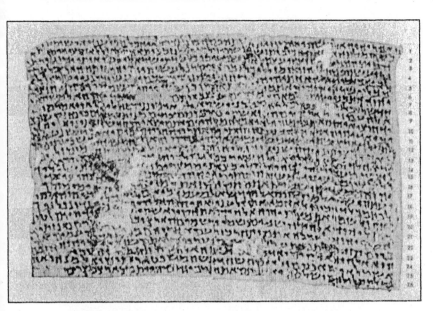

Tefillin, Text This manuscript is of one of the biblical sections found inside the tefillin. Since it contains additional biblical material not required by the later rabbinic tradition, these can be considered sectarian tefillin. The small, crowded script would certainly not have been acceptable by the standards of the later rabbis, but we cannot assume that all Jews fulfilling this commandment would have necessarily done so in accord with rabbinic norms. *Courtesy of the Shrine of the Book of the Israel Museum.*

quired by rabbinic law later on: Exodus 13:1–10, Exodus 11–16, Deuteronomy 6:4–9, and Deuteronomy 11:13–21. We can assume that at least for the Pharisees and the sectarians, these passages were required in Second Temple times. In addition, many of the tefillin contain other passages as well.

Rabbinic tradition testifies to disputes over the order of the passages enclosed in the tefillin. The evidence of the Qumran tefillin as a whole reveals fluidity in this regard: different phylacteries follow different sequences. We find the same situation in the Bar Kokhba caves, although here we find no additional passages besides the required ones. It seems that in Second Temple times, the order was not yet fixed as rigidly as it is today. And we cannot establish whether the tefillin from Qumran followed the order of the two major types known from later times

Order of Biblical Passages in Tefillin

Qumran Tefillin

Deut. 11:13–21	Ex. 13:11–16	Deut. 6:4–9	Ex. 13:1–10
[והיה אם שמע]	והיה כי יביאך	שמע ישראל	קדש לי כל בכור
4	3	2	1
Strap-passage			

Rashi Tefillin

Deut. 11:13–21	Deut. 6:4–9	Ex. 13:11–16	Ex. 13:1–10
והיה אם שמע	שמע ישראל	והיה כי יביאך	קדש לי כל בכור
4	3	2	1
Strap-passage			

Rabbenu Tam Tefillin

Deut. 6:4–9	Deut. 11:13–21	Ex. 13:11–16	Ex. 13:1–10
שמע ישראל	והיה אם שמע	והיה כי יביאך	קדש לי כל בכור
4	3	2	1
Strap-passage			

Adapted from Yadin, *Tefillin from Qumran*, 14.

as Rashi or Rabbenu Tam, named after the protagonists who continued this argument into the medieval period.

Because the Rabbis forbade insertion of additional passages to those required, scholars have theorized that those tefillin found at Qumran containing only required passages are Pharisaic-type tefillin. The Qumran sectarian tefillin are those which contain additional passages. Although this conclusion seems plausible, we have no way of proving such a contention.

When we examine how the Qumran tefillin passages are written we discover that the letters are not formed according to the halakhot found in later rabbinic texts, although corrections and other aspects of writing generally do follow rabbinic law. We cannot be sure whether this is because these laws did not yet exist, even among Pharisaic Jews, or because the sectarian users of these tefillin observed practices different from those of the Pharisaic-rabbinic movement.

These same findings about the formation of letters also apply to the biblical scrolls and mezuzot from Qumran. Since we now know that the biblical scrolls represent various communities in Israel during this period, we can conclude that these scribal regulations were either not yet in force or were not widely observed. If that were the case, then the tefillin from Qumran would be typical of those used in this period, even by Pharisees.

These tefillin raise another interesting issue: Only twenty to twenty-five have been found at Qumran. According to rabbinic sources, tefillin were not originally worn by all Jews, despite the Pharisaic-rabbinic claim that the Torah requires it. With time, however, more and more Jews began to wear them. Our specimens, then, probably date from a period before all Jews wore tefillin, which accounts for the relatively small number found at Qumran. But it is also possible that the small size and the fragility of the tefillin explain why a large number of specimens would not have survived.

A small number of mezuzot have also been found at Qumran. We learn from these that the same passages required by later rabbinic halakhah were also required here, namely Deuteronomy 6:4–9 and 11:13–21—the first two paragraphs of the Shema. But the Qumran mezuzah texts have some additional material, for example, the Ten Commandments (Exodus 20:1–14, Deuteronomy 5:6–18).

Again, we cannot be certain from the small number of samples how widely mezuzot were used by Jews then. All we can establish is that some Jews observed this commandment in the manner required by later tradition. The Rabbis constantly discussed the issue of additional passages, which some mezuzot contained.

The liturgy and ritual of rabbinic Judaism have roots in the traditions of the Second Commonwealth period, which the mishnaic Rabbis inherited. More than a century before the Destruction of the Temple, organized liturgical practices already were in place, at least among those Jews whose texts have survived among

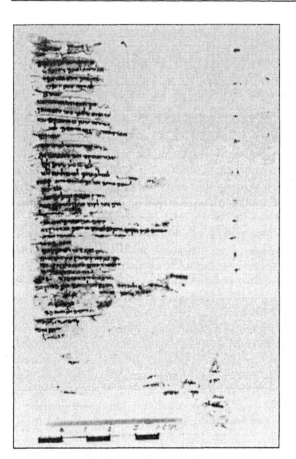

Mezuzah A number of mezuzot—biblical passages affixed to the doorpost— were found in the Qumran collection. As in the case of tefillin, scholars have questioned how early the observance of these commandments became widespread. The Qumran materials provide the earliest examples, reaching into the Hellenistic and early Roman periods. This poorly preserved exemplar contains Deuteronomy 10:12–11:21. *Courtesy of the Israel Antiquities Authority.*

the manuscripts of the Qumran library. Prayer was becoming increasingly important. Purification rituals were being observed. We can document that tefillin and mezuzot were used in that early period. By the time the Temple was destroyed, bringing to a close the age of sacrifice, the mishnaic sages, drawing on inherited traditions, began to standardize and develop the system of prayer and ritual embodied in the Jewish prayer book and in the life of Torah as it came to be understood by generations of Jews.

Our discussion now turns from the contemporary life of Qumran Jews to their vision of the End of Days. Indeed, we will see that the sect practiced its unique way of life in large measure as preparation for the soon-to-dawn messianic era.

PART V

Mysticism, Messianism, and the End of Days

CHAPTER 19

The Messianic Idea

The messianic idea has been central to the development of postbiblical Judaism in all its various forms. Generally speaking, the concept envisions the eventual coming of a redeemer, a descendant of David, who will bring about major changes in the world, leading to world peace, prosperity, and the end of evil and misfortune. Essential to the messianic idea in Judaism is the expectation that when the time comes, the ancient glories of the Davidic kingdom will be reestablished in the Land of Israel. Unquestionably this-worldly, Jewish messianism expresses its ideas in concrete terms. It looks forward to the messianic era, when the spiritual level of humanity will rise, resulting in and from the ingathering of Israel and the universal recognition of Israel's God. Of course, that definition is a sweeping generalization. In reality, the messianic idea in Judaism has a complex history, further complicated by the simultaneous existence, even within the same strain of Judaism, of various views of messianism. Within this history, we can distinguish certain patterns or trends of messianic thought.

Two basic ideals of Jewish messianism can be identified: the restorative and the utopian. The restorative seeks to bring back the ancient glories; the utopian, to bring about an even better future surpassing all that ever came before. The restorative represents a much more rational messianism, anticipating only the improvement and perfection of the present world. The utopian, on the other hand, is much more apocalyptic, looking forward to vast, catastrophic changes with the coming of the messianic age. The perfect world of the future can be built only upon the ruins of this world, after the annihilation of its widespread evil and transgression.

Neither approach can exist independent of the other; rather, both are found in the messianic aspirations of the various Jewish groups. The balance, or creative tension, between these tendencies is what determines the character of the various messianic strands.

Biblical Background

Although we are concerned mainly with the messianism of the Second Temple period, we first need to examine briefly how the concept was understood in the Hebrew Bible. Indeed, we can view all Jewish concepts of messianism as interpretations of biblical traditions.

The messianic ideal emerges from the biblical doctrine that David and his descendants were chosen by God to rule over Israel until the end of time (II Samuel 7; 23:1–3, 5). God also gave the Davidic house dominion over alien peoples (II Samuel 22:44–51 = Psalm 18:44–51; Psalm 2). In II Samuel 22:50–51 (= Psalm 18:50–51), we read of King David as the "anointed one" (*mashiaḥ*, messiah), whose descendants shall rule forever.

After the Israelite kingdom split when Solomon died and the size of the kingdom dwindled, a hope arose among the people that the ancient glories of the past would one day be restored. Such a reunited Davidic monarchy would also control the neighboring territories that were originally part of the Davidic and Solomonic empires. Isaiah describes the qualities of the future Davidic king, especially the justness of his rule (Isaiah 11:1–9).

Related to the concept of messianism is the biblical notion of the Day of the Lord. As expressed in prophetic literature, this notion states that at some certain but as yet unrevealed time, God will punish the wicked and bring about the triumph of justice and righteousness. The most prominent feature of this concept is its underlying sense of doom, including motifs of wailing and darkness.

The prophets proclaim that this day is near. By the time of Amos, in the earliest years of the literary prophets, the concept was already well established. The prophets warn the people that on that day, the wicked will be punished, justice will be established, and the destiny of the world will be changed. God will act in a sudden and decisive manner to destroy evil and exalt righteousness. The vision of this widespread destruction filled the prophets with intense dread.

The idea of a return to the bygone days of Davidic rule and to Israel's place as a world power typifies the restorative tendency: That which was and is no more will be again. On the other hand, the notion of the Day of the Lord—that catastrophic upheaval that will usher in a new age—is utopian, calling for the utter destruction of all evil and wickedness, something never before seen in the history of humanity: That which never was will be. These two approaches together molded the eschatological speculation on the part of all Jewish groups.

It is important to note that in the Hebrew Scriptures these ideas were still separate. It was their combination in Second Temple times that unleashed the powerful forces that eventually propelled the Jews to revolt against Rome and led the Christians to embrace a messianic figure.

THE SECOND TEMPLE PERIOD

These two messianic trends both could be found in the Second Temple period. Restorative views and utopian views of the Jewish future vied with one another as part of the melting pot of ideologies forging the varieties of Judaism in this era. The restorative trend emphasized primarily the reconstitution of the Davidic dynasty; the more utopian and apocalyptic varieties, taking their cue from the biblical notion of the Day of the Lord, focused mainly on the destruction of the wicked.

In early Second Temple times, the prophets Haggai and Zechariah anticipated that the Davidic kingdom would be renewed under Zerubbabel, a scion of King David who governed Judaea in the Persian period. At the same time, Zechariah prophesied about two "messianic" figures—the high priest and the messianic king (Zechariah 6:9–16). This essentially restorative approach would eventually be combined with more apocalyptic ideas in the thought of the Dead Sea sect.

The Book of Ben Sira (c. 180 B.C.E.), a text known at Qumran and at Masada, expresses the hope for a better future (Ben Sira 36:11–14):

> Gather all the tribes of Jacob,
> and give them their inheritance as at the beginning.
> Have mercy, O Lord,
> upon the people called by Your name,
> upon Israel whom You have likened to a firstborn son.
> Have pity on the city of Your sanctuary,
> Jerusalem, the place of Your rest.
> Fill Zion with the celebration of Your wondrous deeds,
> and Your Temple with Your glory.

Here the text speaks only of a return to the ancient glories. No messianic king is mentioned. The notion that the priesthood will be continued is much more prominent than the reestablishment of the Davidic dynasty (Ben Sira 45:24–25). We also see here the notion of Elijah as harbinger of the messiah (Ben Sira 48:10–11).

The Psalms of Solomon, composed in Greek probably in the time of Pompey (63–48 B.C.E.), focus on the figure of the messianic king. The author emphasizes the kingship of God as well as the permanent nature of the Davidic house (*Psalms of Solomon* 17:1, 5). Most probably, the Roman domination of Jerusalem at that time encouraged the author's longing for a Davidic king, to rule over Israel, crush its enemies, and cleanse Jerusalem of the gentiles (*Psalms of*

Solomon 17:23–27). Then righteousness will reign and the land will again be returned to the tribal inheritances (Psalms of Solomon 17:28–31). The gentiles will serve the Davidic king and come up to Jerusalem to see the glory of the Lord. This righteous king will bless his people with wisdom and be blessed by God. The text describes the king as the "anointed of the Lord." Despite God's providential intervention on his behalf, this messiah is seen here strictly as a worldly ruler, a flesh-and-blood king of Israel.

Extremely significant, but at the same time elusive, is the relationship of the Pharisees and the Sadducees to the question of messianic belief. Josephus relates that these two groups were divided over the eternal nature of the soul—the Pharisees accepting this idea, the Sadducees rejecting it. However, we have no reason to believe that the Sadducees similarly rejected the notion of a restorative messianism in accord with the biblical traditions. Neither can we determine the nature of Pharisaic messianism during this period. As in so many other cases, the views of the Pharisees and Sadducees must remain shrouded in mystery.

The Second Temple views we have discussed so far are essentially restorative. We find the more utopian view first expressed in the Book of Daniel and in later sources following its approach, most of which combine the Davidic messiah with the victory of the righteous, a motif found in Daniel. The Book of Daniel anticipates a time of deliverance following the present age of distress (Daniel 12:1). At that time God will judge the kingdoms of this world, taking away their temporal powers. The "holy ones of the Most High" will inherit eternal dominion. The righteous and the evildoers both will be resurrected to receive their just desserts. However, Daniel's vision does not include a messianic king.

Sibylline Oracles 3:652–795, composed in Greek and usually dated to about 140 B.C.E., is almost exclusively messianic in content. Yet only at the beginning does it briefly mention the messianic king, who will put an end to war, in obedience to God's command. When this king arises, the gentile kings will attack the Temple and the Land of Israel. But God will cause them to perish. As in descriptions of the biblical Day of the Lord, various natural phenomena will accompany these events. The attackers will ultimately die, and the children of God will live in peace and tranquillity with God's help.

Although the older strata of I Enoch have little messianic material, it is useful to examine that text's vision of the end of history expressed in 90:13–38. In a section of the book found in the Qumran collection, the author anticipates a final attack by the gentiles, who will be defeated by means of God's miraculous intervention. God will then replace the old Jerusalem with a new one:

> And I saw until the Lord of the sheep brought a new house greater and loftier than the first and set it up in place of the first. . . . All its pillars were new and larger than those of the first, the old one which He had taken away, and all the sheep (the people of Israel) were within it. (I ENOCH 90:29)

Then the messiah will appear, and all the gentiles will adopt the Lord's ways. In this vision, the messiah enters only at the end of a process ushered in by God Himself.

The Parables of Enoch (chs. 37–71) primarily follow the approach of Daniel—with one notable exception: In this text, the expression "son of man" is now applied to the messiah, who is assumed literally to come from heaven and to be preexistent. Scholars have devoted considerable attention to this section of Enoch, focusing on the parallel use of the term "son of man" in the New Testament to describe Jesus. But this section of the text, not found in any of the Qumran manuscripts of Enoch, is believed not to have been part of the original book. Thus, the scrolls provide no evidence that the term "son of man" had an earlier messianic connotation.

The Assumption of Moses, written in either Hebrew or Aramaic most probably around the turn of the era, mentions no messiah but expresses a wish for the destruction of the wicked (ch. 10). The same vision of the future can be found in Jubilees. The Assumption of Moses speaks of a messianic figure, an angel of God, but mentions no human agent of salvation.

This second group of sources—Sibylline Oracles, Parables of Enoch, Jubilees, and Assumption of Moses—reflects the utopian trend, with its expectation that the wicked will eventually be destroyed. These sources are closely linked to dualistic ideas about the struggle between good and evil. Although each messianic approach includes elements of the other, it was left for the Qumran sect to integrate both trends coherently into one system, thus creating at the same time tremendous tension and tremendous power.

MESSIANISM AMONG THE DEAD SEA SECTARIANS

From the very beginning of Dead Sea Scrolls scholarship, it has been clear that the documents of the Qumran sect placed great emphasis on eschatology. A number of documents are dedicated almost completely to issues relating to the End of Days. From the *Scroll of the War of the Sons of Light against the Sons of Darkness,* we learn that the sect expected to participate in the battle that would usher in the final age.

This vision of a cataclysmic battle and the ensuing radical changes in the world order have earned the Qumran group the label "apocalyptic." The notion of a great battle, similar in many ways to the Day of the Lord found in the Hebrew Bible, typifies apocalyptic sects. Various other texts from the Qumran corpus, including the *Florilegium,* have greatly added to our understanding of the messianic age in the ideology of the Qumran sect.

According to the dominant view in the sectarian texts from Qumran, two messiahs were to lead the congregation in the End of Days, one priestly and the other lay. At the same time, the sect expected a prophet who was a quasi-messianic figure. The idea of a priestly messiah reflects the central role of the priesthood in the origins, leadership, and organization of the Qumran sect.

The messiah of Aaron would dominate religious matters; the messiah of Israel would rule over temporal and political matters. Both messiahs would preside over the eschatological banquet. This messianic paradigm of two leaders, based on the Moses/Aaron and Joshua/Zerubbabel model, would later be applied to Bar Kokhba and the High Priest Eleazar in the Bar Kokhba revolt (132–135 C.E.). To the sect, the coming of the messiahs of Israel and Aaron and the eschatological prophet augured the restoration of the old order.

So far we have described restorative tendencies based on the biblical prophetic visions. But the Qumran sect went much further. Reflecting the apocalyptic trend, it anticipated that the advent of the messianic age would be heralded by the great war described in the *War Scroll*, leading to the victory of the forces of good over those of evil, in heaven above and on earth below. After forty years the period of wickedness would come to an end; then the elect would attain glory.

The messianic banquet, which will be treated in detail in the next chapter, is described in *Rule of the Congregation*. Presided over by the two messiahs, it would usher in the new age that would include worship at the eschatological Temple. Sacrificial worship would be conducted according to sectarian law.

In essence, Jews in the messianic age would surpass their current level of purity and perfection in observing Jewish law. Here in the sphere of Jewish law we again find the utopian trend. Only in the future age will it be possible properly to observe the Torah as interpreted by the sect.

Equally important to the sectarians was the immediacy of the End of Days. They anticipated that the old order would soon die. The sect lived on the verge of the End of Days, with one foot, as it were, in the present age and one foot in the future. They were convinced that the messianic era would happen in their lifetime. Their move to the desert from the main population centers of Judaea and their establishment of a center at Qumran had marked the dawn of the new order. Their lives were dedicated to preparing for that new age by living as if it had already come. It is within such a framework that we must approach *Rule of the Congregation*, for it sets out the nature of the future community of perfect holiness.

We cannot precisely date the elements of Qumran messianic doctrine or their crystallization except to place them sometime in the Hasmonaean period. The combination of the two trends, restorative and utopian, that appeared for the first time at Qumran, later exercised a powerful role in the future of Jewish messianic speculation.

MESSIANIC FIGURES IN THE QUMRAN SECTARIAN TEXTS

Among the documents of the Qumran sect, quite a number refer explicitly to messianic figures. Many of the texts speak of two messianic figures; others speak of only one. The former texts assume that the priestly messiah—the messiah of Aaron—will preside over the rebuilt and reconstituted Temple, and a lay messiah will reign as king over the Land of Israel. Others, specifically alluding to a Davidic messiah—a descendant of King David—anticipate only one messiah, whose primary role will be to conduct the temporal affairs of the nation.

The scrolls mention a number of other eschatological figures along with these messiahs. Especially important is the Teacher of Righteousness expected to arise in the End of Days to interpret the law. The Prince of the Congregation, on the other hand, will serve as the sect's military leader at that time. It is also possible that "prince" simply represents an alternative name for the king who will rule in the messianic era, as this term is used in the Book of Ezekiel. Some texts also speak about an eschatological prophet who will announce the coming of the messiah, a figure similar to Elijah in the rabbinic tradition.

Scholarly debate about the sectarian concept of messiah began when the *Zadokite Fragments* was discovered at the end of the past century. In that scroll, the phrase "those anointed with His holy spirit (of prophecy)" parallels the phrase "true prophets" (*Zadokite Fragments* 2:12). Clearly in this text, the Hebrew term "*mashiah*" has not yet acquired its later, unequivocal meaning of "messiah," but rather retains its earlier meaning—a person appointed for a specific leadership role—derived from the widespread custom in the ancient Near East of anointing priests and kings.

Yet the text may also suggest someone other than an earthly authority. It asserts that the "period of evil" will come to an end when:

> there shall arise the one who teaches righteousness in the End of Days.
> (*ZADOKITE FRAGMENTS* 6:10–11)

Does this passage refer to the teacher of the sect himself, whose lifetime will extend into the End of Days, or does it refer to an eschatological Teacher of Righteousness who is yet to arise? Unfortunately, the syntax of this passage is sufficiently difficult that we cannot be certain.

In another passage, the text describes an eschatological era yet to arrive, alluded to in the phrase "with the coming of the messiah" or "messiahs" "of Aaron and of Israel" (*Zadokite Fragments* 19:10–11). Some scholars claim that this text refers to one messianic figure, representing both the priesthood and the people of Israel. Others argue, however, that the text refers to two messiahs—the Aaronide, high-priestly messiah, and the lay, temporal messiah.

Later on in the scroll we encounter the phrase "until the rise of a messiah from Aaron and from Israel" (*Zadokite Fragments* 20:1). Again we are faced with two possible interpretations. The text envisages either only one messiah—"from Aaron *and* from Israel"—or two—one from Aaron, the other from Israel.

When *Rule of the Community* became known after the first Qumran scrolls were discovered, this ambiguity was substantially clarified. In its most significant passage regarding messianism, the text states that in the End of Days, sect members will still be prohibited from mingling property with those outside the sect:

> lest they be judged by the former regulations by which the men of the community began to be judged until the coming of a prophet and the messiahs of Aaron and Israel. (*RULE OF THE COMMUNITY 9:11–12*)

Unlike the case of the *Zadokite Fragments*, this text unquestionably refers to two messiahs, who will be announced by an eschatological prophet.

Based on the cave 4 manuscripts of *Rule of the Community*, the original publication team argued that this passage was added to the text later in the history of the sect. However, the evidence in these manuscripts does not sufficiently support such an assertion. As far as we can tell, the two-messiah concept was part of *Rule of the Community* from the time it was composed.

Furthermore, because the priestly role was more prominent in the sect's earliest history, gradually weakening as lay power increased, we would expect to encounter this notion of priestly preeminence in the End of Days in earlier sectarian documents, not later ones. Significantly, the two-messiah concept is also known from various other Second Temple sources, most notably the Testaments of the Twelve Patriarchs. Thus, it could have entered into the sect's thinking at any time.

These texts nowhere identify the lay messiah of Israel as Davidic. And in addition to the two messiahs, they mention an eschatological prophet who will join the messiahs in settling unresolved controversies in Jewish law, a role assigned to Elijah by later rabbinic tradition.

Apparently, the scribe of the *Rule Scroll* saw strong enough links between *Rule of the Community* and *Rule of Benedictions* to include them in the same manuscript (along with *Rule of the Congregation*, to be discussed in detail below). Opinions differ about who is being blessed in the various fragmentary poems in *Rule of Benedictions*. One benediction definitely refers to the Prince of the Congregation, an eschatological leader (*Rule of Benedictions* 5:20). A short excerpt follows:

> [And there shall rest upon him the spirit of coun]sel and eternal valor, a spirit of knowledge and reverence for God. And justice shall be the girdle of [your loins,] [and faithful]ness the girdle of your wa[is]t.
> (*RULE OF BENEDICTIONS 5:25–26*)

Deposits of Animal Bones Buried around buildings in the Qumran settlement were various deposits of animal bones, containing the remains of cooked—and apparently eaten—sheep, goats, and cattle. The bones were buried in jars covered with lids. Even though some scholars have argued that these are remains of sacrifices, there is no evidence for animal sacrifice at Qumran. *Courtesy of the Israel Antiquities Authority.*

This passage, clearly alluding to Isaiah's famous prophecy about the Davidic messiah (Isaiah 11:2–5), suggests that the Prince of the Congregation designates this figure. If so, then the term "prince" is clearly based on the Ezekiel tradition.

Thus we find that to the extent it can be reconstructed, *Rule of Benedictions* assumes that a Davidic messiah will arise in the End of Days. The text does not explicitly mention a priestly messiah, but it is possible that the full text, in a portion not preserved, did refer to such a figure.

We might have expected that the *War Scroll,* itself a description of a messianic battle between the forces of good and evil, would specifically mention the messiah. But although Israel and Aaron appear on the banner of the entire congregation along with the names of the twelve tribes (*War Scroll* 3:12), the term *"mashiah"* in the phrase "your anointed ones, the seers of things ordained" (*War Scroll* 11:7–8) refers only to prophets. Indeed, the text never explicitly mentions a messiah, perhaps because it describes only events leading up to the messianic era, not events unfolding during that era itself. On the other hand, if the Prince of the Congregation mentioned in the text refers to the lay messiah, then the prince would stand together with the high priest also described in that text. In that case, the scroll would express the two-messiah concept.

Pesher Isaiah A refers to the Prince of the Congregation who will participate in an eschatological battle. The same text interprets Isaiah 11:1–5 as referring to a Davidic messiah, who will arise in the End of Days to rule over the nations. The text of *Florilegium* describes the messianic era when the shoot of David:

> will arise in the End of Days with the Interpreter of the Law who [will rule] over Zi[on in] the End of Days. (*FLORILEGIUM 1:11–12*)

This clearly alludes to a Davidic messiah, who will save Israel. Alongside him will be the Interpreter of the Law, identified by some scholars as a priestly messianic figure.

Here again we encounter explicit references to a Davidic messiah. But the text does not explicitly mention the priestly messiah, unless we identify the messiah of Aaron with the Interpreter of the Law. However, elsewhere in the scroll, the eschatological priest plays a cultic, rather than an educational or exegetical, role.

What emerges from the preceding discussion is that, contrary to the popular view, Qumran sectarian literature expressed two competing messianic ideas: the notion of a single, Davidic messiah and the notion of two complementary messiahs—the Aaronide, priestly leader and the lay messiah of Israel. We must resolutely resist the temptation to conflate these two ideas by first trying to force all Qumran texts into the two-messiah rubric and then falsely identifying the messiah of Israel as Davidic. As in every religious group, sectarians did not always agree, and certainly not in the case of messianic ideology.

LITERARY EVIDENCE OF MESSIANISM IN THE DEAD SEA SCROLLS

It is clear by surveying the scrolls that a variety of motifs and beliefs are distributed throughout many different texts in what may appear to be random fashion. Two possible explanations can be suggested for this pluralism of ideas: Either several parallel approaches coexisted within the group, or the ideas evolved gradually over time. Thus, certain messianic ideas may be earlier, and others later. Most likely, both dynamics operated in the Qumran community. It is virtually impossible to separate coexisting trends from those developing over time, except in certain particular cases. It is also significant that in certain texts, messianism is absent altogether.

More difficult to reckon with, and certainly the case at Qumran, is the confluence of both the restorative and utopian trends found in the literature. The traditions of pre-Hasmonaean Judaism, the new ideas evolving both within the sect and in the general community outside, and the momentous historical forces at work during the period all joined together to produce a set of related but differing concepts. Those concepts, distributed throughout both time and text, express certain common elements, yet testify to diversity and pluralism even within the Dead Sea sect.

It was once thought that a history of the messianic idea at Qumran could be constructed that would go hand in hand with the archaeological reconstruction of the site's history of occupation. However, it has proven impossible to stratify the sect's messianic beliefs historically, as scholars have discovered from surveying the texts. It is clear that in every period, a variety of ideas coexisted within the group. It is far more helpful to analyze the scrolls according to the two dominant trends in Jewish messianism—the restorative and the utopian.

At Qumran those texts that espouse the Davidic messiah tend toward the restorative, emphasizing the prophecies of peace and prosperity and not expecting the cataclysmic destruction of all evil. The more catastrophic, utopian, or even apocalyptic tendencies usually exclude a Davidic messiah. They seek instead to invest authority in a dominant, priestly, religious leader and a temporal prince who will be subservient to the priestly figure. They give no evidence of Davidic allegiance. Instead, they transpose the prominent role of the priesthood in sectarian life onto the End of Days. Sometimes the utopians sought to limit the leadership to one messianic figure. We occasionally encounter both the restorative and utopian trends side by side in the same text, demonstrating that these two trends were beginning the long process of merging into what later would become the messianic ideal of rabbinic Judaism.

We will never be able to construct an exact historical sequence for the messianic ideas and texts found at Qumran. The best we can do is to understand them within the framework just proposed: a matrix of history on one axis and the restorative-utopian dichotomy on the other. Only through such a dynamic perspective can we make sense of the rich and variegated eschatological ideas and approaches represented in the Dead Sea Scrolls. Above all, we cannot approach these materials as a monolithic corpus.

The eschatological nature of many of the Qumran texts gives us an idea of the kind of world the sectarians envisioned in the future: how they would prepare for the End of Days, what events would occur to precipitate it, what battles the sect would fight against its enemies, and what the ultimate, perfected world would be like. These concepts were intimately connected with the sectarian laws and practices that were designed to cultivate purity and perfection. In the next chapter, we will study how the sect hoped to realize its goals in the messianic community that would emerge immediately after the great eschatological war.

CHAPTER 20

The Community at
the End of Days

In the messianic vision of the Dead Sea sect, the approaching End of Days would inaugurate an era of perfection and engender the fulfillment of the rituals and regulations the sect was currently practicing. The resulting eschatological community would reflect the perfection of the present community at Qumran. Men, women, and children who had attained the highest standards of ritual purity would participate in the new community's holy convocations. Assemblies of these deserving persons would conduct the affairs of the sect, pass judgment, and declare war. As in the period of the Israelites' desert wandering, the Levites would assume defined leadership roles in the sect's future life. The Zadokite priesthood would emerge as its dominant force.

FUNCTIONS AND PURITY OF THE ASSEMBLY IN THE END OF DAYS

Rule of the Congregation specifies the functions of the assembly in the End of Days, emphasizing that all who attend must be ritually pure.

> And if there shall be a convocation of all the congregation for judgment or for a council of the community, or for a convocation of war, they shall sanctify them(selves) for three days, so that everyone who comes shall be pre[pared for the coun]cil. *(RULE OF THE CONGREGATION 1:25–27)*

This future council was to perform the same function as performed by the sectarian legislative and judicial assembly, which was the highest court in the daily life of the Qumran sect.

The second function of the assembly was to oversee observance of the law, in accord with sectarian interpretation, and codification of the law, as decided by the sect. The assembly would make decisions pertaining to the sect's organization and structure as well as the status of members. Although all Israel would become members of the community in the End of Days, status within the sect would still have to be determined, a function performed by the assembly.

The final purpose of the assembly was to declare war. This detail is significant because it identifies the stage in the unfolding messianic era when the assembly was to emerge. According to the *War Scroll*, a series of battles and a cycle of victories were to lead to the final End of Days. Thereafter, when all the enemies of Israel had been destroyed and all Israel had either repented and become part of the sect or had been extirpated, eternal peace would reign.

Therefore, our text, in discussing how the assembly will decide whether or not to go to war, must be describing the period inaugurating the End of Days. After receiving some sign that the End of Days had dawned, this assembly would then decide to initiate the series of events announced in the *War Scroll* and would preside over the sect's role in those final battles.

The three functions of the assembly—conducting the sect's affairs, passing judgment, and declaring war—parallel the functions assigned to the later mishnaic Sanhedrin, the court of seventy-one. Like the sectarian assembly in the End of Days, the rabbinic Sanhedrin was to serve as final arbiter in matters of law. Only the Great Sanhedrin could declare war, since only that body could decide if a war would be justified and permitted according to the law of the Torah.

A special state of purity, attained by means of a three-day purification ritual, was required before attendance at a session of the eschatological assembly of the Qumran sect. No doubt this rite was modeled on the three days of preparation observed by the children of Israel before the revelation at Sinai (Exodus 19:10–11, 14–15). According to the biblical account, during this preparation period the Israelites abstained from sexual relations, washed their garments, and performed purification rites, most probably ablutions.

Joining in the messianic convocation required the same level of sanctity and purification, since the sect regarded the actions of the assembly as a continuation of the revelation at Sinai. Indeed, the concept of inspired biblical interpretation that underlay Qumran law assumed that sect members would be acting under divine inspiration at assembly sessions.

THE MESSIANIC WAR

At the onset of the messianic war, the sect would be mustered to fight battles against evildoers and against those who did not know the correct interpretation of the Torah expounded by the sect:

> And th[is is the book of the disposition of] the war. The first engagement of the Sons of Light shall be to attack the lot of the Sons of Darkness, the army of Belial, the troop of Edom and Moab, and the sons of Ammon and the army [of the inhabitants of] Philistia and the troops of the Kittim of Assyria, and in

league with them the violators of the covenant. . . . [That shall be] a time of deliverance for the people of God, an appointed time of dominion for all men of His lot, and eternal annihilation for all the lot of Belial. There shall be [great] panic [among] the sons of Japheth, Assyria shall fall, and no one will help him. And the dominion of the Kittim shall depart, so that wickedness will be subdued without a remnant, and none shall escape of [all the Sons of] Darkness. *(WAR SCROLL 1:1–2, 5–7)*

This graphic description of the beginning of the messianic war identifies the traditional enemies of the Jewish people and marks them for destruction. The names of the nations, originally designating biblical enemies, now refer to the surrounding nations on all sides during this period. Belial is the archangel of evil, the heavenly leader of the lot (the preordained group) of evildoers. The Sons of Darkness are all those who represent evil and oppose the sect. The text continues by describing in detail the fanfare of trumpets, banners, qualifications of officers, battle formations, weapons and horsemen, the progress of the battles, and slain enemies.

Ultimately the sect would overcome its enemies and be victorious. Numbered among the blessed who would survive the battles would be the righteous of Israel, who will have turned to God and adopted the sectarian way of life. Together with the original sectarians, they would constitute the eschatological community.

This new community would then gather together for the messianic banquet, presumably in the aftermath of the great war between the Sons of Light and the Sons of Darkness. Under the leadership of the Zadokite priestly messiah and the renewed king of Israel, they would reconstitute the life of Israel on its land in accord with sectarian views. Together the people of Israel would then live a life of purity and perfection.

From the very beginning, the sect would conduct the war of the End of Days in a state of absolute ritual purity, in accord with the sect's interpretation of the Torah's requirements (Deuteronomy 23:10–15). The *War Scroll* specifies that:

No young boy or woman shall enter their encampments when they go forth from Jerusalem to go forth to battle until they return. Any one who is halt or blind or lame, or a man in whose body there is a permanent defect, or a man affected by an impurity of his flesh, all these shall not go forth to battle with them. All of them shall be volunteers for battle and sound in spirit and flesh, and ready for the day of vengeance. *(WAR SCROLL 7:3–5)*

Those to be excluded from this final battle parallel a list found in *Rule of the Congregation*, enumerating those barred from the council of the community. Here are included the crippled, lame, blind, deaf, dumb, men with blemishes, and the "tottering old man" (2:3–11). These prohibitions were derived from Leviticus 13 and 21, which discusses the disqualification of priests from Temple service. Since the sect saw itself as constituting a sanctuary through its dedication to a

War Scroll The *Scroll of the War of the Sons of Light against the Sons of Darkness* was one of the first seven scrolls recovered. It sets out a schematized plan for a messianic war in which the members of the sect, and those who join them in the End of Days, destroy all their enemies and capture Jerusalem. The scroll describes the military tactics and religious rituals expected to accompany such a messianic battle. *Courtesy of the Shrine of the Book of the Israel Museum.*

life of holiness and purity, it accordingly extended the Torah's legislation for the priesthood to its own eschatological assembly.

The *War Scroll* specifically explains why the messianic assembly requires that those attending be pure and excludes the aged and those with specific deformities: in the End of Days, sectarians would wage war in the presence of the holy angels. A poetic passage (*War Scroll* 12:7–8) describes this awesome array:

> For the Lord is holy, and the King of Glory is with us.
>
> A people of holy ones, her[oes and] a host of angels is mustered with us,
>
> and the Mighty One of w[ar] is in our congregation,
>
> and the host of His spirits marches with us.

The sect firmly believed that just as the world below was divided into the domains of the two spirits, those of good and evil, so too was the world of the angels

Just as the Teacher of Righteousness and the Wicked Priest represented the forces of good and evil in the present age, so too the Prince of Light (the angel Michael) and his enemy Belial represented the same forces on high. In the End of Days, these forces would be arrayed against each other, just as they were in the present, premessianic age.

The great eschatological battle would therefore be fought both in heaven and on earth. In this simultaneous common battle, men would fight alongside angelic comrades-in-arms. After the long series of engagements described in the *War Scroll*, the forces of good would triumph. The sect believed that in the End of Days the angels would be present in the military camp described in the *War Scroll*. And the eschatological council would also include both earthly and heavenly Sons of Light.

After the final battle, the eschatological community would be set up with the Zadokite priests and two messiahs at its head. In perfect purity they would then conduct the messianic banquet for those who were worthy, that is, those predestined to belong to the sect.

MEAL OF THE END OF DAYS

The Dead Sea sect envisaged an eschatological meal at which the priestly messiah together with the messiah of Israel would eat bread and wine amidst the entire congregation of Israel. The messianic banquet is described in *Rule of the Congregation:*

> [The ses]sion of the men of renown, [invited to] the feast for the council of the community when [at the end] (of days) the messiah [shall assemble] with them. [The priest] shall enter [at] the head of all the congregation of Israel, and [all his brethren the sons of] Aaron, the priests, [who are invited] to the feast, the men of renown, and they shall sit be[fore him, each] according to his importance. Afterwards, [the messiah] of Israel [shall enter] and the heads of the [thousands of Israel] shall sit before him, [ea]ch according to his importance, according to [his station] in their encampments and their journeys. And all of the heads of the [households of the congrega]tion, [their] sag[es and wise men,] shall sit before them, each according to his importance. [When they] mee[t at the] communal [tab]le, [to set out bread and wi]ne, and the communal table is arranged [to eat and] to dri[nk] wine, [no] one [shall extend] his hand to the first (portion) of the bread and [the wine] before the priest. Fo[r he shall] bless the first (portion) of the bread and the win[e and shall extend] his hand to the bread first. Afterwa[rds,] the messiah of Israel [shall exten]d his hands to the bread. [Afterwards,] all of the congregation of the community [shall ble]ss, ea[ch according to] his importance. [They] shall act according to this statute whenever (the meal) is ar[ranged] when as many as ten [meet] together. *(RULE OF THE CONGREGATION 2:11–22)*

The banquet was to be presided over by the two messianic figures anticipated by the sectarians: the priest, under whose administration and direction the sacrificial worship would be restored in the New Jerusalem, and the messiah of Israel, who would serve as the temporal and military leader. Because the priesthood and the future restoration of the purified Temple ritual were so important at Qumran, the priestly messiah was accorded the higher status.

Before continuing our discussion of this passage, one detail must be noted. The words translated previously as "shall assemble" (placed in brackets because they are virtually illegible), have been translated by some scholars as "will be born," based on an alternative reading of the traces of the letters. That reading has spawned considerable speculation that this text parallels the accounts of the birth of Jesus found in the New Testament. However, such an interpretation is problematic for two reasons. First, new photographs taken in Amman, where this scroll was on exhibit during the 1967 war and where it has therefore remained, indicate that the reading I have proposed is correct. Second, the context here does not support a description of the birth of the messiah, but rather it describes the assembly of the End of Days that could logically take place only during the adulthood of both messianic figures.

The bread and wine mentioned here would not constitute the entire menu. They are singled out only because benedictions would have to be recited over them at the eschatological meal. The benediction over bread would cover all other foods except for the wine brought to the table during the meal, which would require its own benediction. Whereas the sect's communal meal described in *Rule of the Community* (6:2–5) required either bread or wine, the messianic banquet would include both. The priest would recite the benediction first and would also receive the first portion. All others present would recite the benediction after the priestly messiah in the order of their rank. The meals would require a quorum of ten men. Together with the court of ten that functioned in the sect, this quorum reminds us of the minyan—the minimum of ten adult males required for public worship in Jewish tradition.

The ultimate perfection of the messianic era would fulfill the sect's ambition to achieve total ritual purity. Indeed, such total purity might be regarded as a catalyst that could turn the ordinary communal meal into a foretaste of the great messianic banquet at the End of Days.

THE SECTARIAN COMMUNAL MEAL

Although the messianic banquet of rabbinic sources was envisioned as a onetime affair inaugurating the messianic era, the Dead Sea community looked forward to a regular series of such banquets, as is evident from the words "whenever (the meal) is ar[ranged] when as many as ten [meet] together." The sectarian practice of acting out the future messianic banquet in their everyday lives indicates the messianic overtones that were ever present during their frequent communal meals.

Rule of the Community alludes to the communal meal eaten during the present age. Wherever members of the group reside:

> Together they shall eat; together they shall bless; and together they shall take counsel. *(RULE OF THE COMMUNITY 6:2–3)*

While this passage clearly indicates that communal meals were to be a part of the activities of the sect, it gives no specific information regarding them. There is no mention here of how often such meals should occur or whether all or only some meals were to be eaten communally.

Furthermore, the actions described here—eating, blessing, and taking counsel—are independent of one another. The community held various gatherings to fulfill each purpose. Blessing was apparently part of a fixed regimen of daily prayers such as those known from cave 4, which we have investigated in an earlier chapter. The blessing mentioned in the foregoing passage refers not to the blessings recited over food, but rather to the liturgical worship by the group. Taking counsel occurred in the sectarian legislative and judicial assembly.

What, then, actually happened when sectarians ate together at a communal meal?

THE NONSACRAL NATURE OF THE COMMUNAL MEAL

Rule of the Community specifies that whenever there are ten members of the group, there must always be a priest (6:3–4). As in the messianic banquet, the members were to sit before the priest according to rank and in that order are asked for their counsel. At this point comes the only direct mention in this text of a meal:

> Whenever they arrange the table to eat or the wine to drink, the priest shall extend his hand first to bless the first (portion) of the bread or the wine. *(RULE OF THE COMMUNITY 6:4–5)*

Claiming an analogy between this description and the Christian Eucharist, dominant scholarly opinion has tended to characterize the sect's communal meals as sacral. In fact, some even consider the sacral meal of bread and wine central to Qumran fellowship, tracing its origins back to the priestly traditions of the Temple. By that analogy, the communal meal would effectively have replaced the sacrificial rituals in the Temple from which the sectarian Zadokite priests had withdrawn.

However, let us take a closer look at the passage. First, it indicates no obligation that all meals be communal. Second, it is clear that the priest is accorded special honors strictly because of position, not because of the performance of a substitute sacrifice. Third, bread and wine are mentioned simply because they were the usual food and drink at meals. As we can see from many literary sources, bread was the staple food in that region and period. Wine was a weak, diluted, and often unfermented grape wine, similar to modern grape juice. This passage from *Rule of the Community* does not describe meals at which both bread and wine are required, but rather occasions at which the table is set for bread or wine. The purpose of these occasions is not specified.

We have no evidence that the Qumran authors regarded their meals as a substitute for the sacrificial service. The required purity of food and drink and the rituals associated with grace before and after meals were certainly widespread by that time, but such practices in no way prove that every meal was sacral. All the motifs—purity, benedictions, bread and wine, role of the priest—can be explained within the context of contemporary Jewish ceremonial and ritual practice.

First and foremost among the so-called sacral features of this meal is the singular role of the priest, who blesses and eats first. However, we know that during Second Temple times, priests were called to read the first portion of the Torah (which includes the recitation of the initial benediction), to pronounce the grace after meals first, and to receive the best portion of food first. Such procedures were probably ancient customs that demonstrated no more than people's deep reverence for priest, Temple, and sacrificial service. Showing this respect for the priest in no way transformed the meal into a sacral occasion. Rather, the priest is simply being granted the privilege of being the first to perform rituals permitted to each and every Jew present. In fact, if the meal were indeed sacral, only the priest would be privileged to perform these rituals by virtue of his special status.

The second motif usually seen as sacral is ritual purity. Of course, there is no question that the members of the sect ate their communal meals in a state of ritual purity. However, as we saw in our earlier discussion of initiation rites, the sect placed substantial emphasis on ritual purity relative to food. As new recruits' state of purity rose, they were allowed increasing contact with pure food and drink, moving progressively closer to full membership in the sect.

These purity laws, however, did not designate meals as sacred. First, the laws of purity were to be observed by members at all times, whether they ate alone or communally. Indeed, these laws represent the ancient heritage of the priesthood, and like the Pharisees, the Qumran sect extended them to a wider range of adherents. Second, purity of food was an obligation and did not impart any sacral character to the act of eating. One might even argue that these purity laws were, from a functional point of view, similar to the laws of kosher food, although, of course, according to Jewish law, they constitute two distinct categories.

Nor do the benedictions recited by the priest render the meal sacral. By early rabbinic times, blessings both before and after meals were most probably part of the life of the *havurah*, the table fellowship group described in talmudic sources. In fact, these benedictions were to be recited over anything one ate; they bear no sacral connotations.

The benedictions mentioned in Josephus's description of the Essenes should be understood in the same spirit. There the priest says grace before and after the meal (*War* 2, 131). Correctly interpreting this practice in light of Palestinian Jewish custom of his day, Josephus notes that "at the beginning and at the close they do homage to God as the bountiful giver of life."

Thus, the rules of purity and benedictions had a character and importance all their own. In fact, by this time they were totally divorced from the Temple context. They were now part of the daily life of many pious Palestinian Jews, whether Essene, Pharisee, Sadducee, or sectarian at Qumran.

ARCHAEOLOGICAL EVIDENCE OF THE COMMUNAL MEAL

For the Dead Sea group we are fortunate in having not only written remains in the form of the scrolls but also archaeological materials, which shed additional light on life at Qumran. Those archaeological remains include the site of communal meals and remnants of foodstuffs. As may be expected, there is no evidence for the offering of sacrifices. There is no archaeological or historical support for recent contentions that sacrifices were conducted at Qumran.

Already during period Ib of Qumran's occupation, extending approximately from the reign of John Hyrcanus (135–104 B.C.E.) until the earthquake of 31 B.C.E., the largest room of the Qumran buildings was a hall 72 feet (22 meters) long and 15 feet (4.5 meters) wide with a system for washing and draining the floor. The more than one thousand pottery vessels stacked according to type and located in a pantry next door, together with the nearby kitchen, containing several fireplaces, have indicated that the group using these facilities held communal meals at Qumran.

Connected with the problem of characterizing meals at Qumran is the finding (primarily from period Ib) of deposits of animal bones buried between or around the buildings, which were placed in large shards of pitchers or pots or in intact jars with their lids on. These deposits are usually flush with the ground level. Examination of the bones shows that no deposit contained an entire skeleton. Rather, the bones had been taken apart and the flesh removed before burial. Many of the deposits contain the bones of a single type of animal; the remainder represent two, three, or four types. Animals included are adult sheep, adult goats, lambs or kids, calves, cows, and oxen. Without question these are bones of animals used for food. The meat was generally boiled and less often roasted.

Numerous attempts have been made to explain why these bones were buried.

None is satisfactory because we have neither literary evidence nor archaeological parallel for the burial of bones in any Jewish sacrificial or religious rite. However, the practice may relate to a passage in the *Halakhic Letter:*

> And one may not bring dogs into the holy camp because they eat some of the bones of the Tem[ple while] the meat is (still) on them.
> (*Halakhic Letter B58–59*)

The text goes on to extoll Jerusalem as the "holy camp."

Apparently, the authors of the letter were displeased that dogs were allowed in Jerusalem because dogs might scavenge the bones of sacrificial animals. Elsewhere in the text, bones are described as a source of ritual defilement. Perhaps the sectarians at Qumran buried bones to prevent dogs or other animals from scattering the bones throughout the settlement and potentially defiling the members. However, this interpretation must remain tentative until new discoveries provide a more definite explanation for the unusual practice.

The sect's communal meals, conducted regularly as part of its everyday life, were preenactments of the final messianic banquet at the End of Days. Thus, we again see that the contemporary life of the sect reflected its dreams for the age to come.

The Future as a Mirror of the Present

Rule of the Congregation describes the eschatological community in terms that clearly mirror the sect's regulations for the present age. Its prescriptions coincide in many instances with those found in the *War Scroll*, which describes the great final battle before the messianic congregation was to assemble. In linking its present-day laws and procedures with the eschatological battle and the End of Days, the sect was seeking to fulfill in the present its dreams for the better days to come, thus anticipating the perfect holiness that would soon unfold.

Further, the sect saw itself as the embodiment of its leadership, the Zadokite priesthood. It even referred to itself as the Sons of Zadok, accenting over and over again the leadership and decision-making role of this group of priests. Even if that role had become virtually ceremonial by the later period of the sect's history, as some scholars have argued, the identity was still ingrained in the sect's self-image. Sectarians clearly expected this priestly role to continue in the End of Days.

In seeking to achieve the highest standards of purity and perfection in the End of Days, the Dead Sea sect resolved to exclude certain classes from the eschatological war and assembly: those afflicted with impurity, physical deformities, or old age. Since the sect lived in preparation for and expectation of the imminent End of Days, it is probable that these same regulations were in force in the Qumran community.

Reflecting its deep messianic consciousness, the sect participated in the communal meals as a central eschatological ritual, enacting daily the messianic banquets expected to be presided over by the priest and the messiah of Israel. These meals were viewed as a foretaste of the world to come.

In looking forward to the messianic era, the sect borrowed from the terminology of the biblical Exodus and the desert-wandering period in Israelite history. This period served as the prototype of ultimate redemption, for it represented the closest possible relationship to God, involving direct divine intervention in history and revelation of God's law. Also at that time, Israel had been faithful to the Torah's correct teachings. Because the sectarians expected this ancient grandeur to be renewed in the messianic era, it is not surprising to find such biblical terminology and, specifically, allusions to the military encampment and organization of the desert period, everywhere evident in *Rule of the Congregation*.

The author of this text looked to the End of Days for the restoration of Israel's ancient glories: the monarchy, the legitimate high priesthood, and the tribal organization. At the same time, he looked forward to a level of sanctity and purity impossible in the present age. For him, the ideal would be attained when all of Israel observed perfectly the law of the Torah. In his vision, as in the Qumran sect's eschatology as a whole, the restorative and utopian trends of Jewish messianism share an equal role. The coming cataclysm would inaugurate both a return to the past and a new and previously unachievable future characterized by observance of the law, ritual purity, and perfection. It is that combination of trends that generated the messianic fervor and expectancy typical of the Dead Sea sect.

For sectarians, the redemption from Egypt and the period of desert wandering, crowned by the revelation at Sinai, served as a paradigm of the future. They themselves would soon experience the great battles and tribulations at the End of Days. Until that day came, they would strive to live in perfect holiness. And as a result, they would eventually merit the revelation of God's glory in the End of Days, a promise they felt certain would be fulfilled in their lifetime.

CHAPTER 21

The "Pierced Messiah" and Other Controversial Texts

Most of the messianic ideology presented so far has been based on material available to scholars for years. The recent release of the cave 4 documents, previously monopolized by the publication team, has made available a number of texts that either actually or allegedly contain messianic references. In some cases, these texts had already been published, but the intense interest occasioned by their release focused renewed attention upon them. Because of the shrill public debate surrounding these texts and because their import may significantly transform our understanding of both Jewish and Christian history, it is necessary to give them particular attention. These documents confirm that in addition to expecting an apocalyptic messianic cataclysm, the Qumran sect shared with other Jews of that period the traditional Jewish hope for messianic redemption at the End of Days.

THE SON OF GOD TEXT

The biblical Book of Daniel has often been the subject of later additions and adaptations. The Septuagint Daniel, for instance, contains several additions found in Greek Bibles that were not part of the Hebrew original. Scholars have identified a variety of Qumran texts as pseudo-Danielic because they resemble the biblical book in both style and content. In the manuscripts found at Qumran, these materials and the canonical Book of Daniel are each preserved separately, without any hint of overlap or confusion. Yet these texts cannot be understood without referring back to the biblical Daniel.

Perhaps the most significant of these manuscripts is the Son of God text that contains in it an Aramaic expression translated as "son of God." As we will see, the meaning of this term is highly debatable. Although originally designated as *Pseudo-Daniel D*, the text is now generally known as the *Aramaic Apocalypse.*

The manuscript has been dated to the first century B.C.E. and must be assigned to the pre-Qumranic stage of Second Temple Jewish literature.

In the case of this text, it is probable that the entire Son of God passage is based on the elusive text of Daniel 7:13–14: "As I looked on, in the night vision, one like a human being came with the clouds of heaven. . . . Dominion, glory and kingship were given to him; all peoples and nations of every language must serve him. His dominion is an everlasting dominion that shall not pass away, and his kingship, one that shall not be destroyed." In this passage, Daniel sees a vision of an apocalyptic redeemer, who is assigned everlasting rule.

After a break in the manuscript, the *Aramaic Apocalypse* mentions a king. Thereafter, someone, understood by scholars to be the prophet Daniel in the broken text, falls before the throne of the king, presumably the ruler of Babylonia. Apparently the king has had a dream that is to be interpreted here in an apocalyptic manner. The speaker then says to the king:

> You have been angry from eternity and your years (have been spent) [in fear.
> I will interpret (?)] your vision and all that is to come to pass unto eternity.
> (ARAMAIC APOCALYPSE I 2–3)

In this passage, we encounter the classic form of Danielic apocalyptic visions. Here, following the biblical model, the prophet becomes a conduit of revelation for a king. The text then proceeds to give its vision of the war to come:

> [Because of the g]reat [kings (there will be)] great distress on the earth, [there will be war among the peoples] and a great slaughter in the cities. [The kings will arise and do battle,] the king of Assyria and Egypt. [Then there will arise the final king and he] will be great upon the earth. [The nations will] make [peace with him] and all will serve [him]. (ARAMAIC APOCALYPSE I 4–9)

Here the text foretells a great war between the kings of the northern and southern empires, a scenario greatly resembling the expected eschatological battle. Then, in describing the "final king," the text mentions the son of God:

> The [son of the] G[reat Master] shall he be called, and by His name he will be called. He will be said (to be) the son of God, and they will call him the son of the Most High. (ARAMAIC APOCALYPSE I 9–II 1)

The foregoing passage is clearly the key to the entire document. It seems to speak of a figure, arising in connection with the final messianic battle, who will be called the son of God. Not surprisingly, this text has given rise to a number of interpretations. Of course, it is impossible to determine the precise meaning of this phrase outside the context of the entire passage. But for the moment, let us posit several primary possibilities: First, the term "son of God" could in fact designate a messianic figure, evidence that at that time some Jews expected a messiah who would be called the son of God. If this were the case, then the designation, found later in Christianity, appears to have derived from the messianism of a particular Jewish group whose approach is represented in this document.

We can find a close parallel to the passage in two verses from the New Testament (Luke 1:32–33), wherein the angel Gabriel, speaking about the newborn Jesus, proclaims, "He will be great and will be called the son of the Most High . . . and he will reign over the house of Jacob forever; and of his kingdom there will be no end." This parallel lends support to the claim that in pre-Christian times some Jews considered "son of God" a designation for the messiah. However, it is irresponsible to conclude from this evidence that the analogy points to some particularly strong link between the Qumran sectarians, who included this earlier text in their collection, and the Christian faith, which emerged only later.

Alternatively, we might argue that the passage describes a boastful ruler of the entire world, who will arise and declare himself the son of God, only to be later defeated. If so, we would expect to find further on in the text a description of the messianic war but no designation of the messiah as the son of God. Scholars have suggested two candidates for this ruler: Antiochus IV Epiphanes (175–164 B.C.E.), villain of the Maccabean revolt, or his son Alexander Balas (152–145 B.C.E.).

Another theory, one much less likely, is that the text is referring to a kind of anti-Christ, a Belial-like figure who heads the lot of evildoers, the Sons of Darkness. If this were the case, the text would first describe this figure's dominion and then would describe the rule by the leader of the lot of good, the Sons of Light, a figure such as Michael, Melchizedek, or the like.

Let us now examine the next passage in the text. It describes the period of the reign of kings, most probably those of Assyria and Egypt:

> Like the comets which are seen, thus shall their rule be. They shall rule for years upon the earth and shall trample everything. Nation shall trample nation and city (shall trample) city, until there arises the people of God, and all will (then) rest from the sword. *(ARAMAIC APOCALYPSE II 1–4)*

Here is where the confusion starts. The text seems to say that the people of God will arise and usher in a period of world peace. If we identify the people collectively as the redeemer, a notion that in fact can be found in certain Second Temple period texts, then "son of God" must refer to the boastful king, not to a messianic figure. On the other hand, if we assume that the text does not really follow a logical order, then we can still identify the son of God as a messianic figure in whose time the people of God arise to bring peace to the earth.

There follows, in the remaining preserved portion of this text, a description of the End of Days and the role of the redeemer:

> His kingship shall be eternal kingship and all his rule shall be in truth. He will judg[e] the earth with truth and will entirely make peace. The sword

shall cease from the earth, and all the cities shall bow down to him. The great
God will be his strength and will make war for him. The nations He will give
into his hand, and all of them He will cast (down) before him. His dominion
shall be an eternal dominion and all of the boundaries . . .

(*Aramaic Apocalypse II 5–9*)

Here the text breaks off; we know nothing more of its contents. This last passage
clearly describes the End of Days. But who will usher it in? Will it be the son of
God understood as a messianic figure, or will it be the people of God—Israel—
here described in the singular, who will collectively play that role? Because it is
difficult to maintain that the son of God can be at the same time both the boastful king and the ruler presiding over the redeemed world, we must conclude that
the term "son of God," refers to a messianic agent.

Taken in its entirety, this passage fits well into the context of the pseudo-
Danielic literature and in the apocalyptic context of Second Temple Judaism.
The description of the messianic era conforms precisely to the vision embraced by
virtually all Jews both then and throughout the ages: the ultimate reign of the
messiah in an everlasting period of truth and righteousness. In this respect, it
conforms to the restorative trend in Jewish messianism, although the battles it
anticipates take their cue from utopian, cataclysmic ideas. The son of God
imagery, indeed new to Jewish texts of that period, finds its source in the Hebrew
Bible, wherein the Jewish people is identified as the firstborn son of God. Since
the New Testament uses this imagery, we can assume that it was current among
some Second Temple period Jews. Read this way, the text does not contradict the
basic premise that the scrolls are Jewish texts that, for the most part, share the
common Jewish beliefs of the Hellenistic period.

The So-called Pierced Messiah Text

Perhaps the most curious of all of these texts is the one that some have claimed
speaks of an executed messiah. Press reports have repeated the claim that the
text mentions the piercing of the messiah and refers to his death by crucifixion.
Behind these reports, of course, is the assumption that finding such a messianic
description in a Qumran text would link the Qumran corpus intimately with
Christianity. Upon examination of the entire document, however, this claim
proves to be utterly false.

The fragment in question is part of the *War Rule*, which in turn is part of a
larger, interrelated group of documents, most prominent among which is the *War
Scroll*, available in two versions at Qumran. This group of texts depicts the war
at the End of Days, the great cataclysm inaugurating the messianic era. For the
sect, the Roman invasion of Judaea was understood to signal the onset of the End
of Days. Indeed, the sectarians, like other Jews in the Hasmonaean period, were

painfully aware that the Romans would soon attempt to conquer their land. The sectarians hoped that this war would be the last, ushering in eternal peace.

The *War Rule* survives in ten fragments of various sizes. A look at all the fragments together reveals that the claim concerning a reference in this text to a pierced messiah falls apart.

The first fragment preserves a poem of blessing, an expansion of the Priestly Blessing (Numbers 6:24–26). Another manuscript of this poem, known as *Blessings*, has been preserved in cave 11. In this text, God is asked to give his blessings from heaven and to provide fruitful agricultural produce. It concludes with:

> . . . God is with you and His [holy] angels [take their stand] in your congregation, and His holy name is called u[pon you].
> *(WAR RULE 1 9–10 = BLESSINGS 1–2 13–14)*

The presence of angels among the community is reminiscent both of the *War Scroll*, which envisions angels in the military camp of the End of Days, and of *Rule of the Congregation*, which foretells their presence in the community in the End of Days. Another fragment actually mentions the four archangels, a motif also found in the *War Scroll*. Thus, these benedictions clearly relate to an Israel on the verge of the messianic era and to the eschatological military community. In this respect we are here clearly in the world of sectarian thought.

Other fragments of the *War Rule* mention graves and corpses and the return of troops to their base. They also mention the destruction of evil and horns known to have been used for military commands. The enemy is specifically identified as the Kittim, a code word in the scrolls that always designates the Romans.

One fragmentary passage partially describes the extensive scope of the war that will ensue on the verge of the End of Days:

> . . . [the Pr]ince of the Congregation, until the [great] sea (the Mediterranean) . . . [and] they [will flee] before Israel at that time . . . will stand against them and array themselves for battle against them . . . and they will return to the dry land at th[at] time. *(WAR RULE 4 2–5)*

Here we encounter the Prince of the Congregation, whom some identify as the messiah, who will lead the sectarians in the End of Days. In this text and in the *War Scroll*, the Prince of the Congregation plays the role of a military leader. Opposite this leader is an enemy leader who according to this text was to be captured:

> . . . and they will bring him before the Prince [of the Congregation].
> *(WAR RULE 4 6)*

Now that the full content of the other *War Rule* fragments has been established, we turn finally to the smoking gun—that fragment released to the news media that allegedly describes the execution of the messiah. Although the passage is again fragmentary, we can restore parts of it by referring to the biblical verse that serves as its basis:

> [. . . as it is written in the Book of] Isaiah the prophet, "[The thickets of the forest] shall be hacked away [with iron, and the Lebanon trees in their majesty shall] fall. But a shoot shall grow out of the stump of Jesse, [a twig shall sprout from his stock (Isaiah 10:34–11:1) . . .] shoot of David, and they will be judged, the . . . and the Prince of the Congregation will kill him, the arm[y] of . . . [with drum]s and with dances. And the [high] priest commanded . . . [the c]orpse[s] of the Kittim . . . *(War Rule 5 1–5)*

The beginning of this passage is an interpretation of Isaiah that parallels that found in *Pesher Isaiah A*. The passage speaks of the sprout from Jesse, the branch of David, an expression based on biblical usage (Jeremiah 23:5, 33:15), meaning the Davidic messiah. According to some Second Temple period views, this figure alone would be the messiah.

The rest of the passage has been the subject of fierce debate. In light of its context and the rules of Hebrew grammar, there can only be one possible interpretation. I have translated "and the Prince of the Congregation will kill him" to mean that the prince will kill someone, most probably the leader of the opposition who is discussed in the fragment just prior to this. Others, ignoring the rules of Hebrew grammar and syntax, have translated the same clause as "and he shall kill the Prince of the Congregation," incorrectly reversing the subject and object of the verb. Then, by misreading the text that follows, these others have claimed that the prince is to be identified with the branch of David. Based upon these misreadings, they then took one easy but impossible step: they interpreted the word that I have translated as "dances" (*meḥollot*, cf. Exodus 15:20) as if it meant "pierced" (*meḥollal*), in accord with Christian interpretation of the suffering-servant passage in Isaiah 53:5. Jewish interpreters have understood this passage in Isaiah to refer to Israel, God's servant, "disgraced (*meḥollal*) because of our sins." Christians, on the other hand, have read it as "pierced in atonement for our sins."

None of this, however, has anything to do with the *War Rule* because here neither killing nor suffering, let alone "piercing," of the Prince of the Congregation is even discussed. Rather, the reference to drums and dances must have to do with the celebration of victory anticipated in the *War Rule* and presented in much more extensive detail in the *War Scroll*. Furthermore, those who released this fragment as a pierced messiah text did not realize that the last line contains a direct reference to "the corpses of the Kittim," that is, the Romans, thus making clear that it is neither the sect's leader nor the Jewish people who will perish in the messianic battle, but rather the Kittim and, apparently, their leader.

When we compare the *War Rule* passage with a parallel section in *Pesher Isaiah A*, we find definitive proof that mine is the correct interpretation. This parallel passage interprets the same text in Isaiah (10:33–11:5). After quoting

10:34, "The thickets of the forest shall be hacked away with iron, and the Lebanon trees in their majesty shall fall," the *pesher* continues:

> [These are the] Kittim wh[o] will fa[ll] into the hand of Israel . . . these are the mighty ones of the Kit[tim] . . . *(PESHER ISAIAH A 7–10 III 7–9)*

The text then interprets the "shoot of Jesse" (Isaiah 11:1):

> [The interpretation of the text concerns the branch] of David who will arise in the en[d of days to save Israel and to destroy its en]emies. . . . And he will rule over all the na[tion]s . . . [al]l the nations will his sword judge.
> *(PESHER ISAIAH A 7–10 III 22–26)*

This passage leaves no doubt that the parallel in the *War Rule* refers to the defeat of the Romans at the hands of the sect and its leader, the Prince of the Congregation. The eschatological expectations of the sectarians previous to the Roman conquest of 63 B.C.E. looked forward to such a victory in the great battle that would occur. Far from describing the piercing of a messiah, the *War Rule* foretells the hoped for sectarian defeat of the Romans, including the killing of their leader and his soldiers, whose corpses are explicitly mentioned in the text.

THE MESSIANIC APOCALYPSE

Perhaps one of the most beautiful messianic descriptions is the *Messianic Apocalypse* from Qumran. The manuscript of this text has been dated to between 100 and 80 B.C.E. The text's largest fragment contains the clearest messianic material. Poetic in quality and lacking any sectarian character, the passage reflects the messianic hopes of the people of Israel as a whole. Here again, we see the blending of the restorative and utopian varieties of Jewish messianism. Most important, the text foretells the resurrection of the dead, a notion rare in the Qumran corpus. Because of its poetic character, it is translated here in its entirety, following the poetic lines of the manuscript (*Messianic Apocalypse* 2 ii + 4, 1–15):

> [For the hea]vens and the earth will harken to His messiah,
> [And all w]ho are in them shall not retreat from the commandment of the holy ones.
> Make effort, O seekers of the Lord, in His service,
> For is it not in this that you will find the Lord, all who hope in their hearts?
> For the Lord will visit the pious and call the righteous by name,
> And over the humble His spirit will hover and He will renew the faithful with His strength.
> For He will honor the pious upon the eternal royal throne.
> He frees the captives, makes the blind see, and makes the ben[t over] stand straight.

So for[ev]er I will cleave [to those who h]ope, and He will [repay] His pious ones,

And the frui[t of a] good dee[d] to a person He will not delay.

Glorious deeds such as have never been will the Lord do as He has pro[mised,]

For He will heal the sick, revive the dead, and give good news to the humble,

And the [po]or He will satis[fy], the abandoned He will lead, and the hungry He will make rich,

And the wi[se . . .] and all of them, like holy [ones]. . . .

Some scholars have attempted to bring this poem into the sphere of early Christianity. Somehow, they seem to have forgotten that messianism—the beliefs in the coming restoration of the ancient glories of Israel and in a utopian future age—was widespread and almost normative among Jews of the Hasmonaean and Roman periods. Even though there existed various approaches to messianism, the basic principles were shared by most Jews. This text, then, offers a glimpse into early Jewish messianic thought.

Some of the phrases are recognizable from the traditional Jewish liturgy that itself traces its roots back to Second Temple and rabbinic times. One such prayer, dating to early rabbinic times, says of God, "He awakens the slumberers, makes the dumb speak, frees the captives, gives support to those who have fallen, and causes the bent over to stand upright." Elsewhere God "frees the captives, saves the poor, and helps the destitute." In one of the opening paragraphs of the Amidah prayer we read, "You restore the dead to life in Your great mercies, give support to those who have fallen, heal the sick and free the captives." Certainly, in ascribing such actions to God in the End of Days, our text is expressing nothing more than the common Jewish beliefs of the period, views in fact that have remained central to Judaism up until our own day.

According to the *Messianic Apocalypse,* the messiah has ultimate authority over the heavens and earth and calls upon those who seek God to observe the Torah even more vigilantly. Such seekers are enjoined to concentrate on God's service, for only through proper observance of the commandments can one achieve closeness to the divine. God reciprocates by establishing a special relationship with the pious, protecting those who are faithful to him. It is God who helps the downtrodden, the captives, the blind, and the bent over. In the End of Days, God will perform miracles—healing the sick, reviving the dead, and feeding the hungry. The wise will live like angels. Every one of these ideas can be found in traditional Judaism.

But in an effort to render a Christianized reading of this material, the text has been misinterpreted to suggest that the messiah, not God, will revive the dead. That interpretation, however, is difficult to defend. The pseudo-Ezekiel texts from Qumran (*Pseudo-Ezekiel A* 2 5–8), adapting material from Ezekiel 37:1–14

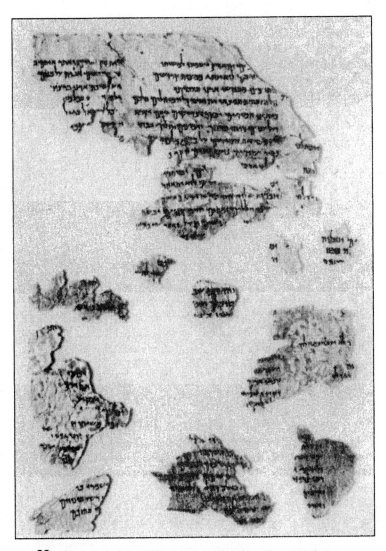

Messianic Apocalypse This document describes the messiah, emphasizing the great works to be done by God in the End of Days. Among those works is the resurrection of the dead. Some have misinterpreted this document, however, claiming that it speaks of resurrection that is effected by the messiah, but that view cannot be sustained. The text fits squarely within Jewish tradition and has important parallels in later Jewish liturgy. *Courtesy of the Israel Antiquities Authority.*

(especially verses 12–14), emphasize that God himself will revive the dead, demonstrating that the sect did not expect a messianic surrogate to perform this miracle.

The dominant Christian conception of resurrection asserts that the messiah himself will die and be resurrected. In the *Messianic Apocalypse*, however, the resurrection of the dead refers to the people, not to the messiah. Even if it were to be interpreted as referring to the resurrection of the dead *by* the messiah, such a notion still would not be comparable to the resurrection of Jesus in Christian belief.

This text, therefore, has no connection to Christianity at all, except that it indicates the presence of the messianic idea in Judaism before Christianity emerged. It is understandable that those Jews who started the early Jesus movement brought with them the teachings of Judaism that they had learned. This beautiful poem sums up these beliefs, calling on human beings to observe God's Torah in order to bring about the eternal redemption.

The texts examined here in some detail have occasioned considerable controversy in the media because they allegedly espouse messianic views somehow connected with Christianity. While some parallels do exist, they merely demonstrate that early Christianity borrowed its messianic ideals from Judaism, specifically, the kinds of apocalyptic notions contained in some of the texts preserved at Qumran. Some of these documents were authored by the sectarians; some were composed by their predecessors even before the Maccabean Revolt.

In these texts, as in those examined in previous chapters, we find expressed the fervent Jewish hope for messianic redemption, usually coupled with the notion of one or two redeemers. Jews hoped, then as now, that the messianic era would both put an end to all the evils besetting the Jewish people and bring lasting peace to the world. For some, this meant utter destruction of the wicked as a prelude to the coming messianic era; for others, indeed for the restorative rabbinic tradition that would long outlive sectarian apocalyptic trends, it meant repentance by the wicked and their return to the commandments of God that would bring about the End of Days.

The messianic views of the Qumran sectarians and of other Jews of the period were focused on creating a world hospitable to the perfect observance of God's Torah. Yet even in the present world, Jews strove for closer contact with God. In the next chapter we address the mystical side of Qumran literature as well as the magical tradition that has always played some part in the Jewish community.

CHAPTER 22

Mysticism and Magic

Throughout their long history, Jews have continually striven to gain greater access to the realm of the divine. When such attempts have included an experiential element, for example, a personal vision or other religious experience, they can rightly be called mystical. The texts we will look at in this chapter cannot really be defined as mystical in the full sense of the word, since they are descriptive rather than truly experiential. They disclose no real sense of mystical experience, nor do they show adepts undergoing mystical transformation. Nonetheless some texts found at Qumran reflect motifs and subjects, as well as language and style, that are more typical of later Jewish mystical texts. We therefore will call them mystical, because they point directly forward to the development of Jewish mysticism as a profound phenomenon in Jewish religious thought and history.

Although mysticism is often linked with magic, we must be careful to distinguish between the two. Magic is intended to elicit God's help in warding off the forces of evil; mysticism, on the other hand, is intended to draw human beings close to God. Yet despite the significant differences between these two forms of religious behavior, we find in many Jewish mystical texts considerable interaction between the two phenomena. So, too, in the literature from Qumran, which is why we will examine these two aspects together.

Before discovery of the Qumran scrolls, various theories abounded about the sources of Jewish mysticism. Most scholars assumed that certain foreign traditions had somehow merged with the Jewish tradition to produce this "aberrant" phenomenon. A number of theories were proposed: Some suggested the influence of Gnosticism, a religious movement that stresses the relation of the self to a transcendent source of being through secret knowledge and that often designates a creator god distinct from that source of being. Others pointed to the influence of Zoroastrianism that taught that the good and evil aspects of the world had arisen as a consequence of the existence of rival gods. Still others proposed that

Hellenism had brought with it a variety of religious models, ranging from the pantheon of Greek gods to the various mystery cults.

These theories are misguided in assuming that Jewish mysticism developed outside the traditional Jewish yearning for closeness to God. They have failed to see that these phenomena can be encountered in ancient biblical traditions and Second Temple sources—including prominently the Dead Sea Scrolls—and that they can be traced through certain rabbinic traditions into the early Jewish mystical literature known as *Hekhalot* or *Merkavah* mysticism. This literature, dating back to rabbinic and early medieval times, stresses the contemplation of God's palaces (*hekhalot*) and God's heavenly throne (*merkavah*).

Once such a history is recognized and studied, it becomes clear that the origins of Jewish mysticism can be found in the inner workings of Judaism itself. Although other traditions may have periodically interacted with the developing Jewish mystical tradition, influenced it, and even been influenced by it, it is not necessary to seek foreign origins for such phenomena. In fact, the failure to understand this ancient material properly can in large measure be attributed to the prejudices of those modern scholars who regard mysticism as a blemish on Judaism and so look to foreign sources for its origins.

BIBLICAL BACKGROUND

Because the Qumran materials draw extensively on biblical texts for many of their ideas, we should expect to find in these ancient sources the original motifs that then appeared in later mystical speculation or description. Essentially four biblical texts provide this raw material: the Books of Exodus, Isaiah, Ezekiel, and Daniel, which describe mystical encounters.

The first source is a short passage from Exodus 24:10–11 that, according to many later views, describes the divine vision experienced by Moses, Aaron, Nadab, and Abihu immediately after God's revelation at Sinai. At that moment, the Torah states, "they saw the God of Israel, and under His feet there was the likeness of a pavement of sapphire, as pure as the sky itself." Despite the fact that they had drawn so near to God, they were not punished, "but they beheld God and they ate and drank," presumably of the sacrifices they had offered (verse 5). Here we already find the ingredients of later mystical visions: the use of terms such as "likeness" to escape anthropomorphism, the vision of what was beneath God and His throne, and the great light beneath Him, symbolic of His presence.

The second significant biblical description is the vision of Isaiah (6:1–4) that many commentators view as Isaiah's initiation into prophecy. The prophet sees a vision of the divine throne with the Lord upon it. The angels antiphonally recite praises to God. This angelic utterance, called the *kedushah* (sanctification) in later rabbinic tradition, can be found in verse 3: "Holy, holy, holy! The Lord of Hosts! His presence fills all the earth!" Here we have the vision of a divine throne with an angelic retinue reciting praises to God—another motif that was to play a significant part in the Qumran text known as *Songs of the Sabbath Sacrifice.*

Perhaps the most significant text for the later history of Jewish mysticism is the vision of the divine throne found in Ezekiel 1, 3:12–13, and 10. In this vision, Ezekiel sees a chariot-throne of God, supported by four animals. The entire scene is engulfed by fire and bright lights. The throne moves in all directions as if on wheels. The prophet hears the sounds of angels' wings. Above the heads of the beasts is a firmament of pure white and above that, the likeness of a throne of sapphire, the same sapphire previously described in Exodus. A manlike form sits upon the throne surrounded by visions of fire, and Ezekiel then hears the words "Blessed is the Presence of the Lord in His place" (Ezekiel 3:12).

The final passage of significance is found in the Book of Daniel (7:9–14). Daniel sees the Ancient of Days, white-haired and clothed in white, sitting on His fiery throne. As in Ezekiel, the throne has wheels, and streams of fire flash out before it. Myriads of angels stand before God to serve Him. The books of Judgment are open; before God stands the son of man. Although it is possible that aspects of this vision draw on the Ezekiel material, we cannot establish a definite connection.

The exegesis of these passages and their expression in mystical experience set the agenda for early Jewish mysticism. Such biblical accounts of mystical visions are reflected in Second Temple literature, including texts preserved at Qumran.

DESCRIPTIONS OF THE DIVINE CHARIOT-THRONE (*MERKAVAH*)

Certainly the most prominent element of Jewish mystical tradition in late rabbinic and early medieval times focuses on the divine throne. In all four biblical passages already discussed, themselves key sources for later mystical traditions, speculation about this throne is the central theme. The mystical interpretation of these biblical passages, especially of Ezekiel 1, was prominent in a number of texts unearthed at Qumran as well as in other texts from the Second Commonwealth period.

The divine throne motif appears already in the pre-Qumranic, probably third-century B.C.E. Enoch materials in fragments preserved at Qumran. In chapter 14 of I Enoch, preserved fully in Ethiopic, Enoch describes the upper world. He sees a wall of crystals and tongues of fire, as well as a crystal palace surrounded by fire. Inside is another house of even greater splendor in which stands a lofty throne described in a manner reminiscent of Ezekiel 1. Streams of fire come forth from the throne. The description of the Great Glory recalls Daniel 7:9–14. The text then describes, in terms similar to that same passage in Daniel, the greatness of the divine presence and the angels surrounding the throne. Finally, as in Ezekiel (1:28), Enoch prostrates himself before the throne.

A fragmentary section about this throne mysticism, fusing Ezekiel and

Danielic sources, is found among the preserved Enoch fragments from Qumran. In the Aramaic text of I Enoch 14:18–20, the throne is described as follows:

> . . . [like crystal. And its wheels were like the wheel (orb) of the shining sun. And its wings were ch]erub[im. And from beneath the throne came forth] streams o[f fire that I was not able to look at (because of the brightness). The great Great One sat on this throne, and His garment was shining more than the sun and whiter than] the grea[t sn]ow. *(Enoch C 1 vii 1–2 = Enoch 14:18–20)*

Despite its extensively reconstructed condition, the evidence from this small fragment, as well as from other parts of this section of I Enoch found at Qumran, proves that this entire literary unit was available to the members of the Qumran sect. In fact, we know that it predated the Qumran sect. The passage in question is certainly a harmonization of the vision of Ezekiel 10 with that of Daniel 7:9–10, a practice typical to later Jewish mysticism.

In the Ethiopic version of I Enoch 18, Enoch is taken on a journey to the heavens. He comes to the treasury of the winds and to a place of seven mountains, the middle one of which is the mountain of the Lord. There he sees that:

> the middle one (mountain) reached to heaven like the throne of God, of alabaster, and the summit of the throne was of sapphire.
>
> *(I Enoch 18:8, Ethiopic text)*

A small fragment of this text found at Qumran proves that the sectarians also knew this text. The passage reads:

> The throne w[as of sapphire]. *(Enoch C 1 viii 27)*

Again we find an allusion to the sapphire mentioned in Exodus 24:10 and in Ezekiel 1:26 and 10:1.

So far, we have looked only at Enoch materials that parallel the Aramaic fragments from Qumran. Only through such parallels could we determine beyond a doubt that the texts we discussed were pre-Qumranic and that they were known to the sectarians (or at least to some of them). However, as explained before, we can prove that four of the five sections of I Enoch found in Qumran fragments also roughly resemble the form of the Ethiopic text that survives in its entirety. With the exception of the Parables (chs. 37–71) the entire book can be considered representative of the pre-Maccabean period. If this is so, then we can safely conclude that even more material related to later Jewish mystical tradition preexisted the Qumran sect and found its way into the sect's collection of texts.

The concept of the divine throne is also represented indirectly in the Book of Ben Sira. In his narration about the ancient heroes of Israel, he says of the prophet Ezekiel:

> It was Ezekiel who saw the vision of glory which God showed him from above the chariot of the cherubim. *(Ben Sira 49:8)*

This is the first reference, again in a text known to the Qumran community, of the term "*merkavah*," literally "chariot," to describe the divine throne seen by Ezekiel. It was this vision that set the pattern for so much of later Jewish mysticism.

Related to these throne visions is a short reference to a vision of the divine presence in a liturgical poem from Qumran, *Liturgical Prayer* II 6–7 = *Prayers for Festivals C* 97–98 I 8–10:

> And You shall renew Your covenant with them with visions of the gl[o]ry,
> and the words of Your holy [spirit] with Your creatures,
> and the writing of Your right hand,
> to make known to them the glorious teachings,
> and the deeds of eternity.

In other words, just as God had first revealed to Israel visions of the glory—that is, the divine presence—when giving His covenant, the Torah, written in His own hand, so too when that covenant is renewed, these visions will recur.

THE ANGELIC LITURGY

The foregoing material concerning Enoch and Ben Sira shows that even before the rise of the Qumran sect, Jewish mystical fascination with the throne of God was already being reflected in Jewish thought. Perhaps the most significant text for this discussion, however, is *Songs of the Sabbath Sacrifice*, also called the *Angelic Liturgy*. This text is preserved in nine manuscripts found at Qumran and one found at Masada. Although we have only incomplete manuscripts, the combination of these fragments provides a substantial text that preserves quite a number of beautiful hymns. The oldest of the manuscripts dates to 75–50 B.C.E.

When a manuscript of this text was found at Masada, it was initially suggested that some Qumran sectarians who had taken part in the Great Revolt escaped to Masada after Qumran's destruction, bringing this text with them. However, study of the remaining Masada texts makes it clear that the Masada corpus contained a number of texts parallel to those found in the Qumran collection. Apparently, these were commonly known works that circulated widely in Palestine during this period, at least in the case of the apocryphal texts. Although we cannot be sure who read this text at Masada, we can speculate that, if this text circulated outside the Qumran community in the first century C.E., then some of the ideas contained therein may in fact have been preserved in later traditions.

Songs of the Sabbath Sacrifice is a set of angelic hymns designated for the various Sabbaths of the year, although some scholars have suggested that the full text included poems for only the first thirteen Sabbaths, the first quarter of the Qumran annual cycle. Each poem generally begins with a first line such as:

> By a sage. The song of the Sabbath sacrifice for the seventh Sabbath on the 16th of the 2nd month. Praise the exalted God . . .
> (SONGS OF THE SABBATH SACRIFICE D 1 I 30).

The poem then goes on to exhort the angels, called by various designations, to offer different forms of exaltation and praise to God. Each song describes the angelic praise, the heavenly Temple, and the angelic priesthood.

The first five songs deal with the angelic priesthood. Songs 6 and 8 are formulaic descriptions of the praises of the seven chief priests and the deputy priests. The seventh song contains seven calls-to-praise, which are addressed to seven councils of angels, followed by a description of praises of the heavenly Temple itself. Songs 9–13 describe the heavenly Temple and praise of God. Song 12 describes the divine throne, the _merkavah_, to which we shall return presently. The last song describes the garments of the heavenly high priest.

Characteristic of this poetry is the following excerpt from the sixth song (_Songs of the Sabbath Sacrifice D_ 1 I 16–26):

> The fourth of the chief princes
> shall invoke blessing in the name of the majesty of the King,
> upon all those who live uprightly,
> with seven majestic words.
> And bless those who recite majesty
> with seven wondrous words.
> And bless all the angels who exalt in His true knowledge
> with seven righteous words for those who cherish His glory.
> The fifth of the chief princes
> shall invoke blessing in the name of His wonders,
> upon all who know the secrets of the most pure,
> with seven words of His true exaltation.
> And bless all who hasten to do His will
> with seven wondrous words,
> and bless all who acknowledge Him
> with seven majestic words for those who acknowledge (His) wondrousness.
> The sixth of the chief princes
> shall invoke blessing in the name of (God's) mighty deeds through the angels,
> upon all those distinguished for (their) knowledge,
> with seven words of His mighty wondrousness.

And bless all of the perfect path
with seven wondrous words as a daily offering with the eternal beings,
and bless all who wait for Him
with seven wondrous words for the restoration of His mercies.
The seventh of the chief princes
shall invoke blessing in His holy name,
upon all the Holy ones who recite His knowledge
with seven words of His holy wondrousness.
And bless all who exalt His laws
with seven wondrous words as impregnable shields,
and bless all who have banded together for righteousness
who praise His glorious kingdom . . . eternity,
with seven wondrous words for eternal well-being.
And all the wondrous chief princes
shall together bless the God of all the angels
in the name of . . . and all. . . .

We can see from this poem, and from many others in this work, with what awe
and sense of majesty the poet looks at the heavens and the angelic hosts arrayed
in them. Yet although the poet witnesses this angelic drama, the text does not
suggest that he joins in this process himself.

A second excerpt, taken from the twelfth song, describes a vision of the heavenly chariot-throne. Like other compositions such as Enoch, the description is
based on an interpretation of Ezekiel's vision and other relevant biblical sources.
Because it contains a description of the divine chariot, the *merkavah*, this
excerpt is perhaps the most significant from this text:

> The cherubim fall before Him and utter blessing. When they rise up, the gen-
> tle voice of the angels (is heard) on high. And there is much song when their
> wings lift up, the gentle voice of the angels, blessing the figure of the chariot-
> throne above the firmament of the cherubim. Then they sing the praise of the
> firmament of light from beneath His glorious throne. And when the wheels
> move back and forth, the holy angels go forth. And from between its glorious
> wheels, like the appearance of fire, are the spirits of the holy ones (angels). All
> around are the appearances of paths of fire in the likeness of the electrum and
> shining creatures (dressed) in glorious embroidery of wondrously refined pure
> colors. Spirits of the living God move to and fro continuously with the won-
> drous glory of the chariot-thrones, and the gentle voice of blessing (is heard)
> with the sound of their going. And they praise the Holy One when they re-
> turn. When these rise up, those (also) rise up. When these stand still, those
> (also) stand still. The quiet voice of songs of joy and the gentle blessing of

> God (are heard) in all the camps of the angels. . . . And the voice of praises
> . . . and from among all their cohorts. . . . All their troops, singing one after
> another in position. *(Songs of the Sabbath Sacrifice F 20–22 7–14)*

Here the visionary is not taken on a "guided tour" of the chariot-throne by some angelic docent, but instead appears as a stationary observer. Perhaps the character of this depiction reflects the intellectual rather than experiential orientation of the interpreter of this biblical material. In this respect, the text is not really mystical, but it does contain many motifs that presage the full flowering of *Merkavah* speculation later on.

The peculiar literary style of these texts is typical of later *Hekhalot* literature, demonstrating that behind these later mystical texts is a long tradition reaching back to material like the passage cited above. When we analyze the text's sentence structure, characteristic of later *Hekhalot* texts as well, we find frequent use of participles, a startling paucity of verbs, and chains of nouns that frequently defy efforts to parse them into discrete phrases and clauses. Such unstructured syntax leaves a strange impression on the reader, a sense of spiritual intoxication stimulated largely by the constant flow of praise. Clearly, this special syntactic style developed in order to convey the awesome nature of the throne as well as to express the effusive praise and grandiose descriptions inspired by its presence.

Scholars have debated how these texts were actually used. Some have suggested that they were a liturgy meant to be recited on a weekly basis, perhaps as a substitute for the Sabbath offerings that the sect no longer offered, having removed themselves from participation in the Jerusalem Temple. Others have considered them merely descriptive hymns, with no particular function in sectarian ritual.

We cannot determine whether and to what extent the material preserved in this text was used liturgically. What we can learn from these poems, however, is that the heavenly Temple reflects the earthly one. As in the Bible and later Jewish literature as well, these Qumran texts assume that the service below is patterned on the ideal service performed in the heavenly Temple above.

The earliest speculative literature describing the chariot-throne depicts only the angelic praise of God. Not until the rabbinic period does this literature link the celestial and earthly liturgies with the idea that human worshipers should imitate such angelic praise. Most probably our text is merely a kind of description—in the form of praise recited by the heavenly angels on this particular Sabbath—rather than a prescribed sectarian liturgy. Indeed, it is most likely that *Songs of the Sabbath Sacrifice* represents a speculative description of what goes on in heaven.

Many phrases in our text describe the angels. It is difficult to know whether these terms designate different classes of angels or are simply multiple names for the same angels. At Qumran, as in later *Hekhalot* literature, complicated angelologies divided the angels in respect to class (nature) and function. In addition, the text mentions seven archangels. Although we cannot determine whether each archangel is assigned to a separate heaven, as in the later *Hekhalot* texts, we find this idea expressed in Second Temple times in the Greek text of the Testament of Levi and in one Armenian recension of that text.

The *Psalms Scroll* from Qumran cave 11 may help us identify to whom the sectarians attributed authorship of the songs in our text. In the section entitled by the editor David's Compositions, already discussed in a previous chapter, the author of this scroll states that besides 3,600 psalms and four songs of uncertain purpose, David composed:

> songs to sing before the altar over the daily burnt offering every day, for all the days of the year, 364; and for the sacrifice of the Sabbaths, 52 songs . . .
> (PSALMS SCROLL 27:5–7)

Thus, the sect may have believed that David composed the angelic liturgy.

Songs of the Sabbath Sacrifice is replete with expressions and motifs also encountered in later Jewish mystical traditions. Among the most prominent: the seven archangels, the idea that the angelic hosts regularly praise God, the heavenly sanctuary and cult, the "gentle voice," association of fire with the angels, variegated colors, the "living God," multiple chariot-thrones, and the military organization of the heavenly hosts. Further, the language, terminology, and style of our text strongly resemble what we encounter in later *Hekhalot* literature.

However, this material also reflects some significant differences from the later mystical texts. When depicting what transpires in heaven, the sectarian texts do not describe an ascent or present a guided tour, as is typical in later texts. Rather the sectarian authors simply describe what might be perceived from their own vantage point. Because the sectarians derived this knowledge primarily by interpreting the visions of the divine throne in Ezekiel and related biblical texts, they prescribed no special ritual to prepare them for a mystical "journey." Thus, the songs of praise in our text were not intended, as in later materials, as a means to bring about ecstasy or a mystical experience but were uttered exclusively by those on high. In addition, the angels in our text bear epithets, which are quite different from the numerous and often incomprehensible names developed in later mystical tradition.

The text we have examined, composed by at least the second half of the first century B.C.E., is certainly the earliest-known postbiblical Hebrew text containing mystical speculation about the divine throne (*merkavah*) and the associated retinue of angelic beings. The text clearly shows that the *Merkavah* tradition began with such interpretations of Ezekiel in light of other relevant texts. This form of early midrash was supplemented with angelic songs. Only later, perhaps under foreign influence, did magical and incubation techniques and angelic names become part of this mystical speculation, transforming *Merkavah* mysticism into an esoteric tradition. These developments did not appear in our sources until the rabbinic period. They probably were fused with the descriptions of heavenly praise after the composition of *Songs of the Sabbath Sacrifice*, perhaps after the extinction of the Qumran sect itself.

THE ANGELIC HOSTS

One of the themes expressed in the *War Scroll* is the motif depicting angels as warriors. The sectarians expected that the angels would fight at their side in the war at the End of Days. Therefore, the sect needed to observe the laws of ritual purity within the military camp (Deuteronomy 23:10–15), "for the holy angels are with their armies together" (*War Scroll* 7:6). The most important angels who were to fight with the sect were Michael, Gabriel, Sariel, and Raphael (*War Scroll* 9:15–16).

Michael, Gabriel, and Raphael appear in all lists of the archangels, including those found in *Hekhalot* literature. Uriel appears in the midrashic literature and the apocryphal books, although I Enoch usually has the name Penuel. This alternative designation occurs only in the section called the Parables, not included in the Aramaic fragments found at Qumran. In any case, when the *War Scroll* was composed, the list of four archangels had not yet been totally fixed. Probably, since Michael represented the Prince of Light in the *War Scroll*, there was no role for Uriel—literally, "the light of God"; hence, his absence from the *War Scroll's* angelology. Instead, Sariel—the "Prince of God"—became the fourth archangel.

The angels play a central role in the songs of the *War Scroll*. Literary analysis of the scroll shows that the author drew these poems from some preexistent source rather than composing them himself. One poetic passage (*War Scroll* 12:1–5) delineates the role of the angels:

> For You have many angels in heaven,
> and hosts of angels in Your holy habitation to p[raise] Your [name].
> And the elect ones of the holy nation You placed for Yourself in a
> co[mmunity,
> and the num]ber of the names of all their hosts is with You in Your holy
> abode,
> and the en[umeration of the an]gels is in Your holy habitation.
> And blessed kindness [for Your thousands] and Your covenant of peace You
> engraved for them with the stylus of life,
> to rule o[ver them] in all appointed times forever,
> and to muster the armies of Your el[ect] ones,
> in their thousands, their myriads, together with Your holy ones,
> [and the army of] Your angels for strength in battle,

[to subdue] those who have arisen in the land against Your judgments.
And with the elect of heaven are [Your] blessings.

In this poem the angels are organized as an army, just as the men of the sect are mustered and listed in rosters according to military units. Just as the members of the sect are God's elect, so too are the angels chosen. Just as membership in the sect has been predestined, so from eternity the angels have been predestined for their assigned tasks.

The organization of the angels in military units is a typical motif in *Hekhalot* literature. What primarily distinguishes the concept as expressed here from that presented in later *Hekhalot* texts is that the sectarians envisioned that opposite themselves and their angelic comrades-in-arms would stand the angels of destruction led by Belial. Such an opposing camp also appears in the magical literature associated with the *Hekhalot*.

We find this motif of the angels as military units also in the Babylonian Jewish Aramaic magic bowls, incantation texts written in the sixth to eighth centuries C.E., and in the Palestinian Jewish magical text *Sefer ha-Razim* (*Book of the Mysteries*), dated to the same period or somewhat later. This kind of magic found its home among the common people, who preserved traditions like these, pitting demonic forces against the angels. In rabbinic literature, these forces of evil appear as demons. Various later Jewish magical texts give instructions about how to banish such demons.

The notion that angels fight alongside sectarian soldiers appears repeatedly in the *War Scroll*. Further down on the same column (*War Scroll* 12:7–8), mighty warriors, the host of the angels, and the host of God's spirits all stand on the side of the sect. This description accords with the sectarian notion that the holy angels will be present in the End of Days, when the council of the sectarian community will assemble (*Rule of the Community* 13:10–12).

The heavenly leader of the angels of God is Michael, the Prince of Light, who stands opposite Belial and his angels of destruction:

> And the Prince of Light You appointed from of old to assist us, and in [his] lo[t are all the sons of righteous]ness, and all the spirits of truth are in his dominion. And You made Belial for corruption, the angel of animosity, and in the dark[ness is] his [dominion] and his counsel is to do evil and to render guilty. And all the spirits of his lot, his angels of destruction, walk according to the laws of darkness, and for it (darkness) is their [de]sire altogether.
> (*WAR SCROLL 13:10–12*)

Michael is clearly designated as the Prince of Light:

> He has exalted the authority of Michael with eternal light to enlighten with joy the h[ouse of I]srael, (with) peace and blessing for the lot of God, to increase among the angels the authority of Michael and the dominion of Israel over all flesh. (*WAR SCROLL 17:6–8*)

In the biblical Book of Daniel, Michael appears as the angel of Israel (Daniel 10:21, 12:1). This is also his role in the *War Scroll*. But in the *Hekhalot* literature, Michael has been replaced by Metatron as archangel and assistant to God. Metatron never appears in the scrolls. For the sectarian, it is Michael, the Prince of Light, who presides over the holy angels.

PHYSIOGNOMY AND CHIROMANCY

Before the Dead Sea Scrolls were discovered, it was already known that a Jewish esoteric tradition of physiognomy and chiromancy existed. Physiognomy assumes that we can discover people's nature and future by "reading" the physical features of their face. Chiromancy promises the same results from reading the lines of the palm. In these early medieval esoteric texts, the Hebrew word *toledot*—literally, "generations"—carries the sense of the Latin *natura*, that is, one's particular character, or nature. The term conveys the same meaning in *Rule of the Community*. The sectarian use of the term clearly influenced its later use in Jewish esoteric circles.

Other early medieval texts discuss how to determine a person's fate based on the shape of the feet and the sexual organs. Two Qumran fragments, one a *Horoscope* and the second the *Elect of God* text, discuss the same technique, mentioning some of the very signs that later appear in early medieval texts. The first fragment, the *Horoscope*, is written left to right, and is composed partially in a cryptic alphabet. A few samples of the fragmentary text will make clear its contents:

> . . . and if his legs are long and slender and his toes are slender and long, then he is of the second column. His spirit consists of six (parts) in the house of light and three in the pit of darkness. And this is the birth sign under which he was born, in the foot of Taurus he will be poor. And this is his animal, the Bull. (*HOROSCOPE 1 II 5–9*)

People are somehow classified into "columns," depending upon the shape of their legs and toes, and perhaps also of other parts of the body. Personalities are apparently compound; thus, the person described here belongs two-thirds to the good lot, one-third to the evil. The text places one under one's zodiac sign and describes one's nature. Among the other documents found at Qumran is a *Zodiac* text, providing a full catalog of the signs.

Another section of the *Horoscope* text contains the following description:

> . . . echo of his voice is weak, and his teeth are thin and sit in a straight line, and he is neither tall nor short. (*HOROSCOPE 2 I 1–4*)

Again, a person's physical characteristics are taken as indicative of true inner nature. In the case of the person just described, these and other features place him eight parts in the house of light and one in darkness.

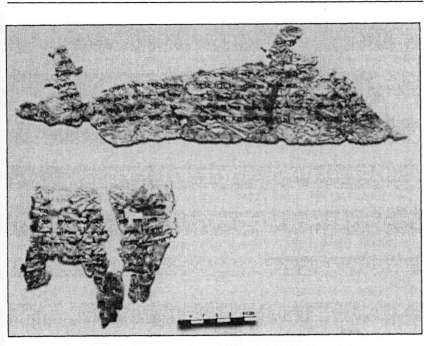

Horoscope Among the Qumran documents is a peculiar
set of horoscopes designed to determine, based on physical
characteristics, the extent to which an individual belongs to
the Sons of Light and the extent to which that same individual
belongs to the Sons of Darkness. The horoscope material is
extremely significant because it indicates that the spirits of
good and evil are understood to be in competition within the
personality of each individual, an approach similar to that of
the rabbinic good and evil inclinations. *Courtesy of the Israel
Antiquities Authority.*

The ideas expressed in this text are intimately linked to the sectarian concept
of predestination. Accordingly, physical characteristics could reveal whether a
person had been predestined to the camp of light or the camp of darkness. Although this notion resembles the idea of the two spirits expressed in *Rule of the
Community,* the two texts differ in that the *Rule* describes everything as black or
white, and the author of *Horoscopes* paints people as more complex, consisting
of both light and dark elements. It is the dominant element that ultimately determines a person's nature.

The second composition we will consider here is the *Elect of God* text. Although this Aramaic document was first believed to describe the birth of the

messiah, scholars have now concluded that it most probably describes the miraculous birth of Noah. Its text may represent part of an ancient Book of Noah referred to by other Qumran texts in Hebrew or Aramaic. If that is the case, the manuscript would belong to the literature the sectarians inherited from previous generations. In the following passage, the elect of God is recognized by the features of his body:

> ... of his hand, two ... a mark ... a mark like barley and lentils ... and tiny marks on his thigh. *(ELECT OF GOD I 1–3)*

These marks indicate that this child is special, someone who "will become wise and will be endowed with discretion" (line 6).

These texts, reflecting key sectarian notions about human nature and destiny, prove that physiognomy and chiromancy played an important role in the sect's thought and practice. From the Dead Sea sect and similar groups, the notions then passed into the hands of circles that eventually contributed these ideas to the Jewish esoteric tradition.

Mysticism and Magic

Despite the fact that mysticism and magic are decisively different religious phenomena, they often appear together in esoteric manuscripts, one aspect often reflecting the other. Thus, to achieve the vision of God's chariot, the *Merkavah* mystics engaged in a number of practices that can only be described as magical. We also find this phenomenon in the Qumran text called *Songs of the Sage*, preserved in two manuscripts from cave 4 dating to the late first century B.C.E.

Songs of the Sage contains an interesting mixture of poetry and magic. On one hand, it has hymns and praises to God very close in style and form both to *Songs of the Sabbath Sacrifice* and to the hymns in the *Hekhalot* texts. On the other hand, it includes magical material similar to early Jewish incantation texts. Some parallels also exist between *Songs of the Sage* and the *Thanksgiving Hymns*.

The *Songs of the Sage* text informs us that it was composed by the *maskil* (a sectarian "instructor"), in order to exorcise demons. Apparently, sectarians believed they could be magically protected from demonic forces by praising God. One such poem, preserved in two fragmentary manuscripts, will illustrate this notion. The poem begins with praise of God (*Songs of the Sage A* 1 1–4):

> Bene[dictions for the Ki]ng of glory,
> words of thanks with psalms of . . . to the God of knowledge.
> The glory of mi[ght]y deeds, God of (all) gods, Master of all the angels.
> and [Whose] dom[inion] is over all the powerful and mighty.

And by Whose powerful mi[gh]t all would be terrified and scatter,
and flee from the splendid dwel[ling] of His glorious majesty.

The poem first sets the stage: God, as the true power over all the angels, must also rule over the powers of evil. Therefore, praising this all-powerful God can serve as a means to banish demons. The magical poem begins by establishing that God's glory, that is, his divine presence, can make all the forces of evil shudder and flee from before him. Then the text turns to the actual spell:

> And I, the *maskil*, proclaim his splendid glory in order to frighten and to ter[rify] all the spirits of the angels of destruction and spirits of bastards, (male) demons, (female) liliths, howlers, and [yellers . . .].
> (*SONGS OF THE SAGE A 1 4–5*)

Here the *maskil* banishes all the forces of evil: the spirits of bastards (*mamzerim*, technically those born of forbidden unions), as well as other demonic forces, male and female. These spirits bear the same names as those in later Jewish magical texts. Likewise, the formulas of banishment, known technically as exorcisms, are very similar.

Further on, the text links the forces of evil with the sectarian notions of successive periods of history. Because the sectarians believed they were still living in the period of evil, the author describes these demonic forces as still operative:

> at the time of the period of the domini[on] of evil, and the appointed times for the affliction of the Sons of Li[ght], in the guilt of the periods of [those] afflicted with transgression, but not for eternal destruction, but for the period of the affliction of transgression. (*SONGS OF THE SAGE A 1 6*)

These antidemonic *Songs of the Sage* are certainly sectarian compositions, reflecting in both their praise and their exorcisms the ideology of the sect. The *Songs* express the need to control evil forces in the present age until such are finally destroyed in the war ushering in the End of Days.

Clearly, the Qumran sect had an extensive and developed demonology that shared many of the characteristics recognizable in later Jewish magical literature: angels of destruction, demons, liliths, female demons, and various other forces of evil. To ward off these demonic forces, the sectarians used hymns of praise to God together with spells. The poems not only served a magical function but also expressed many of the mystical ideas found in other sectarian poetry and the poetry of later Jewish mystical literature.

Thus, we have discovered intimate links between certain material in the Dead Sea Scrolls—some composed by the sect and some inherited by them—and the early Jewish *Hekhalot* literature. We have also found connections between the early magical tradition and this mystical material. If we had uncovered these links only in literature composed by the sect, we might have concluded that the ideas had originated in the Qumran group and then influenced the development of other esoteric trends in rabbinic and early medieval Judaism. Yet we have seen that the Qumran collection demonstrates that mystical and magical ideas were widespread in the Second Temple Jewish community. Far from being some late import into Judaism, these ideas represent a continuation of approaches already present in biblical texts that then developed throughout Second Temple times, eventually achieving final written form only at the start of the Middle Ages.

However, despite these internal developments within Judaism, the Dead Sea Scrolls and the ideas they express were not composed or gathered in a vacuum. We have now examined the ways the sectarians interacted with a variety of other contemporary Jewish groups and have studied various sectarian approaches to the major issues of Jewish thought. We now turn to what the scrolls tell us about a topic of great importance in every period of Jewish history: how Jews interacted with their non-Jewish neighbors.

PART VI

Sectarianism,
Nationalism,
and Consensus

CHAPTER 23

Israel and the Nations

Throughout the ages, most Jews have in large measure defined themselves over and against non-Jewish majorities. More often than not, those majorities have been hostile to Jews, thus compelling Jews to erect barriers in order to define themselves and maintain their group identity. Although the sectarians waged a fierce polemic against other Jews who deviated from their views, they never blurred the distinction between Jews and non-Jews, nor did they ever accuse their Jewish opponents of non-Jewish status. And although they defined themselves primarily over and against these other Jews—particularly the Pharisees and the later Sadducees, in addition to the Hasmonaean establishment and the Hellenized Jews—they also partially defined their identity in response to the nations that surrounded them and to the pagans who populated the Land of Israel in the Greco-Roman period.

It must be stressed at the outset that the scrolls contain no references to Christianity. Christianity is a movement that began as a Jewish sect and then developed into a separate religious group. Because the sectarian documents were authored before the careers of John the Baptist and Jesus, the scrolls make no mention nor do they even allude to these New Testament figures—notwithstanding specious claims to the contrary. This is the case even though the sectarian settlement at Qumran continued to be occupied until 68 C.E. and even though some of the manuscripts may have been copied in the early first century C.E.

The scrolls contain numerous references to non-Jews. Quite prominent among these are texts dealing with the halakhic status of non-Jews regarding Sabbath law, purity regulations, and commerce. Other passages discuss how the sect should implement biblical laws banning idolatrous practices. Another major theme is the role gentiles were to play in the forthcoming eschatological battle during which the sectarians would defeat them. Here, the nations are assigned a central role in the unfolding divine plan. A number of these texts, basing themselves on biblical precedent, describe how God demonstrates His might in the presence of the nations. Other texts speak of the chosen people. We will also look at the status of proselytes as described in the Qumran texts. All of these aspects will be touched upon so that we can come to a fuller understanding not only of the overall history of relations between Jews and non-Jews during this period but also of the self-image constructed by the Qumran sect.

NON-JEWS IN THE SECTARIAN LAW OF THE *ZADOKITE FRAGMENTS*

Although the Qumran corpus contains neither specific information about what constitutes Jewish identity nor, hence, how to define a non-Jew, it does offer numerous laws relating to non-Jews. The regulations of the *Zadokite Fragments* on this topic begin by legislating:

> Let him not put forth his hand to shed the blood of anyone from among the non-Jews for the sake of wealth and profit. *(ZADOKITE FRAGMENTS 12:6–7)*

The text makes no reference to any penalty for such actions. Certainly killing for self-defense would have been permitted by Jewish law. Rather, this particular law is meant as a polemic against the Hasmonaean rulers, warning against military campaigns undertaken only to add territory or to accumulate spoils of war. A similar view is expressed in *Pesher Habakkuk*, which condemns:

> the last priests of Jerusalem who gather wealth and property from the spoil of the nations. *(PESHER HABAKKUK 9:4–6)*

The text goes on to prohibit the carrying off of the property of non-Jews:

> And furthermore, let him not carry off any of their property so that they not blaspheme, except in accord with the decision of the Community of Israel. *(ZADOKITE FRAGMENTS 12:7–8)*

This law prohibits stealing from non-Jews, specifically by taking their property through military action. Most interesting is the explanation given: lest they blaspheme God. The same idea is expressed in the talmudic ruling (T. Bava Qamma 10:15) that prohibits stealing from non-Jews because it leads to profaning God's name. In reflecting badly on the Jewish people, such actions impugn Israel's God. This proscription also makes clear that war could be undertaken only with the council's permission. Only under that condition could such a war be considered just, that is, more than simply an excuse to plunder the enemy.

This series of laws then turns to two matters pertaining to animals and produce:

> Let no one sell pure (kosher) animals and fowl to non-Jews in order that they not sacrifice them. And from his threshing floor and from his wine press let him not sell to them (the non-Jews) at any price. *(ZADOKITE FRAGMENTS 12:8–10)*

The first ruling, prohibiting the sale of pure (kosher) animals and fowl to non-Jews lest they sacrifice them, also existed in rabbinic law. It was intended to make certain that Jews did not support idolatrous worship even indirectly. Also prohibited here is the sale to non-Jews of sectarian produce processed on the threshing floor or in the wine press. This law prohibits selling the produce directly from these installations, that is, before it has been tithed. In other words, selling to non-Jews does not exempt produce from tithing—the obligation to set aside one-tenth of the produce for the Levites, for the poor, or for eating in Jerusalem, depending on the particular year.

The final law in this series prohibits selling male or female servants to non-Jews:

> And his man-servant and his maid-servant, let him not sell to them (the non-Jews), since they (the servants) have entered with him into the covenant of Abraham. (ZADOKITE FRAGMENTS 12:10–11)

This law clearly concerns servants who would come under the rabbinic classification of 'eved kena'ani, literally "Canaanite slave," that is, non-Jewish servants who have begun a process of conversion to Judaism. The same regulation exists in mishnaic law wherein such slaves automatically gained their freedom if sold to non-Jews (M. Gittin 4:6). This law was intended to ensure that slaves preparing themselves to convert would be able to fulfill the commandments they were undertaking. Another text, Ordinances A, prohibits a Jew from being the servant of a non-Jew (2–4 2).

In the area of Jewish/non-Jewish relations, the Zadokite Fragments presents a summary of laws enshrined by later rabbinic tradition in the Mishnah tractate Avodah Zarah (Foreign Worship). The laws in this scroll simply reflect those followed by a number of Jewish groups, including the Pharisees. Like other non-Hellenized Jews of the Second Temple era, the sectarians eschewed killing or robbing gentiles, yet they also were careful to avoid in any way supporting or encouraging idolatrous worship.

As mentioned in an earlier chapter, the Zadokite Fragments discusses non-Jews with reference to Sabbath law. Again, in another exact parallel to mishnaic law, the text prohibits assigning a non-Jewish surrogate to do labor prohibited on the Sabbath, for doing so would make the non-Jew the Jew's agent, thereby implicating the latter in an indirect violation of Sabbath law (Zadokite Fragments 11:2). Indeed, a similar prohibition applies to male and female servants (Zadokite Fragments 11:12). This second law certainly concerns Canaanite slaves in the process of conversion, because Jewish servants would be already obligated to observe the Sabbath under Jewish law.

A strange proscription, possessing no known parallel in rabbinic law but perhaps parallel to some later Karaite views, prohibits spending the Sabbath "in a place close to the gentiles" (*Zadokite Fragments* 11:14–15). This law was most probably intended to ensure ritual purity on the Sabbath, a matter important in sectarian circles. On the other hand, the law might have been meant to forbid sectarians, seeking to circumvent the Sabbath ban on carrying or traveling, from creating a technical residency in partnership with non-Jews for this purpose. Such an interpretation would accord fully with later rabbinic law.

Here we see that although non-Jews are not obligated to observe the Jewish Sabbath, neither are Jews permitted to employ non-Jews to do prohibited labor, whether they are free or Canaanite slaves. Here again, the sect's views on this topic are sufficiently close to the Pharisaic-rabbinic tradition to suggest that they were views held by many observant Jews in this period.

A fragmentary law preserved in three Qumran manuscripts of the *Zadokite Fragments* seems to outlaw bringing (perhaps to the Temple or to the sectarian communal meals) meat slaughtered by non-Jews:

> Let no one bring [meat] with the blood of their sacrifice [from the nations . . .] and from an[y] of the gold, silver, brass, [and the] tin and the le[ad of which] the nations have made an idol, let no one bring it . . .
> (Zadokite Fragments D^f 1 II 8–10; D^d 10 3–5)

Metals—gold, silver, brass, tin, and lead—used by non-Jews to make an idol were likewise prohibited. Such vessels were to be free of all contact with idolatrous worship.

According to *Words of Moses* (III 6) and in line with Deuteronomy 15:3, it is permissible to take interest from non-Jews, but not from Jews. The *Zadokite Fragments* (D^d 6 10–11) castigates anyone who takes interest from a fellow Jew.

Extremely important, especially in light of material to be cited later from the *Temple Scroll*, is an enigmatic passage stating:

> Any man who shall condemn (or destroy) any man according to the laws of the nations is to be put to death. (Zadokite Fragments 9:1)

Scholars have debated the meaning of this passage, found in two of the Qumran manuscripts as well as in the medieval copy. It clearly is based on Leviticus 27:29 and Genesis 9:6. The Leviticus passage, translated literally, states: "No man who has been condemned for the Lord can be ransomed; he shall be put to death." In light of this verse, we can interpret our passage to mean that a man who condemns—that is, singles out for death—another shall be put to death. Genesis 9:6 provides that "whoever sheds the blood of man, by man shall his blood be shed," that is, one who causes another to lose his life shall lose his own. It is most probable that in our passage, we are dealing with a law condemning to death one who turns to non-Jewish courts to accuse a fellow Jew of a crime, since in so doing one has informed against one's fellow Jew.

Preserved only in a Qumran copy is a passage that appears to be a list of offenses, including:

> the person who reveals the secret of his people to the nations, or one who curses o[r speaks] slanderously against those anointed with His holy spirit, or leads [his people astray]. *(ZADOKITE FRAGMENTS D^e 9 II 12–15)*

As we know also from somewhat later rabbinic texts, informing on Jews to non-Jewish authorities was such a problem during this period that strong measures were considered necessary to prevent it. In context, this passage probably listed the punishment or procedures for those committing this offense.

PROHIBITIONS AGAINST IDOLATRY

We have already seen that the *Zadokite Fragments* prohibits the support of idolatrous practices. The *Temple Scroll*, in recapitulating biblical legislation on this topic, also addresses the issue. In the introduction to the scroll, the author, basing himself on Exodus 34:10–17, restates the obligation to destroy idolatrous cult objects and to avoid idolatrous worship *(Temple Scroll 2:6–12)*. His extensive treatment begins with the prohibition of idolatrous practice:

> Do not do in your land as the nations do: Everywhere they sacrifice, and plant for themselves *Asherot*, and erect for themselves pillars, and set up for themselves figured stones to bow down to (or: on) them. . . . You may not plant [for yourself any tree as an *Asherah* next to my altar which you shall make for] yourself. Nor may you erect for yourself a pillar [which I despise], n[or] shall you make for yourself (anywhere) in your entire land a [fi]gured [st]one to bo[w] down to (or: on). *(TEMPLE SCROLL 51:19–52:3)*

This passage, based on Deuteronomy 16:21–22 (cf. Leviticus 26:1), outlaws decentralized sacrifice throughout the land, planting *Asherot*, and erecting cultic pillars and figured stones. Note that the sectarian version of this law adds nothing to biblical law, except in its particular reformulation.

The scroll next paraphrases the law of the idolatrous prophet stated in Deuteronomy 13:2–6 *(Temple Scroll 54:8–18)*. Here, too, although the text includes minor variations in the textual traditions behind it, as well as a few changes to eliminate ambiguities, the passage simply repeats the biblical law mandating the death penalty for what is termed a "prophet" who advocates worship of other gods. Similar is the way the scroll reviews the law of the enticer to idolatry, found in Deuteronomy 13:7–12 *(Temple Scroll 54:19–55:1)*. As in Deuteronomy, such a person is to be put to death. Here again, the scroll introduces no significant legal innovations.

More significant variants appear in a paraphrase of the law of the idolatrous city, found in Deuteronomy 13:13-19:

> If you hear regarding on[e of your cities which] I give you [in which] to dwe[ll], the following: "Some worth[less] peo[p]le among you have gone out and have led astray all the [in]habitants of their city, saying, 'Let us go and worship gods' which you have not known," then you must ask, inquire and investigate carefully. If the accusation turns out to be true (and) correct, (that) this abominable transgression has been committed among (the people of) Israel, you must kill all the inhabitants of that city by the sword, destroying it and all (the people) that are in it. And all its domesticated animals you must kill by the sword. Then you must gather all the spoil (taken) from it into its town square and burn the city and the spoil (taken) from it with fire as a whole burnt offering to the Lord your God. It shall be an eternal mound never to be rebuilt. None of the property to be destroyed should remain in your possession. (You shall do all this) in order that I shall be appeased from My anger and show you mercy, and have compassion on you and increase you as I promised to your forefathers, provided that you obey My voice to observe all My commandments which I command you this day so as to do what is right and good before the Lord your God. (Temple Scroll 55:2-14)

The biblical legislation requires that a city that has gone astray and worshiped idols be totally destroyed, its inhabitants killed, and its spoils burned.

Our passage modifies some of these requirements: For the city to be entirely destroyed, all its inhabitants must have worshiped idols—in contrast to the mishnaic requirement that only the majority must have transgressed (M. Sanhedrin 4:1). Conversely, although the rabbinic view exempts the city's children from death (T. Sanhedrin 14:3), the scroll condemns all the inhabitants. Similarly, the rabbinic interpretation spares animals dedicated for certain sacrificial offerings (T. Sanhedrin 14:5; Sifre Devarim 94), whereas the Temple Scroll mandates that all the animals be destroyed.

The final law on idolatry in the Temple Scroll is the law of the idolatrous individual, based on Deuteronomy 12:2-7 (Temple Scroll 55:15-56:04). While the text eliminates some ambiguities found in the original passage, it is essentially a recapitulation of the Deuteronomic prescription that idolaters be put to death if they can be convicted in court under the applicable rules of testimony.

In formulating all these laws—with the exception of the law of the idolatrous city—the sectarian text simply adheres to the biblical prohibitions with little addition or modification. In the one case in which there are extensive changes, the law may have been formulated in response to Hasmonaean attempts to eradicate idolatry in the country, a campaign that sometimes led to the destruction of entire cities, without prior investigation or trial. Our author may have wanted to argue that Hellenistic Jews, no matter how errant, should not be destroyed unless the entire city had participated in idolatrous worship.

What emerges from this discussion is that the author/redactor of the *Temple Scroll* had little if anything to add to the Torah's legislation on idolatry. Furthermore, he says nothing about non-Jews who worship idols except that their cult objects and cult places are to be destroyed. Thus, following the lead of Deuteronomy, he is concerned almost exclusively with eliminating idolatrous worship from among the Jews, an agenda that fits both the author of Deuteronomy and the author/redactor of the scroll.

OTHER LAWS IN THE *TEMPLE SCROLL*

At the beginning of the preserved portion of the *Temple Scroll* (2:1–15), in the same context as the requirement to destroy pagan cult objects, we find restated the biblical prohibition against making covenants with the nations of Canaan, who are to be destroyed (Exodus 34:10–16). Both the Bible and the scroll state explicitly that such a restriction is intended to prevent intermarriage with these nations. This passage adheres so closely to its biblical source that we cannot determine if the sect expanded the law in Exodus to ban intermarriage with all nations, as was already done in the biblical period (I Kings 11:1–2, Ezra 9:1–2, Nehemiah 10:31). However, passages elsewhere in the scroll seem to indicate that all marriage between Jews and gentiles was prohibited (*Temple Scroll* 57:15–17).

No doubt non-Jews would have been prohibited from entering the Temple since even proselytes were forbidden entry into the middle court until the fourth generation (*Temple Scroll* 39:5–7). Indeed, in the End of Days, non-Jews as well as proselytes were to be excluded from the sanctuary described in *Florilegium* (1–2 I 4).

Another law, concerning burial, is unique to the scroll, although the text's literary style reflects the phraseology of biblical language. Because the dead impart impurity, Jews are to bury their dead in specially set-out cemeteries, one for every four cities, in order to maintain the ritual purity of the Land of Israel. In contrast, the nations bury their dead everywhere (*Temple Scroll* 48:11–14). They similarly offer sacrifices and erect cult places everywhere, a practice condemned by the scroll (*Temple Scroll* 15:19–21). The unstated (or perhaps unpreserved) implication here is that Israel is to perform sacrificial worship only at its central Temple complex in Jerusalem.

The scroll also lists the abominations of the nations: passing children through fire as part of Molekh worship, divination, augury, sorcery, and necromancy. Israel is told that because of these abominations, the Canaanite nations have been expelled from the land (*Temple Scroll* 60:16–61:02). This passage, however, is no more than a verbatim quotation of Deuteronomy 18:9–14, with minor textual variation.

The nations are mentioned several times in the Law of the King, a separate source that the author/redactor of the scroll incorporated into his text. Although Israel is to have a king "like all the (other) nations," that king must be Jewish (*Temple Scroll* 56:13–15), an exact echo of Deuteronomy 17:14–15. He may marry only a Jewish woman (*Temple Scroll* 57:15–16). He must be protected by a guard of twelve thousand chosen Jewish men, lest he be kidnapped by "the nations" or by "a foreign nation" (*Temple Scroll* 57:5–11). The repetition within this passage, undoubtedly intended for emphasis, suggests that kidnapping by foreigners was a central concern. (A passing reference in *Zadokite Fragments* 14:15 similarly mentions redeeming hostages "captured by a foreign nation." Furthermore, the sect considered no longer fit for priestly service any priest captured by non-Jews.) A fundamental duty of the king was to defend the Land of Israel against foreign attackers in quest of booty (*Temple Scroll* 58:3–10).

After the conclusion of the Law of the King, we find another recapitulation of the Deuteronomic laws of war, obligating Israel to kill all the Canaanites lest Israel learn from the Canaanites' abominable ways (*Temple Scroll* 62:11–16). Here again we are dealing with a Deuteronomic text (20:15–18), rather than with independent Second Temple period material.

Two final examples from the *Temple Scroll* concern those to be punished by hanging:

> If a man has informed and has delivered his people up to a foreign nation, and has inflicted harm on his people, you shall hang him on a tree and he shall die. . . . If a man has committed a crime punishable by death and has fled to the midst of the non-Jews and cursed his people and the children of Israel, you shall hang him also on a tree and he shall die . . . (Temple Scroll 64:6–11)

The first law prescribes that one who informs against his people or delivers them to "a foreign nation" shall be executed, apparently by crucifixion (*Temple Scroll* 64:6–9). This law is based on an interpretation of Leviticus 19:16: "Do not go about slandering your people." Like the Targumim and the Rabbis, and the *Zadokite Fragments*, the *Temple Scroll* regarded informing to non-Jews a particularly heinous crime, as indeed it has always been regarded in Jewish tradition.

The second law concerns those subject to the death penalty who flee "to the midst of the nations" and there curse their people, the Israelites. If caught, they are to be put to death, apparently by crucifixion as well (*Temple Scroll* 64:9–13). The prohibition against execrating the Jewish people and the prescribed punishment by what was termed "hanging," but was most probably crucifixion, is based on an interpretation of Deuteronomy 21:22–23, "If a man is guilty of a capital offense . . . and you impale him on a stake. . . . For an impaled body is an affront to God. . . ." This verse is understood by the scroll to mean that one who affronts God, by cursing the Jewish people, is to be impaled, that is, crucified.

This passage has given rise to heated discussion because it seems to legitimize punishment by crucifixion, according to the scroll's own interpretation of the Torah. However, some scholars have argued that "hanging from a tree" refers no to crucifixion, but to hanging after death, which is the original intent of the Torah. Whatever the term's precise meaning, the *Temple Scroll* condones this punishment only in the limited circumstance of informers whose actions threaten to expose the Jewish people to serious danger.

In general, in the *Temple Scroll*, most mentions of non-Jews ("the nations") occur in material taken almost verbatim from Scripture. Particularly significant are those passages the author composed on his own: the rejection of non-Jewish burial practices to ensure the purity of the land, the requirement that the king marry only a Jewish bride, fear of enemy attack by non-Jews, fear that the king might be kidnapped, and the problem of informers and execrators against the Jewish people. Here we see the special concerns of the author/redactor or his sources, writing in the Second Temple period. Indeed, the issues of purity, especially of the land; intermarriage; treason; and the complex web of Hasmonaean and pagan military activity were major concerns during this period.

Non-Jews in the *Halakhic Letter*

The *Halakhic Letter* contains (of a total of twenty-two) two laws relating to non-Jews.

The founders of the sect, writing to their former priestly colleagues in Jerusalem soon after 152 B.C.E., criticize them for accepting grain offerings (*terumah*) from the produce of non-Jews:

> [And regarding the g]rain of the [non-Jews, which they bring] and cause to come into cont[a]ct wi[th their . . .] and render [it] im[pure, but one is not permitted to eat] of the grain of [the non-J]ews [and one is not permitted] to bring (it) to the Temple. (*HALAKHIC LETTER B3–5*)

Such produce, the sectarians assert, is not to enter the Temple lest it defile the offerings collected from Jews. In fact, it is forbidden even to eat of such produce. Sectarians also oppose accepting sacrificial offerings from non-Jews, which was the current practice in the Temple:

> And regarding the sacrifice of the non-Jews, [we say that they] sacrifice [. . .].
> (*HALAKHIC LETTER B8*)

Certainly, the continuation of this fragment would condemn this practice. No such laws are known from the Pharisaic-rabbinic tradition.

These two cultic matters were certainly important to the sect's founders. The exclusionist views expressed here fit well with their eschatological ideas: they expected the nations ultimately to disappear from the face of the earth. The alternative approach of the Pharisaic-rabbinic tradition envisioned the nations coming to Jerusalem to recognize God's sovereignty and to participate in the worship of the Lord.

NON-JEWS IN SECTARIAN TEACHING

The long Admonition at the beginning of the *Zadokite Fragments* is almost entirely directed to intra-Jewish issues, especially to the sect's self-image and polemic with the Pharisees. The only time that non-Jews appear here is in a *pesher*-like exegesis of Deuteronomy 32:33 ("Their wine is the venom of asps, the pitiless poison of vipers") that mentions the "kings of the peoples," their evil ways, and the "king of Greece" (that is, Rome), who will take vengeance, most probably on the other kings (*Zadokite Fragments* 8:9–12 = 19:21–25). This passage certainly reflects the circumstances during the Hasmonaean period, when the Romans were slowly gobbling up the various local kings of the Mediterranean Basin and the Near East. The same circumstances are referred to in *Pesher Habakkuk* (3:2–13, 3:17–4:9).

A strange passage in the *Zadokite Fragments*, preserved only in the Qumran manuscripts, appears as part of a ritual for expelling miscreants from the sect. There we read that God created the various peoples of the earth:

> . . . and You led them astray in confusion, and with no path, but You chose our forefathers . . . (ZADOKITE FRAGMENTS D⁴ 18 V 10–11)

Here we are told that God caused the other nations to go astray. That is, the nations were predestined to go astray, a view consonant with the sect's predestinarian outlook and its extreme ethical dualism. We will encounter the chosen people motif in other texts later.

According to *Pesher Hosea A* (II 12–13), the Jews will be punished for their transgressions in the presence of the nations. The same text lists as a primary transgression the scheduling of feasts "according to the appointed times of the nations" (*Pesher Hosea A* II 15–16), a reference to following the wrong calendar. This passage most probably alludes to the sect's adoption of a solar calendar, as opposed to the calendar of lunar months adjusted to solar years followed by most of the Jewish community.

THE DESTRUCTION OF THE NATIONS

The Dead Sea sect expected that the End of Days would soon dawn. Their apocalyptic, messianic tendencies led them to develop a body of literature outlining the eschatological battle that would usher in the final age. The *War Scroll* presents a very schematized view of these battles: The sectarians are the Sons of Light, destined to emerge victorious in the End of Days. The place of their exile before this battle is called "the desert of the peoples." The nations, on the other hand, are grouped with the Sons of Darkness, including also those Jews whose behavior has revealed that they are not predestined to be among the Sons of Light but are to be assigned to the lot of Belial. No remnant of these evil nations is to survive in the End of Days.

In the author's scheme, the nations bear names drawn from the biblical table of nations in Genesis 10. Most prominent of these are Assyria (Seleucid Syria) and Kittim (Rome); the destruction of both is high on the author's agenda. The battles will take place in "all the lands of the nations." Indeed, as one of their banners testified, the sect expected the "annihilation by God of all nations of vanity" (*War Scroll* 4:12). The final battle would exact retribution on these nations for their wickedness, killing all of them.

The text echoes the chosen people motif of the Bible (Deuteronomy 7:6, 14:2), when it declares:

> Who is like unto Your people Israel which You have chosen for Yourself from all the nations of the lands, a people of those holy through the covenant!"
> (*WAR SCROLL* 10:9–10; Me FRAG. 1)

The passage goes on to explain that Israel has expressed its chosenness through being willing to receive revelation and to probe the depths of God's commands (lines 10–11). This passage, like other poetic and liturgical sections of the scroll, probably predated its final authorship. When the author compiled the scroll as a whole, he included in it various poems previously composed. Further on, the sectarians themselves are designated as "the chosen ones of the holy nation" (12:1).

One particular poem, included twice in the scroll, seems to contradict the document's premise that all the nations are to be destroyed in the End of Days. Addressed primarily to God, who is asked to crush the nations, his adversaries, the poem (*War Scroll* 12:12–14) turns to the city of Jerusalem and calls on it to:

> Open your gates forever,
> to let enter in to you the wealth of the nations,
> and their kings shall serve you . . .
> and rule over the king[dom of the Kittim].

We will discuss this poem in the next chapter when we investigate the place of Jerusalem in the scrolls. For now it is enough to remark that this passage, based almost entirely on Isaiah 60:10–14, anticipates that the nations, including the Romans, will survive into the messianic era when they will be subservient to Israel. That the nations will continue to exist, this time under the rule of the Davidic messiah, is also expected in *Pesher Isaiah A* (7 25).

This idea may also lie behind the expression "to subdue the nations," found in the messianic *Rule of the Congregation* (1:21), although the phrase may, alternatively, refer to their destruction. And we might be encountering this approach also in a related text in a blessing for the Prince of the Congregation, when we are told:

> be[fore you will bow all peoples, and all the nat]ions will serve you.
> (RULE OF BENEDICTIONS 5:28–29)

Despite these few exceptions, however, the dominant theme of the *War Scroll* is that the nations are predestined to be destroyed in the great war that will usher in the End of Days. At that time, the sectarians, aided by angelic forces, will defeat and kill all the nations. Even those Jews who do not join the group will be destroyed. Thus, in the End of Days, the world will be populated only by members of the sect.

ISRAEL AND THE NATIONS IN LITURGICAL TEXTS

The *Lament* from cave 4 asks God "not to give our inheritance to strangers nor our property (or possessions) to foreigners" (line 1). This text envisions that Rome will soon conquer and destroy the Land of Israel. The author clearly understood that Rome was interested in the affairs of the Near East in the first century B.C.E. only because it eventually wanted to conquer Judaea.

The chosen people motif appears again in a fragmentary prayer, most probably for the Festival of Passover, in which God is praised "[W]ho cho[se] us from among [the] nations" (*Daily Prayers* 24–25 VII 4). The same idea is asserted in the *Non-canonical Psalms* (76–77 15).

Words of the Luminaries A appeals to God to remember "Your wonders which You did before the nations" (1–2 II 12), referring to the miracles of biblical times that had demonstrated God's power to the nations. The text also recalls "that (God) took us out (of Egypt) in the presence of all the nations" (1–2 V 10). Yet these nations are to be regarded as "[no]thing before You" (1–2 III 3). Indeed, God has created the Jewish people, made them his children, and called them, "My son, My firstborn" before the nations (lines 4–6).

The chosen people motif is also prominent in this text:

> You have loved Israel more than the (other) peoples. . . . All the nations saw Your glory in that You were sanctified among Your people Israel.
> (WORDS OF THE LUMINARIES A 1–2 IV 4–9)

Because God has loved Israel and chosen it as his people and Israel has sanctified him, the nations have recognized God's sovereignty.

This motif also occurs in *Prayers for Festivals*. In one prayer we hear that:

> You chose a people at the time of Your favor, for You remembered Your covenant. You set them aside for Yourself as holy from all the peoples and You renewed for them Your covenant with visions of (Your) glory and the words of Your holy [spirit].
> (LITURGICAL PRAYER II 5–7 = PRAYERS FOR FESTIVALS C 97–98 I 7–10)

Israel is indeed God's chosen nation, but the text makes clear that what it has been chosen for is to receive a vision of God's glory, His divine presence, and the revelation of his Torah, the divine law. Israel, in turn, has responded by accepting the obligations of the covenant.

PROSELYTES IN THE DEAD SEA SCROLLS

Despite the sect's notions of predestination and their view that the nations—the non-Jews—would be destroyed in the End of Days, it nonetheless recognized the institution of proselytism—religious conversion to Judaism—that apparently existed by that time. Proselytes appear in the lists of the classes making up the sect:

> They shall all be mustered by their names, the pr[ies]ts first, and the Levites second, and the children of Israel third, and the proselyte fourth. And they shall be written down by their na[mes], each after his brother. . . . Thus shall they sit and shall they be asked about everything. (ZADOKITE FRAGMENTS 14:3–6)

During the sect's occupation of Qumran, sectarian officials maintained written documents that the sect used for the purposes of its mustering ceremony. Some of the lists of names found among the documentary texts from Qumran may be remnants of such lists. In another passage, the *Zadokite Fragments* mentions that the proselyte may be in need of economic help (6:21).

The sectarians assigned proselytes a status different from that of full Israelites. In this respect, they conformed to an approach held by a minority of early Rabbis (T. Kiddushin 5:1). Accordingly, the *Temple Scroll* expected that proselytes would be permitted to enter the Temple only in the fourth generation. The author of *Florilegium* wanted to exclude converts altogether from his messianic sanctuary.

We have previously noted that slaves who had entered the status called by the Rabbis "the Canaanite slave"—that is, who were already involved in the process of conversion—could not be sold to non-Jews. Clearly, then, the sect recognized converts and conversion and probably included converts in its ranks.

The material studied here represents a paradox. On one hand, we have encountered non-Jews in what may be considered the classic position assigned to them by the Jewish legal system. Although they are not obligated to observe specifically Jewish precepts such as the Sabbath laws or other Jewish commandments, they are nevertheless forbidden to worship idols or to blaspheme God. Hence, our texts go out of their way to note laws pertaining to idolaters and idolatry. Of course, some of these laws indirectly address the problems of how pagan religious behavior affects Jews. Yet non-Jews, even idolaters, are to be protected from depredation and pillage by Jewish armies solely intent on enriching Jewish rulers or their subjects.

On the other hand, some of the sectarian documents express an eschatological view that anticipates the future destruction of the non-Jews, together with those

Jews who reject (or who are predestined to reject) sectarian doctrine and practice. For the Qumran sect, the messianic redemption was not to be the universal experience foretold by the prophet Isaiah; it was to be theirs and theirs alone.

Ultimately, Judaism accepted many aspects of the laws commonly held during the Second Temple period as well as specifically Pharisaic teachings. Together, these laws formed the basis for rabbinic halakhah. Although Qumran law shares many of the presuppositions and rulings of this Pharisaic-rabbinic tradition, the sectarians were less willing than the Rabbis to embrace the vision of Israel's prophets, who anticipated that all the nations would one day come to worship God under Israel's leadership. To the Pharisees and their rabbinic successors, this universal homage at Israel's holy mountain would represent the true fulfillment of the ideals and aspirations of the messianic future.

That holy mountain, of course, was located in Jerusalem. We now turn our attention to the nature and significance of the holy city, which, to the Qumran sect, as for all Jews, is the center of the Jewish world.

CHAPTER 24

Jerusalem, the Holy City

Despite its self-imposed exile from the Temple and from the holy city itself, Qumran sectarians accorded Jerusalem a special place in their mind and heart. The Dead Sea Scrolls, especially the *New Jerusalem* texts and the *Temple Scroll*, offer us a remarkable opportunity to see how Jerusalem was viewed in the Second Temple period, both by the Qumran sect and by the various earlier authors represented in the Qumran library. We will see that throughout this period, Jews of all kinds affirmed the sanctity and centrality of the Temple and its sanctuary, regarded as the religious epicenter of the Jewish world.

We will look at two types of material on this topic. The first consists of a substantial body of texts that mention Jerusalem or Zion by name. Another group of prominent texts, whether for literary reasons or due to natural decay, do not explicitly mention the city, but instead allude to it extensively. In these materials we will find Jerusalem cast in three central roles: the Jerusalem of history, experienced by the authors of our texts; the Jerusalem consonant with the ideals of Jewish law; and the Jerusalem of the future.

THE JERUSALEM OF HISTORY

Although the Jerusalem most often mentioned in the scrolls is the city of Hasmonaean times, some texts allude to the Jerusalem of the First Temple period. Indeed, the destruction of the First Temple was still being mourned even after the Jews had replaced it with the Second Temple. Such a text is the *Lamentation* from cave 4, which adapts the biblical Book of Lamentations with explanatory expansions. In this text we hear of the destruction of Jerusalem by the Babylonians (586 B.C.E.) and the end of its sacrifices as well as the suffering of the "children of Zion," the inhabitants of the city. Jerusalem is depicted mourning the destruction of its suburbs. This text, not in any way peculiar to the Qumran sect, may express the nation's general sorrow over the loss of the ancient glories of

First Temple times. The pseudoprophetic texts mention Jews taken into captivity by the Babylonians (*Pseudo-Ezekiel A* 16 I 3–4) and the worship of other gods by "priests of Jerusalem" (*Pseudo-Ezekiel C* 3 III 5–7). The latter reference, however, may be an extrapolation by the author, reflecting his censure of the current priestly establishment.

The destruction of Jerusalem is also the theme of the cave 4 *Consolations* text, essentially a series of biblical passages, mostly from Isaiah, comforting the people of Israel and foretelling the future rebuilding of Zion. Because we find no sectarian elements in this text either, we can assume it reflects sentiments typical of the committed Palestinian Jew of Second Temple times. Also, the *Halakhic Letter* (C19) explicitly alludes to "the exile of Jerusalem" in the time of Zedekiah.

Yet despite the love for Jerusalem expressed in these texts, it is clear that members of the Qumran sect stood apart from the Jerusalem of their own times, since they regarded it as the seat of an illegitimate priesthood. *Pesher Habakkuk* states that:

> the last priests of Jerusalem gather great wealth and property from the spoil of the nations. But in the End of Days their property will be delivered along with their spoil into the hands of the army of the Kittim. (PESHER HABAKKUK 9:4)

The Kittim are, of course, the Romans, whose imminent attack on Palestine, expected by the *pesher*, will signal the dawn of the End of Days. In that attack, the priests will pay their just penalty, losing all the wealth they have gathered by attacking non-Jews. *Pesher Psalms* (9 1–2) also alludes to the city's impending destruction at the hands of the Kittim.

According to the fragmentary *Pesher Micah* (11 1), these are the same priests who had led the people astray. The continuation of the broken text would probably have contained a description of the priests' punishment. It is likely that these are the priests described in *Pesher Isaiah B* (2 6–8) as the "men of scoffing who are in Jerusalem":

> those who despised the Torah of the Lord and reviled the word of the holy One of Israel. (ISAIAH 5:24)

And they were probably allied with the Wicked Priest, the archenemy of the Teacher of Righteousness.

Also centered in Jerusalem was another group inimical to the sect's approach to Judaism: the "seekers of smooth things," that is, the Pharisees. Their sobriquet can more precisely be understood as "those who derive false laws through interpretation."

Almost the entire surviving portion of *Pesher Nahum* (3–4 I) refers to Jerusalem. According to the author, the holy city has become a dwelling place for gentiles. The author recounts the alliance of the Pharisees with the Seleucids under Demetrius III Eukerus (96–88 B.C.E.), who together attempted to overthrow the Hasmonaean Alexander Janneus (103–76 B.C.E.), the Lion of Wrath, and his council. The text makes specific reference to Janneus's garrison in Jerusalem as well as to the large amounts of money accumulated by the "priests of Jerusalem," no doubt a reference to the Sadducees described as wealthy elsewhere in the text.

Testimonia (21–30) and the *Psalms of Joshua B* (22 II 7–14) contain identical passages ascribed pseudepigraphically to Joshua. In this passage based on the canonical Joshua 6:26, Joshua foretells the rebuilding of Jericho and the disastrous consequences. There in the rebuilt city, a Hasmonaean ruler, whose identity has been widely debated:

> will [spill bl]ood like water upon the barrier of the Daughter of Zion and in the precincts of Jerusalem. *(TESTIMONIA 29)*

This text reflects the sect's generally negative views about the Hasmonaeans and their military exploits.

Pesher Habakkuk describes Jerusalem itself as:

> the city in which the evil priest has undertaken abominable actions so as to render the Temple impure. *(PESHER HABAKKUK 12:7)*

Here is a clear reference to Hasmonaean Jerusalem and its polluted Temple.

Thus, although sectarians continued to mourn the Destruction of the First Temple as did their fellow Jews in this period, they regarded the contemporary city, together with its priestly government and its Temple, as anathema. Yet an exceptional passage mentions the Jerusalem of this period in a positive context. *Pesher Micah* 10 4–7 interprets "Jerusalem," mentioned in Micah 1:5, as referring to the Teacher of Righteousness and the sect who will be saved from the final destruction. Indeed, although sectarians condemned virtually every feature of the Jerusalem of their times, they continued to place the city at the center of their halakhic and eschatological ideals.

THE JERUSALEM OF RELIGIOUS LAW

All Jewish groups in the Second Temple period assigned Jerusalem special sanctity in Jewish law, because the Temple located there was the religious center of the Jewish people. Despite the Dead Sea sectarians' condemnation of and abstention from the Temple rituals of their own day, the Judaism they espoused did not in any way renounce these rituals in principle. Rather, they objected to specific practices being currently performed at the Temple, fully expecting that both in the present and in the eschatological future, such improprieties would be corrected.

According to Jewish tradition, Jerusalem was central in Jewish ritual because God had chosen the city as the final resting place for the ark of His covenant. Indeed, in a broken passage in *Words of the Luminaries*, referring to the placement of the ark and Temple in Jerusalem, the text declares:

> Its Ta[ber]nacle [. . .] rest in Jerusa[lem, the city which] You [ch]ose from the entire land so that Y[our name] would be there forever.
>
> *(Words of the Luminaries A 1–2 IV 2–4)*

According to this text, the placing of the ark and Tabernacle in Jerusalem in David's time secured the city's future role as the spiritual center of the Jewish people. The passage goes on to recount the political and economic effects precipitated when the religious capital was established in Jerusalem:

> Then all the nations saw Your glory in that You were sanctified among Your people Israel, as well as Your great name, and they brought their tribute of silver and gold and precious stone(s) with all the treasure of their countries, to honor Your people and Zion Your holy city, and Your glorious Temple. And there was no adversary or misfortune, but rather peace and blessing . . .
>
> *(Words of the Luminaries A 1–2 IV 8–13)*

To this author, the time of David was an ideal period, when Jerusalem, the city of Zion, was simultaneously the religious, political, and economic capital of the nation.

A hymn from *Non-canonical Psalms A Scroll* (1 I 1–8) also focuses on the chosenness of Jerusalem:

> [Jeru]salem [the city which the Lo]rd [chose] from eternity,
> [as a place of residence for] the holy ones.
> [For the na]me of the Lord has been invoked upon it,
> [and His glory] has appeared over Jerusalem [and] Zion.
> Who can declare the renown of the Lord,
> and announce all of [His] praise.

The fragment containing the *Prayer for King Jonathan*, probably a prayer for the welfare of Alexander Janneus, also includes a section (A10), paralleled in Psalm 154 from the *Psalms Scroll*, that has been restored to read:

> His habitation is in Zion,
> He ch[ooses Jerusalem forever].

The poem at the end of Ben Sira (51:12) in the Hebrew version expresses a similar notion:

> Give thanks to the One Who chooses Jerusalem,
> for His mercy endures forever.

Perhaps the most direct statement on the halakhic status of Jerusalem comes from the *Halakhic Letter*. The writers criticize their opponents in the Jerusalem establishment for slaughtering animals outside the "camp," referring to nonsacrificial slaughter—that is, meat to be eaten—that was performed outside the Temple in close proximity to Jerusalem. The *Halakhic Letter* counters that all slaughter is to take place "in the north of the camp," a ruling probably derived from Leviticus 1:11, wherein sacrifice is prescribed on "the north side of the altar, before the Lord." Apparently the authors of this sectarian foundation document required even whole-offerings—those sacrifices offered for eating purposes—to be sacrificed on the north side of the altar, as prescribed in the Torah. This view is directly opposite to mishnaic procedure (M. Zevaḥim 5:7), which permits these offerings to be slaughtered anywhere in the inner court.

Then the writers state:

> But we hold the view that the Temple is [the (equivalent of) the Tabernacle of the Tent of Meeting, and Je]rusalem is the camp, and outside of the camp [is (equivalent to) outside of Jerusalem]; it is the camp of their cities.
> (*HALAKHIC LETTER B29–31*)

Here the sanctuary is regarded as equivalent to the Israelite camp in the wilderness period: the Temple in the center corresponds to the Tabernacle; and the city of Jerusalem, to the entire camp in the desert. Since it was permissible to slaughter only in the Israelite camp, not outside, so it is similarly permissible to slaughter only in the city of Jerusalem. Those outside, presumably those living close by, should be required to offer their animals as whole-offerings in the Jerusalem Temple.

Further on in the text is a second reference to this same matter. After banning dogs from Jerusalem because they might gnaw on the bones of sacrificial meat, the text states:

> For Jerusalem is the camp of holiness, and it is the place which He (God) chose from all the tribes of Israel, for Jerusalem is the chief of the camps of Israel. (*HALAKHIC LETTER B58–62*)

Only Jerusalem has this exalted status since God chose it. Furthermore, for legal purposes the city is the equivalent of the wilderness camp. All offerings and restrictions that pertained to the entire camp here pertain to the entire city of Jerusalem.

In the *Temple Scroll*, we find a vision for the reform of religious and political life in Hasmonaean Judaea, including, among other things, a new Temple of enormous proportions. Rather than being messianic, the scroll envisions an ideal society for the present, premessianic age. But it presents itself as a Torah, with the author's views represented as the word of God. Because of this literary conceit, the *Temple Scroll*, like the Book of Deuteronomy, never mentions Jerusalem, but instead refers to the "place which God will choose to make His name dwell therein." Yet we can confidently assume that this scroll refers directly to Jerusalem as the site of a future Temple that the author/redactor hoped to see constructed in his own day.

If that is the case, then this text should provide us with a description of that "Jerusalem." We have already seen in a previous chapter that the scroll's author regards the Temple as the central building not only of the city, but of the nation as a whole. Unlike the actual Temple of his day, which had two concentric courts, this new Temple would have three concentric courts. Like Ezekiel, he designed the third court to increase the stringency of the purity regulations for the Temple and to further limit access by those who did not attain the necessary levels of purity.

Our detailed analysis of the architecture of this Temple complex, and specifically of its gates and chambers, has shown that its planner conceived of it as a replica of the desert camp. Accordingly, the Temple and the inner court were taken as equivalent to the Tabernacle. The middle court represented the area in which the Levites dwelled, immediately around the Tabernacle. The outer court was the equivalent of the entire camp assigned as the dwelling place of the Israelite tribes.

The scroll calls this Temple complex "the city of the sanctuary." Since the *Temple Scroll* was published, scholars have debated whether that term covers the entire city of Jerusalem or only the Temple complex—what the Rabbis called the Temple Mount. Since it was originally taken to refer to the entire residential area of Jerusalem, it was assumed that Temple purity restrictions would apply throughout the city, thereby elevating earthly Jerusalem to the status of a Temple with its attendant rules and regulations. Other scholars then proposed that "the city of the sanctuary" referred only to the Temple complex itself; in this case, the residential area of Jerusalem would surround the Temple but not be considered part of it.

The enlarged platform on which the Temple would stand was to approximate the size of the entire city in the author's own day. In my view, the author of that section of the scroll, who was also the planner of the future Temple, expected the entire city of Jerusalem to become the Temple complex that would represent the wilderness camp of Israel. It was, after all, during this early period of Israel's history that the people showed uncompromising loyalty to God and his law.

These three courtyards basically accord with the later rabbinic conception of the "camp" in biblical law. The Rabbis understood the various laws about the camp to refer to three concentric camps: the camp of the divine presence, namely, the Tabernacle; the camp of the Levites, the area of their encampment around the Tabernacle; and the camp of Israel, the rest of the desert camp. Although the *Temple Scroll* differs about some of the particular regulations, it adopted for its projected Temple the same system found in the rabbinic sources.

The authors of these documents clearly regarded Jerusalem as the religious center of their universe, the place God had chosen as his own. Worship was to be conducted there according to the sectarian interpretation of the Torah—if not in the present age, then soon, when the End of Days was to dawn. To prepare for this approaching time, the sectarians continued to study sacrificial laws and to dream of a new Temple, purer and more holy than the one they had abandoned.

THE JERUSALEM OF THE END OF DAYS

The *Scroll of the War of the Sons of Light against the Sons of Darkness*, in describing the great cosmic battle to take place before the End of Days, outlines the tactics and rituals to be followed during the war.

The war will start:

> ... when the exiles of the Sons of Light return from the Wilderness of the Nations to encamp in the Wilderness of Jerusalem. *(WAR SCROLL 1:3)*

During the first phase of the war, the Qumran sectarians will be deployed somewhere in the Judaean wilderness close to Jerusalem. The scroll alludes to this base of operations, or perhaps to Jerusalem itself after its conquest, in a description of the battle trumpets that will signal:

> the way of returning from battle with the enemy so as to come to the congregation at Jerusalem. *(WAR SCROLL 3:10–11)*

These trumpets were to be inscribed with the words "Rejoicings of God upon returning in peace."

A similar motif appears in a chain of biblical verses about the messianic era that are given a sectarian interpretation. In a passage apparently referring to the victory of the Sons of Light in the eschatological battle, the text declares:

> and they shall enter Zion with gladness and Jerusalem [with eternal joy].
> *(CATENA A 12–13 I 10)*

The author is paraphrasing Isaiah 35:10 and 51:11. According to the sectarian view, the Sons of Light, after destroying Belial and the people of his lot, will all be gathered together, presumably in the holy city *(Catena* A 12–13 I 10–11).

Further on, in describing the purity rules for the military camp, the *War Scroll* specifies that "no young boy and no woman shall enter their encampments when they go forth from Jerusalem to go to battle" *(War Scroll* 7:3–4). The battle clearly starts from Jerusalem.

A beautiful poetic passage, actually a pastiche of biblical phrases, is found in the *War Scroll* (12:12–14). We have already discussed a section of this poem, but we present here the entire unit:

> Zion, rejoice exceedingly,
> and shine forth in songs of joy, O Jerusalem,
> and be joyful, all (you) cities of Judah.
> Open [your] gates forever,
> to let enter into you the wealth of the nations,
> and their kings shall serve you.
> All who afflicted you shall bow down to you,
> And the dust [of your feet they shall lick.]

In the End of Days Jerusalem will rejoice as its children triumph over their enemies. Those who afflicted Jerusalem will then be forced to pay tribute.

Very similar is the beautiful prayer termed Apostrophe to Zion, preserved in the *Psalms Scroll* (22:1–15), a pastiche of biblical phrases in the same style as the shorter poem from the *War Scroll* cited earlier:

> I will remember you for a blessing, O Zion,
> I have loved you with all my might;
> may your memory be blessed for ever!
> Great is your hope, O Zion,
> that peace and your longed-for salvation will come.
> Generation after generation will dwell in you,
> and generations of the pious will be your glory.
> Those who yearn for the day of your redemption,
> that they may rejoice in your great glory.
> They are nourished from the abundance of your glory,
> and in your beautiful squares they walk.
> You will remember the kindness of your prophets,
> and in the deeds of your pious ones you will glory.
> Purge violence from your midst,
> falsehood and dishonesty should be eradicated from you.
> Your children will rejoice in your midst,
> and your friends will join together with you.
> How many have hoped for your redemption,
> and your pure ones have mourned for you.
> Your hope, O Zion, shall not perish,
> nor will your longing be forgotten.
> Who is it who has ever perished in righteousness,
> or who is it that has ever escaped in his iniquity?
> A person is tested according to his way(s),

one will be requited according to his deeds.

All around your enemies are cut off, O Zion,

and all those who hate you have scattered.

Praise of you is pleasing, O Zion,

cherished throughout the world.

Many times will I remember you for a blessing,

with all my heart I will bless you.

May you attain everlasting justice,

and may you receive the blessings of magnates.

May you merit the fulfillment of the vision prophesied about you,

the dream of the prophets which was sought for you.

Be exalted and spread far and wide, O Zion,

praise the Most High, your Redeemer;

may my soul rejoice at (the revelation of) your glory!

It is difficult to add any comment to this stirring poem that so eloquently expresses the Jewish people's dreams for the city of Jerusalem, from the time of King David until the present. The poem's inclusion in the liturgically oriented *Psalms Scroll* demonstrates that the Qumran sect shared in the fundamental Jewish loyalty to the holy city.

Most important, Jerusalem is to be a spiritual center for the sect in the End of Days. *Florilegium* describes the rebuilding of the Temple by God himself, as well as the stricter purity standards for admission to this new Temple. Then the shoot of David, certainly a messianic figure (in accord with Amos 9:11), will:

> arise together with the Interpreter of the Law who [will rule] in Zi[on in] the End of Days. (*FLORILEGIUM 1:11–12*)

In the future age, Zion, that is, Jerusalem, will be the seat of the messianic king and a center of authoritative interpretation of the Torah.

A number of important Aramaic manuscripts, mostly very fragmentary, and one Hebrew fragment, together constitute the *New Jerusalem* texts, so-called because they describe a new Jerusalem, presumably in the End of Days. However, the name of the city never appears in these texts; the name has been derived based on a New Testament parallel (Revelations 21:1–22:5). Clearly eschatological in nature, the text does not specifically reflect the ideals of the sect, but neither does it contradict sectarian views in any way. Although this text most probably belongs to the literary heritage known to the sect in its early years, its composition cannot predate the Hellenistic period.

Written in the form of a guided tour under the direction of a heavenly figure, the *New Jerusalem* describes an ideal town plan for a rebuilt Jerusalem of gargantuan proportions. All measurements are minutely recorded. According to the substantial fragments from cave 5, the tour begins with the exterior walls that are fitted with gates bearing the names of the tribes of Israel, similar to the outer court of the Temple complex described in the *Temple Scroll*. The city gates are described in detail. This future Jerusalem is to be laid out in a symmetrical manner, like the Greek cities of late antiquity. Throughout the city run major and minor cross streets, creating large blocks of houses in the style of the later Roman apartment blocks, which included smaller houses within them. Led by the guide into one of these blocks, the visionary begins with a detailed account of the gate complex:

> [And he showed me the measurements of the gates of the blocks, and their width] was two reeds which are fo[urte]en cubits. . . . [And he measured] the wid[th of every th]reshold, two reeds which are fourteen cubits. [And its lintel was one cubit . . .] [And he measured at every] threshold the do[or on] it. He measured inside the thr[esh]old. Its length was [thirteen] cubits [and its width ten cubits]. *(NEW JERUSALEM D 1 I 15–17)*

Winding staircases lead to the upper story of each house. Although the city is of great proportions, the houses are of normal size.

Following this description is an account of the Temple located within this ideal city. In the fragments from cave 11, the visionary reports seeing the sacrificial practices of the Temple being performed:

> [And I watched until it was di]vided among the eighty-four priests [. . . Two (loaves of) bre]ad upon which was incense [. . . . I kept watching until one of the two loaves] was given to the [high] priest . . . [and the other was given to the assistant (priest) who was stan]ding apart . . . *(NEW JERUSALEM E VII 3–7)*

The visionary observes a variety of sacrificial rites and animals. Obviously, the *New Jerusalem* texts expected the Temple to be a part of the future Jerusalem.

Despite their common themes, the *Temple Scroll* and the *New Jerusalem* do not really complement one another. But they share in common the aspiration that Jerusalem would fulfill the visions of the prophets and constitute a giant metropolis in the End of Days. God himself would build a new Temple in the midst of a well-planned city, a place of sacrificial perfection and ritual purity.

To the Dead Sea sect, the city of Jerusalem represented three things: the polluted society and sanctuary from which they had chosen to withdraw; the dwelling place of the divine presence, regulated by specific legal requirements regarding the Temple and its service; and the sect's final destination in the End of Days, where a perfect Temple, built by God, would arise in the heart of a perfect city spreading out in all directions.

CHAPTER 25

The Decline of Sectarianism
and the Emergence
of Rabbinic Judaism

The Jewish world in which the Dead Sea sectarians lived was marked by sectarianism and schism. Differing ideologies and approaches to Jewish practice and belief competed for adherents. When this rivalry led to thoughtful debate about the correct interpretation of the Torah and the shape of Jewish life and law, it played a positive role in the developing traditions of Judaism. Unfortunately, however, much of the strife had just the opposite effect, eventually leading the Jewish people into an unsuccessful war with Rome. Only after that war did the Jewish people come together again around the consensus of Pharisaic-rabbinic Judaism. The emergence of this consensus is a process that can best be understood with the help of two sister collections to the Qumran library—the Masada texts and the Bar Kokhba documents. These materials, together with the historical sources of the period, allow us to trace the evolution of the Jewish people from sectarian strife to the new reality of rabbinic consensus.

QUMRAN IN THE ROMAN PERIOD

For many years, the Dead Sea sect had expected the Roman conquest of Palestine. The Dead Sea sectarians felt confident that the coming of the Kittim—as they called the Romans—would trigger the great eschatological battle. But this final, expected war failed to materialize after the Romans easily defeated the divided Hasmonaean state in 63 B.C.E. By the time Jewish resistance developed into the full-scale revolt of 66–73 C.E., the Dead Sea sect had stabilized and had completed the gathering—with some possible exceptions—of its manuscript collection at Qumran.

We do know something about the history of the Qumran settlement in the almost century and a half between the Roman conquest and the Jewish revolt. Archaeological evidence has suggested that Qumran was abandoned at about the time an earthquake shook Judaea in 31 B.C.E., but it was soon reinhabited once

The Roman Period

63–40 B.C.E.	Hyrcanus High Priest and Ethnarch
40	Parthian invasion
39	Herod lands in Palestine
37	Siege and capture of Jerusalem
37–4	Herod rules Judaea
34	Herod defends himself before Antony
31	Earthquake in Palestine
22–9	Caesarea built
20/19	Building of Herodian Temple begun
4 B.C.E.–6 C.E.	Archeleus Ethnarch
6 C.E.	Archeleus deposed
26–36	Pontius Pilate
29	John the Baptist executed by Herod Antipas
30	Jesus crucified by Romans
66–73	Great Revolt
68	Destruction of Qumran
70	Destruction of the Temple
73	Capture of Masada
c. 80	Sanhedrin at Yavneh
115–117	Diaspora Revolt
132–135	Bar Kokhba Revolt
135–138	Hadrianic Persecutions
c. 200	Editing of the Mishnah

the settlement had been rebuilt and expanded. Even after the bulk of the sectarian literary texts had been composed, the sect continued to gather and copy texts. Many of the manuscripts found at Qumran were copied during this "Herodian" period, as scholars have somewhat inaccurately labeled the early Roman era. Because the sectarians would have certainly disapproved of the moral and religious state of the nation during the Roman occupation—whether under Herod or under the procurators—they would have continued to value and consult the older compositions in their collection. Apparently, the Roman period did not yield much in the way of new compositions at Qumran.

After the Roman conquest had failed to launch the final apocalypse, the sectarians undoubtedly revised their messianic scenario, shifting the End of Days forward to the impending war of revolution. Rebellious sentiment had been gathering steam during the entire period of Roman domination, fueled by Roman insensitivity to Jewish law and practice. As time passed, sectarian expectations mounted, as members awaited the great battles that would usher in the End of Days.

When the rebellion finally moved into full swing, the Essenes joined the rebel forces. Josephus records that Essenes fully participated in military action, thus disproving the false notion that members of this group were pacifists. And whether or not the Qumran sect was identified with the Essenes, we can assume, in light of their eschatological views, that members of this group joined the revolt as well.

Qumran soon fell during Roman military operations along the shore of the Dead Sea. Because this area formed part of the vital border region, the Romans had quickly dispatched units there after the start of the revolt in 66 C.E. By 68 C.E., the war had reached Qumran, where the defenders fell amidst a great conflagration. We cannot be certain whether those who occupied the site were killed or captured; we know only that the site was abandoned. From that moment on, the sect ceased to exist as a defined group, although its echoes persisted into later Jewish history and memory. With the fall of Qumran, and indeed, with the destruction of the Jewish nation as a whole, all sectarian and apocalyptic groups faded from view.

Throughout the period when the sect occupied the Qumran site, cave 4 was filled with manuscripts, most probably functioning as a library for regular sectarian use. As the war neared Qumran, the sectarians opened some of the other caves to hide additional manuscripts, either because they expected a Roman onslaught or because the Romans had already put them to flight. As a result, the Qumran caves became depositories for these ancient Jewish scrolls that two thousand years later would speak to us of ancient priests, prophets, and holy men.

Despite earlier claims by some scholars, it is now known that the Roman conquerors, who briefly occupied the Qumran site after its destruction, did not enter cave 4 and did not tear up its manuscripts. Rather, cave 4 remained hidden from the Romans' sight and thus basically intact, only to be ravaged by nature and time over a period of almost two millennia.

THE *COPPER SCROLL*

The priests and sectarians of Qumran never cut off entirely their relations with the priests of Jerusalem, despite their strenuous opposition to and criticism of the views and practices of those priests. As a result of this ongoing contact, the strange document known as the *Copper Scroll* reached Qumran. This scroll, engraved on copper sheets, contains a list of buried treasures hidden in the Judaean Desert at various locations. The text mentions some sixty-four items, specifying the amount of treasure and the hiding place of each one.

Copper Scroll The *Copper Scroll* was chiseled into copper by a scribe who did not understand its Hebrew text. Extremely difficult to read, it seems to be a list of buried treasures— most probably from the Jerusalem Temple—that are said to have been buried in the Judaean wilderness. Although it was found in Qumran cave 3, it is difficult to determine the exact relationship of this document to the rest of the Qumran corpus. For its decipherment, it was cut into vertical strips, one of which is seen here. *Photograph by Bruce and Kenneth Zuckerman, West Semitic Research, in collaboration with Princeton Theological Seminary. Courtesy of the Department of Antiquities of Jordan.*

Because this scroll was composed in a Hebrew dialect somewhat closer to mishnaic Hebrew than the rest of the texts authored or preserved at Qumran, scholars have concluded that the *Copper Scroll* originated in different circles, most likely from Jerusalem. Apparently, as the war approached, or soon after the Temple was destroyed, some persons put together a list of treasures that they either buried, or intended to bury, in the desert. No one has yet located any of these treasures despite many attempts to find them.

Certain scholars have argued that the *Copper Scroll* is entirely a fabrication, a fantasy concocted by some powerless sectarian who could never approach these great treasures of the Temple. The basis for this claim is that the amounts of silver and gold cataloged in the scroll seem inconceivable. However, recent studies have shown that although the amounts do appear large, they are not impossibly so. Furthermore, certain terms in the text link the scroll intimately with the system of tithes and offerings that existed in the Jerusalem Temple.

Others have suggested that the moneys recorded here were collected after the destruction as tithes and other offerings and were then buried in the desert. But that interpretation also cannot be supported. First of all, such substantial funds would never have survived the Roman pillage of Jerusalem. Second, no sources report that offerings were disposed of through burial after the Destruction of the Temple.

Yet another theory claims that the *Copper Scroll* constitutes the central document of the Qumran collection, a hypothesis that would require a radical reinterpretation of the entire Qumran collection. According to this view, the scroll records the placement of Temple documents throughout Judaea, including the scrolls placed in the caves of Qumran. However, though the *Copper Scroll* does mention that a copy of itself was deposited in another location, that statement cannot be interpreted to refer to numerous written texts that were then deposited throughout the Judaean Desert. Other passages, taken to refer to the deposit of numerous scrolls in the Judaean Desert, have been both incorrectly read and misinterpreted. It is entirely unlikely that the Qumran documents would have constituted the hidden library of the Jerusalem Temple, since these documents uniformly object to the conduct of the Jerusalem Temple and its priests.

If indeed the items on this list referred to treasures from the Temple, then the document could not have been created by the sectarians, who had separated themselves from the Temple and the Jerusalem priesthood. It must have been brought in to Qumran, probably by some priests who fled there before the destruction of Qumran in 68 and of the Temple in 70 C.E.

MASADA AND ITS SCROLLS

The texts found at Masada provide us with additional information about the state of Judaism on the eve of the revolt and in the early years thereafter. In this fortress, located south of Ein Gedi and facing the Dead Sea atop an isolated rock cliff, the Jewish rebels made their last stand against Rome in 73 C.E. Josephus's detailed account describes how the last of the *sicarii* (dagger-bearers) took the lives of their families and their comrades in a mass suicide, foreshadowing some of the accounts of medieval Jewish martyrdom. The ongoing debate over the historicity of Josephus's story is not important for our purposes. Rather, we will turn our attention to the manuscripts from Masada as well as to its synagogue and *mikveh* that tell the story of the Judaism of its defenders.

Masada was first built as a fortress by the Hasmonaean priest Jonathan, either the brother of Judah the Maccabee (152–143 B.C.E.) or Alexander Janneus (103–76 B.C.E.). In this fortress, Herod protectively ensconced his family when he traveled to Rome in 40 B.C.E. to convince the Senate to make him king of the Jews. Between 37 and 31, he built it into a beautiful winter palace. After his death, the site was occupied at some point by a Roman garrison, from whom it was captured in 66 C.E. by the rebel forces. In 73 C.E., the fortress fell to the Romans after a protracted siege. With the fall of Masada, the last flame of the Jewish revolt was extinguished.

In order to observe Jewish law as they understood it, the rebels who occupied Masada had to adapt it for their needs. They also had to modify a number of buildings to serve as their living quarters. Two ritual baths—*mikva'ot*—have been identified from this period. Significantly, these baths show definite evidence of having been constructed in the manner prescribed by later rabbinic halakhah. One room at the site has been described as a house of study—*bet midrash*—although because no such structures are known from this early period, this identification is questionable.

More significant is the Masada synagogue, one of the earliest such structures together with Herodion and Gamla, which were also rebel fortresses during the Great Revolt. The synagogue faced northwest, toward Jerusalem, with bleacher seating lining the inside walls. Found there was an ostracon referring to tithes given to the priests, as well as fragments of two scrolls hidden in pits under the floor. Remains of additional scrolls were found in two locations in the casemate walls, one in close proximity to the synagogue.

In all, parts of fifteen biblical and apocryphal scrolls were found in the Masada excavations, including fragments of two scrolls of Leviticus, one each of Deuteronomy and Ezekiel, and two manuscripts of the Psalms. Because the general character of these texts is almost identical to the Masoretic text, we can conclude that this text had essentially become the only recognized biblical text by the period of the revolt.

Yet this same community, whose biblical texts had by this time become standardized, also made use of apocryphal compositions. Very substantial portions of the Book of Ben Sira found at Masada prove beyond a doubt that the medieval fragments preserved in the Cairo *genizah* were derived from the original text, which was composed in Hebrew. This apocryphal composition, we should note, is the only one actually quoted by the talmudic Rabbis. Also found were a small fragment of Jubilees, as well as a number of miscellaneous texts, one perhaps paralleling the *Genesis Apocryphon*.

Masada Perched as it was atop so high a natural platform, Masada was a virtually impregnable fortress. Originally a Hasmonaean winter palace, it was used by Herod to hide his family while he traveled to Rome to seek appointment as king; eventually, it was a winter retreat. Later it was taken over by the *sicarii*, who held it until 73 C.E., when it fell to the Romans, thus bringing to an end the Jewish revolt of 66–73 C.E. *Photograph by Werner Braun. Courtesy of the Biblical Archaeology Society.*

Masada Fragment of *Songs of the Sabbath Sacrifice* A number of
nonbiblical fragments were found at Masada. Among them were a
manuscript of *Songs of the Sabbath Sacrifice*, pictured here; the
Ben Sira Scroll, a text referring to Joshua; and fragments that
resemble the book of Jubilees. These fragments are similar to the
apocryphal material found at Qumran, indicating that these
were not particularly sectarian texts, but rather were part of the
literature of the Jewish people in Second Temple times. *Courtesy
of the Shrine of the Book of the Israel Museum.*

These texts show that in this period, the Jewish people shared a common heritage of apocryphal literature. Although the Rabbis would later try to root out these nonbiblical texts, during Second Temple times these books still enjoyed considerable popularity, which is why they make up approximately one-third of the Qumran collection and were also found at Masada. Furthermore, since most of the apocryphal-type texts found in the Qumran caves were probably copied elsewhere, we can see that these texts were indeed widespread. So, although the defenders of Masada possessed proto-Masoretic Bibles, they still read apocryphal and, most probably, apocalyptic texts. Indeed, we can surmise that the apocalyptic tradition, with its messianic urgency, helped to drive the revolt.

Extremely interesting is the presence at Masada of the quasi-mystical angelic liturgy called *Songs of the Sabbath Sacrifice*, found at Qumran in nine manuscripts. When this text was first identified among the Masada scrolls, the other Masada scroll fragments had not yet been fully investigated. Accordingly, scholars assumed that this document, together with other sectarian writings, had been brought to Masada by fleeing sect members after Qumran was destroyed in 68 C.E. In fact, at that point in the history of scrolls research, the prevailing theory held that any texts found in the Qumran caves had been composed by the sectarians and copied in the Qumran scriptorium.

However, these assumptions have been overturned in light of the Masada materials published since then. We now believe that the reason these sites share literary remains is simply because the texts were widespread in Judaea at the time. Hence, it may be that this angelic liturgy and the mystical approach it follows were not limited to the Qumran sectarians in the last years of the Second Temple but had spread much farther among the Jewish community of Palestine. If so, we can now understand why ideas such as those reflected in this text appeared in rabbinic literature and in the *Merkavah* mysticism of the third through eighth centuries C.E. In light of the evidence, we have to view the common heritage of Qumran and Masada as typical of the literature read by the intellectual and religious elites of Second Temple Judaism.

What the Masada material demonstrates, therefore, is that by the period of the revolt, the biblical text had been essentially standardized in favor of the Masoretic text, even among groups that still read apocryphal texts. But we also see that this apocryphal material continued to constitute part of the heritage of the Second Temple Jewish community as a whole and was only later rooted out by the Rabbis. Finally, we learn from the synagogue and ritual baths—basically constructed according to the Pharisaic-rabbinic tradition documented somewhat later—that this group's views on such matters were becoming normative among Jews even before the revolt. It should not surprise us, therefore, that the Pharisaic-rabbinic approach to Judaism became dominant after the final defeat of Masada's defenders and the crushing of the revolt by the Roman legions.

The Rise of Christianity

Ironically, what also encouraged the shift from sectarianism to Jewish consensus in the first century C.E. was the rise of Christianity. Although I have intentionally confined my study to issues bearing primarily on the history of Judaism, I have occasionally mentioned how the scrolls relate to Christianity. We have seen that quite a few notions found in the New Testament that were previously considered derivative of either Eastern or Hellenistic influence really evolved from the various sectarian and apocalyptic ideas expressed in the Qumran scrolls. Some of these notions actually derive from the Dead Sea sect itself; others, from the literature the sect inherited from its forebears and apparently read with great interest.

While I completely reject the simplistic assumption that Jesus or John the Baptist was actually a member of the sect, I recognize that these men shared certain ideas and a common religious milieu with the sectarians at Qumran. When the movement centered on Jesus began, and after his death developed into a collection of traditions that were then embellished in the Gospels, the fledgling religion was the inheritor of certain ideas abandoned by the emerging rabbinic consensus. Thus, notions found in Second Temple texts that were not continued into talmudic Judaism influenced the emerging church. As Christianity absorbed these ideas, the Jewish community saw further reason to reject them. Hence, Jewish self-definition crystallized as Jews identified certain ideas as being "Christian." In effect, the Jewish community reacted to this rival religion by eliminating certain Second Temple period options from the emerging Jewish consensus.

The rise of Christianity radically altered the way Jews saw themselves and their faith. Whereas in Second Temple times divergent Jewish groups vied with one another for the mantle of the true Israel, which they each claimed, Jews now vied with the Christians, a competing group that made the same claim. By the time of the Bar Kokhba Revolt (132–135 C.E.), the new Jewish consensus stood over against Christianity. The separation of the two faiths was essentially complete.

The internal Jewish polemic of the Second Temple period, dominated in its last stage by the argument between the early Jewish Christians and other Jewish groups—the Pharisees and the Sadducees—was now replaced by the argument with the "other." Henceforth, the newly unified Jewish people faced off against the church that now saw itself as a distinct religious group.

The Bar Kokhba Documents

The emergence of the new consensus becomes even clearer when we look at the documents found in the Bar Kokhba caves located along the shore of the Dead Sea, south of Qumran and north of Masada, primarily at Wadi Murabba'at and

Nahal Hever. Some of these documents, which allegedly came from Wadi Seyyal (Nahal Seelim), were actually stolen by Bedouin from Nahal Hever and smuggled across to Jordan. These texts had been left behind by those who rebelled against Rome under the messianic pretender Simeon bar Kosiba, called Bar Kokhba, in the second Jewish revolt of 132–135 C.E. During the revolt, the rebels hid in caves overlooking the wadis above the Dead Sea. Very recently, a number of other such documents were found in a cave near Jericho, suggesting that such hideaways were located all along the Dead Sea.

After the failure of the Great Revolt and the fall of Masada in 73 C.E., Rome empowered the Pharisaic-rabbinic leaders to manage the internal affairs of the Jews in Palestine. Needless to say, this political authority allowed the emerging rabbinic movement to make its own tradition—a continuation of Second Temple period Pharisaic Judaism—the norm for virtually all Jews in the Land of Israel.

Yet despite this political alliance, some Jews, both among the Pharisaic-rabbinic leaders and outside this elite, continued to believe that the Roman yoke had to be thrown off, for both religious and nationalistic reasons. These ideas were certainly linked with the belief that overthrowing Roman rule would usher in the messianic era. In this sense, the second Jewish revolt carried forward the distinct eschatology of the *War Scroll*. By about 125 C.E., preparation for the revolt was in full swing, no doubt spurred on by the unsuccessful Diaspora revolt of 115–117 C.E.

Until the letters in the caves near the Dead Sea were discovered, Bar Kokhba's real name was not known. The letters contain the first mention of his full name, "Simeon bar Kosiba." We now realize that the talmudic Rabbis were hinting at this name in connecting the rebel leader with the Hebrew root *kzv* (to be false), referring to his false messiahship. But to some of the Rabbis, he was known as Bar Kokhba (son of a star), an allusion to the star prophecy of Numbers 24:17, "A star rises from Jacob, a scepter comes forth from Israel," which was interpreted as prophesying a future messianic redeemer. In the *Zadokite Fragments* (7:18–21), this same prophecy had been considered a reference to the Interpreter of the Law, a quasi-messianic figure.

Yet despite these messianic hopes, the revolt, after initial successes, eventually failed. By the time it was crushed by the Romans, the Jewish insurgents had appointed a high priest, perhaps because sacrifices had been reinstituted, and minted their own coins. Substantial numbers of documents, both from Bar Kokhba's government and from private individuals, survived in the caves. The human remains found in the caves reveal that the rebels hiding there fell to the Roman sword. The texts demonstrate the continuing rise of the rabbinic consensus, even within a context of interaction with and influence from non-Jewish neighbors.

These documents mention the first rabbi known to us from nonrabbinic sources, suggesting that the rabbinic class did extend beyond the teachers named

Bar Kokhba Coins During the Bar Kokhba revolt, coins were minted as a sign of Jewish independence. No. 165 pictures the facade of the Temple and is inscribed with "Jerusalem." On the other side is a *lulav*, with the inscription "Year One of the Redemption of Israel." No. 166 is inscribed with "Eleazar the Priest," the high priest appointed by Bar Kokhba. Both Nos. 169 and 170 mention "Simeon, the Prince of Israel"—referring to Bar Kokhba—and "Jerusalem." No. 169A was broken apart in order to create coins of smaller denomination. Nos. 165–167 are silver, and the others are bronze. *From Y. Meshorer,* Jewish Coins of the Second Temple Period, *plate XXI. With permission of the author.*

in the Mishnah and other rabbinic works. We also learn that Bar Kokhba encouraged his followers to observe the holiday of Sukkot, commanding that he be sent the *lulav* and *etrog* (palm branch and citron), as well as the myrtle and willow branches used for this holiday, and requiring that produce be properly tithed.

But the finds tell us much more. From the numerous contracts in the collection, we learn that the Jews of the Dead Sea region, most prominently those who lived in the oasis of Ein Gedi, practiced both in general terms and in many specifics the legal system sketched out in the Mishnah and early rabbinic sources. In this legal category we find trade documents as well as marriage, divorce, and various other types of contracts. On the other hand, we find some contracts using Greek law and others that are syntheses of Jewish law and Greek law. Some documents reveal economic and social interaction between Jews and Greek-speaking pagans or Arabs. We find evidence of some Hellenization among the Jews in language and other affairs. Yet despite such outside influences, it is clear that by the time of the revolt, the normative Jewish legal system, later represented in the Mishnah, was already in use, albeit in an earlier and less standardized form.

These materials also indicate that the biblical text was becoming increasingly standardized. Biblical material such as the *Twelve Prophets Scroll* from Wadi Murabba'at is essentially identical to the Masoretic text. Indeed, the Masoretic text had become so well established by that time that other text types are not in evidence at all. The competition had been entirely eliminated. The early Masoretic text that at Qumran had been dominant among other textual forms, and at Masada had been almost the exclusive biblical text, by this time had truly become the authorized Jewish Bible.

But the process had gone even further. The *Greek Twelve Prophets Scroll* from Nahal Hever (part of the so-called Seiyal collection) shows evidence that Septuagint texts of the Bible were being revised to conform to the Masoretic text, for those Jews who demanded Greek Bibles equivalent to the Masoretic Hebrew. So thoroughly in fact had the Masoretic Bible triumphed over competing texts that all Jews, even those speaking Greek, insisted on the text type that was accepted and required by the Rabbis.

In the wake of the Bar Kokhba Revolt, the Rabbis ruled that the emerging Christian community was not to be considered part of the Jewish people. Their decision rested largely on nontheological grounds, namely, that the church, even in the Land of Israel, had become largely gentile. Furthermore, the Christians had refused to support the Jewish revolt, spurning its messianic overtones. Thus, the earlier schism that had merely separated the two communities finally became irreparable.

The Bar Kokhba period represented a watershed in the shaping of Jewish identity. Not only the Christians but also the Samaritans—the surviving remnant of

Biblical Psalms from Masada Among the biblical texts found at
Masada were fragments of two or three partial manuscripts of the
Book of Psalms. Shown here is *Masada Psalms B*, a manuscript
virtually identical to the Masoretic text and demonstrating the
extent to which that text had become standardized by the first
century C.E. The Psalms are written here in columns, indicating
an understanding of the poetic structure of the text. *Courtesy of
the Shrine of the Book of the Israel Museum.*

ancient North Israelites—were now regarded for all intents and purposes as non-
Jews. The rules of Jewish identity were firmly in place. Overall, the Bar Kokhba
documents testify to the continued triumph of the rabbinic consensus, which,
though not eliminating all other forms of Jewish thought entirely, certainly became the dominant form of Judaism by the end of the second century.

The Qumran corpus, with its varied sectarian literature, richly represents the
complex tapestry of competing Jewish approaches in the Second Temple period.
By the time of the Great Revolt, the Qumran group had completed its original
compositions. In the revolt itself, the Essenes and sectarian groups such as the
Dead Sea sect disappeared as independent entities, as did the Sadducees, who lost
their natural power base when the Temple was destroyed.

As a result of the elimination of its Jewish competition, the continuing standardization of the biblical text and of Jewish law, and a political alliance with the Romans, the Pharisaic-rabbinic movement was able to strengthen its dominant position within Judaism. By this time, Christianity had absorbed certain apocalyptic ideas of the Second Temple period; Judaism, intent on defining itself against the newly emerging religion, accordingly wrote these ideas out of its tradition. By the time of the Bar Kokhba revolt, the last vestiges of Second Temple sectarianism were gone from Judaism. The new consensus was essentially complete. From the crucible of sectarianism, revolt, and restoration had emerged the mature Judaism of the Mishnah and Talmud, which came to serve as the foundation of the Judaism we know today.

List of Abbreviations

ANRW	*Aufstieg und Niedergang der Römischen Welt.*
B.	Babylonian Talmud.
BA	*Biblical Archaeologist.*
BAR	*Biblical Archaeology Review.*
BASOR	*Bulletin of the American Schools of Oriental Research.*
CBQ	*Catholic Biblical Quarterly.*
DJD 1	Barthélemy, D., and J. T. Milik. *Qumran Cave I.* Discoveries in the Judaean Desert 1.
DJD 2	Benoit, P., J. T. Milik, and R. de Vaux. *Les Grottes de Murabba'ât.* Discoveries in the Judaean Desert 2.
DJD 3	Baillet, M., J. T. Milik, and R. de Vaux. *Les "Petites Grottes" de Qumran.* Discoveries in the Judaean Desert 3.
DJD 4	Sanders, J. A. *The Psalms Scroll of Qumrân Cave 11 (11QPs^a).* Discoveries in the Judaean Desert 4.
DJD 5	Allegro, J. M. *Qumrân Cave 4, I.* Discoveries in the Judaean Desert 5.
DJD 6	Vaux, R. de, and J. T. Milik. *Qumrân Cave 4, II.* Discoveries in the Judaean Desert 6.
DJD 7	Baillet, M. *Qumrân Cave 4, III.* Discoveries in the Judaean Desert 7.
DJD 8	Tov, E. *The Greek Minor Prophets Scroll from Naḥal Ḥever.* Discoveries in the Judaean Desert 8.
DJD 9	Skehan, P. W., E. Ulrich, and J. Sanderson. *Qumran Cave 4, IV: Palaeo-Hebrew and Greek Manuscripts.* Discoveries in the Judaean Desert 9.
DJD 10	Qimron, E., and J. Strugnell. *Qumran Cave 4, V: Miqṣat Ma'ase ha-Torah.* Discoveries in the Judaean Desert 10.
DSD	*Dead Sea Discoveries.*
ETL	*Ephemerides Theologicae Lovanienses.*

FO	*Folia Orientalia.*
HAR	*Hebrew Annual Review.*
HTR	*Harvard Theological Review.*
HUCA	*Hebrew Union College Annual.*
IEJ	*Israel Exploration Journal.*
JANES	*Journal of Ancient Near Eastern Studies.*
JBL	*Journal of Biblical Literature.*
JBTh	*Jahrbuch für Biblische Theologie.*
JETS	*Journal of the Evangelical Theological Society.*
JJS	*Journal of Jewish Studies.*
JNES	*Journal of Near Eastern Studies.*
JQR	*Jewish Quarterly Review.*
JSJ	*Journal for the Study of Judaism.*
JSS	*Journal of Semitic Studies.*
JTS	*Journal of Theological Studies.*
M.	Mishnah.
MGWJ	*Monatsschrift für Geschichte und Wissenschaft des Judentums.*
NRT	*La Nouvelle Revue Théologique.*
NTS	*New Testament Studies.*
P.	Palestinian Talmud (Yerushalmi).
PAAJR	*Proceedings of the American Academy for Jewish Research.*
PEQ	*Palestine Exploration Quarterly.*
RB	*Revue Biblique.*
REJ	*Revue des Études Juives.*
RJ	*Reform Judaism*
RQ	*Revue de Qumran.*
Shnaton	*Shnaton la-Miqra' u-le-Ḥeqer ha-Mizraḥ ha-Qadum.*
Suppl. to VT	*Supplements to Vetus Testamentum.*
T.	Tosefta.
TZ	*Theologische Zeitschrift.*
VT	*Vetus Testamentum.*
ZAW	*Zeitschrift für die Alttestamentliche Wissenschaft.*

REFERENCE NOTES

INTRODUCTION

PAGE xvii

Halakhic Letter—See notes to chapter 2.

PAGE xviii

Finds in the Judaean Desert—Pfann, "Sites in the Judean Desert," 109–19.

PAGE xx

Aramaic Documents—Wacholder, "Ancient Judaeo-Aramaic Literature," 257–81. See also Reed, "Preliminary List of Aramaic Documents from Qumran Cave 4."

PAGE xxi

Library—As in the title of Cross, *The Ancient Library of Qumran and Modern Biblical Studies.*

Causes of Scroll Damage—Stegemann, "Methods for the Reconstruction of Scrolls," 193–94.

What the Scrolls Are Not—The hypothesis that the scrolls are the library of the Jerusalem Temple is put forward by Golb in "Who Wrote the Dead Sea Scrolls?" "The Dead Sea Scrolls," and "Khirbet Qumran." For a critique of Golb's position, see García Martínez and van der Woude, "'Gröningen' Hypothesis," 521–41. Shanks, "Qumran Settlement," also disputes his view. Eisenman states his views relating the scrolls to the early Christian community in *Maccabees, Zadokites, Christians and James the Just.* Thiering's similar but even more extreme approach has most recently been set forth in *Jesus and the Riddle.* Her earlier works are *Redating the Teacher of Righteousness* and *Gospels and Qumran.* For a critique of Eisenman, see García Martínez, "Notas al margen." Thiering's book is reviewed by Shanks in "Did Jesus Really Die on the Cross?" and Shanks convincingly refutes Thiering's claims. We must also reject on chronological and substantive grounds the identification of the scrolls with the Zealots, as put forward in Driver, *Judean Scrolls,* and Roth, *Dead Sea Scrolls.* Cf. the survey of scrolls theories in Cook, *Solving the Mysteries,* 82–126. Christianizing theories are put into the proper perspective by Cook on 127–51. A sense of the recent debate on the scrolls can be gotten from the collection edited by Shanks, *Understanding the Dead Sea Scrolls.* See also VanderKam, *Dead Sea Scrolls Today,* which appeared after this volume went to press, and Stegemann, *Die Essener,* which has also just appeared.

Dating the Scrolls—The classic discussion of the paleography of the scrolls is Cross, "Development of the Jewish Scripts." For the results of the latest carbon-14 tests, see Bonani et al., "Radiocarbon Dating of the Dead Sea Scrolls," and Shanks, "Carbon-14 Tests Substantiate Scroll Dates."

Page xxiii

The Scrolls and the History of Judaism—For a summary, see Vermes, "Impact of the Dead Sea Scrolls," and Schiffman, "Sadducean Origins" and "Dead Sea Scrolls and the History of Judaism."

History of Research—See Schiffman, "Confessionalism." Cf. Broshi, "Religion, Ideology, and Politics."

Consensus—That there is no consensus is noted in Feldman, "Traveling Scrolls Debate." Note his conclusion, "The only consensus in Dead Sea Scroll studies is that there is no consensus," 72. A variety of provocative challenges to the perceived consensus and their methodological basis are presented in Davies, *Behind the Essenes.*

Page xxv

Methodology—General considerations of method for the study of this period are discussed in Schiffman, *From Text to Tradition,* 1–16. For our approach to the study of Qumran legal texts, see Schiffman, *Halakhah at Qumran,* 1–3, and *Sectarian Law,* 1–3 and 17–19.

Chapter 1

Page 3

Premodern Discoveries—For information on the discovery of scrolls in the Jericho region in both antiquity and the Middle Ages, see Lieberman, "Light on the Cave Scrolls," 402–3.

Zadokite Fragments from the Cairo Genizah—Schechter, *Documents of Jewish Sectaries.* Extremely important is the work of Ginzberg, which originally appeared in a series of articles published in *MGWJ* 55 (1911)–58 (1914), collected and published by the author as *Eine unbekannte jüdische Sekte;* English translation with additional chapters: *An Unknown Jewish Sect.* See, in addition, Schiffman, "[Review of] L. Ginzberg, *An Unknown Jewish Sect.*" A related *genizah* fragment that is still unexplained is published in Lévi, "Document." On the relationship of the two medieval manuscripts of the Zadokite Fragments, see White, "Comparison." See also notes to chapter 5.

Page 6

The Story of the Finds—The chronological outline of scrolls discoveries in our century and much of the account we have outlined are drawn from Pfann, "History of the Judean Desert Discoveries." A fascinating account of the attempts of Sukenik and Yadin to purchase the seven scrolls found in cave 1 is contained in Yadin, *Message of the Scrolls,* 19–52. Other important accounts are found in Allegro, *Dead Sea Scrolls,* 15–40, and Trever, *Dead Sea Scrolls;* however, the work of both of these scholars has been quite controversial, and their accounts disputed orally by others involved in the discovery. Cf. also Brownlee, "Edh-Dheeb's Story," which argues for 1945 as the date of the discovery.

Trever, "When Was Qumran Cave 1 Discovered?" argues convincingly for 1947. A recent review of the discovery of the scrolls, including the rediscovery in our own time, is found in Cook, *Solving the Mysteries*, 11–81.

PAGE 10

Photography—Two memoirs of the team at the Rockefeller are Cross, "On the History of the Photography," and Strugnell, "On the History of the Photographing of the Discoveries." Information on the earlier American School of Oriental Research photographs is scattered throughout Trever, *Dead Sea Scrolls*, 38–80. Those made in Israel are discussed in Broshi, "Negatives Archive." See also Pfann, "Chronological List."

PAGE 11

International Team of Editors and the Scrollery—Cross, *Ancient Library of Qumran*, 28; Allegro, *Dead Sea Scrolls*, 41–43. Much interesting information concerning Allegro is found in the otherwise exaggerated and tendentious account by Baigent and Leigh, *The Dead Sea Scrolls Deception*, 45–63. Our chronological account of the discoveries and the work at the Rockefeller follows Pfann, "History of the Judean Desert Discoveries," especially 99–104.

First Scrolls Publications—The scrolls that were brought to the American School of Oriental Research and later bought by the Syrian Metropolitan were the first to be published; they appeared in a two-volume set edited by Burrows, *The Dead Sea Scrolls of St. Mark's Monastery*. Both volumes contain only black-and-white photographs. Trever's color photographs appear in Cross, Freedman, and Sanders, *Scrolls from Qumrân Cave I*, a volume that also contains an account by Trever on the procedure he followed to produce the photographs.

PAGE 12

The Second Israeli Scrolls Purchase—Yadin tells this story in *Message of the Scrolls*, 39–52. The wider context is related in Silberman, *Prophet from Amongst You*, 212–18. A fascinating account is given by Orlinsky, "Dead Sea Scrolls and Mr. Green."

PAGE 14

Important Publications of the Fifties and Sixties—In 1955, Sukenik published in *Dead Sea Scrolls of the Hebrew University* three of the scrolls he had acquired. Avigad and Yadin published *Genesis Apocryphon* in 1956, but were able to edit only part of the scroll. Sanders published the *Psalms Scroll* of cave 11 in *DJD 4* in 1965. This was followed shortly by his more popular book, *Dead Sea Psalms Scroll*. In 1968, with the publication of *DJD 5*, Allegro became the first editor of cave 4 fragments to complete his assignment. However, the book was devastated in the review article by Strugnell, "Notes en marge."

Concordance—Brown, Fitzmyer, Oxtoby, and Teixidor, *Preliminary Concordance*, 5 vols., published in about 30 copies in 1988 for internal use by scrolls scholars, distributed mostly to members of the International Team.

PAGE 15

Masada—A popular account is Yadin, *Masada*. Full excavation reports are appearing now. See Yadin, Naveh, and Meshorer, *Masada I*; Cotton and Geiger, *Masada II*; and Netzer,

Masada III. For a historical account of the role of Masada in Israeli archaeology, see Silberman, *Prophet from Amongst You,* 270–93. For the texts found at Masada, see Yadin, *Ben Sira Scroll;* Talmon, "Qiṭʻe Ketavim"; "Fragments of a Psalms Scroll from Masada"; and "Qetaʻ mi-Megillah Ḥiṣṣonit." See also notes to chapter 25.

Copper Scroll—Allegro, *The Treasure of the Copper Scroll.* See also the slanted account by Baigent and Leigh, *The Dead Sea Scrolls Deception,* 51–56. Official publication: Milik, *DJD 3,* 201–302. A complete discussion of scholarship on this scroll is available now in Lefkovits, *Copper Scroll—3Q15.* See also Goranson, "Sectarianism, Geography, and the Copper Scroll"; Mandel, "On the 'Duplicate Copy' of the Copper Scroll"; Pixner, "Unravelling the Copper Scroll Case"; and Wolters, "Copper Scroll" and "Literary Analysis."

Page 16

Temple Scroll Purchase—Yadin's account in *Temple Scroll, The Hidden Law of the Dead Sea Sect,* 9–15, 24–32, and 38–44; a summary in *The Temple Scroll* 1:1–4; Shanks, "Intrigue and the Scroll"; and Silberman, *Prophet from Amongst You,* 304–6. In a lecture at the Annenberg Research Center (now the Center for Judaic Studies of the University of Pennsylvania) on March 17, 1993, F. M. Cross related that this scroll was offered to him for sale by Kando in Beirut shortly before the 1967 war.

Conquest of Palestine Archaeological Museum (Rockefeller)—Yadin, *Temple Scroll, The Hidden Law of the Dead Sea Sect,* 44–46; Silberman, *Prophet from Amongst You,* 303–4.

Page 17

Christian Interpreters of the Scrolls—Prominent among the early works that present a Christianized interpretation of the scrolls are Burrows, *Dead Sea Scrolls* and *More Light,* and Dupont-Sommer, *The Dead Sea Scrolls, The Jewish Sect of Qumran,* and *Les Écrits esséniens.* A critique of this approach may be found in LaSor, *Dead Sea Scrolls and the New Testament,* 22–27. For an example of a more careful methodology, see Fitzmyer, *Essays,* which deals in large measure with Qumran material.

Early Attempts at Identifying the Sect—See, for example, Sukenik, *Megillot Genuzot,* especially 16; Cross, *Ancient Library,* 37–79.

Page 19

Early Jewish Contributions to Scrolls Studies—Lieberman, "Light on the Cave Scrolls" and "Discipline of the So-Called Dead Sea Manual of Discipline"; Lehmann, "Talmudic Material"; Licht, *Megillat ha-Hodayot* and *Megillat ha-Serakhim;* and Rabin, *Zadokite Documents* and *Qumran Studies.*

Work of Yigael Yadin—In addition to many articles and several more popular books, note especially the following: *Scroll of the War; Genesis Apocryphon* (published with Avigad); and *Megillat ha-Miqdash,* whose updated English translation is *Temple Scroll.* For the latter, see Schiffman, "[Review of] Yadin's *The Temple Scroll,*" 122–26. A full account of Yadin's life and work may be found in Silberman, *Prophet from Amongst You.*

CHAPTER 2

PAGE 22

Works of Baumgarten and Schiffman—Baumgarten, *Studies in Qumran Law* and Schiffman, *Halakhah at Qumran, Sectarian Law, The Eschatological Community,* and *Halakhah, Halikhah u-Meshiḥiyut.*

PAGE 23

Publication Delays in the Wake of the Six-Day War—See Benoit's Preface in *DJD* 6.

Important Publications after 1967—Milik, *Books of Enoch* and *DJD* 6; Baillet, *DJD* 7; Freedman and Mathews, *Paleo-Hebrew Leviticus Scroll* (on which see Puech, "Notes en marge de 11Qpaléolévitique").

Scrolls Still Unpublished—For a calculation of the percentage of material not yet published when the controversies began, see Stegemann, "Methods for the Reconstruction of Scrolls," 209, n. 13. An annotated listing of all scrolls either published or mentioned in print was provided by García Martínez, "Lista de MSS." In addition, Reed prepared a full catalog of scroll materials and photographic plates entitled *Dead Sea Scrolls Inventory Project;* an abbreviated form is printed as part of *Dead Sea Scrolls on Microfiche,* edited by Tov. This list served as the basis of Reed's work. Upon his appointment as editor, Tov issued two lists of scrolls, both entitled "The Unpublished Qumran Texts from Caves 4 and 11," which appeared in *BA* and *JJS.* See also Ulrich, "Biblical Scrolls from Qumran Cave 4," and Tov, "Expanded Team of Editors."

Suppression of the Scrolls—The accusations by Baigent and Leigh, *The Dead Sea Scrolls Deception,* 99–126, are unfounded. For a correct response, see Shanks, "Is the Vatican Suppressing the Dead Sea Scrolls?"

Causes of Dissatisfaction—The timetable that Strugnell submitted to the Israel Antiquities Authority, and failed to keep, was subsequently published by Shanks. See his "Publisher's Foreword" in Eisenman and Robinson, *Facsimile Edition,* 1:xxvi (fig. 3). In the pages of *BAR,* one can follow clearly the growing dissatisfaction of an ever larger number of people interested in the scrolls. The exact extent of the unpublished material was revealed in the catalog of materials published by Reed, *Dead Sea Scrolls Inventory Project.* Cf. also Kapera, "Present State," which describes the perceived failures of the field of Qumran studies up until 1989.

Announcement of the *Halakhic Letter* (4QMMT)—The initial description of this important document is found in two different articles of the same name, both of them by Qimron and Strugnell, entitled "An Unpublished Halakhic Letter." Before its importance was known, however, Milik had published several lines of it in *DJD* 3:225.

PAGE 26

New York University Conference—The conference, sponsored by the Hagop Kevorkian Center for Near Eastern Studies, produced a volume edited by Schiffman, *Archaeology and History.* Yadin had been a member of the organizing committee, and after his death the conference was dedicated to his memory.

Reorganization of the Team of Editors—The anti-Semitic remarks by Strugnell that led to his dismissal are printed in Hebrew in *Haaretz*, November 9, 1990. For a transcription of the original interview in English, see Katzman, "Chief Dead Sea Scroll Editor Denounces Judaism." Three new volumes of texts have been published since Tov became editor in chief: Tov, *The Greek Minor Prophets Scroll from Naḥal Ḥever (8ḤevXIIgr)* (*DJD* 8), and Skehan, Ulrich, and Sanderson, *Qumran Cave 4, IV: Palaeo-Hebrew and Greek Biblical Manuscripts (DJD 9)*. The third text, by Strugnell and Qimron, *DJD* 10, an edition, translation, and commentary on the *Halakhic Letter*, has just appeared.

PAGE 27

Full Release of the Scrolls—The first publication that attempted to break the deadlock was the volume of reconstructed texts entitled *A Preliminary Edition of the Unpublished Dead Sea Scrolls*, published by Wacholder and Abegg (a second fascicle has since appeared). These reconstructions are based on *A Preliminary Concordance*, printed from a card index prepared by Brown, Fitzmyer, Oxtoby, and Teixidor. The title page stated that the copies were distributed by H. Stegemann on behalf of J. Strugnell. Actual photographs of almost all of the unpublished material from Qumran appeared in Eisenman and Robinson, *Facsimile Edition*. The text of the *Halakhic Letter* (4QMMT) had already been circulated by Z. J. K[apera], in "An Anonymously Received Pre-Publication of the 4QMMT." For reflections on the release of the scrolls, see Vermes, "Present State."

PAGE 31

Brill Edition—The fullest and best set of photographs is the official publication, edited by Tov, *Dead Sea Scrolls on Microfiche*. This edition includes all of the Judaean Desert photographs from all the sites, prepared in high-quality positive images. Provided with it are a *Companion Volume*, ed. Tov with the collaboration of Pfann, and an *Inventory List of Photographs*, compiled by Reed and edited by Lundberg. This edition includes about 6,000 photographs.

Contents of the Library—Much of this section is based on the exhaustive study by Dimant, "Qumran Manuscripts: Contents and Significance." The distinction between those texts brought to Qumran and those actually composed there was first noted by Sparks in "Books of the Qumran Community." For an earlier survey of the nonbiblical materials, see Dimant, "Qumran Sectarian Literature." Many texts are discussed in Schürer, *History of the Jewish People*, 3.1:1–479. Texts of the community are found on 380–479, whereas other nonbiblical texts appear among the materials surveyed earlier in the book. A good guide to the texts and bibliography is Fitzmyer, *Dead Sea Scrolls: Major Publications and Tools for Study*. The most comprehensive English translation is still Vermes, *Dead Sea Scrolls*, but García Martínez, in *Textos de Qumrân*, has translated a much larger number of texts into Spanish, and an English version is soon to appear.

PAGE 32

Languages of Palestine—On Qumran Hebrew, see Qimron, *Hebrew of the Dead Sea Scrolls*; cf. idem, "Observations on the History of Early Hebrew." On the question of the languages in use in Palestine during the Second Temple Period, see Schürer, *History of the Jewish People*, ii, 2:20–28, and Fitzmyer, *Wandering Aramean*, 29–56.

CHAPTER 3

PAGE 37

Excavation Reports—At the present time, the three most important works that deal with the archaeology of Qumran are de Vaux, *Archaeology and the Dead Sea Scrolls;* Laperrousaz, *Qoumrân: l'établissement essénien,* which carried out a sustained polemic with de Vaux regarding all kinds of minor matters, the effect of which is to confirm the relative merit of de Vaux's judgments in most cases; and Davies, *Qumran.* In all the references that follow for this chapter, we suggest that the reader also consult the three aforementioned works for the valuable information they contain. Shorter accounts may be found in Cross, *Ancient Library of Qumran,* 38–52, and Milik, *Ten Years of Discovery,* 45–56. Numerous photographs from the excavations appear in Tov, *Dead Sea Scrolls on Microfiche,* although these are not cataloged there. De Vaux summarized his research in "Qumran, Khirbet and 'Ein Feshkha," 1235–41, which has been supplemented by Broshi, ibid., 1241. Interesting in light of recent debates is Bar-Adon, "Bissure ha-Hashmona'im," which discusses Qumran in the context of the Hasmonaean fortresses. See also Broshi, "Archaeology of Qumran—A Reconsideration." On the recent attempt to publish de Vaux's excavation reports, see Donceel, "Reprise des travaux." Humbert, "L'espace sacré à Qumrân," has revived the Maccabean theory for the site and proposes a radical reevaluation of the archaeology of Qumran. For the conclusions of Magen and Drori, see Rabinovich, "Operation Scroll."

PAGE 40

The Water System—North, "Qumran Reservoirs" and Magen and Patrich, "'Amat ha-Mayyim." For a general discussion of *mikva'ot* in Second Temple times, with a few brief remarks about Qumran, see Sanders, *Jewish Law from Jesus to the Mishnah,* 214–27. Also note Wood, "To Dip or to Sprinkle?"

Pottery—An important, though now somewhat dated, work that describes the Qumran pottery finds in the context of finds from other, contemporaneous sites, is Lapp, *Palestinian Ceramic Chronology.* See the forthcoming papers by Magness, "The Community at Qumran," and for a very different view, Donceel-Voute, "Archaeology of Qumran."

Coins—Unfortunately, many of the coins discovered at Qumran were misplaced before having been published. Numismatic evidence is discussed throughout de Vaux, *Archaeology,* 5–48, and in Laperrousaz, *Qoumrân,* 149–54, which contains a complete catalog of what is known.

PAGE 47

Scriptorium—Much controversy has surrounded interpretation of the plaster fragments generally believed to have formed a sort of writing table and accompanying bench or footstool. An important study is Metzger, "Furniture in the Scriptorium." On the inkwells discovered at Qumran, see Goranson, "Qumran—The Evidence of the Inkwells."

Page 51

Cemeteries—De Vaux, *Archaeology*, 45–48; Haas and Nathan, "Anthropological Survey"; and Steckoll, "Preliminary Excavation Report." Cf. Eshel and Greenhut, "Ḥiam el-Sagha."

Page 53

Caves—The results of the excavation carried out in cave 1 are reported by Lankester Harding et al. in *DJD* 1:3–40. The finds from the other caves (with the exception of cave 4) are discussed by de Vaux in *DJD* 3:1–36. The finds from all of the caves are surveyed in Pfann, "Sites in the Judean Desert," 110–15. Recently, the caves have been reexplored by Patrich, whose results will appear in "Khirbet Qumran."

Page 57

Ein Feshka and Ein el-Ghweir—Ein Feshka is described in de Vaux, *Archaeology and the Dead Sea Scrolls*, 60–83, and Lapperousaz, *Qoumrân*, 65–90. On the tannery, see Poole and Reed, "'Tannery' of Ain Feshka." The excavations at Ein el-Ghweir are reported by Bar-Adon, "Another Settlement of the Judean Desert Sect."

Page 60

Local Economy of the Qumran Area—Farmer, "Economic Basis" and "Postscript." Although describing a later time period, a good description of the economy of the area may be found in Hirschfeld, *Judean Desert Monasteries in the Byzantine Period*, 102–11.

Chapter 4

Page 65

Jews in the Persian Period—Schiffman, *From Text to Tradition*, 33–59, and Stern, "Persian Empire" and "Archaeology of Persian Palestine."

Page 66

Ptolemies and Seleucids—A useful account of both history and culture is Koester, *Introduction to the New Testament*, vol. 1. For the impact on Palestine and the Jewish people, see Tcherikover, *Hellenistic Civilization and the Jews*, 1–89, and Schiffman, *From Text to Tradition*, 62–70.

Page 67

Hellenism—Schiffman, *From Text to Tradition*, 60–62. A study of the results of this synthesis is Peters, *Harvest of Hellenism*. The classic work on the Greek city is Jones, *Greek City from Alexander to Justinian*. A historical account is Kasher, *Jews and Hellenistic Cities in Eretz-Israel.*

Page 68

Hellenistic Trends in Palestinian Judaism—Schiffman, *From Text to Tradition*, 70–72. Hengel, *Judaism and Hellenism*, is both fundamental and provocative. Cf. the important review of this work by Millar, "Background to the Maccabean Revolution." See also Tcherikover, *Hellenistic Civilization and the Jews*, 90–116; Bickerman, *Jews in the Greek Age*; Cohen, *From the Maccabees to the Mishnah*, 34–46.

PAGE 69

The Maccabean Revolt, Causes and History—Schiffman, *From Text to Tradition*, 72–79. Fundamental for the entire period is the revision of Schürer's *History of the Jewish People* by Vermes et al., 1:137–73, and Tcherikover, *Hellenistic Civilization and the Jews*, 117–234. See also Bickerman, *God of the Maccabees*.

PAGE 71

Hasmonaean Dynasty—Schiffman, *From Text to Tradition*, 99–103; Schürer, *History of the Jewish People*, 1:174–242; Tcherikover, *Hellenistic Civilization and the Jews*, 235–65.

PAGE 72

Jewish Sects in the Second Commonwealth—See Schiffman, "Jewish Sectarianism in Second Temple Times" and *From Text to Tradition*, 103–19, for a general survey. Cf. also Rofé, "Onset of Sects"; Smith, "Palestinian Judaism in the First Century"; and Cohen, *From the Maccabees to the Mishnah*, 124–73. Important historical issues regarding sectarianism in this period are raised in Baumgarten, "Qumran ve-ha-Kitatiut ba-Yahadut bi-Tequfat Bayit Sheni."

PAGE 73

Sadducees—The complete history of the Sadducees has yet to be written. For the present, see Schürer, *History of the Jewish People*, 2:404–14.

PAGE 76

Pharisees—Schürer, *History of the Jewish People*, 2:388–403. Finkelstein, *Pharisees*, is outdated methodologically, but still provides much information and insight. For rabbinic materials, see Neusner, *Rabbinic Traditions about the Pharisees*. A summary of this work is Neusner, *From Politics to Piety*. See also Baumgarten, "Name of the Pharisees," which provides a good review of the various approaches. We cannot, however, accept Baumgarten's conclusions. A recent study of the Pharisees and Sadducees that makes use of a sociological approach is Saldarini, *Pharisees, Scribes and Sadducees in Palestinian Society*.

PAGE 78

Essenes and Essene Hypothesis—Schürer, *History of the Jewish People*, 2:555–74, and Schiffman, "Essenes." A recent study that seeks to evaluate the connection between the Essenes and the documents found at Qumran is Beall, *Josephus' Description of the Essenes*. See also Buchanan, "Role of Purity," and Vermes, "Essenes and Therapeutae." Stegemann, "Qumran Essenes—Local Members of the Main Jewish Union," greatly exaggerates the role of the Essenes in Second Temple times. On the name, see Kampen, "Reconsideration of the Name 'Essene'"; Goranson, "'Essenes': Etymology"; and Vermes, *Post-Biblical Studies*, 8–36.

Chapter 5

Page 83

Publication of the *Halakhic Letter*—The existence and contents of the *Halakhic Letter* were first reported by Qimron and Strugnell in two separate articles, both entitled "An Unpublished Halakhic Letter." Further discussion may be found in Schiffman, "New *Halakhic Letter.*" The entire text, in an early version of the edition by Qimron and Strugnell, was published—without the permission of the editors—in Eisenman and Robinson, *Facsimile Edition*, in the Publisher's Foreword, by Shanks, as figure 8. This edition was in turn based on Kapera, *Anonymously Received Pre-Publication*. Figure 8 appeared only in the first edition of Eisenman and Robinson, but was subsequently removed in accord with the ruling of an Israeli court. This text was the cause of the lawsuit by Qimron against Shanks.

Page 86

Halakhah of the Letter—General discussion of the various systems of Jewish law observed during the Second Temple period, together with a more detailed discussion of the *Halakhic Letter*, may be found in Schiffman, "Temple Scroll and the Systems of Jewish Law" and "Qumran and Rabbinic Halakhah," and Baumgarten, "Recent Qumran Discoveries and Halakha." Extremely important is Sussmann, "Ḥeqer Toldot ha-Halakhah." The first to realize the Sadducean halakhic tendencies of the *Halakhic Letter*, when only a short passage from it was known, was Baumgarten, "Pharisaic-Sadducean Controversies," 163–64. A thorough study of the law of the document is found in Qimron and Strugnell, *DJD* 10:123–77. The text of Sussmann's Hebrew article appears in translation with selected footnotes in that same volume, on 129–200.

Page 87

The Origin of the Sect—The *Halakhic Letter* confirms the priestly origins of the sect, which fact had been suggested by, among others, Cross, "Early History of the Qumran Community." Cf. also Schwartz, "On Two Aspects of a Priestly View of Descent at Qumran" and "Law and Truth." The historical relevance of the *Halakhic Letter* to the founding of the sect is discussed in Schiffman, "New Halakhic Letter." On this issue, see Qimron and Strugnell, *DJD* 10:109–21, who see the letter as originating during the leadership of the Teacher of Righteousness. We, however, see the letter as dating to before his career.

Page 89

Confirmation of the Sadducean Connection—In addition to the *Halakhic Letter*, another Qumran text, the *Temple Scroll*, also shows some affinity with Sadducean halakhah, as shown in Schiffman, "Temple Scroll and the Systems of Jewish Law." Attention was called to Sadducean elements in the *Temple Scroll* by Lehmann, "Temple Scroll as a Source for Sectarian Halakhah." (This and other articles by Lehmann on the scrolls are collected in his *Massot u-Massa'ot*.) It was also proposed early in Qumran research by North, "Qumran Sadducees." Burgmann, "11QT: The Sadducean Torah," also alleges a Sadducean background for this scroll, but Burgmann fails to argue his thesis in a sustained manner, dealing only with the Levitical favoritism in the *Temple Scroll*.

This connection is also prominent in Wacholder, *Dawn*, 99–169, on which see Basser, "Rabbinic Citations," which raises some of the fundamental problems in Wacholder's argumentation.

PAGE 90

Zadokite Fragments—The *Zadokite Fragments* provides important information for determining the history of the sect's establishment. This text was first published by Schechter, in *Documents of Jewish Sectaries*, and has recently been reedited by Qimron, "Text of CDC," in Broshi, *Damascus Document Reconsidered*. For a description of the manuscripts of this document that were discovered in Qumran cave 4, see Baumgarten, "Laws of the Damascus Document." The text of these manuscripts has now been published from preliminary transcriptions by Milik in *Preliminary Concordance*, by Wacholder and Abegg in fascicle 1 of *A Preliminary Edition*. On the reliability of the medieval copies, see Baumgarten, "Laws of the *Damascus Document*," 62. See also Rowley, *Zadokite Fragments and the Dead Sea Scrolls*, for the relationship of the *genizah* find to the Qumran corpus. The best commentary remains Rabin, *Zadokite Documents*. Extremely important is Ginzberg, *Unknown Jewish Sect*, which was a pathbreaking study of this text. See Davies, *Damascus Covenant*, for a study of the Admonition, which, however, ignores the legal section of the text. Davies shares the notion of Babylonian origins for the Essenes with Murphy-O'Connor, who analyzes this text in "Critique of the Princes," "Literary Analysis," and "Damascus Document Revisited." See also Davies, "Ideology of the Temple." For a discussion of the sectarians' viewing themselves as the direct heirs of biblical Israel, see Talmon, *World of Qumran from Within*, 11–52.

Three Hundred Ninety Years—See Rabinowitz, "Reconsideration."

PAGE 92

Well Midrash—See Brooke, "Amos-Numbers Midrash."

PAGE 93

"Damascus" in the *Zadokite Fragments*—Wieder, *Judean Scrolls and Karaism*, 1–52; North, "Damascus of Qumran Geography"; Iwry, "Was There a Migration?"; Milikowsky, "Again: DAMASCUS"; and Davies, "Birthplace of the Essenes." Cf. also Knibb, "Exile in the Damascus Document."

PAGE 94

Proposal That Qumran Is Called Secacah in the Bible—This identification has been suggested by Bar-Adon, "Another Settlement of the Judean Desert," and Allegro, *The Treasure of the Copper Scroll*, 68–74. Cross and Milik, "Explorations in the Judaean Buqê'ah," suggest that Qumran is to be identified with "The City of Salt." A useful discussion of both views may found in Davies, *Qumran*, 36–40.

PAGE 95

Desert—See Talmon, "Desert Motif," and Schwartz, *Studies*, 29–43, on the significance of the desert and the exodus to it in the thought of the Qumran sectarians. On the influence of the Bible in general, see Freedman, "Old Testament at Qumran."

CHAPTER 6

PAGE 97

Initiation Rites—Rabin, *Qumran Studies*, 1–21, and Lieberman, "Discipline." On the nature of the sect, see Wernberg-Møller, "Nature of the YAḤAD."

PAGE 99

Rule of the Community—The text was first published in Burrows, *Dead Sea Scrolls*, vol. 2, fascicle 2. See also the commentaries of Brownlee, "Dead Sea Manual of Discipline"; Leaney, *Rule of Qumran*; Licht, *Megillat Ha-Serakhim*, 1–237; Guilbert, in Carmignac, *Textes* 1:1–80; and Wernberg-Møller, *Manual of Discipline*. Important studies on the structure of the text include Guilbert, "Le Plan," and Pouilly, *La Règle de la communauté*. For the cave 4 variants that are still not fully published, see Milik, "[Review of] P. Wernberg-Møller, *Manual of Discipline*"; Vermes, "Qumran Corner: Preliminary Remarks" and "Qumran Forum Miscellanea I," 300–301; Qimron, "Ketav Yad D shel Serekh ha-Yahad"; and Metso, "Primary Results."

Food and Drink of the Community—On liquid food being more susceptible to impurity than solid food, see Licht, *Megillat Ha-Serakhim*, 294–303, and Schiffman, *Sectarian Law*, 163–64. For the reasons for not understanding *ṭoharah* as ritual purification but as pure food, see *Sectarian Law*, 162–63.

PAGE 100

Evidence of the *Zadokite Fragments*—Forkman, *Limits of the Religious Community*, 52–57.

PAGE 103

Essene Comparison—See above to chapter 4.

PAGE 104

Ḥavurah—See Lieberman, "Discipline"; Neusner, *Fellowship in Judaism*, 11–59; and Oppenheimer, *'Am ha-'Aretz*, 118–56.

PAGE 105

Hellenistic Parallels—Weinfeld, *Organizational Pattern*, which in our view fails to demonstrate its thesis that Hellenistic influence accounts for the presence of these features in Qumran sectarian life. Cf. Puech, "[Review of] M. Weinfeld, *Organizational Pattern*."

PAGE 106

Communal Property at Qumran—Rabin, *Qumran Studies*, 22–36. Regarding the sale of slaves, see Schiffman, "Legislation Concerning Relations with Non-Jews," 388–89. For a discussion which argues that the practice of the early church described in Acts was similar to the one we have argued for at Qumran, see Black, *Scrolls and Christian Origins*, 32–39. Cf. Hengel, *Property and Riches in the Early Church*.

PAGE 108

Penal Code—Schiffman, *Sectarian Law*, 155–73; Baumgarten, "Cave 4 Versions of the Qumran Penal Code"; Weinfeld, *Organizational Pattern*, 23–43.

CHAPTER 7

PAGE 113

Priestly Leadership at Qumran—See Schiffman, *Halakhah at Qumran*, 70–75; Liver, "Sons of Zadok"; and Baumgarten, "Heavenly Tribunal," 233–36. Baumgarten, ibid., 236–39, discussed the relations of the Qumran Zadokites with the Sadducees. On the Zadokites' continued leadership role even at the End of Days, see Schiffman, *Eschatological Community*, especially 11–13, 28–29, and 32–35. On the *Rule of Benedictions*, see ibid., 72–76. Cf. also Baumgarten, "Disqualifications of Priests," and Brooke, "Levi and the Levites."

PAGE 117

The Teacher of Righteousness—All attempts at identifying the Teacher of Righteousness with a person otherwise known in Jewish history have ended in failure. The scrolls themselves offer little help here. As discussed in this chapter and in chapter 14, somewhat more is known about the teacher's role in the formation of the Qumran sect and its struggles with its opponents. On the teacher, see Jeremias, *Der Lehrer der Gerechtigkeit*; Lambert, *Le Maître de justice*; Bruce, *Second Thoughts*, 92–97; Buchanan, "Office of Teacher of Righteousness"; Gluskina, "Teacher of Righteousness in Joseph Amussin's Studies"; and Schiffmann, "Teacher of Righteousness in the Soviet Qumran Studies." See also Bregman, "Another Reference," and Siegel, "Two Further Medieval References." A recent maximalist view of the teacher is Schweitzer, "Teacher of Righteousness."

PAGE 121

***Mevaqqer* (Examiner)**—See Priest, "*Mebaqqer, Paqid* and the Messiah," and Marcus, "*Mebaqqer* and *Rabbim*."

PAGE 123

Paqid—Some scholars have been inclined to identify the *paqid* with the *mevaqqer*; for a representative of this view, see Cross, *Ancient Library*, 175–76. Milik, however, in *Ten Years of Discovery*, 99–100, argued persuasively for the distinction of the two offices.

PAGE 124

Maskil—See Kosmala, "*Maskil*."

PAGE 125

Jewish Leadership—On the lay Pharisaic-rabbinic sages, see Schürer, *History of the Jewish People*, 2:322–80, and for a later period, Levine, *Rabbinic Class of Roman Palestine*.

Chapter 8

Page 127

Celibacy of the Dead Sea Sect—A balanced early account is Cross, *Ancient Library*, 96–98. More recent discussions of this issue are listed in Baumgarten, "Qumran-Essene Restraints on Marriage," 20–21, n. 1. See also Qimron, "Celibacy," and Elder, "Female Ascetics."

Celibacy of the Essenes—Schürer, *History of the Jewish People*, 2:570, and the literature cited in n. 55.

Page 130

Attack on Polygamy—See Vermes, *Post-Biblical Jewish Studies*, 50–56; Baumgarten, "Qumran-Essene Restraints on Marriage," 14–15; and Yadin, "L'Attitude essénienne." See also the reference to fornication with one's wife in Baumgarten, "Cave 4 Versions of the Qumran Penal Code," 270–71.

Page 131

Oaths and Vows—Schiffman, "Law of Vows and Oaths."

Page 133

Twenty as the Age of Maturity—Schiffman, *Sectarian Law*, 55–60 and 63–65, and *Eschatological Community*, 16–20.

Page 134

Testimony of Women—Baumgarten, *Studies*, 183–86, whose emendation we follow; Schiffman, *Sectarian Law*, 52–53.

Page 135

Ritual of Marriage—Baumgarten, "4Q502, Marriage or Golden-Age Ritual" has proposed that this is an old-age ritual.

Page 136

Women in the *Temple Scroll*—Schiffman, "Laws Pertaining to Women."

Page 139

Wiles of the Wicked Woman—See Licht, "Ra'atah shel ha-'Ishah ha-Zarah," and Broshi, "Beware the Wiles." Broshi incorrectly takes the poem as reflecting misogyny, the sect's hatred of women, not realizing that this poem is directed against a particular kind of woman. Many have taken this text as allegorical, since it is assumed that the Qumran community, which was thought to be celibate, would have no need for such advice otherwise. Our objections to this approach should by now be obvious. See Allegro, "Wiles of the Wicked Woman" and *DJD* 5:82–85; Strugnell, "Notes," 263–68; Carmignac, "Poème allégorique"; Gazov-Ginsburg, "Double Meaning"; Burgmann, "Wicked Woman," which takes it as referring to Simon the Hasmonaean; and the detailed analysis of this poem by Moore, "Personification." Baumgarten, "On the Nature of the Seductress," takes this poem as referring to a female demon.

PAGE 140

Ben Sira Poem—The translation is from Sanders, *The Dead Sea Psalms Scroll*, 114–15. See his full discussion, 112–17. Cf. also Trenchard, *Ben Sira's View of Women*, which makes mention of this poem only in a list of passages involving the personification of wisdom as a woman (207, n. 215). Cf. also Lehmann, "11Q Ps^a and *Ben Sira*."

PAGE 142

Sarai's Beauty in the *Genesis Apocryphon*—See Fitzmyer, *The Genesis Apocryphon*, 119–24, and VanderKam, "Poetry of 1 Q Ap Gen XX, 2–8a." An additional text of interest in the context of this chapter is the "Song of Miriam," which is preserved in *Pentateuch Reworked*. See White, "4Q364 & 365," 320–24, and Brooke, "Power to the Powerless."

CHAPTER 9

PAGE 145

Sectarian Theology—This chapter leans heavily on the excellent work of Ringgren, *Faith of Qumran*, 47–151, from which the order of our discussion is derived. See Sanders, *Paul and Palestinian Judaism*, 239–328, which is written from the point of view of the author's interest in covenant—an emphasis also followed by Talmon, "New Covenanters of Qumran" and *The "Dead Sea Scrolls" or the "Community of the Renewed Covenant."*

PAGE 146

Thanksgiving Hymns—The first edition is Sukenik, *Dead Sea Scrolls of the Hebrew University*, 35–58. For commentary, see Carmignac, *Les Textes*, 1:129–280; Delcor, *Les Hymnes de Qumran (Hodayot)*; Holm-Nielsen, *Hodayot Psalms from Qumran*; Mansoor, *Thanksgiving Hymns*; and Licht, *Megillat ha-Hodayot*. The cave 4 manuscripts have been published from Strugnell's preliminary readings in the *Preliminary Concordance*, by Wacholder and Abegg, *Preliminary Edition*, 2:254–84. Schuller, "A Hymn from a Cave 4 *Hodayot* Manuscript," publishes, translates, and comments on one of the new hymns. Stegemann, "Methods for the Reconstruction," 204, and Puech, "Quelques aspects," propose a reordering of the text in accord with the cave 4 material. On the theology of the *Thanksgiving Hymns*, see Licht, "Doctrine of the Thanksgiving Scroll." For a discussion of the poetry, see Kittel, *The Hymns of Qumran*. Cf. also Carmignac, "Les Éléments historiques."

Writing of Divine Names—Schiffman, *Sectarian Law*, 135–36; Siegel, "Employment of Palaeo-Hebrew Characters"; Birnbaum, *Qumran (Dead Sea) Scrolls and Palaeography*, 11–15 and 25–26; and Stegemann, "Religionsgeschichtliche Erwägungen."

Angels—Ringgren, *Faith of Qumran*, 81–93, and Yadin, *Scroll of the War*, 229–42.

PAGE 147

Predestination and Dualism—Ringgren, *Faith of Qumran*, 68–80; Licht, "Analysis of the Treatise of the Two Spirits"; Wernberg-Møller, "Reconsideration of the Two Spirits"; Duhaime, "Le Dualisme" and "Dualistic Reworking"; and Nickelsburg, *Resurrection*,

144–69. For the rabbinic good and evil inclinations, see Schechter, *Aspects,* 242–92, which remains an excellent survey of the material, and Urbach, *Sages,* 1:471–83. On the term "lot," see Licht, "Ha-Munaḥ Goral."

Page 150

Lowliness of Man—Ringgren, *Faith of Qumran,* 94–104.

Page 152

Election—Ringgren, *Faith of Qumran,* 104–12.

Knowledge—See Gruenwald, "Knowledge and Vision," and de Caevel, "La Connaissance religieuse."

Eternal Life—The exhaustive study of Puech, *La Croyance des Esséniens en la vie future,* 2 vols., arrived only after this book was already in press.

Chapter 10

Page 161

Definition and Extent of the Canon—See Sarna, "Canon"; Leiman, *Canonization of the Hebrew Scripture;* and Beckwith, *Old Testament Canon.* Cf. also Sarna, "Order of the Books." Sanders, "Cave 11 Surprises" and *Torah and Canon,* argue for an open canon at Qumran. Cf. also Ulrich, "Canonical Process."

Page 163

Lists of Biblical Manuscripts—The biblical material published as of 1990 was listed in Fitzmyer, *Dead Sea Scrolls.* For cave 4, see the report by Ulrich, "Biblical Scrolls from Qumran Cave 4." The major manuscripts are surveyed in a popular format in Scanlin, *Dead Sea Scrolls and Modern Translations.* Even though no copy of Esther has been found, the scrolls show knowledge of this book. See especially Milik, "Les Modèles araméens du livre d'Esther."

Page 165

Halakhic Letter—The passage quoted in the foregoing discussion is based on the edition by Qimron and Strugnell, *DJD* 10:58–9; cf. also 111–12. See also Sarna, *Songs of the Heart,* 11.

Page 168

Book of Daniel and Its Additions—Manuscripts of the Book of Daniel have been found in caves 1, 4, and 6 at Qumran; none contains any of the additions found in the Greek Bible nor, for that matter, the so-called *Pseudo-Daniel* materials from Qumran. The cave 1 manuscripts of Daniel have been published by Trever, "Completion of the Publication"; those of cave 4 by Ulrich, "Daniel Manuscripts from Qumran" (parts 1 and 2); and that of cave 6 by Baillet, *DJD* 3:114–16. See also Trever, "1 Q Danª."

Pseudo-Daniel—A number of texts have been considered to be imitations or extensions of the Book of Daniel. Prominent among these is the *Aramaic Apocalypse,* the so-called *Son of God* text, which is dealt with later. Also important is the *Prayer of Nabonidus,* on which see Milik, "Prière de Nabonide"; Grelot, "La Prière de Nabonide"; and van der Woude, "Bemerkungen zum Gebet des Nabonid."

PAGE 169

Evidence of the *Psalms Scroll*—The differing content and arrangement of this scroll from the canonical book of Psalms have led Sanders, *Torah and Canon*, to argue that the Qumran sect had an open-ended canon. On the other hand, Talmon, *World of Qumran*, 244–72, and Goshen-Gottstein, "Psalms Scroll," argue that this scroll is a collection of biblical and nonbiblical material compiled for liturgical purposes. According to that view, with which we agree, the scroll offers no real evidence concerning the biblical canon at Qumran. Cf. also Sarna, "[Review of] the *Psalms Scroll.*" The text was published first by Sanders as *DJD* 4 and republished by him in a more popular format, *The Dead Sea Psalms Scroll*. The latter includes a "Postscriptum" regarding fragment E, which came into the possession of Yadin. The additional material was published by Yadin in "Another Fragment." On the apocryphal Psalm 151, see Smith, "Psalm 151," and Baumgarten, "Perek Shirah." Talmon, "Mizmorim Ḥiṣṣoniyim," and Greenfield, "Two Notes," also deal with the apocryphal psalms material. See also Brownlee, "Significance of 'David's Compositions.' " Probably to be considered with the apocryphal psalms are the so-called *Non-Canonical Psalms*, published in Schuller, *Non-Canonical Psalms from Qumran*. See also idem., "4Q380 and 381."

Primary Witnesses of the Biblical Text—A clear and comprehensive introduction to the various textual witnesses of the Bible is Tov, *Textual Criticism of the Hebrew Bible*, 21–197. The ancient account of the events surrounding production of the Greek version of the Torah is contained in *Letter of Aristeas*, a translation of which may be found in Charlesworth, *Old Testament Pseudepigrapha*, 2:7–34, and in B. Megillah 9a–b. On the harmonizing tendency of the Samaritan Pentateuch, cf. Tov, "Nature and Background of Harmonizations."

PAGE 170

Textual Families—The theory that the various types of biblical text originated in different localities was first proposed by Albright, "New Light on Early Recensions of the Hebrew Bible," and further developed by Cross, "Contribution of the Qumran Discoveries," "Evolution of a Theory of Local Texts," and *Ancient Library*, 163–94. For an evaluation of this theory, see Tov, *Textual Criticism*, 185–87. Tov has shown the need to completely reevaluate this question, and our discussion largely follows his research and conclusions.

PAGE 171

Biblical Texts from Qumran—The theory that those biblical manuscripts among the Dead Sea Scrolls that were actually written at Qumran (as opposed to those imported from elsewhere) may be identified by certain orthographic and morphological features was developed by Tov, "Hebrew Biblical Manuscripts from the Judaean Desert." On understanding certain of these texts as vulgar texts, cf. Kutscher, *Language and Linguistic Background*, 77–89, and Tov, *Textual Criticism*, 193. The classification of the Qumran biblical manuscripts vis-à-vis the Masoretic, Samaritan, and Septuagintal text types is undertaken in Tov, "Groups of Biblical Texts." For a different perspective, see also Ulrich, "Pluriformity in the Biblical Text." Some important articles are reprinted in Cross and Talmon, *Qumran and the History of the Biblical Text*. Cf. also Skehan, "Scrolls and the Old Testament Text."

PAGE 172

Biblical Manuscripts from Masada—A survey of the scrolls found at Masada is found in Yadin, *Masada*, 168–89, although nonbiblical texts are also discussed there. Texts are published in Nebe, "Die Masada-Psalmen-Handschrift," and Talmon, "Fragments of a Psalms Scroll." See also notes to chapter 1.

Biblical Texts from the Bar Kokhba Period—The biblical texts from Murabba'at were published by Milik in *DJD* 3:75–86 and 181–205. For an example of a Greek manuscript from this period that has been corrected toward the Masoretic Hebrew text, see Tov, *Greek Minor Prophets Scroll*, especially 99–158.

PAGE 173

Isaiah Texts—*Isaiah A* was edited by Burrows, *Dead Sea Scrolls of St. Mark's Monastery*, vol. 1. Beautiful color photographs by Trever are published in Cross, Freedman, and Sanders, *Scrolls from Qumran Cave I*. This text is studied in depth in Kutscher, *Language and Linguistic Background*. See also Talmon, "DSIa as a Witness to Ancient Exegesis." For a detailed list of Isaianic material preserved in *Isaiah B*, see Sukenik, *Dead Sea Scrolls of the Hebrew University*, 43. The example we cite from Isaiah 38 is from Tov, *Textual Criticism*, 340–42.

PAGE 174

Samuel—The date of 4QSam^b has been discussed by Cross, "Oldest Manuscripts from Qumran," 152–59 and 165. In another article, "New Qumran Biblical Fragment," he maintains that 4QSam^a is close to the type of Hebrew text that must underlie the Septuagint version of this book. Tov, "Groups of Biblical Texts," however, classifies this text as nonaligned. Cf. also Tov, "Textual Affiliations," and Polak, "Statistics and Textual Filiation." Rofé, "Nomistic Correction," shows that *Samuel A* exhibits changes intended to bring it into harmony with the laws of the Torah. Exceedingly important is Ulrich, *Qumran Text of Samuel and Josephus*, especially 39–164. See also Barthélemy, Gooding, Lust, and Tov, *Story of David and Goliath*; Tov, *Textual Criticism*, 334–37 and "Composition of 1 Samuel 16–18"; Rofé, "Battle of David and Goliath"; Trebolle, "Story of David and Goliath"; and Anderson and Freedman, "Another Look at 4QSam^b."

Nahash Addition—Cross, "Ammonite Oppression," and Rofé, "Acts of Nahash." Our discussion follows the presentation in Tov, *Textual Criticism*, 342–44. Interesting in this context are the secondary additions in *Numbers B*, on which see Jastram, "Text of 4QNum^b."

PAGE 175

Jeremiah—The various manuscripts of the Book of Jeremiah are described in Tov, "Jeremiah Scrolls" and "Three Fragments." The close connection between *Jeremiah B* and the Septuagint is explored in Tov, "Some Aspects of the Textual and Literary History of the Book of Jeremiah," 145–47. The proto-Masoretic character of *Jeremiah A* and

Jeremiah C is noted in Tov, "Jeremiah Scrolls," 198–99. See also Tov, "Literary History." Tov's work is conveniently brought together in *Textual Criticism*, 319–27.

PAGE 176

Paleo-Exodus—For a general discussion of those biblical scrolls written in Paleo-Hebrew script, see Ulrich, "Paleo-Hebrew Biblical Manuscripts," and Mathews, "Background of the Paleo-Hebrew Texts." See also Freedman and Mathews, *Paleo-Hebrew Leviticus Scroll* (on which see Puech, "Notes en marge de 11Qpaléolévitique"). For the dating of Paleo-Exodus, see McLean, *Use and Development of Palaeo-Hebrew*, 78 and Skehan, Ulrich, and Sanderson, *DJD* 9:61–62. For a full study of the text of this manuscript, see Sanderson, *Exodus Scroll from Qumran*, and "Contribution of 4QpaleoExod^m."

PAGE 178

Psalms—On the cave 11 *Psalms Scroll*, see above, notes to this chapter. *Psalms F* has been published by Starcky, "Psaumes apocryphes de la grotte 4," and *Psalms B*, by Skehan, "Psalm Manuscript from Qumran." Many of the Psalms manuscripts are described by Skehan in "Qumran Manuscripts and Textual Criticism"; cf. idem, "Qumran and Old Testament Criticism." See also van der Ploeg, "Fragments" and "Le Psaume XCI"; Milik, "Fragment d'une source du Psautier"; and Ouellette, "Variantes qumrâniennes."

CHAPTER 11

PAGE 181

Apocryphal Literature from Second Temple Times—For a general description of this literature, see Schürer, *History of the Jewish People*, vols. 3.1 and 3.2, and Stone, ed., *Jewish Writings of the Second Temple Period*. English translations of these works may be found in Charles, *Apocrypha and Pseudepigrapha of the Old Testament*; Sparks, *Apocryphal Old Testament*; and Charlesworth, *Old Testament Pseudepigrapha*. See also Stone, "Apocrypha and Pseudepigrapha and the Dead Sea Scrolls," and his *Selected Studies in Pseudepigrapha and Apocrypha*. For the apocryphal material from Masada, cf. Talmon, "Qit'e Ketavim." On the Aramaic literature from Qumran that predates the sect, see Wacholder, "Ancient Judaeo-Aramaic Literature." Much of the identification of apocryphal works at Qumran has been guided by James, "Lost Apocrypha."

PAGE 182

Enoch—A brief description of the contents of this work may be found in the introduction of Isaac's translation, "1 (Ethiopic Apocalypse of) Enoch." For a description of the Aramaic fragments found at Qumran, see Black, "Fragments of the Aramaic Enoch." On the history of the Book of Enoch, see Milik, *Books of Enoch*, 1–88, whose views are at times rejected in our discussion. Extremely important are VanderKam, *Enoch*, and García Martínez, *Qumran and Apocalyptic*, 45–96. Knibb, *The Ethiopic Book of Enoch*, 2 vols., provides an authoritative text and commentary, as does Black, *Books of Enoch*. Greek fragments are available in Black, *Apocalypsis Henochi Graeci*. Still useful is the commentary by Charles, *Book of Enoch*. See also Milik, "Écrits prééssèniens" and

"Problèmes de la littérature hénochique"; Greenfield and Stone, "Enochic Pentateuch and the Date of the Similitudes"; Levine, "From the Aramaic Enoch Fragments"; Sokoloff, "Notes on the Aramaic Fragments of Enoch"; and Nickelsburg, "Epistle of Enoch."

PAGE 184

Book of Noah—García Martínez, *Qumran and Apocalyptic*, 24–44.

PAGE 185

Book of Giants—Milik, *Books of Enoch*, 298–339, and García Martínez, *Qumran and Apocalyptic*, 97–115.

Jubilees—A detailed summary of this composition is given by Wintermute, "*Jubilees*," 35–36. The Ethiopic text has been critically edited by VanderKam, *Book of Jubilees*, 2 vols. Still useful is the commentary by Charles, *Book of Jubilees*. VanderKam offers a general survey of the cave 4 texts in "*Jubilees* Fragments." See also Kister, "Newly Identified Fragments." For the Jewish law material, see Albeck, *Das Buch der Jubiläen und die Halacha*.

PAGE 188

Genesis Apocryphon—The most complete study is that by Fitzmyer, *Genesis Apocryphon*. Extremely important is Kutscher, "Language of the *Genesis Apocryphon*." See also Lehmann, "*1 Q Genesis Apocryphon*"; and Bernstein, "Harmonizations in the *Genesis Apocryphon*."

PAGE 191

Tobit—Milik, *Ten Years*, 31–32. These texts prove that the longer recension of the Codex Sinaiticus and Vetus Latina was the original. Cf. Schürer, *History of the Jewish People*, 3.1:229. For lists of the preserved passages, see Milik, "La Patrie de Tobie," 521, n. 3, and Schürer, 3.1:222–32.

PAGE 192

Testament of Levi—The Aramaic text found in the Cairo *genizah* was published by Charles and Cowley, "Early Source of the Testaments," and Charles, *Greek Versions of the Testaments*, 53*–57* and 245–56. Qumran material appears in Milik, "Testament de Lévi" and *DJD* 1:87–91, and Puech, "Fragment d'un apocryphe de Lévi." Cf. Brooke, "4QTestament of Levi^d," and Stone and Greenfield, "Prayer of Levi."

PAGE 193

Testament of Naphtali—Schürer, *History of the Jewish People*, 3.2:776–77.

Testament of Kohath—Puech, "*Le Testament de Qahat*." See also Cook, "Remarks on the *Testament of Kohath*." This text first appeared in Shanks and Eisenman (writing separately), "Long Secret Plates from the Unpublished Corpus." *Testament of Kohath* turned out to be partly published with Puech's complete edition already in the mail; a second text had been published years before in *DJD* 7; and one text, the *Messianic Apocalypse*, was indeed new.

PAGE 195

Other Testaments—Milik, "4Q Visions de 'Amram et une citation d'Origène.*"*

CHAPTER 12

PAGE 197

Ancient Near Eastern Wisdom Literature—For the Mesopotamia evidence, see Lambert, *Babylonian Wisdom Literature.* For ancient Egypt, see Pritchard, *Ancient Near Eastern Texts*, 412–25. For ancient Israel, see Crenshaw, ed., *Studies in Ancient Israelite Wisdom.*

PAGE 198

Ben Sira—All of the Hebrew texts, ancient and medieval, are available in Historical Dictionary of the Hebrew Language, *Sefer Ben Sira.* The best commentary is that by Segal, *Sefer Ben Sira ha-Shalem.* The Introduction deals thoroughly with the original language of the book, the name of the author, and the rabbinic attitude to it. See also the comments of Kister, "Le-Ferusho." Yadin, *Ben Sira Scroll*, published the Masada material, and the Qumran fragments appeared in Sanders, *Dead Sea Psalms Scroll* and *DJD* 4. For the debate over the original language, and a general survey on this book, see Schürer, *History of the Jewish People*, 3.1:198–212. See also Lehmann, "*Ben Sira* and the Qumran Literature" and "Yom Kippur at Qumran," 119–20. On the medieval adaptations, see Yassif, *Sippure Ben Sira.* For his attitude to women, see Trenchard, *Ben Sira's View of Women*, which discusses 42:9–14 on 146–62. The identification of wisdom and Torah is taken up in Rylaarsdam, *Revelation in Jewish Wisdom Literature.*

PAGE 203

Sapiential Works—See the introduction to this material in Wacholder and Abegg, *Preliminary Edition*, 2:xii–xiv, and Elgvin, "Admonition Texts." That none of this material was known is clear from the brief section on Qumran wisdom literature in Schürer, *History of the Jewish People*, 3.1:213–14, which deals with none of these texts. Another *Sapiential Work* was published without a title by Allegro in *DJD* 5:85–87. See Tobin, "4Q185 and Jewish Wisdom Literature."

PAGE 206

Mysteries Texts—De Vaux, "La Grotte des manuscrits hébreux," 605–9; Milik, *DJD* 1:102–7; and Rabinowitz, "Authorship, Audience and Date," all pertain to the *Book of Mysteries* from cave 1. See also Schiffman, "4QMysteries[a], a Preliminary Edition," and "4QMysteries[b], a Preliminary Edition." An edition of *Mysteries C* will soon go to press.

The Term "Mystery"—Brown, *Semitic Background*, and Rigaux, "Révélation des mystères," discuss the relevance of the term at Qumran to the New Testament use. Cf. also Ringgren, *Faith of Qumran*, 60–63, which in light of the new texts is seriously outdated.

Chapter 13

Page 211

Interpretation of Scripture in the Qumran Corpus—On exegesis and study in the scrolls, see Betz, *Offbarung und Schriftsforschung;* Lowy, "Some Aspects of Normative and Sectarian Interpretation"; Gabrion, "L'Interprétation"; Vermes, "Qumran Interpretation of Scripture"; Dimant, "Use and Interpretation"; and Fraade, "Interpreting Authority." Helpful background is found in Fishbane, *Biblical Interpretation.*

Page 212

Septuagint—See Tov, *Textual Criticism,* 134–42; "Septuagint"; "Contribution of the Qumran Scrolls"; and *Text Critical Use of the Septuagint.* For an excellent introduction, see Jellicoe, *Septuagint in Modern Study.* The cave 7 Septuagint texts are published in Baillet, *DJD* 3:142–43. Those from cave 4 appear in Skehan, Ulrich, and Sanderson, *DJD* 9:161–97. On these texts, see Skehan, "Qumran Manuscripts and Textual Criticism," "Biblical Scrolls from Qumran" (90–95), and "4QLXXNUM"; Ulrich, "Greek Manuscripts of the Pentateuch" and "Septuagint Manuscripts from Qumran."

Page 214

Targum—See Tov, *Textual Criticism,* 148–51, and Alexander, "Jewish Aramaic Translations."

Leviticus Targum—Milik, *DJD* 6:86–89, and the extremely important "Appendix" there by Kasher, 92–93; Fitzmyer, "Targum of Leviticus."

Job Targum—The first edition by van der Ploeg and van der Woude, with Jongeling, *Le Targum de Job,* cannot be used without the important edition and commentary by Sokoloff, *Targum to Job.* Our following examples are drawn from his discussion on 6–8. A small fragment of a *Job Targum* is published in Milik, *DJD* 6:90. See also Jongeling, "Contributions" and "Job Targum," and Weiss, "Further Notes."

Page 215

Rabbinic Tradition on the Targum of Job—T. Shabbat 13:2; P. Shabbat 16:1 (16c); B. Shabbat 115a; Sofrim 5:15. Cf. Sokoloff, *Targum to Job,* 4–5.

Page 216

Genesis Commentary—This text has attracted tremendous attention. It was first discussed by Allegro, "Further Messianic References." On this fragment, see Schwartz, "Messianic Departure," and Stegemann, "Weitere Stücke," 211–17. More recent studies have been based on the entire document. These include Glessmer, "Antike und Moderne Auslegungen"; Bernstein, "4Q252: From Re-Written Bible to Biblical Commentary"; Lim, "Chronology" and "Notes on 4Q252"; Jacobson, "4Q252: Addenda" and "4Q252 fr. 1: Further Comments"; and Kister, "Notes on Some New Texts," 287–89. It appears in Wacholder and Abegg, *Preliminary Edition,* 2:212–15. Other Pesher Genesis material appears there on 217–22.

PAGE 217

Retelling the Bible—Some of the many additional texts of this type are the *Flood Apocryphon*, on which see Newsom, "4Q370: An Admonition Based on the Flood"; *Moses Apocryphon A*, on which see Newsom, "4Q374: A Discourse"; *David Apocryphon (?)*, on which see Schuller, "Preliminary Study of 4Q373"; *Joseph Apocryphon B*, on which see Schuller, "Text about Joseph"; and *Exposition on the Patriarchs*, on which see Stone and Eshel, "Exposition." See also the *Zedekiah Fragment*, on which see the forthcoming edition of Larson, Schiffman, and Strugnell, "4Q470 with a Fragment Mentioning Zedekiah," and the analytical article by Larson, "New Apocryphal Text."

Genesis Apocryphon—See notes to chapter 11. For this text as a type of rewritten Bible, see Evans, "*Genesis Apocryphon*."

PAGE 218

Harmonizing Interpretation—Yadin, *Temple Scroll*, 1:74–77. See Schiffman, "Deuteronomic Paraphrase," 553–54, and Tov, "*Deut* 12 and *11QTemple*." On the spring New Year Festival, see Yadin, *Temple Scroll* 1:89–91.

PAGE 219

Halakhic Midrash—See Schiffman, "Deuteronomic Paraphrase," 558–61, and *Halakhah at Qumran*, 54–60. The sectarian requirement of reproof is discussed in detail in Schiffman, *Sectarian Law*, 89–98.

PAGE 221

Decrees of Reproof—The reproof document from cave 4 was first analyzed by Eisenman and Wise, *Dead Sea Scrolls Uncovered*, 269–73, who read it incorrectly. See now the excellent edition by Eshel, "4Q477: The Rebukes of the Overseer." This reading shows that the document contained the record of a series of rebukes to different individuals for violating the sectarian codes. On the prohibition of planning on the Sabbath to labor afterward, see the detailed discussion in Schiffman, *Halakhah at Qumran*, 90–91.

CHAPTER 14

PAGE 223

Pesher Exegesis and Literary Form—A good introduction is found in Dimant, "Qumran Sectarian Literature," 503–8, and "*Pesharim*, Qumran." See also Horgan, *Pesharim*, 229–59; Nitzan, *Megillat Pesher Habakkuk*, 29–80; and Brownlee, "Biblical Interpretation," *Midrash Pesher* (23–36), and "Background of Biblical Interpretation." We cannot accept, however, the confusion of the genres of Midrash and Pesher that takes place in his work. This position is also followed by Brooke, "Qumran Pesher." Cf. his "Pesharim and the Origins of the Dead Sea Scrolls." On the quotation formulas, see most recently Bernstein, "Introductory Formulas for Citation." See also Fröhlich, "Le Genre littéraire"; Rabinowitz, "*Pêsher/Pittârôn*"; Collins, "Prophecy and Fulfillment"; and Fishbane, "Use, Authority and Interpretation," 360–61.

PAGE 226

Pesher Habakkuk—This was one of the original seven scrolls found at Qumran and it was part of the lot bought by Yadin from Mar Athanasius Samuel. It was first published by Burrows (with the photographs by Trever) in *Dead Sea Scrolls of St. Mark's Monastery* I, plates LV–LXI. Together with color photos, also by Trever, it appeared again in Cross, Freedman, and Sanders, *Scrolls from Qumrân Cave I*, 150–63. Major commentaries are by Carmignac, *Textes* 2:93–117; Dupont-Sommer, "Le 'Commentaire d'Habacuc'"; Brownlee, *Midrash Pesher*; Horgan, *Pesharim*, 10–55; and Nitzan, *Megillat Pesher Habakkuk*. Nitzan is certainly the most comprehensive resource on this text. A full study of the text is Elliger, *Studien*. See recently, Lim, "Eschatological Orientation."

PAGE 228

Pesher Nahum—Published by Allegro, *DJD* 5:37–42. This edition can be used only with the corrections of Strugnell, "Notes," 204–10. See also Allegro, "Further Light." The best edition and commentary available is Horgan, *Pesharim*, 158–91 (with the accompanying "Texts," 46–50). A number of earlier studies are worthwhile. See especially Licht, "Dappim Nosafim"; Flusser, "Kat Midbar Yehudah ve-ha-Perushim"; Carmignac, *Textes*, 2:85–92; Dupont-Sommer, "Le Commentaire de Nahum"; Amoussine, "Éphraïm et Menassé"; Dupont-Sommer, "Lumières nouvelles"; Maier, "Weitere Stücke"; and Schiffman, "Pharisees and Sadducees in *Pesher Nahum*."

Pesher Psalms—Published by Allegro, *DJD* 5:42–43. This edition can be used only with the corrections of Strugnell, "Notes," 211–19. The best edition and commentary is that of Horgan, *Pesharim*, 192–228 (with the accompanying "Texts," 51–61). See also Carmignac, *Textes*, 2:119–28. Important studies are Pardee, "Restudy"; Stegemann, "Der Pešer Psalms 37" and "Weitere Stücke," 207–10; and Yadin, *Message of the Scrolls*, 99–102. Note also the comments of Amoussine, "Observatiunculae," 533–35.

PAGE 229

Pesher Isaiah—First published by Allegro, *DJD* 5:11–30. This edition must be read with the corrections of Strugnell, "Notes," 183–99. Cf. also Allegro, "More Isaiah Commentaries." The best edition is that of Horgan, *Pesharim*, 70–138 (with accompanying "Texts," 15–37). See also Carmignac, *Textes*, 2:65–76. Important studies are Amoussine, "À Propos de l'interprétation"; Burrows, "Ascent from Acco" (cf. Allegro, "Addendum"); Rosenthal, "Biblical Exegesis"; and Yadin, "Ḥadashot," 49–52, and "Some Notes." The issue of the relationship of *Pesher Isaiah D* to the twelve apostles is discussed in Baumgarten, *Studies*, 145–71, and Flusser, *Yahadut*, 283–304 and *Judaism and the Origins of Christianity*, 173–85.

PAGE 230

Other Continuous Pesharim—See the editions, commentaries, and bibliographies in Horgan, *Pesher Hosea* and *Pesharim*, 138–58 ("Texts," 38–45); Allegro, "Recently Discovered Fragment"; Amoussine, "Observatiunculae," 545–52; and Horgan, *Pesher Micah*, 55–63 ("Texts," 55–63).

Florilegium—This text is exhaustively studied in Brooke, *Exegesis at Qumran*. More recently, Steudel, in *Der Midrash zur Eschatologie* and in "4QMidrEschat," has analyzed it thoroughly again while making the case that it and the so-called *Catena* constitute one eschatological midrash. Cf. also Steudel, "Eschatological Interpretation." *Florilegium* was originally published by Allegro, *DJD* 5:53–174. (Cf. idem, "Fragments of a Qumran Scroll.") This edition can be used only with the corrections of Strugnell, "Notes," 220–25, and Yadin, "Midrash on 2 Sam. vii and Ps. 1–11." See also Dimant, "Qumran Sectarian Literature," 518–21; Schwartz, "Three Temples"; Blidstein, "4 Q Florilegium"; Baumgarten, "Exclusion"; and Wise, "4QFlorilegium and the Temple of Man."

PAGE 231

Melchizedek—This document was first published by van der Woude, "Melchisedek," and again by de Jonge and van der Woude, "11QMelchizedek." The most extensive study is Kobelski, *Melchizedek and Melchireša'*. Important studies are Brooke, *Exegesis at Qumran*, 319–23; Carmignac, "Le Document"; Delcor, "Melchizedek"; Fitzmyer, *Essays*, 245–67; Milik, "*Milkî-ṣedeq et Milkî-reša'*"; Puech, "Notes sur le manuscrit de XIQMelkîsédek"; Sanders, "Old Testament in 11QMelchizedek"; and Yadin, "Note on Melchizedek." Central to the debate has been the relationship of this material to the priestly Melchizedek of the New Testament Epistle to the Hebrews (5:5–10 and 7:1–7).

Historical Relevance of the Pesharim—Nitzan, *Megillat Pesher Habakkuk*, 11–28 and 123–45; Cross, *Ancient Library*, 107–60 and "Early History"; Stegemann, *Entstehung*; Dupont-Sommer, "Lumières nouvelles"; Amusin, "Reflection of Historical Events"; Charlesworth, "Origin and Subsequent History"; Callaway, *History of the Qumran Community*, 135–71; García Martínez and van der Woude, "'Groningen' Hypothesis"; and Lim, "Wicked Priests of the Groningen Hypothesis." It goes without saying that we disagree with many of the details in these accounts, which tend to make definite identifications that in our view cannot be sustained by the available evidence.

PAGE 235

Testimonia—This text is published by Allegro, *DJD* 5:57–60, and must be read with the corrections of Strugnell, "Notes," 225–29. Studies of this document include Amusin, "4QTestimonia," 15–19; Brooke, *Exegesis at Qumran*, 309–19; Callaway, *History of the Qumran Community*, 173–83; Fitzmyer, *Essays*, 59–89; and Lübbe, "Reinterpretation of 4 Q Testimonia."

Psalms of Joshua—The text is published and discussed in Newsom, "Psalms of Joshua." See the important study of Eshel, "Historical Background," and Lim, "Psalms of Joshua."

Historical Events of the Hasmonaean Period—For a survey of the Hasmonaean dynasty, see Schiffman, *From Text to Tradition*, 99–103. On Simon, see Schürer, *History of the Jewish People*, 1:189–99. John Hyrcanus's rule is discussed in Schürer, *History of the Jewish People*, 1:200–215. On Aristobulus I and Antigonus, see Schürer, *History of the Jewish People*, 1:216–18.

PAGE 236

Demetrius and Alexander Janneus—The reign of Alexander Janneus is discussed in Schürer, *History of the Jews*, 1:219–28. The invasion by Demetrius III Eukerus is analyzed there on 223–24. Our story here shows that Janneus cannot have been the Wicked Priest. See the detailed discussion of our passage in *Pesher Nahum* (apparently by Vermes) in

Schürer, *History of the Jewish People,* 1:224–25, n. 22. Eshel and Kister, in "Polemical Qumran Fragment," see the *Polemical Fragment* as belonging to this same period.

Page 238

Prayer for King Jonathan—The presence of the name Jonathan in this text was deciphered properly by Yardeni, and it was subsequently published and analyzed in Eshel, Eshel, and Yardeni, "A Qumran Composition" and "Rare DSS Text." See also Vermes, "So-Called King Jonathan Fragment," which argues for identification of Jonathan here with Jonathan the Hasmonaean, and Alexander, "Note on the Syntax." The edition of this text in Eisenman and Wise, *Dead Sea Scrolls Uncovered,* 273–81, is unreliable and depends on the *Jerusalem Post* report of the decipherment by Yardeni (281, n. 50). The attempt by Eisenman and Wise to use this text to characterize the Qumran sect as a pro-Maccabean corpus cannot be accepted by us.

Chapter 15

Page 245

Cave 4 Halakhic Texts—See the survey of the newly released material in Schiffman, "New Halakhic Texts." A legal text mentioned only briefly in this book but of great interest is *Ordinances.* On *Ordinances A,* see Allegro, "Unpublished Fragment of Essene Halakhah," and *DJD* 6–9. His edition only can be used with the corrections of Strugnell, "Notes," 175–79. For *Ordinances B* and *Ordinances C,* see Baillet, *DJD* 7:287–98. Schiffman, "4QOrdinances^{a,b}," provides new editions, translations, and commentary to *Ordinances A* and *Ordinances B.* Important articles are Yadin, "Note on 4Q 159," and Weinert, "4Q159: Legislation for an Essene Community." Other legal issues are discussed in Baumgarten, "Halakhic Polemics."

Page 246

Extrabiblical Laws—See Schiffman, *Sectarian Law,* 14–17. See also Fishbane, "Use, Authority and Interpretation," which provides important background for this section.

Lists of Sectarian Laws—See Schiffman, *Halakhah at Qumran,* 60–68.

Page 247

Hidden and Revealed Law—Schiffman, *Halakhah at Qumran,* 22–32; cf. Wieder, *Judean Scrolls and Karaism,* 53–85; Wacholder, "'Sealed' Torah"; and VanderKam, "Zadok."

Page 249

Pharisees—See Schiffman, "New Light on the Pharisees." The polemic against the "builders of the wall" renders impossible the interpretation of Finkelstein, "Maxim," 461–63, to M. Avot 1:1. On the "interpreters of false laws," see Schiffman, "Pharisees and Sadducees in *Pesher Nahum,*" 276–77. On the "talmud," see Wacholder, "Qumran Attack." For the identifications of Ephraim and Menasseh as the Pharisees and Sadducees, see Flusser, "Perushim, Şeduqim ve-'Issiyim."

Page 252

Sadducees—Schiffman, "Pharisees and Sadducees in *Pesher Nahum,*" 284–88. See Schürer, *History of the Jewish People,* 2:408, on the Sadducean attitude to Jewish law.

PAGE 253

Halakhic Letter and the Temple Scroll Sources—See notes to chapter 16; Schiffman, *"Miqṣat Maʿase ha-Torah* and the *Temple Scroll."* See also Schiffman, "Theology of the *Temple Scroll."* Numerous parallels to the *Temple Scroll* are cited in Qimron and Strugnell, *DJD* 10:148–75 in the discussion of individual laws found in the *Halakhic Letter.*

CHAPTER 16

PAGE 257

Temple Scroll—Initial impressions are conveyed in Yadin, "Temple Scroll," *BA,* and "Temple Scroll," *New Directions.* A popular volume is Yadin, *Temple Scroll, The Hidden Law of the Dead Sea Sect.* The text was fully published in a Hebrew edition in Yadin, *Megillat Ha-Miqdash,* and in English, Yadin, *Temple Scroll,* each 3 vols. Cf. my review in *BA* 48, in which I surveyed the outlines of the debate as it had then taken shape, and Brooke, "Temple Scroll." For a more recent survey, see Schiffman, "Temple Scroll and the Nature of Its Law." On the acquisition of the scroll, see Shanks, "Intrigue and the Scroll." Numerous corrections to the edition by Yadin have been made by Qimron in a series of articles: Qimron, "Le-Nushah shel Megillat ha-Miqdash," "New Readings in the Temple Scroll," "Shalosh Heʿarot le-Nushah shel Megillat ha-Miqdash," "Heʿarot le-Nusah Megillat ha-Miqdash," "Further New Readings," "Column 14 of the Temple Scroll," and "Need for a Comprehensive Critical Edition." Also important is the evidence of the other copy or copies of the scroll. See Wacholder, "Fragmentary Remains of 11QTorah," and García Martínez, "11QTemple[b]." Qimron is hoping to publish a new edition of the scroll soon.

Language of the Scroll—Tov, "Orthography and Language"; Schiffman, "Temple Scroll in Literary and Philological Perspective"; and Qimron, "Le-Millonah shel Megillat Ha-Miqdash."

PAGE 258

Sadducean Sources—On the sources of the scroll, see Wilson and Wills, "Literary Sources"; Wise, *Critical Study of the Temple Scroll,* 195–98; García Martínez, "Sources et rédaction"; Schiffman, "Deuteronomic Paraphrase"; and Callaway, "Source Criticism." Cf. letter from J. Strugnell, published in Wacholder, *Dawn of Qumran,* 205–6; White, "4Q364 and 365"; and Tov, "Textual Status of 4Q364–367." In our view, these sources are Sadducean. Sadducean aspects of the law of the *Temple Scroll* have certainly been noticed by others. Cf. Lehmann, "Temple Scroll as a Source of Sectarian Halakhah"; Baumgarten, "Pharisaic-Sadducean Controversies about Purity"; Sussmann, "Heqer Toldot Ha-Halakhah."

Idolatry; Oaths and Vows—Schiffman, "Laws Pertaining to Idolatry" and "Laws of Vows and Oaths."

Temple Scroll and Qumran Sect—The relation of this text to the Qumran sect has been debated in a series of studies: Levine, "Temple Scroll"; Milgrom, "'Sabbath' and 'Temple City'"; Yadin, "Is the *Temple Scroll* a Sectarian Document?"; Schiffman, *Sectarian Law,* 13–17; and Stegemann, "Origins of the Temple Scroll" and "Institutions of Israel."

Contents of the Scroll—See the survey in Milgrom, "*Temple Scroll*" and the full listing of Yadin, *Temple Scroll,* 1:39–70. That the scroll is not messianic is clear from *Temple Scroll* 29:2–10. See Schiffman, "Theology"; contra Wacholder, *Dawn of Qumran,* 21–30; and Wise, "Eschatological Vision." On *Temple Scroll* 29:2–10, cf. Wise, "Covenant of the Temple Scroll"; Callaway, "Exegetische Erwägungen"; and Wentling, "Unraveling the Relationship."

PAGE 260

Exegesis—Yadin, *Temple Scroll,* 1:71–88; Schiffman, "Deuteronomic Paraphrase"; and Schiffman, "Septuagint and the Temple Scroll." Very important for the scroll's exegesis are the two articles by Milgrom "Studies in the Temple Scroll" and "Further Studies." The biblical text that underlies the scroll is discussed in Tov, "Megillat ha-Miqdash," and Brooke, "Textual Tradition."

PAGE 262

Theology of the *Temple Scroll*—A fuller presentation of much of the same material in this and the next section will be found in Schiffman, "Theology." On the elimination of Moses from the text, see Yadin, *Temple Scroll,* 1:71–73; Levine, "*Temple Scroll,*" 17–18.

PAGE 263

Dating of the Scroll—Yadin, *Temple Scroll,* 1:386–90; Schiffman, "King, His Guard and the Royal Council," 257–58. Cf. Hengel, Charlesworth, and Mendels, "Polemical Character," 28–38, who date the scroll to 103–88 B.C.E. The earlier dating of Wacholder, *Dawn of Qumran,* 202–12, cannot be accepted in light of the clear impression that the Law of the King of the scroll reacts to events that occurred in the early years of the Hasmonaean dynasty.

PAGE 264

Purity Regulations—Yadin, *Temple Scroll,* 1:277–307 and 321–43; Schiffman, "Impurity of the Dead"; Schiffman, "Exclusion from the City"; Milgrom, "Scriptural Foundations"; and Harrington, *Impurity Systems,* 47–110.

Sacrificial Festival Calendar—Yadin, *Temple Scroll,* 1:89–136 and Schiffman, "Sacrificial Calendar."

PAGE 266

Land and Temple —On the architecture of the Temple, see Yadin, *Temple Scroll,* 1:177–276; Schiffman, "Architecture and Law," "Furnishings of the Temple," and "Sacred Space"; and Broshi, "Gigantic Dimensions." Note also that much architectural discussion is found in Maier, *Temple Scroll* and "Temple Scroll and Tendencies in the Cultic Architecture." Bean, *Theoretical Construct,* 265–359, is an interesting study that, unfortunately, does not base itself on new textual scholarship. On the land, see Schiffman, "Sacred Space" and Stegemann, "'Das Land' in der Tempelrolle."

PAGE 268

Law of the King—Yadin, *Temple Scroll,* 1:344–62; Schiffman, "King, His Guard and the Royal Council" and "Laws of War"; Weinfeld, "Megillat Miqdash" and "Royal Guard"; and Hengel, Charlesworth, and Mendels, "Polemical Character."

CHAPTER 17

PAGE 273

Zadokite Fragments—See notes to chapters 1 and 5.

PAGE 274

Topics Covered in the Fragments—These are surveyed in Milik, *Ten Years*, 151–52; Fitzmyer, "Prolegomenon," in Schechter, *Documents*, 17–19; and Baumgarten, "Laws of the *Damascus Document*," 52–55. See also Stegemann, "Gesetzkorpus." Cf. Schiffman, "New Halakhic Texts," 24–29, for a survey of the material in the newly released fragments.

Rule of the Community and War Scroll—On the *Rule of the Community*, see notes to chapter 6; on the *War Scroll*, see notes to chapter 20.

PAGE 275

Sabbath Code—A complete study is Schiffman, *Halakhah at Qumran*, 84–133. That study was updated in Schiffman, *Halakhah, Halikhah u-Meshihiyut*, 90–135. The earlier study by Ginzberg, *Unknown Jewish Sect*, 58–70 and 107–15, originally published before the Dead Sea Scrolls were discovered, remains extremely important. We cannot accept the views of Zahavy, "Sabbath Code."

Beginning of the Day at Sunset—Schiffman, *Halakhah at Qumran*, 84–87, and Gilat, *Peraqim*, 258–61. The claim that the Sabbath began at sunrise on Saturday is put forward by Talmon, "Calendar Reckoning," 192–4, and "Le-'Inyan ha-Luah." Those supporting the notion that the Sabbath in this text began at sunset Friday evening—the view we accept—are Wieder, *Judean Scrolls and Karaism*, 54–55; Leibel, "Shabbatah shel Kat Midbar Yehudah"; and Baumgarten, *Studies*, 124–30.

PAGE 276

Sabbath Limits—Schiffman, *Halakhah at Qumran*, 91–98 and 111–13; Gilat, *Peraqim*, 249–55; and Rosenthal, "'Al Hishtalshelut Halakhah."

PAGE 277

Carrying on the Sabbath—Schiffman, *Halakhah at Qumran*, 113–15.

PAGE 278

Delivering or Saving an Animal—Schiffman, *Halakhah at Qumran*, 121–23.

PAGE 279

Saving a Human Life—Schiffman, *Halakhah at Qumran*, 125–28, and the revision in *Halakhah, Halikhah u-Meshihiyut*, 129–31. Herr, "Li-Va'ayot Hilkhot Milhamah be-Shabbat," discusses the problem of defensive war on the Sabbath in Second Temple times. On the relevant New Testament material and its historical context, see Sanders, *Jewish Law*, 19–23.

PAGE 282

Judiciary—Schiffman, *Sectarian Law*, 23–40.

Page 283

Witnesses—Schiffman, "Qumran Law of Testimony" and *Sectarian Law*, 55–65 and 73–81; Levine, "*Damascus Document*"; Neusner, "By the Testimony of Two Witnesses" and "*Damascus Document* IX, 17–22"; Jackson, "Damascus Document" and *Essays*, 171–75; and Rabinovitch, "*Damascus Document* IX, 17–22." Cf. also Wacholder, "Rules of Testimony," which sees the *Zadokite Fragments* as dependent on the law of testimony in the *Temple Scroll*, a view we cannot accept.

Page 285

Recovery of Lost or Stolen Property—Schiffman, *Sectarian Law*, 111–24.

Chapter 18

Page 289

Prayer in Second Temple Times—See Elbogen, *Jewish Liturgy*, 187–99, and Heinemann, *Ha-Tefillah*, 78–98, for the rabbinic evidence. See also Levine, "Second Temple Synagogue."

Prayer in the Dead Sea Scrolls—Much of the material we present in this chapter is available in a more technical form in Schiffman, "Dead Sea Scrolls and the Early History of Jewish Liturgy." Cf. also Talmon, "Emergence of Institutionalized Prayer"; Weinfeld, "Prayer and Liturgical Practice" and "'Aqavot shel Qedushat Yoṣer"; and Chazon, "Prayers from Qumran." A full-length study is Nitzan, *Qumran Prayer and Religious Poetry*. Weinfeld, "Grace after Meals," proposes to identify a grace for mourners in the still unpublished *Barkhi Nafshi* texts, but we cannot accept that conclusion. On this excerpt, see also Reed, "What Is a Fragment?"

Sacrifice and the Qumran Sect—See Baumgarten, *Studies*, 39–74; Carmignac, "L'Utilité"; and Bowman, "Did the Qumran Sect Burn the Red Heifer?" On the sect's self-image as a sanctuary, see Gärtner, *The Temple and the Community*. For the parallel experience in rabbinic Judaism after the destruction of the Temple, see Schiffman, *From Text to Tradition*, 164–66.

Page 291

House of Prostration—For recent discussion, see Steudel, "House of Prostration."

Page 292

Prayer Times—Following Dupont-Sommer, "Contribution." We cannot accept the larger number of daily prayers found by Talmon, "Manual of Benedictions," 481–84. Talmon wrote before the publication of the *Daily Prayers*, which is discussed later. Parallels with the *Shema* and *Amidah* are noted by him on 488–93.

Page 293

Daily Prayers—Baillet, *DJD* 7:105–36; Baumgarten, "4 Q 503 (*Daily Prayers*)"; and Weinfeld, "Morning Prayers." On rabbinic practices regarding the *Shema* and its benedictions, see Elbogen, *Jewish Liturgy*, 16–24. On the benedictions over the Torah, see ibid., 140–41. On the benediction formula in Dead Sea Scrolls texts, see Schuller, "Some Observations on Blessings of God."

PAGE 296

Supplication Texts—On the rabbinic *Taḥanun* prayers, see Elbogen, *Jewish Liturgy,* 66–72. *Lament* appears in Baillet, *DJD* 7:79–80; *Words of the Luminaries* is on 137–75. See also Baillet, "En Recueil liturgique." *Words of the Luminaries* was first compared to the *Taḥanun* by Lehmann, "Re-Interpretation." The problems with the edition are highlighted by the editor, in Baillet, "Remarques." This text has been reedited by Chazon in her Hebrew University dissertation, and she has reordered the text with the help of Stegemann. See Chazon, "Is *Divrei ha-me'orot* a Sectarian Prayer?" and "4QDibHam."

PAGE 297

Festival Prayers—Milik, *DJD* 1:136 and 152–55, and Baillet, *DJD* 7:175–215.

PAGE 299

Purification Rituals—Baillet, *DJD* 7:262–86, and Baumgarten, "Purification Rituals."

PAGE 300

Psalms Scroll—See notes to chapter 10.

PAGE 301

Thanksgiving Hymns—See notes to chapter 9.

Songs of the Sabbath Sacrifice—See notes to chapter 22.

Calendar—The basic outline of the sectarian calendar was deduced from partial evidence by Talmon, "Calendar Reckoning." See also Jaubert, "Les Calendriers de Jubilés et de la secte de Qumran" and "Les Calendriers de Jubilés et les jours liturgiques de la semaine"; Morgenstern, "Calendar of the Book of Jubilees"; VanderKam, "Origins" and "Twenty-eight Day Month"; Davies, "Calendrical Change"; and Beckwith, "Modern Attempt," "Essene Calendar," and "Significance of the Calendar." This seems to be the calendar assumed by the *Temple Scroll.* See Yadin, *Temple Scroll,* 1:116–19, and Baumgarten, "Calendars." Contrast Levine, "Temple Scroll," 7–11, and "Further Look." Calendar texts have now appeared in preliminary publications. The editions of Milik were published from *Preliminary Concordance* in Wacholder and Abegg, *Preliminary Edition,* 1:60–101 (see the appendix on 104–18). Eisenman and Wise, *Dead Sea Scrolls Uncovered,* 106–33, published much of the same material, apparently utilizing the readings of *Preliminary Concordance* as well as the work of Talmon, which is not acknowledged. Talmon is readying the official edition of this material. See Talmon and Knohl, "Qeta'im shel Megillat Luaḥ mi-Qumran."

PAGE 305

Tefillin—Phylacteries are published in Kuhn, *Phylacterien;* Barthélemy, *DJD* 1:72–76; Baillet, *DJD* 3:149–57; Milik, *DJD* 6:48–79; and Yadin, *Tefillin from Qumran.* Discussion of the halakhic issues is found in Yadin. Milik, *DJD* 6:34–47, deals with textual and historical issues. See also Habermann, "'Al ha-Tefillin bi-Yeme Qedem," and Baillet, "Nouveaux phylactères."

PAGE 311

Mezuzot—Mezuzot are published in Baillet, *DJD* 7:158–61, and Milik, *DJD* 6:80–85. See also the introductory material on 35–47.

Chapter 19

Page 317

Messianic Idea—The distinction between restorative and utopian messianism is put forth in Scholem, *Messianic Idea*, 1–36. Its application to the Qumran materials is suggested in Talmon, *King, Cult and Calendar*, 203–5. Contrast the approach of Green, "Introduction: Messianisms in Judaism." Our remarks in this section are continued into the rabbinic period in Schiffman, "Concept of the Messiah," 235–46.

Page 318

Biblical Background—The most comprehensive study is Mowinckel, *He That Cometh*, 2–186. On the Day of the Lord, see von Rad, "Origin of the Concept of the Day of Yahweh."

Page 319

Messianism in the Second Temple Period—See Schürer, *History of the Jewish People*, 2:488–561. While this discussion has much valuable information, it does not make adequate distinction between the types of messianism, and it projects an artificially constructed systematic presentation. See also Collins, "Messianism in the Maccabean Period," and Charlesworth, "Concept of the Messiah in the Pseudepigrapha."

Page 321

Messianic Ideas in the Qumran Scrolls—Schürer, *History of the Jewish People*, 2:550–54; Talmon, *World of Qumran*, 273–300; and García Martínez, "Messianische Erwartungen." For treatment of the wider issue of apocalypticism at Qumran, see Newsom, "Apocalyptic"; Stegemann, "Die Bedeutung der Qumranfunde"; and Collins, *Apocalyptic Imagination*, 115–41, and "Was the Dead Sea Sect an Apocalyptic Movement?" Contrast Davies, "Qumran and Apocalyptic." See also Licht, "Torat ha-'Ittim," for the sectarian understanding of time and chronology. An attempt to construct a chronological history of the messianism in the Qumran texts is Starcky, "Les Quatres étapes."

Two-Messiah Concept—Of the many studies on this topic, see, for example, LaSor, "Messiah of Aaron and Israel"; Liver, "Doctrine of the Two Messiahs"; Kuhn, "Two Messiahs of Aaron and Israel"; Silberman, "Two Messiahs"; Laurin, "Problem of the Two Messiahs"; and Brooke, "Messiah of Aaron."

Messianic Figures—See Schiffman, "Messianic Figures and Ideas," for a full survey of all the material that was available before the full release of the scrolls. For the use of Hebrew *mashiah* in the *Zadokite Fragments*, see Yadin, "Three Notes," 158–59. Cf. Ginzberg, *Unknown Jewish Sect*, 209–56, on the messianic ideas of this text.

Chapter 20

Page 329

Rule of the Congregation—First published by Barthélemy, *DJD* 1:108–18. For analysis and commentary see Carmignac, *Textes*, 2:11–27; Licht, *Megillat ha-Serakhim*, 241–70; and the full-length study by Schiffman, *Eschatological Community*. Cf. also Richardson,

"Some Notes on 1QSa"; North, "Qumran 'Serek A'"; Smith, "God's Begetting the Messiah"; and Yadin, "Crucial Passage."

Assembly at the End of Days—Schiffman, *Eschatological Community*, 37–52, and "Purity and Perfection." Cf. Bokser, *Approaching Sacred Space*, 279–87.

PAGE 330

War Scroll—The *War Scroll* was first published in Sukenik, *Dead Sea Scrolls of the Hebrew University*, 16–34. An important early study is Segal, "Qumran *War Scroll*." The scroll was later reedited with detailed introduction and commentary in Yadin, *Scroll of the War*. Yadin defends this volume (in its original Hebrew edition) in "Ha-Milḥamah." Additional commentaries are Carmignac, *La Règle de la guerre*, and van der Ploeg, *Le Rouleau de la guerre*. Davies, *IQM*, shows that the scroll is in fact a composite work. See also Duhaime, "*War Scroll*," which compares the text to ancient military manuals. Cave 4 yielded further manuscripts of this text indicating it circulated in at least two recensions. *War Scrolls A–F* are published by Baillet in *DJD* 7:12–68. On those texts see Baillet, "Les manuscrits." The scheme of the messianic war is set out in detail and discussed in Yadin, *Scroll of the War*, 18–37. A number of texts are closely related to the *War Scroll* and may even be parts of other recensions. See Duhaime, "Étude comparative"; Eshel and Eshel, "4Q471 Fragment 1"; and the discussion of the *War Rule*, later, in chapter 21. See also Carmignac, "Les Kittim," and Smith, "Ascent to the Heavens."

PAGE 333

Meal of the End of Days—Schiffman, *Eschatological Community*, 53–56. Previous literature on this topic was aimed primarily at comparison to the Last Supper. For a sampling of these studies, some of which make major contributions to the understanding of the text, see Priest, "Messiah and the Meal," and Kuhn, "Lord's Supper." On the messianic banquet, cf. Ginzberg, *Legends*, 1:27–28 and 5:43–46, n. 127, and Moore, *Judaism*, 2:363–64. A list of references is also found under "Messianic banquet" in the index to Charles, *Apocrypha and Pseudepigrapha*, 2:859.

PAGE 334

Sectarian Communal Meal—Schiffman, "Communal Meals," revised and expanded in *Eschatological Community*, 56–64. Cf. van der Ploeg, "Meals of the Essenes"; Ringgren, *Faith of Qumran*, 217–20; and Cross, *Ancient Library*, 85–91, which relates the communal meals to the meal of the End of Days. Cf. Delcor, "Repas cultuels."

PAGE 337

Archaeological Evidence for Communal Meals—Schiffman, *Eschatological Community*, 64–67, and de Vaux, *Archaeology*, 11–14 and, especially, 14–16, nn. 2 and 3. Cf. also Laperrousaz, *Qoumrân*, 215–18, and "A Propos des dépôts," and Duhaime, "Remarques."

CHAPTER 21

PAGE 341

Aramaic Apocalypse (Son of God)—This text was first published (based on a lecture by Milik) in Fitzmyer, "Contribution of Qumran Aramaic." This article is reprinted in Fitzmyer, *Wandering Aramean*, 90–93, with additional discussion (not in the original publication) on 102–7. For some reason, Baigent and Leigh, *Dead Sea Scrolls Deception*, 66, talk about a 1990 leak of this text, unaware that it had been available in the Fitzmyer publication since 1974. It has now been fully published in a detailed study by Puech, "Fragment d'une apocalypse." A discussion of the various interpretations is available in García Martínez, *Qumran and Apocalyptic*, 162–79, whose own view (178–79) is that the Son of God is identified with Michael, Melchizedek, or the Prince of Light, who will unleash the war of the End of Days. See also Flusser, *Judaism and the Origins of Christianity*, 207–13, and the short discussion by Vermes, "Qumran Forum Miscellanea I," 301–3.

PAGE 344

War Rule—The debate about this text was first joined in the press and then in several articles in *BAR*: Vermes, "'Pierced Messiah' Text—An Interpretation Evaporates"; Tabor, "A Pierced or Piercing Messiah?"; Wise and Tabor, "Messiah at Qumran"; and Eisenman and Vermes (writing separately), "More on the Pierced Messiah from Eisenman and Vermes." Vermes, "Oxford Forum for Qumran Research: Seminar on the Rule of War from Cave 4 (4Q285)," decisively proved that there was no mention of a pierced messiah in the text. The same view is conclusively proven in Abegg, "Messianic Hope." The full text, which was published based on the readings of Milik by Wacholder and Abegg, *Preliminary Edition*, 2:223–27, can only be a document closely related to the *War Scroll*, hence the name *War Rule*. Part of the text is paralleled by a manuscript from cave 11 published by van der Woude "Ein neuer Segensspruch." Small fragments had been published in Milik, "*Milkî-ṣedeq* et *Milkî-reša'*," 143. Eisenman and Wise, *Dead Sea Scrolls Uncovered*, 24–27, seems to back away somewhat from the exaggerated claims reported in the press.

PAGE 346

Pesher Isaiah A—See notes to chapter 14. For our passage, see the commentary by Horgan, *Pesharim*, 83–4 and 85–86.

PAGE 347

Messianic Apocalypse—This text was first published by Eisenman, "Messianic Vision," and again in Eisenman and Wise, 19–23, who take the incorrect view that this text attributes the resurrection to the messiah. A thorough, scholarly edition was then published by Puech, "Une Apocalypse messianique." Cf. also Vermes, "Qumran Forum Miscellanea I," 303–4. See also Collins, "Works of the Messiah." For the general background, see Nickelsburg, *Resurrection*, which was written before direct allusions to resurrection in the scrolls corpus were known.

CHAPTER 22

PAGE 351

Jewish Mysticism—On early Jewish mysticism, see Scholem, *Major Trends*, 40–79, and *Jewish Gnosticism*; Gruenwald, *Apocalyptic and Merkavah Mysticism*; and Schäfer, *Hidden and Manifest God*. In *Major Trends*, 3–10, Scholem tackles the difficult task of defining Jewish mysticism. This debate will probably never be concluded. Hesitation about calling nonexperiential materials such as those discussed here "mystical" is voiced in Wolfson, "Mysticism and the Poetic-Liturgical Compositions." Scholem, *Jewish Gnosticism*, 3–4 and 128, already pointed to the relevance of the Dead Sea Scrolls to the study of early Jewish mysticism. A more detailed presentation of much of the material in this chapter appears in Schiffman, "Sifrut ha-Hekhalot."

Magic—On Jewish magic, see Schiffman and Swartz, *Hebrew and Aramaic Magical Texts*, 1–62. Early magical materials are published ibid., 64–164, and in Naveh and Shaked, *Amulets and Magic Bowls* and *Magic Spells and Formulae*. These materials reflect the Jewish magical traditions of the late Talmudic and early medieval periods, but they have much in common with late antique traditions such as those preserved in Margaliot, *Sefer Ha-Razim*.

PAGE 353

Divine Throne—On Enoch, see notes to chapter 11. On Ben Sira, see notes to chapter 12.

PAGE 355

Songs of the Sabbath Sacrifice—Excerpts of this text were first published in Strugnell, "Angelic Liturgy." Based on this, Schiffman, "Merkavah Speculation," showed the close links between this text and the motifs and language of the Hekhalot texts. The same was shown by Baumgarten, "Qumran Sabbath Shirot." The entire corpus of manuscripts of this text, including the Masada manuscript, was published by Newsom, *Songs of the Sabbath Sacrifice*. (See Qimron, "Review Article of *Songs of the Sabbath Sacrifice*.") The Masada fragment had originally been published in Newsom and Yadin, "Masada Fragment," which argued that the presence of this text at Masada indicated that members of the sect had fled there after Qumran was destroyed. Earlier, we reject this view. Roth, "Qumran and Masadah," in connection with his Zealot identification of the Qumran sect, also argued for a connection between Qumran and Masada. For other studies on this text, see also Newsom, "He Has Established for Himself Priests" and "Merkabah Exegesis"; Allison, "Silence of Angels"; Carmignac, "Roi, royauté et royaume"; Maier, "Shîrê 'Olat hash-Shabbat"; and Segert, "Observations on the Poetic Structures."

PAGE 359

Psalms Scroll—See notes to chapter 10.

PAGE 360

Angelic Hosts—On the *War Scroll*, see notes to chapter 20. On the angels, see Yadin, *Scroll of the War*, 229–42, and Ringgren, *Faith of Qumran*, 81–93 (which discusses also evil spirits). Schiffman, *Eschatological Community*, 49–51, discusses the presence of the angels in the eschatological war and assembly.

PAGE 362

Physiognomy and Chiromancy—See Scholem, "Hakkarat Panim," and Gruenwald, "Qeta'im Ḥadashim." On *toldot*, see Scholem, "Hakkarat Panim," 477–79. The *Horoscope*, first published in Allegro, *DJD* 6:88–91, must be read with Strugnell, "Notes," 274–76. Cf. also Carmignac, "Les Horoscopes"; Delcor, "Recherches sur un horoscope"; and Licht, "Shoqayim."

Page 363

Elect of God—First published by Starcky, "Un Texte messianique." For discussion, see Fitzmyer, *Essays*, 127–60, which suggests that rather than being messianic, this text should be connected with the birth of Noah, on which see VanderKam, "Birth of Noah." Fitzmyer's detailed commentary, 140–57, is extremely important. García Martínez, *Qumran and Apocalyptic*, 1–44, presents a thorough analysis of the text and concludes that it is part of the lost book of Noah.

Page 364

Songs of the Sage—Baillet, *DJD* 7:215–62; Nitzan, "Hymns from Qumran," 53–63; Baumgarten, "'Al Shire ha-Pega'im"; and Ta-Shma, "He'arot." Other Qumran texts have been understood as exorcisms as well. See Dupont-Sommer, "Exorcismes et guérisons," and Puech, "Les deux derniers Psaumes davidiques."

Chapter 23

Page 371

Jews and Non-Jews—It seems most likely that there was already a consensus by this time on the definitions of Jewish status, and for that reason, we encounter no argument on this question. See Schiffman, *Who Was a Jew?* 1–39.

Page 372

Non-Jews in the *Zadokite Fragments*—Schiffman, "Legislation." On the "Canaanite Slave," see Schiffman, *Who Was a Jew?* 36–37. On the prohibition of a Jew's being a servant of a non-Jew, see my edition, translation, and commentary, "4QOrdinances[a,b]."

Page 373

Non-Jews in Sabbath Law—Schiffman, *Halakhah at Qumran*, 104–6, 120–21, and 123–24.

Page 374

Words of Moses—Published by Milik, *DJD* 1:91–97. Cf. Strugnell, "Moses-Pseudepigrapha," 245–54. Dimant, "New Light," 413–31, identifies and publishes another Mosaic pseudepigraphon, *Pseudo-Moses*, although we find her view unproven.

Page 375

Prohibitions against Idolatry—See Schiffman, "Laws Pertaining to Idolatry," for a thorough study of these laws.

Page 377

Prohibition on Entering the Sanctuary—See Schiffman, "Exclusion from the Sanctuary," 305.

Burial—Yadin, *Temple Scroll*, 1:322–24, and Schiffman, "Impurity of the Dead," 137–38.

Law of the King—See notes to chapter 16.

PAGE 378

"Hanging"—Yadin, *Temple Scroll*, 1:373–79, and *"Pesher Nahum"*; Baumgarten, *Studies*, 172–82, and "Hanging and Treason"; Bernstein, "Midrash Halakhah" and "Study in Early Jewish Exegesis"; Schiffman, *Sectarian Law*, 76–77 (and additional bibliography, 85, n. 56); and Schwartz, *Studies*, 81–88.

PAGE 383

Proselytes—On rabbinic views of conversion, see Schiffman, *Who Was a Jew?* 19–39. On this passage, cf. Schiffman, *Halakhah at Qumran*, 66.

CHAPTER 24

PAGE 385

Jerusalem of History—For an overview of the history of the city in our period, see Jeremias, *Jerusalem*, and Peters, *Jerusalem*, 42–130.

PAGE 386

Pseudo-Ezekiel—This text was originally called *Second Ezekiel*, and its contents were regarded as including material pertaining to Jeremiah and even Moses as well. The material has now been divided into several texts, on which see Dimant, "New Light," 408–13. For the material relating to Ezekiel, see Strugnell and Dimant, "4Q Second Ezekiel," and Dimant and Strugnell, "Merkabah Vision." See also Kister, "Barnabas 12:1," and Kister and Qimron, "Observations." The wider exegetical context is discussed in Dimant, "Apocalyptic Interpretation of Ezekiel"; Brooke, "Ezekiel in Some Qumran and New Testament Texts"; and García Martínez, "L'Interprétation." Wacholder, "Ezekiel and Ezekielianism," is in our view much exaggerated.

PAGE 389

Israelite Wilderness Camp and the Jerusalem Temple—See Schiffman, "Exclusion from the City," which uses this scheme to explain a variety of laws in the *Temple Scroll*, and "Architecture and Law." Cf. Broshi, "Gigantic Dimensions." David's construction of the Tabernacle at the rock of Zion is the subject of *Rock of Zion*, on which see Puech, "La Pierre de Sion." On the architecture of the Temple, see notes to chapter 16.

PAGE 391

Trumpets—On the role of trumpets in the tactics of the war at the End of Days, see Yadin, *Scroll of the War*, 87–113.

PAGE 392

Apostrophe to Zion—Studies on this poem include Auffret, "Structure," and Delcor, "L'Hymne à Sion."

PAGE 393

New Jerusalem Texts—These texts have been published in various places and have yet to receive the attention they deserve. For a summary of the issues pertaining to this composition, see García Martínez, *Qumran and Apocalyptic*, 180–213, which lists the manuscripts in n. 1, and "Last Surviving Columns." See also Jongeling, "Publication provisoire," and Starcky, "Jerusalem." For the architecture of these texts, see Licht, "Ideal Town Plan"; Broshi, "'Adrikhalut"; and Chyutin, "New Jerusalem." The links with the *Temple Scroll* are discussed in Wise, *Critical Study*, 66–86, which we regard as vastly exaggerated.

CHAPTER 25

PAGE 396

Herodian Rule—On the Herodian period, see Schürer, *History of the Jewish People*, 1:287–329, and Schalit, *Hordos ha-Melekh*, which is a full-length study of Herod and his reign. Also useful, though dated, is the collection of studies edited by Avi-Yonah, *Herodian Period*. Eisenman, *James the Just*, sees much of the invective of the scrolls as directed against Herodians, that is, those closely associated with the king and his family. Eisenman, of course, dates these compositions later than we do. He collects what he sees as Herodian parallels on 87–94. In our view, the parallels he finds result from the Herodians' continuation of the very same kind of Hellenizing behavior in which the later Hasmonaeans indulged.

Procurators—On the period of procuratorial rule see Schürer, *History of the Jewish People*, 1:357–98 and 455–70.

Rebellion against Rome—On the Great Revolt of 66–73 C.E., see Schürer, *History of the Jewish People*, 1:484–513; Rhoads, *Israel in Revolution*; Goodman, "First Jewish Revolt" and *Ruling Class*; and Smallwood, *Jews under Roman Rule*, 293–330. An important collection of studies that helps to illuminate the background of the revolt is Kasher, *Ha-Mered ha-Gadol*. On the aftermath of the revolt and its effects on the history of Judaism, see Schiffman, *From Text to Tradition*, 161–70.

PAGE 397

Josephus on Essene Participation in the Revolt—John the Essene was one of the revolutionary generals according to *War* 2, 567. *War* 2, 152–53, speaks of the torture of Essenes during the war, which in our view indicates that they were participants. For a somewhat different view, see Rhoads, *Israel in Revolution*, 156, which discusses the relation of the Qumran sect to the revolt on 156–58.

Destruction of Qumran—De Vaux, *Archaeology*, 38–43. The subsequent Roman occupation, known as period III, is discussed on 41–44.

Copper Scroll—See notes to chapter 1. On the values, see Lefkovits, *Copper Scroll—3Q15*, 1:34–44 and 2:1055–99, and Harper, "Too Much to Believe?" The suggestion that these funds were collected after the destruction was made by Lehmann, "Identification of the Copper Scroll" and "Where the Temple Tax Was Buried." See also McCarter, "Mystery."

PAGE 399

Masada—See notes to chapter 1. Josephus's story of the Roman conquest of Masada is related in *War* 7, 275–406. Cf. Netzer, "Last Days and Hours at Masada," and Magness, "Arms and the Man."

PAGE 400

Synagogue and Ritual Baths—For the ritual baths, see Yadin, *Masada*, 164–67, and a technical description in Netzer, *Masada*, 3:14–17 and 507–10. On the synagogue, see Yadin, *Masada*, 180–85, and Netzer, *Masada*, 3:402–13 (and the photograph of the entire area on 389).

Scrolls—For a list of the published scrolls from Masada, see notes to chapters 1 and 10. Other written materials were found at Masada as well. Yadin, Naveh, and Meshorer, *Masada*, 1:12–81, provide an edition by Yadin and Naveh of Aramaic and Hebrew ostraca and jar inscriptions. Cotton and Geiger, *Masada*, 2:27–221, provide Latin and Greek documents left by the Romans who occupied the site after it fell in 73 C.E.

PAGE 404

Scrolls and Christianity—Cross, *Ancient Library*, 195–243; LaSor, *Dead Sea Scrolls and the New Testament*, 142–264; Fitzmyer, "Qumran Scrolls and the New Testament"; VanderKam, "Dead Sea Scrolls and Christianity"; Charlesworth, *Jesus within Judaism*, 54–75; Yadin, "Dead Sea Scrolls and the Epistle to the Hebrews"; Filson, "Dead Sea Scrolls and the New Testament"; Kuhn, "Impact of the Qumran Scrolls"; García Martínez, "Les Limites de la communauté"; Lichtenberger, "Dead Sea Scrolls and John the Baptist"; Stegemann, "Some Aspects of Eschatology"; and Schwartz, "Qumran ben Kohaniut la-Nasrut." Important collections of studies are Black, *Scrolls and Christianity*; Stendahl, *Scrolls and the New Testament*; Murphy-O'Connor and Charlesworth, *Paul and the Dead Sea Scrolls*; and Charlesworth, *John and the Dead Sea Scrolls*. Many of the essays by Flusser on this topic are collected in *Judaism and the Origins of Christianity*, 3–225. See also his "Sons of Light." Numerous important studies by Fitzmyer are collected in *Essays* and *Wandering Aramaean*. A summary is provided by Cook, *Solving the Mysteries*, 152–77. On parallels to the Beatitudes, see Puech, "4Q525 et les péricopes de béatitudes" and "Un Hymne essénien," and Viviano, "Beatitudes Found among Dead Sea Scrolls." All of the foregoing, even those that exaggerate similarities, are to be distinguished from attempts to identify the scrolls as Christian. The claim that there are Greek New Testament texts in the Qumran corpus has been made by O'Callaghan, "Papiros neotestimentarios," but he has been thoroughly disproven. See the discussion in Cook, *Solving the Mysteries*, 145–48, and the extremely learned attempt to defend the claim of O'Callaghan by Thiede, *Earliest Gospel Manuscript?*

PAGE 405

Bar Kokhba Revolt—Schürer, *History of the Jewish People*, 1:534–57; Smallwood, *Jews under Roman Rule*, 428–66, and Abramsky, *Bar Kokhba*. An important collection of studies on the revolt is Oppenheimer, *Mered Bar-Kokhba*.

Bar Kokhba Documents—Benoit and Milik, *DJD* 2:67–280 (including biblical material as well); Yadin, "New Discoveries," "More on the Letters," and *Bar-Kokhba*, 113–39, 172–83, and 222–53; Aharoni, *Judean Desert Caves 1960*, 21–24; Yadin, ibid., 40–52; Lifshitz, ibid., 53–62; Lifshitz, *Judean Desert Caves 1961*, 201–7 and 235–57; Polotsky, ibid., 258–62; Lewis, Yadin, and Greenfield, *Documents* (publishing the Greek papyri from the Cave of Letters as well as the Aramaic and Nabatean signatures and inscriptions); and Lehmann, "Studies." Quite a number of these texts are still unpublished. For collections of the published Aramaic materials, see Fitzmyer and Harrington, *Manual*,

136–68, and Beyer, *Die aramäischen Texte*, 304–23. Beyer, however, did not make use of the corrections other scholars provided for the editions of Milik. His texts are therefore unreliable.

PAGE 407

Twelve Prophets Scroll from **Murabba'at**—Published by Milik, *DJD* 2:181–205.

Greek Twelve Prophets Scroll from **Nahal Hever**—Published by Tov, *DJD* 8. The subtitle, "The Seiyâl Collection I," is misleading, for the scroll comes from Nahal Hever. Tov, 99–158, discusses the translation technique and the revision of the text to accord with the Masoretic Hebrew version. This treatment is put into wider context in Schiffman, "[Review of] E. Tov, *Greek Minor Prophets Scroll*." See also Puech, "Notes en marge de 8KhXIIgr."

PAGE 409

Judaism of the Mishnah and Talmud—For a survey of the development and content of rabbinic Judaism, see Schiffman, *From Text to Tradition*, 177–265.

GLOSSARY

Aggadah, *adj.* **aggadic** The portion of rabbinic literature and tradition that consists of stories about biblical and rabbinic figures, ethical teachings, or interpretations of Scripture that teach the principles of Jewish thought and theology.

'am ha-'aretz Literally, "people of the land," the term designates the common people in the Land of Israel in Second Temple times who were not members of any specific Jewish sect.

Amidah Hebrew for "the standing (prayer)"; the Eighteen Benedictions, which constituted the core of the rabbinic daily prayer service.

Amoraim, *adj.* **Amoraic** The teachers of the Talmud or Gemara (ca. 200–500 C.E.) whose main activity was interpreting the Mishnah and tannaitic traditions.

apocalyptic Pertaining to a genre of literature that divulges otherworldly secrets about the nature of God and the heavens and the End of Days. Also used to describe the immediate messianism that is often part of these texts.

Apocrypha Technically, the books found in the Septuagint Greek Bible but not in the canon of the Hebrew Bible. More loosely, the term refers to pseudobiblical books composed in the Second Temple period.

Aramaic A northwestern Semitic language used throughout the Near East in late antiquity, in which many important Jewish texts were composed.

Asherah, *pl.* **Asherot** A Canaanite goddess often worshiped in the form of a fertility statue. Asherah is often represented as the consort of the god Baal.

Bar Kokhba Literally, "Son of the Star," it is the designation of Simeon bar Kosiba, who led the second Jewish revolt against Rome in 132–135 C.E.

Bar Kokhba Revolt The second revolt of the Jews of the Land of Israel against Rome, which took place in 132–135 C.E.

berakhah Hebrew for "blessing" or "benediction," usually referring to specific prayer texts.

bet midrash Literally, "house of study," the term refers to a building set aside for the study of the Torah in rabbinic circles.

Boethusians A sect of Jews closely linked to the Sadducees in their ideology and interpretation of Jewish law.

Canaanite slave A non-Jewish servant who is in the process of conversion to Judaism.

canon The authoritative corpus of Holy Scriptures.

canonization The process by which the contents of the Holy Scriptures, and, specifically, each of the sections of the Hebrew Bible, were closed and determined to be authoritative.

chiromancy A type of divination involving foretelling a person's future or determining one's nature based on either the lines in the palm or other features of the hand.

corpus, *pl.* corpora Referring to a body of texts or manuscripts that have been grouped together, either in antiquity or by modern scholars.

diadochi The successors to Alexander the Great, referring to his generals who split up his kingdom after his death in 323 B.C.E.

Diaspora Greek for "dispersion," referring to the Jewish population outside the Land of Israel.

doreshe halaqot Literally, "those who seek smooth things," this refers to "interpreters of false laws." It was used by the Dead Sea sect to describe the Pharisees who derived by midrashic interpretation laws that the sect believed were invalid.

End of Days A biblical term that later Jewish tradition understood to refer to the messianic era.

eruv A rabbinic legal institution that allows the extension of the immediate home area for purposes of walking beyond the Sabbath limits of the town or of carrying outside one's house on the Sabbath.

eschatology Doctrines concerning the End of Days or the messianic era.

Essenes A sect of Jews distinguished by its withdrawal from the mainstream of society, its piety, and its ascetic ideals. Many scholars identify this group with the sect of the Dead Sea Scrolls.

exegesis, *adj.* exegetical Interpretation, used in this book primarily to refer to interpretation of the Bible.

First Temple The Jerusalem Temple erected by Solomon ca. 960 B.C.E., which was destroyed by the Babylonians in 586 B.C.E.

genizah A storeroom for old Hebrew books no longer used for holy purposes. The famous Cairo *genizah* yielded up a treasure of manuscripts of Second Temple, rabbinic, and medieval texts.

Gnosticism A variety of religious movements of the first centuries C.E. that offered salvation from material existence through knowledge (Greek *gnosis* = "knowledge").

Great Revolt The revolt of the Jews of the Land of Israel against Rome in 66–73 C.E.

halakhah, *pl.* **halakhot,** *adj.* **halakhic** A Hebrew designation for Jewish law.

Hasidim Hebrew for "pious ones," a loosely organized group of pietists known from the Maccabean period through Mishnaic times.

Hasmonaean Pertaining to the dynasty of Maccabean descendants and the period of their rule (152–63 B.C.E.).

haverim Literally, "associates," the term used in rabbinic sources to designate Jews who observe the strict laws of ritual purity and tithing.

havurah, *pl.* **havurot** Groups of Jews who, according to rabbinic sources, banded together to foster the observance of strict rules of ritual purity and tithing and who occasionally held communal meals.

Hekhalot literature A group of texts that collect the traditions of early Jewish mysticism, emphasizing speculation about the nature of God's heavenly throne. The Hebrew term *hekhalot* refers to God's heavenly palaces.

Hellenism The amalgamation of the Greek and native Near Eastern cultures that swept over the entire Near East in the wake of Alexander the Great's conquest.

hermeneutic Pertaining to a system of interpretation. This term often refers to specific rules for interpretation of biblical text.

Jubilee The last year in a cycle of fifty. The Jubilee is preceded by seven units of seven years, each culminating in a Sabbatical year.

Karaism, *adj.* **Karaite** A movement in medieval Judaism that rejected the authority of the rabbinic tradition. The Karaites claimed instead to base themselves entirely on interpretation of the written Torah.

Kedushah Literally, "sanctification," the term designates a rabbinic prayer in which Isaiah 6:3 ("Holy, holy, holy! The Lord of Hosts!") figures prominently.

Khirbeh Arabic for "ruin." The term is often used in place-names in which Arabic usage preserves the name of a place that has been destroyed.

Kittim A place-name in the Aegean Islands, perhaps Kition in Cyprus, that in Dead Sea Scrolls texts serves as a code word for "Romans."

late antiquity The period between the rise of Alexander the Great (ca. 330 B.C.E.) and the Moslem conquest (ca. 638 C.E.).

Maccabean Revolt The revolt of the Jews led by the Maccabean family against the Seleucid rulers of Syria in 168–164 B.C.E. The victory of the Jews is celebrated on the holiday of Hanukkah.

Maccabees The family of Judah the Maccabee. The term is often used imprecisely to designate later members of the Hasmonaean dynasty as well.

mamzer, *pl.* **mamzerim** The Jewish offspring of a forbidden marriage, that is, the offspring of an incestuous or adulterous union. A *mamzer* is disqualified from marriage with free, native-born Jews.

Manichaeanism A dualistic religious system, founded in Mesopotamia by Mani in the third century C.E. It combines elements of Gnostic Christianity with Eastern religions, yielding a doctrine based on the conflict of light and darkness.

Masada A site on the western shore of the Dead Sea, the destruction of which brought to an end the Jewish revolt against Rome of 66–73 C.E.

mashiah Literally, "anointed," this Hebrew word has given rise to the English "messiah." The word derives from the fact that kings and priests in ancient Israel were anointed as a sign of God's confirmation of their appointment and of His attendant blessing.

maskil A person well schooled in the doctrines of the Qumran sect who was expected both to communicate those doctrines to fellow sectarians and to exemplify the sectarian way of life.

Masoretic Text The traditional, received Hebrew text of the Bible, which has been considered authoritative by Jews from mishnaic times until the present. The term derives from Hebrew *mesorah*, "tradition."

Men of the Great Assembly The sages who, according to rabbinic tradition, played a prominent role in the spiritual leadership of the people of Israel in the Persian and early Hellenistic periods.

Merkavah **mysticism** A form of early Jewish mysticism that emphasized speculation about the nature of God's heavenly throne (Hebrew *merkavah*, lit. "chariot" = divine throne).

messianism The belief that a messiah will come to bring redemption to the world in the End of Days.

mevaqqer The sectarian "examiner," an official who supervised the day-to-day life of the Dead Sea sect and kept its legal and financial records.

mezuzah, *pl.* **mezuzot** A manuscript of specific biblical verses—affirming God's sovereignty over the world and the obligation to observe His law—that is affixed to the doorpost of a Jewish home in accord with the command of the Torah.

Midrash, *adj.* **midrashic** A Hebrew term for the method of biblical interpretation that was current in rabbinic times and earlier. The term can also designate a collection of such interpretations produced by the rabbis.

mikveh, pl. *mikva'ot* A ritual bath that may be used to fulfill the Jewish requirement of immersion after contraction of ritual impurity.

minyan A quorum of ten adult male Jews (over the age of Bar Mitzvah), which makes possible the recitation of certain public prayers according to talmudic law.

Mishmarot The twenty-four courses into which the Jewish priests were divided. The courses were the subject of various Qumran texts that, while setting out the schedule for officiating in the Temple, set forth the solar calendar proposed by the sect and related groups.

Mishnah, *adj.* **mishnaic** The great collection of early rabbinic law edited by Rabbi Judah the Prince, ca. 200 C.E. The term can also designate a particular paragraph of that code.

Musaf An additional service recited on Sabbaths and Festivals in commemoration of the additional sacrifice that was offered on those days in the Jerusalem Temple.

Nezikin Literally, "damages," this Hebrew term refers to an order (section) of the Mishnah and Talmud dealing with damages, property law, other matters of civil law, and courts and testimony.

nigleh A term used by the sectarians to refer to the "revealed" law, which was clearly stated in the Torah for all Jews to follow.

nistar A term used by the sectarians to refer to the "hidden" law, which was known only to the sect and which resulted from sectaries' divinely inspired biblical study sessions.

numismatic Pertaining to coins and coinage. Numismatic evidence is often used to date archaeological finds.

oral law A second Torah (law), consisting of interpretations of the written Torah, which was studied and passed down by oral tradition. In rabbinic Judaism, this oral Torah, believed to have been given by God at Sinai along with the written Torah, constitutes the authoritative interpretation of the written law.

ostracon, *pl.* **ostraca** A piece of broken pottery (a potsherd) used in antiquity for the writing of short texts or quick notes.

paleography The study of the shapes of letters and their history, usually to facilitate the dating of inscriptions and manuscripts.

paqid A priestly official of the Dead Sea sect.

Passover A Jewish springtime Festival commemorating the Exodus of the Jews from Egyptian bondage in biblical times. It is celebrated with the eating of matzah—unleavened bread.

Pentateuch The first five books of the Bible, also termed the Torah, or the Five Books of Moses.

peshat The plain or simple meaning of the biblical text, as opposed to midrashic or aggadic interpretation, which may add layers of meaning not immediately apparent.

pesher, *pl.* **pesharim** The unique biblical interpretations and commentaries of the Dead Sea sect, which understood the words of the biblical prophets as referring to the experiences of sectarians in the Second Temple period.

Pharisees A group of Jews in Second Temple times who constituted the spiritual forebears of the talmudic rabbis. Led by lay teachers of the Torah, they became the dominant sect. The word derives from Hebrew *perushim,* "separate."

phylacteries Cubical compartments of leather that contain biblical passages emphasizing God's sovereignty and the obligation of the Jew to observe His commandments, which are affixed to the head and arm with leather thongs. They are known in Hebrew as tefillin.

physiognomy A type of divination that involves foretelling a person's future or determining one's nature based on the form or features of the body or, more specifically, the face.

proselyte A non-Jew who formally converts to Judaism.

pseudepigrapha, *adj.* **pseudepigraphic** Literally, referring to books written in the Hellenistic age in the name of an ancient biblical figure. More generally, the term is used to designate much of the religious literature of the various groups within Second Temple Judaism.

Ptolemies The rulers of Egypt and its empire in the Hellenistic era. This dynasty took its name from Ptolemy, the general of Alexander the Great who retained control of Egypt after Alexander's death.

Qumran A site on the western shore of the Dead Sea. The Dead Sea Scrolls were uncovered in nearby caves. Qumran itself preserves the ruins of a building complex, which served as the headquarters of the sect in the Second Temple period.

rabbi Hebrew for "my master, my teacher," referring to the teachers and judges of the Jews of Palestine in the Roman and Byzantine periods. The rabbis who shaped the texts of talmudic Judaism are collectively termed "the Rabbis."

rabbinic consensus The consensus reached by the Jewish people in the aftermath of the destruction of the Second Temple in 70 C.E., when the Jews unified around the Rabbis who taught the approach of the Pharisees. That consensus eventually resulted in the editing of the Mishnah ca. 200 C.E.

raz Hebrew for "mystery," referring to the mysteries of creation and the history of the universe. Such secrets could be understood, in the view of the Qumran sect, only with the help of divine guidance.

revelation The process by which God is believed to have revealed His will to the people of Israel and the world.

Rosh Hashanah The Jewish New Year Festival, which is observed in the fall. In postbiblical Judaism, it is a time for celebration of God's kingship and for introspection and repentance.

Sabbatical The designation for every seventh year, in which the Bible commands the remission of debts and prescribes leaving the land fallow.

Sadducees A sect of Second Temple period Jews, connected primarily with the priestly aristocracy, which accepted only the authority of teachings based strictly on the Bible and its interpretation. The word derives from the name "Zadok," the high priest in the time of King Solomon.

Samaritans A mixed people inhabiting certain parts of the Land of Israel, descended from those original northern Israelites who were not exiled in 722 B.C.E. and the tribes introduced into the area by the Assyrians.

Sanhedrin The highest court or council of the Jews in the last years of the Second Temple.

ṣaraʿat A disease of the skin that is normally mistranslated in English Bibles as "leprosy." (Leprosy is a disease with much more permanent and more serious symptoms.)

Second Commonwealth   The political organization of the Jewish people in the Land of Israel beginning with the return from exile in the sixth century B.C.E. and ending with the final dismantling of the Herodian dynasty in the first century C.E.

Second Temple   The Jerusalem Temple that was in use from 522 B.C.E. until its destruction by the Romans in 70 C.E. The term can also designate the period during which this Temple stood.

sect, *adj.* **sectarian.**   The terms designate the various groups of Jews and their particular approaches to Judaism in Second Temple times. Such usage does not imply that any one of the groups is to be considered a mainstream.

Seleucids   The dynasty that ruled Syria in Hellenistic times, tracing itself back to Seleucus, a general of Alexander the Great.

Septuagint   The Greek translation of the Bible produced in Egypt in the Hellenistic period.

serekh, *pl.* ***serakhim***   A list of laws or regulations compiled by the Dead Sea sect as part of its regular formal study sessions.

Shavuot   The Jewish holiday of Pentecost, which in biblical times was connected with the offering of the first fruits of the wheat harvest. Later, Shavuot came to commemorate the giving of the Torah at Sinai as well.

Shema   The Jewish prayer consisting of various passages from the Torah, recited morning and night, proclaiming acceptance of God's kingdom and His commandments.

Shemoneh Esreh   The "eighteen" benedictions (now actually nineteen) that constitute the central prayer in Jewish services. Known also as the *Amidah.*

Sicarii   A group of revolutionaries against Rome in first-century C.E. Palestine known for the dagger (Latin *sica*) they carried.

soferim   Hebrew for "scribes," referring to the early Pharisaic sages.

Sukkah   Literally, "booth," this term designates the temporary shelter Jews erect in observance of the fall Festival of Sukkot.

Sukkot   The Jewish holiday of Tabernacles, which is connected with the fall harvest and which also commemorates both the Exodus from Egypt and God's protection of the people of Israel during the period of their wandering in the desert.

synagogue   A Jewish house of worship. In Hellenistic usage, the term also referred to a Jewish community.

Tahanun   A rabbinic supplication recited in Jewish services daily, except on Sabbaths, Festivals, and other special occasions. A special longer version is recited on Mondays and Thursdays, since these are understood to be days of divine favor.

Talmud, *adj.* **talmudic**   Referring to the Mishnah and Gemara, the literary results of the rabbinic discussions of Jewish law and tradition. Talmudic Judaism is that defined by the rabbis in the first two centuries C.E. and further expounded until the end of the fifth century.

Tannaim, *adj.* **tannaitic** The teachers of the Mishnah, Tosefta, and halakhic Midrashim who flourished ca. 50 B.C.E.–200 C.E.

Targum Aramaic translations of the Hebrew biblical books.

Teacher of Righteousness A sectarian leader who was apparently active soon after the founding of the Dead Sea sect. It is possible there was a series of teachers who filled this role.

tefillin Cubical compartments of leather that contain biblical passages emphasizing God's sovereignty and the obligation of the Jew to observe His commandments, which are affixed to the head and arm with leather thongs. They are also known as phylacteries.

terumah A grain offering of one-fiftieth, given to the priests according to the Torah's legislation.

tetragrammaton The four-lettered name of God, YHVH. Already in Late Antiquity this name was not pronounced because of the great reverence in which it was held. It was therefore also called *the ineffable name.*

Torah The Five Books of Moses, the Pentateuch. The Hebrew word "torah" literally means "instruction, teaching."

Tosefta A collection of early rabbinic traditions that were not included in the Mishnah. The Tosefta is the earliest commentary to the Mishnah and is organized in approximately the same manner.

Urtext A German word meaning "original text" that scholars use to designate the original text of a biblical book as it existed immediately after composition and editing.

Vorlage A German word designating the Hebrew text that "lay before" an ancient copyist or translator of the Bible or an author who composed a text adapted from biblical material.

Wicked Priest A Hasmonaean priestly leader seen by the sect as its arch enemy. This priest apparently came to Qumran, where he had a confrontation with the Teacher of Righteousness.

wisdom literature A genre of literature known throughout the ancient Near East, that preaches common sense wisdom and values designed to result in a happier and more just life.

Yom Kippur The Day of Atonement, held in the fall ten days after the Jewish New Year. In postbiblical tradition, the theme of the day is human repentance, which leads to divine forgiveness.

Zadok, *adj.* **Zadokite** Zadok was one of the high priests of King Solomon in the tenth century B.C.E. His Zadokite priestly line dominated the high priesthood for most of Jewish history.

Zoroastrianism An Iranian religion supposedly founded ca. 600 B.C.E. Zoroastrianism is dualistic, believing in a struggle between the cosmic forces of good and evil.

GUIDE TO
DEAD SEA SCROLLS
TEXTS CITED

Introductory Note: The list that follows is intended to provide readers access to the original texts quoted or cited in this book. In no way should this be seen as a list of all the Dead Sea Scrolls—some of these texts may have been published in their entirety; others may be partially published, unpublished, or published in editions of poor quality.

Some scholars have raised serious questions about some of the unauthorized editions published as part of the movement to "liberate" the scrolls. These editions made available texts previously entrusted for publication only to members of the official editorial team. The editions of Wacholder and Abegg, *Preliminary Edition*, 1–2, acknowledged the work of these editors and their dependency on the *Preliminary Concordance*. A public debate ensued about the work of Eisenman and Wise, *Dead Sea Scrolls Uncovered*, since many scholars were of the opinion that the editions in that book, which had been prepared by Wise, made use of the work of other scholars without giving sufficient credit. Despite profound reservations, whenever these works provide the only available editions or English translations of texts that are discussed in this book, they are cited here.

These editions and translations must be regarded as extremely preliminary. Further, the editions and translations of Allegro cited here can only be used with the corrections of Strugnell, "Notes en marge." Readers have only to look at the various editions and translations to see that many scholarly diagreements exist— and probably always will exist—about the meaning of the texts.

For each Qumran text quoted or cited in this book, I attempt to list here the best available edition of the original text in Hebrew, Aramaic, or Greek and a translation into English, French, or Spanish. Where only partial translations are available in English, I refer also to a full translation into another language. Readers should be aware that to avoid confusing titles, I often had to modify the official titles used for these texts. For this reason, in using other translations, some of which will appear soon after this book, the official numbers of these texts should be noted and these should be used when necessary to be certain that the correct text has been located. Qumran scroll numbers are based on cave numbers, e.g., 1Q = cave 1 and so forth. As in the Reference Notes, all references are by short title. Full information is available in the bibliography.

✺

Admonition Based on the Flood (4Q370) Hebrew and English: Newsom, "4Q370: An Admonition Based on the Flood," 23–41.

Angelic Liturgy See *Songs of the Sabbath Sacrifice.*

Aramaic Apocalypse (4Q246) Aramaic and French: Puech, "Fragment d'une apocalypse," 106–109; Aramaic and English: Eisenman and Wise, *Dead Sea Scrolls Uncovered*, 70–71.

Aramaic Levi Document (1Q21) Aramaic and English: Fitzmyer and Harrington, *Manual of Palestinian Aramaic Texts*, 80–89.

Aramaic Levi Document A (4Q213) Partial Aramaic and English: Stone and Greenfield, "Prayer of Levi," 255–60; Aramaic and English: Eisenman and Wise, *Dead Sea Scrolls Uncovered*, 137–41.

Aramaic Levi Document B (4Q214) Aramaic and English: Eisenman and Wise, *Dead Sea Scrolls Uncovered*, 139–41.

Aramaic Levi Document D (4Q541) Aramaic and French: Puech, "Fragments d'un apocryphe de Lévi," 454–79.

Aramaic Messiah See *Elect of God.*

Ben Sira Scroll Hebrew and English: Yadin, *Ben Sira Scroll*, 12–49.

Blessings (11Q14) Hebrew and German: van der Woude, "Einer neuer Segensspruch aus Qumran," 253–8.

Book of Mysteries (1Q27) Hebrew and French: Milik, *DJD* 1:102–7; Partial English: Vermes, *Dead Sea Scrolls*, 239. See also *Mysteries A–C.*

Catena A (4Q177) Hebrew and German: Steudel, *Der Midrasch zur Eschatologie*, 71–80; Hebrew and English: Allegro, *DJD* 5:67–73.

Consolations (4Q176) Hebrew: Allegro, *DJD* 5:60–67; Spanish: García Martínez, *Textos de Qumrán*, 258–60; partial English: Vermes, *Dead Sea Scrolls*, 302.

Copper Scroll (3Q15) Hebrew and French: Milik, *DJD* 3:284–99; English: Allegro, *Treasure of the Copper Scroll*, 33–55.

Daily Prayers (4Q503) Hebrew and French: Baillet, *DJD* 7:105–36; Partial English: Vermes, *Dead Sea Scrolls*, 234.

Damascus Document See *Zadokite Fragments*

David Apocryphon (?) (4Q373) Hebrew and English: Schuller, "Preliminary Study of 4Q373," 515–30.

Decrees of Reproof (4Q477) Hebrew and English: Eshel, "4Q477: The Rebukes of an Overseer," 112–4.

Elect of God (4Q534) Aramaic and English: García Martínez, *Qumran and Apocalyptic*, 3–5.

Enoch A–C (4Q201, 202, 204) Aramaic and English: Milik, *Books of Enoch*, 141–78, 184–217.

Exposition on the Patriarchs (4Q464) Hebrew and English: Stone and Eshel, "Exposition on the Patriarchs," 243–64.

Ezekiel Scroll (11Q4) Partial Hebrew (unopened scroll): Brownlee, "Scroll of Ezekiel," 14–16.

Florilegium (4Q174) Hebrew and English: Brooke, *Exegesis at Qumran*, 86–97.

Fragment Mentioning Zedekiah (4Q470) Hebrew and English: Larson, Schiffman and Strugnell, "4Q470 with a Fragment Mentioning Zedekiah."

Genesis Apocryphon (1Q20) Aramaic and English: Fitzmyer, *Genesis Apocryphon*, 48–75.

Genesis Commentary (4Q252) Hebrew: Wacholder and Abegg, *Preliminary Edition*, 2:212–5; partial Hebrew and English: Allegro, "Further Messianic References," 174–6; Lim, "Chronology of the Flood Story," 289–91.

Giants (1Q23) Aramaic and English: Fitzmyer and Harrington, *Manual of Palestinian Jewish Aramaic*, 68–72.

Giants (2Q26) Aramaic and English: Fitzmyer and Harrington, *Manual of Palestinian Jewish Aramaic*, 72–3.

Giants (6Q8) Aramaic and English: Fitzmyer and Harrington, *Manual of Palestinian Jewish Aramaic*, 76–9.

Giants A (4Q530) Partial Aramaic and English: Milik, *Books of Enoch*, 311–17.

Giants B (4Q531) Partial Aramaic and English: Fitzmyer and Harrington, *Manual of Palestinian Jewish Aramaic*, 74–77.

Giants C (4Q532) Partial Aramaic and English: Fitzmyer and Harrington, *Manual of Palestinian Jewish Aramaic*, 76–77.

Greek Twelve Prophets Scroll (8ḤevXIIgr) Greek: Tov, *DJD* 8:28–78.

Halakhic Letter (4Q394-399) Hebrew and English: Strugnell and Qimron, *DJD* 10.

Hodayot See *Thanksgiving Hymns*.

Horoscope (4Q186) Hebrew and English: Allegro, *DJD* 5:88–91; English: Vermes, 306.

Isaiah A (1QIsᵃ) Hebrew: Burrows, *Dead Sea Scrolls of St. Mark's Monastery*, 1:1–54.

Isaiah B (1QIs^b) Hebrew: Sukenik, *Dead Sea Scrolls of the Hebrew University*, 1–15.

Jeremiah (2Q13) Hebrew: Baillet, *DJD* 3:62–69.

Jeremiah A (4Q70) Hebrew: Tov, "Jeremiah Scrolls from Qumran," 196, plate III.

Jeremiah B (4Q71) Hebrew: Tov, "Jeremiah Scrolls from Qumran," 192, plate I; Tov, to appear in *RQ* 16.

Jeremiah C (4Q72) Hebrew: Tov, "4QJer^c (4Q72)," 248–76 and plates I–VII.

Jeremiah D (4Q71a) Hebrew: Tov, "Jeremiah Scrolls from Qumran," 196, plate III; Tov, to appear in *RQ* 16.

Jeremiah E (4Q71b) Hebrew: Tov, "Jeremiah Scrolls from Qumran," 196, plate III; Tov, to appear in *RQ* 16.

Job Targum (11Q10) Aramaic and English: Sokoloff, *Targum to Job*, 28–103.

Job Targum (4Q157) Aramaic: Milik, *DJD* 6:90; Spanish, García Martínez, *Textos de Qumrán*, 193–4.

Joseph Apocryphon B (4Q372) Hebrew and English: Schuller, "Text about Joseph," 349–76.

Jubilees (1Q17–18) Hebrew and French: Milik, *DJD* 1:82–4.

Jubilees (2Q19–20) Hebrew and French: Baillet, *DJD* 3:77–79.

Jubilees (3Q5) Hebrew and French: Baillet, *DJD* 3:96–8 (mislabeled as a prophetic apocryphon).

Jubilees (11Q12) Hebrew and German: van der Woude, "Fragmente des Buches Jubiläen," 140–46.

Jubilees A (4Q216) Hebrew and English: VanderKam and Milik, "First *Jubilees* Manuscript from Qumran Cave 4," 246–67.

Lament (4Q501) Hebrew and French: Baillet, *DJD* 7:79–80; English: Vermes, 216.

Lamentation (4Q179) Hebrew and English: Allegro, *DJD* 5:75–7.

Leviticus Targum (4Q157) Aramaic: Milik, *DJD* 6:87; Spanish, García Martínez, *Textos de Qumrán*, 193.

Liturgical Prayers See *Prayers for Festivals*.

Manual of Discipline See *Rule of the Community*.

Melchizedek (11Q13) Hebrew and English: Kobelski, *Melchizedek*.

Messianic Apocalypse (4Q521) Hebrew and French: Puech, "Une Apocalypse messianique," 482–513; English: Collins, "Works of the Messiah," 99.

Messianic Aramaic See *Elect of God*.

Mezuzot A–G (4Q149–155) Hebrew: Milik, *DJD* 6:80–85.

Miqṣat Maʿase ha-Torah   See *Halakhic Letter*.

Mishmarot A–H   (4Q320–330) Hebrew: Wacholder and Abegg, *Preliminary Edition*, 1:60–95; partial Spanish: García Martínez, *Textos de Qumrán*, 466–70; partial Hebrew and English: Eisenman and Wise, 109–28.

Mishmarot Bᵃ   (4Q321) Hebrew: Talmon and Knohl, "Qetaʿim shel Megillat Luaḥ mi-Qumran," 507–12.

MMT   See *Halakhic Letter*.

Moses Apocryphon A   (4Q374) Hebrew and English: Newsom, "4Q374: A Discourse," 40–52.

Mysteries   (1Q27) See *Book of Mysteries*.

Mysteries A   (4Q299) Hebrew: Wacholder and Abegg, *Preliminary Edition* 2:1–28; Hebrew and English: Schiffman, "Preliminary Edition of 4QMysteriesᵃ.

Mysteries B   (4Q300) Hebrew: Wacholder and Abegg, *Preliminary Edition* 2:29–34; Hebrew and English: Schiffman, "Preliminary Edition of 4QMysteriesᵇ.

Mysteries C   (4Q301) Hebrew: Wacholder and Abegg, *Preliminary Edition* 2:35–7; Hebrew and English: Schiffman, "Preliminary Edition of 4QMysteriesᶜ.

New Jerusalem A   (1Q32) Aramaic and English, Fitzmyer and Harrington, *Manual of Palestinian Aramaic Texts*, 46–9.

New Jerusalem B   (2Q24) Aramaic and English, Fitzmyer and Harrington, *Manual of Palestinian Aramaic Texts*, 50–54.

New Jerusalem C   (4Q554) Aramaic and English, Eisenman and Wise, *Dead Sea Scrolls Uncovered*, 41–6.

New Jerusalem D   (5Q15) Aramaic and English, Fitzmyer and Harrington, *Manual of Palestinian Aramaic Texts*, 54–64.

New Jerusalem E   (11Q18) Aramaic and English: García Martínez, "Last Surviving Columns of *11QNJ*," 183–92.

Non-Canonical Psalms A–B   (4Q380–381) Hebrew and English: Schuller, *Non-Canonical Psalms*, 61–265.

Ordinances A   (4Q159)   Hebrew and English: Allegro, *DJD* 5:6–9; Schiffman, "4QOrdinancesᵃ'ᵇ"; English: Vermes, *Dead Sea Scrolls*, 298.

Ordinances B   (4Q513) Hebrew and French: Baillet, *DJD* 7:287–95; Hebrew and English: Schiffman, "4QOrdinancesᵃ'ᵇ"; English: Vermes, *Dead Sea Scrolls*, 298.

Ordinances C   (4Q514) Baillet, *DJD* 7:295–8; English: Vermes, *Dead Sea Scrolls*, 298–9.

Paleo-Exodus   (4Q22) Hebrew: Shehan, Ulrich and Sanderson, *DJD* 9:72–130.

Paleo-Leviticus   (11Q1) Hebrew: Freedman and Mathews, *Paleo-Hebrew Leviticus Scroll*, 26–49, 83–88.

Pesher Genesis   See *Genesis Commentary.*

Pesher Habakkuk   (1QpHab) Hebrew: Nitzan, *Megillat Pesher Ḥabakkuk*, 150–98; English: Vermes, *Dead Sea Scrolls,*

Pesher Hosea A   (4Q166) Hebrew: Horgan, *Pesharim*, Texts, 38; English: Horgan, *Pesharim*, 140–41.

Pesher Isaiah B   (4Q162) Hebrew: Horgan, *Pesharim*, Texts, 19–20; English: Horgan, *Pesharim*, 87–9.

Pesher Isaiah A   (4Q161) Hebrew: Horgan, *Pesharim*, Texts, 15–18; English: Horgan, *Pesharim*, 73–6.

Pesher Isaiah B   (4Q162) Hebrew: Horgan, *Pesharim*, Texts, 19–20; English; Horgan, *Pesharim*, 87–9.

Pesher Isaiah C   (4Q163) Hebrew: Horgan, *Pesharim*, Texts, 20–33; English: Horgan, *Pesharim*, 96–106.

Pesher Isaiah D   (4Q164) Hebrew: Horgan, *Pesharim*, Texts, 34; English: Horgan, *Pesharim*, 126.

Pesher Micah   (1Q14) Hebrew: Horgan, *Pesharim*, Texts, 10–12; English: Horgan, *Pesharim*, 56–58.

Pesher Nahum   (4Q169) Hebrew: Horgan, *Pesharim*, Texts, 46–50; English: Horgan, *Pesharim*, 162–6.

Pesher Psalms   (1QpPs) Hebrew: Horgan, *Pesharim*, Texts, 13–15; English: Horgan, *Pesharim*, 65–70.

Pesher Psalms A   (4Q171) Hebrew: Horgan, *Pesharim*, Texts, 51–7; English: Horgan, *Pesharim*, 194–200.

Pesher Psalms B   (4Q172) Hebrew: Horgan, *Pesharim*, Texts, 57; English: Horgan, *Pesharim*, 226–7.

Phylacteries   See *Tefillin.*

Prayer for King Jonathan   (4Q448) Hebrew and English: Eshel, Eshel and Yardeni, "A Qumran Composition Containing Part of Ps. 154 and a Prayer for the Welfare of King Jonathan and His Kingdom," 201.

Prayers for Festivals A   (4Q507) Hebrew and French, Baillet, *DJD*, 7:175–7; partial English: Vermes, *Dead Sea Scrolls*, 232.

Prayers for Festivals B   (4Q508) Hebrew and French, Baillet, *DJD*, 7:177–84; partial English: Vermes, *Dead Sea Scrolls*, 232.

Prayers for Festivals C   (1Q34, 1Q34[bis], 4Q508) Hebrew and French, Milik, *DJD* 1:154–5; Baillet, *DJD*, 7:184–215; partial English: Vermes, *Dead Sea Scrolls*, 231, 233.

Proto-Esther   (4Q550) Aramaic and French: Milik, "Les Modèles araméen du livre d'Esther," 324–63.

Psalms A (4Q83) Hebrew: to appear in Skehan and Ulrich, *DJD* 12.

Psalms B (4Q84) Hebrew: to appear in Skehan and Ulrich, *DJD* 12.

Psalms C (4Q85) Hebrew: to appear in Skehan and Ulrich, *DJD* 12.

Psalms F (4Q88) Partial Hebrew: Starcky, "Psaumes apocryphes," 355–7; to appear in Skehan and Ulrich, *DJD* 12.

Psalms of Joshua A–B (4Q378, 4Q379) Newsom, "Psalms of Joshua," 61–9.

Psalms Scroll (11Q5) Hebrew and English: Sanders, *DJD* 4:19–49; idem, *The Dead Sea Psalms Scroll*, 28–89, 160–65.

Pseudo-Daniel A–C (4Q243–245) Aramaic and English: Fitzmyer and Harrington, *Manual of Palestinian Aramaic Texts*, 4–9.

Pseudo-Daniel D See *Aramaic Apocalypse*.

Pseudo-Ezekiel A (4Q385) Partial Hebrew and English: Strugnell and Dimant, "4QSecond Ezekiel," 45–58; Dimant and Strugnell, "Merkabah Vision in *Second Ezekiel*," 331–48.

Pseudo-Jubilees A (4Q225) Hebrew: Wacholder and Abegg, *Preliminary Edition*, 2:204–6.

Pseudo-Jubilees B (4Q226) Hebrew: Wacholder and Abegg, *Preliminary Edition*, 2:207–10.

Pseudo-Jubilees C (4Q227) Hebrew: Wacholder and Abegg, *Preliminary Edition*, 2:211; Hebrew and English, Eisenman and Wise, *Dead Sea Scrolls Uncovered*, 96–7.

Purification Rituals (4Q512) Hebrew and French: Baillet, *DJD* 7:262–86; partial English: Vermes, *Dead Sea Scrolls*, 238.

Rewritten Pentateuch (4Q364–367) Partial Hebrew: White, "4Q364 & 365"; Partial Spanish: García Martínez, *Textos de Qumrán*, 274–6.

Ritual of Marriage (4Q502) Hebrew and French: Baillet, *DJD* 7:82–105.

Rule of Benedictions (1Q28b) Hebrew: Licht, *Megillat ha-Serakhim*, 277–89; English: Vermes, *Dead Sea Scrolls*, 235–7.

Rule of the Community (1QS) Hebrew: Licht, *Megillat ha-Serakhim*, 59–237; English: Vermes, *Dead Sea Scrolls*, 61–80.

Rule of the Community A–J (4Q255–264) Partial Hebrew: Qimron, "Ketav Yad shel Serekh ha-Yaḥad," 435–6; Vermes, "Preliminary Remarks on Unpublished Fragments," 250–55; Spanish: García Martínez, *Textos de Qumrán*, 66–79.

Rule of the Congregation (1Q28a) Hebrew: Licht, *Megillat ha-Serakhim*, 251–70; English: Vermes, *Dead Sea Scrolls*, 100–102.

Rule Scroll See *Rule of the Community*, *Rule of the Congregation*, and *Rule of Benedictions*.

Samuel A–C (4Q51–53 = 4QSam[a–c]) Hebrew: to be published by Cross and Ulrich in *DJD* 11.

Sapiential Works (4Q410, 412–413, 415–21, 423–426, 476) Hebrew: Wacholder and Abegg, *Preliminary Edition* 2:40–184, 297–8.

Scroll of the War of the Sons of Light Against the Sons of Darkness. See *War Scroll.*

Septuagint Exodus (7Q1) Greek: Baillet, *DJD* 3:142.

Septuagint Letter to Jeremiah (7Q2) Greek: Baillet, *DJD* 3:143.

Septuagint Leviticus A (4Q119) Greek: Skehan, Ulrich and Sanderson, *DJD* 9:162.

Septuagint Leviticus B (4Q120) Greek: Skehan, Ulrich and Sanderson, *DJD* 9:169–86.

Septuagint Numbers (4Q121) Greek: Skehan, Ulrich and Sanderson, *DJD* 9:189–94.

Septuagint Deuteronomy (4Q122) Greek: Skehan, Ulrich and Sanderson, *DJD* 9:195–7.

Serekh-Damascus (4Q265) Eisenman and Wise, *Dead Sea Scrolls Uncovered*, 202–5 (mislabeled as *Halakhah A*).

Songs of the Sabbath Sacrifice (4Q400–407, 11Q17, MasShirShabb) Hebrew and English: Newsom, *Songs of the Sabbath Sacrifice*, 85–387.

Songs of the Sage A–B (4Q510–511) Hebrew and French: Baillet, *DJD* 7:215–62; Vermes, *Dead Sea Scrolls*, 244–7.

Tefillin (XQPhyl 1–4) Hebrew and English: Yadin, *Tefillin from Qumran.*

Tefillin A–U (4Q128–148) Hebrew: Milik, *DJD* 6:48–79.

Temple Scroll (11Q19) Hebrew and English: Yadin, *Temple Scroll*, vol. 2.

Temple Scroll B (11Q20) Hebrew: García Martínez, "*11QTemple[b].*"

Testament of Kohath (4Q542) Aramaic and French: Puech, "Le Testament de Qahat," 33–50; partial Aramaic and English, Cook, "Remarks on the Testament of Kohath," 205–7.

Testament of Levi See *Aramaic Levi Document.*

Testament of Naphtali (4Q215) Eisenman and Wise, *Dead Sea Scrolls Uncovered*, 159–60.

Testimonia (4Q175) Hebrew: Allegro, *DJD* 5:57–8; Vermes, *Dead Sea Scrolls*, 295–6.

Thanksgiving Hymns (1QH) Hebrew: Licht, *Megillat ha-Hodayot*, 57–241; English: Vermes, *Dead Sea Scrolls*, 166–207.

Thanksgiving Hymns A–F (4Q427–432) Hebrew: Wacholder and Abegg, *Preliminary Edition*, 2:254–84; partial Hebrew and English: Schuller, "Hymn from a Cave 4 *Hodayot* Manuscript," 608–12.

Tobit A–D (4Q196–199) Aramaic and English: submitted for publication in *DJD* by Fitzmyer.

Tobit (Hebrew) (4Q200) Hebrew and English: submitted for publication in *DJD* by Fitzmyer.

Twelve Prophets Scroll Hebrew: Milik, *DJD* 2:181–205.

Visions of Amram A–E (4Q543–547) Partial Aramaic and English: Fitzmyer and Harrington, *Manual of Palestinian Aramaic Texts*, 90–97; English: Vermes, *Dead Sea Scrolls*, 262–3.

War Rule (4Q285) Hebrew: Wacholder and Abegg, *Preliminary Edition*, 2:223–7; Spanish: García Martínez, *Textos de Qumrán*, 174–5.

War Scroll (1Q33) Hebrew and English: Yadin, *Scroll of the War*, 256–353; English: Vermes, *Dead Sea Scrolls*, 105–27.

War Scroll (4Q491–496) Hebrew and French: Baillet, *DJD* 7:12–68; partial English: Vermes, *Dead Sea Scrolls*, 125–7.

Wiles of the Wicked Woman (4Q184) Hebrew and English: Allegro, *DJD* 5:82–5; English: Vermes, *Dead Sea Scrolls*, 240–41.

Words of Moses (1Q22) Hebrew and French: Milik, *DJD* 1:91–7; partial English: Vermes, *Dead Sea Scrolls*, 264–5.

Words of the Luminaries A–C (4Q504–506) Hebrew and French: Baillet, *DJD* 7:138–77.

Zadokite Fragments (CD) Hebrew: Qimron, "Text of CDC"; Hebrew and English: Rabin, *Zadokite Documents*, 2–77.

Zadokite Fragments (5Q12) Hebrew and French: Milik, *DJD* 3:181.

Zadokite Fragments (6Q15) Hebrew and French: Baillet, *DJD* 3:128–31.

Zadokite Fragments D^{a-h} (4Q266–273) Hebrew: Wacholder and Abegg, *Preliminary Edition*, 1:1–56; partial Hebrew and English: Baumgarten, "4Q Zadokite Fragments on Skin Disease," 153–8; idem, "Disqualifications of Priests," 506–7; partial Hebrew and French: Milik, "Fragment d'une source du Psautier," 103–5; Spanish: García Martínez, *Textos de Qumrán*, 95–119.

Zodiac (4Q318) Aramaic and English: Eisenman and Wise, *Dead Sea Scrolls Uncovered*, 261–3.

BIBLIOGRAPHY

Abegg, M. G. "Messianic Hope and 4Q285: A Reassessment." *JBL* 113 (1994):81–91.

Abramsky, S. *Bar-Kokhba: Nesi Yisra'el.* Tel Aviv: Massadah, 1961.

Aharoni, Y. "Expedition B." In *Judean Desert Caves: Survey and Excavations, 1960,* 11–24. Jerusalem: Israel Exploration Society, 1961.

Albeck, C. *Das Buch der Jubiläen und die Halacha.* Berlin, 1934.

Albright, W. F. "New Light on Early Recensions of the Hebrew Bible." *BASOR* 140 (1955):27–33.

Alexander, P. S. "Jewish Aramaic Translations of Hebrew Scriptures." In *Mikra: Text, Translation, Reading, and Interpretation of the Hebrew Bible in Ancient Judaism and Early Christianity,* edited by M. J. Mulder with H. Sysling, 217–53. Corpus Rerum Iudaicarum ad Novum Testamentum II.1. Assen/Mastricht and Minneapolis: Van Gorcum, Fortress Press, 1990.

——— "A Note on the Syntax of 4Q448." *JJS* 44 (1993):301–2.

Allegro, J. M. "Addendum to Professor Millar Burrows' Note on the Ascent from Accho in 4QpIsaᵃ." *VT* 7 (1957):183.

———. *The Dead Sea Scrolls.* Harmondsworth: Penguin, 1958.

———. "Fragments of a Qumran Scroll of Eschatological Midrash." *JBL* 77 (1958):350–54.

———. "Further Light on the History of the Qumran Sect." *JBL* 75 (1956):89–95.

———. "Further Messianic References in Qumran Literature." *JBL* 75 (1956):174–77.

———. "More Isaiah Commentaries from Qumran's Fourth Cave." *JBL* 77 (1958):215–21.

———. *Qumrân Cave 4, I (4Q158-4Q186).* In collaboration with A. A. Anderson. Discoveries in the Judaean Desert of Jordan 5. Oxford: Clarendon, 1968.

———. "A Recently Discovered Fragment of a Commentary on Hosea from Qumran's Fourth Cave." *JBL* 78 (1959):142–47.

———. "Some Unpublished Fragments of Pseudepigraphical Literature from Qumran's Fourth Cave." *Annual of the Leeds Oriental Society* 4 (1962–3):1–5.

———. *The Treasure of the Copper Scroll.* Garden City, NY: Doubleday, 1960.

———. "An Unpublished Fragment of Essene Halakhah (4Q Ordinances)." *JSS* 6-7 (1961–62):71–74.

———. "The Wiles of the Wicked Woman." *PEQ* 96 (1964):53–55.

Allison, D. C. "The Silence of Angels: Reflections on the *Songs of the Sabbath Sacrifice.*" *RQ* 13 (1988):189–98.

Amoussine, J. D. "Éphraïm et Manassé dans le Péshèr de Nahum (4Q p Nahum)." *RQ* 4 (1964):389–96.

———. "Observatiunculae Qumranae." *RQ* 28 (1971):533–52.

———. "À Propos de l'interprétation de 4 Q 161 (fragments 5–6 et 8)." *RQ* 8 (1974): 381–92.

Amusin, J. D. "4Q Testimonia, 15–17." In *Hommages à André Dupont-Sommer*, edited by A. Caquot and M. Philonenko, 357–61. Paris: Adrien-Maisonneuve, 1971.

———. "The Reflection of Historical Events of the First Century B.C. in Qumran Commentaries." *HUCA* 48 (1978):123–52.

Anderson, F. I., and D. N. Freedman. "Another Look at 4QSamᵇ." *RQ* 14 (1989):7–30.

Auffret, P. "Structure littéraire de l'Hymne à Sion de 11 Q Psª XXII, 1–15." *RQ* 10 (1980):203–12.

Avi-Yonah, M., ed. *The Herodian Period*, vol. I.7. The World History of the Jewish People. New Brunswick, NJ: Rutgers University Press, 1975.

Avigad, N. "The Palaeography of the Dead Sea Scrolls and Related Documents," edited by C. Rabin and Y. Yadin. In *Aspects of the Dead Sea Scrolls*, 56–87. Scripta Hierosolymitana. Jerusalem: Magnes Press, 1958.

Avigad, N., and Y. Yadin. *A Genesis Apocryphon: A Scroll from the Wilderness of Judaea*. Jerusalem: Magnes and Heikhal Ha-Sefer, 1956.

Baigent, M., and R. Leigh. *The Dead Sea Scrolls Deception*. New York: Summit, 1991.

Baillet, M. "En Recueil liturgique de Qumrân, grotte 4: 'Les Paroles des Luminaires'" *RB* 68 (1961):195–250.

———. "Les Manuscrits de la Règle de la guerre de la grotte 4 de Qumran." *RB* 79 (1972):217–26.

———. "Nouveaux phylactères de Qumran (X Q Phyl 1–4): à propos d'une édition récente." *RQ* 7 (1970):403–16.

———. *Qumrân Grotte 4, III (4Q482-4Q520)*. Discoveries in the Judaean Desert of Jordan 7. Oxford: Clarendon Press, 1982.

———. "Remarques sur l'édition des *Paroles des luminaires*." *RQ* 5 (1964):23–42.

Baillet, M., J. T. Milik, and R. de Vaux. *Les 'Petites Grottes' de Qumran*. Discoveries in the Judaean Desert of Jordan 3. Oxford: Clarendon Press, 1962.

Bar-Adon, P. "Another Settlement of the Judean Desert Sect at 'En El-Ghuweir on the Shores of the Dead Sea." *BASOR* 227 (1977):1–25.

———. "Bissure ha-Hashmona'im u-Ma'amadah shel Qumran bi-Sefon Yam ha-Melah." *Eretz-Israel* 15 (1981):349–52, Plates 64–67.

Barthélemy, D., D. Gooding, J. Lust, and E. Tov. *The Story of David and Goliath: Textual and Literary Criticism*. Orbis biblicus et orientalis 73. Fribourg: Editions Universitaire; Göttingen: Vandenhoeck & Ruprecht, 1986.

Barthélemy, D., and J. T. Milik. *Qumran Cave I*. Discoveries in the Judaean Desert 1. Oxford: Clarendon Press, 1964.

Basser, H. W. "The Rabbinic Citations in Wacholder's *The Dawn of Qumran*." *RQ* 11 (1984):549–60.

Baumgarten, A. I. "The Name of the Pharisees." *JBL* 102 (1983):411–28.

———. "Qumran ve-ha-Kitatiut ba-Yahadut bi-Tequfat Bayit Sheni." In *Megillot Midbar Yehudah: 'Arba'im Shenot Mehqar*, edited by M. Broshi, S. Talmon, S. Japhet, and D. Schwartz, 139–51. Jerusalem: Bialik Institute, Israel Exploration Society, 1992.

Baumgarten, J. M. "4Q502, Marriage or Golden Age Ritual?" *JJS* 35 (1983):125–35.
———. "4 Q 503 (Daily Prayers) and the Lunar Calendar." *RQ* 12 (1986):399–408.
———. "'Al Shire ha-Pega'im mi-Qumran." *Tarbiz* 55 (1986):442–45.
———. "The Calendars of the Book of Jubilees and the Temple Scroll." *VT* 37 (1987):71–77.
———. "The Cave 4 Versions of the Qumran Penal Code." *JJS* 43 (1992):268–76.
———. "The Disqualifications of Priests in 4Q Fragments of the 'Damascus Document,' a Specimen of the Recovery of Pre-Rabbinic Halakha." In *The Madrid Qumran Conference: Proceedings of the International Congress on the Dead Sea Scrolls, Madrid, 18–21 March, 1991*, edited by J. Trebolle Barrera and L. Vegas Montaner, vol. 2, 503–13. Studies on the Texts of the Desert of Judah 11, 2. Leiden: E. J. Brill, 1992.
———. "The Exclusion of 'Netinim' and Proselytes in 4 Q *Flor.*" *RQ* 8 (1972):87–96.
———. "Exclusions from the Temple: Proselytes and Agrippa I." *JJS* 33 (1982):215–25.
———. "Halakhic Polemics in New Fragments from Qumran Cave 4." In *Biblical Archaeology Today: Proceedings of the International Congress on Biblical Archaeology, Jerusalem, April 1984*, edited by J. Amitai, 390–99. Jerusalem: Israel Exploration Society, the Israel Academy of Sciences and Humanities, in cooperation with the American Schools of Oriental Research, 1985.
———. "Hanging and Treason in Qumran and Roman Law." *Eretz-Israel* 16 (1985):7–16.
———. "The Heavenly Tribunal and the Personification of Ṣedeq in Jewish Apocalyptic." *ANRW* II.19.1 (1979):219–39.
———. "The Laws of the *Damascus Document* in Current Research." In *The Damascus Document Reconsidered*, edited by M. Broshi, 51–62. Jerusalem: Israel Exploration Society and the Shrine of the Book, Israel Museum, 1992.
———. "On the Nature of the Seductress in 4Q184." *RQ* 15 (1991):133–44.
———. "Perek Shirah, an Early Response to Psalm 151." *RQ* 9 (1978):575–78.
———. "The Pharisaic-Sadducean Controversies about Purity and the Qumran Texts." *JJS* 31 (1980):157–70.
———. "The Purification Rituals in *DJD* 7." In *The Dead Sea Scrolls*, edited by D. Dimant and U. Rappaport, 199–209. Leiden and Jerusalem: E. J. Brill, Magnes Press, Yad Izhak Ben-Zvi, 1992.
———. "The Qumran-Essene Restraints on Marriage." In *Archaeology and History in the Dead Sea Scrolls: The New York University Conference in Memory of Yigael Yadin*, edited by L. H. Schiffman, 13–24. Journal for the Study of the Old Testament Supplement Series 8; JSOT/ASOR Monographs 2. Sheffield: JSOT Press, 1990.
———. "The Qumran Sabbath Shirot and Rabbinic Merkabah Traditions." *RQ* 13 (1988):199–214.
———. "Recent Qumran Discoveries and Halakha in the Hellenistic-Roman Period." In *Jewish Civilization in the Hellenistic-Roman Period*, edited by S. Talmon, 147–58. Philadelphia: Trinity Press International, 1991.
———. *Studies in Qumran Law*. Studies in Judaism in Late Antiquity 24. Leiden: E. J. Brill, 1977.
Beall, T. S. *Josephus' Description of the Essenes Illustrated by the Dead Sea Scrolls*. Society for New Testament Studies Monograph Series. Cambridge: Cambridge University Press, 1988.

Bean, P. B. *A Theoretical Construct for the Temple of the Temple Scroll.* Dissertation, University of Oregon, 1987.

Beckwith, R. T. The Essene Calendar and the Moon: A Reconsideration. *RQ* 15 (1992):457–66.

———. "The Modern Attempt to Reconcile the Qumran Calendar with the True Solar Year." *RQ* 7 (1970):379–96.

———. *The Old Testament Canon of the New Testament Church.* Grand Rapids: Eerdmans, 1985.

———. "The Significance of the Calendar for Interpreting Essene Chronology and Eschatology." *RQ* 10 (1980):167–202.

Benoit, P., J. T. Milik, and R. de Vaux. *Les Grottes de Murabbaʿât.* Discoveries in the Judaean Desert 2. Oxford: Clarendon Press, 1960.

Bernstein, M. J. "4Q452: From Re-written Bible to Biblical Commentary." *JJS* 45 (1994):1–27.

———. "Harmonizations in the *Genesis Apocryphon.*" *Maarav,* forthcoming.

———. "Introductory Formulas for Citation and Re-citation of Biblical Verses in the Qumran Pesharim: Observations on a Pesher Technique." *DSD* 1 (1994).

———. "Midrash Halakhah at Qumran?" *Gesher* 7 (1979):145–66.

———. "A Study in Early Jewish Exegesis." *JQR* 74 (1983):21–45.

Betz, O. *Offbarung und Schriftforschung in der Qumransekte.* Wissenschaftliche Untersuchungen zum Neuen Testament 6. Tübingen: J. C. B. Mohr (Paul Siebeck), 1960.

Beyer, K. *Die aramäischen Texte vom Toten Meer.* Göttingen: Vandenhoeck & Ruprecht, 1983.

Bickerman, E. J. *The God of the Maccabees: Studies on the Meaning and the Origins of the Maccabean Revolt.* Studies in Judaism in Late Antiquity 32. Leiden: E. J. Brill, 1979.

———. *The Jews in the Greek Age.* Cambridge, MA: Harvard University, 1988.

Birnbaum, S. A. *The Qumrân (Dead Sea) Scrolls and Palaeography. BASOR* Supplementary Studies 13–14. New Haven, CT: American Schools of Oriental Research, 1952.

Black, M. *Apocalypsis Henochi Graeci in Pseudepigrapha Veteris Testamenti.* Pseudepigrapha Veteris Testamenti graece 3. Leiden: E. J. Brill, 1970.

———. *The Books of Enoch or 1 Enoch: A New English Edition with Commentary and Textual Notes.* Studia in Veteris Testamenti pseudepigrapha 7. Leiden: E. J. Brill, 1985.

———. "The Fragments of the Aramaic Enoch from Qumran." In *La Littérature juive entre Tenach et Mischna,* edited by W. C. van Unnik, 15–28. Leiden: E. J. Brill, 1974.

———. *The Scrolls and Christian Origins: Studies in the Jewish Background of the New Testament.* Brown Judaic Studies 48. Chico, CA: Scholars Press, 1983.

Blidstein, G. "4 Q *Florilegium* and Rabbinic Sources on Bastard and Proselyte." *RQ* 8 (1974):431–36.

Bokser, B. "Approaching Sacred Space." *HTR* 78 (1985):279–99.

Bonani, G. [et al.]. "Radiocarbon Dating of the Dead Sea Scrolls." *Atiqot* 20 (1991):27–32.

Bowman, J. "Did the Qumran Sect Burn the Red Heifer?" *RQ* 1 (1958):73–84.

Bregman, M. "Another Reference to 'A Teacher of Righteousness' in Midrashic Literature." *RQ* 10 (1979):95–96.

Brooke, G. J. "4QTestament of Levi^d(?) and the Messianic Servant High Priest." In *From Jesus to John: Essays on Jesus and New Testament Christology in Honour of Marinus de Jonge*, edited by M. C. de Boer, 83–100. Journal for the Study of the New Testament Supplement Series 84. Sheffield: JSOT Press, 1993.

———. "The Amos-Numbers Midrash (CD 7^{13b}–8^{1a}) and Messianic Expectations." *ZAW* 92 (1980):397–404.

———. "The Biblical Texts in the Qumran Commentaries: Scribal Errors or Exegetical Variants?" In *Early Jewish and Christian Exegesis: Studies in Memory of William Hugh Brownlee*, edited by C. A. Evans and W. F. Stinespring, 85–100. SBL Homage Series 10. Atlanta: Scholars Press, 1987.

———. *Exegesis at Qumran: 4Q Florilegium in Its Jewish Context*. Journal for the Study of the Old Testament Supplement Series 29. Sheffield: JSOT Press, 1985.

———. "Ezekiel in Some Qumran and New Testament Texts." In *The Madrid Qumran Congress: Proceedings of the International Congress on the Dead Sea Scrolls, Madrid, 18–21 March, 1991*, edited by J. Trebolle Barrera and L. Vegas Montaner, vol. 1, 317–38. Leiden and Madrid: E. J. Brill, Editorial Complutense, 1992.

———. "Levi and the Levites in the Dead Sea Scrolls and the New Testament." In *Mogilany 1989*, edited by Z. J. Kapera, 105–29. Kraków: Enigma Press, 1993.

———. "The Messiah of Aaron in the Damascus Document." *RQ* 15 (1991):215–31.

———. "The Pesharim and the Origin of the Dead Sea Scrolls." In *Methods of Investigation of the Dead Sea Scrolls and the Khirbet Qumran Site: Present Realities and the Future Prospects*, edited by J. J. Collins, N. Golb, D. Pardee, and M. Wise. *Annals of the New York Academy of Sciences*. New York: New York Academy of Sciences, 1994.

———. "Power to the Powerless—a Long-Lost Song of Miriam." *BAR* 20 (May/June 1994):62–65.

———. "Qumran Pesher: Towards the Redefinition of a Genre." *RQ* 10 (1981):483–504.

———. "The Temple Scroll: A Law unto Itself?" In *Law and Religion: Essays on the Place of the Law in Israel and Early Christianity*, edited by B. Lindars, 34–43. Cambridge: James Clark, 1988.

———. "The Textual Tradition of the *Temple Scroll* and Recently Published Manuscripts of the Pentateuch." In *The Dead Sea Scrolls: Forty Years of Research*, edited by D. Dimant and U. Rappaport, 261–82. Leiden and Jerusalem: E. J. Brill; Magnes Press, Yad Izhak Ben-Zvi, 1992.

Broshi, M., ed. "'Adrikhalut u-Vinyan 'Arim ba-Megillot ha-Genuzot." *Eretz-Israel* 23 (1992):286–92.

———. "The Archeology of Qumran—A Reconsideration." In *The Dead Sea Scrolls: Forty Years of Research*, edited by D. Dimant and U. Rappaport, 103–15. Leiden and Jerusalem: E. J. Brill, Magnes Press, Yad Izhak Ben-Zvi, 1992.

———. "Beware the Wiles of the Wanton Woman." *BAR* 9 (July/Aug. 1983):54–56.

———. "The Credibility of Josephus." *JJS* 33 (1982):379–84.

———. *The Damascus Document Reconsidered*. Jerusalem: Israel Exploration Society and the Shrine of the Book, Israel Museum, 1992.

———. "The Gigantic Dimensions of the Visionary Temple in the Temple Scroll." *BAR* 13 (Nov./Dec. 1987):36–37.

———. "The Negatives Archive of the Shrine of the Book." In *The Dead Sea Scrolls on Microfiche: A Comprehensive Facsimile Edition of the Texts from the Judean*

Desert. Companion Volume, edited by E. Tov, with the collaboration of S. J. Pfann, 135–36. Leiden: E. J. Brill and IDC, 1993.

―――. "Religion, Ideology, and Politics and Their Impact on Palestinian Archaeology." *Israel Museum Journal* 17 (1987):17–32.

Brown, R. E. *The Semitic Background of the Term "Mystery" in the New Testament.* Biblical Series 21. Philadelphia: Fortress Press, 1968.

Brown, R. E., J. A. Fitzmyer, W. G. Oxtoby, and J. Teixidor. *A Preliminary Concordance to the Hebrew and Aramaic Fragments from Qumrân Caves II–X, Including Especially the Unpublished Material from Cave IV.* Prepared and arranged by H.-P. Richter. 5 vols. Göttingen: Privately printed, 1988.

Brownlee, W. H. "The Background of Biblical Interpretation at Qumrân." In *Qumrân: sa piété, sa théologie et son milieu,* edited by M. Delcor, 183–93. Bibliotheca ephemeridum theologicarum lovaniensium 46. Paris-Gembloux and Leuven: Duculot, Leuven University Press, 1978.

―――. "Biblical Interpretation among the Sectaries of the Dead Sea Scrolls." *BA* 14 (1951):54–76.

―――. "The Dead Sea Manual of Discipline." BASOR Supplementary Studies 10–12 (1951):4–60.

―――. "Edh-Dheeb's Story of His Scroll Discovery." *RQ* 3 (1962):483–94.

―――. *The Midrash Pesher of Habakkuk.* SBL Monograph Series 24. Missoula, MO: Scholars Press, 1979.

―――. "The Scroll of Ezekiel from the Eleventh Qumran Cave." *RQ* 4 (1963):11–28.

―――. "The Significance of 'David's Compositions.'" *RQ* 5 (1966):569–74.

Bruce, F. F. *Second Thoughts on the Dead Sea Scrolls.* Grand Rapids, MI: Eerdmans, 1977.

Buchanan, G. W. "The Office of Teacher of Righteousness." *RQ* 9 (1977):237–40.

―――. "The Role of Purity in the Structure of the Essene Sect." *RQ* 4 (1963):397–406.

Burgmann, H. "11QT: The Sadducean Torah." In *Temple Scroll Studies,* edited by G. J. Brooke, 257–63. Sheffield: Sheffield Academic Press, 1989.

―――. "'The Wicked Woman': Der Makkabäer Simon." *RQ* 8 (1974):323–60.

Burrows, M., "The Ascent from Acco in 4Q p Isaᵃ." *VT* 7 (1957):104–5.

―――. *The Dead Sea Scrolls.* New York: Viking, 1956.

―――, ed. *The Dead Sea Scrolls of St. Mark's Monastery.* 2 vols. New Haven, CT: American Schools of Oriental Research, 1950–51.

―――. *More Light on the Dead Sea Scrolls.* London: Secker and Warburg, 1958.

Caevel, J. de. "La Connaissance religieuse dans les hymnes d'action de grâces de Qumrân." *ETL* 38 (1962):435–60.

Callaway, P. R. "Exegetische Erwägungen zur Tempelrolle XXIX, 7–10." *RQ* 12 (1985):95–104.

―――. *The History of the Qumran Community: An Investigation.* Journal for the Study of the Pseudepigrapha Supplementary Series 3. Sheffield: JSOT Press, 1988.

―――. "Source Criticism of the *Temple Scroll:* The Purity Laws." *RQ* 12 (1986):213–22.

Caquot, A. "Le Livre des Jubilés, Melkisedeq et les dîmes." *JJS* 33 (1982):257–64.

Carmignac, J. "Le Document de Qumran sur Melkisedeq." *RQ* 7 (1970):343–78.

―――. "Les Éléments historiques des Hymnes de Qumrân." *RQ* 2 (1960):205–22.

―――. "Les Horoscopes de Qumran." *RQ* 5 (1965):199–217.

———. "Les Kittim dans la 'Guerre des fils de lumière contre les fils de ténèbres.'" *NRT* (1955):737–48.

———. "Poème allégorique sur la secte rivale." *RQ* 5 (1965):361–74.

———. *La Règle de la guerre des fils de lumière contre les fils de ténèbres.* Paris: Letouzey et Ané, 1958.

———. "Roi, royauté et royaume dans la liturgie angélique." *RQ* 12 (1986):177–87.

———. "L'Utilité ou l'inutilité des sacrifices sanglants dans la 'Guerre de la Communauté' de Qumrân." *RB* 63 (1956):524–32.

Carmignac, J., É. Cothenet, and H. Lignée. *Les Textes de Qumran traduits et annotés,* vol. 2. Autour de la Bible. Paris: Letouzey et Ané, 1963.

Carmignac, J., and P. Guilbert. *Les Textes de Qumran traduits et annotés,* vol. 1. Autour de la Bible. Paris: Letouzey & Ané, 1961.

Charles, R. H. *The Apocrypha and Pseudepigrapha of the Old Testament in English.* 2 vols. Oxford: Clarendon Press, 1913.

———. *The Book of Enoch, or 1 Enoch.* Jerusalem: Makor, 1973.

———. *The Book of Jubilees, or the Little Genesis.* Jerusalem: Makor, 1972.

———. *The Greek Versions of the Testaments of the Twelve Patriarchs.* Oxford, 1908.

Charles, R. H., and A. Cowley. "An Early Source for the Testaments of the Patriarchs." *JQR* O. S. 19 (1907):566–83.

Charlesworth, J. H. "The Concept of the Messiah in the Pseudepigrapha." *ANRW* II.19.1 (1979):187–219.

———. *Jesus within Judaism: New Light from Exciting Archaeological Discoveries.* New York: Doubleday, 1988.

———, ed. *John and the Dead Sea Scrolls.* New York: Crossroad, 1990.

———, ed. *The Old Testament Pseudepigrapha.* 2 vols. Garden City, NY: Doubleday, 1983–85.

———. "The Origin and Subsequent History of the Authors of the Dead Sea Scrolls: Four Transitional Phases among the Qumran Essenes." *RQ* 10 (1980):213–34.

———. "The Pseudepigrapha as Biblical Exegesis." In *Early Jewish and Christian Exegesis,* edited by C. A. Evans and W. F. Stinespring, 139–52. Atlanta: Scholars Press, 1987.

Chazon, E. G. "4QDibHam: Liturgy or Literature?" *RQ* 15 (1992):447–56.

———. "Is *Divrei Ha-me'orot* a Sectarian Prayer?" In *The Dead Sea Scrolls: Forty Years of Research,* edited by D. Dimant and U. Rappaport, 3–18. Leiden and Jerusalem: E. J. Brill, Magnes Press, Yad Izhak Ben-Zvi, 1992.

———. "Prayers from Qumran and Their Historical Implications." *DSD* 1 (1994): in press.

Chyutin, M. "The New Jerusalem: Ideal City." *DSD* 1 (1994):71–97.

Cohen, S. J. D. *From the Maccabees to the Mishnah.* Philadelphia: Westminster, 1987.

———. "Masada, Literary Tradition, Archaeological Remains, and the Credibility of Josephus." *JJS* 33 (1982):385–405.

Collins, J. J. *The Apocalyptic Imagination.* New York: Crossroad, 1984.

———. "Messianism in the Maccabean Period." In *Judaisms and Their Messiahs at the Turn of the Christian Era,* edited by J. Neusner, W. S. Green, and E. S. Frerichs, 97–109. Cambridge: Cambridge University Press, 1987.

———. "Prophecy and Fulfillment in the Qumran Scrolls." *JETS* 30 (1987):267–78.

———. "Was the Dead Sea Sect an Apocalyptic Movement?" In *Archaeology and History* in the Dead Sea Scrolls: The New York University Conference in Memory of Yigael Yadin, edited by L. H. Schiffman, 25–51. Journal for the Study of the Pseudepigrapha Supplement Series 8; JSOT/ASOR Monographs 2. Sheffield: JSOT Press, 1990.

———. "The Works of the Messiah." DSD 1 (1994):98–112.

Cook, E. M. "Remarks on the Testament of Kohath from Qumran Cave 4." JJS 44 (1993):205–19.

———. Solving the Mysteries of the Dead Sea Scrolls: New Light on the Bible. Grand Rapids, MI: Zondervan, 1994.

Cotton, H. M., and J. Geiger. Masada II: The Yigael Yadin Excavations 1963–1965, Final Reports. Jerusalem: Israel Exploration Society, The Hebrew University of Jerusalem, 1989.

Crenshaw, J., ed. Studies in Ancient Israelite Wisdom. New York: Ktav, 1976.

Cross, F. M. "The Ammonite Oppression of the Tribes of Gad and Reuben: Missing Verses from 1 Samuel 11 Found in 4QSamuelª." In History, Historiography and Interpretation: Studies in Biblical and Cuneiform Literatures, edited by H. Tadmor and M. Weinfeld, 148–58. Jerusalem: Magnes Press, 1983.

———. The Ancient Library of Qumran and Modern Biblical Studies. Garden City, NY: Doubleday, 1958.

———. The Ancient Library of Qumran and Modern Biblical Studies. Grand Rapids, MI: Baker Book House, 1980.

———. "The Contribution of the Qumran Discoveries to the Study of the Biblical Text." IEJ 16 (1966):81–95.

———. "The Development of the Jewish Scripts." In The Bible and the Ancient Near East, edited by G. E. Wright, 170–264. Garden City, NY: Doubleday, 1961.

———. "The Early History of the Qumran Community." In New Directions in Biblical Archaeology, edited by D. N. Freedman and J. C. Greenfield, 70–89. Garden City, NY: Doubleday, 1971.

———. "The Evolution of a Theory of Local Texts." In Qumran and the History of the Biblical Text, edited by F. M. Cross and S. Talmon, 306–20. Cambridge, MA: Harvard University Press, 1975.

———. "A New Qumran Biblical Fragment Related to the Original Hebrew Underlying the Septuagint." BASOR 132 (1953):16–18.

———. "The Oldest Manuscripts from Qumran." JBL 74 (1955):147–72.

———. "On the History of the Photography." In The Dead Sea Scrolls on Microfiche: A Comprehensive Facsimile Edition of the Texts from the Judean Desert. Companion Volume, edited by E. Tov, in collaboration with S. J. Pfann, 121–22. Leiden: E. J. Brill and IDC, 1993.

———. "Papyri of the Fourth Century B.C. from Dâliyeh." In New Directions in Biblical Archaeology, edited by D. N. Freedman and J. C. Greenfield, 45–69. Garden City, NY: Doubleday, 1971.

Cross, F. M., D. N. Freedman, and J. A. Sanders, eds. Scrolls from Qumrân Cave I: The Great Isaiah Scroll, the Order of the Community, the Pesher to Habakkuk, from Photographs by J. C. Trever. Jerusalem: Albright Institute of Archaeological Research, Shrine of the Book, 1972.

Cross, F. M., and J. T. Milik. "Explorations in the Judaean Buqêàh." BASOR 152 (1956):5–17.

Cross, F. M., and S. Talmon. *Qumran and the History of the Biblical Text*. Cambridge, MA: Harvard University Press, 1975.

Davies, P. R. *1QM, the War Scroll from Qumran: Its Structure and History*. Biblica et Orientalia 32. Rome: Biblical Institute Press, 1977.

———. *Behind the Essenes: History and Ideology in the Dead Sea Scrolls*. Atlanta: Scholars Press, 1987.

———. "The Birthplace of the Essenes: Where Is 'Damascus'?" *RQ* 14 (1990):503–19.

———. "Calendrical Change and Qumran Origins: An Assessment of VanderKam's Theory." *CBQ* 45 (1983):80–89.

———. *The Damascus Covenant: An Interpretation of the "Damascus Document."* Journal for the Study of the Old Testament Supplement Series 25. Sheffield: JSOT Press, 1983.

———. "The Ideology of the Temple in the *Damascus Document*." *JJS* 33 (1982):287–301.

———. "Oumran and Apocalyptic or *Obscurum Per Obscurius*." *JNES* 49 (1990): 127–34.

———. *Qumran*. Cities of the Biblical World. Grand Rapids: Eerdmans, 1982.

Delcor, M., ed. and trans. *Les Hymnes de Qumran (Hodayot)*. Autour de la Bible. Paris: Letouzey et Ané, 1962.

———. "L'Hymne à Sion du *Rouleau des psaumes* de la grotte 11 de Qumrân (*11 Q Ps a*)." *RQ* 6 (1967):71–88.

———. "Melchizedek from Genesis to the Qumran Texts and the Epistle to the Hebrews." *JSJ* 2 (1971):115–35.

———. "Recherches sur un horoscope en langue hébraïque provenant de Qumran." *RQ* 5 (1966):521–42.

———. "Repas cultuels esséniens et thérapeutes: Thiases et Haburoth." *RQ* 6 (1968):401–26.

Dimant, D. "The Apocalyptic Interpretation of Ezekiel at Qumran." In *Messiah and Christos: Studies in the Jewish Origins of Christianity Presented to David Flusser*, edited by I. Gruenwald, S. Shaked, and G. G. Stroumsa, 31–51. Tübingen: J. C. B. Mohr (Paul Siebeck), 1992.

———. "New Light from Qumran on the Jewish Pseudepigrapha—4Q390." In *The Madrid Qumran Conference: Proceedings of the International Congress on the Dead Sea Scrolls, Madrid, 18–21 March, 1991*, edited by J. Trebolle Barrera and L. Vegas Montaner, vol. 2, 405–48. Studies on the Texts of the Desert of Judah 11, 2. Leiden: E. J. Brill, 1992.

———. "Pesharim, Qumran." In *Anchor Bible Dictionary*, vol. 5, 244–51. New York: Doubleday, 1992.

———. "The Qumran Manuscripts: Contents and Significance." In *"Time to Prepare the Way in the Wilderness:" Papers on the Qumran Scrolls by Fellows of the Institute for Advanced Studies of the Hebrew University, Jerusalem, 1989–90*, edited by D. Dimant and L. H. Schiffman, 23–58. Studies on the Texts of the Desert of Judah. Leiden: E. J. Brill, 1994.

———. "Qumran Sectarian Literature." In *Jewish Writings of the Second Temple Period*, edited by M. E. Stone, 483–550. Compendia Rerum Iudaicarum ad Novum Testamentum II, ii. Assen and Philadelphia: Van Gorcum, Fortress Press, 1984.

———. "Use and Interpretation of Mikra in the Apocrypha and Pseudepigrapha." In *Mikra: Text, Translation, Reading, and Interpretation of the Hebrew Bible in Ancient Judaism and Early Christianity,* edited by M. J. Mulder with H. Sysling, 379–419. Corpus Rerum Iudaicarum ad Novum Testamentum II. 1. Assen/Mastricht and Minneapolis: Van Gorcum, Fortress Press, 1990.

Dimant, D., and J. Strugnell. "The Merkabah Vision in Second Ezekiel (4Q385 4)." *RQ* 14 (1990):331–48.

Donceel, R. "Reprise des travaux de publication des fouilles au Khirbet Qumrân." *RB* 99 (1992):557–73.

Donceel-Voute, P. "The Archaeology of Qumran." In *Methods of Investigation of the Dead Sea Scrolls and the Khirbet Qumran Site: Present Realities and Future Prospects,* edited by J. J. Collins, N. Golb, D. Pardee, and M. Wise. *Annals of the New York Academy of Sciences.* New York: The New York Academy of Sciences, 1994.

Driver, G. R. *The Judean Scrolls.* Oxford: Basil Blackwell, 1965.

Duhaime, J. "Le Dualisme de Qumrân et la littérature de sagesse vétérotestamentaire." *Église et Théologie* 19 (1988):401–22.

———. "Dualistic Reworking in the Scrolls from Qumran." *CBQ* 49 (1987):32–56.

———. "Étude comparative de 4QM⁴ fgg. 1–3 et 1QM." *RQ* 14 (1990):459–72.

———. "Remarques sur les dépôts d'ossements d'animaux à Qumrân." *RQ* 9 (1977–78):245–51.

———. "The *War Scroll* from Qumran and the Greco-Roman Tactical Treatises." *RQ* 13 (1988):133–52.

Dupont-Sommer, A. "Le Commentaire de Nahum découvert près de la Mer Morte (4Q P NNah): traduction et notes." *Semitica* 13 (1963):55–88.

———. "Le 'Commentaire d'Habacuc' découvert près de la Mer Morte." *Revue de l'Histoire des Religions* 137 (1950):129–71.

———. "Contribution à l'exégèse du Manuel de Discipline X, 1–8." *VT* 3 (1952):229–43.

———. *The Dead Sea Scrolls,* translated by E. M. Rowley. Oxford: Basil Blackwell, 1952.

———. *Les Écrits esséniens découverts près de la Mer Morte.* Paris: Payot, 1964.

———. "Exorcismes et guérisons dans les écrits de Qoumrân." Suppl. to *VT* 7 (1960): 246–61.

———. *The Jewish Sect of Qumran and the Essenes: New Studies on the Dead Sea Scrolls.* London: Vallentine, Mitchell, 1955.

———. "Lumières nouvelles sur l'arrière-plan historique des écrits de Quomrân." *Eretz-Israel* 8 (1967):25–36.

Eisenman, R. H. *James the Just in the Habakkuk Pesher.* Leiden: E. J. Brill, 1986.

———. *Maccabees, Zadokites, Christians and Qumran.* Leiden: E. J. Brill, 1983.

———. "A Messianic Vision." *BAR* 17 (Nov./Dec. 1991):65.

———. "The Testament of Kohath; a War Prayer; a Messianic Vision." *BAR* 17 (Nov./Dec. 1991):64–65.

Eisenman, R. H., and J. M. Robinson. *A Facsimile Edition of the Dead Sea Scrolls, Prepared with an Introduction and Index.* Publisher's Foreword by H. Shanks. 2 vols. Washington, DC: Biblical Archaeology Society, 1991.

Eisenman, R. H., and G. Vermes. "More on the Pierced Messiah Text from Eisenman and Vermes." *BAR* 19 (Jan./Feb. 1993):66–67.

Eisenman, R. H., and M. O. Wise. *The Dead Sea Scrolls Uncovered*. Rockport, MA: Element, 1992.

Elbogen, I. *Jewish Liturgy: A Comprehensive History*, translated by R. P. Scheindlin. Philadelphia and New York: Jewish Publication Society, Jewish Theological Seminary of America, 1993.

Elder, L. B. "Female Ascetics among the Essenes." Unpublished paper.

Elgvin, T. "Admonition Texts from Qumran Cave 4." In *Methods of Investigation of the Dead Sea Scrolls and the Khirbet Qumran Site: Present Realities and Future Prospects*, edited by J. J. Collins, N. Golb, D. Pardee, and M. Wise. *Annals of the New York Academy of Sciences*. New York: New York Academy of Sciences, in press.

Elliger, K. *Studien zum Habakkuk-Kommentar vom Toten Meer*. Beitrage zur historischen Theologie 15. Tübingen: J. C. B. Mohr, 1953.

Eshel, E. "4Q477: The Rebukes by the Overseer." *JJS* 45 (1994):111–22.

Eshel, E., and H. Eshel. "4Q471 Fragment I and Ma'amadot in the War Scroll." In *The Madrid Qumran Conference: Proceedings of the International Congress on the Dead Sea Scrolls, Madrid, 18–21 March, 1991*, edited by J. Trebolle Barrera and L. Vegas Montaner, vol. 2, 611–20. Studies on the Texts of the Desert of Judah 11, 2. Leiden: E. J. Brill, 1992.

Eshel, E., H. Eshel, and A. Yardeni. "A Qumran Composition Containing Part of Ps. 154 and a Prayer for the Welfare of King Jonathan." *IEJ* 42 (1992):199–229.

———. "Rare DSS Text Mentions King Jonathan." *BAR* 20 (Jan./Feb. 1994):75–78.

Eshel, E., and M. Kister. "A Polemical Qumran Fragment." *JJS* 43 (1992):277–81.

Eshel, H. "The Historical Background of the Pesher Interpreting Joshua's Curse on the Rebuilder of Jericho." *RQ* 15 (1992):409–20.

Eshel, H., and Z. Greenhut. "Ḥiam El-Sagha, a Cemetery of the Qumran Type, Judaean Desert." *RB* 100 (1993):252–59.

Evans, C. A. "The *Genesis Apocryphon* and the Rewritten Bible." *RQ* 13 (1988):153–66.

Farmer, W. R. "The Economic Basis of the Qumran Community." *TZ* 11 (1955):295–308.

———. "A Postscript to 'The Economic Basis of the Qumran Community.'" *TZ* 12 (1956):56–58.

Feldman, S. "Traveling Scrolls Debate Touches down in Washington." *BAR* 19 (July/Aug. 1993):69–70, 72–73.

Filson, F. V. "The Dead Sea Scrolls and the New Testament." In *New Directions in Biblical Archaeology*, edited by D. N. Freedman and J. C. Greenfield, 142–55. Garden City, NY: Doubleday, 1971.

Finkelstein, L. "The Maxim of the *Anshe Keneset Ha-Gedolah*." *JBL* 59 (1940):455–69.

———. *The Pharisees*. 2 vols. Philadelphia: Jewish Publication Society, 1962.

Fishbane, M. *Biblical Interpretation in Ancient Israel*. Oxford: Clarendon Press, 1985.

———. "Use, Authority and Interpretation of Mikra at Qumran." In *Mikra: Text, Translation, Reading, and Interpretation of the Hebrew Bible in Ancient Judaism and Early Christianity*, edited by M. J. Mulder, with H. Sysling, 339–77. Corpus Rerum Iudaicarum ad Novum Testamentum II.1. Assen/Mastricht and Minneapolis: Van Gorcum, Fortress Press, 1990.

Fitzmyer, J. A. "The Contribution of Qumran Aramaic to the Study of the New Testament." *NTS* 20 (1973–74):382–407.

———. *The Dead Sea Scrolls: Major Publications and Tools for Study*. SBL Resources for Biblical Study 20. Atlanta: Scholars Press, 1990.

———. *Essays on the Semitic Background of the New Testament.* London: Geoffrey Chapman, 1971.

———. *The Genesis Apocryphon of Qumran Cave 1.* Biblica et Orientalia 18A. Rome: Biblical Institute Press, 1971.

———. "The Qumran Scrolls and the New Testament after Forty Years." *RQ* 13 (1988):609–20.

———. "The Targum of Leviticus from Qumran Cave 4." *Maarav* 1 (1978):5–23.

———. *A Wandering Aramaean: Collected Aramaic Essays.* SBL Monograph Series 25. Missoula, MO: Scholars Press, 1979.

Fitzmyer. J. A., and D. J. Harrington. *A Manual of Palestinian Aramaic Texts (Second Century B.C.–Second Century A.D.).* Biblica et Orientalia 34. Rome: Biblical Institute Press, 1978.

Flusser, D. *Judaism and the Origins of Christianity.* Jerusalem: Magnes Press, 1988.

———. "Kat Midbar Yehudah ve-ha-Perushim." *Molad* 19 (1961):456–58.

———. "Perushim, Ṣeduqim ve-'Issiyim be-Fesher Naḥum." In *G. Alon Memorial Volume,* 133–68. Tel Aviv, 1960.

———. "The Sons of Light in Jesus' Teaching and in the New Testament." In *Biblical Archaeology Today: Proceedings of the International Congress on Biblical Archaeology, Jerusalem, April 1984,* edited by J. Amitai, 427–28. Jerusalem: Israel Exploration Society, Israel Academy of Sciences and Humanities, in cooperation with the American Schools of Oriental Research, 1985.

———. *Yahadut u-Meqorot ha-Naṣrut,* edited by H. Safrai. Tel Aviv: Sifriat Po'alim, 1979.

Forkman, G. *The Limits of the Religious Community.* Coniectanea Biblica New Testament Series 5. Lund: CWK Gleerup, 1972.

Fraade, S. T. "Interpreting Authority in the Studying Community at Qumran." *JJS* 44 (1983):46–69.

Freedman, D. N. "The Old Testament at Qumran." In *New Directions in Biblical Archaeology,* edited by D. N. Freedman and J. C. Greenfield, 131–41. Garden City, NY: Doubleday, 1971.

Freedman, D. N., and K. A. Mathews. *The Paleo-Hebrew Leviticus Scroll (11 QpaleoLev).* Winona Lake, IN: American Schools of Oriental Research, 1985.

Fröhlich, I. "Le Genre littéraire des Pesharim de Qumrân." *RQ* 12 (1986):383–98.

Gabrion, H. "L'Interprétation de l'écriture dans la littérature de Qumran." *ANRW* II.19.1 (1979):779–848.

García Martínez, F. "11QTemple[b]: A Preliminary Publication." In *The Madrid Qumran Conference: Proceedings of the International Congress on the Dead Sea Scrolls, Madrid, 18–21 March, 1991,* edited by J. Trebolle Barrera and L. Vegas Montaner, vol. 2, 363–91. Studies on the Texts of the Desert of Judah 11, 2. Leiden: E. J. Brill, 1992.

———. "L'Interprétation de la Torah d'Ezéchiel dans les MSS de Qumrân." *RQ* 13 (1988):441–52.

———. "The Last Surviving Columns of 11QNJ." In *The Scriptures and the Scrolls: Studies in Honour of A. S. Van der Woude on the Occasion of His 65th Birthday,* edited by F. García Martínez, A. Hilhorst, and C. J. Labuschagne, 178–92, + plates. Leiden: E. J. Brill, 1992.

————. "Les Limites de la communauté: pureté et impureté à Qumrân et dans le Nouveau Testament." In *Text and Testimony: Essays on New Testament and Apocryphal Literature in Honour of A. F. J. Klijn*, edited by T. Baarda, 111–22. Kampen: H. J. Kok, 1988.

————. "Lista de MSS procedentes de Qumran." *Henoch* 11 (1989):149–232.

————. "Los Mesías de Qumrán: problemas de un traductor." *Sefarad* 53 (1993):345–60.

————. "Messianische Erwartungen in den Qumranschriften." *JBTh* 8 (1993):171–208.

————. "Notas al margen de 'The Dead Sea Scrolls Uncovered.'" *RQ* 16 (1993):123–50.

————. "Nuevos textos mesiánicos de Qumrán y el Mesías del Nuevo Testamento." *Communio* 26 (1993):3–31.

————. *Qumran and Apocalyptic: Studies on the Aramaic Texts from Qumran*. Studies on the Texts of the Desert of Judah 9. Leiden: E. J. Brill, 1992.

————. "Sources et composition du *Rouleau du temple*." *Henoch* 13 (1991):219–32.

————, trans. *Textos de Qumrân*. Colección estructuras y procesos, serie religión. Madrid: Editorial Trotta, 1993.

————. "Texts from Qumran Cave 11." In *The Dead Sea Scrolls: Forty Years of Research*, edited by D. Dimant and U. Rappaport, 18–26. Leiden and Jerusalem: E. J. Brill, Magnes Press, Yad Izhak Ben-Zvi, 1992.

García Martínez, F., and E. J. C. Tigchelaar. "The Books of Enoch (1 Enoch) and the Aramaic Fragments from Qumran." *RQ* 14 (1989):131–46.

García Martínez, F., and A. S. van der Woude. "A 'Groningen' Hypothesis of Qumran Origins and Early History." *RQ* 14 (1990):521–41.

Gärtner, B. *The Temple and the Community in Qumran and the New Testament*. Cambridge: Cambridge University Press, 1965.

Gazov-Ginzberg, A. M. "Double Meaning in a Qumran Work ('The Wiles of the Wicked Woman')." *RQ* 6 (1967):279–87.

Geiger, A. *Urschrift and Übersetzungen der Bibel und ihre Abhängigkeit von der innern Entwicklung der Judenthums*. Breslau: Julius Hainauer, 1857.

Gilat, Y. D. *Peraqim be-Hishtalshelut ha-Halakhah*. Ramat Gan: Bar-Ilan University Press, 1992.

Ginzberg, L. *Eine unbekannte jüdische Sekte*. New York: L. Ginzberg, 1922.

————. *The Legends of the Jews*. 6 vols. Philadelphia: Jewish Publication Society, 1968.

————. *An Unknown Jewish Sect*. New York: Jewish Theological Seminary of America, 1976.

Glessmer, U. "Antike und moderne Auslegungen des Sintflutberichtes Gen 6–8 und der Qumran-Pesher 4Q252." *Mitteilungen und Beiträge* 6 (1993):2–81.

Gluskina, L. "The Teacher of Righteousness in Joseph Amussin's Studies." In *Mogilany 1989: Papers on the Dead Sea Scrolls*, edited by Z. J. Kapera, vol. 2, 7–21. Kraków: Enigma Press, 1991.

Golb, N. "The Dead Sea Scrolls: A New Perspective." *The American Scholar*, Spring 1989, 177–207.

————. "Khirbet Qumran and the Manuscripts of the Judaean Wilderness: Observations on the Logic of Their Investigations." *JNES* 49 (1990):103–14.

————. "Who Wrote the Dead Sea Scrolls?" *The Sciences*, May/June 1987, 40–49.

Goodman, M. "The First Jewish Revolt: Social Conflict and the Problems of Debt." *JJS* 33 (1982):419–27.

———. *The Ruling Class of Judaea: The Origins of the Jewish Revolt against Rome.* Cambridge: Cambridge University Press, 1993.

Goranson, S. "'Essenes': Etymology from '*sh.*" *RQ* 11 (1984):483–98.

———. "Qumran—The Evidence of the Inkwells." *BAR* 19 (Nov./Dec. 1993):67.

———. "Sectarianism, Geography, and the *Copper Scroll.*" *JJS* 42 (1992):281–87.

Goshen-Gottstein, M. H. "The *Psalms Scroll* (11QPs^a): A Problem of Canon and Text." *Textus* 5 (1966):22–33.

Green, W. S. "Introduction: Messiah in Judaism: Rethinking the Question." In *Judaisms and Their Messiahs at the Turn of the Christian Era,* edited by J. Neusner, W. S. Green, and E. S. Frerichs, 1–13. Cambridge: Cambridge University Press, 1987.

Greenfield, J. C. "Ahiqar in the Book of Tobit." In *De la Tôrah au Messie: études d'exégèse et bibliques offertes à Henri Cazelles,* edited by M. Carrez, J. Doré, and P. Grelot, 329–36. Paris: Desclée, 1981.

———. "*Ben Sira* 42.9 and Its Talmudic Paraphrase." In *A Tribute to Geza Vermes: Essays on Jewish and Christian Literature and History,* edited by P. R. Davies and R. T. White, 167–73. Journal for the Study of the Old Testament Supplement Series 100. Sheffield: JSOT Press, 1990.

———. "Two Notes on the Apocryphal Psalms." In *"Sha'arei Talmon": Studies in the Bible, Qumran, and the Ancient Near East Presented to Shemaryahu Talmon,* edited by M. Fishbane and E. Tov, 309–14. Winona Lake, IN: Eisenbrauns, 1992.

———. "The Words of Levi Son of Jacob in *Damascus Document* IV, 15–19." *RQ* 13 (1988):319–22.

Greenfield, J. C., and E. Qimron. The *Genesis Apocryphon* Col. XII." *Abr-Nahrain* Suppl. 3 (1992):70–77.

Greenfield, J. C., and M. E. Stone. "The Enochic Pentateuch and the Date of the Similitudes." *HTR* 70 (1977):50–65.

———. "Two Notes on the Aramaic Levi Document." In *Of Scribes and Scrolls: Studies on the Hebrew Bible, Intertestamental Judaism, and Christian Origins, Presented to John Strugnell,* edited by H. W. Attridge, J. J. Collins, and T. H. Tobin, 153–61. College Theology Society Resources in Religion 5. Lanham, MD: University Press of America, 1990.

Greenleaf Pedley, K. "The Library at Qumran." *RQ* 2 (1959):53–68.

Grelot, P. "Notes sur le testament araméen de Lévi." *RB* 63 (1956):391–406.

———. "La Prière de Nabonide (4 Q Or Nab)." *RQ* 9 (1978):483–96.

Gruenwald, I. *Apocalyptic and Merkavah Mysticism.* Leiden: E. J. Brill, 1980.

———. "Knowledge and Vision: Towards a Clarification of Two 'Gnostic' Concepts in the Light of Their Alleged Origins." *Israel Oriental Studies* 3 (1973):63–107.

———. "Qeta'im Ḥadashim mi-Sifrut Hakkarat Panim ve-Sidre Sirṭuṭin." *Tarbiz* 40 (1970/1).

Guilbert, P. "Le Plan de la *Règle de la communauté.*" *RQ* 1 (1959):323–44.

Haas, N., and H. Nathan. "Anthropological Survey on the Human Skeletal Remains from Qumran." *RQ* 6 (1968):345–52.

Habermann, A. M. "'Al ha-Tefillin bi-Yeme Qedem." *Eretz-Israel* 3 (1954):174–77.

Haran, M. "11QPs^a and the Canonical Book of Psalms." In *Minḥah Le-Naḥum: Biblical* and Other Studies Presented to Nahum M. Sarna in Honour of His 70th Birthday, edited by M. Brettler and M. Fishbane, 193–201. Sheffield: JSOT Press, 1993.

———. "The Two Text-Forms of Psalms 151." *JJS* 39 (1988):171–82.

Harper, J. E. "26 Tons of Gold and 65 Tons of Silver." *BAR* 19 (Nov./Dec. 1993):44–45.

Harrington, H. K. *The Impurity Systems of Qumran and the Rabbis: Biblical Foundations.* SBL Dissertation Series 143. Atlanta: Scholars Press, 1993.

Heinemann, J. *Ha-Tefillah bi-Tequfat ha-Tanna'im ve-ha-Amora'im.* Jerusalem: Magnes Press, 1966.

Heisey, T. M. "Paradigm Agreement and Literature Obsolescence: A Comparative Study in the Literature of the Dead Sea Scrolls." *Journal of Documentation* 44 (1988):285–301.

Hengel, M. *Judaism and Hellenism: Studies in Their Encounter in Palestine in the Early Hellenistic Period.* 2 vols. Philadelphia: Fortress Press, 1974.

———. *Property and Riches in the Early Church.* Philadelphia: Fortress Press, 1974.

Hengel, M., J. H. Charlesworth, and D. Mendels. "The Polemical Character of 'On Kingship' in the Temple Scroll: An Attempt at Dating 11QTemple." *JJS* 37 (1986):28–36.

Herr, M. D. "Li-Ve'ayat Hilkhot Milḥamah be-Shabbat bi-Yeme Bayit Sheni u-vi-Tequfat ha-Mishnah." *Tarbiz* 30 (1961):242–56, 341–56.

Hirschfeld, Y. *The Judean Desert Monasteries in the Byzantine Period.* New Haven, CT: Yale University, 1992.

Historical Dictionary of the Hebrew Language. Sefer Ben Sira: ha-Makor, Qondordansiyah ve-Nituah Oṣar ha-Millim. Jerusalem: Academy of the Hebrew Language, the Shrine of the Book, 1973.

Holm-Nielsen, S. *Hodayot Psalms from Qumran.* Acta Theologica Danica 2. Denmark: Universitetsforlaget I Aarhus, 1960.

Horgan, M. P. *Pesharim: Qumran Interpretations of Biblical Books.* CBQ Monograph Series 8. Washington, DC: Catholic Biblical Association of America, 1979.

Humbert, J.-B. "L'espace sacré à Qumrân: Propositions pour l'archéologie." *RB* 101–2 (1994):161–211. With Annexe by S. J. Pfann, 212–4.

Ilan, Z., and D. Amit. "'Amat ha-Mayyim shel Qumran." In *'Amot ha-Mayyim ha-Qedumot be-'Ereṣ Yisrael,* edited by D. Amit, Y. Hirschfeld, and J. Patrich, 283–88. Jerusalem: Yad Izhak Ben-Zvi, 1989.

Isaac, E. "1 (Ethiopic Apocalypse of) Enoch (Second Century B.C.–First Century A.D.): A New Translation and Introduction." In *The Old Testament Pseudepigrapha,* edited by J. H. Charlesworth, vol. 1, 5–89. Garden City, NY: Doubleday, 1983.

Iwry, S. "Was There a Migration to Damascus? The Problem of *šby yšr'l.*" *Eretz-Israel* 9 (1969):80–88.

Jackson, B. S. "*Damascus Document IX,* 16–23 and Parallels." *RQ* 9 (1978):445–50.

———. *Essays in Jewish and Comparative Legal History.* Studies in Judaism in Late Antiquity 10. Leiden: E. J. Brill, 1975.

Jacobson, H. "4Q252: Addenda." *JJS* 44 (1993):118–20.

———. "4Q252 fr. 1: Further Comments." *JJS* 44 (1993):291–93.

James, M. R. *The Lost Apocrypha of the Old Testament.* London: Society for Promoting Christian Knowledge, 1936.

Jastram, N. "The Text of 4QNum[b]." In *The Madrid Qumran Congress: Proceedings of* the *International Congress on the Dead Sea Scrolls, Madrid, 18–21 March, 1991,* edited by J. Trebolle Barrera and L. Vegas Montaner, Vol. 1, 77–98. Studies on the Texts of the Desert of Judah 11, 1. Leiden and Madrid: E. J. Brill, Editorial Complutense, 1992.

Jaubert, A. "Le Calendrier des Jubilés et de la secte de Qumrân: ses origines bibliques." *VT* 3 (1953):250–64.

———. "Le Calendrier des Jubilés et les jours liturgiques de la semaine." *VT* 7 (1957):35–61.

Jellicoe, S. *The Septuagint and Modern Study.* Winona Lake, IN: Eisenbrauns, 1989.

Jeremias, G. *Der Lehrer der Gerechtigkeit.* Göttingen: Vandenhoeck & Ruprecht, 1963.

Jeremias, J. *Jerusalem in the Time of Jesus.* Philadelphia: Fortress Press, 1969.

Jones, A. H. M. *The Greek City from Alexander to Justinian.* Oxford: Clarendon Press, 1940.

Jonge, M. de, and A. S. van der Woude. "11QMelchizedek and the New Testament." *NTS* 12 (1966):301–26.

Jongeling, B. "Contributions of the Qumran Job Targum to the Aramaic Vocabulary." *JSS* 17 (1972):191–96.

———. "The Job Targum from Qumran Cave 11 (11QtgJob)." *FO* 15 (1974):181–96.

———. "Publication provisoire d'un fragment provenant de la grotte 11 de Qumrân (11q jér nouv^ar)." *JSJ* 1 (1970):57–64.

Kampen, J. "A Reconsideration of the Name 'Essene' in Greco-Jewish Literature in Light of Recent Perceptions of the Qumran Sect." *HUCA* 57 (1986):61–81.

Kapera, Z. J. "An Anonymously Received Pre-publication of the 4QMMT." *The Qumran Chronicle* Appendix A, no. 2 (1990).

———. "The Present State of Qumranology." In *Mogilany 1989: Papers on the Dead Sea Scrolls,* edited by Z. J. Kapera, vol. 1, 181–228. Kraków: Enigma Press, 1993.

Kasher, A. *Jews and Hellenistic Cities in Eretz-Israel: Relations of the Jews in Eretz-Israel with the Hellenistic Cities during the Second Temple Period (332 B.C.E.– 70 C.E.).* Texte und Studien zum Antiken Judentum 21. Tübingen: J. C. B. Mohr (Paul Siebeck), 1990.

———, ed. *Ha-Mered ha-Gadol: ha-Sibbot ve-ha-Nesibbot li-Ferisato.* Sugyot be-Toldot 'Am Yisra'el 13. Jerusalem: Merkaz Shazar, 1983.

Katzman, A. "Chief Dead Sea Scroll Editor Denounces Judaism, Israel; Claims He's Seen Four More Scrolls Found by Bedouin." *BAR* 17 (Jan./Feb. 1991):64–65, 70, 72.

Kister, M. "Barnabas 12:1; 4:3 and 4Q Second Ezekiel." *RB* 97 (1990):63–67.

———. "Le-Ferusho shel Sefer *Ben-Sira.*" *Tarbiz* 59 (1990):303–78.

———. "Newly Identified Fragments of the Book of Jubilees: *Jub. 23:21–23, 30–31.*" *RQ* 12 (1987):529–36.

———. "Notes on Some New Texts from Qumran." *JJS* 44 (1993):280–90.

Kister, M., and E. Qimron. "Observations on 4QSecond Ezekiel (*4Q385 2–3*)." *RQ* 15 (1992):595–602.

Kittel, B. P. *The Hymns of Qumran.* SBL Dissertation Series 50. Chico, CA: Scholars Press, 1981.

Knibb, M. A. *The Ethiopic Book of Enoch: A New Edition in the Light of the Aramaic Dead Sea Fragments.* 2 vols. Oxford: Clarendon Press, 1978.

———. "Exile in the *Damascus Document.*" *JSOT* 99 (1983):99–117.

Kobelski, P. *Melchizedek and Melchireša'*. CBQ Monograph Series 10. Washington, DC: Catholic Biblical Association of America, 1981.

Koester, H. *Introduction to the New Testament*. 2 vols. Philadelphia: Fortress Press, 1982.

Kosmala, L. "Maskil." *Journal of the Ancient Near Eastern Society of Columbia University* 5 (1973):235–41.

Kuhn, H. W. "The Impact of the Qumran Scrolls on the Understanding of Paul." In *The Dead Sea Scrolls: Forty Years of Research*, edited by D. Dimant and U. Rappaport, 327–39. Leiden and Jerusalem: E. J. Brill, Magnes Press, Yad Izhak Ben-Zvi, 1992.

Kuhn, K. G. "The Lord's Supper and the Communal Meal at Qumran." In *The Scrolls and the New Testament*, edited by K. Stendahl, with an introduction by J. H. Charlesworth, 65–93. New York: Crossroad, 1992.

——. *Phylakterien aus Höhle 4 von Qumran*, 1–31. Abhandlungen der Heidelberger Akademie der Wissenschaften, Philosophisch-historische Klasse. Heidelberg: Carl Winter Universitätsverlag, 1957.

——. "The Two Messiahs of Aaron and Israel." In *The Scrolls and the New Testament*, edited by K. Stendahl, with an introduction by J. H. Charlesworth, 54–64. New York: Crossroad, 1992.

——. "The Two Messiahs of Aaron and Israel." In *The Scrolls and the New Testament*, edited by K. Stendahl. London: SCM Press, 1958.

Kutscher, E. Y. *The Language and Linguistic Background of the Isaiah Scroll (1QIsaᵃ)*. Studies on the Texts from the Desert of Judah 6. Leiden: E. J. Brill, 1974.

——. "The Language of the *Genesis Apocryphon*: A Preliminary Study." In *Aspects of the Dead Sea Scrolls*, edited by C. Rabin and Y. Yadin, 1–35. Scripta Hierosolymitana. Jerusalem: Magnes Press, 1958.

Lambert, G. *Le Maître de justice et la communauté de l'alliance*. Analecta Lovaniensia Biblica et Orientalia II.28. Louvain: Publications Universitaires, 1952.

Lambert, W. G. *Babylonian Wisdom Literature*. Oxford: Clarendon Press, 1960.

Laperrousaz, E. M. "À Propos des dépôts d'ossements d'animaux trouvés à Qoumrân." *RQ* 9 (1978):569–74.

——. *Qoumrân, l'établissement essénien des bords de la Mer Morte: histoire et archéologie du site*. Paris: A. & J. Picard, 1976.

Lapp, P. W. *Palestinian Ceramic Chronology 200 B.C.–A.D. 70*. New Haven, CT: American Schools of Oriental Research, 1961.

Larson, E. "A New Apocryphal Text from Qumran." *DSD* 1 (1994):in press.

Larson, E., L. H. Schiffman, and J. Strugnell. "4Q470: With a Fragment Mentioning Zedekiah." *RQ* (1994):in press.

LaSor, W. S. *The Dead Sea Scrolls and the New Testament*. Grand Rapids: Eerdmans, 1972.

——. "The Messiah of Aaron and Israel." *VT* 6 (1956):425–29.

Laurin, R. B. "The Problem of Two Messiahs in the Qumran Scrolls." *RQ* 4 (1963):39–52.

Leaney, A. R. C. *The Rule of Qumran and Its Meaning*. Philadelphia: Westminster Press, 1966.

Lefkovits, J. *The Copper Scroll—3Q15, a New Reading, Translation, and Commentary (Parts 1 & 2)*. Dissertation, New York University, 1993.

Lehmann, M. R. "11 Q Psᵃ and Ben Sira." *RQ* 11 (1983):239–52.

————. "*1 Q Genesis Apocryphon* in the Light of Targumim and Midrashim." *RQ* 1 (1958):249–64.

————. "*Ben Sira* and the Qumran Literature." *RQ* 3 (1961):103–16.

————. "Identification of the *Copper Scroll* Based on Its Technical Terms." *RQ* 5 (1964):97–105.

————. *Massot u-Massa'ot*. Jerusalem: Mosad Harav Kook, 1982.

————. "Midrashic Parallels to Selected Qumran Texts." *RQ* 3 (1962):545–52.

————. "New Light on Astrology in Qumran and the Talmud." *RQ* 8 (1975):599–602.

————. "A Re-interpretation of *4 Q Dibrê Ham-Me'oroth*." *RQ* 5 (1964):106–10.

————. "Studies in the Murabba'ât and Naḥal Ḥever Documents." *RQ* 4 (1963):53–82.

————. "Talmudic Material Relating to the Dead Sea Scrolls." *RQ* 1 (1959):391–404.

————. "The *Temple Scroll* as a Source of Sectarian Halakhah." *RQ* 9 (1978):579–88.

————. "Where the Temple Tax Was Buried: The Key to Understanding the Copper Scroll." *BAR* 19 (Nov./Dec. 1993):38.

————. "'Yom Kippur' in Qumran." *RQ* 3 (1961):117–24.

Leibel, D. "Shabbatah shel Kat Midbar Yehudah." *Tarbiz* 29 (1960):296.

Leiman, S. Z. *The Canonization of the Hebrew Scripture: The Talmudic and Midrashic Evidence*. Transactions 47. Hamden, CT: Published for the Connecticut Academy of Arts and Sciences by Archon Books, 1976.

Lévi, I. "Document relatif a la 'Communauté des fils de Sadoq.'" *REJ* 65 (1913):24–31.

Levine, B. A. "*Damascus Document* IX, 17–22. A New Translation and Comments." *RQ* 8 (1973):195–96.

————. "From the Aramaic Enoch Fragments: The Semantics of Cosmography." *JJS* 33 (1982):311–26.

————. "A Further Look at the *Mo'adim* of the *Temple Scroll*." In *Archaeology and History in the Dead Sea Scrolls: The New York University Conference in Memory of Yigael Yadin*, edited by L. H. Schiffman, 53–66. Journal for the Study of the Pseudepigrapha Supplement Series 8; JSOT/ASOR Monographs 2. Sheffield: JSOT Press, 1990.

————. "The *Temple Scroll*: Aspects of Its Historical Provenance and Literary Character." *BASOR* 232 (1978):5–23.

Levine, L. I. *The Rabbinic Class of Roman Palestine in Late Antiquity*. Jerusalem and New York: Yad Izhak Ben-Zvi, Jewish Theological Seminary of America, 1989.

————. "The Second Temple Synagogue: The Formative Years." In *The Synagogue in Late Antiquity*, edited by L. I. Levine, 7–31. Philadelphia: American Schools of Oriental Research, 1987.

Lewis, N., Y. Yadin, and J. C. Greenfield, eds. *The Documents from the Bar Kokhba Period in the Cave of Letters*. Jerusalem: Israel Exploration Society, 1989.

Licht, J. "An Analysis of the Treatise of the Two Spirits in DSD." In *Aspects of the Dead Sea Scrolls*, edited by Rabin C. and Y. Yadin, 88–100. Scripta Hierosolymitana. Jerusalem: Magnes Press, 1958.

————. "Dappim Nosafim le-Fesher Naḥum." *Molad* 19 (1961):454–56.

————. "The Doctrine of the *Thanksgiving Scroll*." *IEJ* 6 (1956):1–13, 89–101.

————. "Ha-Munah Goral be-Khetaveha shel Kat Midbar Yehudah." *Beth Miqra* 1 (1955/6):90–99.

————. "An Ideal Town Plan from Qumran—The Description of the New Jerusalem." *IEJ* 29 (1979):45–59.

————. *Megillat ha-Hodayot mi-Megillot Midbar Yehudah.* Jerusalem: Bialik Institute, 1957.

————. *Megillat ha-Serakhim mi-Megillot Midbar Yehudah.* Jerusalem: Bialik Institute, 1965.

————. "Ra'atah shel ha-'Ishah ha-Zarah: Shir she-Nimṣa bi-Seride Khetavehah shel Kat Midbar Yehudah (4Q184)." In *Ha-Miqra' ve-Toldot Yisrael: Mehkarim le-Zikhro shel Y. Liver,* edited by B. Uffenheimer, 289–96. Tel Aviv: Tel-Aviv University, 1972.

————. "Shoqayim Siman le-Behirah." *Tarbiz* 35 (1965/6):18–26.

————. "Torat ha-'Itim shel Kat Midbar Yehudah ve-shel Meḥashve Qiṣin 'Aḥerim." *Eretz-Israel* 8 (1967):65–70.

Lichtenberger, H. "The Dead Sea Scrolls and John the Baptist: Reflections on Josephus' Account of John the Baptist." In *The Dead Sea Scrolls: Forty Years of Research,* edited by D. Dimant and U. Rappaport, 340–46. Leiden and Jerusalem: E. J. Brill, Magnes Press, Yad Izhak Ben-Zvi, 1992.

Lieberman, S. "The Discipline in the So-Called Dead Sea Manual of Discipline." *JBL* 71 (1951):199–206.

————. "Light on the Cave Scrolls from Rabbinic Sources." *PAAJR* 20 (1951):395–404.

Lifshitz, B. "The Greek Documents from Nahal Seelim and Nahal Mishmar." In *Judean Desert Caves: Survey and Excavations 1960,* 53–62. Jerusalem: Israel Exploration Society, 1961.

————. "The Greek Documents from the Cave of Horror." In *Judean Desert Caves: Survey and Excavations, 1961,* 201–6. Jerusalem: Israel Exploration Society, 1962.

Lim, T. H. "The Chronology of the Flood Story in a Qumran Text (4Q252)." *JJS* 43 (1992):288–98.

————. "Eschatological Orientation and the Alteration of Scripture in the *Habakkuk Pesher.*" *JNES* 49 (1990):185–94.

————. "Notes on 4Q252 fr. 1, cols. i–ii." *JJS* 44 (1993):121–26.

————. "The 'Psalms of Joshua' (4Q379 fr. 22 col. 2): A Reconsideration of Its Text." *JJS* 44 (1993):309–12.

————. "The Wicked Priests of the Groningen Hypothesis." *JBL* 112 (1993):415–25.

Liver, J. "The Doctrine of the Two Messiahs in Sectarian Literature in the Time of the Second Commonwealth." *HTR* 52 (1959):149–85.

————. "The 'Sons of Zadok the Priests' in the Dead Sea Sect." *RQ* 6 (1967):3–32.

Lowy, S. "Some Aspects of Normative and Sectarian Interpretation of the Scriptures (the Contribution of the Judean Scrolls Toward Systematization)." *The Annual of Leeds University Oriental Society* 6 (1969):98–163.

Lübbe, J. "A Reinterpretation of 4 Q Testimonia." *RQ* 12 (1986):177–86.

Magness, J. "The Community at Qumran in Light of Its Pottery." In *Methods of Investigation of the Dead Sea Scrolls and the Khirbet Qumran Site: Present Realities and Future Prospects,* edited by J. J. Collins, N. Golb, D. Pardee, and M. Wise. *Annals of the New York Academy of Sciences.* New York: The New York Academy of Sciences, 1994.

————. "Masada—Arms and the Man." *BAR* 18 (July/Aug. 1992):58–67.

Maier, J. "Shîrê 'Ôlat Hash-Shabbat: Some Observations on Their Calendric Implications and on Their Style." In *The Madrid Qumran Conference: Proceedings of the International Congress on the Dead Sea Scrolls, Madrid, 18–21 March, 1991,* edited by J. Trebolle Barrera and L. Vegas Montaner, vol. 2, 543–60. Studies on the Texts of the Desert of Judah 11, 2. Leiden: E. J. Brill, 1992.

———. "The *Temple Scroll* and Tendencies in the Cultic Architecture of the Second Commonwealth." In *Archaeology and History in the Dead Sea Scrolls: The New York University Conference in Memory of Yigael Yadin*, edited by L. H. Schiffman, 67–82. Journal for the Study of the Pseudepigrapha Supplement Series 8; JSOT/ASOR Monographs 2. Sheffield: JSOT Press, 1990.

———. *The Temple Scroll*. Journal for the Study of the Old Testament Supplement Series 34. Sheffield: JSOT Press, 1985.

———. "Weitere Stücke zum Nahumkommentar aus der Höhle 4 von Qumran." *Judaica* 18 (1962):215–50.

Mandel, P. "On the 'Duplicate Copy' of the *Copper Scroll* (3Q15)." *RQ* 16 (1993):69–76.

Mansoor, M. *The Thanksgiving Hymns*. Studies on the Texts of the Desert of Judah 3. Grand Rapids: Eerdmans, 1961.

Marcus, R. "*Mebaqqer* and *Rabbim* in the *Manual of Discipline* VI, 11–13." *JBL* 75 (1956):398–402.

Margalioth, M. *Sefer ha-Razim*. Jerusalem: American Academy for Jewish Research, 1966.

Mathews, K. A. "The Background of the Paleo-Hebrew Texts at Qumran." In *The Word of the Lord Shall Go Forth*, edited by C. Meyers and M. O'Connor, 549–68. Winona Lake, IN: Eisenbrauns, 1983.

McCarter, K. P. "The Mystery of the *Copper Scroll*." In *Understanding the Dead Sea Scrolls*, edited by H. Shanks, 227–41. New York: Random House, 1992.

McLean, M. D. *The Use and Development of Palaeo-Hebrew in the Hellenistic and Roman Periods*. Dissertation, Harvard University, 1982.

Metso, S. "The Primary Results of the Reconstruction of 4QS^e." *JJS* 44 (1993):303–8.

Metzger, B. M. "The Furniture in the Scriptorium at Qumran." *RQ* 1 (1959):509–16.

Milgrom, J. "Further Studies in the *Temple Scroll*." *JQR* 71 (1980–81):1–17, 89–106.

———. "'Sabbath' and 'Temple City' in the *Temple Scroll*." *BASOR* 232 (1978):25–27.

———. "The Scriptural Foundations and Deviations in the Laws of Purity of the *Temple Scroll*." In *Archaeology and History in the Dead Sea Scrolls: The New York University Conference in Memory of Yigael Yadin*, edited by L. H. Schiffman, 83–99. Journal for the Study of the Pseudepigrapha Supplement Series 8; JSOT/ASOR Monographs 2. Sheffield: JSOT Press, 1990.

———. "Studies in the *Temple Scroll*." *JBL* 97 (1978):501–23.

———. "The *Temple Scroll*." *BA* 41 (1978):105–20.

Milik, J. T. "4Q Visions de Amram et une citation d'Origène." *RB* 79 (1972):77–97.

———. *The Books of Enoch: Aramaic Fragments of Qumrân Cave 4*. Oxford: Clarendon Press, 1976.

———. "Daniel et Susanne à Qumrân." In *De la Tôrah au Messie*, edited by M. Carrez, J. Doré, and P. Grelot, 337–59. Paris: Desclée, 1981.

———. "Écrits préesséniens de Qumrân: d'Hénoch à Amram." edited by M. Delcor. In *Qumrân: Sa piété, sa théologie et son milieu*, 91–106. Bibliotheca ephemeridum theologicarum lovaniensium 46. Paris-Gembloux and Leuven: Duculot, Leuven University Press, 1978.

———. "Fragment d'une source du Psautier (4Q Ps 89)." *RB* 73 (1966):94–106.

———. "*Milki-ṣedeq* et *Milki-reša'* dans les anciens écrits juifs et chrétiens." *JJS* 23 (1972):95–144.
———. "Les Modèles araméens du livre d'Esther dans la grotte 4 de Qumrân." *RQ* 15 (1992):321–99, plates I–VII.
———. "La Patrie de Tobie." *RB* 73 (1966):522–30.
———. "'Prière de Nabonide' et autres écrits d'un cycle de Daniel: fragments araméens de Qumrân 4." *RB* 63 (1956):407–15.
———. "Problèmes de la littérature hénochique à la lumière des fragments araméens de Qumrân." *HTR* 64 (1971):333–78.
———. *Qumran Cave 4 II: I. Archaeologie II. Targums (4Q128–4Q157).* Discoveries in the Judaean Desert of Jordan 6. Oxford: Clarendon Press, 1987.
———. "[Review of] P. Wernberg-Møller, *The Manual of Discipline*, 1957." *RB* 67 (1960):410–16.
———. *Ten Years of Discovery in the Wilderness of Judaea.* Studies in Biblical Theology 26. London: SCM Press, 1959.
———. "Le Testament de Lévi en araméen." *RB* 62 (1955):398–406.
Milikowsky, C. "Again: DAMASCUS in *Damascus Document* and in Rabbinic Literature." *RQ* 11 (1982):97–106.
Millar, F. "The Background to the Maccabean Revolution: Reflections on Martin Hengel's 'Judaism and Hellenism.'" *JJS* 29 (1978):1–26.
Moore, G. F. *Judaism in the First Centuries of the Christian Era: The Age of the Tannaim.* 3 vols. Cambridge, MA: Harvard University Press, 1927–30.
Moore, R. D. "Personification of the Seduction of Evil: 'The Wiles of the Wicked Woman.'" *RQ* 10 (1981):505–20.
Morgenstern, J. "The Calendar of the Book of Jubilees: Its Origin and Its Character." *VT* 5 (1955):34–76.
Mowinckel, S. *He That Cometh,* translated by G. W. Anderson. Oxford: Basil Blackwell, 1956.
Murphy-O'Connor, J. "A Critique of the Princes of Judah (CD VIII, 3–19)." *RB* 79 (1972):200–216.
———. "The *Damascus Document* Revisited." *RB* 92 (1985):223–46.
———. "A Literary Analysis of *Damascus Document* XIX, 33-XX, 34." *RB* 79 (1972):544–64.
Murphy-O'Connor, J., and J. H. Charlesworth, eds. *Paul and the Dead Sea Scrolls.* New York: Crossroad, 1990.
Naveh, J., and S. Shaked. *Amulets and Magic Bowls: Aramaic Incantations of Late Antiquity.* Jerusalem: Magnes Press, 1985.
———. *Magic Spells and Formulae: Aramaic Incantations of Late Antiquity.* Jerusalem: Magnes Press, 1993.
Nebe, G. W. "Die Masada-Psalmen-Handschrift M1039–160 nach einem jüngst veröffentlichten Photo mit Text von *Psalm* 81:2–85:6." *RQ* 14 (1989):89–98.
Netzer, E. "The Last Days and Hours at Masada." *BAR* 17 (Nov./Dec. 1991):20–32.
———. *Masada III: The Yigael Yadin Excavations 1963–1965, Final Reports.* Jerusalem: Israel Exploration Society, The Hebrew University of Jerusalem, 1991.
Neusner, J. "'By the Testimony of Two Witnesses' in the *Damascus Document* IX, 17–22 and in Pharisaic-Rabbinic Laws." *RQ* 8 (1973):197–218.

———. "Damascus Document IX, 16–23 and Parallels." RQ 9 (1978):441–44.

———. Fellowship in Judaism. London: Vallentine, Mitchell, 1963.

———. From Politics to Piety: The Emergence of Pharisaic Judaism. Englewood Cliffs, NJ: Prentice Hall, 1973.

———. "HBR and N'MN." RQ 5 (1964):119–22.

———. The Rabbinic Traditions about the Pharisees before 70. 3 vols. Leiden: E. J. Brill, 1971.

Newsom, C. A. "4Q370: An Admonition Based on the Flood." RQ 13 (1988):23–43.

———. "4Q374: A Discourse on the Exodus/Conquest Tradition." In The Dead Sea Scrolls: Forty Years of Research, edited by D. Dimant and U. Rappaport, 40–52. Leiden and Jerusalem: E. J. Brill, Magnes Press, Yad Izhak Ben-Zvi, 1992.

———. "Apocalyptic and the Discourse of the Qumran Community." JNES 49 (1990):135–44.

———. "'He Has Established for Himself Priests': Human and Angelic Priesthood in the Qumran Sabbath Shirot." In Archaeology and History in the Dead Sea Scrolls: The New York University Conference in Memory of Yigael Yadin, edited by L. H. Schiffman, 101–20. Journal for the Study of the Pseudepigrapha Supplement Series 8; JSOT/ASOR Monographs 2. Sheffield: JSOT Press, 1990.

———. "Merkabah Exegesis in the Qumran Shabbat Shirot." JJS 38 (1987):11–30.

———. "The 'Psalms of Joshua' from Qumran Cave 4." JJS 39 (1988):56–73.

———. Songs of the Sabbath Sacrifice: A Critical Edition. Harvard Semitic Studies 27. Atlanta: Scholars Press, 1985.

Newsom, C. A., and Y. Yadin. "The Masada Fragment of the Qumran Songs of the Sabbath Sacrifice." IEJ 34 (1984):77–88 and plate.

Nickelsburg, G. W. E. "The Epistle of Enoch and the Qumran Literature." JJS 33 (1982):333–48.

———. Resurrection, Immortality, and Eternal Life in Intertestamental Judaism. Harvard Theological Studies 26. Cambridge, MA: Harvard University, 1972.

Nitzan, B. "Hymns from Qumran—4Q510–4Q511." In The Dead Sea Scrolls: Forty Years of Research, edited by D. Dimant and U. Rappaport, 53–63. Leiden and Jerusalem: E. J. Brill, Magnes Press, Yad Izhak Ben-Zvi, 1992.

———. Megillat Pesher Habakkuk. Jerusalem: Bialik Institute, 1986.

———. Qumran Prayer and Religious Poetry. Studies on the Texts of the Desert of Judah 12. Leiden: E. J. Brill, 1994.

North, R. "The Damascus of Qumran Geography." PEQ 87 (1955):34–38.

———. "The Qumran Reservoirs." In The Bible in Current Catholic Thought, edited by J. L. McKenzie, 100–132. New York: Herder and Herder, 1962.

———. "The Qumran 'Sadducees.'" CBQ 17 (1955):44–68.

———. "Qumran 'Serek A' and Related Fragments." Orientalia N. S. 25 (1956):90–99.

Oppenheimer, A., ed. Mered Bar-Kokhba. Sugyot be-Toldot 'Am Yisra'el 10. Jerusalem: Merkaz Shazar, 1980.

———. The 'Am ha-Aretz: A Study in the Social History of the Jewish People in the Hellenistic-Roman Period. Arbeiten zur Literatur und Geschichte des hellenistischen Judentums 8. Leiden: E. J. Brill, 1977.

Orlinsky, H. "The Mysterious Mr. Green." RJ 20 (Spring 1992):47–48.

Ouellette, E. "Variantes qumrâniennes du Livre des psaumes." RQ 7 (1969):105–24.

Pardee, D. "A Restudy of the Commentary on Psalm 37 from the Qumran Cave 4." *RQ* 8 (1973):163–94.

Patrich, J. "'Amat ha-Mayim me-'Eṭam le-Vet ha-Miqdash ve-Halakhah Ṣeduqit 'Ahat." *Cathedra* 17 (1981):11–23.

———. "Khirbet Qumran in Light of New Archaeological Explorations in the Qumran Caves." In *Methods of Investigation of the Dead Sea Scrolls and the Khirbet Qumran Site: Present Realities and Future Prospects,* edited by J. J. Collins, N. Golb, D. Pardee, and M. Wise. *Annals of the New York Academy of Sciences.* New York: New York Academy of Sciences, 1994.

Peters, F. E. *The Harvest of Hellenism.* New York: Clarion, 1970.

———. *Jerusalem: The Holy City in the Eyes of Chroniclers, Visitors, Pilgrims, and Prophets from the Days of Abraham to the Beginnings of Modern Times.* Princeton NJ: Princeton University Press, 1985.

Pfann, S. J. "Chronological List of the Negatives of the PAM, IAA, and Shrine of the Book." In *The Dead Sea Scrolls on Microfiche: A Comprehensive Facsimile Edition of the Texts from the Judean Desert. Companion Volume,* edited by E. Tov, with the collaboration of S. J. Pfann, 73–95. Leiden: E. J. Brill and IDC, 1993.

———. "The History of the Judean Desert Discoveries." In *The Dead Sea Scrolls on Microfiche: A Comprehensive Facsimile Edition of the Texts from the Judean Desert. Companion Volume,* edited by E. Tov, with the collaboration with S. J. Pfann, 97–108. Leiden: E. J. Brill and IDC, 1993.

———. "Sites in the Judean Desert Where Texts Have Been Found." In *The Dead Sea Scrolls on Microfiche: A Comprehensive Facsimile Edition of the Texts from the Judean Desert. Companion Volume,* edited by E. Tov, with the collaboration of S. J. Pfann, 109–19. Leiden: E. J. Brill and IDC, 1993.

Pixner, B. "Unravelling the *Copper Scroll* Case: A Study on the Topography of 3Q15." *RQ* 11 (1983):323–66.

Ploeg, J. van der. "Fragments d'un manuscrit de psaumes de Qumran." *RB* 74 (1967):408–13.

———. "The Meals of the Essenes." *JSS* 2 (1957):163–75.

———. "Le Psaume XCI dans une recension de Qumran." *RB* 22 (1965):210–17.

———. *Le Rouleau de la guerre.* Studies on the Texts of the Desert of Judah 2. Leiden: E. J. Brill, 1959.

Ploeg, J. van der, and A. S. van der Woude. *Le Targum de Job de la grotte XI de Qumrân,* in collaboration with B. Jongeling. Koninklijke Nederlandse Akademie van Wetenschappen. Leiden: E. J. Brill, 1971.

Polak, F. "Statistics and Textual Filiation: The Case of 4QSamᵃ/LXX (with a Note on the Text of the Pentateuch)." In *Septuagint, Scrolls, and Cognate Writings,* edited by G. Brooke and B. Lindars, 215–76. Septuagint and Cognate Studies 33. Atlanta: Scholars Press, 1992.

Polotsky, H. J. "The Greek Papyri from the Cave of the Letters." In *Judean Desert Caves: Survey and Excavations, 1961,* 258–62. Jerusalem: Israel Exploration Society, 1962.

Poole, J. B., and R. Reed. "The 'Tannery' of Ain Feshka." *PEQ* 93 (1961):114–23.

Pouilly, J. *La Règle de la communauté de Qumrân: son évolution littéraire.* Cahiers de la Revue Biblique 17. Paris: J. Gabalda, 1976.

Priest, J. F. "*Mebaqqer, Paqid* and the Messiah." *JBL* 81 (1962):55–61.

———. "The Messiah and the Meal in 1QS^a." *JBL* 82 (1963):95–100.

Pritchard, J. B., ed. *Ancient Near Eastern Texts Relating to the Old Testament.* Princeton, NJ: Princeton University Press, 1969.

Puech, É. "11QPsAp^a: un rituel d'excorcisme: essai de reconstruction." *RQ* 14 (1990):377–408.

———. *La Croyance des Esséniens en la vie future: Immortalité, résurrection, vie éternelle?* Études bibliques 21. 2 vols. Paris: J. Gabalda, 1993.

———. "4Q525 et les péricopes des béatitudes en *Ben Sira* et Matthieu." *RB* 97 (1991):80–106.

———. "Une Apocalypse messianique (4Q521)." *RQ* 15 (1992):475–522.

———. "Les Deux derniers Psaumes davidiques du rituel d'exorcisme, 11QPsAP^a IV4-V14." In *The Dead Sea Scrolls: Forty Years of Research*, edited by D. Dimant and U. Rappaport, 64–89. Leiden and Jerusalem: E. J. Brill, Magnes Press, Yad Izhak Ben-Zvi, 1992.

———. "Fragment d'une apocalypse en araméen (4Q246 = pseudo-Dan^d) et al 'Royaume de Dieu.'" *RB* 99, no. 98–131 (1992).

———. "Fragments d'un apocryphe de Lévi et le personnage eschatologique: 4QTestLévi^c–d(?) et 4QAJa." In *The Madrid Qumran Conference: Proceedings of the International Congress on the Dead Sea Scrolls, Madrid, 18–21 March, 1991*, edited by J. Trebolle Barrera and L. Vegas Montaner, vol. 2, 449–501. Studies on the Texts of the Desert of Judah 11, 2. Leiden: E. J. Brill, 1992.

———. "Un Hymne essénien en partie retrouvé et les Béatitudes. 1QH V 12-VI 18 (= col. XIII–XIV 7) et 4QBéat." *RQ* 13 (1988):59–88.

———. "Notes en marge de 8KhXIIgr." *RQ* 15 (1992):583–94.

———. "Notes en marge de 11QPaléoLévitique: Le Fragment L, des fragments inédits et une jarre de la grotte 11." *RB* 96 (1989):161–83.

———. "Notes sur le manuscrit de 11QMelkîsédeq." *RQ* 12 (1987):483–515.

———. "La Pierre de Sion et l'autel des holocaustes d'après un manuscrit hébreu de la grotte 4 (4Q522)." *RB* 99 (1992):676–96.

———. "Quelques aspects de la restauration du *Rouleau des hymnes*." *JJS* 39 (1988):38–55.

———. "[Review of] Moshe Weinfeld, *The Organizational Pattern and the Penal Code of the Qumran Sect*, 1986." *RQ* 14 (1989):147–48.

———. "Le Testament de Qahat en araméen de la grotte 4 (4QTQah)." *RQ* 15 (1991):23–54.

Qimron, E. "Celibacy in the Dead Sea Scrolls and the Two Kinds of Sectarians." In *The Madrid Qumran Congress: Proceedings of the International Congress on the Dead Sea Scrolls, Madrid, 18–21 March, 1991*, edited by J. Trebolle Barrera and L. Vegas Montaner, vol. 1, 287–94. Studies on the Texts of the Desert of Judah 11, 1. Leiden and Madrid: E. J. Brill, Editorial Complutense, 1992.

———. "Column 14 of the Temple Scroll." *IEJ* 38 (1988):44–46.

———. "He'arot le-Nusaḥ Megillat ha-Miqdash." *Tarbiz* 53 (1983/4):139–41.

———. *The Hebrew of the Dead Sea Scrolls.* Harvard Semitic Studies 29. Atlanta: Scholars Press, 1986.

———. "Ketav Yad D shel Serekh ha-Yaḥad mi-Ma'arah 4 be-Qumran: Pirsum Muqdam shel Turim 7–8." *Tarbiz* 60 (1991):435–37.

———. "Le-Millonah shel Megillat ha-Miqdash." *Shnaton* 4 (1980):239–61.

———. "Le-Nushah shel Megillat ha-Miqdash." *Leshonenu*, no. 42 (1978):136–45.

———. "The Need for a Comprehensive Critical Edition of the Dead Sea Scrolls." In *Archaeology and History in the Dead Sea Scrolls: The New York University Conference in Memory of Yigael Yadin*, edited by L. H. Schiffman, 121–31. Journal for the Study of the Pseudepigrapha Supplement Series 8; JSOT/ASOR Monographs 2. Sheffield: JSOT Press, 1990.

———. "New Readings in the *Temple Scroll*." *IEJ* 28 (1978):161–72.

———. "Observations on the History of Early Hebrew (1000 B.C.E.–200 C.E.) in the Light of the Dead Sea Scrolls." In *The Dead Sea Scrolls: Forty Years of Research*, edited by D. Dimant and U. Rappaport, 349–62. Leiden and Jerusalem: E. J. Brill, Magnes Press, Yad Izhak Ben-Zvi, 1992.

———. "A Review Article of *Songs of the Sabbath Sacrifice: A Critical Edition*, by Carol Newsom." *HTR* 79 (1986):349–71.

———. "Shalosh He'arot le-Nushah shel Megillat ha-Miqdash." *Tarbiz* 51 (1981/2): 135–37.

———. "The Text of CDC." In *The Damascus Document Reconsidered*, edited by M. Broshi, 9–49. Jerusalem: Israel Exploration Society, The Shrine of the Book, Israel Museum, 1992.

Qimron, E., and J. Strugnell. "An Unpublished Halakhic Letter from Qumran." In *Biblical Archaeology Today: Proceedings of the International Congress on Biblical Archaeology, Jerusalem, April 1984*, edited by J. Amitai, 400–407. Jerusalem: Israel Exploration Society, The Israel Academy of Sciences and Humanities, in cooperation with the American Schools of Oriental Research, 1985.

———. "An Unpublished Halakhic Letter from Qumran." *Israel Museum Journal* 4 (1985):9–12.

Qimron, E. and J. Strugnell, with contributions by Y. Sussman and A. Yardeni, *Miqsat Ma'ase ha-Torah*. Discoveries in the Judaean Desert 10. Oxford: Clarendon Press, 1994.

Rabin, C. *Qumran Studies*. Scripta Judaica 2. Oxford: Oxford University, 1957.

———. *The Zadokite Documents*. Oxford: Clarendon Press, 1954.

Rabinovich, A. "Operation Scroll: Recent Revelations about Qumran Promise to Shake Up Dead Sea Scroll Scholarship." *Jerusalem Post Magazine* (May 6, 1994):6–10.

Rabinovitch, N. L. "*Damascus Document IX, 17–22* and Rabbinic Parallels." *RQ* 9 (1977):113–16.

Rabinowitz, I. "The Authorship, Audience, and Date of the de Vaux Fragment of an Unknown Work." *JBL* 71 (1952):19–32.

———. "*Pêsher/Pittârôn*: Its Biblical Meaning and Its Significance in the Qumran Literature." *RQ* 8 (1973). 219–32.

———. "A Reconsideration of 'Damascus' and '390 Years' in the 'Damascus' ('Zadokite') Fragments." *JBL* 73 (1954):11–35.

Rad, G. von. "The Origin of the Concept of the Day of Yahweh." *JSS* 4 (1959):97–108.

Reed, S. A. *Dead Sea Scrolls Inventory Project: Lists of Documents, Photographs and Museum Plates*. 14 fascicles. Claremont, CA: Ancient Biblical Manuscript Center, 1991–93.

———. "Preliminary List of Aramaic Documents from Qumran Cave 4." *The Comprehensive Aramaic Lexicon (CAL) Newsletter*, no. 9 (February 1992):1–4.

———. "What Is a Fragment?" *JJS* 45 (1994):123–25.

————, comp., M. J. Lundberg, ed. *The Dead Sea Scrolls on Microfiche: A Comprehensive Facsimile Edition of the Texts from the Judean Desert, Inventory List of Photographs.* Leiden: E. J. Brill, IDC, 1993.

Rhoads, D. *Israel in Revolution: 6–74 C.E.* Philadelphia: Fortress Press, 1976.

Richardson, H. N. "Some Notes on 1QSa." *JBL* 76 (1857):108–22.

Rigaux, B. "Révélation des mystères et perfection à Qumran et dans le Nouveau Testament." *NTS* 4 (1957–58):237–62.

Ringgren, H. *The Faith of Qumran: Theology of the Dead Sea Scrolls,* translated by E. P. Sanders. Philadelphia: Fortress Press, 1963.

Rofé, A. "Acts of Nahash According to 4QSamᵃ." *IEJ* 32 (1982):129–33.

————. "The Battle of David and Goliath—Folklore, Theology, Eschatology." In *Judaic Perspectives on Ancient Israel,* edited by J. Neusner, 117–51. Philadelphia: Fortress Press, 1987.

————. "The Nomistic Correction in Biblical Manuscripts and Its Occurrence in 4QSamᵃ." *RQ* 14 (1989):247–54.

————. "The Onset of Sects in Postexilic Judaism: Neglected Evidence from the Septuagint, Trito-Isaiah, *Ben Sira,* and Malachi." In *The Social World of Formative Christianity and Judaism: Essays in Tribute to Howard Clark Kee,* edited by J. Neusner, E. S. Frerichs, P. Borgen, and R. Horsley, 39–49. Philadelphia: Fortress Press, 1988.

Rosenthal, J. M. "'Al Hishtalshelut Halakhah be-Sefer Berit Dameseq." In *Sefer ha-Yovel Mugash li-Khvod ha-Rav Shim'on Federbush,* edited by J. L. Maimon, 293–303. Jerusalem: Mosad Harav Kook, 1960.

————. "Biblical Exegesis of 4QpIs." *JQR* 60 (1969/70):27–36.

Roth, C. *The Dead Sea Scrolls: A New Historical Approach.* New York: W. W. Norton, 1965.

————. "Qumran and Masadah: A Final Clarification Regarding the Dead Sea Sect." *RQ* 5 (1964):81–88.

Rowley, H. H. *The Zadokite Fragments and the Dead Sea Scrolls.* Oxford: Basil Blackwell, 1952.

Rylaarsdam, J. C. *Revelation in Jewish Wisdom Literature.* Chicago: University of Chicago Press, 1974.

Saldarini, A. *Pharisees, Scribes and Sadducees in Palestinian Society.* Wilmington, DE: Michael Glazier, 1988.

Sanders, E. P. *Jewish Law from Jesus to the Mishnah.* Philadelphia: Trinity Press International, 1990.

————. *Paul and Palestinian Judaism: A Comparison of Patterns of Religion.* Philadelphia: Fortress Press, 1977.

Sanders, J. A. "Cave 11 Surprises and the Question of Canon." In *New Directions in Biblical Archaeology,* edited by D. N. Freedman and J. C. Greenfield, 113–30. Garden City, NY: Doubleday, 1971.

————. *The Dead Sea Psalms Scroll.* Ithaca, NY: Cornell University, 1967.

————. "The Old Testament in 11QMelchizedek." *JANES* 5 (1973):373–82.

————. *The Psalms Scroll of Qumrân Cave 11 (11QPsᵃ).* Discoveries in the Judaean Desert 4. Oxford: Clarendon Press, 1965.

————. *Torah and Canon.* Philadelphia: Fortress Press, 1972.

Sanderson, J. E. "The Contribution of 4QpaleoExod^m to Textual Criticism." *RQ* 13 (1988):547–60.

———. *An Exodus Scroll from Qumran: 4Qpaleo-Exod^m and the Samaritan Tradition.* Harvard Semitic Studies 30. Atlanta: Scholars Press, 1986.

Sarna, N. M. "Canon." In *Encyclopaedia Judaica*, vol. 4, cols. 816–36. Jerusalem: Keter, 1971.

———. "The Order of the Books." In *Studies in Jewish Bibliography History and Literature, in Honor of I. Edward Kiev*, edited by C. Berlin, 407–13. New York: Ktav, 1971.

———. "[Review of] The *Psalm Scroll* in Cave 11." *Conservative Judaism* 20 (1966):63–66.

———. *Songs of the Heart.* New York: Schocken Books, 1993.

Scanlin, H. *The Dead Sea Scrolls and Modern Translations of the Old Testament.* Wheaton, IL: Tyndale House, 1993.

Schäfer, P. *The Hidden and Manifest God: Some Major Themes in Early Jewish Mysticism.* SUNY Series in Judaica. Albany, NY: State University of New York Press, 1992.

Schalit, A. *Hordos ha-Melekh: ha-'Ish u-Fo'alo.* Jerusalem: Mosad Bialik, 1964.

Schechter, S. *Aspects of Rabbinic Theology.* New York: Macmillan, 1909.

———. *Documents of Jewish Sectaries: Fragments of a Zadokite Work.* Prolegomenon by J. A. Fitzmyer. 2 vols. New York: Ktav, 1970.

Schiffman, L. H. "4QMysteries^a: A Preliminary Edition." In *Jonas Greenfield Jubilee Volume*, in press.

———. "4QMysteries^b: A Preliminary Edition." *RQ*: in press.

———. "4QOrdinances^a,b." In *The Rule of the Community and Related Documents*, edited by J. H. Charlesworth, vol. 1, 145–75. The Princeton Theological Seminary Dead Sea Scrolls Project. Tübingen: J. C. B. Mohr (Paul Siebeck), 1994.

———, ed. *Archaeology and History in the Dead Sea Scrolls: The New York University Conference in Memory of Yigael Yadin.* Journal for the Study of the Pseudepigrapha Supplement Series 8; JSOT/ASOR Monographs 2. Sheffield: JSOT Press, 1990.

———. "Architecture and Law: The Temple and Its Courtyards in the *Temple Scroll*." In *From Ancient Israel to Modern Judaism: Intellect in Quest of Understanding, Essays in Honor of Marvin Fox*, edited by J. Neusner, E. S. Frerichs, and N. M. Sarna, vol. 1, 267–84. Brown Judaic Studies 159. Atlanta: Scholars Press, 1989.

———. "Communal Meals at Qumran." *RQ* 10 (1979):45–56.

———. "The Concept of the Messiah in Second Temple and Rabbinic Literature." *Review and Expositor* 84 (1987):235–46.

———. "Confessionalism and the Study of the Dead Sea Scrolls." *Jewish Studies* 31 (1991):3–14.

———. "The Dead Sea Scrolls and the Early History of Jewish Liturgy." In *The Synagogue in Late Antiquity*, edited by L. I. Levine, 33–48. Philadelphia: American Schools of Oriental Research, 1987.

———. "Dead Sea Scrolls and the History of Judaism." In *Proceedings of the Library of Congress Symposium on the Dead Sea Scrolls.* Washington, DC: Library of Congress, in press.

———. "The Deuteronomic Paraphrase of the *Temple Scroll*." *RQ* 15 (1992):543–68.

———. *The Eschatological Community of the Dead Sea Scrolls: A Study of the Rule of the Congregation.* SBL Monograph Series 38. Atlanta: Scholars Press, 1989.

———. "Essenes." In *The Encyclopedia of Religion, vol. 5,* edited by M. Eliade, 163–66. New York: Macmillan, 1987.

———. "Exclusion from the Sanctuary and the City of the Sanctuary in the *Temple Scroll.*" *HAR* 9 (1985):301–20.

———. *From Text to Tradition: A History of Second Temple and Rabbinic Judaism.* Hoboken, NJ: Ktav, 1991.

———. "The Furnishings of the Temple According to the *Temple Scroll.*" In *The Madrid Qumran Conference: Proceedings of the International Congress on the Dead Sea Scrolls, Madrid, 18–21 March, 1991,* edited by J. Trebolle Barrera and L. Vegas Montaner, vol. 2, 621–34. Studies on the Texts of the Desert of Judah 11, 2. Leiden: E. J. Brill, 1992.

———. *The Halakhah at Qumran.* Leiden: E. J. Brill, 1975.

———. *Halakhah, Halikhah u-Meshihiyut be-Khat Midbar Yehudah.* Jerusalem: Merkaz Shazar, 1993.

———. "The Impurity of the Dead in the *Temple Scroll.*" In *Archaeology and History in the Dead Sea Scrolls: The New York University Conference in Memory of Yigael Yadin,* edited by L. H. Schiffman, 135–56. Journal for the Study of the Pseudepigrapha Supplement Series 8; JSOT/ASOR Monographs 2. Sheffield: JSOT Press, 1990.

———. "Jewish Sectarianism in Second Temple Times." In *Great Schisms in Jewish History,* edited by R. Jospe and S. Wagner, 1–46. New York: Center for Judaic Studies, Ktav, 1981.

———. "The King, His Guard and the Royal Council in the *Temple Scroll.*" *PAAJR* 54 (1987):237–59.

———. "Laws Concerning Idolatry in the Temple Scroll." In *Uncovering Ancient Stones: Essays in Memory of H. Neil Richardson,* edited by L. M. Hopfe. Winona Lake, IN: Eisenbrauns, 1994, 159–75.

———. "Laws Pertaining to Women in the *Temple Scroll.*" In *The Dead Sea Scrolls: Forty Years of Research,* edited by D. Dimant and U. Rappaport, 210–28. Leiden and Jerusalem: E. J. Brill, Magnes Press, Yad Izhak Ben-Zvi, 1992.

———. "Legislation Concerning Relations with Non-Jews in the *Zadokite Fragments* and in Tannaitic Literature." *RQ* 11 (1983):379–89.

———. "*Merkavah* Speculation at Qumran: the 4Q *Serekh Shirot 'Olat ha-Shabbat.*" In *Mystics, Philosophers and Politicians: Essays in Jewish Intellectual History in Honor of Alexander Altmann,* edited by J. Reinharz, D. Swetschinski, and in collaboration with K. P. Bland, 15–47. Duke Monographs in Medieval and Renaissance Studies no. 5. Durham, NC: Duke University Press, 1982.

———. "*Miqsat Ma'aseh ha-Torah* and the *Temple Scroll.*" *RQ* 14 (1990):435–57.

———. "The New *Halakhic Letter* (4QMMT) and the Origins of the Dead Sea Sect." *BA* 53 (1990):64–73.

———. "New Halakhic Texts from Qumran." *Hebrew Studies* 34 (1993):21–33.

———. "Pharisees and Sadducees in *Pesher Nahum.*" In *Minhah Le-Nahum: Biblical and Other Studies Presented to Nahum M. Sarna in Honour of His 70th Birthday,* edited by M. Brettler and M. Fishbane, 272–90. Sheffield: JSOT Press, 1993.

————. "A Preliminary Edition of 4QMysteries^c," forthcoming.

————. "Purity and Perfection: Exclusion from the Council of the Community." In *Biblical Archaeology Today: Proceedings of the International Congress on Biblical Archaeology, Jerusalem, April 1984*, edited by J. Amitai, 373–89. Jerusalem: Israel Exploration Society, The Israel Academy of Sciences and Humanities, in Cooperation with the American Schools of Oriental Research, 1985.

————. "Qumran and Rabbinic Halakhah." In *Jewish Civilization in the Hellenistic-Roman Period*, edited by S. Talmon, 138–46. Philadelphia: Trinity Press International, 1991.

————. "The Qumran Law of Testimony." *RQ* 8 (1975):603–12.

————. "[Review of] *An Unknown Jewish Sect* by L. Ginzberg." *JAOS* 99 (1979):113–14.

————. "[Review of] E. Tov, *The Greek Minor Prophets Scroll from Naḥal Ḥever.*" *JBL* 111 (1992):532–35.

————. "[Review of] Yadin's *The Temple Scroll.*" *BA* 48 (1985):122–26.

————. "Sacred Space: The Land of Israel in the *Temple Scroll.*" In *Biblical Archaeology Today 1990*, edited by A. Biran and J. Aviram, 398–410. Jerusalem: Israel Exploration Society, 1993.

————. "The Sacrificial System of the *Temple Scroll* and the *Book of Jubilees.*" In *Society of Biblical Literature 1985 Seminar Papers*, edited by K. H. Richards, 217–33. Atlanta: Society of Biblical Literature, 1985.

————. "The Sadducean Origins of the Dead Sea Scroll Sect." In *Understanding the Dead Sea Scrolls*, edited by H. Shanks, 35–49. New York: Random House, 1992.

————. *Sectarian Law in the Dead Sea Scrolls: Courts, Testimony, and the Penal Code.* Chico, CA: Scholars Press, 1983.

————. "The Septuagint and the *Temple Scroll:* Shared 'Halakhic' Variants," edited by G. Brooke and B. Lindars. In *Septuagint, Scrolls, and Cognate Writings*, 277–97. Septuagint and Cognate Studies 33. Atlanta: Scholars Press, 1992.

————. "Sifrut ha-Hekhalot ve-Khitve Qumran." *Meḥqere Yerushalayim Be-Maḥshevet Yisra'el* 6 (1987):121–38.

————. "The *Temple Scroll* and the Nature of Its Law: The Status of the Question." In *The Community of the Renewed Covenant: The Notre Dame Symposium on the Dead Sea Scrolls*, edited by E. Ulrich and J. C. VanderKam. Notre Dame, IN: University of Notre Dame Press, 1994.

————. "The *Temple Scroll* and the Systems of Jewish Law of the Second Temple Period." In *Temple Scroll Studies*, edited by G. J. Brooke, 246–50. Sheffield: Sheffield Academic Press, 1989.

————. "The *Temple Scroll* in Literary and Philological Perspective." In *Approaches to Ancient Judaism*, edited by W. S. Green, vol. 2, 143–55. Brown Judaic Studies 9. Chico, CA: Scholars Press, 1980.

————. "The Theology of the *Temple Scroll.*" In *The Dead Sea Scrolls: Proceedings of a Conference at the Center for Judaic Studies of the University of Pennsylvania* (JQR Supplement). Philadelphia: Center for Judaic Studies, 1994.

————. *Who Was a Jew? Rabbinic and Halakhic Perspectives on the Jewish Christian Schism.* Hoboken, NJ: Ktav, 1985.

Schiffman, L. H., and M. D. Swartz. *Hebrew and Aramaic Incantation Texts from the*

Cairo Genizah: Selected Texts from Taylor-Schechter Box K1. Semitic Texts and Studies 1. Sheffield: JSOT Press, 1992.

Schiffmann, I. "The Teacher of Righteousness in the Soviet Qumran Studies." In *Mogilany 1989: Papers on the Dead Sea Scrolls,* edited by Z. J. Kapera, vol. 2, 47–52. Kraków: Enigma Press, 1991.

Scholem, G. G. "Hakkarat Panim ve-Sidre Sirṭutin." In *Sefer Assaf,* edited by U. Cassuto, 459–95. Jerusalem, 1952/3.

———. *Jewish Gnosticism, Merkabah Mysticism, and Talmudic Tradition.* New York: Jewish Theological Seminary of America, 1965.

———. *Major Trends in Jewish Mysticism.* New York: Schocken Books, 1977.

———. *The Messianic Idea in Judaism: And Other Essays on Jewish Spirituality.* New York: Schocken Books, 1971.

Schuller, E. M. "4Q380 and 4Q381: Non-Canonical Psalms from Qumran." In *The Dead Sea Scrolls: Forty Years of Research,* edited by D. Dimant and U. Rappaport, 90–100. Leiden and Jerusalem: E. J. Brill, Magnes Press, Yad Izhak Ben-Zvi, 1992.

———. "A Hymn from a Cave Four *Hodayot* Manuscript 4Q427 7 i + ii." *JBL* 112 (1993):605–28.

———. *Non-Canonical Psalms from Qumran: A Pseudepigraphic Collection.* Harvard Semitic Studies 28. Atlanta: Scholars Press, 1986.

———. "A Preliminary Study of 4Q373 and Some Related (?) Fragments." In *The Madrid Qumran Conference: Proceedings of the International Congress on the Dead Sea Scrolls, Madrid, 18–21 March, 1991,* edited by J. Trebolle Barrera and L. Vegas Montaner, vol. 2, 515–30. Studies on the Texts of the Desert of Judah 11, 2. Leiden: E. J. Brill, 1992.

———. "Some Observations on Blessings of God in Texts from Qumran." In *Of Scribes and Scrolls: Studies on the Hebrew Bible, Intertestamental Judaism, and Christian Origins Presented to John Strugnell,* edited by H. W. Attridge, J. J. Collins, and T. H. Tobin, 133–43. College Theology Society Resources in Religion 5. Lanham, MD, and London: University Press of America, 1990.

———. "A Text about Joseph." *RQ* 14 (1990):349–76.

Schürer, E. *The History of the Jewish People in the Age of Jesus Christ (175 B.C.–A.D. 135),* edited by G. Vermes, F. Millar, and M. Goodman, in collaboration with P. Vermes and M. Black. 3 vols. Edinburgh: T. & T. Clark, 1973–87.

Schwartz, D. R. "The Messianic Departure from Judah (4Q Patriarchal Blessings)." *TZ* 37 (1981):257–66.

———. "On Two Aspects of a Priestly View of Descent at Qumran." In *Archaeology and History in the Dead Sea Scrolls: The New York University Conference in Memory of Yigael Yadin,* edited by L. H. Schiffman, 157–79. Journal for the Study of the Pseudepigrapha Supplement Series 8; JSOT/ASOR Monographs 2. Sheffield: JSOT Press for ASOR, 1990.

———. "Qumran ben Kohaniut la-Naṣrut." In *Megillot Midbar Yehudah: 'Arba'im Shenot Meḥqar,* edited by M. Broshi, S. Talmon, S. Japhet, and D. Schwartz, 176–81. Jerusalem: Bialik Institute, Israel Exploration Society, 1992.

———. *Studies in the Jewish Background of Christianity.* Wissenschaftliche Untersuchungen zum Neuen Testament 60. Tübingen: J. C. B. Mohr (Paul Siebeck), 1992.

———. "The Three Temples of 4 Q *Florilegium*." *RQ* 10 (1979):83–92.

Schweitzer, F. M. "The Teacher of Righteousness." In *Mogilany 1989: Papers on the Dead Sea Scrolls*, edited by Z. J. Kapera, vol. 2, 53–97. Kraków: Enigma Press, 1991.

Segal, M. H. "The Qumran *War Scroll* and the Date of Its Composition." In *Aspects of the Dead Sea Scrolls*, edited by C. Rabin and Y. Yadin, 138–43. Scripta Hierosolymitana. Jerusalem: Magnes Press, 1958.

———. *Sefer Ben Sira ha-Shalem*. Jerusalem: Mosad Bialik, 1972.

Segert, S. "Observations on the Poetic Structures in the Songs of the Sabbath Sacrifice." *RQ* 13 (1988):215–24.

Shanks, H., ed. *Understanding the Dead Sea Scrolls*. New York: Random House, 1992.

———. "Carbon-14 Tests Substantiate Scroll Dates." *BAR* 17 (Nov./Dec. 1991):72.

———. "Did Jesus Really Die on the Cross? [Review of] *Jesus & the Riddle of the Dead Sea Scrolls* by B. Thiering." *BAR* 18 (Sept./Oct. 1992):69–70.

———. "Intrigue and the Scroll." In *Understanding the Dead Sea Scrolls*, edited by H. Shanks, 116–25. New York: Random House, 1992.

———. "Is the Vatican Suppressing the Dead Sea Scrolls?" *BAR* 17 (Nov./Dec. 1991): 66–71.

———. "Long Secret Plates from the Unpublished Corpus." *BAR* 17 (Nov./Dec. 1991):64.

———. "The Qumran Settlement: Monastery, Villa or Fortress?" *BAR* 19 (May/June 1993):62–65.

Siegel, J. P. "The Employment of Palaeo-Hebrew Characters for the Divine Name at Qumran in Light of Tannaitic Sources." *HUCA* 42 (1971):159–72.

———. "Two Further Medieval References to the Teacher of Righteousness." *RQ* 9 (1978):437–40.

Silberman, L. "The Two Messiahs of the Manual of Discipline." *VT* 5 (1955):77–82.

Silberman, N. A. *A Prophet from Amongst You: The Life of Yigael Yadin, Soldier, Scholar, and Mythmaker of Modern Israel*. Reading, MA: Addison-Wesley, 1993.

Skehan, P. W. "4QLXXNUM: A Pre-Christian Reworking of the Septuagint." *HTR* 70 (1977):39–50.

———. "The Biblical Scrolls from Qumran and the Text of the Old Testament." *BA* 28 (1965):87–100.

———. "A Psalm Manuscript from Qumran (4QPSb)." *CBQ* 26 (1964):313–22.

———. "Qumran and Old Testament Criticism." In *Qumrân: Sa piété, sa théologie et son milieu*, edited by M. Delcor, 163–82. Bibliotheca ephemeridum theologicarum lovaniensium 46. Paris-Gembloux and Leuven: Duculot, Leuven University Press, 1978.

———. "The Qumran Manuscripts and Textual Criticism." *Suppl. to VT* 4 (1957):148–60.

———. "The Scrolls and the Old Testament Text." In *New Directions in Biblical Archaeology*, edited by D. N. Freedman and J. C. Greenfield, 99–112. Garden City, NY: Doubleday, 1971.

Skehan, P. W., E. Ulrich, and J. Sanderson. *Qumran Cave 4, IV: Palaeo-Hebrew and Greek Biblical Manuscripts*. Discoveries in the Judaean Desert 9. Oxford: Clarendon Press, 1992.

Smallwood, E. M. *The Jews under Roman Rule: From Pompey to Diocletian*. Studies in Judaism in Late Antiquity 20. Leiden: E. J. Brill, 1991.

Smith, M. "Ascent to the Heavens and Deification in 4QM^a." In *Archaeology and*

History in the Dead Sea Scrolls: The New York University Conference in Memory of Yigael Yadin, edited by L. H. Schiffman, 181–88. Journal for the Study of the Pseudepigrapha Supplement Series 8; JSOT/ASOR Monographs 2. Sheffield: JSOT Press, 1990.

———. "'God's Begetting the Messiah' in 1QSa." *NTS* 5 (1958/9):218–24.

———. "Palestinian Judaism in the First Century." In *Israel: Its Role in Civilization,* edited by M. Davis, 67–81. New York: Harper & Row, 1956.

———. "Psalm 151, David, Jesus, and Orpheus." *ZAW* 93 (1981):247–53.

Smith, M. S. "*4Q462* (Narrative) Fragment 1: A Preliminary Edition." *RQ* 15 (1991):55–77.

Sokoloff, M. "Notes on the Aramaic Fragments of Enoch from Qumran Cave 4." *Maarav* 1/2 (1978/79):197–225.

———. *The Targum to Job from Qumran Cave XI.* Bar-Ilan Studies in Near Eastern Languages and Culture. Ramat-Gan: Bar-Ilan University, 1974.

Sparks, H. F. D., ed. *The Apocryphal Old Testament.* Oxford: Clarendon Press, 1984.

———. "The Books of the Qumran Community." *JTS* 6 (1955):226–29.

Starcky, J. "Jerusalem et les manuscrits de la Mer Morte." *Le Monde de la Bible* 1 (1977):39–40.

———. "Psaumes apocryphes de la grotte 4 de Qumrân (4QPs^f vii–x)." *RB* 73 (1966):353–71.

———. "Les Quatre étapes du messianisme à Qumran." *RB* 70 (1963):481–505.

———. "Un Texte messianique araméen de la grotte 4 de Qumrân." In *Ecole des langues orientales anciennes de l'Institut Catholique de Paris: mémorial du cinquantenaire 1914–1964,* 51–66. Travaux de l'Institut Catholique de Paris 10. Paris: Bloud & Gay, 1964.

Steckoll, S. H. "Preliminary Excavation Report in the Qumran Cemetery." *RQ* 6 (1968):323–44.

Stegemann, H. "Die Bedeutung der Qumranfunde für die Erforschung der Apokalyptik." In *Apocalypticism in the Mediterranean World and the Near East: Proceedings of the International Colloquium on Apocalypticism,* edited by D. Hellholm, 495–530. Tübingen: J. C. B. Mohr, 1983.

———. *Die Entstehung der Qumrangemeinde.* Bonn: Rheinische Friedrich-Wilhelms-Universität, 1971.

———. *Die Essener, Qumran, Johannes der Täufer und Jesus.* Freiburg: Herder, 1993.

———. "Das Gesetzekorpus der 'Damaskusschrift' (CD IX–XVI)." *RQ* 14 (1990):409–34.

———. "The Institutions of Israel in the *Temple Scroll.*" In *The Dead Sea Scrolls: Forty Years of Research,* edited by D. Dimant and U. Rappaport, 156–85. Leiden and Jerusalem: E. J. Brill, Magnes Press, Yad Izhak Ben-Zvi, 1992.

———. "'Das Land' in der *Tempelrolle* und in anderen Texten aus den Qumranfunden." In *Das Land Israel in biblischer Zeit,* edited by G. Strecker. 154–71. Göttingen: Vandenhoeck & Ruprecht, 1983.

———. "Methods for the Reconstruction of Scrolls from Scattered Fragments." In *Archaeology and History in the Dead Sea Scrolls: The New York University Conference in Memory of Yigael Yadin,* edited by L. H. Schiffman, 189–220. Journal for the Study of the Pseudepigrapha Supplement Series 8; JSOT/ASOR Monographs 2. Sheffield: JSOT Press, 1990.

———. "The Origins of the *Temple Scroll." Suppl. to VT* 40 (1988):235–56.

———. "Der Pešer Psalm 37 aus Höhle 4 von Qumran." *RQ* 4 (1963):235–70.

———. "The Qumran Essenes—Local Members of the Main Jewish Union in Late Second Temple Times." In *The Madrid Qumran Congress: Proceedings of the International Congress on the Dead Sea Scrolls, Madrid, 18–21 March, 1991,* edited by J. Trebolle Barrera and L. Vegas Montaner, vol. 1, 83–166. Studies on the Texts of the Desert of Judah 11, 1. Leiden and Madrid: E. J. Brill, Editorial Complutense, 1992.

———. "Religionsgeschichtliche Erwägungen zu den Gottesbezeichnungen in den Qumrantexten." In *Qumrân: sa piété, sa théologie et son milieu,* edited by M. Delcor, 195–217. Bibliotheca ephemeridum theologicarum lovaniensium 46. Paris-Gembloux and Leuven: Duculot, Leuven University Press, 1978.

———. "Some Aspects of Eschatology in Texts from the Qumran Community and in the Teachings of Jesus." In *Biblical Archaeology Today: Proceedings of the International Congress on Biblical Archaeology, Jerusalem, April 1984,* edited by J. Amitai, 408–26. Jerusalem: Israel Exploration Society; The Israel Academy of Sciences and Humanities, in cooperation with the American Schools of Oriental Research, 1985.

———. "Weitere Stücke von 4 Q p Psalm 37, von 4 Q Patriarchal Blessings, und Hinweis auf eine unedierte Handschrift aus Höhle 4 Q mit Exzerpten aus dem Deuteronomium." *RQ* 6 (1967):193–28.

Stendahl, K., ed. *The Scrolls and The New Testament.* New York: Crossroad, 1992.

Stern, E. "The Archaeology of Persian Palestine." In *The Cambridge History of Judaism,* edited by W. D. Davies and L. Finkelstein, 88–114. Cambridge: Cambridge University Press, 1984.

———. "The Persian Empire and the Political and Social History of Palestine in the Persian Period." In *The Cambridge History of Judaism,* edited by W. D. Davies and L. Finkelstein, 70–87. Cambridge: Cambridge University Press, 1984.

Steudel, A. "4QMidrEschat: 'A Midrash on Eschatology' (4Q174 + 4Q177)." In *The Madrid Qumran Congress: Proceedings of the International Congress on the Dead Sea Scrolls, Madrid, 18–21 March, 1991,* edited by J. Trebolle Barrera and L. Vegas Montaner, vol. 2, 531–41. Studies on the Texts of the Desert of Judah 11, 2. Leiden: E. J. Brill, 1992.

———. "Eschatological Interpretation of Scripture in 4Q177 (4QCatena[a])." *RQ* 14 (1990):473–82.

———. "The House of Prostration CD xi 21–xii 1—Duplicates of the Temple." *RQ* 16 (1993):49–68.

———. *Der Midrasch zur Eschatologie aus der Qumrangemeinde (4QMidrEschat[a,b]).* Studies on the Texts of the Desert of Judah 13. Leiden: E. J. Brill, 1994.

Stone, M. E. "The Apocrypha and Pseudepigrapha and the Dead Sea Scrolls." In *Biblical Archaeology Today 1990,* edited by A. Biran and J. Aviram, 383–90. Jerusalem: Israel Exploration Society, 1993.

———, ed. *Jewish Writings of the Second Temple Period: Apocrypha, Pseudepigrapha, Qumran Sectarian Writings, Philo, Josephus.* Compendia Rerum Iudaicarum ad Novum Testamentum II, ii. Philadelphia and Assen: Fortress Press, Van Gorcum, 1984.

———. *Selected Studies in Pseudepigrapha and Apocrypha.* Leiden: E. J. Brill, 1991.

Stone, M. E., and E. Eshel. "An Exposition on the Patriarchs (4Q464) and Two Other Documents (4Q464ᵃ and 4Q464ᵇ)." *Le Muséon* 105, no. 3–4 (1992):243–64.

Stone, M. E., and J. C. Greenfield. "The Prayer of Levi." *JBL* 112 (1993):247–66.

Strugnell, J. "The Angelic Liturgy at Qumrân—4Q Serek Šîrôt 'Ôlat Haššabbat." *Suppl. to VT* 7 (1959):318–45.

———. "Moses-Pseudepigrapha at Qumran: 4Q375, 4Q376, and Similar Works." In *Archaeology and History in the Dead Sea Scrolls: The New York University Conference in Memory of Yigael Yadin*, edited by L. H. Schiffman, 221–56. Journal for the Study of the Pseudepigrapha Supplement Series 8; JSOT/ASOR Monographs 2. Sheffield: JSOT Press, 1990.

———. "Notes en marge du volume V des 'Discoveries in the Judean Desert of Jordan.'" *RQ* 7 (1970):163–276.

———. "On the History of the Photographing of the Discoveries in the Judean Desert for the International Group of Editors." In *The Dead Sea Scrolls of Microfiche: A Comprehensive Facsimile Edition of the Texts from the Judean Desert. Companion Volume*, edited by E. Tov, in collaboration with S. J. Pfann, 123–24. Leiden: E. J. Brill and IDC, 1993.

Strugnell, J., and D. Dimant. "4Q Second Ezekiel (4Q385)." *RQ* 13 (1988):45–58.

Sukenik, E. L. *The Dead Sea Scrolls of the Hebrew University.* Jerusalem: Magnes Press, 1955.

———. *Megillot Genuzot mi-Tokh Genizah Qedumah she-Nimṣe'ah be-Midbar Yehudah: Seqirah Rishonah.* Jerusalem: Bialik Institute, 1948.

Sussmann, J. "Ḥeqer Toldot ha-Halakhah u-Megillot Midbar-Yehudah: Hirhurim Talmudiyim Rishonim le-'Or Megillat 'Miqṣat Ma'ase ha-Torah.'" *Tarbiz* 59 (1989/90):11–77.

Ta-Shma, Y. M. "He-'arot le-Shire Shevaḥ mi-Qumran." *Tarbiz* 55 (1986):440–42.

Tabor, J. D. "A Pierced or Piercing Messiah? The Verdict Is Still Out." *BAR* 18 (Nov./Dec. 1992):58–59.

Talmon, S. "The Calendar Reckoning of the Sect from the Judean Desert." In *Aspects of the Dead Sea Scrolls*, edited by C. Rabin and Y. Yadin, 162–99. Scripta Hierosolymitana. Jerusalem: Magnes Press, 1958.

———. *The "Dead Sea Scrolls" or the "Community of the Renewed Covenant."* The Albert T. Bilgray Lecture, 1993. Tucson: University of Arizona, 1993.

———. "The 'Desert Motif' in the Bible and in Qumran Literature." In *Biblical Motifs, Origins, and Transformations*, edited by A. Altmann, 31–63. Cambridge, MA: Harvard University, 1966.

———. "DSIa as a Witness to Ancient Exegesis of the Book of Isaiah." In *Qumran and the History of the Biblical Text*, edited by F. M. Cross and S. Talmon, 116–26. Cambridge, MA, and London: Harvard University Press, 1975.

———. "The Emergence of Institutionalized Prayer in Israel in the Light of the Qumrân Literature." In *Qumrân: sa piété, sa théologie et son milieu*, edited by M. Delcor, 266–84. Bibliotheca ephemeridum theologicarum lovaniensium 46. Paris-Gembloux and Leuven: Duculot, Leuven University Press, 1978.

———. "Fragments of a *Psalms Scroll* from Masada, MPsᵇ (Masada 1103–1742)." In *Minḥah Le-Naḥum: Biblical and Other Studies Presented to Nahum M. Sarna in*

Honour of His 70th Birthday, edited by M. Brettler and M. Fishbane, 318–27. Journal for the Study of the Old Testament Supplement Series 154. Sheffield: JSOT Press, 1993.

———. *King, Cult and Calendar in Ancient Israel*. Jerusalem: Magnes Press, 1986.

———. "Le-'Inyan ha-Luah shel Kat Midbar Yehudah." *Tarbiz* 29 (1960):394–95.

———. "The 'Manual of Benedictions' of the Sect of the Judean Desert." *RQ* 2 (1959–60):475–500.

———. "Mizmorim Hissoniyim bi-Leshon ha-'Ivrit mi-Qumran." *Tarbiz* 35 (1965/6):214–34.

———. "The New Covenanters of Qumran." *Scientific American* 225 (1971):73–81.

———. "Qet'a mi-Megillah Hissonit le-Sefer Yehoshua' mi-Mesadah." In *Shai le-Chaim Rabin: Asuppat Mehqere Lashon li-Khevodo bi-Melot Lo Shiv'im ve-hamesh*, edited by M. Goshen-Gottstein, S. Morag, and S. Kogut, 147–57. Jerusalem: Academon, 1990.

———. "Qit'e Ketavim Ketuvim 'Ivrit Mi-Mesadah." *Eretz-Israel* 20 (1989):278–86.

———. *The World of Qumran from Within: Collected Studies*. Jerusalem: Magnes Press, 1989.

Talmon, S., and I. Knohl. "Qeta'im shel Megillat Luah mi-Qumran: Mishmarot Ba (4Q321)." *Tarbiz* 60 (1991):505–21.

Tcherikover, V. *Hellenistic Civilization and the Jews*. Philadelphia: Jewish Publication Society, 1959.

Thiede, C. P. *The Earliest Gospel Manuscript? The Qumran Papyrus 7Q5 and Its Significance for New Testament Studies*. [England]: Paternoster Press, 1992.

Thiering, B. E. *The Gospels and Qumran: A New Hypothesis*. Australian and New Zealand Studies in Theology and Religion. Sydney: Theological Explorations, 1981.

———. *Jesus and the Riddle of the Dead Sea Scrolls*. San Francisco: HarperCollins, 1992.

———. *Redating the Teacher of Righteousness*. Australian and New Zealand Studies in Theology and Religion 1. Sydney: Theological Explorations, 1979.

———. "Suffering and Asceticism at Qumran as Illustrated in the Hodayot." *RQ* 8 (1974):393–406.

Tobin, T. H. "4Q185 and Jewish Wisdom Literature." In *Of Scribes and Scrolls: Studies on the Hebrew Bible, Intertestamental Judaism, and Christian Origins Presented to John Strugnell*, edited by H. W. Attridge, J. J. Collins, and T. H. Tobin, 145–52. College Theology Society Resources in Religion 5. Lanham, MD, and London: University Press of America, 1990.

Tov, E. "4QJer^c (4Q72)." In *Tradition of the Text*, edited by G. Norton and S. Pisano, 248–76. Göttingen: Vandenhoeck & Ruprecht, 1991.

———. "The Composition of 1 Samuel 16–18 in the Light of the Septuagint Version." In *Empirical Models for Biblical Criticism*, edited by J. H. Tigay, 97–130. Philadelphia: University of Pennsylvania, 1985.

———. "The Contribution of the Qumran Scrolls to the Understanding of the LXX." In *Septuagint, Scrolls, and Cognate Writings*, edited by G. Brooke and B. Lindars, 11–47. Septuagint and Cognate Studies 33. Atlanta: Scholars Press, 1992.

———. ed. *The Dead Sea Scrolls on Microfiche*. With the collaboration of S. J. Pfann. Leiden: E. J. Brill, 1993 (microfiche).

————. "*Deut* 12 and *11QTemple* LII-LII: A Contrastive Analysis." *RQ* 15 (1991):169–74.

————. "Expanded Team of Editors Hard at Work on Variety of Texts." *BAR* 18 (July/Aug. 1992):69, 72–75.

————. *The Greek Minor Prophets Scroll from Naḥal Ḥever (8ḤevXIIgr)*. Discoveries in the Judaean Desert 8. Oxford: Clarendon Press, 1990.

————. "Groups of Biblical Texts Found at Qumran." In *"Time to Prepare the Way in the Wilderness:" Papers on the Qumran Scrolls by Fellows of the Institute for Advanced Studies of the Hebrew University, Jerusalem, 1989–90*, edited by D. Dimant and L. H. Schiffman, 85–102. Studies on the Texts from the Desert of Judah. Leiden: E. J. Brill, 1994.

————. "Hebrew Biblical Manuscripts from the Judaean Desert: Their Contribution to Textual Criticism." *JJS* 39 (1988):5–37.

————. "The Jeremiah Scrolls from Cave 4." *RQ* 14 (1989):189–206.

————. "The Literary History of the Book of Jeremiah in the Light of Its Textual History." In *Empirical Models for Biblical Criticism*, edited by J. Tigay, 211–27. Philadelphia: University of Pennsylvania, 1985.

————. "'Megillat ha-Miqdash' u-Viqqoret Nusaḥ ha-Miqra'." *Eretz-Israel* 16 (1981/82):100–111.

————. "The Nature and Background of Harmonizations in Biblical Manuscripts." *JSOT* 31 (1985):3–29.

————. "The Orthography and Language of the Hebrew Scrolls Found at Qumran and the Origin of These Scrolls." *Textus* 13 (1986):32–57.

————. "The Septuagint." In *Mikra: Text, Translation, Reading, and Interpretation of the Hebrew Bible in Ancient Judaism and Early Christianity*, edited by M. J. Mulder with H. Sysling, 161–88. Corpus Rerum Iudaicarum ad Novum Testamentum II.1. Assen/Mastricht and Minneapolis: Van Gorcum, Fortress Press, 1990.

————. "Some Aspects of the Textual and Literary History of the Book of Jeremiah." In *Le Livre de Jérémie*, edited by P.-M. Bogaert, 145–67. Bibliotheca ephemeridum theologicarum lovaniensium 54. Leuven: Leuven University Press, 1981.

————. "The Textual Affiliations of 4QSamᵃ." *JSOT* 14 (1979):37–53.

————. *Textual Criticism of the Hebrew Bible*. Minneapolis: Fortress Press, 1992.

————. "The Textual Status of 4Q364–367 (4QPP)." In *The Madrid Qumran Congress: Proceedings of the International Congress on the Dead Sea Scrolls, Madrid, 18–21 March, 1991*, edited by J. Trebolle Berrara and L. Vegas Montaner, vol. 1, 43–82. Studies on the Texts of the Desert of Judah 11, 1. Leiden and Madrid: E. J. Brill, Editorial Complutense, 1992.

————. "Three Fragments of Jeremiah from Qumran Cave 4." *RQ* 15 (1992):531–42.

————. "The Unpublished Qumran Texts from Caves 4 and 11." *BA* 55 (1992):94–104.

————. "The Unpublished Qumran Texts from Caves 4 and 11." *JJS* 43 (1992):101–36.

Trebolle, J. "The Story of David and Goliath (1 Sam 17–18): Textual Variants and Literary Composition." *Bulletin of the International Organization for Septuagint and Cognate Studies* 23 (1990):16–30.

Trenchard, W. C. *Ben Sira's View of Women: A Literary Analysis*. Brown Judaic Studies 38. Chico, CA: Scholars Press, 1982.

Trever, J. C. "1 Q Danᵃ, the Latest of the Qumran Manuscripts." *RQ* 7 (1970):277–86.

———. "The Completion of the Publication of Some Fragments from Qumran Cave I." *RQ* 5 (1965):323–44.

———. *The Dead Sea Scrolls: A Personal Account.* Grand Rapids: Eerdmans, 1977.

———, photographer. *Scrolls from Qumrân Cave I: The Great Isaiah Scroll, the Order of the Community, the Pesher to Habakkuk,* with an introduction by F. M. Cross. Jerusalem: Albright Institute of Archaeological Research, Shrine of the Book, 1972.

———. "When Was Qumran Cave 1 Discovered?" *RQ* 3 (1961):135–42.

Ulrich, E. "The Biblical Scrolls from Qumran Cave 4: A Progress Report of Their Publication." *RQ* 14 (1989):207–28.

———. "The Canonical Process, Textual Criticism, and Latter Stages in the Composition of the Bible." In *"Sha'arei Talmon": Studies in the Bible, Qumran, and the Ancient Near East Presented to Shemaryahu Talmon,* edited by M. Fishbane and E. Tov, 267–91. Winona Lake, IN: Eisenbrauns, 1992.

———. "Daniel Manuscripts from Qumran. Part 1: A Preliminary Edition of 4QDanᵃ." *BASOR* 268 (1987):17–37.

———. "Daniel Manuscripts from Qumran. Part 2: Preliminary Editions of 4QDanᵇ and 4QDanᶜ." *BASOR* 274 (1989):3–26.

———. "The Greek Manuscripts of the Pentateuch from Qumrân, Including Newly-Identified Fragments of Deuteronomy (4QLXXDeut)." In *De Septuaginta: Studies in Honour of John William Wevers on His Sixty-fifth Birthday,* edited by A. Pietersma and C. Cox, 71–82. Mississauga, ON: Benben, 1984.

———. "The Palaeo-Hebrew Biblical Manuscripts from Qumran Cave 4." In *"Time to Prepare the Way in the Wilderness": Papers on the Qumran Scrolls by Fellows of the Institute for Advanced Studies of the Hebrew University, Jerusalem, 1989–90,* edited by D. Dimant and L. H. Schiffman, 103–30. Leiden: E. J. Brill, 1994.

———. "Pluriformity in the Biblical Text, Text Groups, and Questions of Canon." In *The Madrid Qumran Congress: Proceedings of the International Congress on the Dead Sea Scrolls: Madrid, 18–21 March, 1991,* edited by J. Trebolle Barrera and L. Vegas Montaner, vol. 1, 23–42. Studies on the Texts of the Desert of Judah 11, 1. Leiden and Madrid: E. J. Brill, Editorial Complutense, 1992.

———. "The Septuagint Manuscripts from Qumran: A Reappraisal of Their Value." In *Septuagint, Scrolls, and Cognate Writings,* edited by G. Brooke and B. Lindars, 49–80. Septuagint and Cognate Studies 33. Atlanta: Scholars Press, 1992.

Urbach, E. E. *The Sages: Their Concepts and Beliefs.* 2 vols. Jerusalem: Magnes Press, 1987.

VanderKam, J. C. "The Birth of Noah." In *Intertestamental Essays in Honour of Józef Tadeusz Milik,* edited by Z. J. Kapera, 213–31. Kraków: Enigma Press, 1992.

———. *The Book of Jubilees.* 2 vols. Corpus scriptorum christianorum orientalium 510–11; Scriptores Aethiopici 87–88. Louvain: Peeters, 1989.

———. "The Dead Sea Scrolls and Christianity." In *Understanding the Dead Sea Scrolls,* edited by H. Shanks, 181–202. New York: Random House, 1992.

———. *The Dead Sea Scrolls Today.* Grand Rapids: Eerdmanns, 1994.

———. *Enoch and the Growth of an Apocalyptic Tradition.* CBQ Monograph Series 16. Washington, DC: Catholic Biblical Association of America, 1984.

———. "The Jubilees Fragments from Qumran Cave 4." In *The Madrid Qumran*

Congress: Proceedings of the International Congress on the Dead Sea Scrolls, Madrid, 18–21 March, 1991, edited by J. Trebolle Barrera and L. Vegas Montaner, vol. 2, 635–48. Studies on the Texts of the Desert of Judah 11, 2. Leiden: E. J. Brill, 1992.

———. "The Origin, Character, and Early History of the 364-Day Calendar: A Reassessment of Jaubert's Hypotheses." *CBQ* 41 (1979):390–411.

———. "The Poetry of 1 Q Ap Gen XX, 2–8a." *RQ* 10 (1979):57–66.

———. "A Twenty-eight Day Month Tradition in the Book of Jubilees?" *VT* 32 (1982):504–6.

———. "Zadok and the SPR HTWRH HHTWM in Dam. Doc. V, 2–5." *RQ* 11 (1984):561–70.

VanderKam, J. C., and J. T. Milik. "The First *Jubilees* Manuscript from Qumran Cave 4: A Preliminary Publication." *JBL* 110 (1991):243–70.

Vaux, R. de. *Archaeology and the Dead Sea Scrolls.* The Schweich Lectures 1959. London: Oxford University Press for the British Academy, 1973.

———. "La Grotte des manuscrits hébreux." *RB* 56 (1949):586–609.

———. "Qumran, Khirbet and 'Ein Feshka," with an afterword by M. Broshi. In *The New Encyclopedia of Archaeological Excavations in the Holy Land,* edited by E. Stern, vol. 4, 1235–41. Jerusalem: Israel Exploration Society, Carta, 1993.

Vaux, R. de, and J. T. Milik. *Qumrân Grotte 4, II.* Discoveries in the Judaean Desert 6. Oxford: Clarendon Press, 1977.

Vermes, G. *The Dead Sea Scrolls in English.* London: Penguin Books, 1987.

———. "Essenes and Therapeutai." *RQ* 3 (1962):495–504.

———. "The Etymology of 'Essenes.'" *RQ* 2 (1960):427–44.

———. "The Impact of the Dead Sea Scrolls on Jewish Studies during the Last Twenty-five Years." In *Approach to Ancient Judaism: Theory and Practice,* edited by W. S. Green, 201–14. Brown Judaic Studies 1. Missoula, MT: Scholars Press, 1978.

———. "The 'Pierced Messiah' Text—An Interpretation Evaporates." *BAR* 18 (July/Aug. 1992):80–82.

———. *Post-Biblical Jewish Studies.* Studies in Judaism in Late Antiquity 8. Leiden: E. J. Brill, 1975.

———. "Preliminary Remarks on the Unpublished Fragments of the Community Rule from Qumran Cave 4." *JJS* 42 (1991):250–55.

———. "The Present State of Dead Sea Scrolls Research." *JJS* 45 (1994):101–10.

———. "Qumran Corner: Preliminary Remarks on the Unpublished Fragments of the Community Rule from Qumran Cave 4." *JJS* 42 (1991):250–55.

———. "Qumran Forum Miscellanea I." *JJS* 43 (1992):299–305.

———. "The Qumran Interpretation of Scripture in Its Historical Setting." *The Annual of Leeds University Oriental Society* 6 (1969):85–97.

———. *Scripture and Tradition in Judaism.* Studia Post-Biblica 4. Leiden: E. J. Brill, 1973.

———. "The So-called King Jonathan Fragment (4Q488)." *JJS* 44 (1993):294–300.

Viviano, B. T. "Beatitudes Found among Dead Sea Scrolls." *BAR* 18 (Nov./Dec. 1992):53–55, 66.

Wacholder, B. Z. "The Ancient Judaeo-Aramaic Literature (500–165 B.C.E.): A Classification of Pre-Qumranic Texts." In *Archaeology and History in the Dead Sea*

Scrolls: The New York University Conference in Memory of Yigael Yadin, edited by L. H. Schiffman, 257–81. Journal for the Study of the Pseudepigrapha Supplement Series 8; JSOT/ASOR Monographs 2. Sheffield: JSOT Press, 1990.

———. *The Dawn of Qumran: The Sectarian Torah and the Teacher of Righteousness.* Cincinnati: Hebrew Union College Press, 1983.

———. "Ezekiel and Ezekielianism as Progenitors of Essenianism." In *The Dead Sea Scrolls: Forty Years of Research*, edited by D. Dimant and U. Rappaport, 186–96. Leiden and Jerusalem: E. J. Brill, Magnes Press, Yad Izhak Ben-Zvi, 1992.

———. "The Fragmentary Remains of 11Q Torah (Temple Scroll): 11Q Torah[b] and 11Q Torah[c] 4QparaTorah Integrated with 11Q Torah[a]." *HUCA* 62 (1991):1–116.

———. "A Qumran Attack on the Oral Exegesis? The Phrase *'šr btlmwd šqrm* in 4 Q Pesher Nahum." *RQ* 5 (1966):575–79.

———. "Rules of Testimony in Qumranic Jurisprudence: CD 9 and 11Q Torah 64." *JJS* 40 (1989):163–74.

———. "The 'Sealed' Torah vs. the 'Revealed' Torah: An Exegesis of Damascus Covenant V, 1–6, and Jeremiah 32, 10–14." *RQ* 12 (1986):351–69.

Wacholder, B. Z., and M. G. Abegg. *A Preliminary Edition of the Unpublished Dead Sea Scrolls: The Hebrew and Aramaic Texts from Cave Four.* 2 fascicles. Washington, DC: Biblical Archaeology Society, 1991–92.

Weinert, F. D. "4Q159: Legislation for an Essene Community outside of Qumran." *JSJ* 5 (1974):179–207.

Weinfeld, M. "'Aqavot shel Qedushat Yoṣer u-Fesuqqe de-Zimra' bi-Megillot Midbar Yehudah u-ve-Sefer Ben Sira." *Tarbiz* 45 (1975/6).

———. "Grace after Meals in Qumran." *JBL* 111 (1992):427–40.

———. "'Megillat Miqdash' 'o 'Torah la-Melekh.'" *Shnaton* 7 (1978/9):214–37.

———. "The Morning Prayers (Birkhoth Hashachar) in Qumran and in the Conventional Jewish Liturgy." *RQ* 13 (1988):481–94.

———. *The Organizational Pattern and the Penal Code of the Qumran Sect.* Novum Testament et Orbis Antiquus 2. Fribourg and Göttingen: Editions Universitaires, Vandenhoeck & Ruprecht, 1986.

———. "Prayer and Liturgical Practice in the Qumran Sect." In *The Dead Sea Scrolls: Forty Years of Research*, edited by D. Dimant and U. Rappaport, 241–58. Leiden and Jerusalem: E. J. Brill, Magnes Press, Yad Izhak Ben-Zvi, 1992.

———. "The Royal Guard According to the Temple Scroll." *RB* 87 (1980):394–96.

Weiss, R. "Further Notes on the Qumran Targum to Job." *JSS* 19 (1974):13–18.

Wentling, J. L. "Unraveling the Relationship between 11QT, the Eschatological Temple, and the Qumran Community." *RQ* 14 (1989):61–74.

Wernberg-Møller, P. *The Manual of Discipline.* Studies on the Texts of the Desert of Judah 1. Leiden: E. J. Brill, 1957.

———. "The Nature of the YAḤAD According to the *Manual of Discipline* and Related Documents." *The Annual of Leeds University Oriental Society* 6 (1969):56–81.

———. "A Reconsideration of the Two Spirits in the *Rule of the Community*." *RQ* 3 (1961):413–42.

White, S. A. "4Q364 & 365: A Preliminary Report." In *The Madrid Qumran Congress: Proceedings of the International Congress on the Dead Sea Scrolls, Madrid, 18–21*

March, 1991, edited by J. Trebolle Barrera and L. Vegas Montaner, vol. 1, 217–28. Studies on the Texts of the Desert of Judah 11, 1. Leiden and Madrid: E. J. Brill, Editorial Complutense, 1992.

———. "A Comparison of the 'A' and 'B' Manuscripts of the *Damascus Document*." *RQ* 12 (1987):537–54.

Wieder, N. *The Judean Scrolls and Karaism*. London: East and West Library, 1962.

Wilson, A. M., and L. Wills. "Literary Sources of the Temple Scroll." *HTR* 75 (1982):275–88.

Wintermute, O. S. "Jubilees (Second Century B.C.): A New Translation and Introduction." In *The Old Testament Pseudepigrapha*, edited by J. H. Charlesworth, vol. 2, 35–142. Garden City, NY: Doubleday, 1985.

Wise, M. O. "4QFlorilegium and the Temple of Man." *RQ* 15 (1991):103–32.

———. "The Covenant of *Temple Scroll* XXIX, 3–10." *RQ* 14 (1989):49–60.

———. *A Critical Study of the Temple Scroll from Qumran Cave 11*. Studies in Ancient Oriental Civilization 49. Chicago: Oriental Institute of the University of Chicago, 1990.

———. "The Eschatological Vision of the *Temple Scroll*." *JNES* 49 (1990):155–72.

Wise, M. O., and J. D. Tabor. "The Messiah at Qumran." *BAR* 18 (Nov./Dec. 1992):60–61, 65.

Wolfson, E. R. "Mysticism and the Poetic-Liturgical Compositions from Qumran." In *Center for Judaic Studies Colloquium on the Dead Sea Scrolls*. Philadelphia: Center for Judaic Studies, 1994.

Wolters, A. "The *Copper Scroll* and the Vocabulary of Mishnaic Hebrew." *RQ* 14 (1990):483–95.

———. "Literary Analysis and the *Copper Scroll*." In *Intertestamental Essays in Honour of Józef Tadeusz Milik*, edited by Z. J. Kapera, 239–52. Kraków: Enigma Press, 1992.

Wood, B. G. "To Dip or to Sprinkle? The Qumran Cisterns in Perspective." *BASOR* 256 (1984):45–60.

Woude, A. S. van der. "Bemerkungen zum Gebet des Nabonid." In *Qumrân: Sa piété, sa théologie et son milieu*, edited by M. Delcor, 121–29. Bibliotheca ephemeridum theologicarum lovaniensium 46. Paris-Gembloux and Leuven: Duculot, Leuven University Press, 1978.

———. "Fragmente de Buches Jubiläen aus Qumran Höhle XI (11QJub)." In *Tradition und Glaube: Das frühe Christentum in seiner Umwelt*, edited by J. Jeremias, et al., 140–46. Göttingen: Vandenhoeck & Ruprecht, 1971.

———. "Melchisedek als himmlische Erlösergestalt in den neugefundenen eschatologischen Midraschim aus Qumran Höhle XI." *Oudtestamentlische Studien* 14 (1965):354–73.

———. "Ein neuer Segensspruch aus Qumran (11 Q Ber)." *Bibel und Qumran* (1968):253–58.

Yadin, Y. "Another Fragment (E) of the *Psalms Scroll* from Qumran Cave 11 (11QPsᵃ)." *Textus* 5 (1966):1–10.

———. "L'Attitude essénienne envers la polygamie et le divorce." *RB* 79 (1972):98–100.

———. *Bar-Kokhba: The Rediscovery of the Legendary Hero of the Second Jewish Revolt against Rome*. New York: Random House, 1971.

———. *The Ben Sira Scroll from Masada*. Jerusalem: The Israel Exploration Society and the Shrine of the Book, 1965.

———. "A Crucial Passage in the Dead Sea Scrolls." *JBL* 78 (1959):238–41.

———. "The Dead Sea Scrolls and the Epistle to the Hebrews." In *Aspects of the Dead Sea Scrolls*, edited by C. Rabin and Y. Yadin, 36–55. Scripta Hierosolymitana. Jerusalem: Magnes Press, 1958.

———. "Expedition D." In *Judean Desert Caves: Survey and Excavations 1960*, 36–52. Jerusalem: Israel Exploration Society, 1961.

———. "Expedition D—The Cave of the Letters." In *Judean Desert Caves: Survey and Excavations 1961*, 227–57. Jerusalem: Israel Exploration Society, 1962.

———. "Ha-Milḥamah 'al 'Milḥemet Bene 'Or bi-Vene Ḥoshekh.'" *Molad* 14 (1956):192–99.

———. "Hadashot me-'Olaman shel ha-Megillot." In *'Iyunim Bi-Megillot Midbar Yehudah*, edited by J. Liver, 40–54. Jerusalem: Kiryat Sepher, 1957.

———. "Is the *Temple Scroll* a Sectarian Document?" In *Humanizing America's Iconic Book: Society of Biblical Literature Centennial Addresses: 1980*, edited by G. M. Tucker and D. A. Knight, 153–69. Chico, CA: Scholars Press, 1982.

———. *Masada: Herod's Fortress and the Zealots' Last Stand*. New York: Random House, 1966.

———. *Megillat ha-Miqdash*. 3 vols. Jerusalem: Israel Exploration Society, 1977.

———. *The Message of the Scrolls*. New York: Simon & Schuster, 1957.

———. "A Midrash on 2 Sam. vii and Ps. i–ii (4Q *Florilegium*)." *IEJ* 9 (1959):95–98.

———. "More on the Letters of Bar Kochba." *BA* 24 (1961):86–95.

———. "New Discoveries in the Judean Desert." *BA* 24 (1961):34–50.

———. "A Note on 4Q 159 (Ordinances)." *IEJ* 18 (1968):250–52.

———. "A Note on Melchizedek and Qumran." *IEJ* 15 (1965):152–54.

———. "*Pesher Nahum* (4Q PNahum) Reconsidered." *IEJ* 21 (1971):1–12.

———. *The Scroll of the War of the Sons of Light against the Sons of Darkness*, translated by B. Rabin and C. Rabin. Oxford: Oxford University Press, 1962.

———. "Some Notes on the Newly Published *Pesharim* of Isaiah." *IEJ* 6 (1959):39–42.

———. *Tefillin from Qumran*. Jerusalem: Israel Exploration Society, Shrine of the Book, 1969.

———. "The Temple Scroll." In *New Directions in Biblical Archaeology*, edited by D. N. Freedman and J. C. Greenfield, 156–66. Garden City, NY: Doubleday, 1971.

———. "The Temple Scroll." *BA* 30 (1967):135–39.

———. *The Temple Scroll*. 3 vols. Jerusalem: Israel Exploration Society, 1983.

———. *The Temple Scroll, the Hidden Law of the Dead Sea Sect*. New York: Random House, 1985.

———. "Three Notes on the Dead Sea Scrolls." *IEJ* 6 (1956):158–62.

Yadin, Y., J. Naveh, and Y. Meshorer. *Masada I: The Yigael Yadin Excavations 1963–1965, Final Reports*. Jerusalem: Israel Exploration Society, the Hebrew University of Jerusalem, 1989.

Yassif, E. *Sippure Ben Sira bi-Yeme ha-Benayim*. Jerusalem: Magnes Press, 1984.

Zahavy, T. "The Sabbath Code of *Damascus Document* X,14–XI,18: Form Analytical and Redaction Critical Observations." *RQ* 10 (1981):589–91.

INDEX

Italic page numbers refer to illustrations; page numbers followed by t refer to tables; those followed by n refer to notes.